THE BOOK OF ENOCH

OR

1 ENOCH

TRANSLATED FROM THE EDITOR'S
ETHIOPIC TEXT

AND EDITED WITH THE INTRODUCTION NOTES AND
INDEXES OF THE FIRST EDITION WHOLLY
RECAST ENLARGED AND REWRITTEN

TOGETHER WITH A REPRINT FROM THE EDITOR'S TEXT OF
THE GREEK FRAGMENTS

By R. H. CHARLES, D.Litt., D.D.

FELLOW OF MERTON COLLEGE
FELLOW OF THE BRITISH ACADEMY

OXFORD
AT THE CLARENDON PRESS
1912

HENRY FROWDE, M A
PUBLISHER TO THE UNIVERSITY OF OXFORD
LONDON, EDINBURGH, NEW YORK
TORONTO AND MELBOURNE

TO

THE WARDEN AND FELLOWS
OF MERTON COLLEGE

PREFACE

THIS is not so much a second edition as a new book   A brief comparison of the first edition and the present work will make this clear even to the cursory reader.   Alike in the translation and in the commentary it forms a vast advance on its predecessor. I cannot claim to be satisfied with it even as it stands, and yet twenty additional years spent in Apocalyptic and Biblical studies have not, I would fain hope, been fruitless with regard to the present work.

The translation in the first edition was made from Dillmann's edition of the Ethiopic text, which was based on five MSS. With a view to this translation the present editor emended and revised Dillmann's text in accordance with nine hitherto uncollated Ethiopic MSS in the British Museum, and the Greek and Latin fragments which had just come to light, but notwithstanding every care he felt his work in this respect to be of a wholly provisional character.   From the date of the publication of the first edition in 1893 he steadily made preparation for an edition of the Ethiopic text and of the Greek and Latin fragments.   This text, which is exhaustive of existing textual materials in these languages, was published by the University Press in 1906, and from this text the present translation is made. A new and revolutionary feature in the translation is due to the editor's discovery of the poetical structure of a considerable portion of the work   I call it revolutionary; for such it proves to be in respect of the critical problems of the text.   By its means the lost original of the text is not infrequently recovered, phrases and clauses recognized as obvious interpolations, and not a few lines restored to their original context, whose claims to a place in the text were hitherto ignored on the ground of the weakness of their textual attestation.

During the past eighteen years the criticism of the book has made undoubted headway, and that, I am glad to say, mainly in the direction defined in the first edition.   The idea of a *Grund-schrift*, which was accepted by most of the chief scholars in this field till its appearance, and to which I strove and not in vain to give the *coup de grâce*, is now universally abandoned.   The critical advance made in the present volume is not of a revolutionary character, but consists rather in a more detailed application of the principles of criticism pursued in the first edition.

In my first edition I said that a knowledge of 1 Enoch was indispensable to N.T students. The further study of Apocalyptic and Biblical literature, Jewish and Christian, in the score of years that have since elapsed, has convinced me still more fully of this fact. And I might add here that to the O.T. student it is likewise indispensable, if we would understand many of the problems underlying O.T prophecy. To the biblical scholar and to the student of Jewish and Christian theology 1 Enoch is the most important Jewish work written between 200 B.C and 100 A D. For a short account of the book the reader should consult the Introduction, § 1

I cannot help expressing here my deep regret that Jewish scholars are still so backward in recognizing the value of this literature for their own history. Apocalyptic is the true child of Prophecy, and became its true representative to the Jews from the unhappy moment that the Law won an absolute autocracy in Judaism, and made the utterance of God-sent prophetic men impossible except through the medium of Pseudepigraphs, some of which, like Daniel, gained an entrance despite the Law into the O T Canon. It is true that eminent Jewish scholars in America and elsewhere have in part recognized the value of Apocalyptic literature, but, as a whole, Orthodox Judaism still confesses and still champions the one-sided Judaism, which came into being after the Fall of Jerusalem in 70 A D., a Judaism lopped in the main of its spiritual and prophetic side and given over all but wholly to a legalistic conception of religion It is not strange that since that disastrous period Judaism became to a great extent a barren faith, and lost its leadership in the spiritual things of the world.

I cannot close this Preface without recording my deep obligations to the officials of the University Press for the skill, care and expedition with which they have carried this work through; and likewise acknowledging the very helpful service rendered to me by a promising scholar, the Rev. A. L Davies, in the correction of proofs, the verification of references, and at times the acquisition of fresh materials.

24 BARDWELL ROAD, OXFORD
June 1, 1912

CONTENTS

THE BOOK OF ENOCH

ı e 1 ENOCH

INTRODUCTION

§ 1. Short Account of the Book.

It is seldom that authors attain to the immortality which they hope for, and it is still more seldom that anonymous authors achieve this distinction. And yet it is just such a distinction that the authors of the Book of Enoch have achieved That such should be ultimately his lot was the deep-rooted conviction of one of this literary circle. He looked forward (104^{11-12}) to the time when his writings would be translated into various languages, and become to the righteous 'a cause of joy and uprightness and much wisdom'. This hope was to a large degree realized in the centuries immediately preceding and following the Christian era, when the currency of these apocalyptic writings was very widespread, because they almost alone represented the advance of the higher theology in Judaism, which culminated in Christianity.[1] But our book contained much of a questionable character, and from the fourth century of our era onward it fell into discredit, and under the ban of such authorities as Hilary, Jerome, and Augustine, it gradually passed out of circulation, and became lost to the knowledge of Western Christendom till over a century ago, when an Ethiopic version of the work was found in Abyssinia by Bruce, who brought home three MSS of it, from one of which Laurence made the first modern translation

---

[1] Nearly all the writers of the New Testament were familiar with it, and were more or less influenced by it in thought and diction It is quoted as a genuine production of Enoch by St Jude, and as Scripture by St Barnabas The authors of the Book of Jubilees, the Apocalypse of Baruch, and 4 Ezra, laid it under contribution. With the earlier Fathers and Apologists it had all the weight of a canonical book.

of Enoch. It was not, however, till recent years that the Book of Enoch and similar works have begun to come into their own owing to their immeasurable value as being practically the only historical memorials of the religious development of Judaism from 200 B C to 100 A. D., and particularly of the development of that side of Judaism, to which historically Christendom in large measure owes its existence.

The Book of Enoch is for the history of theological development the most important pseudepigraph of the first two centuries B C Some of its authors—and there were many—belonged to the true succession of the prophets, and it was simply owing to the evil character of the period, in which their lot was cast, that these enthusiasts and mystics, exhibiting on occasions the inspiration of the O.T. prophets, were obliged to issue their works under the aegis of some ancient name. The Law which claimed to be the highest and final word from God could tolerate no fresh message from God, and so, when men were moved by the Spirit of God to make known their visions relating to the past, the present, and the future, and to proclaim the higher ethical truths they had won, they could not do so openly, but were forced to resort to pseudonymous publication.

To describe in short compass the Book of Enoch is impossible. It comes from many writers and almost as many periods. It touches upon every subject that could have arisen in the ancient schools of the prophets, but naturally it deals with these subjects in an advanced stage of development Nearly every religious idea appears in a variety of forms, and, if these are studied in relation to their contexts and dates, we cannot fail to observe that in the age to which the Enoch literature belongs there is movement everywhere, and nowhere dogmatic fixity and finality. And though at times the movement may be reactionary, yet the general trend is onward and upward. In fact the history of the development of the higher theology during the two centuries before the Christian era could not be written without the Book of Enoch.

From what has been already said it is clear that no unity of time, authorship, or teaching is to be looked for. Indeed, certain considerable portions of the book belonged originally not to the Enoch literature at all, but to an earlier work, i. e. the Book of Noah, which probably exhibited in some degree the syncretism of the work into which it was subsequently incorporated. This Book of Noah clearly embraced chapters 6–11, 54^7–55^2, 60, 65–69^{25}, 106–107 [1]

As regards the Enoch elements, the oldest portions of them are likewise pre-Maccabean, i. e. 12–36, and probably 90^{1-10} 91^{12-17}, i e the Apocalypse of Weeks. The Dream Visions, i. e. 83–90, were in all probability written when Judas the Maccabee was still warring, 165–161 B.C., 72–82 before 110 B.C, the Parables, 37–71 and 91–104, 105–64 B.C.

The authors of all the sections belong to the Chasids or their successors the Pharisees.

Conflicting views are advanced on the Messiah, the Messianic kingdom, the origin of sin, Sheol, the final judgement, the resurrection, and the nature of the future life. There is an elaborate angelology and demonology, and much space is devoted to the calendar and the heavenly bodies and their movements. Babylonian influences are here manifest and in a slight degree Greek.

The Book of Enoch, like the Book of Daniel, was written originally partly in Aramaic and partly in Hebrew. From an Aramaic original is derived 6–36, and possibly 83–90, while the rest of the book comes from a Hebrew original. To determine these questions categorically is a task of no little difficulty, seeing that for four-fifths of the text we have only a translation of a translation, and that such close affinities exist between Hebrew and Aramaic. For the resemblances between the two languages are so great that frequently retranslation from the Ethiopic into either is sufficient to explain corruptions in the former. There has accordingly been great divergence of opinion on this question, but in the opinion of the present writer, who

---

[1] Portions have been preserved in Jubilees 7^{20-39} 10^{1-15}, but the date of this Noachic literature is at latest pre-Maccabean.

has spent considerable time on the problem, the balance of evidence is decidedly in favour of the view above stated.

In the course of his studies it suddenly dawned upon the writer that much of the text was originally written in verse. This discovery has frequently proved helpful in the criticism of difficult passages, and the recovery of the original in a multitude of cases

§ 2. THE TITLE.

Our book appears under various titles, which may be briefly enumerated as follows

1°. *Enoch.* Jude 14 ἐπροφήτευσεν   ἕβδομος ἀπὸ Ἀδὰμ Ἐνὼχ λέγων.

Ep. Barn. iv. 3 ὡς Ἐνὼχ λέγει.

Clem. Alex. *Eclog. Proph* (Dindorf, iii. 456) ὁ Δανιὴλ λέγει ὁμοδοξῶν τῷ Ἐνώχ: also in iii. 474.

Origen, *In Ioannem* vi. 25 ὡς ἐν τῷ Ἐνὼχ γέγραπται: *Contra Celsum* v 54 τῶν ἐν τῷ Ἐνὼχ γεγραμμένων

Tertullian, *De Cultu Fem.* ii. 10 'Ut Enoch refert'; *De Idol* iv 'Enoch praedicens', xv 'Spiritus .   praececinit per . . Enoch'.

Anatolius of Laodicaea (cited by Eus. *H E* vii 32. 19 τὰ ἐν τῷ Ἐνὼχ μαθήματα).

2° *The Books of Enoch.* This is probably the oldest title. The fifth Section of the book itself opens with the words . 92[1] 'The book written by Enoch'.   108[1] begins · 'Another book which Enoch wrote.' In 82[1] Enoch says to Methuselah 'All these things I am recounting to thee .   . and given thee books concerning all these· so preserve . . . the books from thy father's hand.' 14[1] 'The book of the words of righteousness' The third Section, i. e. 72[1], begins, 'The book of the courses of the luminaries'.   These passages imply a plurality of books.

But though apparently the oldest title, it has not the oldest independent attestation.   It is found in the following works

T. Jud xviii. 1 (β A S[1]) ἐν βίβλοις Ἐνὼχ τοῦ δικαίου.

T. Lev. x. 5 (A) = καθὼς γέγραπται ἐν βίβλοις Ἐνώχ.

Origen, *Contra Celsum*, v. 54 τὰ ἐπιγεγραμμένα τοῦ 'Ενὼχ βιβλία. *In Num. Homil.* xxviii. 2 'In libellis qui appellantur Enoch'.

Pistis Sophia (ed. Schwartze, p. 245) 'Ea in secundo libro Ieu, quae scripsit Enoch'.

Syncellus (*Chronographia*, ed. Dind.), i. p 20 ἐκ τοῦ πρώτου βιβλίου τοῦ 'Ενώχ. The same phrase reeurs in i p 21, 47. Cf. i. 42 ἐκ τοῦ πρώτου λόγου 'Ενώχ. Here and in the preceding work the division of Enoch into books is clearly recognized. There were five such divisions or books, see § 6.

3°. *Book of Enoch.* This title is found in:

T Lev x. 5 (*a, d e g*) καθὼς περιέχει ἡ (> *a b f*) βίβλος 'Ενὼχ τοῦ δικαίου.

Origen, *De Princ.* i. 3. 3 'In Enoch libro'. iv. 35 'in libro suo Enoch ita ait'.

Hilary, *Comment in Ps.* cxxxii 3 'Fertur id de quo etiam nescio cuius liber exstat'.

Jerome, *De Viris illustr.* iv 'De libro Enoch qui apocryphus est'.

Syncellus, *op. cit.* i. 60 ὡς ἐν τῇ βίβλῳ αὐτοῦ 'Ενὼχ φέρεται. But this title may refer merely to one of the books of Enoch, and so come under 2°

3°. *Words of Enoch.* This title has the oldest external attestation. Jub. 21[10] 'For thus I have found it written in the books of my forefathers and in the words of Enoch, and in the words of Noah'.

T. Benj. ix. 1 ἀπὸ λογίων (= λόγων *β–d*) 'Ενὼχ τοῦ δικαίου. This title finds some justification in 1 Enoch 1[1] 'Words of the blessing of Enoch', 14[1] 'book of the words of righteousness'.

4°. *Writing of Enoch*:

T. Lev. xiv. 1 (*β A*) ἔγνων ἀπὸ γραφῆς 'Ενώχ. See also in T. Sim. v. 4, T. Naph. iv. 1

Tertullian, *De Cultu Fem.* i. 3 'Scio scripturam Enoch . . . cum Enoch eadem scriptura etiam de domino praedicarit'.

§ 3. ITS CANONICITY.

The citations of Enoch by the Testaments of the Twelve Patriarchs and by the Book of Jubilees show that at the close of the second century B.C., and during the first century B.C., this book was regarded in certain circles as inspired. When we come down to the first century A.D., we find that it is recognized as Scripture by Jude. See under § 2, 1°. In the next century this recognition is given amply in the Ep. Barnabas xvi. 5 λέγει γὰρ ἡ γραφή; by Athenagoras, *Legatio pro Christianis* 24 à τοῖς προφήταις ἐκπεφώνηται (referring to Enoch), in the third century by Clem. Alex. *Eclog. Prophet.* ii, see § 2, 1°; by Irenaeus iv. 6. 12 'Enoch . . . placens Deo . . . legatione ad angelos fungebatur', by Tertullian, *De Cultu Fem.* i. 3, *De Idol.* xv, see § 2, 1°, by Zosimus of Panopolis, quoted in Syncellus (Dind. i. 24) τοῦτο οὖν ἔφασαν αἱ ἀρχαῖαι καὶ αἱ θεῖαι γραφαί, ὅτι ἄγγελοί τινες ἐπεθύμησαν τῶν γυναικῶν. After the third century the Book of Enoch fell into discredit and gradually passed out of circulation.

§ 4. THE GREEK VERSIONS. EDITIONS OF THESE VERSIONS.

The Greek Versions have only in part been preserved. Chapters 1–32⁶ and 19³–21⁹ in a duplicate form were discovered in 1886–1887 at Akhmîm by the Mission Archéologique Française at Cairo, and published by M. Bouriant in 1892. These are designated as G^g, and G^{g1} and G^{g2} in the case of the duplicate passage. Large fragments have been preserved in Syncellus, namely 6–10¹⁴ 15⁸–16¹, and 8⁴–9⁴ in a duplicate form. These are designated as G^s and G^{s1}, G^{s2} in the case of the duplicate passage.

The chief literature on these fragments is as follows —

Bouriant, *Fragments grecs du livre d'Énoch. Mémoires publiés par les membres de la Mission archéologique française au Caire*, tom ix, pp. 91–136, 1892. This is praiseworthy as a first edition, but the text is disfigured by many errors.

—— *L'Évangile et l'Apocalypse de Pierre avec le texte grec du livre d'Énoch. Texte publié en fac-similé par l'héliogravure d'après les photographies du manuscrit de Gizeh.* Paris, 1893.

Dillmann, *Sitzungsberichte d. kgl Preuss. Akademie d. Wissenschaften zu Berlin*, 1892, li–liii, pp. 1039–1054, 1079–1092.

These studies are of course good, and several of this scholar's suggestions are excellent. In his comparison of the Ethiopic and Greek Versions he had the benefit of having collations of *q t u* before him These gave him no inconsiderable advantage in dealing with the problems before him, though his article takes cognizance of only a limited number of readings where these MSS furnish a superior text.

Lods, *Le livre d'Hénoch, Fragments grecs découverts à Akhmîm, publiés avec les variantes du texte Éthiopien, traduits et annotés* Paris, 1892. Lods' contribution is learned, scholarly, and judicious, but as he had the misfortune to base his work on the corrupt text published by Dillmann in 1851, a large portion of his conclusions was vitiated from the outset.

Charles, *The Book of Enoch*, pp. 318–370 Oxford, 1893. In this work I attempted an exhaustive comparison of the Greek and Ethiopic texts, and carried the criticism of the materials several stages beyond previous scholars in this department.

Swete, *The Old Testament in Greek, vol. III.*

Radermacher, *Das Buch Henoch, herausgegeben . von J. Flemming und L. Radermacher,* pp 18–60, 113–114. Leipzig, 1901. This text, on the whole, is well edited and forms an advance on preceding editions. But, unless I am greatly mistaken, Dr. Radermacher is not a Semitic scholar. This deficiency in his equipment proved a sore handicap in the task he undertook. How is a purely classical scholar to edit a Greek text which is Greek in vocabulary, but largely Semitic in idiom ? To show that our text is of this character it will be sufficient to adduce the following passages : 22^9 <u>οὖ ἡ πηγὴ τοῦ ὕδατος ἐν αὐτῷ</u> (בו .... אשר) = 'in which there is the spring of water'. 17^1 <u>ἐν ᾧ</u> οἱ ὄντες ἐκεῖ γίγνονται (שם .... אשר) = 'where the dwellers become'. Here, it is true, ἐκεῖ could be taken with οἱ ὄντες. 32^3 <u>οὖ</u> ἐσθίουσιν ἁγίου τοῦ καρποῦ αὐτοῦ (.... אשׁ פריו) = 'whose holy fruit they eat'. The editor's failure to recognize this idiom in 16^1 has led him to emend the text in such a way as to obliterate wholly its original form. The unemended text runs : ἀπὸ ἡμέρας .... θανάτου <u>ἀφ' ὧν</u> τὰ πνεύματα ἐκπορευόμενα ἐκ τῆς ψυχῆς τῆς σαρκὸς αὐτῶν.[1] This Semitic construction is supported by E though in a slightly corrupted form   Hence it must be preserved, though as I pointed out in 1893, there is according to E the loss of τῶν γιγάντων before ἀφ' ὧν   This very phrase, moreover, τῶν γιγάντων is found in G⁸, though this version inserts after it a gloss (?) containing the names of the three orders of giants as they are given in the Targum of Jonathan on Gen. 6¹⁻⁴.

The text and notes are accurately edited, but there are some errors.   In v. 6 Radermacher reads οἱ ἀμίαντοι as an emendation of the corrupt reading which he says is αμα | τοι and not αμαρτητοι, as Bouriant and Lods stated.   Bouriant and Lods were certainly wrong, and Dillmann's edition and mine, which were necessarily based on the work of these scholars, shared in their error.   The autotype reproduction of the text was not published till after the issue of these editions.   But if Bouriant and Lods deciphered the MS wrongly, so also has Radermacher.   It reads αμαρ|τοι. The ρ is partially obliterated, but it is unmistakable in the photographic reproduction of the MS.   Hence we might possibly emend αμαρτοι into ἀναμάρτητοι, but certainly not into ἀμίαντοι. Notwithstanding, this forms a serviceable edition of the Greek.

Another fragment is found in a Vatican Greek MS, No 1809, written in tachygraphic characters.   This was published by Mai, *Patrum Nova Bibliotheca*, tom. ii, and deciphered by Gildemeister in the *ZDMG.*, 1855, pp. 621–624, and studied afresh by von Gebhardt in Merx' *Archiv*, ii 243, 1872.   Besides the above, references to or Greek quotations explicitly or implicitly from Enoch are found in the *Ep of Barnabas* (see iv 3; xvi 4, 6), Justin Martyr, *Apol.* ii 5, Athenagoras in his Πρεσβεία, x; Clement Alex, *Eclogae Prophet* iii 456 (ed Dindorf), iii 474, *Strom* iii. 9, Origen, *Contra Celsum*, v. 52, 54, *In Ioannem*, vi. 25 (Lommatzsch, i. 241); *Clementine Homilies*, viii 12. Since these last afford but slight help in correcting the text, we shall do no more here than refer to Lawlor's article on this subject in the *Journal of Philology*, xxv. 164–225, 1897.

[1] I have given the idiom in Hebrew, though the original was in Aramaic.

§ 5. THE RELATIONS OF THE G^a AND G^g TO EACH OTHER
AND TO E (THE ETHIOPIC VERSION).

(a) *G^s more original than G^g.* These two fragments are closely
related and yet exhibit marks of independence.   They are
closely related, and probably go back to the same Greek translation of the Aramaic text, since they present in so many passages
identically the same text.   On the other hand G^s has in several
passages a different and undoubtedly better order of text.   Thus
G^a rightly places 7$^{3-5}$ of G^g (or rather its equivalent of 7$^{3-5}$)
after 8^3 of G^g.   For manifestly 7$^{1, 2}$ 8$^{1-3}$ precede 7$^{3-5}$.   Thus it
alone preserves the original order.   The angels went in to the
daughters of men, who bare to them three classes of giants
And the angels taught their women sorceries and incantations
(7$^{1, 2}$).   Then follows a detailed account of the art, which each
of the leading twenty angels taught mankind   And after this
the giants turned against men and began to devour their flesh
(G^a 8$^{1-3}$ G^g 8$^{1-3}$ 7$^{3-5}$).   It will be observed that in 8^3 G^g is
very defective compared with G^s in the list of the offices of the
various angels.   The additional elements in G^a here could not
have been written by a Greek, for in every instance the office
constitutes when translated into Aramaic a play on the name of
the angel who discharges the office.   Similarly in 6^7 the order
of the names of the angels is different and G^a is here preferable
to G^g E.

Again, 8^4 of G^a has preserved in all probability a more original
text than G^g E.   For it is natural that the substance of the
prayer of men as they were slain by the giants should be given
when it is first referred to in 8^4.   Here, indeed, G^a presents a
duplicate text, and both texts give the prayer in question.   G^g E,
on the other hand, do not give the words of the prayer till 9^3,
when the angels are presenting it before God.   G^a in Semitic
fashion gives the prayer *in extenso* here also.   Again the additional clauses (πορεύου κτλ.) in G^a 10$^{2, 4}$ belong most probably to
the original work but have been lost in G^g E, see note on 10^2
The same is true of the addition in G^a 9^9 with its peculiar diction,
as is clear from a comparison of 10$^{9, 15}$

Finally G⁸ preserves several right readings over against G⁸ E. Thus δῆσον in 10¹¹ where G⁸ E corruptly read δήλωσον, κατακριθῇ in 10¹⁴ where G⁸ E read κατακαυσθῇ. Cp. also 10⁷

(*b*) *Relations of G⁸ and Gᵍ to E* Even the most superficial study makes it clear that E and G⁸ are more closely related than E and G⁸ or G⁸ and G⁸. Indeed the evidence makes it clear that *E was translated from a MS. which was also the parent or ancestor of Gᵍ* This follows from the fact that *the same corruptions* appear in G⁸ E over against true readings in G⁸ where this exists. Thus they both give impossible readings in 10⁷ †ἐπάταξαν (G⁸ εἶπον); 10¹¹ δήλωσον (G⁸ δῆσον); 10¹⁴ †κατακαυσθῇ (G⁸ κατακριθῇ); 14⁸ †ἐθορύβαζον (a mistranslation of the Aramaic original) Gᵍ; 14¹⁸ †ορος (G⁸. E = ὁπός) (corrupt for ὅρασις?), 15⁹ †ἀνωτέρων (G⁸ ἀνθρώπων), 18⁵ †βαστάζοντας ἐν νεφέλῃ, 22⁴ †ἐποίησαν for ἐποίησησαν, 25⁵ †εἰς ζωήν, 28² †ἀπὸ τῶν σπερμάτων. In 9⁶ all the authorities are corrupt, but G⁸ E agree closely

On the other hand *E preserves certain original readings lost by Gᵍ and vice versa.* Thus E G⁸ rightly add αὐτοῖς after ἐγεννήθησαν in 6¹ and read βασιλεὺς τῶν βασιλευόντων in 9⁴ where G⁸ reads β. τῶν αἰώνων, and πάντων τὴν ἐξουσίαν in 9⁵ where G⁸ reads πᾶσαν τ. ἐξουσίαν, and attest ἐν ταῖς θηλείαις in 9⁸ and εἰς ἀλλήλους ἐξ αὐτῶν εἰς αὐτούς in 10⁹, which G⁸ in both cases omits Moreover, in 9¹¹ the corruption in E = τὰ εἰς αὐτούς (for ἐᾶς αὐτούς so G⁸) is easy of correction, whereas G⁸ offers the corrupt αιας. In the following passages *Gᵍ omits clauses and passages preserved by E.* Thus it omits by hmt clauses in 9¹, ⁵ 10¹⁶ 12⁸ 14⁸ 15² 18⁸, ⁵, ¹¹, and without any such intelligible ground 2³, all 3 and 4 except six words, words and clauses in 6¹, ⁵ 9⁸ 10¹⁰, ¹⁹, ²⁰ 14¹⁴ 15⁴, ⁸ 16¹ 19¹ 22⁵, ⁸ 24¹, ² 27¹. On the other hand *E omits words and clauses preserved by Gᵍ* in 1¹, ⁹ 5¹ ³ 10¹, ² 13⁷ 14²⁵ 15¹¹ 20⁸ 22², ⁵ 26¹.

Naturally G⁸ and E have severally developed corruptions which it is generally possible to emend in either case by the help of the other

In the following passages E presupposes ὁμοῦ μετά for ὁμοῦνται in 5⁶, τὰ μετὰ αὐτά for μέταλλα in 8¹; ἀνάγω for ἀναγνῶ in 13⁴, μυστηρίου for μυρίων in 18¹⁶; ὡς εἰρηναῖαι for εἰς σειρῆνας in 19², λαῷ for χάφ ın 20⁵; κοῖλοι for καλοί ın 22², ³ Corruptions of G⁸ will be found in the following passages. 1², ³, ⁵, ⁸, ⁹ 5¹ 6⁸ 9⁴, ⁶ 10¹⁹ 13¹ 14⁶, ⁸, ¹³, ¹⁵, ¹⁸, ¹⁹ 15⁸, ⁹ 16³ 17³, ⁷ 18⁴, ⁷, ¹¹ 21¹⁰ 22⁵, ⁶, ⁹ 23² 24³ 26² 31³.

(c) From the above facts it follows that *G⁹ and E spring from a common ancestor which we may designate x, and that this x and G⁸ proceed ultimately from the same original, the first Greek translation of the Book of Enoch* [1] Hence the genealogy of the above documents might be represented as follows .—

Original Greek Translation from the Semitic

§ 6. THE LATIN VERSION AND QUOTATIONS

The Latin Fragment, which constitutes a very imperfect reproduction of 106¹⁻¹⁸, was discovered in 1893 in the British Museum by Dr James, the present Provost of King's College, Cambridge, and most kindly placed at my service for publication in my edition of 1 *Enoch* in 1893 In the same year he issued it in the Cambridge Texts and Studies II, No 3, *Apocrypha Anecdota*, pp 146–150

The text has suffered from additions, omissions, and corruptions, and is very seldom a literal rendering of the original for many words together. Notwithstanding, it makes some contribution to the formation of a better text of 106

This MS. further may point to a Latin translation, or at least to a partially completed Latin translation of Enoch, for (1) occurring in the midst of original Latin treatises it appears to have been found in Latin by the collector or scribe of these

---

[1] This conclusion hardly seems adequate to explain all the phenomena mentioned on pp. xvii–xix. These postulate not only the occurrence of duplicate renderings in the Greek translation, but most probably also the occurrence of variants in the Hebrew original

treatises. (2) It has suffered much in the course of tradition, and may, therefore, go back to a date when the Book of Enoch was not reprobated generally, and when a Latin translation would have been acceptable. (3) It does not show signs of being an excerpt from a collection of excerpts, such as we find in the Greek fragment of Enoch, 89$^{42-49}$; but standing as it does without any introductory note or explanation, it looks as if it had been drawn directly from at least a larger Latin fragment of Enoch.

It is possible that the absurd statement with which the fragment opens—'[Cum esset Lamech annorum tricentorum quinquaginta] natus est ei filius'—originally referred to Methuselah, who was 355 years old when Noah was born according to the LXX Chronology. E speaks here of Methuselah taking a wife for his son Lamech and of a son being born to him.

Latin Quotations These have been collected most fully by Dr Lawlor in his article in the *Journal of Classical Philology*, xxv. 164–225

§ 7. THE ETHIOPIC VERSION

The Ethiopic Version has been preserved in twenty-nine MSS. of which fifteen are to be found in England, eight in France, four in Germany, one in Italy, and one in America Of these MSS. there are only three of which my knowledge is indirect and slight, but not yet too slight to enable me to estimate their value and their affinities with the other MSS. These MSS. are p and z, $_1z$. Of these z indeed was most kindly lent to the Bodleian Library for my use, but unhappily I was absent part of the time of its sojourn there, and whilst I was present the officials of the Bodleian did not notify me of its arrival. $_1z$ is of no account as it is merely an exact transcript of b. Next as regards p, this MS. formerly belonged to Lord Crawford, and was lent by him to the editor of the German edition of the Ethiopic text of Enoch which appeared in 1901, but since that date this MS. passed into the hands of a lady, who refused to lend it or any other MS. in her possession to the Bodleian

Library for the use of English editors. Of the remaining MSS I have directly examined twenty-two, i. e. g_1gmqtu, $abfhiklno$, and $suvwy_1a_1b$. Of these I photographed thirteen, i. e. g_1gmqtu, $fhiklno$. Five others, i. e. aby_1a_1b, I had no need to photograph, as the owners of $_1a_1b$ most kindly put these MSS at my service for the space of two years, while aby were always at hand for consultation in the Bodleian, to which y had been lent for that purpose by the Munich Library. Of the Abbadian MSS $rsvw$ I made collations on a number of test passages while at Abbadia These readings are appended in foot-notes on these MSS. in the following list, and are sufficient to show the affinities of these MSS amongst MSS. of the second class. Finally, as regards $cdex$ I have used Dillmann's collation of cde and a photograph of x which I procured from the Vatican. Thus for the construction of the present text I have had at my service photographs of fourteen MSS. g_1gmqtu, the constant use of the five MSS aby_1a_1b, Dillmann's collations of cde, Flemming's collation of p (which I have used sparingly)—in all twenty-three MSS. Four other MSS. $rsvw$ I have collated sufficiently to determine their character. Of the remaining MS. z (for $_1z$ may be ignored as a transcript of b) it is enough that we have Flemming's assurance that it is closely related to $abcde$

The division of Enoch into chapters was made apparently in the sixteenth century. The division into 108 chapters was made by Dillmann without MSS. authority, but as it has been followed by all subsequent scholars it is here adopted for the sake of convenience. The above division is indeed found in one MS., i e h, but this MS was unknown to Dillmann when he made his text. Moreover, the chapters in h vary frequently in length from those in Dillmann's text

§ 8 Ethiopic MSS.

The full list of the MSS. is as follows .—

a. Bodley, No. 4. Large quarto. 40 foll. 3 cols. 105 chapters Latter half of 18th cent. Enoch only.[1]

---

[1] Laurence issued a transcript of this MS in 1838.

b. Bodley, No 5   Large quarto.   141 foll.   3 cols.   18th cent (?).
Enoch (98 chapters), Job, Isaiah, 12 Minor Prophets, Proverbs,
Wisdom, Ecclesiastes, Canticles, Daniel.

c Frankfort MS.   Rupp. II. 1.   34 × 30 cm.   181 foll.   3 cols
18th cent   In several hands.   Enoch (98 chapters), Job,
Octateuch

d Curzon MS.   Quarto.   91 foll   2 cols   Enoch (102 chapters),
Job, Daniel, 4 Ezra, Sirach.

e Curzon MS   Small quarto   101 foll.   2 cols.   Marginal notes
from another hand   Enoch (98 chapters?), Samuel, Kings, and
Apocryphal book.

f. British Museum   Add. 24185 (Wright's Catalogue, 1877 No 5).
2 cols of 23 lines   19th cent   Enoch only   106 chapters

g Brit Mus Orient 485 (Wright, No 6).   190 foll   23 × 19 cm
2 cols. of 23 or 24 lines.   First half of 16th cent.   Enoch
(without division into chapters), Book of Jubilees. On foll 168ᵃ–
177ᵃ a duplicate of chapters 97⁶ᵇ–108¹⁰ is inserted from another
MS akin to *q*   See next MS

₁q. This MS consists only of 97⁶ᵇ–108¹⁰, and is found in foll 168ᵃ–
177ᵃ of *g*   It is inserted between the last word and the last
but one of 91⁵   It is written by the same scribe, but the text
though belonging to the best type differs from *g*

h Brit Mus Orient 484 (Wright, No 7)   3 cols of 50 or 51 lines
18th cent   Enoch (108 chapters), Octateuch, Jeremiah, Daniel,
Ezekiel, 1–4 Ezra, Tobit, Judith, Esther, Sirach

ι Brit Mus Orient. 486 (Wright, No 8)   3 cols of 29 lines
18th cent   Chapters 1–60¹³ᵃ missing   Nos of remaining
chapters erased   Enoch, Samuel, Kings, Jeremiah, Sirach

k Brit Mus Orient. 490 (Wright, No 12)   3 cols of 30 lines.
18th cent   Enoch (107 chapters), Job, Daniel, 1 Ezra, Isaiah,
12 Minor Prophets.

l Brit. Mus. 24990 (Wright, No. 13)   3 cols of 31 lines   18th cent
Enoch (divided into chapters, but no numbers supplied), Job,
Books ascribed to Solomon, Isaiah, 12 Minor Prophets, Daniel

m Brit Mus. Orient 491 (Wright No. 15)   219 foll.   40 × 32 cm.
3 cols of 27 lines   18th cent.   Enoch (without division into
chapters), Job, 12 Minor Prophets, Tobit, Judith, Esther,
Maccabees

n. Brit. Mus. Orient. 492 (Wright, No. 16) 3 cols. of 30 lines
18th cent. Enoch (87 chapters), Books ascribed to Solomon,
Jeremiah, 1 Ezra, Canticles, Sirach, Judith, Esther, Tobit

o. Brit. Mus. Orient. 499 (Wright, No. 23). 3 cols. of 31 lines.
18th cent. Sirach, Daniel, Enoch (106 chapters), Isaiah,
12 Minor Prophets

p. Formerly in the possession of Lord Crawford—now in the
Rylands Collection 67 foll 39 × 33 cm. 3 cols 17th cent
Enoch and other books.

q. Berlin MS. Peterm II. Nachtr. No. 29 (Dillmann's Cat. 1).
167 foll. 17 × 14 cm. 2 cols. of 13 to 14 lines 16th cent.
Without division into chapters. Enoch only.

r. Abbadianus 16 (vid. *Cat. raison. de mss. éthiop. appartenant
à A d'Abbadie*, Paris, 1859). 19th cent. Enoch (77 chapters)
and other works. This is a poor MS., but it exhibits a few
good readings.[1]

s Abbadianus 30. 18th cent Enoch and other works. This is
a poor MS, but has some notably good readings [1]

t Abbadianus 35. 40 × 35 cm 3 cols of 38 to 39 lines 17th cent.
There are many erasures and corrections and marginal notes
The latter belong to the later type of text, and are designated
as t^2 The division into chapters is marked in the margin on
the first few folios Enoch. Job, Samuel I and II, Kings,
Chronicles. Books ascribed to Solomon, Prophets, Sirach,
1–4 Ezra, Tobit, Judith Esther

u. Abbadianus 55. 191 foll 51 × 39 cm 3 cols. of 48 to 50 lines.
Possibly as early as the 15th cent Enoch (without division into
chapters) and other works. Text of Enoch much abbreviated
after chapter 83

v Abbadianus 99 70 foll 23 × 17 cm 2 cols 19th cent.
Copy made for M d'Abbadie from a MS. in high estimation
among the native scholars. This MS has all the bad characteristics of the later type of text, but has some excellent
readings Enoch only.[1]

w Abbadianus 197. 157 foll. 26 × 23 cm. 3 cols. of 29 lines.
17th or 18th cent. Enoch (98 chapters) and other works.[2]

---

[1] For further descriptions see my Ethiopic Text, Introd p xx
[2] See my Ethiopic Text, p xxi

x. Vatican MS 71 (cf. Mai, *Script. veterum nova collectio, Romae,*
   1831, T. v. 2, p 100) 27 foll. 3 cols. of 32 lines. 17th cent.
   Enoch only. 98 chapters.

y. Munich MS. 30 61 foll. 25 × 15 cm 2 cols of 20 to 28 lines.
   17th cent. Division into chapters only at the beginning
   Enoch only

z. Paris MS 50 (see Zotenberg's Cat.) 17th cent Enoch (division
   into chapters only at the beginning) and other works.

$_1z.$ Paris MS 49. 18th cent Copy of *b.*

$_1a$ Garrett MS. 17 × 12 cm 2 cols. of 22 lines. 19th or end of
   18th cent. Enoch only.

$_1b.$ Westenholz MS. 71 foll., of which first and last two are empty
   2 cols of 24 lines. 18th cent. 106 chapters Enoch only.

RELATIONS OF THE ETHIOPIC MSS.

(a) *Two forms of text,* $a, \beta,$ *of which* β *is late and secondary.*
There are two forms of the Ethiopic text. The first is represented
by $g\ _1g\ m\ q\ t\ u$ (and in some degree by *n*), which we shall henceforth designate by a, and the second, which owes its origin to
the labours of native scholars of the sixteenth and seventeenth
centuries, by all the remaining MSS., i. e. β The result of
these labours has been on the whole disastrous; for these scholars
had neither the knowledge of the subject-matter nor yet critical
materials to guide them as to the form of the text. Hence in
nearly every instance where they have departed from the original
unrevised text they have done so to the detriment of the book.
But it is not to be inferred from the above that a always
represents one type of text and β another type opposed to the
former, for the attestation of neither group is wholly uniform,
as each group is divided within itself. This statement holds true
in a much greater degree of a Indeed, the cases are compara-
tively few where a differs as a whole from β. Fifty readings
out of fifty-one which any editor must adopt will have the
support of one MS. singly as g, m, q, t, u, or of groups such as
$g\ m$, $g\ q$, $q\ t$, $g\ u$, $g\ m\ q$, $g\ m\ t$, $g\ m\ u$, &c., and the fifty-first time of

the undivided a.   For instances of the latter see 1^9 (note 23), 8^1 (note 34), 10^3 (note 36), 10^{13} (note 28), 10^{17} (note 7), 10^{22} (note 48), 15^5 (note 24).[1]   Moreover, when the attestation of a is divided, the individual or group of a attesting the right reading will often have the support of β or of groups within β.   The above facts serve to prove that *the recension was not the work of a few years, but was rather a process which culminated in such a text as we find in β, but particularly in the MS. v.*

(*b*) *β or groups in β sometimes preserve the original texts.*   Again it is noteworthy that in a limited number of cases β preserves the original text where a is secondary.[2]

(*c*) *The character and affinities of the chief MSS.*

g.   Of the MSS of a, g is decidedly the best all-round MS This does not mean that it has more unique and right readings than any other MS of the older type of text, but that when all the good points of the various MSS. are summed up, g comes out an easy first.   In the first thirty-two chapters g alone attests the right reading in 6^4 (note 37),[1] 17^3 (note 27), 18^7 (note 33), 21^5 (note 8), 28^3 (note 11).   In 89^{42} (note 4) it has only the support of n, the best of the second class MSS.   This MS has been made the basis, so far as any single MS. can, of my text It exhibits much strange orthography and bad grammar, and many corruptions.   Notwithstanding it is by far the best representative we have of the ancient text.   It was this MS together with m that I used when emending Dillmann's text for my translation and commentary which appeared in 1893.

$_1g$.   This MS, which has already been described, shows certain idiosyncrasies in 108^{9-15}, where it uses the first person over against the third in the other MSS.   Outside this chapter it agrees in turn with g, m, q, t, u or with combinations of these or with one or more of these combined with β, but it is most nearly related to g.

m.   This MS. is in some respects the weakest of the older

---

[1] The references enclosed in brackets are to the critical notes in my edition of the Ethiopic text, 1906.

[2] See further my Ethiopic Text, p. xxii.

group. It attaches itself so closely to g that we must assume its having come under its influence. This fact becomes of importance when we come to chapters 97^{6b}–108^{10}, where we have both g and $_1g$. In the vast majority of its unique readings $_1g$ is unaccompanied by m. Yet somehow m has been influenced by the readings both of g and $_1g$ In 10^2 (note 33)[1] and 17^4 (note 36) it alone attests the primitive text, in 7^3 (note 9) alone with f, and in 15^{11} (note 21) with $b\,x\,y$

q. Though teeming with every form of error incident to the transmission of a text in the way of additions, corruptions, and omissions, this MS. contains a larger number of unique original readings than any other used in our text. Thus it alone preserves the original text in 9^8 (note 21),[1] 10^{11} (note 16), 14^1 (note 39), 21^2 (note 24), 22^9 (note 25), 24^2 (note 41), 26^3 (note 33), 27^4 (note 47), 32^4 (note 31) It approximates more closely to $g\,_1g\,m$ than to $t\,u$.

t This is a most interesting MS.,[2] as it gives the older type of reading in the text and the later either over erasures or above the line or in the margin, with the rejected words in the text bracketed The corrector has not done his work thoroughly Accordingly many of the older readings remain untouched. The work of erasing has been so frequently perfunctory that it is generally possible to decipher the original text. Moreover, in some cases the correction represents a return to the older text Cf 1^6 (note 5)[1] As $g\,_1g\,m$ are closely connected, so are t and u. t is the least original of the MSS. of the first class Thus it is hardly ever right alone For one instance in the first thirty-two chapters see 10^{10} (note 3)

---

[1] The references enclosed in brackets are to the critical notes in my edition of the Ethiopic text, 1906

[2] This MS is notable also from the fact that for the Books of Samuel and Kings it alone exhibits a third type of text diverging from the two types of text in circulation in Abyssinia These were the first and primitive type of text and the later or Vulgate. Where this MS. diverges from these two classes of text it repeatedly agrees with the Hebrew (Massoretic) text Subsequently a corrector worked over this MS and erased readings belonging to the first class, as well as those peculiar to this MS which were derived from the Hebrew, and substituted readings of the second or Vulgate type.

u. This MS. would form a good third to *g* and *q* but that it is so imperfect after chapter 83, for nearly one-seventh of the entire book is omitted in the course of 83–108 These omissions are made in the most capricious way. Sometimes words, sometimes phrases, sometimes whole sentences and paragraphs are excised to the entire destruction of the sense. Notwithstanding as *u* is a valuable MS. I have most faithfully recorded all its omissions and changes. In chapters 1–32 it alone preserves the true text in 3 (note 23),[1] 4 (note 33), 21⁷ (note 40).

n. Of MSS. of the second class *n* is by far the best. Indeed, though in the main embodying the second type of text, it attests more unique and original readings in chapters 1–32 than *m* or *t* or *u*. Thus it stands alone in giving the original text in 9¹¹ (note 15),[1] 10³ (note 37), 10⁷ (note 21), 22⁹ (note 29) (?). Alone of MSS. of the second class it gives along with various MSS. of the first class the true text as in 1³ (note 18),[1] 14²¹ (note 10), 25⁷ (note 19), 89⁴² (note 4), &c. Thus *n* exhibits the characteristics of both types of text

§ 9. Editions of the Ethiopic Version.

Laurence, *Libri Enoch Versio Aethiopica* Oxoniae, 1838. This text was issued simply as a transcript of *a*, one of the MSS. brought to Europe by Bruce, the great Abyssinian traveller, in 1773. The transcription is not very accurate in the early chapters, though the errors are as a rule easy to correct. In chapters 5–10 there are ten, most of these have passed over into Dillmann's *Apparatus Criticus*, and from Dillmann's to Flemming's. As the text advances it becomes more accurate, so that I found its citation by Dillmann to be sufficiently trustworthy for use in the present edition

Dillmann, *Liber Henoch, Aethiopice, ad quinque codicum fidem editus, cum variis lectionibus* Lipsiae, 1851. This edition was based on five MSS., *a b c d e*. No further work on the Ethiopic

---

[1] The references enclosed in brackets are to the critical notes in my edition of the Ethiopic text, 1906.

text appeared till 1892, when Dillmann (*Sitzungsberichte d. kgl. Preuss. Akad. d. Wiss. zu Berlin,* 1892, li–liii, pp 1039–1054, 1079–1092) published some variants from three MSS. on the first thirty-two chapters of Enoch in connexion with his edition of the fragmentary Greek Version.

Charles *The Book of Enoch translated from Professor Dillmann's Ethiopic Text emended and revised in accordance with hitherto uncollated MSS. and with the Gizeh and other Greek and Latin Fragments.* Oxford, 1893. This translation was based on a drastic revision of Dillmann's text Ten new MSS., which belong to the British Museum, were used, three of them, $g_1 g m$, being of primary importance, and seven, $f h i k l n o$, being of only secondary Of these MSS. I collated $m, f h i k l n o$ on about three hundred passages; but $g_1 g$ I collated throughout, on the whole accurately, but defectively, as I now find, in a relatively small number of passages.

Flemming, *Das Buch Henoch · Aethiopischer Text herausgegeben von Joh Flemming* (= *Texte und Untersuchungen,* Neue Folge, VII. 1) Leipzig, 1902. Dr. Flemming's text is based on fifteen MSS., $a b c d c g_1 g m p q t u v w y$. Of these six belong to the first class, $g_1 g m q t u$, and the rest to the second class. This editor has been at no little pains in the preparation of his text. Thus he has himself collated $g m p q y$. His knowledge of $t u$ he owes to photographs taken by Professor Meyer in France, and of $v w$ to collations of the same scholar It was a fatal error on Dr. Flemming's part that he did not photograph $g m q$, or, at all events, revise his collations of them.

Flemming's text naturally constitutes an immeasurable advance on that of Dillmann, and a considerable advance on Dillmann's text as emended in my commentary in 1893. With the help of the three new first-class MSS., $q t u$, this editor was able to point out a few passages where I followed mere idiosyncrasies of g, and also some others where I preferred the less trustworthy of the two texts $g_1 g$ in chapters 97^{6b}–108^{10}.

On the whole, Flemming's text is good, as might be expected from so excellent an Ethiopic scholar, and several of his suggestions have been accepted in the present edition. On close examination, however, Flemming's edition proves unsatisfactory from its frequent inaccuracy in the collation of the MSS. generally, and its inadequate collation of the first-class MSS. In my review of this edition in the *American Journal of Theology*, pp. 689–703, 1903, I have summed up its serious shortcomings under the following heads . (i) *Inaccurate and defective collation of the MSS.* ; (ii) *The adoption of inferior readings into the text where the MSS. evidence for the true text is incontrovertible.* Flemming's treatment of the great Berlin MS q on chapters 10–32 will exemplify his method in dealing with the other MSS. In six passages in these chapters q *alone* amongst the Ethiopic MSS. preserves the true text of E, as is proved by G. Yet in two of them, 21^2 (note 24),[1] 24^2 (note 41), q is not collated at all, and in the remaining four, 10^{11} (note 16), 14^1 (note 39), 22^9 (note 25), 32^4 (note 31), the reading of q is relegated to the notes, and the wrong reading adopted. In 10^7 (note 21) q practically gives the original text (which is preserved by n alone), but the corrupt text is adopted by this editor. (iii) *Corrupt passages are left in the text without any attempt to emend them or even to call attention to their viciousness.* (iv) *Divergencies between G and E are left unexplained.* (v) *Practically no use is made of the Semitic background for purposes of emendation.* Notwithstanding the above shortcomings, Dr Flemming's edition is deserving of the gratitude of Orientalists, as it constitutes a vast advance on that of Dillmann, and forms on the whole a serviceable work for students generally.

Charles, *The Ethiopic Version of the Book of Enoch, edited from twenty-three MSS. together with the fragmentary Greek and Latin Versions*, 1906.

§ 10. TRANSLATIONS

LAURENCE, *The Book of Enoch, an apocryphal production, now first translated from an Ethiopic MS. in the Bodleian Library*, Oxford, 1821.

---

[1] The references enclosed in brackets are to the critical notes in my edition of the Ethiopic text, 1906.

HOFFMANN (A.G.), *Das Buch Henoch in vollstandiger Ubersetzung mit fortlaufendem Commentar, ausfuhrlicher Einleitung und erlauternden Excursen*, 2 vols., Jena, 1833–1838.

DILLMANN, *Das Buch Henoch ubersetzt und erklart*, Leipzig, 1853. (See below under § 11, Critical Inquiries.)

SCHODDE, *The Book of Enoch translated with Introduction and Notes*, Andover, 1882.

CHARLES, *The Book of Enoch translated from Dillmann's Ethiopic Text, emended and revised in accordance with hitherto uncollated Ethiopic MSS. and with the Gizeh and other Greek and Latin Fragments,* Oxford, 1893

BEER, in Kautzsch's *Die Apokryphen und Pseudepigraphen des Alten Testaments*, Tubingen, 1900, ii. 236–310.

FLEMMING and RADERMACHER, *Das Buch Henoch herausgegeben im Auftrage der Kirchenvater-Commission der Koniglich Preussischen Akademie der Wissenschaften*, Leipzig, 1901.

MARTIN, *Le Livre d'Hénoch traduit sur le texte éthiopien*, Paris, 1906.

§ 11. CRITICAL INQUIRIES.

I had intended to give a critical history of all the work done on Enoch since 1850, and had collected almost sufficient materials for that purpose, when I found that my space would not permit of such a large addition to the book I shall therefore content myself with enumerating these inquiries and adding occasional notes

LUCKE, *Einleitung in die Offenbarung des Johannes* (2nd ed. 1852), pp 89 144 · 1071–1073. Lucke regards the book as consisting of two parts, the first embraces 1–35 71–105, written at the beginning of the Maccabaean revolt (p. 142), or, according to his later view, in the reign of J Hyrcanus (p. 1072); the second consists of the Parables and was written in the early years of Herod the Great (p. 142). 59^{7-14} and $64-67^1$ are interpolations of an uncertain date. In his first edition Lucke maintained the Christian authorship of the whole book

HOFMANN (J. Chr K), ' Ueber die Entstehungszeit des Buch Henoch' (*Zeitschr. D. M G* vi. 1852, pp. 87–91); *Schriftbeweis* (2nd ed.), i. 420–423 , *Die heil. Schrift N. T.'s zusammenhängend untersucht*, vii. 2, pp. 205 sqq. Hofmann regards Enoch as the work of a Christian writer of the second century A. D. His chief contribution to the understanding of Enoch is his correct interpretation of the seventy shepherds in 89–90.

DILLMANN, *Das Buch Henoch übersetzt und erklärt*, Leipzig, 1853. This edition at once displaced the two that preceded it, corrected their many ungrammatical renderings, and furnished an excellent translation of a text based on five MSS. So much, however, has been done in the criticism of Enoch since 1853 that the need of a new edition was imperatively needed alike in respect of the text, translation, interpretation, and criticism of the book As for the translation some of the renderings are grammatically impossible, and as regards his interpretation of the book, this has been pressed and strained in order to support the critical views which he then held but which he has long since abandoned. His critical views indeed have undergone many changes, but these undoubtedly are in the right direction.

In his edition of 1853 Dillmann insisted that the book proceeded from one author, with the exception of certain historical additions, 6–16 91^{12-17} 93 106–107, and of certain Noachic interpolations, 54^7-55^2 60 $65-69^{25}$, and also of 20 70 75^5 82^{9-20} 108

In 1860 in Herzog's *R.-E.*, ed. 1, vol. xii. 308–310, and in 1871 in Schenkel's *Bibel-Lex.* iii. 10–13, he recognized the separate authorship of 37–71 and asserted with Ewald its priority to the rest of the book

In 1883 in Herzog's *R.-E.*, ed. 2, vol. xii. 350–352 he abandons his original standpoint so far as to describe the Book of Enoch as a mere ' combination of the Enoch and Noah writings ', and concedes that 37–71 are later than the rest of the book. His final analysis is as follows. (1) 1–36 72–105, with the exception of certain interpolations, form the groundwork and were composed in the time of J. Hyrcanus (2) 37–71,

together probably with 17–19, were written at latest before 64 B. C
(3) The Noachic fragments 6^{3-8} 8^{1-3} 9^7 $10^{1, 11}$ 20 $39^{1, 2 a}$ 54^7–55^2
60 65–69^{25} 106–107. (4) 108.

See also *Zeitschr. D. M. G*, 1861, pp 126–131, for a criticism
by Dillmann of Volkmar's theory.

JELLINEK, *Zeitschr. D. M G.*, 1853, p. 249.

GILDEMEISTER, *Zeitschr. D. M. G.*, 1855, pp. 621–624, gives
the Greek fragment of Enoch from the Codex Vaticanus (Cod. Gr.
1809) and discusses the relative merits of the Greek and Ethiopic
versions.

EWALD, *Abhandlung uber des athiopischen Buches Henokh
Entstehung, Sinn und Zusammensetzung,* 1855 ; *History of Israel,*
v. 345–349 (translated from the German). It was the merit of
Ewald first to discern that Enoch was composed of several
originally independent books. It is, in fact, as he declares,
'the precipitate of a literature once very active which revolved
. . . round Enoch' (*Hist.* v. 349). Though this view was at
once assailed by Kostlin and nearly every other critic since, its
truth can no longer be denied, and Holtzmann's declaration that
'the so-called groundwork (i. e. 1–37 72–105) is composed of
a whole series of sections, some of Pharisaic and others of Essene
origin' (*Theol. Literaturzeitung,* 1890, p. 497), was a notable sign
of the return to Ewald's view. But though future criticism
must confirm Ewald's general judgement of the book, it will
just as surely reject his detailed analysis of its parts. His
scheme is—

(1) Book I, 37–71 (with the exception of certain interpolations),
circ. 144 B C.

(2) Book II, 1–16 81^{1-4} 84 91–105, circ. 135 B. C

(3) Book III, 20–36 72–90 106–107, circ. 128 B. C.; 108
later

(4) Book IV, the Noah book 6^{3-8} 8^{1-3} 9^7 $10^{1-3, 11, 22 b}$ 17–19
54^7–55^2 $60^{1-10, 24, 25}$ 64–69^{16}. Somewhat later than the former.

(5) Finally the editing, compressing, and enlarging of the
former books into one vol.

WEISSE, *Die Evangelien-Frage*, 1856, pp 214–224. Weisse agrees with Hofmann and Philippi in maintaining a Christian authorship of the book, but his advocacy of this view springs from the dogmatic principle that the entire idea of Christianity was in its pure originality derived from the self-consciousness of Christ.

KOSTLIN, ' Ueber die Entstehung des Buchs Henoch' (*Theol. Jahrb*, 1856, pp. 240–279, 370–386). Kostlin, as we have already remarked, contended against Ewald that the book of Enoch did not arise through the editing of independent works, but that by far the larger part of Enoch was the work of one author which through subsequent accretions became the present book. Though this view must be speedily abandoned, it must be confessed that the articles in which it is advocated are masterly performances, and possess a permanent value for the student of Enoch.

HILGENFELD, *Die judische Apokalyptik*, 1857, pp. 91–184. This work, like that of Köstlin, is of lasting worth and indispensable in the study of Enoch. We cannot, however, say so much for the conclusions arrived at. Many of these are, in fact, demonstrably wrong. According to Hilgenfeld, the groundwork consists of 1–16 20–36 72–105 written not later than 98 B. C. The later additions, i. e. 17–19 37–71 106–108 are the work of a Christian Gnostic about the time between Saturninus and Marcion. There are no Noachic interpolations.

There is no occasion to enter on the, for the most part, barren polemic between Hilgenfeld and Volkmar on the interpretation and date of Enoch, to which we owe the following writings of Hilgenfeld :—' Die judische Apokalyptik und die neuesten Forschungen' (*Zeitschr. f. wissenschaftl. Theol.*, iii. 1860, pp. 319–334) : ' Die Entstehungszeit des ursprunglichen Buchs Henoch' (*Z. f w. Theol*, iv. 1861, pp. 212–222) : ' Noch ein Wort über das Buch Henoch' (*Z. f. w. Theol.*, v 1862, pp. 216–221). In *Z. f. w. Theol.*, xv 1872, pp. 584–587, there is a rejoinder to Gebhardt (see below).

VOLKMAR, 'Beiträge zur Erklärung des Buches Henoch' (*Zeitschr. D. M G.*, xiv. 1860, pp. 87–134, 296) · 'Einige Bemerkungen über Apokalyptik' (*Zeitschr. f. w. Theol.*, iv. 1861, pp. 111–186) · 'Ueber die katholischen Briefe und Henoch' (iv. 1861, pp. 422–436 , v. 1862, pp. 46–75). As Hilgenfeld reckoned the periods of the Seventy Shepherds at seven years each, starting from 588 B C., and thus arrived at 98 B c, Volkmar started from the same anterior limit and reckoned each period at ten years. He thus found the entire rule of the shepherds to last 700 years or, through certain refinements, peculiarly Volkmarian, 720 years, and so arrived at the year of Barcochab's rebellion A D. 132—a year which has exercised a strange fascination over him and has been fatal to his reputation as a critic Thus Enoch was written 132 B. c. It was the work of a disciple of Akiba, and was designed to announce the final victory of Barcochab. Volkmar restated his theory in an essay: Eine Neutestamentliche Entdeckung, Zürich, 1862. His views have received more attention than they deserved through the rejoinders of Hilgenfeld, Dillmann, Langen, Sieffert, Gebhardt, Drummond, and Stanton.

GEIGER, *Judische Zeitschr. f. Wissensch. und Leben*, 1864–1865, pp. 196–204 This article deals mainly with the Calendar in Enoch. I have adopted one of his suggestions in 10^4.

LANGEN, *Das Judenthum in Palästina*, 1866, pp. 35–64. Langen regards Enoch as an early but highly composite work put together in its present form about 160 B c. (pp. 36, 64), and emanating from orthodox and patriotic Judaism as a protest against heathen religion and philosophy.

SIEFFERT, *De apocryphi libri Henochi origine et argumento*, Regimonti, 1867. Sieffert (p. 3) takes the groundwork to be 1–16 20–36 72–82 91–105, written by a Chasid in the age of Simon the Maccabee (pp. 11–13) 83–90 is a later addition about the year 108 B. c , and 17–19 37–71 106–108 are of Essene origin and composed before 64 B c. (pp. 27–29)

HOLTZMANN, *Geschichte des Volkes Israel*, 1867, vol. ii, pp. 201, 202.

HALÉVY, 'Recherches sur la langue de la rédaction primitive du livre d'Énoch' (*Journal Asiatique*, 1867, pp. 352–395). This most interesting essay sought to prove that Enoch was originally written in Hebrew. Unhappily the writer lost much time over passages which better MSS. show to be mere corruptions of the text. I have given several of the most probable of Halévy's suggestions in my Notes.

PHILIPPI, *Das Buch Henoch, sein Zeitalter und sein Verhältniss zum Judasbriefe,* Stuttg. 1868 This writer agrees with Hofmann, Weisse and Volkmar, in regarding the book as post-Christian. He thinks it was written in Greek by one author, a Christian, about A D. 100. It is notable that all the four writers, who assign a post-Christian origin to the book, have done so for dogmatic reasons.

WITTICHEN, *Die Idee des Menschen*, 1868, pp. 63–71, *Die Idee des Reiches Gottes,* 1872, pp. 118–133, 145–150. He sees the primitive work in 1–5 17–19 21^1–54^6 55^8–59^3 61–64 69^{26-29} 71^1–82^8 83^1–$91^{11, 18, 19}$ 92 94–105, while he discovers later additions in 6–16 93 91^{12-17} 106–107; still later additions in 20 54^7–55^2 60 65^1–69^{25} 70 82^{9-20}, and the latest in 108.[1]

GEBHARDT, 'Die 70 Hirten des Buches Henoch und ihre Deutungen mit besonderer Rucksicht auf die Barkochba-Hypothese' (Merx' *Archiv fur wissenschaftl Erforschung des A. T.* 1872, vol. ii. Heft ii. pp. 163–246). In this most trenchant criticism of the different explanations of chaps. 89–90 the writer carefully refrains from advancing any theory of his own. Nay more, he holds it impossible with our present text to arrive at a true interpretation of the author's meaning. But this writer's despair of a true interpretation is over-hasty and his condemnation of the text is unwarrantable.

ANGER, *Vorlesungen uber die Geschichte der Messianischen Idee*, 1873, pp. 83–84

VERNES, *Histoire des Idées Messianiques*, 1874, pp. 66–117, 264–271. These sections are composed mainly of a French

[1] The above details regarding Wittichen are due to Martin.

translation of Dillmann's German version. Vernes thinks that the earliest part of Enoch was written in Aramaic by a contemporary of J Hyrcanus ; and that the Parables spring from a Christian and Gnostic circle about the close of the first century A D. (pp 264 sqq.)

KUENEN, *Religion of Israel*, 1874–1875, iii. 265, 266 (translated from the Dutch Edition of 1869-70)

TIDEMAN, 'De Apocalypse van Henoch en het Essenisme' (*Theol. Tijdschrift*, 1875, pp. 261–296). Tideman regards the book as proceeding from different authors living at different periods. His analysis is as follows.—

(1) The oldest book 1–16 20–36 72–82 93 91$^{12-19}$ 92 94–105, from the hand of a Pharisee in the early times of the Maccabees 153-135 B C.

(2) The second book . 83–91^{10}, from an Essene writer who added it to the older book 134–106 B.C.

(3) The Apocalypse of Noah : 17–19 41$^{3-9}$ 43$^{1, 2}$ 44 54$^{.7}$–55^{2} 59–60 65–69^{25} 70 106–107, from an author versed in Jewish Gnosticism A.D 80

(4) The Parables (with the exception of the Noachic interpolations), written by a Christian in the days of Domitian or Trajan, when the Christians were persecuted and the Romans were at war with the Parthians, A.D. 90-100

(5) Chapter 108 by the final editor of the book, a Christian Gnostic of the type of Saturninus, A D. 125.

Christian interpolations are found in 90^{88} 105

Tideman thinks that we have in the Parables a combination of the thought that the Messiah is to be a man in the clouds (Daniel), and of the doctrine that he was to proceed from the community, 1 En 90$^{37, 38}$

DRUMMOND, *The Jewish Messiah*, 1877, pp. 17–73. Drummond gives a concise and able review of the work of former critics on Enoch. He rightly approves and further enforces Hofmann's interpretation of the seventy shepherds as angels. He agrees with the limits assigned by Tideman to the oldest book in Enoch, but concludes, against Hilgenfeld and Tide-man, that the Parables could not *entirely* be the work of a Christian; for if they were such, there would undoubtedly have been some reference to the crucified and risen Christ such as we find in Test. Levi 4[1,4]. The difficulties of the case are met, he believes, by supposing that a Christian Apocalypse has been worked into the tissue of an earlier Jewish production, and that all the Messiah passages are due to the former. His chief arguments are : (i) the title 'son of a woman' could not have been applied by a pre-Christian Jew to a supernatural Messiah ; (ii) a consistent text is possible by an omission of the Messiah passages, a text also which answers to the title placed at the beginning of each Parable, (iii) the closing chap. 71 confirms this view where in the description of a Theophany there is no mention of the Messiah and the title 'Son of Man' is applied to Enoch, (iv) the Book of Jubilees, though using Enoch extensively, does not cite the Messiah passages

Of these arguments the only one that can still be maintained with any show of reason is (ii), and this in itself will have no weight if we bear in mind the want of logical sequence and the frequent redundancy characteristic of Semitic writings generally and of Jewish apocalypses in particular Moreover, in no instance that I am aware of does any superscription in Enoch give an exact account of the chapters it introduces.

HAUSRATH, *Neutestamentliche Zeitgeschichte*, Erster Theil, 3rd ed, 1879, pp. 185–189, 191–193. The oldest book, 1–36 72–105, is referred to the time of J. Hyrcanus. The Parables, with the exception of the Noachic interpolations, were probably composed in the reign of Herod the Great. Hausrath thinks that the Messiah-passages may have won somewhat of a Christian colouring in the process of translation from Hebrew to Greek and Greek to Ethiopic by Christian hands.

LIPSIUS, art. 'Enoch' in Smith and Wace's *Dictionary of Christian Biography*, vol. ii, 1880, pp. 124–128. (1) The oldest book dealt with the Heavenly Luminaries, 17–19 21–36 72–79 82, in which Enoch appears as a teacher of such higher wisdom. This, however, is an unhappy synthesis, for the demonic doctrine of 17–19 connects it peculiarly with the Noachic interpolations, while its Greek colouring as strongly disconnects it with the ultra-Jewish 72–79 82. (2) In the second book, 1–16 80–81 83–105, which never existed independently but only as an expansion of the former, Enoch is represented as a preacher of righteousness. This book belongs to the reign of J. Hyrcanus. (3) The Parables, written under the later Maccabeans or the Herods (4) Noachic interpolations 54^{7}–55^{2} 60^{7-25} 65–68^{1} and probably $10^{1-3,\ 22b}$ 41^{2-9} 43–44 59 $69^{2,\ 8}$ 106–107 Other interpolations and additions 20 108.

This article forms a valuable contribution to the criticism of Enoch, and I welcome it all the more gladly as I arrived at many of its results before I was acquainted with it.

WESTCOTT, *Introduction to the study of the Gospels*, 1881, 6th ed, pp 99–109, *Gospel of St John*, 1882, p 34. In the former work this writer recognizes the probability of the different sections of the book as proceeding from different authors, yet he essays the impossible task of moulding their conflicting features into one consistent whole. In the latter work Dr Westcott asserts that the title in Enoch is ' A Son of Man ', but wrongly, for it is as definitely ' The Son of Man ' as the language and sense can make it. The being so named, further, is superhuman, and not merely human as Dr. Westcott states.

SCHODDE *The Book of Enoch translated with Introduction and Notes*, Andover, 1882. The introduction is interesting and the account of the bibliography though incomplete is helpful, but the arrangement of the text and notes in this edition is most inconvenient. The translation is made from Dillmann's Ethiopic text. But the work as a whole is unsatisfactory All Dillmann's slips and inaccuracies, with one or two exceptions, are perpetuated. Dr Schodde's analysis of 2 Enoch is :—

i. The groundwork 1–36 72–105, before the death of Judas Maccabaeus.

ii. The Parables 37–71, between 37–4 B.C.

iii Noachic interpolations 54^7–55^2 60 65–69^{25} 106–107.

He thinks it probable that 20 70 75^5 82^{9-20} 93^{11-14} are also interpolations.

WIESELER, 'Ueber die Form des jüdischen Jahres um die Zeit Jesu' (*Beiträge zur richtigen Würdigung der Evangelien*, 1869) We have here an interesting and valuable discussion of the Calendar in Enoch.

'Zur Abfassungszeit des Buchs Henoch' (*Zeitschr. D. M. G.*, 1882, pp. 185–193) Wieseler assigns the Parables no less than the rest of the book to the reign of J. Hyrcanus.

SCHÜRER, *1 History of the Jewish People in the Time of Jesus Christ* (translated from the second and Revised Edition of the German), vol. iii, div. ii, pp. 54–73, 1886. This is a most judicious statement of the results already attained by criticism. In accordance with these Schürer divides the book into three parts: (1) 'the original writing' 1–36 72–105, written in the reign of J. Hyrcanus, (2) the Parables, written in the time of Herod the Great; (3) the Noachian Fragments, 54^7–55^2 60 65–69^{25}, and probably 106–107. 108 is a later addition. He is careful, however, to remind us that the 'original writing is composed of very heterogeneous elements'. While he rightly dismisses as idle all attempts to introduce chronological exactness into the interpretation of the Seventy Shepherds, he thinks there can be no doubt as to where the different periods are intended to begin and end. It was Schürer who was the first to recognize the validity of Hoffmann's interpretation of the Shepherds and to give it currency. This article concludes with a very full list of patristic passages referring to Enoch and with an excellent bibliography of the literature In his third edition, 1898, pp. 192–209, he maintains the same position.

STANTON, *The Jewish and the Christian Messiah*, 1886, pp.

44–64, 139–140, 142, 153, 170–175, 286, 305, 311–315, 332, 335, 347.

The analysis of the book given in Schurer is adopted also here. Dr. Stanton agrees likewise with the generality of critics in assigning the first part, i.e 1–36 72–105, to the reign of J Hyrcanus. The Parables must, he thinks, be ascribed to a Jewish Christian or to a Jew influenced by Christian ideas. The fragments of a lost Apocalypse of Noah are probably $39^{1, 2a}$ 54^{7}–55^{2} 60 65–69^{25}

REUSS, *Gesch. der heil. Schriften des A T's*, §§ 498–500.

HOLTZMANN, *Einleitung in das N. T.*, 1886, 109, 110.

FRIEDLIEB, *Das Leben Jesu Christi des Erlosers*, 1887, pp. 126–151. Friedlieb divides the book thus: 1–36 37–64 70–71 72–82, the original work by one and the same author, composed between 141 and 130 B.C. 65–69 are by a second writer; 83–105 by a third, writing between 129 and 125 B C. The two appendices 106–107 and 108 are perhaps by the final editor [1]

HOLTZMANN (OSKAR), in Stade's *Geschichte des Volkes Israel*, ii 1888, pp. 416–429, and 483–490 He resumes, but with more success, the principle laid down by Ewald. He sees in 1 Enoch a whole literature made up of independent fragments which, however, form a complete whole though often mutilated in their existing condition. He distinguishes thus not merely the five constituent books, but even their subdivisions as sections of varied origin. In Book I, for instance, he reckons four sections (i) 1–5, Introduction, of the date of the early Maccabees. (ii) 6–11, Two narratives, of the same date (iii) 12–16 (iv) 17–36, Enoch's journey to the hidden places of the earth. This last section contains various accounts dealing with the same theme, and some fragments about the revolution of the stars are interpolated in it. He separates also the Apocalypse of Weeks in Book V. It is earlier than 20 B.C. The rest of that book goes back to the time of the struggle between the Pharisees on one side and the Sadducees and Hasmonaeans on the other,

---

[1] The above details are due to Martin.

with some Christian insertions at the end. The whole work ends with an appendix containing a Noachic fragment 106–107, and a later addition 108. These views on the whole were on the right lines, but did not meet with immediate acceptance.[1]

PFLEIDERER, *Das Urchristenthum*, 1887, pp 310–318. This writer accepts the traditional view with regard to the groundwork, and approves of Drummond's theory as to the origin of the Messiah-passages in the Parables. This theory he seeks further to substantiate, but without success.

BALDENSPERGER, *Das Selbstbewusstsein Jesu*, 1888, pp. 7–16 This writer assents to the traditional view and date of the groundwork. The Parables he assigns to the years immediately following on the death of Herod the Great. He believes there are many references to the Romans in the Parables, and that Augustus and Herod are designed under the phrase ' the kings and the mighty '.

SALMON, *Introduction to the N. T.*, 4th ed., 1889, pp. 527, 528.

PETER, *Le Livre d'Hénoch. Ses Idées Messianiques et son Eschatologie*, Genève, 1890 This is an interesting little treatise, but by no means free from blemishes. The Parables are pre-Christian, and the traditional view and date of the groundwork are here reproduced.

DEANE, *The Pseudepigrapha*, 1891, pp 49–94 This is a praiseworthy attempt to popularize a knowledge of these works. The writer assigns the traditional groundwork to the years 153–130 B C., and regards the Parables as written a few years later. Many of this writer's statements on the theology and influence of 1 Enoch are to be taken with extreme caution.

THOMSON, *Books that influenced our Lord and His Apostles*, 1891, pp 95, 103, 108, 225–248, 389–411. Mr. Thomson's analysis is as follows —

---

[1] The above details are due to Martin.

(1) Book of the Parables and the Book of the Weeks, 37–71 91^{12}–99, written about the year 210 B.C.

(2) Noachic Fragments, 60 65–69^{24}.

(3) Book of the Fall of the Angels and of the Luminaries, 1–36 72–91^{11} 100–107, written not later than 160 B C.

(4) 108.

Mr. Thomson's chief ground for regarding 37–71 as the oldest Section is derived from the presence of the Noachic interpolations. As he believes that these interpolations are confined to this Section, he infers that 37–71 is therefore the oldest and that 1–36 72–91 were not yet in existence. Even if Mr. Thomson were right in his facts, quite another conclusion would be possible. But this writer's premises are without foundation. Interpolations are found in every section in Enoch and numerously in the sections which Mr. Thomson regards as free from them. It cannot be said that this book contributes much to the better interpretation of Enoch, and this is all the more to be deplored as its author obviously possesses abundant ability for the task.

CHEYNE, *Origin of the Psalter*, 1891, pp. 22, 375, 412–414, 423–424, 448–449, and about fifty references besides. 'Possible Zoroastrian Influences on the Religion of Israel,' *Expository Times*, 1891, p. 207 Dr. Cheyne accepts provisionally the traditional division of Enoch into the groundwork, Parables and Noachic fragments, and regards the Parables as pre-Christian He deals mainly with the dogmatic teaching of the book and its place in the development of Jewish religious thought, and points to the Essene and Zoroastrian elements which have found a place in it.

DE FAYE, *Les Apocalypses juives*, Paris, 1892, pp. 28–33, 205–216.

LODS, *Le Livre d'Hénoch*, 1892, reckons in the original work 1–16 (with certain Noachic interpolations in 6–8) 21 36 72–82 90$^{1-11}$ 94–105.[1]

---

[1] The above details are due to Martin

CHARLES. *The Book of Enoch, translated from Professor Dillmann's Ethiopic Text, emended and revised in accordance with hitherto uncollated Ethiopic MSS. and with the Gizeh and other Greek and Latin Fragments,* Oxford, 1893.

CLEMEN, *Theologische Studien und Kritiken,* 1898, pp. 211–227, 'Die Zusammensetzung des Buches Henoch.' He emphasizes the varied traditions represented by the different portions of the book. These twelve traditions the 'author of the book' either found committed to writing or he collected them from oral transmission. The earliest go back to 167 B C , the latest to 64 B.C. These traditions are (1) 1–5, (2) 6–11, (3) 12–16, (4) 17–19, (5) 20 (?)–36, (6) 37–69, with some interpolations, (7) 70–71, (8) 72^1–$91^{10, 18}$ et sqq. (?), (9) 92 93 91^{12-17} 94–103, (10) 106–107, (11) 108, (12) the Noachic fragments 54^7–55^2 60 65^1–69^{25}. The author found already existing in a written form (9) (11) (12), probably (3), and perhaps even (6). Clemen lays great stress on the changes of person as betraying the composite character of the work [1]

BEER, 'Das Buch Henoch' (*Die Apokryphen und Pseudepigraphen des A T., Kautzsch,* vol. II, 1900, pp. 224–230). Beer thus divides the work :—

(1) 1–5, a work complete in itself and yet forming an introduction in the form of an apologia to the whole book.

(2) 6–11 comprise two different traditions interwoven. The burden of the former is the revelation of mysteries, and the judgement by the Flood: that of the latter is the fall of the angels, their punishment, and the wickedness of the giants. The blending together of the two traditions was made easier by the fact that they both alike dealt with the leading astray of the angels by the daughters of men. This fragment, thus surviving in two mutilated groups, has been drawn from a larger cycle of legends which grew up around the name of Noah. The two groups might be distinguished as follows (a) 6^{2b-8} 7^{3-6} 8^4 $9^{1-5, 9-11}$ 10^4–11^2 and (b) 7^{1b} 8^{1-3} 9^{6-8} 10^{1-3}.

---

[1] The above details are due to Martin.

(3) 12–16 These chapters had originally nothing to do with 6–11. They spring from the Enoch cycle, whereas 6–11 spring from the Noah cycle

(4) 17–36 likewise belong to the Enoch cycle, and contain two accounts which narrate the same journey in different words, 17–19 and 20–36. Possibly, however, 20 was composed after the other chapters. This Section cannot be shown to depend directly on 12–16 or 6–11.

(5) 37–71. This Book, dealing with the Messiah, is nearer to the ruling idea of chapter 1, which centres round the Messianic account of the last times. The Book is not a single homogeneous work in its present form, as it contains Noachic interpolations and other distinct documents. Thus in 40^2 we have 'the angel who went with me', while in 40^8 we have 'the angel of peace'; the Messiah bears the name of the 'Elect One' in 45 and 49, but that of 'the Son of Man' in 46 and 48^{2-7}. Parallel with the use of these names is the title of the two angels who are commissioned to interpret the visions. For instance, the 'angel who went with me' explains that of the Son of Man, 46^2, the 'angel of peace' explains that of the Elect One, 52^5. Beer questions whether these two names and two angels do not suggest two different texts in the Parables. There is the same doubt as to the authenticity of the passages dealing with physical phenomena which are inserted in this Section. These chapters, though like 17–36 betraying a duplicate origin, are not the continuation of those chapters. 37 begins anew and introduces Enoch as a hitherto unknown person. The physical secrets are common to 33–36 and the Parables, but the title 'Lord of Spirits' is peculiar to the latter. 6–11 do not even mention Enoch's name, while 1–5 and 12–16 recount not visions, but an actual journey of Enoch. These chapters therefore are all of distinct origin from 37–71

(6) 70 and 71 belong to an independent tradition, for in 71^{14} Enoch is identified with the Son of Man. This Section is, however, connected with the Parables, as the Messiah is here also, in 70^1, called the Son of Man, but not with 12–16, as 71

would be merely a useless repetition of 14—a description of God's habitation.

(7) 72-82. Chapter 80 gives us the somewhat artificial connexion by which 'the writer' has joined on this treatise on the stars to a book on the Messianic kingdom. the fair order described in 72-82 will change in the days of the sinners. This Section has not come down to us in its original condition. 76-77 deal with the winds, the points of the compass, &c, though these subjects have not been promised in 72^4. Moreover, 79^{1-6} and 82^{1-6} each form a conclusion. 82^{9-20} is incomplete, and ought to come before 79 Despite the partial resemblance in the subject, especially in regard to the second source of 17-36 ($=21$-36), 72-82 is not, at least in its original form, by the same author as 21-36 For instance, the function of Uriel in 72^1 agrees with that in 20^2 21^5; but Uriel writes for Enoch, 33^4, while Enoch writes himself, 74^2.

(8) 83-108. This part is quite in harmony with the subject proposed in 1^1. Beer reckons in this Section six fragments more or less distinct. first, 83-84; second, 85-90; third, the Apocalypse of Weeks, 92 93^{1-14} 91^{12-17}; fourth, the admonitions, $91^{1-11,\ 17,\ 18}$ 94-105; fifth, 106-107; sixth, 108. The Messiah occurs in $90^{37,\ 38}$, but not at all in 1-36 or 72-82. This Messiah, sprung from Abraham, is not the Messiah of the Parables, who is a heavenly, pre-existent being.

Finally, Beer thus assigns the various passages to their different sources A, from the Enoch cycle, (1) 1-5, (2) 12-16, (3) 17-19 (4) 20-26, (5) 37-69, (6) 70-71, (7) 72-82, (8) 83-84, (9) 85-90, (10) 92 93^{1-14} 91^{12-17}, (11) 91^{1-11} 94-105, (12) 108 Of these (5) and (7) may be subdivided, as above. B, from the Noah cycle, (13) 6-11, (14) $39^{1,\ 2a}$ 54^7-55^2 60 65-69^{25}, (15) 106 107.

Martin, *Le Livre d'Hénoch traduit sur le texte éthiopien*, 1906. This scholar (see pp lxxxviii-xcvii) designates the Book of Enoch as a mosaic composed of nine or ten distinct works or traditions emanating from the Enoch cycle. These are 1° 1-5 ; 2° 6-16 20-36, before 166 B.C.; 3° 17-19, before 166 B.C., 4° 37-69, 95-78 B C., 5° 70-71; 6° 72-82, before 185 B.C.;

7° 83–90, 166–161 B. C.; 8° 91–105, 95–78 B C , 9° 93 91^{12-17},
before 170 A D.; 10° 108, before 64 B. C.

A certain number of strange elements have been incorporated
into most of the above works. 1° various fragments, 41^{3-8} 43^{1-2}
44 59 $60^{7-10, \, 11-23, \, 24, \, 25}$ 69^{23} 77 81 89^{31b} 90^{15} 91^{11} 105^{2a}, perhaps
also 52^4 68^1—from the Enoch cycle (with the exception of 105^{2a}) :
2° fragments from the Noah cycle, 10^{1-3} 39^{1-2a} 54^7-55^2 60^{1-0}
65–69^{25} 106 sq.

There are many ingenious suggestions in Professor Martin's
Commentary, some of which I have adopted with due recognition.

§ 12. THE DIFFERENT ELEMENTS IN THE BOOK OF ENOCH.

The Book of Enoch was intended by its final editor to consist
of five Sections, like the Pentateuch, the Psalms, Proverbs,
Sirach, and many other Jewish works (see p. lxiv). These consist
of 1–36 37–71 72–82 83–90 91–108. Behind this apparently
artificial division lies a real difference as to authorship, system
of thought, and date   When I edited my first edition of Enoch
in 1893 it was necessary for me to go at great length into the
differentiae marking these divisions, since the accepted criticism
of the day regarded 1–36 72–104 as forming the groundwork and
proceeding from one and the same author. Since that date this
impossible hypothesis has vanished from the field of criticism
My task here is, therefore, no longer of a polemical nature, but
simply to determine so far as possible the extent, character, and
date of the various independent writings embodied in this work.
The various Sections will now be dealt with in the order of their
occurrence.

Fragments of the Book of Noah   But before we enter on the
criticism of the various elements in the book, we should observe
first of all that it contains fragments of an earlier work—entitled
the Book of Noah. Of the existence of this book we know
independently from the Book of Jubilees, 10^{13} 21^{10}, and later
sources. But even if we had possessed no independent reference
to such a book, we could have had no doubt as to its existence ,
for the contents of chapters 60 65–69^{25} prove conclusively that

they are from this source ; also 106–107. Furthermore, 6–11 [1]
are derived from the same work. These latter chapters never
refer to Enoch, but to Noah. Moreover, where the author of
Jubilees in 7^{20-25} describes the laws laid down by Noah for his
children, and Noah's accounts of the evils that had brought the
Flood upon the earth, he borrows not only the ideas, but at
times the very phraseology of these chapters Finally, we may
observe that chapters 88–89[1] presuppose a minute acquaintance
with chapter 10. 54^7–55^2 probably belong to the same source.
The Noachic fragments preserved in this book are thus: 6–11 54-55[2]
60 65–69[25] 106–107.

These facts throw some light on the strange vicissitudes to
which even the traditional legends were subject. Thus it would
appear that the Noah saga is older than the Enoch, and that
the latter was built up on the débris of the former.

Having now disposed of the earlier materials utilized by the
writers of the different Sections of Enoch, we shall now proceed
to deal with the five Sections or Books in the order of their
occurrence

SECTION I. 1–36 We have already seen that 6–11 belonged
originally to the Book of Noah ; 12–16, on the other hand, are
a vision or visions of Enoch in which he intercedes on behalf of
Azazel and the Watchers. These visions are preserved in a
fragmentary form, and not in their original order—a fact which
is most probably due to the editor of the whole work, since the
same dislocation of the text recurs in 78–80 and 91–93. The
original order of 12–16 was, so far as the present fragmentary
text goes : 14^1 . . . 13^{1-2} 13^3 12^3 13^{4-10} 14^2–16^2 12^{4-6} ‖ 16^{3-4}.
12^{1-2} is an editorial introduction.

This portion of our text began obviously with the words . 14^1
‘ The book of the words of righteousness, and of the reprimand

---

[1] Even these chapters are composite, for they are a conflation of two distinct
cycles of myths relating respectively to Semjaza and Azazel (see later under
the text, pp 13–14 notes), and this conflation was anterior to the date of the
Dream Visions, which presuppose the existence of these chapters in their present
form, or at all events of chapter 10

of the eternal Watchers.' Then came a request on the part of Azazel that Enoch should intercede for him   This request was acceded to on the part of Enoch, who in a vision received God's judgement on Azazel.   But both the request and the vision are lost   In 13¹⁻², however, the answer to Azazel's request is given in the divine doom announced by Enoch. Next Enoch is besought by the Watchers to intercede for them, 13³ 12³ 13⁴⁻⁷.   Thereupon Enoch has a vision regarding them, 13⁸, which he recounts to them, 13⁹⁻¹⁰ 14²⁻16²   Finally the Section closes with the message of doom, which Enoch is bidden to take to the Watchers, 16³⁻⁴   Of 16³⁻⁴ there is a doublet, 12⁴⁻⁶, which is more original than 16³⁻⁴.

17–19 stand by themselves, exhibiting, as they do, strong traces of Greek influences in their description of the underworld, and yet showing a close affinity to 20–36, since 18⁶⁻⁹ is a doublet of 24¹⁻³, 18¹¹ of 21⁷⁻¹⁰, 18¹²⁻¹⁶ of 21¹⁻⁶; 19², moreover, reflects the same view as 10¹⁴

20–36 come apparently from one and the same author. the functions ascribed to the archangels in 20 are tolerably borne out in 21–36 But since only four of the seven archangels mentioned in 20 are dealt with in 21–36, it is possible that a considerable passage was early lost

1–5 now call for treatment. These chapters are connected in phraseology with every section of the book save 72–82. (See p. 2 sq.) Thus the phrase 'he took up his parable', 1², suggests a connexion with 37–71, but this may be a mere coincidence, since the writer is here consciously influenced by Num. 23–24, where the phrase recurs several times. These chapters, moreover, appear to be of composite origin   2–5 seem to be a unity. But I see no satisfactory solution of the problem.

To sum up. 1–36 may be analysed into the following independent elements, 1–5 6–11 12–16 17–19 20–36   When the Book of Jubilees was written we shall see that 6–36 had already been put together.

SECTION II. 37–71. As all critics are now agreed that the Parables are distinct in origin from the rest of the book, I will simply refer the reader here to p 65 sq, for some of the grounds for this conclusion.

37–71 have been handed down in a fragmentary condition, and many of the problems they suggest can only be tentatively solved or merely stated.

37–71 consist in the main of three Parables, 38–44 45–57 58–69 These are introduced by 37 and concluded by 70, which describes Enoch's final translation in terms of that of Elijah. 71, which contains two visions received in his lifetime, belongs to one of the three Parables. We have already seen that 54^7–55^2 60 65–69^{25} are interpolated from the ancient Book of Noah

Behind the Parables there appear to be two sources, as Beer suggested though he did not work out his suggestion. The one was the 'Son of Man' source, in which the angelic interpreter was 'the angel who went with me' i e 40^{3-7} 46–48^7 52^{0-4} 61^{3-4} 62^2 63 69^{26-29} 70–71, and the other 'the Elect One' source, in which the angelic interpreter was 'the angel of peace': i e. 38–39 $40^{1-2, 8-10}$ $41^{1-2, 9}$ 45 48^{8-10} $50-52^{1-2, 5-9}$ $53-54^6$ $55'-57$ $61^{1-2, 5-13}$ 62^1 See pp. 64–65.

Section III. 72–82. Chapter 72 introduces a scientific treatise. In this treatise the writer attempts to bring the many utterances in the O.T. regarding physical phenomena into one system. The sole aim of his book is to give the laws of the heavenly bodies, and this object he pursues undeviatingly to 79^1, where it is said that his treatise is finished. Through all these chapters there is not a single ethical reference. The author's interest is scientific, and, like the author of Jubilees in 6^{32-36}, he upholds the accuracy of the sun and stars as dividers of time, 74^{12} And this order is inflexible and will not change till the new creation, 72^1. But in 80^{2-8} the interest is ethical and nothing else, and though it recognizes an order of nature, this order is more conspicuous in its breach than in its observance. 80^{2-8} appears then to be an addition. Nor, again, can 81 belong to 72–82 Whereas the blessing of 72–79 82 is for the man who knows the right reckoning of the years, the blessing of 81^4

is for the man ' who dies in righteousness'   81 is of the nature
of a mosaic and may come from the hand of the editor of the
complete Enoch.   Finally 82 stood originally before 79⁶ ' Such
is the . .   sketch of every luminary which Uriel .   . showed
unto me'.   After the long disquisition on the stars in 82, the
first words in 79¹ come in most appropriately : 'I have shown
thee everything, *and the law of all the stars of the heaven is
completed.'*   If 82 did not precede, these words could not be
justified.   For like dislocations cf. 12–16 91–93

Thus the original order of this Section was : 72–78 82 79.
For a full discussion of this Section, and its independence of 1–36
and the knowledge it implies of the Calendar, see pp. 147–150.

SECTION IV.   83–90.   This is the most complete and self-
consistent of all the Sections, and has suffered least from the
hand of the interpolator.   For passages that have suffered in
the course of transmission see 90¹⁹, which I have restored before
90¹⁴   also 89⁴⁸   In 90, vv 13–15 are a doublet of vv. 16–18.

83–90 is of different authorship from 6–36.   (1) The descent
of the Watchers in 86¹⁻³ differs from that in 6.   (2) The throne
of judgement is in Palestine in 90²⁰⁻²⁶, but in the N.W. in the
midst of the Seven Mountains in 18⁸ 25³.   (3) The scene of the
kingdom in 83–90 is the New Jerusalem set up by God Himself :
in 1–36 it is Jerusalem and the earth *unchanged* though purified,
10¹⁸, ²⁰   (4) 83–90 are only visions assigned to Enoch's earlier
and unwedded life · 6–36 are accounts of actual bodily translations and are assigned to his later life   If these two Sections
were from one and the same author, and that an ascetic, exactly
the converse would have been the case   For other grounds see
p. 179 sq.

Identity of authorship appears, therefore, to be impossible ;
but the similarities in phraseology and idea (see *loc. cit.*) prove
that one of the authors had the work of the other before him.
Of the two Sections there is no room for doubt that 83–90 is
the later.

SECTION V.   91–104.   *Critical Structure.*   This Section is in the main complete and self-consistent. It has, however, suffered at the hands of the editor of the entire work in the way of direct interpolation and of severe dislocations of the text. We have already seen his handiwork in the case of 12–16 and 78–82. The dislocations of the text are a remarkable feature in this Section, and I cannot see any adequate explanation. The editor incorporated an earlier work—the Apocalypse of Weeks—into his text, 93^{1-10} 91^{12-17}, the former part dealing with the first seven weeks of the world's history and the latter with the last three. Taken together these form an independent whole. But this is not all. Since this Section is of different authorship from the other Sections of the book it is obvious that it began originally with 92^1, 'Written by Enoch the scribe,' &c On 92 follows $91^{1-10, 18-19}$ as a natural sequel, where Enoch summons his children to receive his parting words. Then comes the Apocalypse of Weeks 93^{1-10} 91^{12-17}. Thus the original order of the book is 92 $91^{1-10, 18-19}$ 93^{1-10} 91^{12-17} 94

Relation to 6–36. At first sight the evidence for the unity of authorship of these two Sections is very great They have many phrases in common In each there are references to the law, to the eating of blood, and to the regularity of nature. There is no hint of a Messiah in either. There are other resemblances, but they are seeming and not real On the other hand, in 6–36 the Messianic kingdom is eternal, in 91–104 it is temporary, if the Apocalypse of Weeks is taken to be a constituent part of 91–104 In the former the final judgement is held before the establishment of the kingdom, 10^{12} 16^1, in the latter at the close of the temporary kingdom (93^{1-10} 91^{1-10}). Whereas the resurrection in 6–36 is a resuscitation to a temporary blessedness, 10^{17} 25^6, in the latter it is not to the temporary kingdom spoken of in $91^{13, 14}$ 96^8, but to one of eternal blessedness subsequent to the final judgement, $100^{4, 5}$ Whereas the resurrection in 6–36 is a resuscitation in a physical body, in 91–104 it is a resurrection in a spiritual body, $92^{3, 4}$ $104^{2, 6}$ In the latter there is a resurrection of the righteous only not so in the former. For other grounds see p. 219 sq.

Relation to 83–90. In 91 104 the Messianic kingdom is temporary in duration, but not so in 83–90 · in the former the final judgement is consummated at the close of the kingdom, in the latter at its beginning. In 91–104 there is a resurrection of the righteous only; in 83–90 of the righteous and the apostate Jews. The kingdom to which the righteous rise in 91–104 is not the temporary kingdom on the earth but the new heaven, but in 83–90 it is the Messianic kingdom on the earth.

105. This chapter appears to be an independent fragment.

106–107. These chapters have already been dealt with as part of the Book of Noah

108 This chapter forms an Appendix to the entire work, added not by the editor but by a subsequent writer to confirm the righteous in the face of repeated disappointment in their expectations

§ 13. CHARACTERISTICS AND DATES OF THE DIFFERENT ELEMENTS.

I will here deal with these elements in the order of their age.

Book of Noah. This book was, as we have seen already, laid under contribution by the author of the Book of Jubilees and by the general editor of Enoch. Part of it is embodied in 6–36, and this part is presupposed as already existing by 83–90. Now, since 83–90 cannot be later than 161 B C , it follows that we have here the *terminus ad quem* of this work

6–36 Since 6–16 23–36 were known to the author of the Book of Jubilees (see my edition, p. lxix), this Section must have been written before the latter half of the second century B.C. Since, further, 83–90, written before 161 B.C., show a minute acquaintance with 10, the date of 6–11 must be put back to the first third of that century. Many other points in 83–90 (see p. 179) point to the acquaintance of the author of 83–90 with 6–36. Again, since 6–36 makes no reference to the persecution of Antiochus, the *terminus ad quem* is thus fixed at 170 B. C. The fact that 6–36 was written in Aramaic is in favour of pre-Maccabean date; for when once a nation recovers, or is trying to recover, its independence, we know from history that it seeks to revive its national language.

83–90. The fourth and last of the four periods into which 83–90 divides history between the destruction of Jerusalem and the establishment of the Messianic kingdom began about 200 B C. (see pp. 180 sq., 206 sqq.), and marks the transition of supremacy over Israel from the Graeco-Egyptians to the Graeco-Syrians, as well as the rise of the Chasids. The Chasids, symbolized by the lambs that are borne by the white sheep, 90^6, are already an organized party in the Maccabean revolt. But certain of these lambs became horned, i.e the Maccabean family, and the great horn is Judas Maccabaeus, 90^9. As this great horn is still warring at the close of the rule of the shepherds, 90^{16}, this Section must have been written before the death of Judas, 161 B C

93^{1-10} 91^{12-17}. This—the Apocalypse of Weeks—may have been written before the Maccabean revolt. There is no reference in it to the persecution of Antiochus But the date is wholly doubtful.

72–82. This Section is referred to in Jubilees $4^{17,\ 21}$, where the author tells how Enoch wrote a book of the order of the months, the seasons of the years, and the rule of the sun. Hence the *terminus ad quem* is 110 B.C. or thereabouts.

91–104. In 83–90 the Maccabees were the religious champions of the nation and the friends of the Chasidim. Here they are leagued with the Sadducees and are the foes of the Pharisaic party. This Section was written, therefore, after 109 B.C., when (?) the breach between John Hyrcanus and the Pharisees took place. But a later date must be assumed according to the literal interpretation of $103^{14,\ 15}$, where the rulers are said to uphold the Sadducean oppressors and to share in the murder of the righteous. This charge is not justified before 95 B C. As for the later limit, the Herodian princes cannot be the rulers here mentioned; for the Sadducees were irrevocably opposed to these as aliens and usurpers. The date, therefore, may be either 95–79 B.C. or 70–64 B C., during which periods the Pharisees were oppressed by both rulers and Sadducees. In my edition of Jubilees, pp. lxix–lxxi, I have given various grounds for regarding 91–104 as dependent on Jubilees.

37–71. From a full review of the evidence, which is given and discussed in the notes on 38⁵, it appears that the kings and the mighty so often denounced in the Parables are the later Maccabean princes and their Sadducean supporters—the later Maccabean princes, on the one hand, and not the earlier, for the blood of the righteous was not shed, as the writer complains (47¹, ², ⁴), before 95 B C. the later Maccabean princes, on the other hand, and not the Herodians, for (1) the Sadducees were not supporters of the latter, and (2) Rome was not as yet known to the writer as one of the great world-powers—a fact which necessitates an earlier date than 64 B.C., when Rome interposed authoritatively in the affairs of Judaea. Thus the date of the Parables could not have been earlier than 94 B C or later than 64 B.C. But it is possible to define the date more precisely. As the Pharisees enjoyed unbroken power and prosperity under Alexandra 79–70 B.C., the Parables must be assigned either to the years 94–79 or 70–64.

The varying relations in which the Maccabees stand to the Chasid or Pharisaic party are faithfully reflected in the books of Enoch. In 83–90 the Maccabees are the leaders of the righteous, and their efforts form the prelude to the Messianic kingdom. In 91–104 they are no longer regarded as the chiefs and friends of the Chasids, and yet they have not become their open foes. They are, however, the secret abettors of their Sadducean oppressors. But when we turn to the Parables the scene is wholly changed. The Maccabeans are now the open and declared enemies of the Pharisees and add to their other guilt the slaying of the righteous.

It is still more instructive to observe the conceptions regarding the Messiah to which the writers of these books were led by the events of their times. In 83–90 we have the Messiah coming forth from the bosom of the community. He is a man only, but yet a glorified man and superior to the community from which he springs. So far as he is a man only, he may be regarded as the prophetic Messiah as opposed to the Apocalyptic Messiah of the Parables and yet he is not truly the prophetic Messiah; for he has absolutely no function to perform, and he does not appear till the world's history is finally closed Accordingly his presence here must be accounted for purely through literary reminiscence, and the hope of the Messiah must be regarded as practically dead at this period. The writer felt no need of such a personality so long as the nation had such a chief as Judas Maccabaeus. It was very different fifty years or more later, when the fondest enthusiasts could no longer look to the Asmonaeans for any help or stay in the time of their distress. Accordingly the writer of 91–104 refers only once to the recreant chiefs of the nation as secret upholders of the enemies of the righteous, and directs the thoughts of his readers no longer to a religious monarchy but to a religious commonwealth or restored theocracy established by the righteous themselves, and owning no head but God alone. This Messianic kingdom, further, which was without a Messiah, was to have only a temporary continuance, and heaven was to be the true and final abode of the righteous. Once more, as we turn to a somewhat later book, we find in the Parables that the irremediable degradation and open hostility of the Maccabees have caused the hopes and aspirations of religious thinkers to take various directions. Of these some returned to a fresh study of the Old Testament, and revived, as in the Psalms of Solomon, the expectation of a prophetic Messiah, sprung from the house and lineage of David. Others followed the bold and original thinker of this period, who, starting from a suggestive phrase in Daniel, conceived the Messiah as the supernatural Son of Man, who, possessing divine prerogatives, should destroy the wicked, and justify the righteous, and vindicate a transformed heaven and earth as their habitation for everlasting. For some account of the Messiah of the Parables we must refer the reader to the notes on 46[3] and 38[2].

The teaching of the Parables stands throughout in clear contrast to that of 91–104 Whilst in the latter there is no

Messiah, in the former the conception of the Messiah plays a more important rôle than had ever yet been assigned to him. In the former, again, there was only a resurrection of the righteous, in the latter a resurrection of all Israelites. In the former the Messianic kingdom was only temporary; in the latter it was of everlasting continuance. In the former the final judgement was held at the close of the Messianic kingdom, in the latter at its beginning. In the former there was a resurrection of the spirit only, in the latter of the body also.

§ 14. THE POETICAL ELEMENT IN 1 ENOCH.

In the course of editing the Ethiopic text of 1 Enoch I was fortunate enough to discover that no small proportion of it was written originally in verse. But the full extent of the poetical element was not recognized till the completion of the present edition. This discovery not only adds to the interest of the book, but also illuminates many a dark passage, suggests the right connexions of wrongly disjoined clauses, and forms an admirable instrument of criticism generally. Our recognition of this fact enables us to recognize the genuineness of verses which had hitherto been regarded as interpolations, and to excise others which were often in themselves unmeaning or at variance with their contexts. The very first chapter is the best witness in these respects. There we find that 1^{3b-9} consists of nine stanzas of three lines each. E had lost two of the lines of stanza seven, but happily these had been preserved by G^g. Again, in 5^{4-9} we have eight stanzas of four lines each. The order of the lines has been disarranged as will be seen in 5^{6-7}, but here the parallelism enables us to effect their restoration Ch. 51 would without a recognition of the poetical character be in many respects inexplicable. In other passages it enables us to recognize certain lines as dittographs · cf. 59^{6d} 71^{3c} 80^{7c} 82^{2b} 94^{7d}.

§ 15. Original Language of Chapters VI-XXXVI— Aramaic, of I-V, XXXVII-CIV—Hebrew.

That 1 Enoch was originally written in a Semitic language is now universally admitted. But what that language is is still, as regards portions of the book, a question of dispute. In the past, Murray, Jellinek, Hilgenfeld, Halévy, Goldschmidt, Charles (formerly), Littmann, and Martin have advocated a Hebrew original, while at various times an Aramaic original has been maintained by De Sacy, Lévi, Eerdmans, Schmidt, Lietzmann, Wellhausen, and Praetorius. Ewald, Dillmann, Lods, Flemming could not come to a decision between Hebrew and Aramaic. But of the above scholars only three have really grappled with the subject, i. e. Halévy, Charles, and Schmidt, and three different theses are advanced by them. While Halévy maintains a Hebrew original, and Schmidt an Aramaic, the present writer, as a result of his studies in editing the Ethiopic text and the translation and commentary based upon it, is convinced that neither view can be established, but that each appears to be true in part.[1] In other words, like the Book of Daniel, part of 1 Enoch was written originally in Aramaic and part in Hebrew. The proofs of this thesis amount in certain Sections almost to demonstration in the case of others only to a high probability. The results of the present study of this problem tend to show that chapters 6-36 were originally written in Aramaic, and 37-104, and probably 1-5, in Hebrew.

Chapters 1-5 Probably from a Hebrew original These chapters, as we have shown elsewhere, do not come from the same author or period as 6-36

1[1]. In E the text = ἐξᾶραι πάντας τοὺς πονηρούς whereas G^g has ἐξᾶραι πάντας τοῖς ἐχθρούς The former, as the context shows, as well as Pss. Sol. 4[9] (see note on p. 4 of the Commentary), is original, the latter not. Now the former = בל־הרעים, the latter = בל־הצרים, a corruption of the former. The same corruption is found in the LXX of Prov 20[22] Since E and G^g are in the main derived from the same Greek translation, this fact, unless due to a sheer blunder

---

[1] This view was first advanced in my edition of the Ethiopic text, pp xxvii-xxxiii

of a copyist, points to the presence of alternative readings in the margin of the Hebrew archetype, which were reproduced by the Greek translator Other facts point in the same direction : see note on 5⁹ᵇ below.

1⁹. In ' He cometh with ten thousands of His holy ones ' the text reproduces the Massoretic of Deut 33² in reading אָתָה = ἔρχεται, whereas the three Targums, the Syriac and Vulgate read אתה = μετ' αὐτοῦ Here the LXX diverges wholly The reading אתא is recognized as original The writer of 1–5 therefore used the Hebrew text and presumably wrote in Hebrew

5⁶ᵇ *ἐν ὑμῖν καταράσονται πάντες οἱ καταρώμενοι* = בכם יקללו כל־המקללים is, so far as I am aware a Hebrew idiom, and not an Aramaic See note on p. 12.

5⁹ᵇ. Here Gᵍ reads *ἁμάρτωσιν*, but E = *κριθήσονται* = יאשמו (cf Prov 30¹⁰ Isa. 24⁶ Jer. 2³, &c.). The parallelism shows that Gᵍ is right. Here, as in 1¹ above, we can explain the double rendering by assuming that one of these readings stood in the text and the other in the margin

Since none of the evidence favours an Aramaic original, and whatever linguistic evidence there is makes for a Hebrew, we may provisionally conclude in favour of the latter.

Chapters 6–36. The evidence in favour of an Aramaic original of these chapters is practically conclusive

(*a*) *Aramaic words transliterated in the Greek or Ethiopic.* Amongst the many Semitic words transliterated in these versions the following are Aramaic and Aramaic only in Gᵍ φουκά, 18⁸, i e פיבא, μανδοβαρά, 28¹, and βαβδηρά, 29¹, i e מדברא Another Aramaic form is χερουβίν. 14¹¹, ¹⁸ 20⁷ but this form is indecisive as it is found not infrequently in the LXX In E manzerân[1] for manzerîn, 10⁹, i e ממזרין , 'alwâ, 31² (see note *in loc.*) = אחלא The Hebrew form is אהלים

Other transliterations are βάτους, 10¹⁹, i e בת, which is both Hebrew and Aramaic χαλβάνη, 31¹, i e חלבנה Hebrew or חלבונא Aramaic. On the other hand there are two Hebrew words transliterated, thus σαρράν, 31¹ = צרי, which is not found in Aramaic but which is rendered in Aramaic by קטף : and γῆ, 27² = ניא = ' valley ', which is a pure Hebrew word, the Aramaic being חילא.

---

[1] Here Gᵍ has μαζηρέους and cannot account for E. Hence E here, as in 1¹ 5⁹ᵇ above, presupposes another reading than that in Gᵍ, this reading being in the text or margin of the Greek translation

These last two cases are somewhat strange, but, since נ׳א is here
used as a proper name, its use in an Aramaic document may be
justified.

(b) *Aramaic constructions.* In 19² we have the peculiar Greek
αἱ γυναῖκες αὐτῶν τῶν παραβάντων ἀγγέλων This is a literal reproduction of the Aramaic idiom נשיהון די מלאביא די חטו. The same
construction recurs in E 9⁸ which = συνεκοιμήθησαν μετ᾽ αὐτῶν μετὰ
τῶν θηλειῶν = שביבו עמהון עם נשיא. Here G^g, it is true, has omitted
μετὰ τῶν θηλειῶν. This omission was probably due to the un-
intelligibility of the construction to a Greek scribe. G^a, however,
preserves the missing clause but wrongly connects it with the
following verb—this change being due no doubt to an attempt to
normalize the Greek. Thus G^a reads συνεκοιμήθησαν μετ᾽ αὐτῶν καὶ
ἐν ταῖς θηλείαις ἐμιάνθησαν Here the καί should be restored after
θηλείαις. In 6⁸ we have a third instance of this idiom, though in
a corrupt form οὗτοί εἰσιν ἀρχαὶ αὐτῶν τῶν δεκά⟨δων⟩ = ראשיהון
דעסריתא. This Aramaic idiom has found its way into the O T
as in Cant 3⁷

(c) *Some of the proper names with which paronomasias are connected postulate an Aramaic original* Thus in G^a 8³ we have ὁ δὲ
τρίτος ἐδίδαξε τὰ σημεῖα τῆς γῆς Now the ὁ τρίτος in 6⁷ is Ἀρακιήλ
= ארקיאל, where ארק is Aramaic for ‘earth’. Thus this angel
naturally taught the signs of the earth: ארקיאל יאליף אתי ארקא
Again in G^a 8³ we have ὁ δὲ εἰκοστὸς ἐδίδαξε τὰ σημεῖα τῆς σελήνης,
where ὁ εἰκοστός according to G^a 6⁷ is Σαριήλ = סהריאל Here סהר
is Aramaic for ‘moon’ Again in 8³ the ὁ ὄγδοος in ὁ ὄγδοος ἐδίδαξε
ἀεροσκοπίαν is in G^a 6⁷ Ἐζεκιήλ (G^a Ζακιήλ) = ישחקיאל. שחק (= ἀήρ),
it is true, is Hebrew as well as Aramaic.

In 13⁷ it is said that ‘the angels were mourning in Abilene’,
i. e. אבלין באבילין. In G^a 6⁷ the play on Hermon is possible both in
Aramaic and Hebrew (see note *in loc*), but the play on Jared in the
same verse is only possible in Hebrew. Whence we may infer that
this paronomasia originated in Hebrew and is only reproduced in
this Aramaic document Finally in E G^a 10⁷ the command is given
to Raphael. ἴασαι τὴν γῆν = רפי הארעא, in which there is an obvious
play on Raphael’s name But though Noldeke states that ‘רפא 1st
gemeinsemitisch’ (*ZDMG*, 1886, xl. 723, quoted by Schmidt), it is
not found in the Targums and later rabbinical literature. Here,
therefore, the play may be due to a pre-existing Hebrew document
or myth, just as we are obliged to make the same presupposition in
the case of ‘Jared’ above.

(d) Text restored through retranslation into Aramaic. In this Section there are many corrupt passages, as might be expected, which can be restored through retranslation either into Aramaic or Hebrew, owing to the close affinities of these languages. This may be the case in 9⁴ מלכיא (i. e. τῶν βασιλέων E) corrupt for עלמיא = τῶν αἰώνων, or מלכים for עלמים. similarly in 10⁷ ἐπάταξαν E G⁸ = אברו, which is both Hebrew and Aramaic, and corrupt for אמרו = εἶπον G⁸ [1] In 10¹⁷ τὰ σάββατα αὐτῶν = שַׁבַחהֹן, wrongly vocalized for שבחהון, or = שַׁבְתָם corrupt for שבתם. 14⁸ κατεσπούδαζον καὶ †ἐθορύβαζον† Here the second verb is impossible. The clause in Aramaic = ייחון ויבהלון. Now the pael יבהלון = θορυβάζειν, ταράσσειν, or συνταράσσειν in Dan. 4², ¹⁶ 5⁹, ¹⁰ 7¹⁵, ²⁸, and is rendered by Theodotion by the latter two verbs. On the other hand, the LXX renders the same Aramaic verb by κατασπεύδειν in 4¹⁶ 5⁶. Thus the translator of the LXX, who, as we know from the rest of his translation of the Aramaic section of Daniel, was very familiar with Aramaic, assigns to the pael of the Aramaic verb the same meaning as the piel and hiphil of the Hebrew בהל. Hence we may assume that the pael in Aramaic could mean κατασπεύδειν or θορυβάζειν. Thus we could explain ἐθορύβαζον as a mistranslation in this context of יבהלון. It is also possible that the two verbs are alternative renderings of one and the same verb in the Aramaic. This would have been possible also if the original had been Hebrew; for יבהלי pointed as a piel would mean κατεσπούδαζον and ἐθορύβαζον as a niphal. In 13² 15⁴, ¹¹ 29² also the text can be restored by either language. (See notes *in loc.*)

But there are other passages that apparently defy restoration save through retranslation into Aramaic. In 9¹⁰ ἀνέβη ὁ στεναγμὸς αὐτῶν καὶ οὐ δύναται †ἐξελθεῖν†, the ἐξελθεῖν is meaningless, but by retranslation we discover the origin of the corruption. ἐξελθεῖν = למנפק corrupt for למפסק = 'cease'. The lamentations 'cannot cease because of the lawless deeds which are wrought on the earth'.

In 10⁷ (where see note) the variations of the versions can be explained through the Aramaic, where E has twice 'earth' (= γῇ), G⁸ has once γῇ and once πληγή, and G⁸ πληγή both times. The variations could, of course, have originated in G, but γῇ and πληγή can be readily accounted for as renderings of ארעא, which, punctuated as אַרְעָא = γῇ, and as אַרְעָא = πληγή.

---

[1] Here again the two readings in the Greek versions can be best explained by variants in the margin of the Semitic original. See foot-note under (*a*) above and the paragraphs on 14⁸ (*ad fin*), 17⁷

In 17^7 E $= τὰ ὄρη τῶν γνόφων =$ טורי קבלא The phrase was derived most probably from Jer 13^{16} הרי נשף. But G^g reads ἀνέμους τῶν γνόφων $=$ רוחי קבלא. Here, as we have seen several times already, the Greek translator appears to have found טורי in the text and רוחי in the margin (or vice versa), and to have rendered both, one of which was preserved by G^g and the other by the Greek ancestor of E.

In 18^2 the text ἴδον τοὺς τέσσαρας ἀνέμους τὴν γῆν βαστάζοντας καὶ τὸ στερέωμα (G^g E) is quite impossible. The winds do not bear the earth By retranslation into Aramaic we see that τὴν γῆν arose in the Aramaic through a dittography The clause $=$ חזית רוחיא ארבע ארעא מסוברין, where ארעא is a dittograph of ארבע The winds bear the firmament, not the earth

In 28^2 πλήρης δένδρων καὶ ἀπὸ τῶν σπερμάτων It would be absurd to speak of a plain as being 'full of trees and seeds' Here ἀπὸ τῶν σπερμάτων $=$ ומזרעין, corrupt for וזרעין (cf Dan $1^{12,\,16}$, Mishna, Ail ii. 2, iii 2) $= καὶ τῶν φυτευμάτων$ Or the wrong phrase may be due to a wrong punctuation of the Aramaic word by the Greek translator. See note *in loc*

In 31^3 ὅταν τρίβωσιν refer to certain fragrant trees mentioned in the preceding verse. These trees yielded a fragrant odour when burnt. (See note *in loc*) Hence I assume that ידקקון ($= τρίβωσιν$) is corrupt for ידלקון $= καύσωσιν$.

Chapters 37–71 from a Hebrew original In support of this view Halévy (*op. cit.* pp 364 sqq) criticized over a dozen of passages from the Parables and the interpolations with a view to showing that the meaning of the text could not be recovered unless by retranslation from a Hebrew original. Unhappily Halévy based his work on the corrupt text of Dillmann, and most of his conclusions have thereby been invalidated Some, however, are of permanent value. On the other hand Schmidt (*O. T. and Semitic Studies*, ii. 336–43) strongly contests this view, and maintains the hypothesis of an Aramaic original. I have studied carefully his ingenious essay, but this study has served to confirm me in the belief in a Hebrew original, which I assumed in my edition of 1893, and supported by arguments in my text of 1908. The preparation of my new edition has served to bring fresh evidence on this question to light.

First of all I will give (*a*) *a list of passages which can be restored on the hypothesis of either a Hebrew or an Aramaic original*,

(*b*) *passages which are believed to presuppose an Aramaic only*, and
(*c*) *passages which postulate a Hebrew original*

(*a*) *Passages which can be restored on the hypothesis of a Hebrew or
an Aramaic original*. 37[4] 'Till the present day such wisdom has
never been given by the Lord of Spirits' Here the Ethiopic has
'ĕmqĕdma = ἐκ προσώπου or ἔμπροσθεν = מלפני, 'from before,' or
practically 'by', as I have rendered it This late use of מלפני is
found in Esther 1[19] 4[8] 1 Chron 29[12] The same idiom is found
in Aramaic, i.e מן־קדם cf. Dan 6[27] (‖ 3[29] מִן־). The same idiom
recurs in 65[10], and possibly in 48 [2, 3, 6]

40[9] The play on the names of Raphael and Gabriel is found in
Hebrew it is possible in Aramaic in the case of Gabriel, but a play
on Raphael has never been found in Aramaic In fact, רפא is not
found in the Targums

45[3] 'Shall **try** their works' For 'try' the text reads 'choose'
Now, as I pointed out in 1906, this = יבחר, corrupt for יבחן · or, if
the original had been Aramaic, we have to suppose that the translator
followed the wrong meaning of יבחר Schmidt accepts the latter
supposition

46[4b]. 'Shall †raise up† the kings . from their seats.' A dittograph of this verse reappears in 46[5a] ' shall put down the kings from
their thrones' Here 'raise up' = יטול is corrupt for יפיל = 'put
down' This restoration is possible either in Hebrew or Aramaic.

54[10] 'And **when**' Here the text reads 'and because', but the
context requires 'when'. The wrong rendering can be explained
either from Hebrew or Aramaic (see note *in loc*)

55[3]. In my note I have restored the text by means of Hebrew but
it is possible also through Aramaic, since מן־קדם can also mean
'because of'

65[11]. See note *in loc*

66[2] Here the text reads 'hands הידים or ידיא corrupt for המים
or ימיא

68[2]. Text reads 'provokes me' = ירגיני or יארגוני

69[1] As in 68[2].

69[4]. The corruption can be explained either by Hebrew or Aramaic

69[13]. *Task* Here 'number' = מנין (or מנינא as Schmidt points
out) which seems corrupt for ענין (or ענינא) = 'task'

71[1] Same corruption as in 69[4].

(*b*) *Phrases and passages which are adduced by Schmidt in support
of an Aramaic original*. Some of these have been dealt with already

undei (*a*), i.e. 37⁴ 40⁹ 45⁸ 65¹¹ 68² 69¹³, in which cases Schmidt
suggests that the corrupt passages in question can be best explained
by an Aiamaic original, though possible also by a Hebrew original.
His suggestions on 51³ 41⁵ are unnecessary, as the corruptions are
native to E, and that on 52⁹, as we shall see later, is untenable, and
his transformation of 38² ' whose elect works hang upon the Lord of
Spirits' into ' whose worship has been rendered solely to the Lord
of Spirits' is wholly uncalled for, since there is no difficulty in the
phrase which recurs twice in 40⁵ 46⁸, and has a parallel in Judith 8²⁴.
The plurals Sûiâfên, Kirûbên, Afnin in 61¹⁰ 71⁷ are ceitainly
Aramaic in form, but σεραφείν which occuis only twice in the O T.,
i.e. in Isa 6²ˑ⁶, appears both times in the oldest MSS of the א A of
the LXX in this form, in Isa. 6² and in B in 6⁶. The Aramaic form
χερουβείν is often found in the LXX Hence this evidence for an
Aramaic original is without weight.

But ' the most convincing evidence . of an Aiamaic oiiginal is
furnished by the Ethiopic translations of the term "Son of Man"
They are walda sab'ö 46²ˑ ³ˑ ⁴ 48² 60¹⁰ . walda b'esî 62⁵ 69²⁹ᵃˑ b 71¹⁴
and walda 'êguâla 'êmahijâw 62⁷ˑ ⁹ˑ ¹⁴ 63¹¹ 69²⁶ˑ ᵘ⁷ 70¹ 71¹⁷ . . . .
Of these the last is the most peculiar. Literally it means " the son
of the offspiing of the mothei of the living " and is a rendering
of οἱ ἄνθρωποι, οἱ υἱοὶ τῶν ἀνθρώπων and especially of υἱὸς ἀνθρώπου.'
Schmidt then proceeds to emphasize the impoitance of these different
renderings in the Parables, whereas in the N T. it is the last that is
uniformly used as a iendering of ὁ υἱὸς τοῦ ἀνθρώπου, and observes:
' befoie 62 he uses no other teim than walda sab'ö, the equivalent of
the Aramaic בר נשא. Later he employs foui times the phiase walda
bě'sî which coiiesponds to the Aiamaic ברה דנכרא . . . This title is
found in the Palestinian Lectionary, the Cuietonian Fragments, and
the Sinaitic text' From the above evidence Schmidt concludes
that, if the translatoi had ' a Gieek text befoie him in which the
N.T. title ὁ υἱὸς τοῦ ἀνθρώπου was uniformly used ', it would be
scaicely conceivable that he would have used three distinct Ethiopic
expressions to render it, and ' these of such a natuie as to coiiespond
exactly to the three diffeient Aramaic teims'. He holds, therefoie,
that ' the conclusion seems inevitable that he translated directly from
the Aramaic. . . . General considerations strengthen this conclusion.
If the Parables of Enoch were translated from a Greek text one
would certainly expect to find somewhere a quotation from it or
a reference to it in eaily Christian liteiature '. But Schmidt can
find none.

The last argument I will answer first. The reader has only to refer to the list of parallels between the N T. books and the Parables on pp xcv sqq in order to learn that the Parables did influence, and that directly, the writers of the N T. Further, Tertullian's words, when discussing the authenticity of 1 Enoch, cannot be adequately explained, unless as bearing on passages in the Parables referring to the Son of Man 'Cum Enoch eadem scriptura etiam de domino praedicarit, a nobis quidem nihil omnino reiiciendum est quod pertineat ad nos ... A Iudaeis potest iam videri propterea reiecta, sicut et cetera fere *quae Christum sonant*' (*De Cultu Fem.* 1³). The Noah Apocalypse, moreover, which is interpolated in the Parables, is referred to in Origen, *Contra Celsum* 5³² (i.e. τοὺς ἀγγέλους) γενέσθαι κακούς, καὶ κολάζεσθαι δεσμοῖς ὑποβληθέντας ἐν γῇ· ὅθεν καὶ τὰς θερμὰς πηγὰς εἶναι τὰ ἐκείνων δάκρυα (1 En 67⁶, ¹¹, ¹²). This evidence necessitates the existence of a Greek Version of the Parables.

Let us turn now to the next argument. The Ethiopic must have been made direct from the Aramaic because of the three forms in which the title 'Son of Man' is given in the Ethiopic, since these, according to Schmidt, correspond exactly to the three forms in Aramaic. But here I must join issue. We have, unless I have failed wholly in this study, seen that the evidence adduced by Schmidt for an Aramaic original is quite inconclusive, and that on the contrary the evidence so far points, though not conclusively, to a Hebrew original. For this conclusion other evidence will be adduced later. We are not, therefore, predisposed to accept such an extraordinary thesis as that the Ethiopic must have been made directly from the Aramaic. Before dealing directly with the titles in question we might point to two facts which render this thesis not merely improbable, but incredible. 1°. No known Ethiopic version has been made directly from the Aramaic. 2°. The Book of Enoch, by its artificial division into five books, like the five books of the Pentateuch, the five books of the Psalms, the five Megilloth, the five books in Proverbs, in Sirach, the five divisions in the Pirke Aboth, and the five books of the Maccabean wars by Jason of Cyrene (see Hawkins², *Horae Synopticae*, p. 164), was after its kind a carefully edited work in which the fragments of a literature were put together with just as much fitness and insight as that of the Proverbs or the Pirke Aboth. This fivefold division was thus a well-known Jewish device, and, since according to the use of the book made by the N T writers it existed in its completed form in the first half of the first century A.D , if not nearly a century earlier, we cannot understand how an Ethiopic translator in the sixth or seventh century A.D. could have used the Greek version for the four books of Enoch, 1-36 72-82 83-90 90-108, and an Aramaic for the fifth, i.e. the Parables, 37-71. It is very probable that the entire book was translated early in the first century of the Christian era into Greek. That the Semitic original was early lost is to be inferred from the fact that no evidence of any kind testifies to its existence after the birth of Christianity, whereas multitudinous evidence attests the existence of the Greek version.

We may, therefore, safely relegate to the limbo of impossibilities the hypothesis that chapters 37-71 of the Ethiopic version were translated directly from the Aramaic.

We have now to consider what Schmidt terms ' the most convincing evidence of an Aramaic original', i. e. the Ethiopic translations of the term ' Son of Man '. The Ethiopic translation was made, as we have just seen, from the Greek. Hence whatever explanation we give of the three forms must be justified by a Greek retranslation. This fact at once discounts any attempt to find a Greek prototype for 'ĕguâla 'ĕmahĕjâw ' offspring of the mother of the living '. This Ethiopic phrase is used indifferently as a rendering of ἄνθρωπος, υἱὸς ἀνθρώπου, ἄνθρωποι, υἱοὶ ἀνθρώπων, ἀνήρ. And the full form walda 'ĕguâla 'ĕmahĕjâw = υἱὸς ἀνθρώπου in Dan. 7¹³ Ps. 79¹⁸, in Ezekiel about ninety times, Rev. 1¹³ 14¹⁴, and in the Gospels always = ὁ υἱὸς τοῦ ἀνθρώπου In itself the Ethiopic phrase can mean ' son of man ' or ' the Son of Man '. But if the translator wished to make it clear that the latter title was used, he could do so by prefixing a demonstrative pronoun as a rendering of the Greek article ὁ. This is done in every instance in the Parables save three. In the course of eight verses in 89¹²⁻⁹ the Greek article is so rendered eleven times.

Let us now examine the other two titles walda sab'ĕ and walda b'ĕsî. sab'ĕ distinctively = ἄνθρωπος (though in a few cases it = ἀνήρ). Thus walda sab'ĕ = υἱὸς ἀνθρώπου. It can also = ὁ υἱὸς τοῦ ἀνθρώπου, but to make this unmistakable the translator could prefix the demonstrative pronoun as the equivalent of ὁ.

Next comes walda b'ĕsî. b'ĕsî = ἀνήρ generally, but as Dillmann (*Lex* 519) puts it, it stands *creberrime* for ἄνθρωπος. In fact in the Ethiopic Version of our book it is used as a rendering of ἄνθρωπος in 1² 15¹. If more of the Greek version had survived we should no doubt find many other instances.

The result of the above examination comes to this. The above three renderings do not presuppose three different forms in the Greek. They most probably presuppose merely one, i.e. ὁ υἰὸς τοῦ ἀνθρώπου, but walda b'ěsî may presuppose ὁ υἰὸς τοῦ ἀνδρός But I think the latter improbable. In 62⁵ 69²⁹ (*bis*) 71¹⁴ bě'sî may be a rendering of ἀνθρώπου as in 1² 15¹.

This change of rendering may seem surprising, but we have a perfect parallel in the Curetonian and Sinaitic versions of the Syriac N T.[1] Thus whereas in the Peshitto b'reh dě-našâ (ברה ראנשא) occurs uniformly as a rendering of ὁ υἰὸς τοῦ ἀνθρώπου, in the Curetonian version we have b'reh de-gabrâ (ברה דגברא) in Luke 7³⁴ 9²⁶ 22⁴⁸, and in the Sinaitic version b'reh de-gabrâ in Mark 8³⁸ Luke 7³⁴ John 13³¹, and elsewhere in both these versions b'reh de-našâ. In the Palestinian Lectionary there is still another way of rendering the phrase, but this does not concern us here. We have, however, learnt from these versions that differences in the manner of rendering the title 'Son of Man' in these versions does not imply any difference in the original Greek Similarly we conclude that the three renderings of this title in the Parables do not presuppose corresponding variations in the Greek, but are due to the translator

If, then, these variations in the Parables are due to the translator or translators it follows that these translators were Aramaic-speaking Jews, since the phrases walda b'ěsî and walda sab'ě are respectively equivalents of b'reh de-gabrâ and b'reh dě-našâ [2]

On the above grounds we conclude that ὁ υἰὸς τοῦ ἀνθρώπου stood in all cases in the Greek version of the Parables.[3] That this Greek *phrase* represents the Hebrew בן־האדם, we shall further conclude from the evidence given in the next section.

(c) *Passages which postulate a Hebrew original*

39⁷ᵇ. 'The righteous . . shall †be strong| (*a—m* 'be beautiful† ' *m, β*) as fiery lights' Neither reading is satisfactory. *a—m* = יחזקו which may be corrupt for יזהרו = 'shine' · cf. Dan. 12³ . . יזהרו ככוכבים.

46⁷ 'These are they who |judge† the stars of heaven.' Here, as I have shown, the text appears to be based on Dan 8¹⁰, and should be read (see my note *in loc*) as follows .—

---

[1] See Schmidt in *Encyclo Bibl* iv 4714

[2] The Aramaisms in the Ethiopic version of the O T. are probably due to Aramaean missionaries

[3] There is just a possibility that two forms stood in the Greek version, i.e ὁ υἰὸς τοῦ ἀνθρώπου and ὁ υἰὸς τοῦ ἀνδρός, and that these were due to the translators, who in this case also would be Aramaic-speaking Jews, but this is highly improbable

'These are they who raise their hands against the Most High,
　　And cast down the stars of heaven,
　　And tread them upon the earth.'

Thus 'judge' = יְדִינוּ which the context shows to be corrupt for
יְרִידוּ = 'cast down'.

47[4b]. 'Because the number of the righteous **had been offered.**'
As the context shows (see my note *in loc*) these words mean that the
number of the righteous, 1 e the martyrs, is complete. cf Rev 6[10, 11].
Now α reads qarĕba = ἤγγικε = קָרֵב, which in Mishnaic Hebrew =
' has been offered '. This meaning is not found in the qal of this
verb in Aramaic

52[9]. ' All these things shall be [denied and] destroyed from the
surface of the earth.' Here there were two alternative Greek renderings of יִבָּחֲרוּ. One was originally in the text, and the other in the
argin, but subsequently both were incorporated into the text. Or
the dittograph was native to the Hebrew, 1. e יכחשו and יכחרו.
Schmidt attempts to explain the corruption from an Aramaic basis
by assuming that יתרמאן stood in the original, and that this
received the two renderings in the text. But רמא does not mean
' to destroy ' Moreover, the Ethiopic word kĕhĕda here, which
means ' to deny ', occurs again in 45[1] 46[7] 48[10], in which three
passages Schmidt says it goes back to the Aramaic כפר Thus his
proposal is satisfactory in no respect.

60[6]. I have followed *u* in the text, but the parallelism is in favour
of regarding the text as corrupt in the word ' worship '. This word
is wholly unsatisfactory. It = יִשְׁתַּחֲווּ, which may be corrupt (or
יְשַׁחֲתוּ = ' pervert ' or ' corrupt '). Thus we recover an excellent
parallelism .—

'For those who corrupt the righteous law,
　　And for those who deny the righteous judgement,
　　And for those who take His name in vain '

65[10a]. ' Then judgement has been determined upon and shall not
be **withheld** by me for ever.'

For ' withheld ' the text reads λογισθήσεται or ἀριθμηθήσεται. The
Ethiopic word can mean either The former rendering (as in 52[8d])
is generally followed here. It is, however, unsatisfactory. The true
reading, as I pointed out in my text, can be recovered by retranslation into Hebrew. οὐ λογισθήσεται = לא יחשב, corrupt for לא יחשך
= ' shall not be withheld '. Here Schmidt follows the other possible
meaning of the Ethiopic word ἀριθμηθήσεται = יתמנא—a corruption of
יתמנע.

65[10b]. 'Because of the **sorceries** which they have searched out and learnt, the earth and those who dwell upon it shall be destroyed.' Instead of 'sorceries' the Ethiopic reads 'months' = חדשים, which Halévy rightly recognized as a corruption of חרשים = 'sorceries'. It is true that on an exceptional occasion Aramaic-speaking Jews used חרשיא instead of their own word ירחיא. Hence the evidence for a Hebrew original is slightly weakened here.

The text of this passage as known to Halévy and originally to myself was corrupt, and Schmidt rightly objected to this text even when emended as follows · 'because of the sorceries which they have searched out and (through which) they know that the earth . . will be destroyed' Schmidt observes that it 'is a strange idea that the terrible judgement of the flood would come because men had succeeded in discovering that the earth with its inhabitants would be destroyed' This observation is just, but the remedy lies in the MSS. *g t u*, which omit the 'that'. The omission of this word restores the meaning of the whole verse. See note on p. 131

From the above evidence we infer a Hebrew original. As in the Hebrew chapters of Daniel, so here there were possibly many Aramaisms

Chapters 72–82. *From a Hebrew original.*

76[1, 14]. Here the word in the text 'winds' = רוחות, which should have been rendered 'quarters' This restoration is possible both in Hebrew and Aramaic.

77[1]. In this verse there is a play on the four quarters of the earth It is possible to recover this play by retranslation into either Hebrew or Aramaic in the case of the 'east' and 'north' קדם or קרום and צפון or צפון

But this is not so in the case of the 'south' and 'west'. As regards the first the text reads 'the south, because the Most High will descend there, yea there will He descend' = דרום כי ירד דם. This is possible only in Hebrew.

77[2]. 'And the west quarter is named (lit. 'its name') diminished because there all the luminaries wane' והרוח המערבית שמו אהרון כי שם יאחרו כל־המאורות

78[1] Of the two names of the sun which are transliterated, though corruptly, in this verse, one is Hebrew and not Aramaic, i.e. Orjares = אור חרם The other, Tômâs cf. = תמה, is Hebrew and Aramaic, but if it is corrupt from חמה, as Halévy conjectures, it is Hebrew.

78². Of the four names of the moon which are here transliterated, three are Hebrew only, Asônjâ, i. e אישׁון, Eblâ, i. e לְבָנָה, and Benâsê, i. e בן־כסה

80⁵. See note *in loc.*

82¹⁰ See note *in loc*

82¹⁵ 'Tam'âinî and Sun.' These two names are one, i. e שֶׁמֶשׁ תִּימָנִי. This is Hebrew, and not Aramaic.

Chapters 83–90　　From a Hebrew (or Aramaic?) original

89⁴⁴. The emendation suggested here is possible both in Hebrew and Aramaic

90¹³ᵃ, ¹⁶ᵃ In the duplicate version which we have of these verses, 'shepherds' in 90¹³ corresponds to 'ravens' in 90¹⁶. The latter is right. The corruption can be explained from a Hebrew background, רעים, corrupt for ערבים, or from an Aramaic רעין, corrupt for עורבין.

90¹³ᵇ, ¹⁶ᵇ In the former 'cried to' corresponds to 'were gathered together' in the latter. Now the former = ἔκραζον = יועקי or יצעקי, and the latter יָנְעֲקי or יִצְעֲקי in Hebrew But this explanation is impossible in Aramaic, for though עק and צעק occur in the sense of 'to cry', no mood of this verb is used in the sense of 'to assemble' For this word they use בנשׁ.

90¹⁸ **covered them.** The Ethiopic expression here is not good Ethiopic, but reproduces the Greek ἐκάλυψεν ἐπ᾽ αὐτούς, which in turn is a literal rendering of בסה עליהם (Hebrew), or עליהון (or כסי) חפא in Aramaic

90²⁷. 'I saw those sheep †burning and their bones burning†.' This clause is obviously corrupt. In 'bones' there appears to be a mistranslation of the late Hebrew עצם or the Aramaic גרם, which literally mean 'bone' or 'bones', but which when compounded with a suffix = 'self' or 'selves' The participle is then a doublet Hence we have וארא הצאן הזאת עצמה בערת = 'I saw those very sheep burning' This is possible also in Aramaic

90³⁸ 'The first among them became the **lamb.**' 'The lamb' = הטלה, which was corrupted into המלה, as Goldschmidt has pointed out, whence the corruption in the Ethiopic text 'the word' This explanation is possible also in Aramaic.

Chapters 91–104　　From a Hebrew original

93⁵ Text reads 'after him' = אחריו, which I take to be corrupt for אחיתו = 'his posterity'.

93⁸ᵇ. The Ethiopic has a peculiar form, and = ἀσεβήσουσιν καρδίαι πάντων ἀπὸ τῆς σοφίας, which is pure Hebrew = ירשע לבב כלם מחכמה. Cf Ps. 18²² רשעתי מאלהי

95¹ᵃ. 'Oh that mine eyes were [a cloud of] waters' The bracketed word is either an intrusion and = עַן, a dittograph of עני = 'eyes', or עַן is corrupt for עין = 'fount', the corruption being due to the occurrence of the phrase 'cloud of waters' in 95¹ᶜ. Hence 'Oh that mine eyes were a fount of waters'. This is possible also in Aramaic

96⁷   'Who devour the finest of the wheat
            And drink **wine in large bowls.**'

For the emended phrase E has here the extraordinary words 'strength of the root of the fountain' = ἰσχὺν ῥίζης πηγῆς = כח עיקר עין, corrupt for במזרקי יין (Amos 6⁶)   See my note *in loc.*

96⁶ᵃ. **From every fountain.** E reads 'at every time' = בכל־עת, corrupt for מכל־עין.

97⁸ᵇ⁻⁹. We have here a remarkable series of rhyming verses which arise on retranslation into Hebrew

8ᵇ	עֹשֶׁר עָשַׁרְנוּ	9.	וְנֶעֱשַׂח שֶׁחָשַׁבְנוּ
	וּרְבוּשׁ לָנוּ		כי כסך אסף אספנו
8ᶜ.	וכל קָנינו	9ᵈ	ורבים אברי בתינו
	אשר אוינו	9ᶜ	ומלאים כמים אוצרינו

98⁴ᵃᵇ. See note *in loc*

99⁶. Here E = εἰς ἡμέραν αἵματος ἀδιαλείπτου, but in Tertullian (*De Idol.* iv) the phrase appears as 'in diem sanguinis *perditionis*' = εἰς ἡμέραν αἵματος ἀπωλείας = ליום דם לאיד, where לאיד is corrupt for לעד = ἀδιαλείπτου.

99¹⁶. E (₁ₛ𝑔 β) reads 'the spirit of His indignation' = רוח אפו, corrupt for חרון אפו = 'His fierce indignation'

100⁶ᵃ. See note *in loc,*

101⁴. E reads 'kings' = מַלְכִי, corrupt for מלחי, 'sailors.'   This is also possible in Aramaic.

§ 16. The Influence of 1 Enoch on Jewish Literature.

In the Book of Jubilees, written before 105 B c., 1 Enoch is largely drawn upon, as may be seen from the following parallel passages and phrases :—

Jubilees	*1 Enoch*
1¹¹ 'sacrifice . . to demons'	19¹ 'sacrificing to demons as gods'
12.	89⁵¹⁻⁵³.

Jubilees	1 Enoch
1b 'the plant of uprightness' Cf. 16²⁶.	10¹⁶ 'the plant of righteousness and truth'.
	93² 'the plant of uprightness' Cf. 93⁵, ¹⁰ also 84⁶
2⁶ 'until 1 descend and dwell with them'	25³ 'the Lord of Glory . when He shall come down to visit the earth'.
⁴⁰ 'angel of the presence'.	40², ³ 'four presences'.
⁴⁹ 'the heavens shall be renewed the powers of the heaven ... the luminaries be renewed'.	91¹⁶ 'a new heaven shall appear, and all the powers of the heavens shall give sevenfold light'.
2² 'the spirit of the winds'. 'the spirit of snow'. 'the spirit of hail' 'the spirit of hoar-frost' 'the angels of the voices and of the thunder and of the lightning'.	60¹². ¹⁸ 'the spirit of the snow'. ²¹ 'the spirit of the rain.' ¹⁷ 'the spirit of the hoar-frost'. ¹³⁻¹⁵ 'the thunder—lightning-peals—the spirit'.
2⁴	54⁷, ⁸
3¹⁰ 'the heavenly tablets', and *passim*	81¹, ² 93² 103² 'the heavenly tablets'
4³	22⁵⁻⁷.
15 'Jared, for in his days the angels of the Lord descended on the earth'	6⁶ (the angels) 'descended in the days of Jared'.
'the Watchers' Cf. 10⁵.	1⁵ 12²⁻⁴ the Watchers'.
¹⁷ 'the first who learnt writing'	12³ 'Enoch the scribe'.
'who wrote down the signs of heaven, &c.'	72–82
¹⁹ 'what was and what will be, he saw in a vision of his sleep . until the day of judgement'	83–90. The Dream-Visions.
'placed the testimony on earth for all the children of men and for their generations'.	1² 37²⁻⁴ 92¹ 104¹¹⁻¹³.
²⁰ 'he took to himself a wife, and her name was Ednî'	85³ 'Before I took ... Edna'.

Jubilees	1 *Enoch*
[21] 'he was with the angels of God these six jubilees of years'	$12^{1,\,2}$ 'he was hidden and his activities had to do with the Watchers, &c'
'and they showed, &c'	23–36.
'the rule of the sun'	82^{13-20}
[22] 'testified to the Watchers'	12^{3-6} 13^{1-12} 14^{4-7} 15^2 sqq.
'who had sinned with the daughters of men'. Cf 5^1.	6^2 7^1 9^8 10^{11} 12^4 $15^{3,\,4}$.
'unite themselves, so as to be defiled with the daughters of men'.	10^{11} 'united themselves with women so as to have defiled themselves with them'. Cf $15^{3,\,4}$.
[23] 'we conducted him into the Garden of Eden'	50^8 ' the garden where the elect and righteous dwell where my grandfather was taken up, the seventh from Adam'. Cf. 70^{1-3}.
'there he writes down the condemnation, &c'	12^4 15^1 'scribe of righteousness'
[26] 'the Mount of the East' (one of the four places of the Lord on earth)	$18^{7,\,8}$ 'as for those towards the east; the middle one reached to heaven like the throne of God' Cf 24^3 25^3
5^1 'they bare unto them sons, and they were giants'.	7^2 'they bare great giants'. Cf. $15^{3,\,8}$
[2] 'all of them corrupted their ways and their orders, and they began to devour each other'. Cf. 7^{24}	7^5 'they began to sin against birds and beasts and to devour one another's flesh'.
[6] 'He bade us to bind them in the depths of the earth' Cf. 5^{10} 10^7	10^{12} 'bind them fast **in the valleys** (*emended*) of the earth'.
[7] Destruction of the angels' children by the sword	10^9 $14^{5,\,6}$.
[9] 'that each should slay his neighbour'.	10^9 'that they may destroy each other in battle' Cf. 10^{12} 88^1.
[10] 'and their fathers were witnesses (of their destruction), and after this they were bound	10^{12} 'and when their sons have slain one another, and they have seen the destruction of

Jubilees	1 Enoch

Jubilees

in the depths of the earth for ever, until the day of the great condemnation when judgement is executed, &c '

1 Enoch

their beloved ones, bind them fast for seventy generations in the **valleys** of the earth till the day of their judgement and of their consummation, till the judgement that is for ever and ever is consummated '

12^6 ' the murder of their beloved ones shall† they see '. Cf 14^6

$11, 12$ ' He destroyed all and He made . . a new and righteous nature, &c.'

$10^{13, 16}$ ' destroy all . . and let the plant of righteousness and truth appear, &c.'

^{24} ' seven flood-gates of heaven '.

89^2 ' heaven .. a lofty roof with seven water torrents thereon '

^{25} ' the fountains of the deep also sent up waters '

89^3 ' fountains were opened on the surface of that great enclosure, &c.'

^{29} ' the fountains of the great deep were closed and the flood-gates of heaven were restrained, and . . all the mouths of the abysses of the earth were opened, and the water began to descend into the deep below ' Cf 6^{26}.

89^7 ' those water torrents were removed from that high roof and the chasms of the earth were levelled up and other abysses were opened. ^{8} Then the water began to run down into these, &c.'

$6^{23, 29-32}$ A year of 364 days, four being intercalary days.

$75^{1, 2}$ $82^{4, 6, 11}$

$^{2-38}$ Warning against the use of any other calendar.

82^{4-7}.

7^{21} The deluge due to the Watchers' sin.

10^2.

The Watchers' sin. Cf 4^{22}.

7^1, &c

' against the law of their ordinances '.

15^{3-7}.

' they made the beginning of uncleanness '

8^2 ' there arose much godlessness and they committed fornication '

9^6 ' hath taught all unrighteousness on earth '

10^8 ' . to him ascribe all sin '.

Jubilees

[22] The Giants, the Nâphil, the Eljô

'they devoured one another' Cf. 5[9].

[23] 'shed much blood the earth was filled with iniquity'

[24] 'they sinned, &c.' (*emended*).

[25] 'into Sheol shall they go, and into the place of condemnation shall they descend, and into the darkness' Cf 22[22].

[30] 'the seventh in his generation'.

'whilst still living he testified to his son, &c.'

8[12] 'the middle of the earth' (Shem's lot).

[22] 'the mountains of fire'.

10[1] 'the unclean demons began to lead astray and destroy them' Cf. 11[5].

'hold them fast in the place of condemnation'

[12] 'we explained to Noah the medicines how he might heal'

12[2] 'what help and profit have we from those idols'.

[4] 'who causes the rain and the dew to descend on the earth'.

1 Enoch

7[1] (*Syncellus's Greek Version*) The Giants, Nephilim, the Eliud.

87[1] 'devour each other' Cf. 10[9, 12] 88[1].

9[1] 'much blood being shed . . all lawlessness being wrought upon the earth'.

7[5].

103[7, 8] 'then souls shall be made to descend into Sheol and into darkness and a burning flame where there is grievous judgement

60[8] 'the seventh from Adam'

93[3] 'the seventh in the first week'. 93[1, 2]

26[1] 'the middle of the earth' (Palestine).

Cf. 18[6-9] 24[1-3].

15[8] 'the giants shall be called evil spirits . . .'.

11 ' . afflict, oppress, destroy, attack, do battle' Cf. 16[1].

19[1] 'then (the angels') spirits assuming many different forms are defiling mankind and will lead them astray into sacrificing to demons as gods'.

19[1] 'here shall they stand till the day of the great judgement'.

10[7] 'heal the earth which the angels have corrupted, &c'

99[7] ' shall get no manner of help from them'.

101[2] 'withholds the rain and the dew from descending on the earth'

Jubilees	*1 Enoch*
15³² 'But over Israel He did not appoint any angel or spirit for He alone is their ruler'. This contradicts 1 En. 89⁵⁹.	89⁵⁹ 'and He called seventy shepherds and cast those sheep to them, &c.'
'He will require them at the hands of His angels, &c.'	90¹⁷, ²²
16²⁶ 'plant of righteousness'. Cf. 21.	10¹⁶ 'plant of righteousness' Cf. 93², ⁵
22¹⁷ 'worship evil spirits'.	99⁷ 'worship impure spirits and demons'.
22 'For they will descend into Sheol, &c.' See 7²⁹ above.	103⁷, ⁸.
23¹⁶ ˢqq. Rise of the Chasids.	90⁶⁻⁷.
23—24 Attack of the (?) Syrians	90⁸⁻¹¹.
27—29 A future time of peace and joy and plenty, with long life.	5⁹ 10¹⁷; also 91–104 *passim.*
31 'their spirits will have much joy' (though 'their bones will rest in the earth').	103³ 'all goodness and joy and glory are .. written down for the spirits of them, &c'
	103⁴ 'and the spirits ... shall live and rejoice . and their spirits shall not perish'.
30²² 'the book of life' Cf 36¹⁰	47³ 'the books of the living'.
32¹⁸, ¹⁹ Jacob's seed rule and judge.	95³ 96¹ The righteous rule and judge
35¹⁷ 'the guardian of Jacob'	20⁵ 'Michael . . set over the best part of mankind' [+ 'over the people'. *Eth.*]
36¹⁰ 'the day of turbulence and execration and indignation and anger'	39² 'books of zeal and wrath, and books of disquiet and expulsion'.
'the book of life'. Cf. 30²²	47³ 'the books of the living'
37²⁹ 'the boar' (Esau speaks in reference to himself).	89¹², ⁴², ⁴⁹, ⁶⁶ 'wild boar', 'wild boars' (= Edom)

In the *Testaments of the Twelve Patriarchs,* written between 137 and 105 (possibly 109–107) B.C., there are nine direct references to a book of Enoch.—

T. Lev 10[5] 'the house which the Lord shall choose . . as is contained in the book of Enoch the righteous'	1 En. 89[50] 'the house for the Lord'.
16[1] 'I have learned (in the book of Enoch βA^β S) . . for seventy weeks'	89[59 sqq]
14[1] 'I have learned (from the writing of Enoch βA^β S[1]) &c.'	91[6, 7]

T Dan 5[6] T. Sim 5[4] T Jud 18[1] (β) T. Zeb 3[4] (β) T. Naph. 4[1] T. Benj. 9[1], 10[6]	cannot be traced directly to any passage in 1 Enoch In T Zeb. 3[4] there is a slip, 'Enoch' being written for 'Moses' in β S[1], or else a scribe has changed the reference to Moses as being an anachronism on the lips of Zebulon.

There are also passages in the *Testaments* which are more or less closely parallel to 1 Enoch, e. g. —

T Reub. 5[6, 7] The Watchers, the women and the giants	1 En. 6–9[2]
T. Lev 3[4] 'the Great Glory' ($a \beta A^\beta$ S).	14[20] 102[3]
T Lev. 16[2] 'make void the law and set at naught . . by evil perverseness'.	99[2, 14] 104[9, 10]
18[5] (see note on 1 En. 51[4]).	51[1]
T. Naph. 3[5] 'the Watchers changed the order of their nature'	6–9[2]

1 Enoch was probably used by the author of the *Assumption of Moses*, written between A. D. 7 and 30. Cf. —

Ass. Mos.	1 *Enoch*
4[8] 'sad and lamenting because they will not be able to offer sacrifices to the Lord of their fathers'	89[73] 'they began to place a table . . . but all the bread on it was polluted and not pure'
10[3, 4] 'He will go forth from His holy habitation'	1[3] 'will come forth from His dwelling'

Ass Mos	1 *Enoch*
10⁴ 'And the earth shall tremble. to its confines shall it be shaken. And the high mountains shall be made low, and the hills shall be shaken and fall'.	1⁵˙°'.. unto the ends of the earth ⁶And the high mountains shall be shaken and the high hills . . made low'

2 Baruch (for date see Introd. to my *Apoc. Bar.* § 7, pp. lvii and lxiv) has many affinities with 1 Enoch both in diction and in thought, and is manifestly dependent on it.

2 *Baruch*	1 *Enoch*
10⁶.	38²
10⁸ Sirens.	19² Sirens.
13⁸ 'The judgement of the Lofty One who has no respect of persons'.	63⁸ 'His judgements have no respect of persons'
21²³ 'treasuries of souls'.	100⁵
24¹ 'the books shall be opened in which are written the sins of all those who have sinned'.	90²⁰ 'he took the sealed books and opened those books'
29⁴ A later form of the myth of Behemoth and Leviathan which is found first in En 60⁷⁻⁹	60⁷⁻⁹, ²⁴
29⁵ 'The earth also shall yield its fruit ten thousandfold'.	10¹⁹ 'each measure shall bear a thousand'.
32⁶ 'renew His creation'	45⁴.
35² 'O that mine eyes were springs, and mine eyelids a fount of tears'.	95¹ 'Oh that mine eyes were [a cloud of] waters that I might weep over you and pour down my tears as a cloud †of† waters'
48⁹ 'The spheres . . in their orders'.	2¹ 'The luminaries . . . rise and set in order'
50²	51¹.
51³ 'who have planted in their heart the root of wisdom' (cf 59⁷).	10¹⁶ 'the plant of righteousness'.
51¹⁰ 'they shall be made like unto the angels, and be made equal to the stars'	104²,⁴ 'shine as the lights of heaven . . have great joy as the angels . Cf 69¹¹.

2 *Baruch*	1 *Enoch*
54² 'for Whom nothing is too hard '.	84³ ' nothing is too hard for Thee '
55³ Remiel.	20⁷ Ramiel (*Greek*).
56⁶ ' when he (Adam) transgressed, untimely death came into being '.	69¹¹ 'men were created exactly like the angels—and death could not have taken hold of them '
56¹⁰⁻¹³ · even to the angels became he a danger For, moreover, at that time, when he was created, they enjoyed liberty And some of them descended and mingled with the women. And then those who did so were tormented in chains ·	6–10
59² ' the eternal law '	99² ' the eternal law '
59⁵, ⁸.	18¹¹ 21⁷⁻¹⁰ 40¹¹, ¹² 47⁵
¹⁰ Gehenna.	27², ³ 54 62¹² 90²⁶, ²⁷.
' the station of vengeance '	18¹²⁻¹⁶ 19 21 22¹⁰⁻¹³ 54¹⁻⁶ 90²⁴⁻²⁷.
68⁶.	89⁷³, ⁷⁴.

The dependence of this book on 1 Enoch is still more evident if we may regard it as proceeding from one author; for it reproduces in the main the conceptions of 1 En. 91–104 save that it expects a Messiah. Thus in this Apocalypse of Baruch the Messianic Kingdom is only of temporary duration. The Messiah reigns till sin is at an end 74², ³. During his reign the earth yields ten thousandfold, and there are no premature deaths. At the close of this period the Messiah returns to heaven and the resurrection ensues 50–51⁶. The righteous are then transformed and made like the angels 51⁵, ¹⁰.

The author of 4 Ezra, writing between A.D. 81–96, has made a not infrequent use of 1 Enoch, and this mainly of the Parables.

4 *Ezra*	1 *Enoch*
6⁴⁰⁻⁵² takes up and develops further the myth found in En. 60⁷⁻⁹	60⁷⁻⁹ Leviathan and Behemoth.

<table>
<tr><td>

4 Ezra

$7^{32,\ 33}$ ' Et terra reddet qui in ea
dormiunt, et pulvis qui in eo
silentio habitant, et promptu-
aria reddent quae eis commen-
datae sunt animae.   Et re-
velabitur Altissimus super
sedem iudicii '

7^{37} ' Et dicet tunc Altissimus ad
excitatas gentes videte et in-
tellegite quem negastis, vel cui
non servistis vel cuius diligen-
tias sprevistis '.

</td><td>

1 Enoch

$51^{1,\ d}$ ' And in those days shall the
earth also give back that which
has been entrusted to it, And
Sheol also shall give back that
which it has received, And
hell shall give back that which
it owes   . And the Elect One
shall in those days sit on My
throne '.

62^{1} ' thus the Lord commanded
.. those who dwell on the
earth, and said " Open your
eyes and lift up your horns if
ye are able to recognize the
Elect One ''

60^{6} ' Who worship not the right-
eous law and   who deny
the righteous judgement and
.. who take His name in
vain '.

</td></tr>
</table>

4 Ezra	1 Enoch
7^{36} ' Clibanus gehennae ostende- tur, et contra eum iocundi- tatis paradisus '	$48^{9,\ 10}\ 27^{3}$
7^{75} ' incipies creaturam renovare '.	72^{1}.
$7^{85,\ 95}$. A development of 1 En. 100^{5}	100^{5}
7^{125}. ' Super stellas fulgebunt facies eorum ' Cf. 7^{97}.	104^{2} ' ye shall shine as the lights of heaven '
' . nostrae autem facies super tenebras nigrae '.	62^{10} ' darkness shall grow deeper on their faces '

From the second century A.D. onwards all knowledge of
1 Enoch vanishes from Jewish literature with the exception of
a few references that are given by Jellinek in the *Zeitschr. D M.G* ,
1853, p. 249

§ 17. THE HEBREW BOOK OF ENOCH.

The Hebrew Book of Enoch ספר חניך, of which a complete
but unedited MS. exists in the Bodleian Library, is a work which

must be dated later than the Book of the Secrets of Enoch (or
2 Enoch), as it continually betrays its dependence on that work.
A printed edition of the book is given by Jellinek, *Bet ha-
Midrasch*, 1873, v. 170–190, but in an incomplete form.   It
describes the ascent into heaven of Rabbi Ishmael, who receives
a series of revelations from Metatron, who relates in chaps. 3–5
7–16 (cf. 1 En. 14³ 70²) that he is Enoch the son of Jared, translated to heaven in a chariot of fire at the time of the Deluge, to
bear eternal witness against his sinful contemporaries (1 En. 5⁴⁻⁶
14¹⁻⁷).   He had there been instructed by the Angel of Wisdom
in all wisdom and knowledge, and all the mysteries of creation
(1 En. 93¹⁰ 63¹¹⁻²¹), of heaven and earth, of past and future
things, and of the world to come.   In chap. 6 it is said that
Adam and his generation beheld the heavenly glory, until in the
time of Enoch ' Aza and Azael led men to idolatry '.   Cf. 'in
the days of Jared' (1 En. 6⁶)—'Azazel' (1 En. 8¹ 10⁴ 13¹)—'the
angels . . spirits shall lead them astray into sacrificing to demons
as gods' (1 En. 19¹).

Chaps. 18–22 (not in Jellinek's edition) describe the seven
heavens with their hosts of angels, and the courses of the sun,
moon, and stars (1 En. 72–82).   In chap 23 Metatron describes
the fragrant odours and perfumes wafted into paradise to the
pious and just, for whom paradise and the tree of life are prepared as an eternal inheritance (1 En 24⁴–25⁷).   In 24–26 he
describes the chariot of God, and the many-eyed, radiant, God-
praising Ophannim and Seraphim (1 En. 61¹⁰ 71⁷).   The latter
burn the accusations continually brought by Satan against
Israel (1 En. 40³⁻⁷).   In 27 he tells of a heavenly registrar and
keeper of the archives (cf. 1 En. 89⁶¹⁻⁶⁴, ⁷⁰, ⁷⁶ 98⁶⁻⁸ 104⁷).
Chaps. 35–40 relate how the heavenly hosts pass into God's
presence to praise and glorify Him with the song, ' Holy, Holy,
Holy is the Lord Sabaoth,' and how at that the Ophannim,
Cherubim, Chayyoth, and Seraphim prostrate themselves (cf.
1 En. 39¹⁰⁻¹³ 61¹⁰⁻¹²).   In 41–47 Metatron shows Ishmael the
repositories of the rain, snow, hail, thunder and lightning (cf.
1 En 60¹¹⁻²¹), the spirits of those angels who were punished,

and whose bodies were turned to great fiery mountains (1 En. 18[11-16, 21]), the places of punishment (cf. 1 En. 18[14] 19[1] 21[7] 27[1-3], &c), Meṭaṭron next shows all past and future ages from Adam to the end of time, including the Messiah ben David and his age, and the wars of Gog and Magog (1 En. 56[5]–57[2]), and other events of the Messianic era. In the last chap., 48, he shows Ishmael the glorious future Jerusalem (1 En. 89[29]), where the souls of the righteous stand praying for its advent upon earth (1 En. 97[3, 5] 99[3, 10] 104[3]).

The date of this work cannot be later than the time of the completion of the Babylonian Talmud. An apocalyptic fragment (dealt with in *Jewish Encyc.* i 678, 679), apparently written under the immediate impression of the Hadrianic persecution, seems to supply the link which connects 2 Enoch with this Neo-Hebrew Book of Enoch, which itself must be dated earlier than Talmud *Berachoth* 7 *a* which quotes from it [1]

§ 18. The Influence of Enoch on Patristic Literature.

Epistle of Barnabas (soon after 70 A D)

4[3] τὸ τέλειον σκάνδαλον ἤγγικεν περὶ οὗ γέγραπται, ὡς Ἐνὼχ λέγει

Not in our Enoch

16[5] λέγει γὰρ ἡ γραφή· καὶ ἔσται ἐπ' ἐσχάτων τῶν ἡμερῶν καὶ παραδώσει κύριος τὰ πρόβατα τῆς νομῆς καὶ τὴν μάνδραν καὶ τὸν πύργον αὐτῶν εἰς καταφθοράν

1 En. 89[56] · He forsook that their house and their tower and gave them (those sheep) all into the hands of the lions, to . . devour them' [66] devoured . . . those sheep and they burnt that tower and demolished that house'

16[8].

91[13]

Apocalypse of Peter (early in second century) (ed Robinson and James, 1892).

3 τοὺς πεινῶντας καὶ διψῶντας καὶ θλιβομένους, καὶ ἐν τούτῳ

108[7-9] those who have afflicted their bodies, &c'

[1] This account is based on that given in *Jewish Encyc.* i. 676–679.

τῷ βίῳ τοὺς ψυχὰς ἑαυτῶν
δοκιμάζοντας

3 Description of the 'two   106[2, 10] ' body whiter than snow,
righteous brethren'   &c ' See notes *in loc.*

5 . γῆν . ἀρωμάτων πλήρη   24° 25[4] Fragrant.
καὶ φυτῶν εὐανθῶν καὶ ἀφθάρτων
καὶ καρπὸν εὐλογημένον φερόν-
των.

μιᾷ φωνῇ τὸν Κύριον θεὸν ἀνευφή-   61[9—12] ' one voice .. bless, &c.'
μουν

οἱ δὲ οἰκήτορες τοῦ τόποι ἐκείνου   108[12] ' in shining light '
ἐνδεδυμένοι ἦσαν ἔνδυμα ἀγγέλων
φωτινῶν

6 οἱ κολαζόμενοι .. σκοτινὸν εἶχον   62[10, 15, 16]
αὐτῶν τὸ ἔνδυμα κατὰ τὸν ἀέρα
τοῦ τόπου.

οἱ κολάζοντες ἄγγελοι   Cf 8   53[3] 56[1] 62[11] 63[1] 66[1] ' the angels
ἄγγελοι βασανισταί   of punishment '.

7 πῦρ φλεγόμενον   10[13] 90[24] 98[3] 108[5].

οἱ βλασφημοῦντες   τὴν   ὁδὸν   27[2] ' utter   unseemly words,
τῆς δικαιοσύνης.   Cf [13]   &c ' Cf. 108[6]
                                   91[18] 94[1] ' the paths of righteous-
                                   ness '

15 οἱ πλουτοῦντες καὶ τῷ πλούτῳ   63[10] 94[8—11] 96[4—8] 97[8—10]
αὐτῶν πεποιθότες . . ἀλλ᾽ ἀμελή-
σαντες τῆς ἐντολῆς τοῦ θεοῦ

Justin Martyr (died between A D. 163 and 167),   9[8—9] 15[8, 9].
Apol 11 5 οἱ δὲ ἄγγελοι   γυναικῶν μίξεσιν
ἡττήθησαν καὶ παῖδας ἐτέκνωσαν, οἵ εἰσιν οἱ
λεγόμενοι δαίμονες καὶ εἰς ἀνθρώποις φόνοις,
πολέμους, μοιχείας καὶ πᾶσαν κακίαν ἔσπειραν.
Cf 1. 5.

Tatian (flor. A D. 160), *Oratio adv. Graecos* 8   8[3] ' astrology '.
ὑπόθεσις δὲ αὐτοῖς τῆς ἀποστασίας οἱ ἄνθρωποι
γίνονται. διάγραμμα γὰρ αὐτοῖς ἀστροθεσίας
ἀναδείξαιτες . . .

20 μετῳκίσθησαν οἱ δαίμονες . καὶ οἱ μὲν ἀπ᾽   6[6] ' who descend-
οὐρανοῦ κατεβλήθησαν   ed ', 15[8, 9]

Athenagoras (about A D. 170), *Legatio pro*
Christianis, 24 ' De angelis et gigantibus ',
regards Enoch, though he does not name him,

as a true prophet ἴστε δὲ μηδὲν ἡμᾶς ἀμάρτυρον
λέγειν, ἃ δὲ τοῖς προφήταις ἐκπεφώνηται, μηνύειν.
ἐκεῖνοι μέν, εἰς ἐπιθυμίαν πεσόντες, παρθένων ..   6 7 13⁵ 14, 15⁸⁻¹⁰
ἐκ μὲν οὖν τῶν περὶ τὰς παρθένους ἐχόντων οἱ
καλούμενοι ἐγεννήθησαν γίγαντες   25. οὗτοι
τοίνυν οἱ ἄγγελοι οἱ ἐκπεσόντες τῶν οὐρανῶν περὶ
τὸν ἀέρα ἔχοντες καὶ τὴν γῆν, οὐκέτι εἰς τὰ
ὑπερουράνια ὑπερκύψαι δυνάμενοι· καὶ αἱ τῶν
γιγάντων ψυχαί, οἳ περὶ τὸν κόσμον εἰσὶ πλανώ-
μενοι δαίμονες.

Minucius Felix (second century), *Octavius*, xxvi   8 15⁸⁻¹² 16¹ 19¹
'Isti igitur spiritus, posteaquam simplici-
tatem substantiae suae, onusti et immersi
vitiis, perdiderunt, ad solatium calamitatis
suae non desinunt perditi iam perdere . et
alienati a Deo, inductis pravis religionibus a
Deo segregare. Eos spiritus daemonas esse
poetae sciunt, philosophi disserunt, Socrates
novit . Magi quoque quicquid miraculi
ludunt, per daemonas faciunt.'

Irenaeus (ob. circa A.D. 202).

i 10. 1 (ed Stieren) Πνεῦμα ἅγιον, τὸ διὰ τῶν   1 En. 10¹³, ¹⁴
προφητῶν κεκηρυχὸς . . κρίσιν δικαίαν ἐν τοῖς
πᾶσι ποιήσηται (sc Χριστὸς Ἰησοῦς) τὰ μὲν
πνευματικὰ τῆς πονηρίας, καὶ ἀγγέλους παρα-
βεβηκότας, καὶ ἐν ἀποστασίᾳ γεγονότας, καὶ τοὺς
ἀσεβεῖς καὶ ἀδίκους καὶ ἀνόμους καὶ βλασφήμους   5⁴, &c
τῶν ἀνθρώπων εἰς τὸ αἰώνιον πῦρ πέμψῃ

i. 15. 6 (a quotation from a 'divine elder and   8³ 'enchantments
preacher of the truth ')   .. astrology '
Εἰδωλοποιέ, Μάρκε, καὶ τερατοσκόπε,
Ἀστρολογικῆς ἔμπειρε καὶ μαγικῆς τέχνης,
Δι' ὧν κρατύνεις τῆς πλάνης τὰ διδάγματα,
Σημεῖα δεικνὺς τοῖς ὑπὸ σοῦ πλανωμένοις,
Ἀποστατικῆς δυνάμεως ἐγχειρήματα
Ἃ σοι χορηγεῖ σὸς πατὴρ Σατᾶν ἀεί,
Δι' ἀγγελικῆς δυνάμεως Ἀζαζὴλ ποιεῖν,   8¹ 'Azazel taught
Ἔχων σε πρόδρομον ἀντιθέου πανουργίας.   men, &c '

iv. 16. 2. 'Sed et Enoch, . . cum esset homo,   12⁴, ⁶ 13 14³⁻⁷ 15
legatione ad angelos fungebatur et translatus   16.
est et conservatur usque nunc testis iudicii

Dei, quoniam angeli quidam transgressi
deciderunt in terram in iudicium '

iv 36. 4 'Et temporibus Noe diluvium inducens,   10² ' a deluge is
uti exstingueret pessimum genus eorum qui   about to come
tune erant hominum, qui iam fructificare   upon the whole
Deo non poterant, cum angeli transgressores   earth, &c '   9⁸
commixti fuissent eis '   'slept with the
                                           women '

v 28. 2. ' Et non est mirandum, si daemoniis   99⁷'impurespirits
et apostaticis spiritibus ministrantibus ei,   and demons '
per eos faciat signa, in quibus seducat habi-   19¹ 'lead (man-
tantes super terram ' Cf Tert *De Idol* iv   kind)astray,&c '

Tertullian, writing between 197 and 223, regards
Enoch as Scripture, *Apol* xxii   Cf. 1 En. 15⁸, ⁹

           (Quoted in note on 15⁸, ⁹)

De Cultu Femin i 2.   8¹⁻³

           (Quoted in note on 8¹.)

i 3 'Scio scripturam Enoch quae hunc ordinem angelis
dedit, non recipi a quibusdam, quia nec in arma-
rium Iudaicum admittitur   Opinor, non puta-
verunt illum ante cataclysmum editam post eum
casum orbis omnium rerum abolitorem salvam esse
potuisse.' But Tertullian proceeds to show that this
was possible . ' cum Enoch filio suo Matusalae nihil
aliud mandaverit quam ut notitiam eorum posteris
suis traderet '   He then pronounces the singular
critical canon   ' cum Enoch eadem scriptura etiam
de domino praedicarit, a nobis quidem nihil omnino
reiciendum est quod pertineat ad nos   A
Iudaeis potest iam videri propterea reiecta, sicut
et cetera fere quae Christum sonant . . . Eo accedit
quod Enoch apud Iudam apostolum testimonium
possidet '

ii 10 (quoted in note on 8¹)   8¹

De Idol. iv.   19¹ 99⁶, ⁷

           (Quoted in notes on 19¹ and 99⁶, ⁷.)

De Idol. ix   *De Virg. Veland* vii ' Si enim propter   6 14⁵.
angelos, scilicet quos legimus a Deo et caelo excidisse
ob concupiscentiam feminarum, &c.'

Clement of Alexandria (circa A D. 150–210) *Eclogae
Prophet* (ed Dindorf).

iii. 456 (quoted in note on 19³)   19³

iii 474 (quoted in note on 8², ³)   8², ³

Strom. (ed. Dindorf), iii 9 (quoted in note on 16³).   8¹⁻³ 16³

Bardesanes (?) (154–222) *Book of the Laws of*   6 &c.
Countries. 'If the angels likewise had not been possessed of personal freedom they would not have consorted with the daughters of men and sinned and fallen from their places.

Julius Africanus (ob. circ. 237) *Chronographia.*   7¹ 8, &c
Πλήθους ἀνθρώπων γενομένου ἐπὶ τῆς γῆς ἄγγελοι τοῦ οὐρανοῦ θυγατράσιν ἀνθρώπων συνῆλθον. Ἐν ἐνίοις ἀντιγράφοις εὗρον, ' οἱ υἱοὶ τοῦ Θεοῦ .' Εἰ δὲ ἐπ' ἀγγέλων νοοῖτο ἔχειν τούτους, τοὺς περὶ μαγείας καὶ γοητείας, ἔτι δὲ ἀριθμῶν κινήσεως, τῶν μετεώρων ταῖς γυναιξὶ τὴν γνῶσιν παραδεδωκέναι, ἀφ' ὧν ἐποίησαν τοὺς παῖδας τοὺς γίγαντας, δι' οὓς τῆς κακίας ἐπιγενομένης, &c.

Origen (185–254) does not regard Enoch as inspired, and yet he does not wholly reject it. Cf. *Contra Celsum*, v. 52. Celsus argues that other ἄγγελοι descended to the earth before Christ ἐλθεῖν γὰρ καὶ ἄλλους λέγουσι πολλάκις καὶ ὁμοῦ γε ἑξήκοντα ἢ ἑβδομήκοντα· οὓς δὴ γενέσθαι κακοὺς καὶ κολάζεσθαι δεσμοῖς ὑποβληθέντας ἐν γῇ ὅθεν καὶ τὰς θερμὰς πηγὰς εἶναι τὰ ἐκείνων δάκρυα. In a lengthy rejoinder Origen remarks, v. 54 ἐν ταῖς ἐκκλησίαις οὐ πάνυ φέρεται ὡς θεῖα τὰ ἐπιγεγραμμένα τοῦ 'Ενὼχ βιβλία (cf. 1 En. 6 10¹¹⁻¹² 67⁶⁻⁷). That Origen was undecided as to the value to be attached to Enoch is clearer from the following passages. *In Ioannem*, vi. 25 (Lommatzsch, i. 241) ὡς ἐν τῷ 'Ενὼχ γέγραπται, εἴ τῳ φίλον παραδέχεσθαι ὡς ἅγιον τὸ βιβλίον. *In Num. Homil.* xxviii. 2 (Lommatzsch, x 366) 'De quibus quidem nominibus plurima in libellis, qui appellantur Enoch, secreta continentur, et arcana· sed quia libelli ipsi non videntur apud Hebraeos in auctoritate haberi, interim nunc ea quae ibi nominantur ad exemplum vocare differamus'. *De Princip.* i. 3. 3 (Lommatzsch, xxi. 73) 'Sed et in Enoch libro his similia describuntur'; iv. 35 (Lommatzsch, xxi. 476), quoted on 19³.

In the vision of Perpetua in *Acta SS. Perpet. et Felic.* (early in third century) vii, viii (ed. Robinson, pp. 72 sqq.), we have a remarkable parallel

vii. After prayer for Dinocrates she sees the place once gloomy now bright, and one drawing water from the pool incessantly. 'Then I understood that he was translated from punishment'

xii. 'the house built of light'

1 En. 22. The divisions for the souls of the dead.

9 'this division has been made for the spirits of the righteous in which there is the bright spring of water'.

14^{9-17}.

Pseudo-Tertullian, Five Books against Marcion, iii. ch. ii (Migne, ii. 1070) A summary of Enoch's life is given in which occur the words 'Sacrilegum genus ut fugeret crudele gigantum.'

Commodianus (flor. 250 A D), *Instructiones* (ed. Migne, *P.L.* v. 203, 204), i 3

'(Deus) Visitari voluit terram ab angelis istam Legitima cuius spreverunt illi dimissi

Tanta fuit forma feminarum, quae flecteret illos.

Ut coinquinati non possent caelo redire,

Rebelles ex illo contra Deum verba misere.

Altissimus inde sententiam misit in illis

De semine quorum gigantes nati feruntur

Ab ipsis in terra artes prolatae fucie,

Et tingere lanas docuerunt et quaeque geruntur,

Mortales et illi mortuos simulacro ponebant.

Omnipotens autem, quod essent de semine pravo,

Non censuit illos recipi defunctos e morte.

Unde modo vagi subvertunt corpora multa ·

Maxime quos hodie colitis et deos oratis

Carmen Apologeticum (1011) :

'Stellae cadunt caeli, iudicantur astra nobiscum.'

Cyprian (flor. 250 A.D), *De Hab. Virg* 14 (Hartel, i, p. 197)

Neque Deus . tinguere . docuit . . . lapillis aut margaritis. . conspiciatur id desuper quod diabolus invenit quae omnia peccatores et apostatae angeli suis artibus prodiderunt, quando ad terrena contagia devoluti a caelesti vigore recesserunt illi et oculos

(cf Jub 4^{15}.)

$6^{1,\,2}$

14^{5}.

$1^{9}\ 13^{2}$.

$10^{4sq}\ 12sq$

7^{2}

8^{1}

19^{1}

15^{6}

19^{1}

18^{13-16}

8^{1} &c.

circumducto nigrore fucaie et genas mendacio
ruboris inficere . '

Pseudo-Cyprian (third century), *Ad Novatianum* (ed.
Haitel, *Cyprian*, iii, p. 67)—a citation of 1 En 1⁹.

'ecce venit cum multis milibus nuntiorum suoium   1⁹.
facere iudicium de omnibus et perdere omnes impios
et arguere omnem carnem de omnibus factis impiorum quae fecerunt impie et de omnibus verbis
impiis quae de Deo locuti sunt peccatores'

Hippolytus (floi 220 A D.), *Or.*
adv. Graecos (ed. Bunsen, *Ana-*
lecta Ante-Nicaena, 1 393)

καὶ οὗτος μὲν ὁ περὶ δαιμόνων τόπος.   1 En. 22³ ' all tho souls of the
Περὶ δὲ ″Αιδου, ἐν ᾧ συνέχονται   children of men '.
ψυχαὶ δικαίων τε καὶ ἀδίκων,
ἀναγκαῖον εἰπεῖν. Ὁ ″Αιδης
τόπος ἐστὶν ἐν τῇ κτίσει ἀκατα-   21¹ ' where things were chaotic '
σκεύαστος, χωρίον ὑπόγειον, ἐν ᾧ
φῶς κόσμου οὐκ ἐπιλάμπει.

Anatolius appointed Bishop of Laodicea in 269. Quoted in
Euseb. *Hist. Eccl.* vii. 82 19 τοῦ δὲ τὸν πρῶτον παρ' Ἑβραίοις
μῆνα περὶ ἰσημερίαν εἶναι, παραστατικὰ καὶ τὰ ἐν τῷ Ἐνὼχ
μαθήματα.

Zosimus of Panopolis (third century), quoted in
Syncellus (Dindorf, 1, 1829, p 24) ·

τοῦτο οὖν ἔφασαν αἱ ἀρχαῖαι καὶ αἱ θεῖαι γραφαί. ὅτι   1 En. 6 7
ἄγγελοί τινες ἐπεθύμησαν τῶν γυναικῶν, καὶ κατελ-
θόντες ἐδίδαξαν αὐτὰς πάντα τὰ τῆς φύσεως ἔργα ὧν   8
χάριν, φησί, προσκρούσαντες ἔξω τοῦ οὐρανοῦ ἔμειναν,
ὅτι πάντα τὰ πονηρὰ καὶ μηδὲν ὠφελοῦντα τὴν ψυχήν,
ἐδίδαξαν τοὺς ἀνθρώπους. ἐξ αὐτῶν φάσκουσιν αἱ
αὐταὶ γραφαὶ καὶ τοὺς γίγαντας γεγενῆσθαι.

Clementine Homilies (written perhaps in the fourth century) ·

viii 12–18 The angels before   1 En. 19¹ After the angels' fall—
their fall descended to the   ' their spiits assuming many
earth (cf Jub 4¹⁵) and πρὸς   different forms '
πᾶσαν ἑαυτοὺς μετέβαλον φύσιν,
ἅτε θειωδεστέρας ὄντες οὐσίας,

καὶ ῥᾳδίως πρὸς πάντα μετα-
τρέπεσθαι δυνάμενοι καὶ ἐγίνοντο
λίθος τίμιος, &c. . .

8¹ ' all kinds of costly stones '
6¹, ² 7¹

κρατούμενοι, εἰς γυναικῶν μίξιν
ὤλισθον· αἷς συμπλακέντες. . . .
σαρκὸς γὰρ αὐτοὶ δεσμοῖς πεπε-
δημένοι κατέχονται, καὶ ἰσχυρῶς
δέδενται. οὗ ἕνεκεν εἰς οὐρανοὺς
ἀνελθεῖν οὐκέτι ἐδυνήθησαν

10⁴ 13¹ 14⁵
14⁵ ' You shall not ascend into
heaven unto all eternity'

Μετὰ γὰρ συνουσίαν ὃ τὸ πρῶτον
ἐγίνοντο ἀπαιτηθέντες, καὶ παρασχεῖν μηκέτι δυνηθέντες διὰ τὸ
ἄλλο τι μετὰ μιασμὸν αὐτοὺς
ποιῆσαι μὴ δύνασθαι, ἀρέσκειν
τε ταῖς ἐρωμέναις βουλόμενοι,
ἀνθ' ἑαυτῶν τοὺς τῆς γῆς μιελοὺς
ὑπέδειξαν. λέγω δὲ τὰ ἐκ μετάλλων
ἄνθη, χρυσόν, χαλκόν, ἄργυρον,
σίδηρον, καὶ τὰ ὅμοια, σὺν τοῖς
τιμιωτάτοις ἅπασιν λίθοις σὺν
τούτοις δὲ τοῖς μαγευθεῖσιν λίθοις
καὶ τὰς τέχνας τῶν πρὸς ἕκαστα
πραγμάτων παρέδοσαν, καὶ μαγείας ὑπέδειξαν, καὶ ἀστρονομίαν
ἐδίδαξαν, δυνάμεις τε ῥιζῶν, καὶ
ὅσα ποτὲ ὑπὸ ἀνθρωπίνης ἐννοίας
εὑρεθῆναι ἀδύνατον ἔτι δὲ χρισοῦ
καὶ ἀργύροι καὶ τῶν ὁμοίων
χύσιν, τάς τε τῶν ἐσθήτων
ποικίλας βαφάς καὶ πάνθ' ἁπλῶς
ὅσαπερ πρὸς κόσμου καὶ τέρψεώς
ἐστι γυναικῶν, τῶν ἐν σαρκὶ
δεθέντων δαιμόνων ἐστὶν εὑρή-
ματα ἐκ δὲ τῆς νόθου μίξεως
αὐτῶν, ἄνθρωποι ἐγένοντο νόθοι
. οὓς . γίγαντας ὠνόμασαν
. . πρὸς τὴν ἑαυτῶν πλησμονὴν
τὸν κόσμον οὐκ ἔχοντες αὐτάρκη
τῶν δὲ ἀλόγων ζώων τότε
ἐπιλιπόντων, οἱ νόθοι ἄνθρωποι
καὶ ἀνθρωπίνων σαρκῶν ἐγεύ-

8¹ ' metals and the art of working them . all kinds of
costly stones '

7¹ ' charms and enchantments '

8³ ' enchantments . . astrology '
7¹ ' the cutting of roots '

8¹ ' bracelets ornaments
and all colouring tinctures '

7² &c.

7³ ' **And when** men could no
longer sustain them. ⁴ The
giants turned against them and
devoured mankind. ⁵ And
they began to sin against birds

σαντο　．　　　　　　　　　　　　　and beasts　．and to devour
　　　　　　　　　　　　　　　　　one another's flesh '.

Ἐπεὶ οὖν αἱ τῶν τεθνεώτων γιγάντων　15⁸ 16¹
ψυχαί, . . ὡς καινὸν γένος, καινῷ
καὶ τῷ ὀνόματι προσηγορεύθησαν
　　ἐξεπέμφθη γὰρ αὐτοῖς ὑπὸ　15²
τοῦ θεοῦ ἄγγελός τις, τὴν αὐτοῦ
βουλὴν μηνύων, καὶ λέγων.
Τάδε δοκεῖ　. . a reference to Jub.
4²² not 1 Enoch

There is a parallel but independent passage in the *Clementine Recognitions* (put together in the fourth century). Both the Homilies and the Recognitions are alike indebted for their main ideas to 1 Enoch.

Clem Recog. iv 26, 27 (ed. Cotelier i, p. 543).

' unde colendi idola exordium mundo huic　　1 En. 19¹
Angeli quidam, relicto proprii ordinis cursu,　15³, ⁶, ⁷
hominum favere vitiis coepere, et libidini eorum
illorum opera, suis magis voluptatibus morem　7¹ 8³, &c
gererent. quique　. docuerunt homines quod
daemones artibus quibusdam obedire mortalibus,
id est, magicis invocationibus possent, ac　　totum
mundum, subtracto pietatis lumine, impietatis fumo　8²
repleverunt. Pio his et aliis nonnullis caussis (cf
Jub 7²¹) diluvium mundo introductum est　　.'　10² 106¹³⁻¹⁵

Lactantius (flor. 320), *Instit.* (Migne, *P L.* vi. 330–332; Brandt and Laubmann, i, pp. 162 sqq.), gives quite a long passage which for its main features is indebted to 1 Enoch.

Instit ii 14 ' Deus　. misit an-　(Jub 4¹⁵)
gelos ad tutelam cultumque
generis humani: quibus . .
praecepit, ante omnia, ne　14⁶⁻⁷
terrae contagione maculati substantiae coelestis amitterent
dignitatem. . .　Itaque illos　69⁴ ' Jeqôn . . . who led astray
cum hominibus commorantes　all the sons of God . . . through
dominator ille terrae　. ad　the daughters of men '.

vitia pellexit, et mulierum congressibus inquinavit.   7¹.
Tum in caelum ob peccata quibus se immerserant   14⁵.
non recepti ceciderunt in terram.   Sic eos diabolus   54⁶
ex angelis Dei suos fecit satellites ac ministros.
Qui autem sunt ex his procreati, quia neque angeli
neque homines fuerunt, sed mediam quandam
naturam gerentes, non sunt ad inferos recepti,   15⁸⁻¹¹ 16¹.
sicut in caelum parentes eorum.   Ita duo genera
daemonum facta sunt, unum caeleste, alterum
terrenum.   Hi sunt immundi spiritus malorum,
quae geruntur, auctores, quorum idem diabolus est   54⁶, &c.
princeps   .   Quod idcirco dictum est, quoniam
custodes eos humano generi Deus miserat · sed et
ipsi, cum sint perditores hominum, custodes tamen
se videri volunt, ut ipsi colantur, et Deus non   19¹.
colatur. .. Magorum quoque ars omnis ac potentia
horum adspirationibus constat, a quibus invocati,
visus hominum praestigiis obcaecantibus fallunt
.. Hi, ut dico, spiritus contaminati ac perditi per
omnem terram vagantur, et in solacium perditionis   15⁹⁻¹¹ 16¹
suae perdendis hominibus operantur. .   Hos in
suis penetralibus consecrant, his cotidie vina pro-
fundunt, et, scientes, daemonas venerantur, quasi
terrestres deos   . 15.   . ex caelestibus de-
pravatos, terrenos esse coepisse .. 16 .. Eorum
inventa sunt astrologia et haruspicina   . et ars
magica.   Hi sunt qui fingere imagines et simu-
lacra docuerunt .. Sed eos magi   veris suis
nominibus cient, illis caelestibus, quae in litteris
sanctis leguntur, &c '

vivi non morientur, sed per eosdem mille annos 10^{17} sq.
infinitam multitudinem generabunt . . Terra vero
aperiet fecunditatem suam et uberrimas fruges sua
sponte generabit, rupes montium melle sudabunt,
per rivos vina decurrent, &c '

vii. 26. All the wicked 'shall be burnt for ever in the 1 En. 48⁹
sight of the angels and righteous '.

Priscillian (ob. 380). *De Fide et de Apocryphis*
(Schepss, 1889, p 44), apparently did not know
1 Enoch, but urges from the example of 'Jude' and
'Paul' (Ep. Hebr. 11⁵) that it is admissible to
cite non-canonical works, as they both refer to
Enoch.

Cassianus (360–435), *Collatio* VIII. xxi '. . . illa opinio 1 En 8¹.
vulgi, qua credunt angelos vel maleficia vel diversas
artes hominibus tradidisse '.

Thenceforward the book fails to secure a single favourable
notice. *Hilary*, who died 368 A.D., writes in his *Comment. in Ps*
cxxxii. 3 'Fertur id de quo etiam nescio cuius liber extat, quod
angeli concupiscentes filias hominum, cum de caelo descenderent,
in hunc montem Hermon maxime convenerant excelsum '. Chry-
sostom (346–407) does not indeed mention Enoch, but declares
that the story of the angels and the daughters of men rests on
a false exegesis, *Homil in Gen*. vi. 1, and is a blasphemous fable.

Jerome (346–420) regards Enoch as apocryphal. *De Viris
Illustr.* iv 'Iudas frater Iacobi parvam, quae de septem catho-
licis est, epistolam reliquit. Et quia de libro Enoch, qui
apocryphus est, in ea assumit testimonia a plerisque reicitur
tamen auctoritatem vetustate iam et usu meruit et inter sanctas
computatur '. *Comment. in Ps.* cxxxii. 3 'Legimus in quodam
libro apocrypho, eo tempore, quo descendebant filii dei ad filias
hominum, descendisse illos in montem Hermon, et ibi iniisse
pactum quomodo venirent ad filias hominum et sibi eas sociarent
Manifestissimus liber est et inter apocryphos computatur .
Comment. in Epist. ad Titum, i. 12 'Qui autem putant totum
librum debere sequi eum, qui libri parte usus sit, videntur mihi
et apocryphum Enochi, de quo Apostolus Iudas in Epistola sua
testimonium posuit, inter ecclesiae scripturas recipere '.

Augustine (354–429) pronounces strongly against Enoch. *De Cu. Dei*, xv. 23. 4 'Scripsisse quidem nonnulla divina Enoch illum septimum ab Adam, negare non possumus, cum hoc in Epistola canonica Iudas Apostolus dicat. Sed non frustra non sunt in eo canone Scripturaium . . . Unde illa quae sub eins nomine proferuntur et continent istas de gigantibus fabulas, quod non habuerint homines patres, recte a prudentibus iudicantur non ipsius esse credenda'. Cp also *De Cn. Dei*, xviii. 38.

Enoch is finally condemned in explicit terms in *Constit Apostol.* vi. 16 καὶ ἐν τοῖς παλαιοῖς δέ τινες συνέγραψαν βιβλία ἀπόκρυφα Μωσέως καὶ Ἐνὼχ καὶ Ἀδάμ, Ἠσαΐου τε καὶ Δαβὶδ καὶ Ἡλία καὶ τῶν τριῶν πατριαρχῶν, φθοροποιὰ καὶ τῆς ἀληθείας ἐχθρά· τοιαῦτα καὶ νῦν ἐπενόησαν οἱ δυσώνυμοι, διαβάλλοντες δημιουργίαν, γάμον, πρόνοιαν, τεκνογονίαν, νόμον, προφήτας.

Under the ban of such authorities the book of Enoch gradually passed out of circulation and knowledge in the Western Church, and with the exception of 6–9⁴ 8⁴–10¹⁴ 15⁸–16¹ and another fragment which are preserved by *Syncellus* in his *Chronography*, pp. 20–23, 42–47 (ed. Dind. 1829), it was lost to Western Christendom till the present century. Syncellus adds that the book of Enoch runs counter in some respects to the tradition of the Church, and is untrustworthy through the interpolations of Jews and heretics· καὶ ταῦτα μὲν ἐκ τοῦ πρώτου βιβλίου Ἐνὼχ περὶ τῶν ἐγρηγόρων, εἰ καὶ μὴ τελείως χρὴ προσέχειν ἀποκρύφοις μάλιστα τοὺς ἁπλουστέρους, διά τε τὸ περιττά τινα καὶ ἀτριβῆ τῆς ἐκκλησιαστικῆς παραδόσεως ἔχειν καὶ διὰ τὸ νενοθεῦσθαι αὐτὰ ὑπὸ Ἰουδαίων καὶ αἱρετικῶν (ed. Dindorf, pp. 47, 48).

There are also parallels in Gnostic and Apocryphal Literature to 1 Enoch.

In the Gnostic work, *Pistis Sophia*, composed in Egypt in the third century, we find two apparent references to Enoch.

Pistis Sophia (ed. Schwaitze, 1851–1853, p. 245).

'Invenietis ea in secundo libro Ieu, quae scripsit Enoch, quum	1 En. 32³ 'the Garden of Righteousness . . the tiee of

loquerer cum eo ex arbore cognitionis et ex arbore vitae in παραδείσῳ Adami. (Translated from the Coptic)

(p. 25) 'μυστήρια — quae portarant desuper ἄγγελοι peccatores, quorum (μυστηρίων) sunt μαγία'

knowledge'　⁶ 'thy father old . . ., &c.'

7¹ 8³

In the Gnostic *Acts of Thomas* 1 Enoch may be referred to in the words of the Dragon.—

ch xxxii (Tisch *Acta Apostolorum Apocrypha*, p 218) ·

ἐγώ εἰμι ὁ τοὺς ἀγγέλους ἄνωθεν κάτω ῥίψας καὶ ἐν ταῖς ἐπιθυμίαις τῶν γυναικῶν αὐτοὺς καταδήσας, ἵνα γηγενεῖς παῖδες ἐξ αὐτῶν γένωνται, &c

6⁶ 'they descended, &c.', 86³ 'many stars descend and cast themselves down from heaven, &c'
7², ⁴, &c., 'giants'.

The *Acts of 'the Disputation of Archelaus with Manes'* (written perhaps at the beginning of the fourth century)

ch. xxxii (Routh, *Reliquiae*, iv, p. 211) .

'Angelorum quidam, mandato Dei non subditi, voluntati eius restiterunt, et aliquis quidem de caelo, tanquam fulgur ignis, cecidit super terram, alii vero infelicitate hominum filiabus admixti, a dracone afflicti, ignis aeterni poenam suscipere meruerunt'

86¹ 'a star fell from heaven' ³ 'many stars descend and cast themselves down from heaven'. 7¹ 'they began to go in unto them'. 15³ 18¹¹, ¹²

The Narrative of Joseph of Arimathea (date uncertain) has an unexpected parallel to 1 Enoch.

iii. 3 (Tisch. *Evangelia Apocrypha*, 2nd ed, Lipsiae, 1876, p. 465) The dying thief addresses Christ in the following words.

μὴ ἐν ἐξετάσει σου ποιήσεις τὰ

100¹⁰, ¹² 'from the angels He

ἄστρα ἐλθεῖν κατ' ἐμοῦ ἢ τὴν σελήνην, ὅταν μέλλῃς κρῖναι πᾶσαν τὴν οἰκουμένην, ὅτι ἐν νυκτὶ ἔπραττον τὰς κακάς μου βουλάς μὴ κινήσεις τὸν ἥλιον   οὐδὲν γὰρ ἀφέσεως ἁμαρτιῶν δῶρον δύναμαί σοι παρασχεῖν.

will inquire as to your deeds in heaven, from the sun and from the moon and from the stars in reference to your sins . . And now give presents to the rain that it be not withheld, &c.'

The Apocalypse of Paul has a similar but not identical idea

4 sqq. (Tisch , *Apocal Apocr.*, $100^{10, 12}$.
p. 36).

The sun, and also the moon and the stars, come to the Lord and ask leave to punish men for their sins   As the sun sets πάντες οἱ ἄγγελοι ἔρχονται πρὸς τὸν θεὸν προσκυνῆσαι αὐτῷ, καὶ προσάγουσιν τὰ ἔργα τῶν ἀνθρώπων ἑκάστου ὅ τι ἔπραξεν, &c.

In the Book of Adam and Eve we have references to 1 Enoch as well as to 2 Enoch, and a definite rejection of its teaching.

2^{22} (ed Malan, 1882)
' Enoch to whom many wonders happened and who also wrote a celebrated book '

3^4 ' Certain wise men of old   6–10.
wrote concerning them (the giants) and say in their books, that angels came down from heaven and mingled with the daughters of Cain, who bare unto them these giants   But those err in what they say .
They were children of Seth '

2^{15} ' Jared continued to teach 6^6 ' who descended in the days
his children eighty years , but   of Jared '
after that they began to go down from the Holy Mountain   and to mix with the children of Cain '   Genun had

taught the children of Cain to make musical instruments and induced them to commit all kinds of wickedness, and finally 'took iron and with it made weapons of war' 'Satan taught him (Genun) to make dyeing stuffs for garments of divers patterns, and made him to understand how to dye crimson and purple and what not'	8^1
	8^1. 14^3
'Ye shall not come up hither again for ever'	
2^3 'the middle of the earth' (= Jerusalem) Cf 2^{21} $3^{13,\,14}$ 4^3.	26^1 90^{26}
2^{22} 'the mansions of the righteous and of the chosen'.	39^4 'the mansions of the holy and the resting-places of the righteous'. $6,7$ 'the righteous and the elect'

For further treatment of the subject see H. J. Lawlor's article in the *Journal of Philology*, vol. xxv, pp. 164–225, to which I express my indebtedness.

§ 19. THE INFLUENCE OF 1 ENOCH ON THE NEW TESTAMENT.

The influence of 1 Enoch on the New Testament has been greater than that of all the other apocryphal and pseud-epigraphal books taken together. The evidence for this con-clusion may for the sake of convenience be arranged under two heads. (A) A series of passages of the New Testament which either in phraseology or idea directly depend on or are illustrative of passages in 1 Enoch. (B) Doctrines in 1 Enoch which had an undoubted share in moulding the corresponding New Testament doctrines.

(A) We will begin with the General Epistles. I quote from the Revised Version when a more accurate rendering is desirable.

New Testament	*1 Enoch*
(a) St. Jude [4] Denying our only Master and Lord Jesus Christ.	48^{10} 'Denied the Lord of Spirits and His anointed'. Cf. 38^2 41^2.

New Testament	1 *Enoch*
[6] 'The angels which left their own abode'	12[4] 'the Watchers .. who have left the high heaven, &c'
' reserved . great day'	10[4—6] [11, 12] 'Bind . darkness judgement'
[13] 'Wandering stars'	18[15] 21[2] [3, 6]
[14] 'The seventh from Adam'.	60[5] 'The seventh from Adam'
[14, 15] A direct quotation from	1[9] Cf 5[4] 27[2]
1 St. Peter 3[19, 20]	10[4, 5, 12, 13] 19[1] 20[1]
2 St. Peter 2[4]	10[4—6, 12, 13] 12[5] 13[2]
3[13] 'A new heaven and a new earth'	45[4, 5] 72[1] 91[16]
1 St John 1[7] 'Walk in the light'	92[4] 'The righteous . shall walk in eternal light'

[The contrast between light and darkness in St. John's Epistles repeatedly enforced in 1 Enoch See 38[4] (note)]

2[1] 'Jesus Christ the righteous'.	53[6] 'The Righteous and Elect One'
2[8] 'The darkness is past and the true light already shineth'	58[5] It has become bright as the sun upon earth, and the darkness is past'
2[15] 'Love not the world, nor the things which are in the world'	108[8] 'loved nor any of the good things which are in the world' Cf 48[7]
3[2] 'We shall be like Him'	90[37, 38]
St James 1[8] 'Double-minded man'.	91[4] 'A double heart' See note
5[1—6] Woes against the rich.	94[8—11], also 46[7] 63[10] 96[4—8] 97[8—10]

(*b*) *Book of Revelation.*—The writer or writers of this book are steeped in Jewish apocalyptic literature.

Rev. 1[4] 'Seven spirits which are before His throne' Cf 4[5], also 'the seven angels' 8[2]	90[21] 'those men the seven first white ones' Cf Tobit 12[15]
2[7] 'To him that overcometh will I give to eat of the tree of life'. also 22[2, 14] ('the right to the tree of life') [19].	25[4—6] Only the elect, the righteous and holy, in the Messianic kingdom are allowed to eat of the tree of life

New Testament	*1 Enoch*
3⁵ ' Clothed in white raiment '.	90³¹ ' Clothed in white '
¹⁰ ' Them that dwell upon the earth '.	37⁵ ' Those that dwell on the earth '

[This phrase has always a bad sense in Revelation with the exception of 14⁶ Cf. 6¹⁰ 8¹³ 11¹⁰ 13⁸, ¹⁴ 17⁸, and that in this respect Revelation follows the use of this phrase in the Noachic interpolations, see 1 En 37⁵ (note).]

3¹² ' The New Jerusalem '	90²⁹ ' A new house '.
3¹⁷ ' I am rich and increased with goods '	97⁸ ' We have become rich with riches and have possessions, &c.'
²⁰ ' I will come unto him and sup with him '.	62¹⁴ ' and with that Son of Man shall they (the righteous) eat, and lie down, and rise up for ever and ever '.
²¹ ' Sit with Me on My throne '. Cf 20⁴	108¹² ' I will seat each on the throne of his honour '
4⁶ ' Round about the throne were four living creatures '	40² ' On the four sides of the Lord of Spirits I saw four presences '
4⁸ ' they rest not . saying '.	39¹³ ' who sleep not and say '
5¹¹.	14²² 40¹ 71⁸
6¹⁰ ' How long, O Master, the holy and true, dost thou not judge and avenge our blood on them that dwell on the earth ? '	47² ' that the prayer of the righteous may not be in vain before the Lord of Spirits, That judgement may be done unto them, And that they may not have to suffer for ever '. Cf 97⁸⁻⁷ 99³, ¹⁶ 104³: also 22⁵⁻⁷ where the soul of a righteous man in Hades prays for vengeance.
6¹⁵, ¹⁶ Compare the fear of ' the kings of the earth, and the princes, and the chief captains, and the rich, and the strong ' when they see ' the face of him that sitteth on the throne '	62³, ⁵ ' the kings, and the mighty, and the exalted shall be terrified . And pain shall seize them, When they see that Son of Man sitting on the throne of his glory '.
7¹ The four angels of the winds	69²² ' The spirits of the winds '

New Testament	*1 Enoch*
[15] ' He that sitteth on the throne shall dwell among them '.	45[4] ' I will cause Mine Elect One to dwell among them '.
[17] ' Shall guide them unto fountains of waters of life '	48[1] ' fountain of righteousness fountains of wisdom '
8[3, 4] Angel with golden censer of incense offers it with the prayers of the saints before God. In 5[8] the elders do so also.	This intercession of the angels is found frequently in 1 Enoch, 9[1-3, 11] 15[2] 40[7] 47[2] 99[3].
9[1] ' I saw a star from heaven fallen unto the earth ' [14-15]	86[1] ' And I saw . and behold a star fell from heaven '. 66[1].
[20] ' Repented not of the works of their hands that they should not worship demons, and the idols of gold, and of silver, and of brass, and of stone, and of wood '. 10[5-7].	99[7] ' who worship stones and grave images of gold, and silver, and wood, ⟨and stone⟩ and clay, and those who worship impure spirits and demons '. 16[1].
12[10] ' The accuser of our brethren is cast down '	40[7] ' fending off the Satans and forbidding them to come . . . to accuse them who dwell on the earth '.
13[14] ' Deceiveth them that dwell on the earth '.	54[6] ' Leading astray those who dwell on the earth ' Cf 67[7].
14[9, 10]. The worshippers of the beast are to be ' tormented with fire and brimstone in the . presence of the holy angels, and in the presence of the lamb '	48[9] The unrighteous 'burn before the face of the holy . sink before the face of the righteous'
[10] ' Holy angels '.	*passim* . e g 71[1]
[13] ' Blessed are the dead, &c.'	81[4]
[20] ' Blood came out of the winepress even unto the horses' bridles '	100[3] ' The horse shall walk up to the breast in the blood of sinners '.
16[5] ' Angel of the waters '.	60[16] ' the spirit of the sea '.
17[14] ' Lord of lords and King of kings '.	9[4] ' Lord of lords . . King of kings '
20[12] ' And the books were opened ' and ' another book was opened which is the book of life '.	90[20] ' took the sealed books and opened those books '. 47[3] ' The books of the living '.

New Testament	1 Enoch
13 'The sea gave up the dead which were in it, and death and Hades gave up the dead which were in them'	51¹ 'in those days shall the earth also give back that which has been entrusted to it, and Sheol also shall give back that which it has received, and hell shall give back that which it owes' Cf 61⁵.

20¹¹⁻¹⁵. The last judgement is held after the temporary Messianic kingdom (20⁴, ⁵), just as in 1 En. 91~104   There is, however, no resurrection in the temporary Messianic kingdom of 1 Enoch as there is in Revelation

15 'Cast into the lake of fire'.	90²⁰ 'Cast into this fiery abyss'.

21¹, ² We have here a new heaven and a new earth, and a new Jerusalem coming down from heaven   yet in 22¹⁴, ¹⁵ all classes of sinners are said to be without the gates of the city   But if there were a new earth this would be impossible.   This contradiction may have arisen from combining the divergent Messianic conceptions which appear in 1 Enoch   Cf 45⁴, ⁵ 90²⁹

22⁷ 'no more curse'	25⁶ 'no sorrow or plague or torment or calamity'

(c) We shall next deal with the *Epistles of St. Paul*   This Apostle, as we know, borrowed both phraseology and ideas from many quarters: from the Greek poets; from the apocryphal writings, as the Book of Wisdom; from the lost Revelation of Elias—1 Cor 2⁹ according to Origen, and Eph. 5¹⁴ according to Epiphanius.   We shall find that he was well acquainted with and used 1 Enoch.

Rom 8³⁴ 'Neither angels, nor principalities, nor powers'	61¹⁰ 'angels of power and . angels of principalities'.
9⁵ 'God blessed for ever'	77¹ 'He who is blessed for ever'.
1 Cor. 6¹¹ 'Justified in the name of the Lord Jesus'	48⁷ 'in his (i.e. the Messiah's) name they are saved'.

1 Cor 11¹⁰. Tertullian, *C Marc* v. 8, *de Virg Veland* 7, explains this verse through a reference to the bad angels spoken of in 1 Enoch who would be incited to wantonness by unveiled women

2 Cor. 4⁶ 'To give the light of the knowledge of the glory of God in the face of Jesus Christ'	38⁴ 'The Lord of Spirits has caused His light to appear on the face of the holy, righteous, and elect'

New Testament	1 Enoch
5²⁻⁴	62¹⁵⁻¹⁶.
11³¹ 'He who is blessed for ever .	77¹ ' He who is blessed for ever '
Gal 1⁴ ' This present evil world '.	48⁷ ' this world of unrighteousness '.
Eph. 1²¹ ' Above all principality and power ',	61¹⁰ ' angels of power and angels of principalities '.
⁹ ' According to His good pleasure '.	49⁴ ' according to His good pleasure '.
5⁸ ' Children of light.'	108¹¹ ' the generation of light '
Phil. 2¹⁰ ' At the name of Jesus every knee should bow '.	48⁵ ' shall fall down and worship before Him ' (i e. the Messiah)
Col. 1¹⁶ ' Principalities and powers '	61¹⁰ ' angels of powers and angels of principalities '
2³ ' In whom are hid all the treasures of wisdom and knowledge '.	46³ ' the Son of man . . who reveals all the treasures of that which is hidden '.
1 Thess 5³ 'Then sudden destruction cometh upon them as upon a woman with child '.	62⁴ ' Then shall pain come upon them as on a woman in travail '.

Both these passages refer to the sudden appearing of the Messiah.

5⁵ ' Sons of light '	108¹¹ ' the generation of light '.
2 Thess 1⁷ ' The angels of His power '	61¹⁰ ' the angels of power '.
1 Tim 1⁹ ' Law is not made for a righteous man but for the lawless ', &c	93⁴ ' a law shall be made for the sinners '.
1¹⁵ ' Worthy of all acceptation ' (cf. 4⁹).	94¹ ' worthy of acceptation '.
5²¹ ' The elect angels '	39¹ ' elect and holy children . from the high heaven '.
6¹⁵ ' King of Kings and Lord of Lords '.	9⁴ ' Lord of Lords . . King of Kings '.
¹⁶ ' Dwelling in the light which no man can approach unto, whom no man hath seen '	14²¹ ' None of the angels could enter and could behold His face by reason of the magnificence and glory '

(*d*) *Epistle to the Hebrews.* This Epistle was possibly written by Barnabas. As we have seen above (p lxxxi) this writer cites 1 Enoch as Scripture in the Epistle which goes by his name.

New Testament

Hebrews 4¹³ ' There is no creature that is not manifest in His sight but all things are naked and laid open before the eyes of Him with whom we have to do '

11⁵ ' Enoch was translated . . for before his translation he had this testimony that he pleased God '.

11¹⁰ ' The city which hath foundations whose builder and maker is God ' (cf 13¹⁴)

12⁹ ' Father of spirits '.

¹² ' The heavenly Jerusalem '

(e) Acts of the Apostles.

3¹⁴ ' The Righteous One ', i e. Christ. Cf also 7³² 22¹⁴

4¹² ' There is none other name under heaven .   whereby we must be saved '.

10⁴ ' Thy prayers . . are gone up for a memorial before God '

17³¹ ' He will judge the world in righteousness by the man whom He hath ordained '

(f) The Gospels.

St. John 2¹⁶ The temple is called ' God's house ', but owing to

1 Enoch

9⁵ ' all things are naked and open in Thy sight, and Thou seest all things, and nothing can hide itself from Thee '

The parallel passage must, it seems, depend on the Enoch book where Enoch is always accounted an example of righteousness and therefore translated Cf 15¹ &c In Sirach 44¹⁶ Enoch is translated indeed, but is cited as an example of repentance. Philo, *De Abrahamo*, speaks of the former evil life of Enoch.

90²⁹ God Himself builds the New Jerusalem.

' Lord of Spirits ', 37² and *passim* in Parables

90²⁰.

53⁶ ' the Righteous and Elect One ' (i e the Messiah)

48⁷ ' in His (i.e the Messiah's) name they are saved '

99³ ' raise your prayers as a memorial . . before the Most High '.

41⁹ ' He appoints a judge for them all and he judges them all before Him '.

89⁵¹ Temple = ' house ' of ' the Lord of the sheep '. But in

New Testament	*1 Enoch*
sin of Israel 'your house', i e merely house of Israel in St Luke 13[15] and parallels.	89[56] owing to sin of Israel it is said 'He forsook that their house'.
5[22] 'He hath committed all judgement unto the Son'	69[27] 'the sum of judgement was given unto the Son of Man'.
[27] 'He gave him authority to execute judgement because he is the Son of Man'	
8[12]	48[4]
12[36] 'Sons of light'	108[11] 'the generation of light'
14[2] 'Many mansions'	39[4] 'dwelling-places of the holy and the resting-place of the righteous' Cf. 39[7] 48[1], &c.
	46[4] 'shall †raise up† (Read 'put down') the kings from their seats'.
St Luke 1[52] 'He hath put down princes from their thrones'	
9[35] 'This is My Son, the Elect One' So Greek ὁ ἐκλελεγμένος.	40[5] 'the Elect One', i e the Messiah. Cf. 45[3, 4] ('Mine Elect One'); 49[2, 4], &c.
13[35] See on St John 2[16]	
16[8] 'Sons of the light'.	108[11] the generation of light'.
16[9] 'Mammon of unrighteousness'.	63[10] 'unrighteous gains'
18[7] 'Shall not God avenge His elect which cry to Him day and night, and He is long-suffering over them' Cf 2 Pet 3[9], Sir 32[18]	47[1, 2] 'the prayer of the righteous . that judgement may be done unto them and that they may not have to suffer for ever'
21[28] 'Your redemption draweth nigh'	51[2] 'the day has drawn nigh that they should be saved'.
23[35] 'The Christ of God, the Elect One', ὁ ἐκλεκτός.	40[5] 'The Elect One'.
St Matthew 5[22, 29, 30] 10[28] where Gehenna is the place of final punishment.	27[2] 90[26, 27] where Gehenna first definitely appears as hell.
8[21]	16[1]
13[42]	98[3]
19[28] 'When the Son of Man shall sit on the throne of His glory'	62[5] 'When they see that Son of Man sitting on the throne of his glory'

New Testament	1 Enoch
19^{28} 'Ye also shall sit on twelve thrones'.	108^{12} 'I will seat each on the throne of his honour'.
19^{29} 'Inherit eternal life'.	40^{9} 'inherit eternal life'
21^{13} 23^{38} See St. John 2^{16}	89^{56} 89^{54}.}
25^{41} 'Prepared for the devil and his angels'	$54^{4,\,5}$ 'chains . . . prepared for the hosts of Azazel'.
26^{24} 'It had been good for that man if he had not been born'.	38^{2} 'It had been good for them if they had not been born'
28^{18} 'All authority hath been given to Me in heaven and on earth'.	62^{6} '(the Son of man) who rules over all'.
St. Mark 11^{17} See St John 2^{6}.	89^{54}.

§ 20. Theology.

The books or sections of Enoch were written by orthodox Jews, who belonged to the apocalyptic or prophetic side of Judaism, and by Judaism is here meant, not the one-sided legalistic Judaism that posed as the sole and orthodox Judaism after the fall of Jerusalem in 70 A D., but the larger and more comprehensive Judaism that preceded it. This larger Judaism embraced both the prophetic and the legalistic elements. No religion can make progress without both elements, and, if progress in spiritual development is to be realized, the prophetic element is absolutely indispensable.

Most Jewish writers have ascribed the Book of Enoch and kindred literature to the Essenes. But this is indefensible. For the Essenes, if we are to accept the account of Josephus, *Bell. Iud.* ii. 8. 2 , *Ant.* xviii. 1. 5 , Philo, ii. 633–634 Ἐσσαίων οὐδεὶς ἄγεται γυναῖκα; and Pliny, *Hist. Nat.* v. 17 (see Schürer³, ii. 568), Hippolytus, *Refutatio omnium Haeres.* ix. 18–28, entirely condemned marriage. Now so far is this from being the case in 1 Enoch, that not only is no word said against marriage in any of the sections, but marriage is glorified and fruitful wedlock in 6–36 as having its place in the Messianic kingdom. When later this kingdom became wholly of a spiritual nature, as in 91–104 or 37–71, marriage could no longer be considered as a part of the Messianic blessedness. Again, whereas the Essenes objected to animal sacrifice, no such objection is taken either in 1 or 2 Enoch In the former in 89⁵⁰ the temple sacrifices are referred to with complete approval in the words 'and they offered a full table before Him'. In 89⁷³ the sacrifices are said to be 'polluted', but no condemnation of sacrifice in itself is here implied. The writer uses no stronger words than Mal. 1⁷, 'Ye offer polluted bread upon Mine altar.' In 2 Enoch 59²⁻³ the spiritual value of animal sacrifice is clearly expressed. Furthermore, not a word is said on behalf of certain characteristic beliefs of Essenism—such as the necessity of bathing before meals and at other times, the duty of having all things in common and of having common meals, the rejection of anointing the body, the claim that all were free and that none should be slaves.

The teaching of our books on the chief doctrines of Judaism will now be given under the following heads

Origin of evil. Moral evil is not brought into causal connexion with the transgression of Adam save in one passage, i. e. 69¹¹ (Book of Noah), where it is stated that man was created originally righteous and immortal, but that death got power over him through sin.[1] This thought is not worked out or even touched upon in the other sections. Throughout 6–36 moral evil is traced to the lust of the Watchers 6–7, 15, and the revelations of Azazel 9⁶ 10⁸. The origin of evil is thus carried back into the spiritual world. But even when the Watchers were judged and imprisoned and their children destroyed, the evil set in movement by them was not at an end, for the disembodied spirits of their children became demons 15⁸, ⁹, ¹¹ 16¹ (cf. 99⁷), who were to work moral ruin on the earth without hindrance till the final judgement 16¹. 6–36, here, develops the view propounded in Gen. 6¹⁻³ that evil originated in the angelic world : and the same view is implied in 83–90. The origin of evil is

---

[1] In this same source 69⁶ it is said that the Satan Gadreel seduced Eve cf. 4 Macc. 18⁷ ⁸˙.

carried back one stage further in 37–71. Sin, as affecting mankind at large, did not originate with the Watchers, but with the
Satans, 40[7], who appear to belong to a counter kingdom of evil
ruled by a chief called Satan 53[d]. They existed as evil
agencies before the fall of the Watchers, for the guilt of the
latter consisted in their becoming subject to Satan, and so subsequently leading mankind astray 54[d].

Angelology. The angelology appears in our book in a very
developed form. The subject is too large to enter on here. The
reader can consult the Index. We might, however, shortly
remark that the seven archangels 20[1–8] 81[5] 87[2, 3] 88[1] 90[21, 22] form
the highest order, their names being given in 20[7]. In 40 only four
of these are mentioned as the angels of the presence. Then come
the Cherubim, Seraphim, Ophannim, the angel of peace, angels
of principalities and powers, Watchers, angels of punishment.

Demonology. Two classes can be clearly distinguished here.
(a) The fallen Watchers or the angels who kept not their first
estate 6 15[3] 69[2–3] 86 106[13–14]. These are referred to in Jude 6
and 1 Pet. 2[4]. From the time of their first judgement anterior
to the Deluge they were kept imprisoned in darkness. They
were subject to Satan 54[b]. (b) The demons 15[8, 9, 11] 16[1] 19 99[7].
The demons are, according to 16[1], the spirits which went forth
from the souls of the giants, who were the children of the fallen
angels and the daughters of men. These demons were to work
moral ruin on the earth without hindrance till the final judgement as disembodied spirits.

So in the N T. the demons are disembodied spirits, Matt. 12[43–45]
Luke 11[24–26]. They are not punished till the final judgement.
This is clearly the explanation of Matt 8[29], 'Art thou come
hither to torment us *before the time* ?' They are subject to
Satan, Matt. 12[24–28].

Soul and Spirit On this very complex problem see my
Eschatology, 231–233.

Salvation by works and yet by grace.

The moral ideal is summed up in terms of righteousness and

uprightness. The Son of Man is himself the ideally righteous one 46⁵ :—

> 'This is the Son of Man who hath righteousness
> With whom dwelleth righteousness . . .
> And whose lot hath the pre-eminence before the Lord of
>   Spirits in uprightness for ever.'

Man's duty is to 'love righteousness and walk therein' 94¹. Cf 91¹⁹. The freedom of the will is assumed, and two ways are set before man for his choice, 'the ways of righteousness and the ways of violence' 91¹⁸ 94³. Though the writer of 91–104 acknowledges the activity of the demonic world 99⁷ (cf. 100⁴), yet he maintains that it is in man's power to attain to righteousness and that a man's sin is of his own devising, and attacks in unmeasured terms the immoral view that sin is something original and unavoidable, 98⁴ᶜᵈᵉ —

> 'Even so sin has not been sent upon the earth,
> But man of himself has created it,
> And under a great curse shall they fall who commit it.'

On the other hand, the writer of 37–71 is conscious of the need of a spiritual dynamic. Thus he very frequently calls the righteous 'the elect'—a phrase found only four times outside 37–71 in this book Yet there is no determinism All righteous living is the outcome of dependence on God Thus he speaks of 'the faithful who hang upon the name of the Lord of Spirits' 46⁸ᵇ, 'the elect ones who hang upon the Lord of Spirits' 40⁵, and of 'the righteous whose elect works hang upon the Lord of Spirits' 38²ᵇ Their works are thus wrought in conscious fellowship with God And when by sin they fall from such fellowship, they are forgiven on repentance 40⁹.[1] These works, moreover, shall be tested at the judgement 45⁸ᵇ, they shall be weighed in the balance 41¹ 61⁸ᶜ. But this idea is not incompatible with divine grace. But progress is not limited to this world In the Messianic kingdom they will seek the light and find righteousness, and they will have peace 58⁴ᵃᵇ, and their life

---

[1] The Gentiles also can repent and turn to God 50²′³.

will be a constant progress from light to light and righteousness
to righteousness—which is the heritage that has been preserved
for them by the Messiah 58[5, 6].

Retribution, national and individual. The problem of combining both these types of retribution had been partly solved in
the O.T. With the new solution of the problem of national
retribution we shall deal under the title 'the Kingdom'. But
the more difficult of the two problems had to do with the
individual. Earthly prosperity is no mark of the divine favour,
but only a source of delusion to those who experience it.
In 91–104 the writer denies Ezekiel's doctrine that a man's
earthly condition corresponds to his moral desert. The wicked
often enjoy unbroken prosperity in this life 102[6–11] 103[5d, 6b],
and die in honour 103[6c], and the righteous fare ill 102[6b],
and die in darkness and tribulation 102[7a 11]. But the righteous are bidden to be of good cheer, though their life on
earth be only such as sinners deserved, and their latter end be
full of grief, for in the next life the balance will be redressed,
and 'all goodness and joy and glory are prepared for them and
written down for the spirits of those who have died in righteousness' 103[3] 'The angels remember' them 'for good before the
glory of the Great One' 104[1] for though aforetime they were
'put to shame through ill and affliction', they shall in due time
'shine as the lights of heaven' and 'the portals of heaven shall
be opened' to them 104[2], and they 'shall become companions of
the hosts of heaven' 104[6]. And as for the wicked their recompense is awaiting them, for they shall 'descend into Sheol . .
and into darkness and chains and a burning flame where there
is grievous judgement' shall their spirits enter for all the
generations of the world 103[7, 8].

We cannot leave this subject without confessing 'how nobly
its author maintains the cause of goodness in the face of
triumphant evil, how unhesitatingly he concedes that this
world gives its best to the unrighteous and the sinner, and
that godliness can find no stay or encouragement therein. Yet

though the lot of the latter is thus one of contumely and rebuke and shame, the righteous are not for a moment to regret their high calling, but to be steadfast and hopeful; for the day of their glorification is at hand. It is a noble work, yet falls . . . short of what was noblest in the past. It never reminds the faithful, as do some of the psalmists, that present life and communion with God more than outweigh every temporal blessing' (see my *Eschatology, Hebrew, Jewish, and Christian*, p. 212).

On the teaching of 6–36 see pp 3 sq., 222, and on that of 37–71 see pp. 67 sq.

The Kingdom. On this subject the teaching of our book is most revolutionary. In 6–36 it presents a picture of the kingdom of the O T. prophetic type of a very sensuous character. The Kingdom of God was to be established on the earth, as it is, though purified, with Jerusalem as its centre, the righteous were to live patriarchal lives and have a thousand children each, and God was to come down and dwell with men.

91–104. A great gulf divides as a whole the eschatology of this section from 6–36 and that of the O.T. The hope of an eternal Messianic kingdom on the present earth is now absolutely and finally abandoned. The hopes of the faithful were lifted bodily out of their old materialistic environment that hampered every advance, and were established in a spiritual region of illimitable horizons, and thus the possibility was achieved of endless development in every direction The way was thus made possible for the rise of Christianity.[1]

---

[1] The incident recorded in Matt 22²³⁻³³ Mark 12¹⁸⁻²⁷ Luke 20²⁷⁻³⁸ can hardly be understood apart from Enoch. When the Sadducees said, 'Whose wife shall she be of them? for the seven had her to wife,' they are arguing from the sensuous conception of the Messianic kingdom—no doubt the popular one—given in 1 Enoch 1–36, according to which its members, including the risen righteous, were to enjoy every good thing of earth and have each a thousand children They thought therefore to place Jesus on the horns of a dilemma, and oblige Him to confess either that there was no resurrection or else that polygamy or polyandry would be practised in the coming kingdom But the dilemma proves invalid . and the conception of the future life portrayed in our Lord's reply tallies almost exactly in thought and partially in word with that described in 91–104, according to which there is to be a resurrection indeed, but a resurrection of the spirit, and the risen

This transference of the hopes of the faithful to a spiritual and eternal kingdom necessitated the recasting of many other theological beliefs. There was still a Messianic kingdom on earth looked forward to but it was to be of merely temporary duration—from the eighth to the tenth world week, 91^{12-17}. On this change of conception two others perforce followed. The resurrection and the final judgement could not initiate a temporary Messianic kingdom, but were of necessity adjourned to its close.

The Messiah. There are two very different conceptions of the Messiah in 1 Enoch. In 83–90 he is represented as the head of the Messianic community out of which he proceeds, but he has no special rôle to fulfil.

But in the Parables (37–71) the case is very different. Four titles applied for the first time in literature to the personal Messiah are afterwards reproduced in the N.T.—'the Christ', 'the Righteous One', 'the Elect One', and 'the Son of Man'.

'The Christ' or 'the Anointed One', variously applied in the O T., is for the first time associated in 48^{10} 52^4 with the Messiah.

'The Righteous One.' This title, which occurs in Acts 3^{14} 7^{52} 22^{14}, first appears in 38^2 53^6.

'The Elect One.' This title, likewise appearing first in 40^5 45^{3-4} $49^{2,\,4}$ $51^{3,\,5a}$, &c., passes over into the N.T.—Luke 9^{35} 23^{15}.

'The Son of Man.' This definite title (see notes on $46^{2,\,3}$) is found first in the Parables, and is historically the source of the N.T. designation. See Appendix II on this title.

Conversion of the Gentiles The conversion of the Gentiles is looked for in four Sections of our book, i e. 10^{21} $90^{30,\,33}$ 91^{14} 50^2.

Judgement. Where the eternal Messianic kingdom on earth is expected as in 1–36, the final judgement naturally precedes it, but where, as in 91–104, only a temporary Messianic kingdom is

righteous are to rejoice 'as the angels of heaven' (104^4 Matt 22^{30} Mark 12^{25}), being 'companions of the hosts of heaven', 104^6

expected, the final judgement naturally takes place at its close. In the Parables (37–71), where the kingdom is at once eternal and embraces earth and heaven, it is initiated by the final judgement.

Sheol. This word bears several different meanings in our text, see note on 63^{10}; also my *Eschatology*, 184–188, 236–237. In 91–104 Sheol—or rather a part of it—has for the first time become an abode of fire, so far as the wicked are concerned, and become identical with Gehenna, 98^3 99^{11} 103^7 sqq. Another part of Sheol is the intermediate abode of the righteous, $102^{5, \ 11}$ (cf. 100^5).

The Resurrection. In 6–36 the resurrection is to an earthly Messianic kingdom of eternal duration, and the resurrection is of both soul (or spirit) and body. The body is a physical body The same holds true of 83–90. In 37–71 the resurrection is to a spiritual kingdom, in which the righteous are clothed with a spiritual body—'garments of life', 'garments of glory', 62^{16}. In 91–104 there is only a resurrection of the spirit: see notes on 22^{13} 51^1 61^5 90^{33} 91^{10} 100^5. In this last Section only the righteous attain to the resurrection.

THE BOOK OF ENOCH

ABBREVIATIONS, BRACKETS, AND SYMBOLS
SPECIALLY USED IN THE TRANSLATION
OF 1 ENOCH

a, b, c, d, &c , denote the Ethiopic MSS

a denotes the earlier Ethiopic MSS., i e g ₁g m q t u

β denotes the later Ethiopic MSS , i e a b c d, &c (i.e from a to z a b, with the exception of the earlier MSS.)

$a-g$ denotes all the MSS of the a class but g, and so on.

$\beta-abc$ denotes all the MSS of the β class but a, b, and c, and so on

E denotes the Ethiopic Version

G^s denotes the fragments of the Greek Version preserved in Syncellus in the case of 8^b–9^b there are two forms of the text, G^{s1} G^{s2}

G^g denotes the large fragment of the Greek Version discovered at Akhmim, and deposited in the Gizeh Museum, Cairo.

The following brackets are used in the translation of 1 Enoch

⌐   ⌐   The use of these brackets means that the words so enclosed are found in G^g but not in E.

⌐   ⌐.   The use of these brackets means that the words so enclosed are found in E but not in G^g or G^s.

⟨   ⟩   The use of these brackets means that the words so enclosed are restored.

[   ].   The use of these brackets means that the words so enclosed are interpolations.

(   ).   The use of these brackets means that the words so enclosed are supplied by the editor.

The use of **thick type** denotes that the words so printed are emended

THE BOOK OF ENOCH

SECTION I

INTRODUCTION

A. *Critical Structure and Dates.* B. *Relation of this Section to* (a) 72–82, (b) 83–90; (c) 91–104 C *The Problem and its Solution.*

A. Critical Structure and Dates. This Section is of composite structure and from many hands We shall consider 1–5 last of all. First of all 6–11 stand apart from the rest. These chapters belonged originally to the Book of Noah, many fragments of which are found throughout this book. They never refer to Enoch but only to Noah, 10¹. Since this Section was known to the author of the Book of Jubilees it must have been written before the last quarter of the second century B.C. But since we see that 88–89¹ presupposes a minute acquaintance with 10, and since 83–90 were written before the death of Judas the Maccabee in 161, the date of 6–11 must be put back to the first third of the second century B.C Again, since these chapters and 12–36 make no reference to the persecution of Antiochus, the *terminus ad quem* is thus fixed at 170 B.C. The fact that 4–36 were written in Aramaic is also in favour of a pre-Maccabean date, for when once a nation recovers, or even when it is trying to recover, its independence, we know from history that it seeks to revive its national language, in case it had lost it. Jubilees and the Testaments of the XII Patriarchs which were composed about 107 B C were written in Hebrew, as we might · expect. Later we shall see grounds for regarding 83–90 and other sections of Enoch as having been written in Hebrew

12–16 next call for consideration These chapters preserve in a fragmentary and dislocated form a vision or visions of Enoch The original order, as I have shown on pp. 27, 28, was 14¹ · some verses lost: 13¹⁻³ 12³ 13⁴⁻¹⁰ 14²⁻16² 12⁴⁻⁶ (of which 16³⁻⁴ is a doublet). 12¹⁻² is merely an editorial addition Similar dislocations of the

text will be found in 79–82 and 91–93   Since 12–16 were known
to the author of the Book of Jubilees and were written in Aramaic
they were probably pre-Maccabean.   In these chapters the transcendence of God is pictured in an extreme degree.   He dwells in
heaven in a crystal palace of fire, into which not even an angel
may enter. 14^{9-23}, whereas in 6–11, 20–36 the old Hebrew standpoint is fairly preserved.   The Messianic Kingdom will be established
on earth, and all sin vanish, 10^{17-22}, the chambers of blessing in
heaven will be opened, 11^1, Jerusalem will be the centre of the
Messianic Kingdom. 25^5, and God Himself will come down to visit
the earth with blessing and will sit on His throne on earth, 25^3,
men will enjoy patriarchal lives and die in happy old age, 10^7 25^6

17–19 stand by themselves, exhibiting, as they do, strong traces of
Greek influence in the adoption of Greek conceptions of the underworld (cf. 17^5 ^{sqq})—a thing that a Chasid could not have done
after the Maccabean revolt.   And yet, though these chapters betray
Greek influences, they attest their close relationship with 20–36, for
18^{6-9} is a doublet of 24^{1-3}, 18^{11} of 21^{7-10}, 18^{12-16} of 21^{1-6}, and 19^2
of 10^{11}.

20–36 springs apparently from one and the same hand.   The
connexion of 20 with 21–36 is loose it is true, and yet the functions
ascribed to the Archangels in 20 are tolerably borne out in 21–36.
These chapters also were known to the author of the Book of Jubilees.
They were written in Aramaic   Their date, therefore, is most
probably pre-Maccabean.

Only 1–5 have now to be dealt with.   It is difficult to say anything definite regarding them.   They look like an introduction to
the entire book written by the final editor   Their phraseology
connects them with every Section of the book but 72–82   Thus the
phrases 'the Holy One', 1^2 'the elect', 1^3, 'the Holy Great One', 1^3,
'the eternal God' (or 'the God of the world'), 1^4, 'the Watchers',
1^5, 'the righteous', 1^8, 'His holy ones'. 1^9, 'proud and hard words',
5^4, 'hard-hearted', 5^4, 'Ye shall find no peace', 5^4, are found in some
cases in every Section of the book, and in all cases in one or more.
In 5^9 the righteous look forward to a Messianic Kingdom on earth,
in which they should enjoy patriarchal lives in blessedness and peace.

There is one passage which helps us to determine the *terminus
a quo*.   In 5^9 the words

> ' *They shall complete the number of the days of their life*
> And their lives shall be increased *in peace*
> And the years of their *joy* shall be multiplied '

are most probably derived from Jub. 23[27, 20] :

> ' And the days shall begin to grow many and increase amongst the
> children of men
>
> ... And all their days they shall complete and live in peace and
> joy.'

The *terminus ad quem* cannot be definitely determined It is
possible that there is some connexion between 1-5 and Wisdom.
Thus the resemblance in word and thought between 5[7] καὶ τοῖς
ἐκλεκτοῖς ἔσται φῶς καὶ χάρις καὶ εἰρήνη and 1[8] καὶ ἐπὶ τοὺς ἐκλεκτοὺς
ἔσται συντήρησις καὶ ἐπ' αὐτοὺς γενήσεται ἔλεος and Wisd 4[15]

$$\text{ὅτι χάρις καὶ ἔλεος ἐν τοῖς ἐκλεκτοῖς αὐτοῦ}$$
$$\text{καὶ ἐπισκοπὴ ἐν τοῖς ὁσίοις (ἐκλεκτοῖς A) αὐτοῦ}$$

can hardly be accidental. Since 1-5 is derived from a Semitic
original, the borrowing, if there is any, would naturally be on the
part of Wisdom The date of Wisdom is disputed. It is earlier
than Philo at all events Pss Sol. 4[9] presuppose 1[1 b] (see note)

B. (*a*) **Relation of 1-36 to 72-82.** These two Sections come
from different authors, see Special Introd to 72-82. (*b*) **Relation
of 1-36 to 83-90.** These two Sections are of distinct authorship.
The former, with the exception of chapters 1-5, is older, and was
known in part to the author of the latter, see Special Introd. to
83-90. (*c*) **Relation of 1-36 to 91-104.** These two Sections are
likewise independent , but the author of the latter was acquainted
with 1-36 or some form of it, see Special Introd to 91-104.

C The Problem and its Solution. Under this heading I treat
for convenience sake 1-36 as the work of a single writer The
author essays to justify the ways of God. The righteous will not
always suffer, and the wicked will not always prosper, 1[1]. The
limits thereto are set by death, 22, and by great world judgements.
But the cure of the world's corruption can only be understood by
apprehending its cause, and this cause is to be traced to the lust of
the fallen Watchers for the daughters of men. Original sin stands
not in the following of Adam—whose sin seems limited in its effects
to himself, 32[6]—but in the evil engendered through the Watchers,
9[6, 9, 10] 10[8]. Hence the Watchers, their companions and children
were destroyed, 10[4-10, 12] , and their condemnation and confinement
form the prelude to the first world judgement, of which the Deluge
forms the completion, 10[1-3]. But though only the righteous survived
the Deluge, sin still prevailed in the world through the demons—
the spirits which had gone forth from the slaughtered children of

the Watchers and the daughters of men, and all manner of corruption was wrought through them, 16¹, as they escape punishment till the final judgement. But the recompense of character is not withheld till the last judgement, there is a foretaste of the final doom immediately after death, 22. In the second and last judgement on Sinai, 1⁴, the Watchers, the demons, and godless, 10¹³ 16¹, and all classes of Israel, with one exception, receive their final award, 1⁹. To make this possible, this judgement is preceded by a General Resurrection of Israel, 22. The fallen angels are transferred from their preliminary to their final place of punishment, 10⁶, ¹³⁻¹⁵. A final end is now made of sin on the earth, and the earth cleansed, 10¹⁵, ¹⁶, ²⁰⁻²², the wicked are cast into Gehenna, and their punishment is a spectacle for the righteous to behold, 27², the Messianic kingdom is established, with Jerusalem and Palestine as its centre, 25⁵—there is no Messiah, and God abides with men, 25³; all the Gentiles will become righteous and worship God, 10²¹; the righteous are allowed to eat of the tree of life, 25⁴⁻⁶, and thereby enjoy patriarchal lives, 5⁹ 25⁶, each begetting 1,000 children, 10¹⁷, and enjoying unlimited material blessings, 5⁷ 10¹⁸, ¹⁹ 11².

As to what becomes of the righteous, after the second death, there is no hint in this fragmentary Section. There is much celestial, terrestrial, and subterrestrial geography in 17–19, 21–36.

I–V. *Parable of Enoch on the Future Lot of the Wicked and the Righteous.*

I. 1. The words of the blessing of Enoch, wherewith he blessed the elect ⌐and⌐ righteous, who will be living in the day of tribulation, when all the wicked ⌐and godless⌐ are to be removed. **2.** And he took up his parable and said—Enoch a righteous man, whose eyes were opened by God, saw the vision

---

I. 1. The blessing of Enoch Cf Deut 33¹, 'the blessing of Moses' **The elect and righteous** This designation is found also in 38², ³, ⁴ 39⁶, ⁷ 48¹ 58¹, ² 61¹³ 62¹², ¹³, ¹⁵ 70². **All the wicked.** Here G⁸ reads πάντας τοὺς ἐχθρούς = בל־הצרים corrupt for כל־הרעים Hence E is right here. The same corruption is attested by the

LXX in Prov 20²² This passage appears to have been known by the author of the Pss. Sol 4⁹ τὸ κρίμα τοῦ θεοῦ αὐτῶν ἐν τῷ ἐξαίρεσθαι ἁμαρτωλοὺς ἀπὸ προσώπου δικαίου **Removed.** + 'And the righteous shall be saved' G⁸ **2. Saw.** G⁸ 'had' corrupt The corruption might have arisen in G ie. ἔχων corrupt for ὁρῶν The phrase 'saw the vision' is taken from Num. 24⁴

of the Holy One in the heavens, ⌜which⌝ the angels showed me, and from them I heard everything, and from them I understood as I saw, but not for this generation, but for a remote one which is for to come.   3. Concerning the elect I said, and took up my parable concerning them ·

The Holy Great One will come forth from His dwelling,

4. And the eternal God will tread upon the earth, (even) on Mount Sinai,

מחזה שרי יחזה.   The Holy One. For this and similar designations of God see 1³   The change from the third to the first person in this verse is of frequent occurrence in this book   cf. 12¹⁻³ 37¹, ² 70¹⁻³ 71⁵ 92¹.   Which the angels showed me   G⁵ reads corruptly ' he showed me ', and adds καὶ ἀγιολόγων ἀγίων ἤκουσα ἐγώ   And from them.   (G⁵ ' and when (ὡς) from them '   As I saw   So G⁵ θεωρῶν   E probably implies the same text.   mut²β read ' what I saw ' and gqt '(that) I should see '   To come   + ' do I speak   G⁵ (ἐγὼ λαλῶ em by Swete from ἐγω αλλο).   3. The elect   This designation belongs mainly to the Parables.   It is found in 1⁸ 5⁷ 25⁵ 40⁵ 41² 48¹, ⁹ 51⁵ 56⁶, ⁸ 58⁵ 61⁴, ¹² 62⁷, ⁸, ¹¹ 93²   Before ' concerning ' G inserts ' and '   My   So G⁵ >E.   3ᵇ⁻⁹ A poem consisting of tristichs   The discovery of this structure is helpful in the restoration of the text.   See specially Stanzas 1 and 7   **The Holy Great One**   G⁵ prefixes ' and '.   E reads here and always ' the Holy and Great One ', but G⁵ seems to preserve the original here as in 10¹ 14¹ where it recurs   This title is found in the following passages.   10¹ 14¹ 25⁵ 84¹ 92² 97⁶ 98⁶ 104⁹.   God is designated simply as ' the Holy One ', 1² 93¹¹, and as ' the Great One ', 14² 103⁴ 104¹ (twice).   **Come forth from His dwelling**   Cf Mic 1³   יצא ממקמו, Is 26²¹.   Assumptio Moysis 10³.   **4 The eternal God**

= אלהי העולם, ὁ θεὸς τοῦ αἰῶνος. Cf. Gen 21³³ אל עולם, Is 40²³ אלהי עולם, ὁ αἰώνιος θεός, Rom 16²⁶   Ass Moysis 10¹⁷ Deus aeternus   This could also be translated 'God of the world' as I have shown below, but I have here with Dalman (*The Words of Jesus*, 163 sqq , Eng Transl) adopted the former rendering.   Thus in 25⁸, ⁵, ⁷ 27⁸ we have ὁ βασιλεὺς τοῦ αἰῶνος in the Greek where E renders ὁ βασιλεὺς ὁ αἰώνιος, cf Jer 10¹⁰ מלך עולם   in 12³ ὁ βασιλεὺς τῶν αἰώνων (so 1 Tim 1¹⁷) (where E = ὁ βασ τοῦ αἰῶνος)   in 9⁴ (G⁵) ὁ βασ. τῶν †αἰώνων, for αἰώνων there stood βασιλέων in the original as in G⁸ ¹, ⁹ E   in 9⁴ ὁ κύριος τῶν αἰώνων (G³¹) (where E = ὁ κύριος τῶν † βασιλέων, the corruption originating in the Aramaic (here G⁸,⁸² om))   With ὁ κύρ τῶν αἰώνων compare 22¹⁴ κυριεύων τοῦ αἰῶνος   In 9⁴ we have θεὸς τῶν αἰώνων in G³¹, where G⁸² has θεὸς τῶν ἀνθρώπων.   Here αἰώνων was wrongly read as ‾α‾ν‾π‾α‾ν   This idea of time comes out clearly in 5¹ καὶ ζῇ εἰς πάντας τοὺς αἰῶνας, where E has ὁ ζῶν for καὶ ζῇ   With this we might compare Dan 12⁷ חי העולם (Aram. חי עלמא Dan 4³¹).   Dalman (*op. cit.* 164), however, thinks it probable that עולם, when united with the article in the Book of Enoch, does not merely represent the adjective ‘eternal’   מלך עולם means ‘eternal king , מלך העולם is ‘the king who

[And appear from His camp]

And appear in the strength of His might from the heaven
⌜of heavens⌝.

5. And all shall be smitten with fear,
   And the Watchers shall quake,
   And great fear and trembling shall seize them unto the
   ends of the earth.

6. And the high mountains shall be shaken,
   And the high hills shall be made low,

as ruler controls the immeasurable duration of the world'. Against this view
we might set the fact that E renders
ὁ βασιλεὺς τοῦ αἰῶνος as ὁ βασιλεὺς ὁ
αἰώνιος (see above), and that in 15³ in
Gᵍ τοῦ αἰῶνος can only mean 'eternal'
in τὸν οὐρανὸν τὸν ὑψηλὸν τοῦ
αἰῶνος But the words which I have
rendered 'the eternal God' could also
be rendered 'God of the world' cf.
58⁴ 81¹⁰ 82⁷ 84²: also 12⁸ 81⁹.
Will tread upon the earth So
G From Mic 1³ ארץ . . . על דרך
Here for ἐπὶ τὴν γῆν E reads corruptly
ἐκεῖθεν Sinai, whence the Law was
given, will likewise be the place of
future judgement. Cf Deut 33²
Ps. 68¹⁷ **[And appear from His
camp].** So Gᵍ This I have bracketed
as an addition. It is against the
parallelism It is also against the
sense In 3ᵇ it is already said that 'the
Holy One will come forth from His
dwelling', and the writer has gone on
to speak of God's advent on Sinai. E,
it is true, reads 'And appear with His
hosts' But if Gᵍ originally read ἐν τῇ
παρεμβολῇ it is wholly improbable that
a scribe would change it into ἐκ τῆς
παρεμβολῆς against the context. **5–9**
Dln thinks that we have in 5–9 a
description combining the two great
judgements, but everything from verse 4
to end is perfectly applicable to the final
judgement Yet cf 83⁷. **5 The**

Watchers These are the עירים first
mentioned in Dan 4¹⁰, ¹⁴, ²⁰ (in Hebrew
text) 2 Enoch 18¹. This name belongs
to the fallen angels here and in 10⁹,
¹⁵ 12⁴ 13¹⁰ 14¹, ⁸ 15² 16¹, ² 91¹⁵
In 12², ⁸ 20¹ 39¹², ¹³ 40² 61¹² 71⁷
it designates the archangels. **And
the Watchers shall quake.** So E
But Gᵍ has here 'And the watchers
shall † believe' (i.e. πιστεύσουσιν). This
change seems due to the scribe who
added the following words

'And they shall sing hidden things in
   the ends of the (word omitted)
And all the ends of the earth shall be
   shaken'

The scribe seems to have been thinking
of 2 Enoch 18 where the singing of the
Watchers is mentioned But the text
of E is right and gives a sense which
accords perfectly with 10¹²⁻¹⁴ **Fear
and trembling** So E Gᵍ trans
'trembling and fear' The order of E
is probably original Cf Job 4¹⁴ Ps
2¹¹ Mk 5³² 2 Cor 7¹⁵ Eph 6⁵ Yet
the order here in Gᵇ recurs in Gᵍ in 13³
6 Cf. Judges 5⁵ Ps 97⁵ Is 61¹, ⁵
Mic 1⁴ Hab. 3⁶ Judith 16¹⁵ Assumpt.
Moyseos 10⁴. **Shaken** + 'shall fall
and be dissolved' Gᵍ (πεσοῦνται καὶ
διαλυθήσονται) But this addition of
Gᵍ is against the parallelism **Made
low** + 'so that the mountains shall
waste away' Gᵍ (τοῦ δια⟨ρ⟩ρυῆναι ὄρη).
Another impossible interpolation

And shall melt like wax before the flame.

7. And the earth shall be ⌜wholly⌝ rent in sunder,
And all that is upon the earth shall perish,
And there shall be a judgement upon all (men).

8. But with the righteous He will make peace,
And will protect the elect,
And mercy shall be upon them.

And they shall all belong to God,
And they shall be prospered,
And they shall ⌜all⌝ be blessed.

⌜And He will help them all⌝,
And light shall appear unto them,
⌜And He will make peace with them⌝.

9. And behold ! He cometh with ten thousands of ⌜His⌝ holy
ones

Hills . . . melt like wax. From Ps. 97⁵. **Before the flame** Gᵍ reads 'before the fire in the flame The idea of the destruction of the world by fire may be here hinted at as in Sibyl. Or 3⁵⁴, ⁶⁰, ⁷², ⁸⁴⁻⁸⁷ 4172 sqq. 5211 sqq 2 Pet. 3⁷, ¹⁰ Life of Adam 49³ sq., but it is unlikely. The text does not go beyond Mic. 1⁴ Nah 1⁵ Ps 97⁵ 104³² 7 '**Wholly**'. So Gᵍ σχίσμα [ῥαγάδι] σχίσμα and ῥαγάδι appear to be duplicate renderings of the same Hebrew word διασχισθήσεται . . . σχίσμα a Hebrew construction 8 **Make peace with.** Cf 1 Macc 6⁴⁹, ⁵⁸ for the phrase μετὰ . . . εἰρήνην ποιήσει. On the idea of 5⁴ of the text. See 5⁴ note **The righteous.** This designation is found in all parts of the book · 1⁷, ⁸ 5⁶ 25⁴ 38ʲ 39⁴ 43⁴ 47ʲ, ², ⁴ 48ʲ, ⁴, ⁹ 50² 53⁷ 56⁷ 58³, ⁵ 6(⁲ 61³ 62³ 82⁴ 94³, ¹¹ 95³, ⁷ 96ʲ, ⁸ 97ʲ, ³, ⁵ 98¹²⁻¹⁴ 99³ 100⁶, ⁷, ¹⁰ 102⁴, ¹⁰ 103¹ 104ʲ, ⁶, ¹², ¹³. **With the righteous.** There is a dittography in E here **Will protect, &c** So E.

This is probably a free rendering of Gᵍ ἐπὶ τοὺς ἐκλεκτοὺς ἔσται συντήρησις. Wisdom 4¹⁵ may here be dependent on our text καὶ ἐπισκοπὴ ἐν τοῖς ἐκλεκτοῖς αὐτοῦ. After συντήρησις Gᵍ adds καὶ εἰρήνη. **All belong to God.** Ps 100³ Jer. 31⁶, ⁹ Hos 1⁹, ¹⁰ &c **They shall be prospered.** Gᵍ reads τὴν † εὐδοκίαν δώσει αὐτοῖς, where εὐδοκίαν is corrupt for εὐοδ'αν—a corruption found also in Sir 43²⁶. Here again the active construction in Gᵍ is probably right. ⌜All⌝ **be blessed** Gᵍ reads 'He will bless them all'. ⌜**And He will help them**⌝. So Gᵍ καὶ πάντων ἀντιλήμψεται. Here there is an obvious dittograph in Gᵍ, for it adds καὶ βοηθήσει ἡμῖν. This line is omitted in E quite wrongly. In fact E preserves only the second line of this stanza **Light shall appear unto them** (Gᵍ). E reads 'light (+ ' of God ' *a–g, β–o*) shall shine upon them'. Cf 38⁴. ⌜**And He will make peace with them**⌝ (Gᵍ). E om. but the tristich requires it **9.** This verse is composed of two tristichs.

To execute judgement upon all,
And to destroy ⌐all⌐ the ungodly :

And to convict all flesh
Of all the works ⌐of their ungodliness⌐ which they have
ungodly committed,
⌐And of all the hard things which⌐ ungodly sinners ⌐have
spoken⌐ against Him

II 1. Observe ye every thing that takes place in the heaven,

And behold So E Gᵍ reads ὅτι corrupt for ἰδού. So Jude ἰδοὺ ἦλθεν Κύριος ἐν ἁγίαις μυριάσιν αὐτοῦ Ps. Cypr. *Ad Novatianum* (Hartel's *Cyprian* III 67) 'Ecce venit cum multis milibus nuntiorum suorum' Ps Vigilius (Migne lxii, col 363) 'Ecce veniet Dominus in millibus' Cometh with ten thousands of ⌐His⌐ holy ones. From Deut. 33² ואתא מרבבת קדש. Since the LXX here renders σὺν μυριάσιν Καδής our author has followed the M T. The ⌐His⌐ is found Gᵍ, Jude, and Ps. Cyprian. As Zahn pointed out, the above passage from Ps. Cyprian is derived directly from our text, and not from it indirectly through Jude This entire verse has been quoted by Jude 14, 15 in a compressed form, who in the same passage draws upon 5⁴ 27² 60⁸. Ten thousands of ⌐His⌐ holy ones Cf. Deut 33² Dan 7¹⁰ The angels are so called in 1 2² 14²⁸ 39⁵ 47² 57² 60⁴ 61⁸, ¹⁰, ¹² 65¹² 69¹³ 81⁵ 103² 106¹⁰, as already in Job 5¹ 15¹⁵ Zech 14⁵ Dan 4¹³ 8¹³ They are called 'holy angels' in 20¹⁻⁷ 21⁵, ⁹ 22³ 24⁶ 27² 32⁶ 71⁸ 93². 'Holy ones of heaven' 9³. For other designations see 6² (note) All the ungodly The 'all' is corrupt in E, but recoverable by an easy emendation Which they have ungodly committed (Gᵍ) Here E is corrupt, reading warasaju for zalasse'il ⌐All the hard things which⌐ . ⌐have

spoken⌐ (Gᵍ). The text of Gᵍ here presents a dittograph. σκληρῶν ὧν ἐλάλησαν λόγων καὶ περὶ πάντων ὧν κατελάλησαν.

II The author in 2–5³ emphasizes the order and regularity that prevail in the world of nature in contrast to the disorder that prevails in the world of man. This was a favourite theme with Jewish writers. The noble words of Hooker (*Ecclesiastical Polity*, i. 16 8) express the view of these old writers 'Of Law there can be no less acknowledged than that her voice is the harmony of the world all things in heaven and earth do her homage, the very least as feeling her care, the greatest as not exempted from her power.' In Sir. 43 we have the glorification of the sun, moon, stars, the rainbow, clouds, snow, lightning, thunder, dew, and other natural phenomena. The moon is especially glorified since the Jewish feasts were celebrated in accordance with the moon's phases. This last is, of course, a view in which the author of 72–82 would not have agreed, since he held that the only true divider of time was the sun In Sir 16²⁶⁻²⁸ there is a nearer approximation to our text, though there is no sure ground for recognizing it as a source of it. Sirach runs —

27. ἐκόσμησεν εἰς αἰῶνα τὰ ἔργα αὐτοῦ,
καὶ τὰς ἀρχὰς αὐτῶν εἰς γενεὰς
αὐτῶν

how they do not change their orbits, ⌐and¬ the luminaries which are in the heaven, how they all rise and set in order each in its season, and transgress not against their appointed order. 2. Behold ye the earth, and give heed to the things which take place upon it from first to last, ⌐how steadfast they are¬, how ⌐none of the things upon earth¬ change, ⌐but¬ all the works of God appear ⌐to you¬. 3 Behold the summer and the winter, ⌐how the whole earth is filled with water, and clouds and dew and rain lie upon it¬

καὶ οὐκ ἐξέλιπον ἀπὸ τῶν ἔργων αὐτῶν·

28. ἕκαστος τὸν πλησίον αὐτοῦ οὐκ ἔθλιψεν,

καὶ ἕως αἰῶνος οὐκ ἀπειθήσουσιν τοῦ ῥήματος αὐτοῦ.

The next work that calls for consideration here is the T. Napht. 2⁹ οὕτως οὖν ἔστωσαν, τέκνα μου, πάντα τὰ ἔργα ὑμῶν ἐν τάξει εἰς ἀγαθὸν ἐν φόβῳ θεοῦ, καὶ μηδὲν ἄτακτον ποιήσητε ἐν καταφρονήσει, μηδὲ ἔξω καιροῦ αὐτοῦ 3ᵃ, ᵇ ὁ ἥλιος καὶ ἡ σελήνη καὶ οἱ ἀστέρες οὐκ ἀλλοιοῦσιν τὴν τάξιν αὐτῶν· οὕτω καὶ ὑμεῖς μὴ ἀλλοιώσητε νόμον θεοῦ ἐν ἀταξίᾳ τῶν πράξεων ὑμῶν. 3 ἔθνη πλανηθέντα καὶ ἀφέντα Κύριον ἠλλοίωσαν τὴν τάξιν αὐτῶν. These passages may have been before our writer. From works that preceded our book we now pass to works which were written later. The earliest of these is the Pss. Sol. 18¹²⁻¹⁴.

2 ὁ διατάξας ἐν πορείᾳ φωστῆρας εἰς καιροὺς ὡρῶν ἀφ' ἡμερῶν εἰς ἡμέρας, καὶ οὐ παρέβησαν ἀπὸ ὁδοῦ ἣν ἐνετείλω αὐτοῖς

3 ἐν φόβῳ θεοῦ ἡ ὁδὸς αὐτῶν καθ' ἑκάστην ἡμέραν,

ἀφ' ἧς ἡμέρας ἔκτισεν αὐτοὺς ὁ θεὸς καὶ ἕως αἰῶνος,

4 καὶ οὐκ ἐπλανήθησαν ἀφ' ἧς ἡμέρας ἔκτισεν αὐτούς·

ἀπὸ γενεῶν ἀρχαίων οὐκ ἀπέστησαν ἀπὸ ὁδοῦ αὐτῶν,

εἰ μὴ ὁ θεὸς ἐνετείλατο αὐτοῖς ἐν ἐπιταγῇ δούλων αὐτῶν.

The next writer who deals with the same subject is the author of 1 Apoc. Bar. 48⁹, ¹⁰

'Thou instructest created things in the understanding of Thee,

And Thou makest wise the spheres so as to minister in their orders

Armies innumerable stand before Thee,

And minister in their orders quietly at thy nod.'

In Clement's *Ep. ad Cor.* 20 the same theme is dealt with at length in dependence mainly on the sources already mentioned. 1. **Observe** (G⁵), and so E by a change of a vowel. **Season** + ' and for (or ' in') their own festivals they appear' G⁵　　2 The Hebrews divided the year into two seasons, קיץ embracing Spring and Summer, and חרף embracing Autumn and Winter Gen 8²² Is. 18⁶ Zech. 14⁸ ⌐How steadfast they are ¬ G⁵ reads ὥς εἰσιν φθαρτά. But φθαρτά is impossible in this context The object of the writer is to praise the works of nature Hence φθαρτά is corrupt Possibly it is a rendering of נבלים (as in Is 24⁴) corrupt for נכנים = 'steadfast'. Hence render. 'how steadfast they are.' **How** ⌐none of the things upon earth¬, &c E reads ' how none of the works of God change in appearing '.

III. Observe and see how (in the winter) all the trees ⌜seem as though they had withered and shed all their leaves, except fourteen trees, which do not lose their foliage but retain the old foliage from two to three years till the new comes.

IV. And again, observe ye the days of summer how the sun is above the earth over against it. And you seek shade and shelter by reason of the heat of the sun, and the earth also burns with glowing heat, and so you cannot tread on the earth, or on a rock by reason of its heat.

V. 1. Observe ye⌝ how the trees cover themselves with green leaves and bear fruit. wherefore give ye heed ⌜and know⌝ with regard to all ⌜His works⌝, and recognize how He that liveth for ever hath made them so.

2. And ⌜all⌝ His works go on ⌜thus⌝ from year to year ⌜for ever⌝, and all the tasks ⌜which⌝ they accomplish for Him, and ⌜their tasks⌝ change not, but according as ⌜God⌝ hath ordained so is it done.

3. And behold how the sea and the rivers in like manner accomplish ⌜and change not⌝ their tasks ⌜from His commandments⌝.

III. In the Geoponica 11ᵗ fourteen evergreen trees are mentioned. Δένδρα ἀειθαλῆ ἐστι, μηδέποτε φυλλορροοῦντα ἐν τῷ χειμῶνι ιδ' φοῖνιξ, κίτριον, στρόβιλος, δάφνη, ἐλαία, κυπάρισσος, κερατέα, πίτυς, πρῖνος, πύξος, μυρσίνη, κέδρος, ἰτέα, καὶ ἄρκευθος. The twelve trees enumerated in Jub 21¹² as fitting for use on the altar have nothing to do with this list; for they are not all evergreen Nor have those referred to in T Lev 9¹² (see my edition of the text of the *Test. XII Patr*, pp 248 sq for a full discussion of the twelve trees which are mentioned in Jub 21¹², and the Aramaic and Greek fragments of a still older work) 1 In Gᵍ 3¹ᵇ–5¹ᵃ has been lost through homoeoteleuton

V. 1. The trees . bear fruit Gᵍ reads 'the green leaves on them

cover the trees and all their fruit is for honour and glory'. He that liveth (cf Sir 18¹)... them so. Here I have emended gabaikemmû la'člûntû kuěllômû into gabiômû la'člôntû kamâhû in accordance with Gᵍ. Gᵍ = 'the living God hath made them so and He liveth for ever'. Here there is a manifest dittograph. 2. ⌜All⌝ His works E adds qedměhû = 'before Him' This seems corrupt for kamâhû = 'thus' (οὖτως in Gᵍ) or for kuěllômû = 'all' The tasks which they accomplish for Him. So Gᵍ πάντα ὅσα ἀποτελοῦσιν αὐτῷ τὰ ἔργα Here τὰ ἔργα does not mean 'the works' as in the beginning of the verse, but the 'offices' or 'tasks' discharged by them as the next sentence—καὶ οὐκ ἀλλοιοῦνται αὐτῶν τὰ ἔργα—proves, and likewise the clause

4. But ye—ye have not been steadfast, nor done the command-
   ments of the Lord,

   But ye have turned away and spoken proud and hard
   words

   With your impure mouths against His greatness.

   Oh, ye hard-hearted, ye shall find no peace.

5 Therefore shall ye execrate your days,

   And the years of your life shall perish,

   And ⌜the years of your destruction⌝ shall be multiplied in
   eternal execration,

   And ye shall find no mercy.

6 *a.* In those days ye shall make your names an eternal execration
   unto all the righteous,

καὶ οὐκ ἀλλοιοῦσιν αὐτῶν τὰ ἔργα in
ver 3. But E omits ὅσα before ἀποτελοῦσιν and αὐτῶν τὰ ἔργα, and renders
' all His works serve Him and change
not '   God. > G⁸.   **4. Of the
Lord.** G⁸ reads ' His '.   **Spoken.**
The charge of blasphemy is frequent
in 91-104   (f 91⁷, ¹¹ 94⁹ 96⁷ 100⁹
Proud and hard words   Cf 27²
101³   From these passages the close
of St Jude 15 is drawn   Cf Ps 12⁴
Dan. 7⁸, ¹¹, ²⁰ Rev 13⁶.   **His
greatness.** G⁸ adds a gloss ' for ye
have spoken (κατελαλήσατε) with
your lies '   **Hard-hearted** Cf. 98¹¹
100⁸ ' obstinate of heart '.   **Ye shall
find no peace**   This phrase occurs in
Sects 1-36 and 91-104 only · 1³ 5⁴
12⁵ 13¹ 16⁴ 94⁶ 98¹¹, ¹⁵ 99¹³ 101³
102³ 103⁸.   It is derived from Is
48²² 57²¹   **5. Therefore**   All
MSS of E but *q* prefix ' and '.
Shall perish (G⁸ ἀπολεῖται).   E
tahaguĕlû (= ' ye shall destroy)
corrupt for jahaguĕlû = ἀπολεῖται
Mercy + καὶ εἰρήνη G⁸.   **6-7**
I have been obliged to rearrange
the text of these verses, which is certainly in disorder.   Thus in v. 6 there

are ten lines, one of which—the eighth
(6 *h*)—καὶ αὐτοὶ κληρονομήσουσιν τὴν
γῆν is a doublet of 7 *b*.   Strangely
enough this line is repeated in an impossible place in v 8.   Now when we
excise this line we have in vv 6-7 the
following arrangement   a tristich, a
tetrastich, a distich, and a tristich.
This of course cannot be right.   Re-
moving the tetrastich from consideration, 6 *d e f g*, which is right, we have
a tristich, a distich, and a tristich.   Now
the first tristich deals with the curse
that will befall sinners in many forms.
A fourth line is wanting that deals
with the same subject   There are
actually two suitable, either the last
line of v. 6 ἀλλὰ ἐπὶ πάντας ὑμᾶς καταλύσει κατάρα or the last line of v 7
ὑμῖν δὲ τοῖς ἀσεβέσιν ἔσται κατάρα   But
6 *j* follows closely on 6 *i*, hence we have
found the missing line of the first stanza
in 7 *c*   Thus we have two complete
tetrastichs in v. 6, 1 *c* 6 *a b c*, 7 *c*, and
6 *d e f g*   It is now obvious that the
remaining distich in v 6 belongs to the
distich in v 7, and thus the stanza in
v 7 is completed.   **6 Ye shall
make your names** (where E = δώσετε

b. And by you shall ⌈all⌉ who curse, curse.

c. ⌈And all⌉ the sinners ⌈and godless⌉ shall imprecate by you,

7 *c.* And for you the godless there shall be a curse.

6 *d.* ⌈And all the . . shall rejoice,

e. And there shall be forgiveness of sins,

f. And every mercy and peace and forbearance ·

g. There shall be salvation unto them, a goodly light

i. And for all of you sinners there shall be no salvation,

j. But on you all shall abide a curse⌉.

7 *a.* But for the elect there shall be light and grace and peace,

b. And they shall inherit the earth.

τὰ ὀνόματα ὑμῶν) G^g reads 'your names shall be' (ἔσται) But, since the phrase is clearly from Is 65^15 והנחתם שמכם לשבועה לבחירי, ἔσται may be corrupt for δώσετε. But if we compare Is 65^15, on which this line was modelled, it is probable that instead of תתנו (= δώσετε) there stood originally in the text תנחו (= κατα-λείψετε), as in Is. For in the preceding verse it is said that their life would prematurely come to an end, and so here it is added that they would leave as a kind of inheritance their name to be used in formulas of cursing, i. e. as an example of one cursed This is the meaning of the next two difficult lines, where G^g is to be followed. And by you shall ⌈all⌉ who curse, curse So G^g καὶ ἐν ὑμῖν καταράσονται πάντες οἱ καταρώμενοι E = 'and you shall the sinners curse'. G^g is clearly right and reflects a Hebrew idiom All who curse will introduce the names of these sinners into their formulas of cursing as instances of persons wholly accused. The text = בכם יקללו כל־המקללים. ⌈And all⌉ the sinners ⌈and godless⌉ shall imprecate by you So G^g since

E is corrupt. Here again we have the same idiom as in the preceding line. εν ὑμῖν ὁμοῦνται = בכם ישבעו This idiom is found in Ps 102^9 מהוללי בי נישבעו · 'they who are mad against me swear by me.' See also Is 65^18 and Jer 29^22, 'And of them shall a curse (קללה) be taken by all the captives of Judah . . saying the Lord make thee like Zedekiah . . whom the king of Babylon roasted in the fire' And all the . shall rejoice. The MS. reads οἱ ἁμαρτοι What does this corrupt form stand for ? It may be corrupt for οἱ (ἀν)αμάρ(τη)τοι, a bad rendering of המתחטאים = 'those cleansed' or 'purified'. The piel and hithpael of חטא in this sense means purification from ceremonial and ritual uncleanness in the O T, whereas the context requires spiritual cleansing Forgiveness of sins This forgiveness will fit them for the sinless life spoken of in v 9. But for the Watchers there is no forgiveness 12^6 7 G^g τοῖς ἐκλεκτοῖς ἔσται φῶς καὶ χάρις καὶ εἰρήνη Has this influenced Wisd. 4^15 χάρις καὶ ἔλεος τοῖς ἐκλεκτοῖς αὐτοῦ? Grace So G χάρις E = χαρά They shall inherit the earth From

8. And then there shall be bestowed upon the elect wisdom,
   And they shall all live and never again sin,
   Either through ungodliness or through pride:
   But they who are wise shall be humble.

9. And they shall not again transgress,
   Nor shall they sin all the days of their life,
   Nor shall they die of (the divine) anger or wrath,
   But they shall complete the number of the days of their life.

   And their lives shall be increased in peace,
   And the years of their joy shall be multiplied,
   In eternal gladness and peace,
   All the days of their life.

VI–XI. *The Fall of the Angels: the Demoralisation of Mankind:
the Intercession of the Angels on behalf of Mankind. The
Dooms pronounced by God on the Angels. the Messianic Kingdom* (a Noah fragment).

VI. 1. And it came to pass when the children of men had
multiplied that in those days were born unto them beautiful and

Ps 37¹¹   8 And > Gᵍ Wisdom
see 42¹, ². + φῶς καὶ χάρις, καὶ αὐτοὶ
κληρονομήσουσιν τὴν γῆν. τότε δοθήσεται
πᾶσιν τοῖς ἐκλεκτοῖς Gᵍ. Here φῶς . .
γῆν is a doublet from v. 7, and τότε . . .
ἐκλεκτοῖς a doublet of the first line of
this verse   They who are wise, &c
Here Gᵍ gives ' And there shall be light
in the enlightened man and in the man
of knowledge understanding'   This
line does not seem to be original   9
Cf Is 35¹⁰ 51³¹ 65²⁰ text 25⁴ note   Sin
So Gᵍ ἁμάρτωσιν. But E = κριθήσονται
= יאשׁמו (cf Prov 30¹⁰ Is. 24⁶ Jer.
2³,&c The word means 'reum iudicare'
in Arabic). But this is not the meaning of the word here. The parallelism
requires us to follow the other meaning
of this word as given in Gᵍ.   (The
divine) anger or wrath   Gᵍ reads
ὀργῇ θυμοῦ, ' the anger of (the divine)
wrath ', which may be right.   Cf. Is

42²⁵, &c   They shall complete . . .
in peace, And the years of their
joy   Expanded from Jub. 23²⁹ (?).   Increased . . multiplied   The words
recall the familiar phrase in Gen. 1²², ²⁸
8¹⁷ Jer   23³ ' Increase and multiply '.
But the increase is a spiritual increase
and not a materialistic, as in Joy . . .
gladness.   Cf. Is 35¹⁰.

VI–XI   The abruptness with which
6–11 are introduced is quite in keeping
with the fragmentary and composite
nature of the rest of the Section   As
Dillmann (Herzog, *R. E* ² xii 352) has
already seen, 6³⁻³ 8¹⁻³ 9⁷ 10¹¹ belong to
a Semjaza cycle of myths , for in these
passages Semjaza is represented as chief
and Azazel tenth in command. as also
in 69²   Elsewhere in Enoch Azazel is
chief and Semjaza is not mentioned.
Again 10¹⁻³ belongs to an Apocalypse
of Noah, many fragments of which are

comely daughters   2. And the angels, the children of the

found in Enoch Another fragment of this Apocalypse is preserved by Syncellus in the Greek, but to this there is no corresponding text in the Ethiopic But these myths were already combined in their present form, when 88–89¹ were written. But not only does 10¹⁻³ belong to the Book of Noah but 6–11 as a whole. These never refer to Enoch but to Noah 10¹. Moreover, when the author of Jubilees is clearly drawing on the Book of Noah, his subject matter 7²¹⁻²⁵ agrees closely with that of these chapters in Enoch (see Charles's edition of Jubilees, pp lxxi sq, 61, 264) 12–16 on the other hand belong to the Book of Enoch. And comely (E Gᵇ) > Gˢ.

VI. 2 Children of the heaven Cf 13⁸ 14³ 39¹. See 15¹⁻⁷ Cf 'Sons of the holy angels', 71¹. The entire myth of the angels and the daughters of men in Enoch springs originally from Gen 6¹⁻⁴, where it is said that 'the sons of God came in to the daughters of men' These words are not to be taken as expressing alliances between the Sethites and the Cainites, but as belonging to a very early myth, possibly of Persian origin, to the effect that demons had corrupted the earth before the coming of Zoroaster and had allied themselves with women See Delitzsch, *Neuer Commentar uber d. Genesis* 1887, pp. 146–8 Bousset, *Rel d Jud* ² 382, 560, Gunkel, *Genesis* 56 The LXX originally rendered the words 'sons of God' by ἄγγελοι τοῦ Θεοῦ, and this rendering is found in Philo, *de Gigantibus*, Eusebius, Augustine, and Ambrose This view of Gen 6¹⁻⁴ was held by most of the early fathers That this was the original meaning of Gen. 6¹⁻⁴ Is. 24²¹ is now generally admitted. For a history of the interpretation of this passage in Jewish and Christian writers see my edition of Jubilees 4¹⁵ note On

the myths regarding the intercourse of angels with the daughters of men, see Grünbaum in *ZDMG.* xxxi 225 ff. (Referred to by Delitzsch) For statements of later writers either depending directly on this account in Enoch or harmonizing with it, cf T Reuben 5⁶, Napth. 3⁵, Jub 4¹⁵ 5¹ ˢᵠᵠ., Joseph *Ant* i 3 1, Philo, *de Gigantibus*, 2 Enoch 7, 18; Jude 6, 2 Pet 2⁴, Justin Martyr, *Apol.* i 5, Ps. Clemens, *Hom* viii 13, Clem Alex. *Strom* v. 1 10, Tert *De Virg Veland* vii; *Adv Marc* v.18, *De Idol* ix, Lact *Instit* ii 15; Commodian *Instruct.* i 3. In the *De Ci Dei* xv 23, Augustine combats this view, and denies the inspiration of Enoch, which is upheld by Tertullian I append here a fragment of the Book of Noah, relating not to the fallen angels but to mankind It may have belonged to it. Fragment of the Book of Noah which Syncellus states was derived ἐκ τοῦ πρώτου βιβλίου Ἐνώχ. 'And again· "from the mountain on which they swore and bound themselves by common imprecations, [that] cold shall not depart from it for ever, nor snow nor hoar-frost, and dew shall not descend on it except it descend on it for a curse, until the great day of judgement In that season (time) it shall be consumed and brought low and shall be burnt up and melt as wax before fire, so shall it be burnt up by reason of all the works thereof And now I say to you, sons of men, great wrath is upon you, upon your sons, and this wrath shall not cease from you until the time of the slaughter of your sons And your beloved ones shall perish and your honoured ones shall die from off all the earth, for all the days of their life from henceforth shall not be more than an hundred and twenty years And think not that they may yet live for more years For there is not for them

heaven, saw and lusted after them, and said to one another:
'Come, let us choose us wives from among the children of
men and beget us children.'   3. And Semjâzâ, who was their
leader, said unto them. 'I fear ye will not indeed agree to do
this deed, and I alone shall have to pay the penalty of a great
sin.'   4. And they all answered him and said 'Let us all swear
an oath, and all bind ourselves by mutual imprecations not to
abandon this plan but to do this thing'   5. Then sware they
all together and bound themselves by mutual imprecations upon
it.   6. And they were in all two hundred; who descended ⌜in

---

any way of escape from this time by
reason of the wrath, wherewith the
king of all the ages is wroth with you
Imagine not that you will escape these
things." And these (words) are from
the first book of Enoch concerning the
watchers' Saw and > G⁵   4.
And said (E G²) > G⁶   This
thing   We must with G⁶ omit mëkĕi
(= 'plan') as a gloss on 'thing' in
E   Its presence makes the text ungrammatical   6 And they were
in all   G⁴ ἦσαν δὲ οὖτοι.   Who
descended . . . on Mount Hermon
I have here followed G⁴ οἱ καταβάντες
ἐν ταῖς ἡμέραις Ἰάρεδ εἰς τὴν κορυφὴν
τοῦ Ἑρμονιεὶμ ὄρους   The Ethiopic text
reads 'and they descended on Ardis
which is the summit of Mt. Hermon.'
The name Ardis, otherwise unknown, is
to be explained with Dillmann as a com-
pression of Ἰάρεδ εἰς, the translator not
having found ἐν ταῖς ἡμέραις in his text
Halévy in the *Journal Asiatique*, Avril-
Mai 1867, pp 356-7, reproduces this
verse in Hebrew, whereby we see at a
glance why the angels descended in the
days of Jared—from ירד to descend,
and why it was that they bound themselves by mutual oaths on Hermon—
from חָרַם a curse.

וַיֵּרְדוּ בִּימֵי יֶרֶד עַל רֹאשׁ הַר חֶרְמוֹן
וַיִּקְרְאוּ לָהָר חֶרְמוֹן כִּי בוֹ נִשְׁבְּעוּ וְהֶחֱרִימוּ
בֵּינֵיהֶם ׃

Cf Book of Jubilees 4¹⁵ 'Jared; for
in his days the angels of the Lord
descended on the earth' This play
on Jared shows that the idea originated
in Hebrew. It cannot be reproduced
in Aramaic, which does not possess the
root ירד. The play on Hermon is
possible not only in Hebrew (see above)
but also in Aramaic אחרימו . . . חרמון.
Cf Hilary, *Comm. in Pss* 132³ 'Hermon
autem mons est in Phoenice, cuius in-
terpretatio anathema est. Fertur id de
quo etiam nescio cuius liber exstat,
quod angeli concupiscentes filias hominum, cum de caelo descenderent, in
hunc montem Hermon maxime convenerant excelsum' The reasons for the
descent of the angels in the Book of
Jubilees differ from those given in this
chapter   In 4¹⁵ and 5¹ ᵃ⁹⁹ of that book
it is stated that the watchers were sent
to the earth by God 'to instruct the
children of men to do judgement and
uprightness', and that when so doing
they began to lust after the daughters
of men   This form of the myth seems
to be followed in Test Reuben 5⁶   In
Enoch the angels are said to have
descended through their lust for the
daughters of men, and the same reason is
given in *Jalkut Shim.* Beresh 44. See
Weber, *Jud Theologie* 253   Against
this and other statements of Enoch
there is an implicit polemic in the Book

the days⁷ of Jared on the summit of Mount Hermon, and they called it Mount Hermon, because they had sworn and bound themselves by mutual imprecations upon it.   7. And these are the names of their leaders: Sêmîazâz, their leader, Arâkîba, Râmêêl, Kôkabîêl, Tâmîêl, Râmîêl, Dânêl, Êzêqêêl, Barâqîjâl, Asâêl, Armârôs, Batârêl, Anânêl, Zaqîêl, Samsâpêêl, Satarêl, Tûrêl, Jômjâêl, Sariêl.   8. These are their chiefs of tens.

of Jubilees. In later tradition (Eisenmenger, *Entdeokt. Jud.* ii. 387) the
reason that Azazel could not return to
heaven was that he had outstayed
the limit of time assigned to angelic
visitants to earth—seven days In the
Targ Jon. on Gen. 6³ Shamchazai and
Uziel (i e Azazel) are mentioned in
connexion with this myth   7. This
list is incomplete. A name has been
lost after Tûrêl. Semîazâz Derivation doubtful. Possibly from שמעזיז
'mighty name' or שמחזאי. Râmêêl.
This is probably corrupt for Arakiêl—
'Αρακιήλ as in G². Now in G³ 8³ where
it is speaking of 'Αρακιήλ we have ὁ
δὲ τρίτος ἐδίδαξεν τὰ σημεῖα τῆς γῆς.
Thus 'Αρακιήλ = ארקיאל where ארק
= 'earth'. Thus we see that the duties
of the angel are reflected in his name
This is frequent in Judaism. Arakiêl
is mentioned as unfallen in *Sib Or.*
2²¹⁵⁻¹⁷ Kôkabîêl = כוכביאל = 'star
of God'. Tâmîêl = תומיאל = 'the
perfection of God'. Râmîêl See
1 Apoc. Bar. 55³, *Sib. Or.* 2²¹⁵⁻¹⁷.
Dânêl, i. e. Δανειήλ G² דניאל Êzêqêêl Since G³ 8³ writes ὁ δὲ ὄγδοος
ἐδίδαξεν ἀεροσκοπίαν, this word comes
from שחקיאל. שחק is rendered by
ἀήρ in 2 Kings 22¹² Ps. 18¹¹ (Beer)
Here again the name and functions of
the angel are connected. Barâqîjal

= ברקיאל = 'lightning of God'
Armârôs. This is the form in E, but
G³ gives Φαρμαρός and G⁵ 'Αρεαρώς.
Since G³ 8³ writes in reference to this
angel ἐδίδαξεν ... ἐπαοιδάς ... καὶ
ἐπαοιδῶν λυτήριον the word may go back
to חבר = 'an incantation', 'spell'
If so Armârôs or 'Αρεαρώς would be
corruptions of Abaros or something
similar Anânêl = ענניאל. Samsâpêêl The word should be 'Sham-
shiel'. Since G³ 8³ describes the
functions of this angel as ὁ δὲ ἕβδομος
ἐδίδαξε τὰ σημεῖα τοῦ ἡλίου the name is
from שמש, i e שמשיאל = 'sun of God'.
On Shamash the sun god see *K A.T.³*
367-370. Tûrêl = טוריאל = 'rock
of God'. Jômjâêl = יומיאל = 'day
of God'. Sariêl. E reads corruptly
'Arazjâl. This name recurs as Esdrêêl
in 8³. Since in G³ 8³ this angel ἐδίδαξε
τὰ σημεῖα τῆς σελήνης, these forms are
corrupt for Sariel as in G² (G⁵ 'Ατριήλ
but in 8³ Σεριήλ) Σαριήλ = סהריאל
where סהר = 'moon'. See *K.A.T³*
367. Chiefs of tens = ἀρχαὶ τῶν
δεκάδων. G⁵ reads ἀρχαὶ αὐτῶν οἱ δέκα,
which points to the Aramaic construction ראשיהון דעסריהא = ἀρχαὶ αὐτῶν
τῶν δεκάδων. In 19² αἱ γυναῖκες αὐτῶν
τῶν ... ἀγγέλων there is again the
same Aramaic idiom.

APPENDIX ON VI. 7.

The three lists of the fallen angels given above in E 6², G Syn , and G Giz go back to one and the same original. In E 69² the same list reappears. In the process of transmission, however, many corruptions and transpositions of the text have occurred. In the main the same order is observed in 6^7 69^2 and G^a. But a very different order is presented by G^g As Lods (106-7) has observed the names in G were from the third onward written in four columns. These were read from left to right by E and G^a, but from top to bottom of each column by G^g. Within G^a and G^g certain transpositions have occurred. These will be made clear by the following Table —

(1)	(2)	(3)	(4)
E 69^2 1. Samjâzâ	2. Artâqifâ	3. †Armên	4. Kôkabel
E 6^7 1. Samîazâz	2 Arâkîba	3. †Ramêel	4. Kôkabîel
G^a 1. Σεμιαζᾶς	2. Ἀταρκούφ	3. Ἀρακιήλ	4. Χωβαβιήλ
G^g 1. Σεμιαζά	2. Ἀραθάκ	3. †Κιμβρά	9. †Χωχαριήλ (8^3 Χωχιήλ)

(5)	(6)	(7)	(8)	(9)
5 †Tûraêl	6 Rûmjâl	7 Dânjal	8. †Nêqâel	9. Barâqel
5. Tâmîêl	6. Râtuîel	7. Dânêl	8. Ézêkêêl	9 Barâqîjal
5. †Ὀραμμαμή	6. Ῥαμιήλ	G^a wanting	8. Ζακιήλ	9 Βαλκιήλ
14. Ταμιήλ	18 Ραμιήλ	5. Δανειήλ	10. Εζεκιήλ (8^3 Σαθιήλ)	15 Βαρακιήλ (and in 8^2)

(10)	(11)	(12)	(14)
10. Azâzel	11 Armârôs	13 Batarjâl	14. Hanânel
10 Asâêl	11 Armârôs	12 Batârêl	13 Anânêl
10 Ἀζαλζήλ (8^3 Ἀζαήλ)	11. Φαρμαρός	12 Ἀμαριήλ	13 Ἀναγημάς
19. Ἀσεαλ	6 Ἀρεαρώς (8^3 Ἀρμαρώς)	11 Βατριήλ	16. Ἀνανθρά

(15)	(16)	(17)	(18)
15 Tûrel	16 Sîmîpêsîêl	17 Jêtrêl	18. Tûmâêl
14 Zaqîêl	15. Samsapêêl	16. Satarel	wanting
14 Θαυσαήλ	7 Σαμψίχ	16 Σαριυᾶς	17 Εὐμιήλ
20 Ῥακειήλ	4. Σαμμανή	12 Σαθιήλ	17 Θωνιήλ

(19)	(20)	(21)	(13)
19 Tûrêl	20 Rûmâêl	21 †Azâzel	13 Basasêjal
17 Tûrêl	19. Jômjâêl	19. †Arâzjâl (8^3 Esdrêêl)	wanting
18. Τυριήλ	19. Ἰουμιήλ	20 Σαριήλ	15 Σαμιήλ
21 Τουριήλ	8 Ἰωμιήλ	18 Ἀτριήλ (8^3 Σεριήλ)	7. Σεμιήλ

In the above Table I have followed the order of E 69^2, the names as they appear in that list head each of the twenty-one columns   Next comes the list in E 6^7; then that in G^a, and finally that in G^g On the left of each name is placed a number which gives its place in its own list   Above each column I have put a number in brackets for convenience in references.   Column (13) is placed at the end instead of after (12) since Basasejal has no parallel in E 6^7 and no certain one in G^a or G^g.

As regards E 69^2, (15) which appears again in (19) is certainly corrupt, also (21) which is a repetition of (10). To (13) we have already referred. Thus the twenty-one names are reduced to nineteen

Of E 6^7 (18) is wanting . also (13): (15) is hopeless   This list furnishes nineteen names

Of G^a (7) is wanting, and (15) and (5) are corrupt. This list has twenty names.

Of G^g the list is complete, but (15) is hopeless.

In the above Table the identifications may be regarded as certain in (1), (4), (6), (7-12), (14), (16), (19-20), as probable or possible in (2-3), (5), (17-18), (21), as undeterminable in (13) and (15).

VII. 1 And all the others together with them took unto themselves wives, and each chose for himself one, and they began to go in unto them and to defile themselves with them, and they taught them charms and enchantments, and the cutting of roots, and made them acquainted with plants. 2. And they became pregnant, and they bare great giants, whose height was three thousand ells : 3. Who consumed all the acquisitions of men. And when men could no longer sustain them, 4. The giants turned against them and devoured mankind 5. And they began to sin against birds, and beasts, and reptiles, and fish, and to devour one another's flesh, and drink the blood. 6. Then the earth laid accusation against the lawless ones.

VIII. 1 And Azâzêl taught men to make swords, and knives, and shields, and breastplates, and made known to them the metals ⟨of the earth⟩ and the art of working them, and bracelets, and

VII 1 And all.. with them G⁸ = 'these and all the rest' Defile themselves SoG⁸ᵗ E reads tadammarû (= 'unite themselves') corrupt (?) for jĕtgammanû = Gᵉ¹ Charms and en-chantments Cf Wisd 12⁴ 18¹³, Jos *Ant.* viii. 2. 5, *Bell* vii 6 3 Plants (= βοτάνας Gᵉ) Not 'trees' here The Ethiopic has both meanings 2 Bare great giants. For further references see Sir 16⁷ Jub 7²²⁻²³ Wisd 14⁶ Tob 6¹⁴ 1 Bar. 3²⁸ 3 Macc 2⁴ The text in E Gᵉ is defective here, and must be made good from G⁸, which gives. 'And they bare unto them three kinds first great giants, and the giants †begat the Naphilim, and to the Naphilim were† born the Eliûd, and they grew according to their greatness' That these classes of giants were mentioned here is presupposed by 86⁴ and 88² of our text Moreover Jub 7²¹⁻²² is based on this passage. 'The watchers took unto themselves wives and they begat sons ⟨the giants⟩, the Naphidim ⟨and the Eliô⟩, and they were all alike, and they devoured one another, and the giants slew the Naphil, and the

Naphil slew the Eljô, and the Eljô mankind' In 7²⁴ Jub quotes the greater part of 8⁵ of our text of E Gᵉ. Hence since G⁸ omits 7³, ⁴ᵃ, ⁵ᵃ, ⁶ (7⁴ᵇ, ⁵ᵇ are inserted after 8³) and E Gᵉ omit portions of 7², both texts are here defective The three classes of giants go back to Gen. 6⁴. The γίγαντες = גבורים, the Ναφηλείμ = נפילים, and the 'Ελιουδ = אנשׁי חשׁם. I have obelized 'begat' (ἐτέκνωσαν) as corrupt ἐτέκνωσαν may be corrupt for ἔκτειναν of Jub 7²¹ above Or the corruption may have arisen in the Aramaic : ἐτέκνωσαν = מולידין corrupt for מובדין = 'destroyed'. 3 And when (ὡς δέ Gᵉ E = ὥστε corrupt for ὡς δέ. 5 Blood. The eating of blood with the Jews was a great crime, Gen 9⁴ Acts 15²⁰ Book of Jubilees 7²⁸, ²⁹ 21⁶, ¹⁸, below 98¹¹

VIII. 1 Azâzêl The origin of this word is unknown See *Encyc Bib* in loc Breastplates + διδάγματα ἀγγέλων Gᵉ The metals of the earth. So G⁸. E twice deals with this phrase. First, here it gives only τὰ μετ' αὐτά ornaments, and the use of antimony, and the beautifying of the eyelids, and all kinds of costly stones, and all colouring tinctures. 2. And there arose much godlessness, and they committed fornication, and they were led astray, and became corrupt in all their ways. 3. Semjâzâ taught enchantments, and root-cuttings, 'Armârôs the resolving of enchantments, Barâqîjâl (taught) astrology, Kôkabêl the constellations, **Ezêqêêl the knowledge**

corrupt for τὰ μέταλλα, and then at the end of the verse taulâtₐ, a transliteration of τὰ μέταλλα, and appends τῆς γῆς. Hence the above rendering is to be followed   G⁸ reads only τὰ †μεγάλα. With our text cf. Tertullian, *De Cultu Fem.* 1 2 'Metallorum opera nudaverunt'. Antimony. This mineral is referred to in the following excerpt from Tert. *De Cultu Fem* 1 2, in which he lays under contribution this and the preceding chapter   'Herbarum ingenia tia duxerant et incantationum vires provulgaverant et omnem curiositatem usque ad stellarum interpretationem designaverant, proprie et quasi peculiariter feminis instrumentum istud muliebris gloriae contulerunt, lumina lapillorum quibus monilia variantur et circulos ex auro quibus brachia artantur —et illum ipsum nigrum pulverem quo oculorum exordia producuntur' and in ii 10 'Quodsi idem angeli qui et materias eiusmodi et illecebras detexerunt, auri dico et lapidum illustrium, et operas eorum tradiderunt, et iam ipsum calliblepharum—tincturas—docuerunt, ut Enoch refert.' Cf T. Reub. 5⁵,⁶ also Is. 3¹⁶⁻²⁴ for the ornaments of women. 2. Godlessness. + 'upon the earth' G⁴ And they committed . astray > G⁴.   3. G⁸ gives this verse as follows 'First Azazel—the tenth of the leaders—taught (men) to make swords and breastplates and every kind of warlike arms, and the metals of the earth and the gold, how they were to work them and make them ornaments for the women and the silver. And he showed

them the art of using antimony (l στιβίζειν for στίλβειν) and beautifying the face, and precious stones and colouring tinctures. And the children of men made (them) for themselves and their daughters and transgressed and led astray the holy ones.' This last sentence is alien to the Book of Noah, and belongs rather to the Book of Jubilees and the Testaments. The latter books represent the daughters of men as seducing the angels by their ornaments, &c, whereas the older books declare that such arts were first introduced by the fallen angels. Cf Clem Alex. *Eclog. Proph* (ed. Dindorf, iii 474) ἤδη δὲ καὶ Ἐνώχ φησιν τοὺς παραβάντας ἀγγέλους διδάξαι τοὺς ἀνθρώπους ἀστρονομίαν καὶ μαντικὴν καὶ τὰς ἄλλας τέχνας. Semjâzâ (G⁸ˢ). E corruptly reads Amizârâs—an internal Ethiopic corruption. Armârôs On 6⁷ I have suggested that this word is corrupt, and was originally derived from חבר on the ground of what follows. His function was ἐπαοιδῶν λυτήριον An allied phrase is found in Dan. 5¹² משרא קטרין (= λύων συνδέσμους Theod) ' the resolving of spells' In 95⁴ below we have ' anathemas that cannot be resolved '. Here the word חרם is referred to. Barâqîjâl .. Kôkabêl See notes on 6⁷. Ezêqêêl the knowledge of the clouds E is here very corrupt. Though it gives Ezêqêêl rightly in 6⁷, here it reads ' Tamiel'. G⁸ is also corrupt—Σαθήλ corrupt for Ζακιήλ, as in 6⁷, or Ἐζεκιήλ Again G⁸ E have ἀστεροσκοπίαν, which,

of the clouds, ⟨Araqiêl the signs of the earth, Shamsiêl the signs of the sun⟩, and Sariêl the course of the moon   4. And as men perished, they cried, and their cry went up to heaven. . . .

IX. 1 And then Michael, Uriel, Raphael, and Gabriel looked down from heaven and saw much blood being shed upon the earth, and all lawlessness being wrought upon the earth. 2 And they said one to another: 'The earth made †without inhabitant cries the voice of their crying† up to the gates of heaven.   3. ⌜And now to you, the holy ones of heaven⌝, the souls of men make their suit, saying, "Bring our cause before the Most High ".'   4. And they said to the Lord of the ages : 'Lord of lords, God of gods, King of kings ⟨and God of the ages⟩, the throne of Thy glory ⟨standeth⟩ unto all the generations of the ages, and Thy name holy and glorious and blessed unto all the ages!   5. Thou hast made all things, and power over all things hast Thou · and all things are naked and open in Thy

as I have already pointed out in 6⁷(which see), is corrupt for ἀεροσκοπίαν (so G⁵) ⟨Araqiêl . . . sun⟩ supplied from G⁵, save that for ὁ τρίτος and ὁ ἕβδομος I have given the names these numbers represent.   Sariêl. E = Esdreêl corrupt : Gᵍ Σεριή(λ) See note on 6⁷ on this word   4 And (E Gˢ¹) Gˢ² reads τότε, Gᵍ οὖν.   They cried, and their cry went up to heaven (E) = ἐβόησαν καὶ ἀνέβη ἡ βοὴ αὐτῶν εἰς τὸν οὐρανόν. Gᵍ om. ἐβόησαν καί. Gˢ¹² reads ἐβόησαν εἰς τὸν οὐρανόν Our text, therefore, may be a conflation of these two readings yet of 9¹⁰   To heaven. + 'saying, Bring our cause before the Most High and our destruction before the Great Glory, before the Lord of all the lords in greatness' Gˢ². Cf. Gˢ¹. This fragment most probably preserves part of the original text · cf. 9², ³. The cry of men is not inarticulate, but a prayer for justice.

IX. 1 And then (E) Gᵍ 'then'. + 'the four great archangels hearing' Gˢ¹, ². Michael, &c See 40² note on the four archangels. Looked down

from heaven = אורדיקו משמיא   An echo of Ps 14²   2 The earth †made without inhabitant .   heaven (E). Gᵍ reads 'the voice of them that cry upon the earth to the gates of heaven '. Gˢ¹, ² omit On 'made without inhabitant' cf 67² 84⁶ T. Naph 3⁵.   3. On the intercession of angels see ver 10 note, and my note on T Lev. 3⁵, where the chief passages on this subject from 200 B C to 100 A.D are dealt with. And now .   heaven (E). Lost in Gˢ¹, ² through hmt.   Holy ones See 1⁹ note.   Most High See 99³ note. 4. Lord of the ages (Gˢ¹) ≯ Gˢ² E = κυρίω τῶν βασιλέων, where τ βασιλέων = מלביא corrupt for עלמיא = τῶν αἰώνων.   Lord of lords, God of gods So in Deut 10¹⁷. The prayer of the angels is fuller in Gˢ, and still more in 84², ³   Of kings (E Gˢ ¹, ²). Gᵍ reads τῶν αἰώνων = עלמיא corrupt for מלביא.   ⟨God of the ages⟩ Restored from Gˢ¹, ². In Gˢ² ἀνθρώπων, ι ε αἰνῶν is corrupt for αἰώνων   5. Power over all things (E Gˢ). Gᵍ

sight, and all things Thou seest, and nothing can hide itself from Thee.　6. Thou seest what Azâzêl hath done, who hath taught all unrighteousness on earth and revealed the eternal secrets which were (preserved) in heaven, which men were striving to learn :　7. And Semjâza, to whom Thou hast given authority to bear rule over his associates.　8. And they have gone to the daughters of men upon the earth, and have slept with the women, and have defiled themselves, and revealed to them all kinds of sins.　9. And the women have borne giants, and the whole earth has thereby been filled with blood and unrighteousness.　10 And now, behold, the souls of those who have died are crying and making their suit to the gates of heaven, and their lamentations have ascended : and cannot cease

---

= 'all power'. And nothing can hide itself from Thee　6 Thou seest Lost in G⁸ through hint　6. Revealed the eternal secrets which were .. learn. So G⁸¹ with the correction of ἔγνωσαν into γνῶναι (cf. G⁸ εἰδέναι), for it is untranslatable as it stands. E is very corrupt. 'the eternal secrets which are wrought in the heaven mankind knows' (g). But G⁸ᵃ show that 'ella jetgabarû should be emended into 'ella jetgébarû (= ȃ ἐπιτηδεύουσιν) and transposed after 'in the heaven'. Next 'a'ĕmara (g) (= ἔγνω) should be emended into 'a'ĕmrô = γνῶναι or εἰδέναι. Thus E agrees with G⁸ when ἔγνωσαν in the latter is corrected as above suggested　G⁸ = 'revealed to the world the things that are (preserved) in heaven. And the children of men are practising his (Azazel's) practices in order to know the mysteries'.　7 ⟨And⟩ Supplied from G⁸.　8, 9 Cf. Justin, *Apol.* ii. 5 Οἱ δὲ ἄγγελοι—γυναικῶν μίξεσιν ἡττήθησαν καὶ παῖδας ἐτέκνωσαν, οἵ εἰσιν οἱ λεγόμενοι δαίμονες—καὶ εἰς διθρώπους φόνους, πολέμους, μοιχείας—καὶ πᾶσαν κακίαν ἔσπειραν　8. With the women. Here E = μετ' αὐτῶν μετὰ τῶν θηλειῶν

—the literal rendering of an Aramaic idiom = עמהין עם נשיא = 'with the women'. G⁴ not understanding this idiom divided the phrase into two parts, and connected them with different verbs συνεκοιμήθησαν μετ' αὐτῶν καὶ ἐν ταῖς θηλείαις ἐμιάνθησαν　G⁸ omitted the latter half of the phrase and read αὐταῖς after συνεκοιμήθησαν　All kinds of sins + 'and have taught them to make hate-producing charms' (G⁸). But as Martin suggests μίσητρα is possibly corrupt for μισητίαν. Hence 'taught them to practise lewdness'　9 Giants　G⁸ reads τιτᾶνας, G⁸ γίγαντας 10–11. The intercession of the angels on man's behalf, which appears in this chapter and is found also in 15² 40⁶ 47² 99³, ¹⁶ 104¹, is an O. T. doctrine , cf. Job 5¹ 33²³ Zech. 1¹²　It was evidently a popular doctrine. Cf. Tobit 12¹² Ἐγὼ προσήγαγον τὸ μνημόσυνον τῆς προσευχῆς ὑμῶν ἐνώπιον τοῦ ἁγίου (contrast Acts 10⁴), also 12¹⁶ ἐγώ εἰμι Ῥαφαὴλ εἶς ἐκ τῶν ἐπτὰ ἁγίων ἀγγέλων οἱ προσαναφέρουσι τὰς προσευχὰς τῶν ἁγίων Rev. 8³, Test Levi 3⁵. also 5⁶, ⁷ ἐγώ εἰμι ὁ ἄγγελος ὁ παραιτούμενος τὸ γένος Ἰσραήλ.　10 Cease. EG⁸ᵃ

because of the lawless deeds which are wrought on the earth.
11. And Thou knowest all things before they come to pass, and
Thou seest these things and Thou dost suffer them, and Thou
dost not say to us what we are to do to them in regard to these.'

X. 1. Then said the Most High, the Holy and Great One
spake, and sent Uriel to the son of Lamech, and said to him:
2 '⟨Go to Noah and⟩ tell him in my name " Hide thyself ! ", and
reveal to him the end that is approaching that the whole earth
will be destroyed, and a deluge is about to come upon the whole
earth, and will destroy all that is on it.   3. And now instruct
him that he may escape and his seed may be preserved for all the
generations of the world.'   4 And again the Lord said to

read ἐξελθεῖν = למנפק corrupt for
למפסק = 'cease' The lamentations
must keep ascending to heaven without ceasing because of the deeds of
violence on earth   11 Seest (G^{ᵍˢ}).
E 'knowest' Dost suffer them
(G^{ᵍˢ}). E = τα εἰς αὐτούς corrupt for
ἐᾷς αὐτούς

X 1 Said So G^{ᵍ·ˢ} E om The
Holy and Great One (E). G^{ᵍˢ} 'And
the Great Holy One' Uriel (G^ˢ)
G^ᵍ Ἰσтραήλ E is corrupt   2
⟨Go to Noah and ⟩ Restored from
G^ˢ πορεύου πρὸς τὸν Νῶε καί This
phrase belonged to the original, though
already lost in the archetype of E. It
belongs to the original, for each new
command issued to the angels begins
with the word 'go' Cf G^ˢ 10^{4, 9, 11}
3 And now (E) G^ᵍ 'and' > G^ˢ
G^ˢ is here much fuller 'Instruct the
righteous (man) what he is to do,
(even) the son of Lamech, and he will
preserve his soul unto life and escape
through the world, and from him will
be planted a plant, and it will be
established throughout all the generations of the world.' Of the world
n, G^{ᵍˢ}. > E–n.   4 Azazel is punished in a place by himself. In his
case as in that of his followers the
place of punishment is in the valleys

of the earth *in the Noah sections* of
the book, but in the genuine Enoch
beyond the earth Azazel as the
chief offender and leader is first punished The preliminary punishment of
Azazel is described in vv 4, 5 the
final one in ver 6 Azazel was conceived as chained in the wilderness
into which the scapegoat was led The
Jerusalem Targum (Ps Jonathan) on
Leviticus says that the goat was sent
to die in a hard and rough place in the
wilderness of jagged rocks, i e Beth
Chadure The passage in Ps Jon.
on Lev 16^{1–22} is as follows ויפטור
ביד גבר . . . למהך למדברא דצוק דהוא
בית הדורי . . . ויפטור גברא ית צפירא
למדברא דצוק ויסוק צפירא על טווריא
דבית הדורי. 'And they will send it
by the hand of a man . that it may
go into the precipitous desert, which
is Beth Chadure and the man will
send the goat into the precipitous
wilderness, and the goat will ascend
the mountains of Beth Chadure' In
the Mishna (Joma 6⁸) we find this
word written חדורי 'Chadûdê'. This
Beth Chaduda was three miles (Joma
6⁸), or according to another account,
twelve miles from Jerusalem This is
clearly the Dudael mentioned in this

Raphael · 'Bind Azâzêl hand and foot, and cast him into the darkness: and make an opening in the desert, which is in Dûdâêl, and cast him therein. 5. And place upon him rough and jagged rocks, and cover him with darkness, and let him abide there for ever, and cover his face that he may not see light. 6. And on the day of the great judgement he shall be cast into the fire. 7. And heal the earth which the angels have corrupted, and proclaim the healing of the earth, that they may heal the plague, and that all the children of men may not perish through all the secret things that the Watchers have disclosed and have taught their sons. 8. And the whole earth has been corrupted through the works that were taught by Azâzêl · to him ascribe all sin' 9. And to Gabriel said the Lord:

---

verse, and it is thus a definite locality in the neighbourhood of Jerusalem See Geiger in the *Judische Zeitschrift f. Wissenschaft und Leben* 1864, pp. 196-204 Cf. Lev. 16¹⁰, ²². Again the Lord (E) > Gᵍ. To Raphael + 'go Raphael and' (Gᵃ). Gᵃ is probably right here. **5 Place upon him** The Greek gives ὑπόθες αὐτῷ, but this is probably a slip for ἐπίθες αὐτῷ Cf 54⁵ **For ever** Like εἰς τὸν αἰῶνα, of which the Ethiopic text is an exact rendering, this phrase has no definite meaning in itself It may denote according to the context an unending period · or a period of seventy generations, as here, of ver 12 , or a period of five hundred years, as in ver 10 **6 Day of the great judgement** So Gᵍ. E reads 'great day of judgement' See 45² (note) This judgement inaugurates the final punishment of the angels **The fire** see 18¹¹ 19 21⁷⁻¹⁰ **7** The command given to Raphael is such as his name suggests from רפא 'to heal' Cf. Tob. 3¹⁷ 12¹⁴. **Heal the earth** (E Gᵃ). Gᵍ 'the earth shall be healed'. Healing of the earth (E Gᵍ) Gᵃ 'healing of the plague' **They may heal the plague** (Gᵍᵃ)

E (i e. *gmu*) 'one may heal the earth' The rest of the MSS. of E = 'I may heal', &c. We should observe here that in these two clauses E has both times medr = γῆ, Gᵃ has both times πληγή, and Gᵍ has first γῆ and then πληγή Two explanations are possible Either πληγή was original in both cases, and Gᵍ represents the first stage in the corruption and E the second Or the variations in G arose from two possible renderings of ארעא, which punctuated as אַרְעָא = γῆ and as אַרְעָא = πληγή. **Have disclosed** EGᵍ have here ἐπάταξαν = אבדו corrupt for אמרו = εἶπον which we find in Gᵃ Cf ἐμηνύσατε in 16³ For an analogous corruption see 2 Chron 22¹⁰ Bouriant's conjecture—ἐπέτασαν—which I formerly followed is impossible **8 All sin** is here ascribed to the fallen angels **The works that were taught** (Gᵍᵃ τοῖς ἔργοις τῆς διδασκαλίας) E 'the teaching of the works' **9, 10** The destruction of the giants through Gabriel. The account here is followed closely by the Book of Jubilees 5⁶⁻¹¹. The giants slay each other in the presence of their parents, cf 14⁶ The latter are then bound in the abysses of the

'Proceed against the bastards and the reprobates, and against
the children of fornication: and destroy [the children of fornication and] the children of the Watchers from amongst men: [and
cause them to go forth]: send them one against the other that
they may destroy each other in battle for length of days shall
they not have.   10. And no request that they (i.e. their
fathers) make of thee shall be granted unto their fathers on
their behalf; for they hope to live an eternal life, and that each
one of them will live five hundred years.'   11. And the Lord
said unto Michael: ' Go, bind Semjâzâ and his associates who
have united themselves with women so as to have defiled themselves with them in all their uncleanness.   12. And, when
their sons have slain one another, and they have seen the
destruction of their beloved ones, bind them fast for seventy
generations in the **valleys** of the earth, till the day of their

earth, and their power of hurting the
earth is at an end, cf 14⁵ But this
is not so with the spirits of the giants.
They enjoy an impunity in wrong-doing
till the final judgement see 15¹¹–16¹.
9 [**The children of fornication
and**] > Gᵍˢ. This is a dittograph
from the preceding clause in E It is
against the context also 'The children
of the Watchers' is sufficient this
phrase includes the three classes in the
preceding clause. [**And cause them
to go forth**] A duplicate rendering
in E of πέμψον **One against the
other** (E Gˢ) > Gˢ **That they may
destroy each other in battle** (E)
This is not a paraphrastic rendering of
Gˢ ἐν πολέμῳ, since Gˢ has ἐν πολέμῳ καὶ
ἐν ἀπωλείᾳ. The original was probably
‫קרב מותא‬ = 'a deadly war' or 'a war of
extermination.' Cf Jub. 5⁹   10. **An
eternal life** = 500 years Touching
the prayer of the angels cf 12⁶ 13⁴⁻⁶
14⁷.   11 **The Lord** (E). > Gᵍˢ.
Bind (i.e δῆσον Gᵃ) Gᵍ E read δήλωσον, a corruption native to Gᵍ, for the
original acc μιγέντας remains unchanged, though of course δήλωσον

would require μιγεῖσι   **United
themselves . . defiled themselves with them** Quoted verbally
in Jub 4²²   12. **Their sons** So
Gᵍˢ οἱ υἱοὶ αὐτῶν E reads all these
sons', but kuellû = 'all' is an internal corruption for 'ellû = οἱ here
Slain one another. Cf 12⁶ 14⁶
Jub. 5⁹   **Valleys** (νάπας Gᵍˢ). E
reads ' hills ' νάπαι is used as a rendering of ‫גבעה‬ in Is. 40¹² Ezek 6³. This
fact and the influence of the Greek
myth of the Titans may explain how
the Ethiopic translator attached this
meaning to it. That νάπαι means
valleys in this passage is beyond the
possibility of doubt In 67⁴ ⁵⁹ this
valley (not valleys) in which the fallen
angels are cast is dealt with at length.
Jub 5¹⁰, which is here dependent on
our text, writes ' After this they were
bound in the depths of the earth for
ever until the day of the great condemnation' This verse is referred to
by St Jude 6 ἀγγέλους τε τοὺς μὴ
τηρήσαντας τὴν ἑαυτῶν ἀρχὴν ἀλλὰ ἀπο-
λιπόντας τὸ ἴδιον οἰκητήριον εἰς κρίσιν
μεγάλης ἡμέρας . . ὑπὸ ζόφον τετήρηκεν.

judgement and of their consummation, till the judgement that
is for ever and ever is consummated.   13. In those days they
shall be led off to the abyss of fire : ⟨and⟩ to the torment and
the prison in which they shall be confined for ever.   14. And
whosoever shall be **condemned** and destroyed will from thenceforth be bound together with them to the end of all generations.   15. And destroy all the spirits of the reprobate and the
children of the Watchers, because they have wronged mankind.
16. Destroy all wrong from the face of the earth and let every
evil work come to an end : and let the plant of righteousness
and truth appear ⌜and it shall prove a blessing . the works of
righteousness and truth⌝ shall be planted in truth and joy for
evermore.

17. And then shall all the righteous escape,
    And shall live till they beget thousands of children,
    And all the days of their youth and their **old age** shall they
        complete in peace.

18. And then shall the whole earth be tilled in righteousness,

13 The final place of punishment for
the angels as for Azazel, 10⁶.   **Abyss
of fire.** This is the λίμνη τοῦ πυρός
of Rev. 20¹⁰, ¹⁴⁻¹⁵ which was prepared for the devil and his angels,
Matt 25⁴¹, as here 10⁶, ¹³   Cf 18¹¹ 19
21⁷⁻¹⁰ 90²⁴.   In which they (Eᵍ).
Eᵃ reads 'and they'   The absence
of the relative here in Eᵍ is due to an
Ethiopic idiom.   14 See19² Condemned (Gˢ).   Gᵍ E read κατακαυσθῇ
corrupt for κατακριθῇ   All generations (E)   Gˢ 'the generation', Gᵃ
'their generation'.   15 The writer
is still describing the duties of Gabriel,
i e. the destruction of the giants and
the imprisonment of the fallen Watchers,
as we see from 10⁹, ¹⁰. This verse is
therefore out of place   Possibly it
belongs after 10¹⁰. Thus 10¹⁻³ refers
to Uriel, 10⁴⁻⁸ to Raphael, 10⁸, ¹⁰, ¹⁵ to
Gabriel, and 10¹¹⁻¹² to Michael And 1⁰
(E) >Gˢ.   16 Plant of righteousness, i e. Israel. Israel springs from

a seed that 'is sown' by God, 62⁸ .
hence it is established as 'a plant of
the seed for ever', 84⁶, is called 'the
plant of uprightness', 93², 'the plant
of righteousness', 93⁵, 'the eternal
plant of righteousness', 93¹⁰, and finally
'the plant of righteous judgement', 93⁵
Righteousness and truth   After
these words Gᵍ omits through limit καὶ
ἔσται εὐλογία· τὰ ἔργα τῆς δικαιοσύνης
καὶ τῆς ἀληθείας, which are preserved
by E   17 The writer has here
gone over wholly to a description of
the Messianic times The picture is
a very sensuous one   Their old age
cf 25³, ⁴ (note)   Here Gᵍ E have τὰ
σάββατα αὐτῶν = שבתהון in which the
word is wrongly vocalized for שבתהון
= τὸ γῆρας αὐτῶν   The error could
also be explained in Hebrew   See
Wellhausen, *Skizzen*, vi. 241, 260
18, 19 The future is depicted after
O T prophecy Cf. Amos 9¹³, ¹⁴ Hos
2²², ²³ Jer. 31⁵ Is 25⁶ Ezek. 28²⁶ 34²⁶, ²⁷.

and shall all be planted with trees and be full of blessing. 19. And all desirable trees shall be planted on it, and they shall plant vines on it: and the vine which they plant thereon shall yield wine in abundance, and as for all the seed which is sown thereon each measure (of it) shall bear a thousand, and each measure of olives shall yield ten presses of oil. 20. And cleanse thou the earth from all oppression, and from all unrighteousness, and from all sin, and from all godlessness and all the uncleanness that is wrought upon the earth destroy from off the earth. 21 ⌜And all the children of men shall become righteous⌝, and all nations shall offer adoration and shall praise Me, and all shall worship Me. 22. And the earth shall be cleansed from all defilement, and from all sin, and from all punishment, and from all torment, and I will never again send (them) upon it from generation to generation and for ever

XI. 1. And in those days I will open the store chambers of blessing which are in the heaven, so as to send them down ⌜upon the earth⌝ over the work and labour of the children of men. 2. And truth and peace shall be associated together throughout all the days of the world and throughout all the generations of men.'

18 Shall all be planted with trees (E) G^g 'and a tree shall be planted in it'. Is this 'the plant of righteousness' of v 16? The sequel, however, points to the former The 'all' in E, 1 e kuĕlantâhâ, may be corrupt for halâ'ĕlĕhâ = ἐν αὐτῇ (G^g) 19 And all . be planted (E). G^g is corrupt. 'and all the trees of the earth shall rejoice, shall be planted' (τῆς γῆς ἀγαλλιασονται φυτινθήσεται) Wine in abundance (E) G^g 'pitchers of wine'. As for all the seed . presses of oil (E = πᾶς ὁ σπόρος ὁ σπαρεὶς ἐν αὐτῇ ἕκαστον μέτρον ποιήσει χιλιάδας καὶ ἕκαστον μέτρον ἐλαίας κτλ). G^g is corrupt and defective χιλιάδας καὶ σπύρου ποιήσει καθ' ἕκαστον μέτρον ἐλαιας Each measure shall bear, &c. Cf the chiliastic expectations in

2 Bar 29^5 and Iren adv Haer v 33, and contrast Is. 5^10   20. Oppression (E). G^g 'impurity'. All 4° (E) > G^g From off the earth. 21 And all the children of men shall become righteous (E) > G^g. The conversion of the Gentiles Cf 90^30 (note) 91^14. 22 The earth (E). G^g 'all the earth'. From all 4° (E) > G^g Upon it (E). G^g 'upon them'

XI 1 This chapter concludes an account of the Messianic kingdom Cf. Deut. 28^12. Upon the earth (E) > G^g. 2 Cf 85^10 Is 32^17. Truth and peace shall be associated together (so G^g E save that E reads 'peace and truth') Cf. Ps 85^11. Of men (G^g). E = αἰώνων, a corruption of ανπων = ἀνθρώπων

XII–XVI. *Dream Vision of Enoch: his intercession for Azazel and the fallen Angels. and his announcement to them of their first and final doom.*

XII. 1. Before these things Enoch was hidden, and no one of the children of men knew where he was hidden, and where he

XII–XVI Vision of Enoch, in which he intercedes on behalf of Azazel and the Watchers. The pronouncement of their doom by God, which Enoch announces to them. The vision or rather visions are preserved only in a fragmentary condition, and not in their original order—a fact which is in part due to our editor, as we shall find elsewhere, as in chapters 78–80 and 91–94. The doom pronounced on Azazel and the fallen angels in 10 has not yet been executed, for Enoch is asked to intercede on their behalf. The order of the original visions was as follows. Enoch was asked to intercede for Azazel. This Section is lost, but its presence in the original vision is implied in 13¹⁻², in which he announces the result of his mission on Azazel's behalf and pronounces his doom. Next the Watchers besought him to intercede on their behalf, 13³ 12³ 13⁴⁻⁷ Enoch has a fresh vision, 13⁸. When he awakes from it he proceeds to the Watchers and recounts it to them, 13⁹⁻¹⁰. The vision is related at length, and all that God said relating to the Watchers, their original condition, their sin and their doom, 14²–16². Finally, the section closes with the message of doom which Enoch is bidden to take to the Watchers, 16³⁻⁴ But this message appears in a duplicate form in 12⁴⁻⁶. The latter is more original since it reflects the discourse of God to Enoch in his vision. This repetition is thoroughly Semitic. I will here write out 12⁴⁻⁶, printing the words which are based on 14²–16² in

black type   12⁴ εἶπὲ τοῖς ἐγρηγόροις τοῦ οὐρανοῦ (14⁸) οἵτινες, ἀπολιπόντες τὸν οὐρανὸν τὸν ὑψηλόν, τὸ ἁγίασμα τῆς στάσεως τοῦ αἰῶνος, μετὰ τῶν γυναικῶν ἐμιάνθησαν, καὶ ὥσπερ οἱ υἱοὶ τῆς γῆς ποιοῦσιν, οὕτως καὶ αὐτοὶ ποιοῦσιν, καὶ ἔλαβον ἑαυτοῖς γυναῖκας (15⁸)· ἀφανισμὸν μέγαν †κατηφανίσατε† τὴν γῆν   5 καὶ οὐκ ἔσται ὑμῖν εἰρήνη οὔτε ἄφεσις (16⁴).   6. καὶ περὶ ὧν χαίρουσιν τῶν υἱῶν αὐτῶν, τὸν φόναν τῶν ἀγαπητῶν αὐτῶν ὄψονται (14⁸ 10¹²), καὶ ἐπὶ τῇ ἀπωλείᾳ τῶν υἱῶν αὐτῶν στενάξουσιν καὶ δεηθήσονται (10¹⁰), εἰς τὸν αἰῶνα, καὶ οὐκ ἔσται αὐτοῖς εἰς ἔλεον καὶ εἰρήνην (16⁴)   The original order therefore of this section was, so far as the present fragmentary text goes   1¹¹   13¹⁻² 13³ 12³ 13⁴⁻¹⁰ 14²–16² 12⁴⁻⁶ ‖ 16³⁻⁴   12¹⁻² is an editorial introduction   It is remarkable that whereas *the angels intercede* in the Noah section *on behalf of man*, in this Enoch section *a man intercedes on behalf of the fallen angels*   In the Noah fragment (68²⁻³) the angels are troubled over the doom of the Watchers, but they are afraid to approach God on their behalf

XII. 1–2 An introduction from the final editor. See preceding note 1. Before these things, i e before the intercession of the angels on behalf of mankind and God's judgement on the watchers, 9–10   Was hidden (E) Gᵇ 'was taken'—ἐλήμφθη This is the Ethiopic way of rendering μετέθηκεν (= לקח) in Gen 5²⁴ cf 71¹, ⁵ in our text   It is possible that the editor intends the reader to understand that

abode, and what had become of him. 2. And his activities had to do with the Watchers, and his days were with the holy ones.

3. And I Enoch was blessing the Lord of majesty and the King of the ages, and lo ! the Watchers called me—Enoch the scribe—and said to me · 4. 'Enoch, thou scribe of righteousness, go, †declare† to the Watchers of the heaven who have left the high heaven, the holy eternal place, and have defiled themselves with women, and have done as the children of earth do, and have taken unto themselves wives: " Ye have wrought

Enoch at this date had already been translated, but, if so, this was not the meaning of the vision he has incorporated, for Enoch is still living his final translation from earth has not yet fallen out, for as a man he writes the petition for the angels, 13⁶ receives a vision in sleep and is transported in spirit unto heaven, 14² speaks with a tongue of flesh, 14² and is terrified, like a mortal man, at the presence of God, 14²⁴ Furthermore, the next verse (12²) was apparently before the author of Jub 4²¹, who states that Enoch spent six jubilees of years (ı e 294) with the angels, being instructed in the things of heaven and earth, and that afterwards he was taken from amongst the children of men. 2. His activities. Here E reads 'all his activities', but kuéllû = 'all' is a corruption of 'ĕllû = τά as frequently For 'his' Gᵍ corruptly reads 'their'. His days. E corruptly prefixes 'in'. 3. This verse, which contains the request of the Watchers that Enoch should intercede for them, should be read after 13³ See note on xii-xvi Of majesty (Gᵍ). So E (ı. e. q β) by changing the vocalization of one letter Otherwise E = 'great', 'majestic' King of the ages This title occurs also in Gᵍ 9⁴, where however it is corrupt. Watchers + 'of the Holy Great One', Gᵍ The scribe. cf 92¹. Enoch is further called 'the scribe

of righteousness', 12⁴ 15¹, because he is himself a righteous man, 15¹ 71¹⁴⁻¹⁶, and declares the righteous judgement that is coming, 13¹⁰ 14¹, ³ 81⁸ 82¹, &c. The idea of a heavenly 'scribe' is derived in the main from the Babylonian Nabû He is the man (in Ezek. 9² ᵃᵠᵠ) clad in linen with writer's inkhorn by his side He is accompanied by six other men These go back to the seven gods of the planets. In later Jewish writings this office is fulfilled by Michael in 1 Enoch 89⁶¹ ᵃᵠᵠ , by Enoch in 1 Enoch 12⁸ ᵃᵠ· 15¹ 92¹, and by Vretil, an archangel, in 2 Enoch 22¹¹ ᵃᵠ. The same function was discharged in the ancient Egyptian religion by the god Thoth. See Zimmern in *K A T*,³ 404 sqq. 4-6 These verses form in reality the close of the Section chs 2-16 See introduction to this section, p 27 4. Declare (E) Read with Gᵍ 'and say' Cf 16⁴, where 'say' is preserved in the duplicate account Have left, &c. Cf 15⁸, which contains most of this verse. ἀπολιπόντες is used in the same connexion in Jude 6 The holy eternal place (E). All MSS but *g* insert 'and' before 'eternal' Gᵍ 'the holiness of the eternal place'. Ye have wrought (Gᵍ). This is better than E = 'and they have wrought'. These words begin God's message to the Watchers This reading is supported by the fact that both in Gᵍ and E the

great destruction on the earth : 5. And ye shall have no peace nor forgiveness of sin · and inasmuch as †they† delight them- selves in †their† children, 6. The murder of †their† beloved ones shall †they† see, and over the destruction of †their† children shall †they† lament, and shall make supplication unto eternity, but mercy and peace shall ye not attain." '

XIII. 1. And Enoch went and said : 'Azâzêl, thou shalt have no peace : a severe sentence has gone forth against thee to put thee in bonds : 2 And thou shalt not have toleration nor †request† granted to thee, because of the unrighteousness which thou hast taught, and because of all the works of godlessness and unrighteousness and sin which thou hast shown to men.' 3. Then I went and spoke to them all together, and they were all afraid, and fear and trembling seized them. 4. And they besought me to draw up a petition for them that they might find forgiveness, and to read their petition in the presence of the Lord of heaven. 5 For from thenceforward they could not speak (with Him) nor lift up their eyes to heaven for shame of their sins for which they had been condemned. 6. Then

next verse, which is clearly part of the message, begins with ' and ', and there- fore presupposes something preceding 5 And ye shall (G⁵). E read ' and they shall' No peace Cf 5⁴ 16⁴ Forgiveness Contrast 5⁶ They delight. For ' they ' and ' them ', obelized in this clause and the follow- ing verse, read ' ye' and 'your' 6 Cf 14⁶ 10¹⁰, ¹²

XIII. 1-2. Message of doom to Azazel. This should have been pre- ceded by an account of Enoch's inter- cession to God for Azazel and the divine reply, but these are lost. See intro- ductory note, p 27 Went and said (E). G⁵ reads εἶπεν πορεύου Perhaps the two forms already existed in the Aramaic — אמר אזיל (so G⁵) and אזל ואמר (E)—the corrupt form in the text and the true in the margin, and

being reproduced in the archetype of G E, were followed respectively by G⁵ and the Greek archetype of E Thou shalt have no peace. Cf. 16⁴ 5⁴. In bonds Cf 10⁴. 2 Tolera- tion (G⁵ ἀνοχή). E ' relaxation ', ' quiet'. Request (G⁵ E) Here ἐρώτησις seems corrupt We should expect at least ' thy request'. Perhaps שְׁאֵלְתָא (= ἐρώτησις) was corrupt for שְׁלֵי = ' rest '. 3. Together (E). > G⁵ and α Fear and trembling (E). ∞ G⁵. Cf. 1⁵. 4. Read (G⁵ ἀναγνῶ). E = ἀνάγω, ' take up.' 5. Cf the Apology of Athenagoras xxv 1 οὖτοι οἱ ἄγγελοι οἱ ἐκπεσόντες τῶν οὐρανῶν . οὐκέτι εἰς τὰ ὑπερουράνια ὑπερκύψαι δυνάμενοι. Of their sins for which they had been condemned (E) G⁵ ' of those things in regard to which they had sinned and been condemned '

I wrote out their petition, and the prayer †in regard to their
spirits and their deeds individually and in regard to their requests

(περὶ ὧν ἡμαρτήκεισαν καὶ κατεκρίθησαν).
6 Spirits + And their deeds individually (E). [And.] Though in G⁶ E,
it should be bracketed. The passage
†in regard to their spirits . . length †
is clearly corrupt   First of all 'length'
is corrupt   μακρότης stands in G⁶ and
nûhat in E is an exact rendering of it,
and cannot in any case mean 'patientia'
—the meaning assigned in this solitary
case to it in Dillmann's Lexicon. The
Ethiopic can only = μακρότης. From
the conjunction of the words ἄφεσις καὶ
μακρότης (G⁶ E) it is clear that μακρότης
here represents אוריכותא and that after
it there stood originally either דיומיא
or דרוחא   in the former case we should
have the familiar phrase 'length of
days' (Heb ארך ימים) in the latter
'forbearance' (Heb ארך אפים) Which
of these two restorations is right we cannot decide before a study of the context.
Does the phrase μακρότης   refer to
the Watchers or to their children? If
to the Watchers, then obviously the
phrase must mean 'forbearance', since
they could not supplicate for 'length
of days' 'on behalf of their spirits'
That 'forgiveness' (ἄφεσις) refers to
the Watchers is clear from 12⁵ 13⁴ If
then 'forgiveness and forbearance' have
to do with the Watchers only, then the
clause in E, 'and their works individually and,' as well as the καὶ in G⁶ before
περὶ ὧν must be excised. We should
then have 'in regard to their spirits in
regard to which they besought forgiveness and forbearance'. But this is
not satisfactory. The Watchers were
deeply concerned for their children
(cf 12⁶ 10¹² 14⁶ where they are called
τῶν ἀγαπητῶν αὐτῶν) (cf 10¹²), and
prayed earnestly on their behalf, 12⁶,
and hoped that they would live each
500 years, 10¹⁰ Hence it is highly
improbable that there should be here

no mention of their sons but only of
themselves   Now if originally there
had been a reference in this passage
to the sons of the Watchers, the phrase
behind μακρότης would probably refer
to them as the word ἄφεσις referred to
the Watchers themselves, as we have
seen above   And that there was such
a double request—for themselves and
for their children—is shown by 14⁷
Hence we should read here μακρότης
ἡμερῶν. The Watchers prayed that
their sons might have 'length of days'.
If we turn to 10⁹ we shall actually find
this phrase where God declares regarding the sons of the Watchers   μακρότης
γὰρ ἡμερῶν οὐκ ἔστιν αὐτῶν The concluding clause therefore should run:
'in regard to whom they besought
forgiveness and length of days'   In
the words preceding this clause, therefore, we should find a reference to the
Watchers themselves and to their sons.
The reference to the former must lie
in 'in regard to their (i e. their own)
spirits'. Possibly τῶν πνευμάτων αὐτῶν
is an inaccurate rendering of נפשתיהון
= 'themselves' Hence 'in regard to
themselves'. But in G⁶ there is no
trace of a phrase referring to their
sons Some trace of this lost phrase
may survive—in fact does survive
—in E, which, translated word for
word = καὶ ἑκάστου ἔργου αὐτῶν.
Possibly this may be a corruption of
τῶν ἑκάστου ἀγαπητῶν. Or E may be
corrupt for ba'ënta wĕlûdômû = περὶ
τῶν υἱῶν αὐτῶν. In any case (cf. 14⁷)
there was here a reference to the sons
of the Watchers. Hence the passage
is probably to be read as follows: 'in
regard to themselves and the beloved
ones of each and in regard to their
requests that they should have forgiveness and length ⟨of days⟩ Irenaeus
iv. 16 2 (Stieren's ed.) refers to this

that they should have forgiveness and length†.   7. And I went off and sat down at the waters of Dan, in the land of Dan, to the south of the west of Hermon · I read their petition till I fell asleep.   8 And behold a dream came to me, and visions fell down upon me, and I saw visions of chastisement, ⌐and a voice came bidding (me)¬ to tell it to the sons of heaven, and reprimand them.   9. And when I awaked, I came unto them, and they were all sitting gathered together, weeping in 'Abels-jâil, which is between Lebanon and Sênêsêr, with their faces covered.   10 And I recounted before them all the visions which I had seen in sleep, and I began to speak the words of righteousness, and to reprimand the heavenly Watchers.

XIV. 1. The book of the words of righteousness, and of the reprimand of the eternal Watchers in accordance with the command of the Holy Great One in that vision.   2. I saw in my sleep what I will now say with a tongue of flesh and with the breath of my mouth : which the Great One has given to men to

---

passage . 'Enoch . cum esset homo, legatione ad angelos fungebatur et translatus est et conservatur usque nunc testis iudicii Dei, quoniam angeli quidam transgressi deciderunt in terram in iudicium '   7 Waters of Dan This river is one of the tributaries of the Jordan, and is called 'the little Jordan' in Jos *Ant.* v. 3 1; viii. 8 4   This place—from ‏דין‎ 'to judge'—is chosen because its name is significant of the subject the writer is dealing with, i e the judgement of the angels.   South of the west of Hermon.   Gᵍ reads ' south of Hermon of the west'.   I read. *gmq* prefix 'and'.   8. To tell . . . and reprimand (E). Gᵍ = 'Tell . to reprimand'.   Sons of heaven. See 6² note. 9. 'Abelsjâil is probably a corruption of 'Αβελήνη, a town in the Antilibanus, which could be loosely described as lying between Lebanon and Senir, i.e Hermon   There was a play of words

in the original.   The angels were mourning (‏אבלין‎) in Abilene (‏אבילין‎). Sênêsêr, i e Senir, a name of Hermon (Deut 3⁹) or a part of it, Cant 4⁸. 10. Before them.   Gᵍ transposes before 'and'   Recounted (ἀνήγγειλα Gᵍ) E = 'spake'   And to reprimand (E)   Gᵍ = ' reprimanding'.   In 1 Cor 6³ St Paul speaks of Christians as having hereafter to judge the angels

XIV 1.   This verse gives the title of the section 12–16.   On the original order see note on p 27.   The book of the words.   So *q* Gᵍ.   In *q* the demonstrative, i.e. the article, has been prefixed to the word ' book   The other MSS of E = ' this book is the word '.   Holy Great One (Gᵍ)   E ' Holy and Great One '.   XIV. 2— XVI 2 The Vision   2. And with the breath of my mouth.   So Gᵍ, save that it omits ' and '.   E differs, but by a slight emendation in accordance with Gᵍ and 84¹ we arrive at this reading.

converse therewith and understand with the heart.   3. As He
has created and given ⌜to man the power of understanding the
word of wisdom, so hath He created me also and given⌝ me the
power of reprimanding the Watchers, the children of heaven.
4. I wrote out your petition, and in my vision it appeared thus,
that your petition will not be granted unto you ⌜throughout all
the days of eternity, and that judgement has been finally passed
upon you · yea (your petition) will not be granted unto you⌝.
5. And from henceforth you shall not ascend into heaven unto
all eternity, and ⌜in bonds⌝ of the earth the decree has gone forth
to bind you for all the days of the world.   6. And (that) previously you shall have seen the destruction of your beloved sons
and ye shall have no pleasure in them, but they shall fall before
you by the sword.   7. And your petition on their behalf shall
not be granted, nor yet on your own: even though you weep
and pray and speak all the words contained in the writing

To .. understand with the heart
(E = νοῆσαι καρδίᾳ). Gᵍ νοήσει καρδίας
= 'with understanding of the heart'
3. As (E = ὡς) Gᵍ = ὕς. To man
the power of understanding the
word of wisdom, so hath He created
me also and given (E) > Gᵍ through
hint. 4 Thus, that .. unto
you. Gᵍ is defective: 'this and
neither was your petition accepted'.
5 In bonds of the earth (so Gᵍ
ἐν τοῖς δεσμοῖς τῆς γῆς) This is a
peculiar expression. E has simply 'on
the earth' Perhaps we should read
δεσμοῖς ἐν τῇ γῇ. Cf. Origen (c Celsum
v. 52) κολάζεσθαι δεσμοῖς ὑποβληθέντας
ἐν γῇ, and Jude 6 εἰς κρίσιν μεγάλης
ἡμέρας δεσμοῖς ἀιδίοις ὑπὸ ζόφον τετήρηκεν. On the other hand, if τῆς γῆς is
original, then possibly the error arose
in the Aramaic ἐν τ δεσμοῖς τ. γῆς
=באיסורי ארעה corrupt for כאסירי
ארעה = 'as prisoners of (i e. 'on') the
earth'. Cf Lam 3³⁴ where the phrase
occurs.   6 Cf. 10⁹ 12⁶ Ye
shall have no pleasure in them (Gᵍ).

Here ὄνησις has the meaning of ἀπό-
λαυσις as in the poet Philemon γένοιτό
σοι τέκνων ὄνησις, ὥσπερ καὶ δίκαιον (see
Schleusner in loc.)· a clause which
gives exactly the same sense as that in
our text. Cf. ὀνίνημι, Sir 30², where
the Syriac renders by חרא   The
same idea is expressed in our text with
regard to the sons of the watchers
in 12⁶ περὶ ὧν χαίρουσιν τῶν υἱῶν αὐτῶν.
E here gives a free rendering 'ye shall
not possess them', i.e so as to delight
in them. Previous translators—myself
included—wrongly took ὄνησις as meaning 'profit' here, but 12⁶ is decisive.
7 The twofold petition of the watchers
on their own behalf and that of their
sons. Cf 13⁶ note.   And speak all
the words. So Gᵍ καὶ μὴν λαλοῦντες
πᾶν ῥῆμα, where I have emended μή
into μήν. The converse change of μή
into μήν is found in Gᵍ 10⁷ If, however, the negative is original, καὶ μή
λαλοῦντες may be corrupt for καὶ μή
λαχύντες or λαβόντες = ולא מקבלין,
which should be taken as the apodosis

which I have written.   8. And the vision was shown to me
thus Behold, in the vision clouds invited me and a mist summoned me, and the course of the stars and the lightnings sped
and hastened me, and the winds in the vision caused me to fly
and lifted me upward, and bore me into heaven.   9. And
I went in till I drew nigh to a wall which is built of crystals
and surrounded by tongues of fire · and it began to affright me.
10. And I went into the tongues of fire and drew nigh to a large
house which was built of crystals and the walls of the house
were like a tesselated floor (made) of crystals, and its groundwork was of crystal.   11. Its ceiling was like the path of the
stars and the lightnings, and between them were fiery cherubim,
and their heaven was (clear as) water.   12. A flaming fire
surrounded the walls, and its portals blazed with fire.   13. And
I entered into that house, and it was hot as fire and cold as ice
there were no delights of life therein. fear covered me, and
trembling gat hold upon me.   14 And as I quaked and
trembled, I fell upon my face. And I beheld a vision,

'ye are not to be granted a single
request in the writing', &c   8. The
vision (E). G^b 'in the vision   Sped
(E) G^g reads κατεσπούδαζον. Hastened. G^g E have here ἐθορύβαζον =
יבחלון. In this context the translator should have rendered it by
ἐτάχυνον. בהל has these two meanings
both in Hebrew and Aramaic In
Daniel, conversely, בהל is several times
rendered by κατασπεύδω in the LXX
when it ought to have been rendered
by θορυβάζω or συνταράσσω. Cf 4^5
5^6, &c Here Dillmann's Lexicon and
all previous translations should be
corrected accordingly   Caused me
to fly (E = ἀνεπτέρωσαν)   But G^g
has ἐξεπέτασαν, which E apparently
confused with ἐξέπτησαν, and derived
it from ἐκπέταμαι, to which it ascribed
an active meaning The same wrong
meaning is attached by the Ethiopic
translator to ἐξεπέτασε in Prov 13^{16}

On the whole I am inclined to regard
ἐξεπέτασαν here as a corruption of
ἐξεπέρασαν (so Lods) The idea may
be derived from Num 11^{31} πνεῦμα
ἐξῆλθεν παρὰ Κυρίου καὶ ἐξεπέρασεν
Lifted me upward (G^g)   E = 'hastened me', and connects 'upward'
with the next clause.   9–13 Enoch
is carried up into heaven and passes
within the outer wall that surrounds
the πρόναος or forecourt of the palace
of God   10. Of crystals ^{10} = ἐν
λίθοις χαλάζης Cf Is 30^{30} אבני ברד
Of crystals ^{20} (E), G^g καὶ πᾶσαι ἦσαν ἐκ
χιόνος   13 Delights = τρυφή G^g
has τροφή The words are frequently
confused; cf Gen. 49^{20} On the other
hand τρυφή is used of Sheol in Sir.
14^{16} οὐκ ἔστιν ἐν ᾅδου ζῆτῆσαι τρυφήν
(בשאול לבקש תענוג) Cf also Erubin
54^a, 'Do good to thyself, for there is
no luxury (תענוג) in Sheol'   14 Cf
60^3 71^{11} Ezek 1^{28} Dan 8$^{17, 18}$, &c

15. And lo! there was a second house, greater than the former, and the entire portal stood open before me, and it was built of flames of fire.   16. And in every respect it so excelled in splendour and magnificence and extent that I cannot describe to you its splendour and its extent.   17. And its floor was of fire, and above it were lightnings and the path of the stars, and its ceiling also was flaming fire.   18. And I looked and saw ⌜therein⌝ a lofty throne. its appearance was as crystal, and the wheels thereof as the shining sun, and there was the vision of cherubim.   19. And from underneath the throne came streams of flaming fire so that I could not look thereon.   20 And the Great Glory sat thereon, and His raiment shone more brightly than the sun and was whiter than any snow.   21. None of the angels could enter and could behold His face by reason of the magnificence and glory, and no flesh could behold Him. 22 The flaming fire was round about Him, and a great fire stood before Him, and none around could draw nigh Him ten thousand times ten thousand (stood) before Him, yet He needed

15. Enoch approaches the palace of God but does not enter, as no mortal may behold God. As the doors are open, he can describe what is within. There was a second house . . . before me and So E   G^g seems corrupt ἄλλην θύραν ἀνεῳγμένην κατέναντι μου καὶ ὁ οἶκος μείζων τούτου καὶ ὅλος   16 It so excelled . . that I cannot describe, &c   Cf Targ Jon on Ezek. 1^{27}, ' the appearance of glory such as the eye cannot see and there was no power to look thereon '   18 In this and the following verses the writer draws upon Is 6 Ezek. 1 10 Dan 7$^{9, 10}$. This passage (vv 18–22) is used by the author of 71$^{5-8}$.   Therein > G^g A lofty throne   On a throne in heaven cf. 1 Kings 22^{19} Is. 6^1 Ezek 1^{26} Dan 7^9 Ass. Mos 4^2 Test Lev 5^1 Rev 4^2 sqq The wheels thereof as the shining sun (E)   G^g τροχὸς ὡς ἡλίου λάμποντος

The expression goes back to Dan. 7^9 גלגלוהי נור דלק = τροχοὶ αὐτοῦ πῦρ καιόμενον   Vision of cherubim. G^g reads οφος, corrupt possibly for ὅρασις. E = ὁπός (from ὄψ) ' the voice'   19. Cf Dan. 7^{10}.   Streams of flaming fire (E)   G^g ' flaming streams of fire '   20. The Great Glory   Cf. 102^3 T Lev 3^4 Whiter, &c. On the brightness that surrounds the throne cf. Ps 104^2 Dan 7^9 Jam 1^{17} Rev 4^3 See K A T.^{3} 353   21. Enter. + 'into this house', G^b.   By reason of the magnificence and glory (G^g).   E = ' of the Magnificent and Glorious One ', but it is probably corrupt   22. Could draw nigh.   Cf 3 Macc. 2^{15} 1 Tim. 6^{16} Ten thousand times, &c, Dan 7^{10}. He needed no counsellor.   Cf Sir 42^{21} οὐδὲ προεδεήθη οὐδενὸς συμβούλου = לא צריך לכל מבין   So E by a slight change   As it stands it = ' He needed no counsel '   Here, since G^g has

no counsellor.   23. And the most holy ones who were nigh to Him did not leave by night nor depart from Him.   24. And until then I had been prostrate on my face, trembling . and the Lord called me with His own mouth, and said to me : ' Come hither, Enoch, and hear my word.'   25. ⌜And one of the holy ones came to me and waked me⌝, and He made me rise up and approach the door . and I bowed my face downwards.

XV. 1. And He answered and said to me, and I heard His voice : ' Fear not, Enoch, thou righteous man and scribe of righteousness : approach hither and hear my voice.   2. And go, say to ⌜the Watchers of heaven⌝, who have sent thee to intercede ⌜for them : " You should intercede⌝ for men, and not men for you 3. Wherefore have ye left the high, holy, and eternal heaven, and lain with women, and defiled yourselves with the daughters of men and taken to yourselves wives, and done like the children of earth, and begotten giants (as your) sons.   4. And though ye were holy, spiritual, living the eternal life, you have defiled yourselves with the blood of women, and have begotten (children) with the blood of flesh, and, as the children of men, have lusted

---

πᾶς λόγος αὐτοῦ ἔργον, it is probable that the two texts are both defective and complementary. At all events 2 Enoch 33⁴ has . ' My wisdom is My counsellor, and My word is reality,' and seems dependent on the present passage   23. The most holy ones. So Gᵍ   Eᵃ has 'the holiness of the holy ones'   24. Prostrate (Gᵍ) E = περίβλημα, but is internally corrupt for περιβεβλημένος With ' prostrate on my face, trembling ' cf Dan. 8¹⁷ ' I was affrighted and fell on my face '. 2 Enoch 21² 'I was afraid and fell on my face ' : Luke 24⁶.   Hear my word (Gᵇ). E ' to My holy word ' reading ἅγιον for ἄκουσον.   25 Bowed (Gᵇ). E reads 'ĕnĕser (= ' I looked ') corrupt for 'asânĕn = ' bowed '.

XV. 1. And ²ᵒ Gᵍ > E   Scribe of righteousness. See 12³   2 And go, say (E).   Gᵍ ' go and say '   The Watchers of heaven. > Gᵍ.   For them   You should intercede > Gᵍ through hmt   Cf 9¹⁰ note   3 Cf. 12⁴ Jude 6.   4–7. For man as mortal and dwelling upon the earth wedlock is appointed that so the race may continue to exist   but for the angels who are immortal and dwell in the heaven such commingling is contrary to their nature and involves pollution and guilt.   4 Spiritual, living the eternal life (E). Gᵍ and spirits, living, eternal '. Here E appears to be right 'Living' by itself would be meaningless as qualifying 'spirits'. Cf ver 6. αἰώνια is simply a rendering of לעלם, which latter would is to be connected with חיין before it as in E   With the blood ¹ᵒ (Gᵍ)   E badiba (= ' with ') corrupt for badama = Gᵍ.   As the children of men. Gᵍ E read ἐν αἵματι ἀνθρώπων = בדם   נשי corrupt for כבני נָשֵׁי = ὥσπερ

after flesh and blood as those ⌐also⌐ do who die and perish.
5 Therefore have I given them wives also that they might impreg-
nate them, and beget children by them, that thus nothing might
be wanting to them on earth.   6. But you were ⌐formerly⌐
spiritual, living the eternal life, and immortal for all generations
of the world.   7. And therefore I have not appointed wives
for you; for as for the spiritual ones of the heaven, in heaven is
their dwelling   8 And now, the giants, who are produced
from the spirits and flesh, shall be called evil spirits upon the
earth, and on the earth shall be their dwelling.   9 Evil
spirits have proceeded from their bodies; because they are born
from men, ⌐and⌐ from the holy watchers is their beginning and
primal origin, ⌐they shall be evil spirits on earth, and⌐ evil spirits
shall they be called.   [10. As for the spirits of heaven, in
heaven shall be their dwelling, but as for the spirits of the earth
which were born upon the earth, on the earth shall be their
dwelling]   11. And the spirits of the giants afflict, oppress,

υἱοὶ τῶν ἀνθρώπων. Cf. ὥσπερ υἱοὶ τῆς
γῆς in the preceding verse ἐπεθυμήσατε
cannot be constructed with ἐν τῷ αἵματι
unless it represents some Semitic idiom
as כ בשׁי. If it could, it would mean
bloodthirstiness, an idea quite foreign
to the context   And lusted after
+ 'and done' E.   5. Nothing . . .
to them. E^stu read balâ'ĕlêhôn (= ἐν
αὐταῖς)—corrupt for kuĕllû lômû (as
Flemming suggests) = πᾶν αὐτοῖς
6 Spiritual, living the eternal life
(E) G^g as in v. 4   And immortal
(G^g) E with the exception of *m* omits
'and'.   8, 9. The union of angels
and the daughters of men will give
birth to a new order of beings, i.e
giants, and from these giants when they
die will proceed evil spirits, i e demons,
and these will have the earth for their
habitation   Observe that the evil activities of these demons are not restrained or forbidden as those of their
parents, for the latter were thrown into
chains immediately on the death of the

giants, their children   8. From
the spirits (E^bq G^gs)   All other MSS
of E = 'from the body'.   On these
verses cf. Justin *Apol.* xxii, quoted in
the note on 9^8,9 Tertull. *Apol* xxii
' Quomodo de angelis quibusdam sua
sponte corruptis corruptior gens daemonum evaserit . . . apud litteras
sanctas ordo cognoscitur'.   In Lact.
Instit ii. 15, the demons are regarded
purely as wicked angels.   Shall be
called evil spirits (E G^s).   G^g defective and corrupt πνεύματα ἰσχυρά
9 From men (G^s)   G^g E 'from
those above'.   Beginning (E)   G^gs
read ἡ ἀρχὴ τῆς κτίσεως αὐτῶν.
They shall be . . earth (E G^s).
> G^g   10 Of the earth (E)
G^g 'on the earth'   G^s omits v. 10.
This verse is merely a repetition of
phrases found in verses 7, 8.   11.
Afflict. G^g E read νεφέλας = עננין,
a corruption probably of מעני = 'afflict'
G^s reads νεμόμενα = 'laying waste'
Beer takes νεμόμενα in the sense of

destroy, attack, do battle, and work destruction on the earth,
and cause trouble · they take no food, ⌜but nevertheless hunger⌝
and thirst, and cause offences. 12. And these spirits shall
ıise up against the children of men and against the women,
because they have proceeded ⌜from them⌝.

XVI. 1. From the days of the slaughter and destruction and
death ⌜of the giants⌝, from the souls of whose flesh the spirits,
having gone forth, shall destroy without incurring judgement
—thus shall they destroy until the day of the consummation,
the great ⌜judgement⌝ in which the age shall be consummated,
over the Watchers and the godless, yea, shall be wholly consummated." 2. And now as to the Watchers who have sent
thee to intercede for them, who had been ⌜aforetime⌝ in heaven,
(say to them). 3. "You have been in heaven, but ⌜all⌝ the
mysteries had not yet been revealed to you, and you knew
worthless ones, and these ın the hardness of your hearts you

'pasturing' = רְעִין, a corruption of
רְעִיןֹ, 'laying waste,' which itself was
corrupted into עֲנִין = νεφέλας. Cause
trouble (E) G⁵ˢ δρόμους ποιοῦντα
where perhaps δρόμους is corrupt for
τρόμους ⌜But nevertheless hun-
ger⌝ (Gᵇˢ). Beer quotes Wellhausen,
Reste Arab Heidenthums², 149 sq., to
the effect that the Jinns suffer from a
devouring hunger and yet cannot eat
Instead of ἀσιτοῦντα, λιμώττοντα would
be better. Gˢ adds καὶ φάσματα
ποιοῦντα — possibly rightly Cause
offences Gᵍˢ E is internally corrupt,
but by an easy emendation of Dillmann's = Gᵉˢ. Against the women
(E) Gᵇˢ = 'of the women'

XVI. 1 The demons will not be
punished till the final judgement This
doctrine likewise appears in the Book
of Jubilees 10⁵⁻¹¹, and in the N.T. Cf
Matt. 8²⁹, 'Art Thou come hither to
torment us before the time?' Of the
giants (E Gˢ). > Gᵍ +Ναφηλείμ, οἱ
ἰσχυροὶ τῆς γῆς, οἱ μεγάλοι ὀνομαστοὶ Gˢ
These are derived from Gen 6⁴ Ναφη-

λείμ is a transliteration of נְפִלִים, and
is thus a doublet of τῶν γιγάντων preceding, οἱ ἰσχ. τῆς γῆς is an expansion of
הַגִּבֹּרִים, and οἱ μεγ ὀνομαστοὶ of אַנְשֵׁי
הַשֵּׁם A different nomenclature is
given in Gˢ 7² (see note in loc), but
that passage is derived from a Noah
Apocalypse From the souls of
whose flesh (Eᵉⁿʸ Gᵍ) Here ἐνy in
E alone preserve the true reading
though 'ĕmnafsât must be changed into
'ĕmnafsâta g reads 'ĕmnafseta, which
is an early corruption of the latter.
All the rest are still further corrupt.
We have here a Semitic idiom which
shows itself clearly in Gˢ ἀφ' ὧν . ἐκ
τῆς ψυχῆς τῆς σαρκὸς αὐτῶν = שֶׁנֶפֶשׁ
דִּי מִנְּהוֹן = 'from the souls of whose
flesh'. 2 Aforetime (E) > Gᵍˢ.
3. This statement is the basis of Clem
Alex. *Strom*. ed Dindorf, iii. 9 οἱ
ἄγγελοι ἐκεῖνοι οἱ τὸν ἄνω κλῆρον
εἰληχότες, κατολισθήσαντες εἰς ἡδονάς,
ἐξεῖπον τὰ ἀπόρρητα ταῖς γυναιξὶν ὅσα τε
εἰς γνῶσιν αὐτῶν ἀφίκτο E wrongly inserts 'and now' at the beginning of

have made known to the women, and through these mysteries women and men work much evil on earth."   4. Say to them therefore. "You have no peace."'

XVII–XXXVI. *Enoch's Journeys through the Earth and Sheol.*

XVII–XIX. *The First Journey.*

XVII. 1. And they took ⌐and brought⌐ me to a place in which those who were there were like flaming fire, and when they wished, they appeared as men   2. And they brought me to the place of darkness, and to a mountain the point of whose summit reached to heaven.   3. And I saw the places of the luminaries ⌐and the treasuries of the stars⌐ and of the thunder, ⌐and⌐ in the **uttermost depths**, where were a fiery bow and arrows and their quiver, ⌐and a fiery sword⌐ and all the lightnings. 4. And they took me to the living waters, and to the fire of the

this verse ⌐All⌐ (G^g).>E   4 No peace see 5^4 (note)

XVII—XIX These chapters are certainly foreign to the rest of this section. They are full of Greek elements We have references in 17^{5,5} to the Pyriphlegethon, Styx, Acheron and Cocytus in 17^{5,7,8} 18^{10}, to the Ocean Stream in 17^6 to Hades in the west Again, 18$^{6-9}$ is a duplicate account of 24$^{1-3}$, 18$^{12-16}$ a duplicate account of 21$^{1-6}$, and 18^{11} of 21$^{7-10}$, though in the last case there are important divergencies. Again, according to 15^{12}–16 an end was set to the destructive agencies of the fallen angels by their imprisonment (cf 10$^{11-14}$ 14^5), whereas according to 19^1 the spirits of the fallen angels are represented as reducing mankind to sacrifice to demons Notwithstanding these chapters belong to the Enoch tradition

XVII. 1. ⌐And brought⌐ Supplied from G^g. On the power of assuming different forms cf 19^1 2 Cor. 11^{14}. 2. Of darkness (G^g ζοφώδη) E = γνοφώδη taking γνόφος in the sense of 'whirlwind' or 'tempest' as in Job 27^{20} (LXX). On the idea in E cf Job 37^9. The point of whose summit (E). G^g 'whose summit'. 3 Places of the luminaries These may be the 'chambers of the luminaries', cf. 41^5 ⌐And the treasuries of the stars⌐. Supplied from G^g Of the thunder Cf 41^3 44 59 60$^{13-15}$ and notes In the uttermost depths = εἰς τὰ ἄκρα βάθη. So I emend E which = εἰς τὰ ἄκρα ἐν τῷ βάθει αὐτοῦ (?) G^g reads εἰς τὰ ἀεροβαθῆ, 'in the depths of air' Fiery bow— the bow with which the lightnings are shot; cf Ps. 7^{12} Hab 3^9 Lam 2^4 3^{12}. Arrows, i e the lightnings, cf Ps. 18^{14} 77^{17,18} Their quiver. Cf Lam. 3^{13}. And a fiery sword (E) >G^g. Cf Ps 7^{12} Deut 32^{41}. 4. Took (E) G^g 'brought' Living waters So G^g and superscription in g. All other MSS. of E read 'waters of life'. Cf 'fountain of life' in Ps 36^9 Prov. 10^{11} 13^{14} 14^{27} 16^{22} Rev. 22^{17}. The expression 'water of life' is found in the Babylonian myths. In the

west, which receives every setting of the sun.   5. And I came
to a river of fire in which the fire flows like water and discharges
itself into the great sea towards the west.   6. I saw the great
rivers and came to the great ⌐river and to the great⌐ darkness,
and went to the place where no flesh walks.   7. I saw the
mountains of the darkness of winter and the place whence all
the waters of the deep flow.   8. I saw the mouths of all the
rivers of the earth and the mouth of the deep.

XVIII. 1. I saw the treasuries of all the winds ; I saw how
He had furnished with them the whole creation and the firm
foundations of the earth.   2. And I saw the corner-stone of
the earth · I saw the four winds which bear [the earth and] the

---

Adapa Myth it is parallel to the 'bread
of life', while in the Descent of Ishtar,
Ishtar is sprinkled with it before she
leaves the lower world See *KAT*[3]
524 sq , 562   Fire of the west · see
23 (notes)   Which receives every
setting of the sun. Blau, in the
Jewish Encyc v 582, explains this
fire in the west to be Gehenna He
says the sun receives its fire from it,
and he quotes Baba Bathia 84ᵃ. But
this is quite wrong. Gehenna is not
in the west in Enoch, and the passage
in the Talmud merely says that the sun
is red in the evening because it passes
the gate of Gehenna, just as it is red
in the morning because it passes the
roses of the Garden of Eden   Receives (E)   Gᵍ παρέχον.   5. River
of fire The Πυριφλεγέθων   Great
sea. 'Ωκεανός or the Great Ocean
Stream   Towards the west (E)
Gᵍ 'of the west '.   6. I saw (Gᵍ).
E 'and I saw'   The great rivers
Styx, Acheron, and Cocytus   River
and to the great Supplied from Gᵍ
No flesh (Gᵍ). E ' all flesh '   7. I
saw (Gᵍ) E 'and I saw' This omission of the copula is more in keeping
with Aramaic idiom   The mountains
of the darkness (E) = τὰ ὄρη τῶν
γνόφων—a phrase that is most probably

derived from Jer. 13¹⁶ נֶשֶׁף הרי where
the Targ Jon has קבל טורי In the
original then we should have had
קבלא טורי But in the text before
the translator טורי was corrupted into
רוחי, whence Gᵍ has τοὺς ἀνέμους. We
must suppose that the true reading
was inserted in the margin and was
reproduced as such in the Greek
Hence E The mountains are probably those which the Babylonian
Cosmogony represents as standing at
the ends of the earth in the neighbourhood of the 'springs of the great deep ',
which are referred to in the next line
8. I saw (Gᵍ) E 'and I saw ' See note
on v 7   Mouths of, &c), i. e Oceanus.
XVIII. 1 I saw (Gᵃ)   E 'and I
saw ' So also in the next sentence
Treasuries of all the winds see 41⁴
(note) 60¹¹, ¹², also 34–36. Foundations of the earth A frequent phrase
in the OT Cf 2 Sam 22¹⁶ Job 38⁴
Ps 18¹⁵ 82⁵, &c   I saw ²⁰ (Gᵍ)   E
' and I saw '.   2. The corner-
stone : Job 38⁶   I saw ²⁰ (Gᵍ)   E
' and I saw '   The four winds which
bear [the earth and] the firmament.
Gᵍ E have τοὺς τέσσαρας ἀνέμους τὴν
γῆν βαστάζοντας καὶ τὸ στερέωμα. Gunkel, *Zum religunsgesch. Verständnis,*

firmament of the heaven.   3. ⌜And I saw how the winds stretch out the vaults of heaven⌝, and have their station between heaven and earth . ⌜these are the pillars of the heaven⌝.   4. I saw the winds of heaven which turn and bring the circumference of the sun and all the stars to their setting.   5. I saw the winds on the earth carrying the clouds. I saw ⌜the paths of the angels. I saw⌝ at the end of the earth the firmament of the heaven above.   6. And I proceeded and saw a place which burns day and night, where there are seven mountains of magnificent stones, three towards the east, and three towards the south.   7. And as for those towards the east ⟨one⟩ was of

p 46 (n 6) proposes to read τῆς γῆς instead of τὴν γῆν, and to omit καί. Hence 'the four winds of the earth bearing the firmament' But the τῆς γῆς or τὴν γῆν seems wholly wrong here. It could have arisen in the Aramaic through a dittograph Thus ἰδὸν τοὺς τέσσαρας ἀνέμους τὴν γῆν βαστάζοντας = חזית רוחיא ארבע ארעא מסוברן where ארעא is a dittograph of ארבע Hence 'the four winds which bear the firmament'   3. And I saw . . heaven (E) > Gᵍ through hmt   These are heaven (E) > Gᵇ through hmt Pillars of the heaven   The expression is from Job 26¹¹, but the idea in the text is not biblical nor Babylonian   4. I saw (Gᵍ)   E 'and I saw'.   Turn and bring, &c. Cf. 72⁶ 73²   Bring .. to ... setting (E) = δύνοντας in an active sense   Gᵍ has διανεύοντας, which Dillmann emends into δινεύοντας, 'whirling, but this idea is already conveyed by στρέφοντας Swete proposes διανύοντας, but this would require τρόχον, whereas the context requires τροχόν (cf 73²)   5 Carrying the clouds (t, β), but Gᵍ gmₐu read ἐν τῇ νεφέλῃ. An explanation of the difficulties suggested in Job 36²⁹ 37¹⁶ The paths of the angels I saw (E) > Gᵍ through hmt   At the end of the earth the firmament, &c.

The ends of the firmament of heaven rest on the ends of the earth ; cf 33², the vault of heaven is supported by the winds, 18², ³.   6–9 This is another version of what is recounted in 24¹⁻⁸   6. And saw a place Gᵍ 1 e καὶ εἶδον τόπον for which E corruptly reads εἰς τὸν νότον   The seven mountains are in the NW   Cf 77³⁻⁴ 70³   Indeed the closing words of this verse imply that these mountains are in the NW — three extending towards the south and three towards the east from the NW. corner where the seventh stands   Seven mountains. These mountains, as I have shown in the note preceding, are in the NW   They and the Garden lie in the same quarter, the Garden to the east of the seven mountains, 32¹⁻²: according to 70³ the Garden lies in the NW , and so apparently in 77³   These mountains are bounded by flaming mountain ridges 24¹ (18⁰)   In 24¹⁻³ the seven mountains are as here in the NW , while the verses that follow 24⁴ sqq refer in some way to the Garden , for they speak of the tree of life   Again, it is worth observing that in 77³ the seas of waters are said to adjoin the Garden   The same idea underlies 60²²⁻²³. The Jewish ideas on these matters might be represented therefore thus —

coloured stone, and one of pearl, and one of jacinth, and those
towards the south of red stone   8 But the middle one reached
to heaven like the throne of God, of alabaster, and the summit
of the throne was of sapphire.   9. And I saw a flaming fire.
And beyond these mountains   10. Is a region the end of the

N

The Great Mountain   Three Mountains   Garden of Righteousness   Seas of Waters

Three
Mountains

W   E

With the above sketch, which represents the views of all the Sections of Enoch, it is difficult to reconcile the statement in 60⁸, where a waste wilderness named Dêndâin is said to lie to the east of the Garden. See note on 32¹. This idea of the seven mountains seems to be originally derived from Babylonian sources, and had ultimately to do with the seven planet gods, the seven-fold division of the heaven and the like division of the earth, six-sevenths land and one-seventh sea, 4 Ezra 6⁴², the seven great rivers and seven great islands, 1 Enoch 77⁵, ⁸. See K A T³ 615-619 With the mountains in our text those mentioned in 52² 77⁴ may originally have been connected Three¹⁰ (E) > Gᵇ   7 Ja-cinth (?) E = ἰάσεως This may be corrupt for ἰάσπιδος (= ישפה) 'jasper'. But since ταθεν is the reading of Gᵍ, the Ethiopic translator probably found merely a corrupt form which suggested some derivative of ἰάσθαι as ἰατικοῦ This word taken in conjunction with ταθεν might point to ὑακίνθου or ἰανθίνου as Diels suggests Beer takes it to be a transliteration of פטדה 'topaz'. Where the ideas of the various stones are drawn from cannot be said with certainty Cf Ezek. 28¹³, K A T³ 619, 624. The difficulty of determining

this is enhanced by the difficulty of identifying the stones in question. 8. Like the throne of God. In 25³ it is declared to be the throne of God This mountain of God, which as we have seen was conceived to be in the NW., is already referred to in Is. 14¹³, where it is said to be in the N The throne of God in Ezekiel 1²ᵇ which is borne of cherubim comes from the N, as appears from 1⁴; cf Job 37²². This throne is 'the holy mountain of God' in Ezek. 28¹⁴, ¹⁶, where 'stones of fire' are associated with the mountain of God, as in our text 18⁹ 24¹. Indeed in Ezek 28¹³⁻¹⁴ the Garden or Paradise and the Mountain of God are already associated as in Enoch, or identified. Alabaster. Gᵍ φουκα, ι ϲ פוכא Sapphire. Ezek. 1²⁶   9 And beyond these (Gᵍ κά(πέ)κεινα τῶν . . τούτων). E corrupt καὶ ἃ ἐπὶ ἐκείνων τῶν ὁρέων, for κυèllû is corrupt for 'ellû, but attests the same text The statement in 24¹ would lead us to connect this clause with what precedes, but the καὶ is against it Hence I have combined it with the next verse. But the former may be right. The seven mountains are encircled with fire—according to 24¹ by a mountain range of fire. In the translation I always follow Gᵍ in the case of ἐπέκεινα as it

gieat earth: there the heavens were completed.   11. And I
saw a deep abyss, with columns ⌜of heavenly fire, and among
them I saw columns⌝ of fire fall, which were beyond measure alike
towaids the height and towards the depth.   12. And beyond
that abyss I saw a place which had no firmament of the heaven
above, and no fiimly founded earth beneath it there was no
water upon it, and no birds, but it was a waste and horrible
place.   13. I saw there seven stars like great burning mountains, and to me, when I inquired regarding them,   14. The
angel said: ''This place is the end of heaven and earth: this has
become a piison for the stars and the host of heaven.   15 And
the stars which roll ovei the fiie are they which have trans-
giessed the commandment of the Loid in the beginning of their
rising, because they did not come forth at their appointed times.
16. And He was wroth with them, and bound them till the time
when their guilt should be consummated (even) ⌜for ten thousand
yeais⌝.'

XIX. 1. And Uriel said to me ' Heie shall stand the angels
who have connected themselves with women, and their spirits
assuming many diffeient forms are defiling mankind and shall
lead them astray into sacrificing to demons ⌜as gods⌝, (heie shall

is always misrendered in E, cf 18¹²
24² 30¹, ³ 31²   10 The same idea
as in 18⁶ 33².   11 This may be the
final place of punishment for the fallen
angels If so, cf 10⁶, ¹⁸ 18¹¹ 21⁷⁻¹⁰
90²⁴   Of heavenly fire, cf Gen 1921
Ps 11⁶ Ezek. 38²² > τοῦ πυρὸς τοῦ
οὐρανοῦ καὶ ἴδον ἐν αὐτοῖς στύλους
through hint Gᵉ   Height. . depth
(E) ∞ Gᵍ   12–16 This place of
punishment for the disobedient stars is
again described in 21¹⁻⁶ It is already
occupied.   13–16. The stars are
really personified as animate beings.
13. And to me, when I inquired
regarding them (περὶ ὧν πυνθανομένῳ
μοι Gᵍ). E corrupt = καὶ ὡς πνεύματα
τυνθαιόμενά μου.   14 Host of
heaven, צבא השמים, cf 1 Kings
22¹⁰, but specially Iˢ 24²¹.   15.

The Lord (Gᵍ). E 'God'. The
stars are regarded as conscious beings
and are accordingly punished The
ἀστέρες πλανῆται of Jude 13 iecall
this verse. Rising + ὅτι τόπος ἔξω
τοῦ οὐρανοῦ κενός ἐστιν Gᵍ—a gloss on
the last clause of ver 12   16. Ten
thousand years (Gᵍ ἐνιαυτῶν μυρίων).
E corrupt = ἐνιαντῷ μυστηρίου. Cf
21⁶.

XIX. See introductory note on xvii–
xix, p. 38   1 Sacrificing to demons, cf. Deut 32¹⁷ Ps 106³⁷ Bar.
4⁷ This passage and 99⁷ are probably
the source of Tertullian, *De Idol* iv
' Henoch praedicens omn a elementa,
omnem mundi censum, quae caelo, quae
mari, quae terra continentui, in idola-
tiiam vcisuros daemonas et spiitus de-
sertorum angelorum, ut pro Deo advei-

they stand), till ⌜the day of⌝ the great judgement in which they shall be judged till they are made an end of.   2. And the women also of the angels who went astray shall become sirens.'   3. And I, Enoch, alone saw the vision, the ends of all things . and no man shall see as I have seen.

XX. *Names and Functions of the Seven Archangels.*

XX. 1. And these are the names of the holy angels who watch.   2. Uriel, one of the holy angels, who is over the world and over Tartarus.   3. Raphael, one of the holy angels, who is over the spirits of men.   4. Raguel, one of the holy angels who †takes vengeance on† the world of the luminaries.   5. Michael, one of the holy angels, to wit, he that is set over the best part of mankind ⌜and⌝ over chaos.   6. Sara-

sus Deum consecrarentur'   **As gods** (E) > G⁵   **Day of the great judgement** see 45² (note)   **The day of** (E) > G⁵   2 The women will be subjected to the same punishment as the fallen angels , cf 10¹³   **The women . . of the angels** G⁵ reproduces here literally an Aramaic idiom. αἱ γυναῖκες αὐτῶν τῶν παραβάντων ἀγγέλων = נשיהון די מלאביא די חמו E is corrupt, reading 'ashitôn (ǧmtu, β), which should be emended into lasêhûtân = G⁵   **Sirens** (G⁵ εἰς σειρῆνας)   E = ὡς εἰρηναῖαι, a corruption of G⁵ σειρήν is a rendering in the LXX of יענה in Mic. 1⁸ Jer 27 (50)³⁹, cf. Is 13²¹, and of תן in Job 30²⁹, Is. 34¹³, &c.   3 **The ends of all things**   Quoted by Clemens Alex *Eclog Proph* (Dind in 456) ὁ Δανιήλ λέγει ὁμοδοξῶν τῷ 'Ενὼχ τῷ εἰρηκότι 'καὶ εἶδον τὰς ὕλας πάσας', and by Origen, *De Princ.* iv. 35 'scriptum namque est in eodem libello dicente Enoch " universas materias perspexi "'.   **XX.** Of the seven archangels given in this chapter, only four—Uriel, Raphael, Raguel, and Michael—are mentioned as acting in 21-36   In the original probably all were men-

tioned   Cf 81⁵   1 This verse is defective in G⁵ ¹, ² The latter omits it, while the former reads simply 'angels of the powers '   But part of the verse is preserved in ver. 8 in both, i. e ὀνόματα ζ ἀρχαγγέλων   **Who watch** see 12² (note).   2 The province assigned to Uriel serves to explain such passages as 19 21⁵, ⁹ 27² 33⁸, ⁴. Of his rôle as overseer of the world in 72 sqq., 4 Ezra 4¹   **Tartarus** (G⁵ ¹, ²)   E = τρόμου corrupt   3. **Raphael** see 10⁴, ⁷   The definition here given is vague, but suits admirably in 22⁸, ⁶   In 32⁶, however, Raphael discharges duties which according to 20⁷ should belong to Gabriel   4 **Raguel**   There seems to be no connexion between the name of the angel and the duty assigned to him   Cf. 23⁴   †**Takes vengeance on** †.   See note on 23⁴.   **Of the luminaries** G⁵ ¹, ²)   E 'and on the luminaries'.   5. **Michael** is the guardian angel of Israel, so in Dan. 10¹³, ²¹ 12¹, and likewise universally see Weber, *Jud Theol* 170 . according to this verse Michael is the right speaker in 24-27, where he instructs Enoch on the blessings that are to befall the chosen people   **And over chaos**

qâêl, one of the holy angels, who is set over the spirits, who sin in the spirit.   7. Gabriel, one of the holy angels, who is over Paradise and the serpents and the Cherubim.   8. Remiel, one of the holy angels, whom God set over those who rise.

XXI–XXXVI *The Second Journey of Enoch.*

XXI *Preliminary and final place of punishment of the fallen angels (stars).*

XXI 1. And I proceeded to where things were chaotic.   2. And I saw there something horrible: I saw neither a heaven above nor a firmly founded earth, but a place chaotic and horrible. 3. And there I saw seven stars of the heaven bound together in it, like great mountains and burning with fire   4 Then I said 'For what sin are they bound, and on what account have they been cast in hither?'   5 Then said Uriel, one of the holy angels, who was with me, and was chief over them, and said 'Enoch, why dost thou ask, and why art thou eager for

(G$^{b\,1,\,2}$) E ἐπὶ τῷ λαῷ   6 **Saraqâêl** (E) G$^{g\,1,\,2}$ Saiiel   **Spirits** + 'of mankind' E   7 Gabriel should be the speaker in 32 according to this verse   8 This verse is preserved only in G$^{g\,2}$, but it is genuine as is shown by the preservation of the number ἑπτά in G$^{b\,1,\,2}$ Here G$^{b\,1,\,2}$ add 'seven names of archangels'.   Remiel. Cf 2 Bar. 55³ 4 Ezra 4³⁶ Sibyl. 2²¹⁵ Apoc. El. 10⁵⁻¹¹

XXI 1–6 This place of preliminary punishment of the disobedient stars has been already described in 18¹²⁻¹⁶ There is no material difference between the two accounts   1. Origen. (*De Princ* iv 35) has cited this verse 'Ambulavi usque ad imperfectum'   2 **Chaotic** So G$^{g\,1,\,4}$ so also E by the emendation of zakôna into za'akô (Flemming)   3 **Together** (E) G$^{g1,\,4}$ read instead καὶ ἐρ⟨ρ⟩ιμμένους, 'and cast down'.   5 And was chief over them (G$^{g\,1,\,2}$) In E all MSS but *g* read 'he was chief over me'. *g* reads

'and was chief over me'.   To be emended as in 24⁶ 72¹ 74²   **Why art thou eager for the truth?** (G$^{g\,1,\,2}$— περὶ τίνος τὴν ἀλήθειαν φιλοσπουδεῖς,) G is clearly here a rendering of תצבא יציבא   This is the actual phrase in Dan. 7¹⁶ יַצִּיבָא אֱבְעָה, where both the LXX and Theod. have τὴν ἀκρίβειαν ἐζήτουν   A modified form of the phrase recurs in 25¹ διὰ τί θέλεις τὴν ἀλήθειαν μαθεῖν, = תצבא ליצבא—which construction occurs also in Dan 7¹⁹,i e צבית ליצבא where the LXX rightly has ἤθελον ἐξακριβάσασθαι, and Theod less accurately ἐζήτουν ἀκριβῶς   Now that we have determined the Aramaic and Greek renderings, we turn to E   First of all in 21⁵ E = περὶ τίνος ἀκριβοῖς καὶ φιλοσπουδεῖς ('about whom inquirest thou accurately and art eager?'), and in 25¹ διὰ τί ἀκριβοῖς μαθεῖν ('wherefore dost thou inquire accurately to learn?')   Now if E had the text of G^g before him such renderings would be extraordinary, for E can quite easily and

the truth ?　　6. These are of the number of the stars ⌐of heaven⌐ which have transgressed the commandment of the Lord, and are bound here till ten thousand years, the time entailed by their sins, are consummated.'　　7. And from thence I went to another place, which was still more horrible than the former. and I saw a horrible thing : a great fire there which burnt and blazed, and the place was cleft as far as the abyss, being full of great descending columns of fire. neither its extent or magnitude could I see, nor could I conjecture　　8. Then I said : ' How fearful is the place and how terrible to look upon!'　　9 Then Uriel answered me, one of the holy angels who was with me, and said unto me · 'Enoch, why hast thou such fear and affright?'　　And I answered: ' Because of this fearful place, and because of the spectacle of the pain.'　　10. And he said ⌐unto me⌐ · ' This place is the prison of the angels, and here they will be imprisoned for ever.'

rightly translate ἀλήθεια see 10¹⁶ 11² 15¹ or ἀληθινός 15¹ 27⁵ Hence we must conclude that in 21⁵ he had περὶ τίνος τὴν ἀκρίβειαν φιλοσπουδεῖς, and in 25¹ διὰ τί θέλεις τὴν ἀκρίβειαν μαθεῖν This is the rendering in the Ethiopic version of Dan 7¹⁶. In fact tajaqqa (in 21⁵ 25¹) and its derivations are never, so far as I can discover, used as renderings of ἀλήθεια. Our translator therefore had τὴν ἀκρίβειαν before him and had a difficulty in rendering it exactly, though other Ethiopic translators had not　　6 Of heaven (G⁸¹,²). > E　　Ten thousand years (G⁸¹,²) This period was assigned as one of punishment among the Greeks for sinful souls See Dieterich, *Nekyia*, 118 sq , 156　　But compare Rohde, *Psyche²*, 11 179　　E reads 'ālam = ' age' corrupt for 'ām = ἔτη　　The time entailed by their sins (G⁸¹,² τὸν χρόνον τῶν ἁμαρτημάτων αὐτῶν)　　This is clearer than E ' the number of the days entailed by their sins'　　7-10 This is the final place of punishment for the fallen angels　　It is distinct from that in 18¹²⁻¹⁶ 19¹⁻² 21¹ ⁶, where the seven stars are already undergoing punishment in the preliminary place of punishment　　This final place of punishment is again mentioned in 10⁶ 18¹¹ 54⁶ 90²⁴⁻²⁶　　In it the fallen angels and the faithless angelic rulers are punished for evermore　　7 Conjecture (*mu* G⁸¹,²). All other MSS. give corruptions of 'ajjēnð Before this rare word all MSS add a gloss nasērð = ' to look upon '　　8 The place. Here, as frequently, E renders the Greek article by a demonstrative, 'this place'　　Terrible So G⁸¹,² δεινός E = ὀδυνηρός.　　9 Uriel (E). > G⁸¹,²　　Was with me Seventeen MSS, including four out of the best five, add here ' and (> some MSS.) he answered me '　　This I have emended into ' and I answered', and added it after ' affright', where it occurs in G⁸¹,² but is lost in E　　The spectacle of the pain (E, where again before ' pain ' there is the demonstrative for the Greek article　　G⁸ τῆς προσόψεως τῆς δεινῆς = ' the terrible spectacle'　　10 Unto me (E) > G⁸.　　For ever Here G⁸

Sheol or the Underworld.

XXII. 1. And thence I went to another place, and he showed me in the west ⌐another⌐ great and high mountain [and] of hard rock.

E

2. And there was in it †four†

Gᵃ

2. And there were †four†

has a dittograph, μέχρι ενος (ι. c αἰῶνος) εις τὸν αἰῶνα

XXII This chapter contains a very detailed description of Sheol or Hades. According to this writer Sheol is situated in the far west according to Babylonian (*K A T* ³ 636), Greek, and Egyptian ideas, and in this respect the writer runs counter to the views of the Hebrews who placed Sheol in the underworld In all the other sections of the book the Hebrew conception prevails. This is the most ancient account of the doctrine of Sheol from the Pharisaic or Chasid standpoint, but clearly this doctrine cannot have leaped into life fullgrown as it appears here, but must already have passed through several stages of development Hades is no longer here, as in the O T, a place mainly of a semi-conscious state of existence where the only distinctions that prevailed were social and not moral ; but has already become essentially a place of conscious existence, where everything is determined by moral distinctions and moral distinctions alone See 63¹⁰ for the history of this doctrine, and my *Eschatology*, pp 426-7, for an enumeration of the various stages of development through which this conception passed So far as we may infer from 1-36, the doctrine of this chapter must be limited to Israelites and their progenitors from Adam, just as only Israelites are taken account of in Dan 12   1 [And.] Bracketed as an intrusion in E Not in Gᵍ 2 †Four† There are four divisions, according to the text of this verse, in

Hades : two for the righteous, vv 5-9, and two for the wicked, vv 10-13 But I cannot help regarding the text as here corrupt In 22⁸⁻⁹ in Gᵍ Enoch asks the angel about all the hollow places, and the angel replies 'These *three*,' &c In E, however, owing to the mention of four places in 22², the scribe was conscious of a contradiction in the text, and accordingly added 'regarding it and' before the words 'regarding all the hollow places'. This addition referred presumably to the fourth place *of which there is no description in the text* If we examine the chapter further, our conviction as to the corruption of the numbers of the places grows in strength In 22³⁻⁴ Enoch asks and is told the object of Sheol. In 22⁸⁻⁹ᵃ he asks and is told the object of the separation of the three chambers in Sheol What follows is a detailed account of these chambers . the first for the righteous, 22⁹ᵇ, the second for sinners who have not met with retribution in this life, 22¹⁰⁻¹¹, and the third for those who have, 22¹²⁻¹³ All this is clear and consecutive. But the writer wished to introduce into this passage the idea, which is in some form common to all the sections of the book, that the souls of the righteous, who had fallen at the hands of sinners, claimed retribution in the spirit-world Hence, after asking the object of Sheol, he turns aside for a moment to deal with the martyred righteous, and with a graphic touch draws the attention of the angel to a spirit that was demanding the vengeance of heaven on him

E	G^g

E

hollow places, deep and wide and very smooth. † How † smooth are **the hollow places** and deep and dark to look at.

G^g

hollow places in it, deep and very smooth · † three † of them were dark and one bright and there was a fountain of water in its midst And I said : '† How † smooth are these hollow places, and deep and dark to view.'

3 Then Raphael answered, one of the holy angels who was with me, and said unto me : ' These hollow places have been created for this very purpose, that the spirits of the souls of the dead should assemble therein, yea that all the souls of the children of men should assemble here. 4. And these places **have been made** to receive them till the day of their judgement and till their appointed period [till the period appointed], till the great judgement (comes) upon them '

that wronged him, and asks ' Whose spirit is this ?' Abel stands here for a class—22⁵⁻⁷—whose abode in Sheol is no doubt along with the rest of the righteous, 28⁹ᵃ Hence we conclude that there were originally only three places in Sheol mentioned in this chapter. †Four† . . †three†. Read ' Three . . . two ' See preceding note. **Hollow** Twice in E the text = καλοί corrupt for κοῖλοι. †How† Since the angel, in reply, gives the object of Sheol, ' how ' cannot be right we expect ' why ', ' wherefore ', or ' for what purpose ' Hence, I suggest that מֶה (= πῶς) was corrupt for לָמָה. Hence read ' for what purpose are these hollow places smooth and deep and dark to view ?' **Hollow places** (G^g = κοιλώματα) E = κυκλώματα, a corruption **Dark to view.** This statement comes in strangely after that made in the preceding sentence that there was ' one bright'. 3–4 The object with which Sheol was made a place of assemblage

for all the departed 3 **Hollow** (G^g κοῖλοι) E = καλοί, corrupt **Have been created** (E) G ἐκρίθησαν corrupt for ἐκτίσθησαν **Spirits of the souls of the dead** (G^g E^gᵘ). Other MSS corrupt. 4. **Have been made** G^g E = ἐποίησαν corrupt for ἐποιήθησαν **To receive them** (G^g εἰς ἐπισύναχεσιν αὐτῶν—of which E is a free rendering) This seems to be the equivalent of the ' promptuaria ' for departed souls in 4 Ezra 4⁸⁶ 7⁹⁵, which are called ' habitacula ' in 7⁸⁵ See our text 100⁴, ° note. [**Till the period appointed.**] A dittograph 5–7 These verses have hitherto been supposed to give a description of the first division of Sheol for righteous souls which in their life met with persecution and suffered a violent and undeserved death These cry continually to God for vengeance on those who wronged them. In the time of the author many of the Chasidim must have perished in this way This idea of

E	Gᵍ
5. I saw the spirits of the children of men who were dead, and their voice went forth to heaven and made suit 6. Then I asked Raphael the angel who was with me, and I said unto him · ' This spirit—whose is it whose voice goeth forth and maketh suit ? '	5. I saw (the spirit of) a dead man making suit, and his voice went forth to heaven and made suit 6. And I asked Raphael the angel who was with me, and I said unto him . 'This spirit which maketh suit, whose is it, whose voice goeth forth and maketh suit to heaven ? '

7. And he answered me saying . ' This is the spirit which went forth from Abel, whom his brother Cain slew, and he makes his suit against him till his seed is destroyed from the face of the earth, and his seed is annihilated from amongst the seed of men.'

E	Gᵍ
8. Then I asked regarding it, and regarding all the hollow places ' Why is one separated from the other ? '	8. Then I asked regarding all the hollow places · ' Why is one separated from the other ? '

the righteous or of the angels crying for vengeance on the wicked is in some form common to all the Sections of this book Cf 9^{1-3}, 10, 11 22^{5-8} $47^{1, 2}$ 89^{76} $97^{3, 5}$ $99^{3, 16}$ 104^{3} Cf Rev 6^{10} 4 Ezra 4^{35}. *But these verses contain no description of a division in Sheol*, but only an account of a soul demanding vengeance   **5** **Spirits of the children of men who were dead** (E) G⁵ is defective and corrupt ἀνθρώπους νεκροὺς ἐντυγχά-νοντος Possibly vv 5–6 refer only to a single spirit To this ἐντυγχάνοντος points, and also ἡ φωνὴ αὐτοῦ in the next clause in Gᵍ If this is right, as I have concluded above, there were only three places in all the first for the righteous martyrs, 22^{5-7}, and

other righteous, 22^{9b}, the second for sinners who had escaped punishment in life, 21^{10-11}, and the third for the sinners who had suffered in their life, 22^{12-13}. This view derives support from 22^{9}, 'The three places' The text of 22^{2} has been emended accordingly. **6–7** Abel's spirit cries for the destruction of the seed of Cain. **6. Whose voice** οὗ . ἡ φωνὴ αὐτοῦ = ד . . קֹלֹה   **7 Answered** + 'and said to me' E, a doublet of the following word 'saying'.   **8** Enoch asks with what object was Sheol divided into three parts? His question deals not with three-fourths of Sheol but with all of it, περὶ τῶν κοιλωμάτων πάντων. **Hollow places.** E = κρι-μάτων, and Gᵍ κυκλωμάτων, both corrupt

E

G^g

9 And he answered me and said unto me: 'These three have been made that the spirits of the dead might be separated. And such a division has been made ⟨for⟩ the spirits of the righteous, in which there is the **bright** spring of water. 10. And such has been made for sinners when they die and are buried in the earth and judgement has not been executed on them in their lifetime   11. Here their spirits shall be set apart in this great pain till the great day of judgement and punishment and

9. And he answered me saying: ·These three have been made that the spirits of the dead might be separated. And this division has been made for the spirits of the righteous, in which there is the bright spring of water.   10 And this has been made for sinners when they die and are buried in the earth and judgement has not been executed upon them in their lifetime.   11. Here their spirits shall be set apart in this great pain, till the great day of judgement, scourgings, and torments of the accursed

for κοιλωμάτων   **9** The first division is for the souls of the righteous—both those who have been martyred and those who have not.   **Spirits** In E only *n* reads 'spirits', the rest give 'souls'. But the word nafs in E frequently means spirit as in 15¹² 69¹² 99⁷, as well as in verses 11, 12, 13 of this chapter. Hence I have rendered it 'spirit' in such cases.   **In which Here** G^g has οὗ   ἐν αὐτῷ = בה . . יד   **The bright spring of water** In E for 'bright' the text gives 'brightness' or 'light'   In the underworld, souls, according to the Greek Cults, Jewish, Hellenistic, and Christian literature, suffered from thirst   see Dieterich, *Nekyia*, 97 sqq   In the Greek Hades there was a spring of forgetfulness on the left, while on the right was the spring of memory—the cool water —ψυχρὸν ὕδωρ, by the drinking of which consciousness and memory were quickened, the first condition of the full

or blessed life. See Rohde, *Psyche*, ii 2. 310, 390–391   The expression ' water of life' is found in Babylonian literature in the Adapa Myth and the Descent of Ishtar *KAT*³ 523 sqq   **10–11** The second division is for those sinners who lived prosperously and escaped punishment in life, and finally attained to honourable burial   According to Hebrew and Greek ideas the privation of funeral rites was a great calamity, and involved, at least according to ancient ideas, inevitable suffering for the departed soul.   **10. And this** In E bakama kamâhû is corrupt for wakamâhû = καὶ οὕτως   Here οὕτως is corrupt for οὗτος the demonstrative   The angel points to each division as he describes it. I have introduced this emendation into my translation of G^g in verses 9, 10, 12, 13.   **11. Great pain.** Cf 103⁷˒ ⁸ Luke 16²³⁻²⁵.   **Great day of judgement** Cf. 45² n.   **The accursed** Here τῶν

E

torment of those who | curse †
for ever, and retribution for
their spirits There He shall
bind them for ever. 12 And
such a division has been made
for the spirits of those who
make their suit, who make
disclosures concerning their
destruction, when they were
slain in the days of the sinners 13. Such has been
made for the spirits of men
who were not righteous but
sinners, who were complete in
transgression, and of the transgressors they shall be companions · but their spirits shall
not be slain in the day of
judgement nor shall they be
raised from thence.' 14. Then

Gg

for ever, so that (there may
be) retribution for their spirits.
There He shall bind them for
ever 12. And this division
has been made for the spirits
of those who make their suit,
who make disclosures concerning their destruction, when they
were slain in the days of the
sinners. 13. And this has
been made for the spirits of
men who shall not be righteous
but sinners, who are godless,
and of the lawless they shall
be companions but their spirits
shall not be punished in the
day of judgement nor shall
they be raised from thence.'
14. Then I blessed the Lord
of Glory and said ' Blessed

κατηραμένων, which E takes actively, is
to be taken passively as in Wisd 12²¹
2 Kings 9³⁴ Matt 25⁴¹ So that
(there may be, retribution = ἵν' ἀντ-
απόδοσις Emended by Radermacher
12-13 The third division is for sinners
who suffered in this life, and therefore
incur a less penalty in Sheol For
them Sheol is an everlasting place of
punishment, since they are not raised
from it to be delivered over to a severer
condemnation at the final judgement.
12 These sinners demand vengeance
on those that did violence to them in
life, just as the righteous in the first
division demanded justice against those
that had destroyed them 13
Companions So also E—kamahōmū

Their spirits + ' because those who
suffer affliction here are punished less ',
Gᵍ—a gloss Shall not be punished
(Gᵍ) Here E has ' shall not be slain
= ἀναιρεθήσονται οἱ φονευθήσονται
The same word is found in 99¹¹ 108⁷ in
the same connexion Cf Matt 10²⁸
Nor shall they be raised The resurrection here implied is of Israel only
so the entire Section 1-36 would lead us
to infer Otherwise this declaration of
a General Resurrection is solitary and
unique in pre-Christian Jewish Apocrypha 14 After each fresh revelation Enoch generally bursts forth
into a doxology Cf 25⁷ 27⁵ 36⁴ 39⁹⁻¹³
48¹⁰ 81³ 83¹¹ 84 90⁴⁰ These doxologies
have, as a rule, a close connexion in

E	G^g
I blessed the Lord of glory and said 'Blessed be my Lord, the Lord of righteousness, who ruleth for ever.'	art Thou, Lord of righteousness, who rulest over the world.'

XXIII. *The Fire that deals with the Luminaries of Heaven.*

XXIII. 1. From thence I went to another place to the west of the ends of the earth. 2. And I saw a ⸢⸢burning⸣⸣ fire which ran without resting, and paused not from its course day or night but (ran) regularly. 3. And I asked saying: 'What is this which rests not?' 4. Then Raguel, one of the holy angels who was with me, answered me ⸢⸢and said unto me⸣⸣. 'This course ⸢of fire⸣ ⸢⸢which thou hast seen⸣⸣ is the fire in the west which †persecutes† all the luminaries of heaven.'

XXIV—XXV. *The Seven Mountains in the North-West and the Tree of Life.*

XXIV. 1. ⸢⸢And from thence I went to another place of the

thought with their respective contexts. **Lord of glory**: see 25^3 (note). **Lord of righteousness**, cf. 90^{40} 106^3.

XXIII. 1, 2. Enoch still remains in the west, but proceeds to another quarter of the west where there is a restless river of fire. 17^4 appears to deal with the same subject. **1. West of the ends** (G^b). E = 'west, to the ends'. **2. Burning** (E). $> G^g$. **But (ran) regularly** (E). G^g ἅμα (corrupt for ἀλλὰ) διαμένον. **4. And said unto me** (E). $> G^b$. **Of fire** (G^b) > E. Unless we take coazni (= 'and this is') as a corruption of coâ 'ĕj = 'of fire' (Flemming). But it may = τό before πρὸς δυσμάς. **Which thou hast seen** (E) $> G^g$. **Persecutes** (G^b ἐκδιῶκον). The text is highly doubtful. E certainly supports ἐκδιῶκον though it is corrupt: that is, it reads jĕnadĕd (= 'burns') corrupt for jĕsadĕd = 'persecutes'. But in 20^4, where the functions of Raguel are described, it is said that he 'takes vengeance on the world of the luminaries', i.e. ἐκδικῶν. These verbs are confused elsewhere, cf. Sir. 39^{30}. Both passages clearly embody the same idea. Raguel 'takes vengeance on the world of the luminaries' in 20^4 and 'persecutes all the luminaries of heaven' in 23^4. The idea of 'taking vengeance on' or 'persecuting *all* the luminaries' is inconceivable, and since the object in both passages is the same, the corruption lies in the verb. ἐκδιῶκον is probably secondary to ἐκδικῶν. The latter = בָּרִיעַ, which means either 'to requite in a good or bad sense' or 'to take vengeance on'. Hence I suggest that the meaning 'requite' should be restored here, and in 20^4.

XXIV. Enoch has been in the extreme west in 23: now he goes to the NW. First he sees a mountain range of fire and then the seven great mountains, one of which is the throne of God. **1. And from thence . . . of the earth** (E). $> G^g$. **Day and**

earth⌐, and he showed me a mountain range of fire which buint ⌐day and⌐ night   2. And I went beyond it and saw seven magnificent mountains all differing each from the other, and the stones (thereof) were magnificent and beautiful, magnificent as a whole, of glorious appearance and fair exterior · ⌐three towards⌐ the east, ⌐one⌐ founded on the other, and three towards the south, ⌐one⌐ upon the other, and deep rough ravines, no one of which joined with any other.   3 And the seventh mountain was in the midst of these, and it excelled them in height, resembling the seat of a throne · and fragrant trees encircled the throne.   4 And amongst them was a tree such as I had never yet smelt, neither was any amongst them nor were others like it it had a fragrance beyond all fragrance, and its leaves and blooms and wood wither not for ever . and its fruit ⌐is beautiful, and its fruit⌐ resembles the dates of a palm.   5 Then I said · ' ⌐How⌐ beautiful is this tree, and fragrant, and its leaves are fair, and its blooms ⌐very⌐ delightful in appearance.'   6 Then answered Michael, one of the holy ⌐and honoured⌐ angels who was with me, and was their leader.

XXV 1. And he said unto me   ' Enoch, why dost thou ask me regarding the fragrance of the tree, and ⌐why⌐ dost thou wish to learn the truth ? '   2 Then I answered him ⌐saying⌐

(E) > G⁵.   2. Beyond it (ἐπέκεινα αὐτῶν) E ' towards it '—always wrong in its rendering of this word, cf 18⁹ note.   Differing each from the other, 1 e of seven different precious stones   And beautiful (E) G⁵ ' in beauty'.   Three towards¹⁰ (E) > G⁵ One¹⁰, ²⁰ (E) > G⁵ Rough (G⁵ τραχεῖαι) E = σκολιαί.   3 Excelled them in height (ḳoₗḥ nŏḥŏmû G⁵, save that G⁵ om 'them') All other MSS of E read nûhŏmû = 'their height'   Resembling (G⁵ and E by emending sa jĕtmâsalû into zajĕtmâsal)   Fragrant (E = εὐώδη G⁵ εὐειδῆ, ' of goodly appearance'—corrupt, cf 24⁴, ⁵ 25⁴)   4 The tree described here is the tree of life ; cf 25⁴⁻⁸.   Neither

was any amongst them (E) G⁵ — ' and no one else had enjoyed (ηὐφράνθη) them '   Is beautiful, and its fruit (E) > G⁵ though hmt   5 How (G⁵ > E)   Fragrant (G⁵ εὐῶδες E = εὐειδίς)   Its blooms (G⁵) E reads fĕrĕhû corrupt for sĕgĕhû = G⁵   Very (E > G⁵).   6. Michael, the patron angel of Israel, is in charge of these special treasures of the Messianic kingdom And yet, according to 20⁷, we should expect Gabriel here And honoured (E. > G⁵)

XXV 1   Ask + ' and why didst thou marvel ' G⁵   Why ²⁰ (G⁵) > E Wish to learn the truth (G⁵).   E = ἀκριβῶς μαθεῖν = ' inquire accurately to learn '.   See note on 21⁵   2. Then I

'I wish to know about everything, but especially about this tree.' 3. And he answered saying : 'This high mountain ⌜which thou hast seen⌝, whose summit is like the throne of God, is His throne, where the Holy Great One, the Lord of Glory, the Eternal King, will sit, when He shall come down to visit the earth with goodness.   4. And as for this fragrant tree no mortal is permitted to touch it till the great judgement, when He shall take vengeance on all and bring (everything) to its consummation for ever. It shall then be given to the righteous and holy.   5. Its fruit shall be for food to the elect, it shall be transplanted to the holy place, to the temple of the Lord, the Eternal King 6. Then shall they rejoice with joy and be glad.

+ 'Enoch' *a–q*, β against G⁸, *q*. Saying (E). > G⁸.   3. On this mountain see note on 18⁸ This mountain is the middle one of the seven in 18⁶⁻⁹ 24¹⁻³ **Which thou hast seen** (E). > G⁸.   **The Holy Great One** . Glory (E) G⁸ 'the great Lord, the Holy One of Glory' Holy Great One see 1³ (note) Lord of Glory, cf 22¹⁴ (25⁷) 27³, ⁵ 36⁴ 40³ 63² 83⁸.   **Eternal King**; cf vv 5, 7, 27³; only found in 1–36 When He shall come down, &c. This mountain, as we have seen in 18⁶ note, is in the NW In 77¹ it is said that God will descend in the south   4 **Then** (G⁸) E = τόδε corrupt for τότε   **Holy** (G⁸ ὁσίοις E = 'humble', cf 108⁷) 4, 5 This tree is the tree of life By the eating of this tree after the final judgement men are endowed with long life—not eternal life, cf 5⁹ 10¹⁷ 25⁶ Cf 2 Bar 73², ³, ⁶, ⁷ 74 The writer of 1–36 has not risen to the conception of an eternal life of blessedness for the righteous, and so has not advanced a single step beyond the conceptions found in Is 65 66. This materialistic conception of the tree of life based on Gen 2⁹ 3²², and here published afresh, gained afterwards a wide currency in Jewish and Christian literature though

mainly with a symbolical meaning, cf. Rev 2⁷ 22², ¹⁴ 4 Ezra 8⁵²   5 Its fruit . . to the elect. G⁸ reads ὁ καρπὸς αὐτοῦ τοῖς ἐκλεκτοῖς † εἰς ζωήν † εἰς βοράν The writer had before him Ezek 47¹² וְיהיו פריו למאכל. εἰς ζωήν = לחייא, which I take to be corrupt for לחוא = ἔσται Thus the original possibly ran ואנבה לבחיריא לחוא למיכל. E is here very corrupt = ἐκ τοῦ καρποῦ αὐτοῦ δοθήσεται τοῖς ἐκλεκτοῖς ζωή, καὶ εἰς βοῤῥάν **Transplanted to** (G⁸ μεταφυτευθήσεται ἐν). The μετά reflects probably a separate verb in the original The tree of life, which, according to the Massoretic Text, stood along with the tree of knowledge in the earthly Garden of Eden was, according to our text, removed to the Garden of Righteousness in the NW., whence it was subsequently to be transplanted to the holy place **The holy place**, i. e. Jerusalem. We cannot tell whether the author intended here the New Jerusalem which, according to 90²⁹, was to be set up by God Himself It is, at all events, a Jerusalem cleansed from all impurity, and that is probably all that the author meant   6 In this verse I have followed G⁸ E differs only in

And into the holy place shall they enter ;
And its fragrance shall be in their bones,
And they shall live a long life on earth,
Such as thy fathers lived :
And in their days shall no ⌈sorrow or⌉ plague
Or torment or calamity touch them.'

7 Then blessed I the God of Glory, the Eternal King, who hath prepared such things for the righteous, and hath created them and promised to give to them.

Jerusalem and the Mountains, Ravines, and Streams.

XXVI. 1. And I went from thence to the middle of the earth, and I saw a blessed place ⌈in which there were trees⌉ with branches abiding and blooming [of a dismembered tree].

the second and third lines, where it reads ' Into the holy place shall they enter (*mtu*, β-o,*b*),

Its fragrance shall be in their bones.' But *gq*, *u₁b* read wajâbaw'û = ' and they shall draw the fragrance thereof into their bones', instead of jɪbaw'û = ' shall enter'. If this reading were right ἐν τοῖς ὀστέοις αὐτῶν would = בגרמיהון = ' into themselves Then we should have

' Then shall they rejoice with joy, And be glad in the holy place And they shall draw the fragrance thereof into themselves And they shall live ', &c

The eating of this tree imparts life, cf Test. Lev. 15¹¹ its fruit fills and heals the righteous, 4 Ezra 7¹²³, cf 8⁵² Rev. 2⁷ 22⁴ Since the word used here is ὀσμαὶ αὐτοῦ, Beer thinks there may be an echo of this idea in 2 Cor 2¹⁶ ὀσμὴ ἐκ ζωῆς εἰς ζωήν. No sorrow or plague. Cf Is 65¹⁹, ²⁰. Touch Cf in this sense Job 1¹¹ 2⁵ 1 Chron. 16²², &c With βάσανοι οὐχ ἅψονται αὐτῶν of Wisd 3¹ οὐ μὴ ἅψηται αὐτῶν βάσανος which seems a quotation βάσανος = כיבא
7 On the doxology cf. 22¹⁴ n Who.

So G⁵ ὅς. E = *ds* = ' because'. Created them (G⁵) E ' created such things'
XXVI Enoch visits Jerusalem and its vicinity 1 **The middle of the earth.** The writer regards Jerusalem as the centre of the earth, cf. Ezek 38¹² 5⁸ טבור In the Book of Jubilees 8¹⁹, ¹⁹ it is called the navel or ὀμφαλός of the earth, just as Delphi was regarded amongst the Greeks. This idea reappears in the Talmud—Joma 54ᵇ Sanh 37ᵃ See Weber, *Jüd. Theol* 208 In En 90²⁶ Gehenna is in the middle of the earth **Blessed place.** All MSS. of E except *q* read ' blessed planted place' against G⁵, cf 27¹ 89⁴⁰ Dan 11¹⁶, ⁴¹, ⁴⁵ In which there were trees So G⁵, but lost in E owing to hmt ɪ e. esaw zahôtû fell out after zahôtû. Or it may have been omitted by the translator owing to the final phrase. **Of a dismembered tree** This phrase can only be interpreted of Israel. If it is original, then ' in which there were trees' cannot be original, and the text may refer to the participation of the righteous descendants of Israel in the Messianic Kingdom in Palestine.

2. And there I saw a holy mountain, ⌜and⌝ underneath the mountain to the east there was a stream and it flowed towards the
south.   3. And I saw towards the east another mountain
higher than this, and between them a deep and narrow ravine :
in it also ran a stream ⌜underneath⌝ the mountain.   4. And to
the west thereof there was another mountain, lower than the
former and of small elevation, and a ravine ⌜deep and dry⌝
between them . and another deep and dry ravine was at the
extremities of the three ⌜mountains⌝.   5. And all the ravines
were deep ⌜and narrow⌝, (being formed) of hard rock, and trees
were not planted upon them.   6. And I marvelled ⌜at the
rocks, and I marvelled⌝ at the ravine, yea, I marvelled very much.

The Purpose of the Accursed Valley.

XXVII. 1. Then said I· 'For what object is this blessed land,
which is entirely filled with trees, and this accursed valley

Since, however, the trees here spoken
of are again referred to in 27¹ γῆ
πλήρης δένδρων, we conclude that the
clause 'in which there were trees'
is original and that ' of a dismembered
tree' is a disturbing gloss, which introduces symbolical meanings into a non-
metaphorical passage   Abiding Gᵍ
E μενούσας = קימין.   Cf Jer. Targ.
on Gen 3²² קיים כאילן חייא   2 A
holy mountain, i e Zion.   And ²⁰.
So E > Gᵍ   A stream, i e. the
brook of Siloah.   Flowed (E = τὴν
ῥύσιν εἶχεν)   Gᵍ corruptly reads δίσιν
3 Another mountain, i e the Mount
of Olives.   Between them (E) Gᵇ
'between it'.   Ravine, i. e. the valley
of the Kedron or of Jehoshaphat
A stream, i e. the brook Kedron.
Underneath (Gᵍ)   E 'towards' or
perhaps 'alongside'.   4 Another
mountain, i e. the Mount of Offence
A ravine, i e. the valley of Hinnom at the point where the three
mountains meet.   Deep and dry
(Gᵍ) E 'underneath it'   Mountains
(Gᵇ) > E   Description is accurate

5 And narrow (E) > Gᵍ.   6
The valley of Hinnom   At the rocks,
and I marvelled E > Gᵍ through hmt
XXVII 1 Then (E) Gᵍ 'and'.
Blessed land   See 26¹ n   And this
accursed valley between (E).   Gᵍ =
'and (why is) this valley accursed'
But Gᵍ has probably lost ἡ before
κεκατηραμένη and E is right   The
valley of Hinnom or Gehenna had
three meanings in the O T   1° It
was used merely in a topographi-
cal sense as the boundary between
Judah and Benjamin, Jos. 15⁸ 18¹⁶
2° It was used in a religious significance as implying a place of idolatrous
and inhuman sacrifices   Cf 2 Kings 16³
2 Chron 28³ Jer 7³¹, &c.   3° It signified the place of punishment for rebel-
lious and apostate Jews in the presence
of the righteous, cf. Is 66²⁴ (50¹') Jer
7³² Dan 12²   In Apocalyptic the idea
underwent further development.   1°
Thus it was conceived as a place of
corporal and spiritual punishment for
apostate Jews in the presence of the
righteous for ever, cf 27²˒³ 90²⁶˒²⁷.

⌐between ?⌐ 2. ⌐Then Uriel, one of the holy angels who was
with me, answered and said : ' This⌐ accursed valley is for those
who are accursed for ever   here shall all ⌐the accursed⌐ be
gathered together who utter with their lips against the Lord
unseemly words and of His glory speak hard things.

E	Gᵍ
Here shall they be gathered together, and here shall be their place of judgement. 3. In the last days there shall be upon them the spectacle of righteous judgement in the presence of the righteous for ever · here shall the merciful	Here shall they be gathered together, and here shall be the place of their habitation. 3. In the last times, in the days of the true judgement in the presence of the righteous for ever : here shall the **godly**

In 37-70 there appears to be a modifi-
cation of this idea, for though the
punishment is everlasting, only its
initial stages were to be executed in
the presence of the righteous   On the
expiration of these the wicked were to
be swept for ever from the presence of
the righteous, cf 48⁹ (note) 62¹², ¹³
2° A place of spiritual punishment
only, for apostate Jews in the presence
of the righteous. This new development is attested in 91-104, cf 98⁹
' their spirits shall be cast into a furnace
of fire' also 103⁸ From 99¹¹ 103⁷, ⁸
it is clear that to this writer Gehenna
and Sheol have become equivalent
terms Cf also 100⁹ 108⁶, the latter passage being from a different hand   On
Sheol see note on 56⁸, and on the question
generally my Art on ' Gehenna ' in
Hastings, *B D* , whence these statements are drawn   In the N T. (Matt
5²⁹, ³⁰ 10²⁸ 18⁹ 23¹⁵, &c.) and in 4 Ezra
7³⁶⁻³⁸ Gehenna is no longer the place
of punishment of unrighteous Jews
but of the wicked generally   In later
Judaism the conception underwent a
further change. Gehenna was regarded

as the Purgatory of faithless Jews who
were afterwards to be admitted into
Paradise, but the place of eternal perdi-
tion for the Gentiles, cf Weber, *Jud.
Theol* 341 sq   2 **Then Uriel** .
said ' This (E) > Gᵍ   **Valley** .
Gᵍ has here γῆ which is a transliteration of גַּיְא as in Neh 11³⁵ Ezek 32⁵
in the LXX   It is transliterated as
γέ in 2 Chron 28⁹ Ezek 39¹⁵, γαί in
Jos 18¹⁶ Ezek 39¹¹   **The accursed**
(Gᵍ) > E   Utter unseemly words.
See 5⁴ note. Gehenna is the final
abode of godless Israelites   Place of
their habitation (οἰκητήριον αὐτῶν Gᵍ)
E reads mëkučnanihômû = 'place
of their judgement', which may be a
corruption of makânômû = οἰκητήριον
αὐτῶν. But the corruption may have
arisen in the Greek, i e. οἰκητήριον may
have been corrupted into κριτήριον
2-3 Accordingly as we follow Gᵍ or
E the text differs somewhat.   In the
days (Gᵍ ἐν ταῖς ἡμέραις)   Here E
reads ἔσται αὐτοῖς εἰς τὴν ὅρασιν (οι
ἡ ὅρασις). This introduces the idea
which reappears in 48⁹ 62¹²   See
note on 27¹. The godly = εὐσεβεῖς

E   G^g

E	G^g
bless the Lord of Glory, the Eternal King	bless the Lord of Glory, the Eternal King.

4. In the days of judgement over the former, they shall bless Him for the mercy in accordance with which He has assigned them (their lot).' 5. Then I blessed the Lord of Glory and set forth His ⌐glory⌐ and lauded Him gloriously.

XXVIII—XXXIII. *Further Journey to the East.*

XXVIII. 1. And thence I went ⌐towards the east⌐, into the midst ⌐of the mountain range⌐ of the desert, and I saw a wilderness and it was solitary, full of trees and plants. 2. ⌐And⌐ water gushed forth from above. 3. Rushing like a copious watercourse [which flowed] towards the north-west it caused clouds and dew to ascend on every side.

emended from ἀσεβεῖς Here E reads maḥârjân, which may be corrupt for mêḥûrân = 'those who have obtained mercy' Lord of Glory Cf 25³ Eternal King Cf. 25⁷ 5 His 'glory⌐ (G^g) E om. 'glory' perhaps owing to its occurrence just before Lauded (G^g ὕμνησα) E reads zakaikû = 'remembered', corrupt for zamarkû = ὕμνησα

XXVIII 1 Dillmann takes the plain here referred to to be that of the Jordan, and the mountain range of the desert to be the rocky region which separates this plain from Jerusalem According to Ezek 47⁹, ¹² this desert should one day be well watered and covered with trees 1. Towards the East (E) > G^g Of the mountain range (E) > G^g And plants Here both G^g and E read καὶ (> E) ἀπὸ τῶν σπερμάτων. In no case can σπερμάτων be right in its literal meaning. The difficulty can be explained from a corruption in the Aramaic or from a faulty rendering by the Greek translator In the former case καὶ

ἀπὸ τ σπερμάτων = ומורעין corrupt for וזרעונים (cf Dan 1¹², ¹⁶, Mishna, *Kil* ii 2; iii 2) = καὶ τῶν φυτευμάτων Or the Greek translator may here have found ומזרעין, which he should have read as ומזרעין = καὶ ἀπὸ τ φυτευμάτων, but which he read as ומזרעין = καὶ ἀπὸ τ σπερμάτων Theodotion gives the same misrendering in Dan 1¹², ¹⁶. 2. And (E) > G^g 3 Rushing (G^g φερόμενον) E = φαινόμενον corrupt for φαιρομενον, i e φερόμενον. Which flowed Bracketed as an addition in E It caused . to ascend (G^g ἀνάγει). E = καὶ ἀνάγεται, but by the change of a vowel point we recover ἀνάγει Owing to this internal corruption E reads ὕδωρ καὶ δρόσος Clouds. G^g E read ὕδωρ But water is the subject of the verb, and in no case can it be said that water 'ascends'. Besides, δρόσον shows that we require here some such word as 'mist' or 'cloud' or 'vapour' Now the exact phrase we need is found in Ps 135⁷ Jer 10¹³ 51¹⁶ מעלה נשאים, which the LXX in each case renders

XXIX. 1 And thence I went to another place in the desert, and approached to the east of this mountain range.   2. And ⌐there⌐ I saw aromatic trees exhaling the fragrance of frankincense and myrrh, and the trees also were similar to the almond tree.

XXX. 1. And beyond these, I went afar to the east, and I saw another place, a valley (full) of water.   2. And ⌐therein there was⌐ a tree, the colour (?) of fragrant trees such as the mastic 3. And on the sides of those valleys I saw fragrant cinnamon. And beyond these I proceeded to the east.

XXXI. 1. And I saw other mountains, and amongst them were ⌐groves of⌐ trees, and there flowed forth from them nectar, which is named sarara and galbanum   2. And beyond these mountains I saw another mountain ⌐to the east of the ends of the earth⌐, ⌐whereon were aloe trees⌐, and all the trees were full

by ἀνάγειν νεφέλας and the Targums by מסיק עננין Hence I assume that מיין (= ὕδωρ) is here a primitive corruption of עננין = clouds' The word 'clouds' is to be taken in the sense of 'mist', for so Onkelos renders אד = 'mist' in Gen 2⁶

XXIX. 1 And thence These words F had by a slip transposed before †'water' (i e, 'clouds') in the preceding verse Gᵍ reads ἔτι ἐκεῖθεν 2. There (E) > Gᵍ Aromatic trees (Gᵍ E read κρίσεως δένδρα κρίσεως = דיניא which, as Praetorius and Beer have recognized, is corrupt for דריחא Hence we should have here εὐώδη instead of κρίσεως Exhaling (Gᵇ). E = πλέον corrupt for πνέοντα (Gᵍ) Frankincense and myrrh לבונה וֹמוֹר Almond tree (Gᵇ καρύαις) E omits unless we suppose kuaskuas, which occurs without any sense in the preceding line after πνέοντα, to be a corrupt transliteration of καρύαις = שקד.

XXX. 1 Beyond (Gᵍ ἐπέκεινα) Here, as elsewhere, E is unable to render this word correctly. See 18⁹ note. Went (Gᵍ ᾠχόμην) E has

here dabra (= ὄρη) which seems to be a corrupt remnant of qarabkû = ᾠχόμην Cf 29¹ 30³. Afar (Gᵇ). E 'not afar' Another + 'great' Gᵇ Water + 'like that which fails not ' E—a gloss ? 2 Therein there was a tree (Gᵇ) E = 'I saw a beautiful tree'. The colour (Gᵍ χρύα), E = ὅμοιον — the same in sense For χρύα Radermacher conjectures χλόᾳ 3. Fragrant cinnamon Gᵍ have here the strange phrase κυνάμωμον ἀρωμάτων, which is a rendering of קנמן־בשם. See Exod 30²³. Beyond E misrenders here see 18⁹ note.

XXXI 1 Groves of (Gᵍ) > E. Nectar = נקטר E prefixes 'as it were' Sarara (E) Gᵍ σορράν = a transliteration of צרי a kind of balsam Galbanum = χαλβάνη = חלבנה 2. Beyond E misrenders Cf. 18⁹ note To the east of the ends of the earth (Gᵍ) > E. Whereon were aloe trees (E) > Gᵍ. Observe that Gᵍ and E are complementary The former gives the habitat of the trees—the furthest east—but not their name E omits the habitat but supplies the name.

of stacte, being like almond trees.   3. And when one burnt it, it smelt sweeter than any fragrant odour.

E

XXXII. 1. And after these fragrant odours, as I looked towards the north over the mountains I saw seven mountains full of choice nard and fragrant trees and cinnamon and pepper.

G^g

XXXII. 1. To the north-east I beheld seven mountains full of choice nard and mastic and cinnamon and pepper.

The aloe mentioned here is not 'the common bitter aloes used in medicine to which alone the name is given in classical writers', nor yet what is commonly known as the American aloe, but 'the modern eagle wood, a precious wood exported from South-Eastern Asia, which yields a fragrant odour when burnt' (*Encyc. Bib* i 120—121) In Hebrew its form is אחלים (Num 24⁶ Prov. 7¹⁷) or אהלות (Ps 45⁹ Cant 4¹⁴— in the last passage א in the LXX and Aquila render it by ἀλόη In Aramaic the form is אָתְלָא. All (Gᵍ). E reads 'êlkû corrupt for kuêllu = 'all'   Of stacte. I have with much hesitation emended ἐξ αὐτῆς in Gᵍ into στακτῆς E is very corrupt = στερεός, which is transposed after almond trees.   3 **Burnt.** Gᵍ has τρίβωσιν E = λάβωσιν, but jĕnaš'ewô may be corrupt for jĕhasjĕwô = τρίβωσιν. If my identification of this tree in the note on ver 2 is right, we should expect καύσωσιν here, as eagle wood exhales fragrant odours when burnt. Now τρίβωσιν = ירקקק (Pael) corrupt for ירלקון = καύσωσιν, 'burnt'   It   Gᵍ reads διό, which may be corrupt for αὐτό.   E = τὸν καρπόν   Smelt sweeter (Gᵍ) E = 'was better'.

XXXII The Earthly Garden of Eden and the Tree of Knowledge   1

Gᵍ has lost 'and after these odours' by hmt., and reads 'To the NE I saw seven mountains'.   This statement that the seven mountains are in the NE creates some difficulty, if the text is correct   And that the text of Gᵍ is correct seems to follow from the statement in ver 2 'far towards the east' in both Gᵍ and E   This being so, it seems necessary to conclude that the Garden of Righteousness in 70⁹ 77⁸ in the NW is distinct from the primitive earthly Garden of Righteousness or Eden in the NE., and that the seven mountains mentioned here in connexion with the Garden of Righteousness in 31¹⁻² are distinct from those mentioned in 18⁵ 24² ˢᵠᵠ For the Garden of Righteousness and the Seven Mountains, one of which is the throne of God, are situated in the NW   The tree of knowledge is in the earthly Garden of Righteousness in the NE, 32⁸⁻⁶, and the tree of life among the Seven Mountains, 24²-25⁶, in the NW.   Again, it is noteworthy that whereas the Garden of Righteousness in 61¹² 60⁸, ²³ 65² 70⁸ 77⁸ is the abode of the departed righteous, the earthly Garden of Righteousness seems not to be   A special division in Sheol is assigned to the souls of the righteous in 22⁹   The earthly Garden of Eden, if the above conclusion is right,

2. And thence I went over the summits of ⌜all⌝ these mountains, far towards the east ⌜of the earth⌝, and passed above the Erythraean sea, and went far from it, and passed over ᵐthe angel⌝ Zotîêl.

E

3. And I came to the Garden of Righteousness, and saw beyond those trees many large trees growing there and of goodly fragrance, large, very beautiful and glorious, and the tree of wisdom whereof they eat and know great wisdom

Gᵍ

3. And I came to the Garden of Righteousness, and from afar off trees more numerous than these trees and great—†two† trees there, very great, beautiful, and glorious, and the tree of knowledge, whose holy fruit they eat and know great wisdom.

has no further connexion with the destinies of mankind according to the Book of Enoch The above conclusions appear tenable, although in Gen 2⁸ the Garden of Eden is said to be in the East, while in 3²⁴ it is implied that it lies in the West, and in 2¹⁰⁻¹⁴ in the North See Gunkel, *Genesis*³ 26 These variations in Genesis are due to different sources. **2 All** (Gᵍ) > E **Of the earth** (Gᵍ) > E **Erythraean sea** The Persian and Indian oceans cf 77⁸,⁷ **Went** (Gᵇ) E reads kônkû corrupt for hôïkû = Gᵍ **Far from it** (E = ἀπὸ τούτου μακράν) Gᵍ reads ἐπ' Ἄκρων, καὶ ἀπὸ τούτου = 'towards Akron and from this' **The angel** (E). > Gᵍ **3 Beyond** So E, which so renders μακρόθεν and wrongly takes it as governing the following words in the genitive. **Growing** (E = φυόμενα). Gᵍ reads δύω μέν, but this reading is certainly corrupt If δύω μέν were original, then τὸ δένδρον τῆς ζωῆς would have to be inserted before καὶ τὸ δένδρον τῆς φρονήσεως But the tree of life, according to 24²-25, is in the neighbourhood of the chief of the

Seven Mountains in the NW. See notes 32¹ 25⁵ 18⁶. The passages from the Zohar quoted by Lawrence, and subsequently adduced by Lods and Lawlor in support of δύω μέν cannot, therefore, bear on our text; but may be derived ultimately from 2 Enoch, and in part from Gen 3. These passages are (Lawrence, p xxix) from vol i, Parasha בראשית, p 37ᵇ, ed Mont et Amstel 'Sanctus et Benedictus sustulit eum (Enochum) ex mundo, ut ipsi serviret

Ex eo inde tempore liber tradebatur, qui Enochi dictus est In hora qua Deus eum sustulit, ostendebat ei *omnia repositoria suprema*, ostendebat ei *arborem vitae medio in horto*, folia eius atque ramos' Again (vol ii, Parasha בשלח, p 55ᵃ) 'In Enochi libro narratur, Sanctum et Benedictum, cum ascendere eum iusserit et *omnia ei superiorum et inferiorum regnorum repositoria* ostenderit monstrasse quoque *arborem vitae* et arborem de qua Adamus praeceptum recepit' These passages refer to 2 Enoch. The italicized words *omnia repositoria suprema* refer to Paradise and Hell, which are described

4. ⸢That tree is in height like the fir, and its leaves are⸣ like (those of) the Carob tree : and its fruit is like the clusters of the vine, very beautiful : and the fragrance of the tree penetrates afar.   **5.** Then I said   '⸢How⸣ beautiful is the tree, and how attractive is its look !'   **6.** Then Raphael, the holy angel who was with me, answered me ⸢and said⸣ᵑ: 'This is the tree of wisdom, of which thy father old (in years) and thy aged mother, who were before thee, have eaten, and they learnt wisdom and their eyes were opened, and they knew that they were naked and they were driven out of the garden.'

XXXIII. 1. And from thence I went to the ends of the earth and saw there great beasts, and each differed from the other ; and (I saw) birds also differing in appearance and beauty and voice, the one differing from the other.   **2.** And to the east of those beasts I saw the ends of the earth whereon the heaven rests, and the portals of the heaven open.   **3.** And I saw how the stars of heaven come forth, and I counted the

---

in 2 Enoch 8-10   The next italicized words—*arborem vitae medio in horto*—may be taken directly from 8ᵍ of the same book or from Gen 2⁹, while the phrase *arborem de qua Adamus praeceptum recepit* might possibly refer to 1 Enoch 32³⁻⁶, but much more likely to Gen 2¹⁷   Whose holy fruit = οὖ τοῦ καρποῦ αὐτοῦ—an Aramaic idiom פירה ... די ,   **4** That tree   its leaves are   So Gᵇ > E through hmt   Like the clusters of the vine According to certain Rabbinic authorities the tree of which Adam ate was the vine cf Sanh 70ᵃ אילן שאכל ממנו אדם הראשון גפן   See also Ber 40ᵃ   **The fragrance of the tree penetrates afar.** So E in q *gmu* add asyndetically after 'penetrates' as a variant (?) 'proceeds', while *tβ* subsequently connect the two verbs   Gᵍ reads 'its fragrance penetrates afar from the tree'   **5** Then (Gᵍ) E 'and'   Τότε occurs frequently in 6-32, i. e. 9¹ 10¹, ¹⁸ 11² 13³, ⁸ 21⁴, ⁵, ⁸ 22³, ⁸, ¹⁴ 23⁴ 24⁵, ⁵ 25⁵, ⁷ 27⁵

32⁵, ⁶ This is an Aramaic feature. E in a few cases fails to preserve it.   **How** (Gᵍ ὡς) > E as in 24⁵   The tree (Gᵍ). E reads 'this tree ', but here, as frequently, E renders the Greek article by a demonstrative pronoun. **And how** All MSS of E except *q* add ' beautiful and ' against Gᵍ and *q*   **6.** Adam and Eve seem to be still living   Hence, if 10¹ belongs to this section originally, the writer adopted the Samaritan chronology   See 65² (note).   Observe that Adam's sin is not regarded as the cause of man's fall and destruction in the deluge.   Then (Gᵍ).   E 'and'   See note on 32⁵   **Raphael** We should, according to 20⁷, expect Gabriel here   **And said** (E). > Gᵍ   **Of which**   Gᵍ breaks off with ἐξ οὗ ἔφαγεν ὁ πατήρ σου

XXXIII 2. Whereon the heaven rests See 18⁶ note.   **3** The portals of the stars here mentioned are described at length in 72-82.   If we are to regard the two accounts as in the

portals out of which they proceed, and wrote down all their outlets, of each individual star by itself, according to their number
and their names, their courses and their positions, and their times
and their months, as Uriel the holy angel who was with me
showed me   4. He showed all things to me and wrote them
down for me   also their names he wrote for me, and their laws
and their companies.

Enoch's Journey to the North.

XXXIV. 1 And from thence I went towards the north to
the ends of the earth, and there I saw a great and glorious
device at the ends of the whole earth   2 And here I saw
three portals of heaven open in the heaven : through each of
them proceed north winds. when they blow there is cold, hail,
frost, snow, dew, and rain.   3. And out of one portal they blow
for good. but when they blow through the other two portals,
†it is with violence and affliction on the earth, and they blow
with violence †

XXXV. And from thence I went towards the west to the
ends of the earth, and saw there three portals of the heaven
open such as I had seen in the †east†, the same number of
portals, and the same number of outlets.

The Journey to the South

XXXVI. 1. And from thence I went to the south to the
ends of the earth, and saw there three open portals of the
heaven   and thence there come dew, rain, †and wind†.   2. And

---

main consistent, the portals of the stars
are also those of the sun and moon, 72³
4 This verse conflicts with the preceding   There Enoch writes down
the various statements   here Uriel
Companies or ' companions' So α β
reads 'functions'

XXXIV. Cf 76   1. Device
(α–m), mt²β read ' wonder '   2.
And > q   North winds (baman-
gala mas'č gui, β)   This ought to be
the meaning, but it is questionable

whether the Ethiopic will admit of it.
The text of θℓ²a is practically the same.
q (bamá'čkala mas'š) = 'winds through
the north '   3 They blow (α–m,
chkla₁a).   mt² abdefox₁b ' it blows '
It is   violence. Probably corrupt
for ' they blow with violence and there
is affliction on the earth .

XXXV The †east† Read ' the
north' Otherwise and preferably we
should transpose this chapter after 36ᵈ

XXXVI 1 Come   Here α–q, β

from thence I went to the east to the ends of the heaven, and
saw here the three eastern portals of heaven open and small
portals above them.   3 Through each of these small portals
pass the stars of heaven and run their course to the west on the
path which is shown to them.   4. And as often as I saw
I blessed always the Lord of Glory, and I continued to bless the
Lord of Glory who has wrought great and glorious wonders, to
show the greatness of His work to the angels and to spirits and
to men, that they might praise His work and all His creation .
that they might see the work of His might and praise the great
work of His hands and bless Him for ever.

add 'the south wind', but this cannot
be right, and here again, as several
times before, we must follow q in omitting this phrase   The fact also that *tu,
abchlx₁u* omit the following 'and'
points in the same direction   *u* emends
'the south wind' into 'from the south'.
†And wind†   As Martin remarks these
words are meaningless here   The text
seems imperfect   Possibly there stood
(cf 84²) originally something like
'And from thence came the south
winds, and when they blow there is
dew and rain'   4 To spirits and
to men (*gqu*[1] though reading nafâsat
(-sâtâ *u*))   Other MSS 'to the spirits
of men'   The work of His might
q reads 'the might of His work'

SECTION II

THE PARABLES. INTRODUCTION

A *Critical Structure* B *Relation of* 37–71 *to the rest of the Book.*
C. *Date.* D. *The Problem and its Solution.*

A. This Section is in a fragmentary condition, and many of the
critical questions connected with it can only be tentatively solved
or merely stated   It consists in the main of three Parables—38–44,
45–57, 58–69. These are introduced by 37 and concluded by 70
which records Enoch's final translation.   71 appears to be out
of place, and belongs to one of the three Parables.   The two visions
recorded in it were witnessed in Enoch's lifetime.   See notes *in loc.*
There are many interpolations.   60 65–69^{25} are confessedly from
the Book of Noah.   39^1 ^{2a} 54^7–55^2 are probably from the same
work.   These interpolations are adapted by their editor to their
adjoining contexts in Enoch   This he does by borrowing characteristic terms, such as 'Lord of Spirits', 'Head of Days', to which,
however, either through ignorance or of set intention he generally
gives a new connotation · see Notes for details

There now remain the following chapters and verses 37–41^2 42
45–54^6 55^3–58 62–63 69^{25}–71   But these passages can hardly have
been derived from the same hand originally   There are traces of
a composite origin Beer, in Kautzsch's *Apok und Pseudep* ii 227,
has drawn attention to the fact that behind the Parables there
appear to lie two distinct sources—one dealing with the Elect One
(10^3 45^3 49$^{2, 4}$ 51^3, ^{5} 52^6, ^{9} 53^6 55^4 61^5, ^{8}, ^{10} 62^1) and the other with
the Son of Man (46$^{2, 3, 4}$ 48^2 62$^{7, 9, 14}$ 63^{11} 69$^{26, 27, 29}$ 70^1 71^{17}),
and that in the former the *angelus interpres* was designated 'the
angel of peace who went with me' and in the latter 'the angel who
went with me' (see 40^2 note)   This observation is just, and even
with the present text it is possible, I think, to distinguish these
sources, though Beer has not attempted it. But these two sources do
not account for the whole of the Parables   In 71 there are two distinct
visions, 71$^{1-4}$ and 71$^{5-17}$, where the *angelus interpres* is Michael and
not either of the former angels, unless we identify him with one of

them, which is indeed possible: see my edition of the *Test. XII Patriarchs*, pp. 39–40. Whence 42 is drawn is a difficulty. But returning to the two sources above-mentioned, we might assign to the 'Son of Man' source and the angelic interpreter—'the angel who went with me.'

40^{3-7}.
$46–48^{7}$.
52^{3-4}.
61^{3-4}.
62^{2}–63.
69^{26-29}.
70–71.

And to the source dealing with the Elect One and the angelic interpreter—'the angel of peace'

38–39.
$40^{1-2,\ 8-10}$.
$41^{1-2,\ 9}$.
45.
48^{8-10}.
$50–52^{1-2,\ 5-9}$.
$53–54^{6}$.
55^{3}–57.
$61^{1-2,\ 5-13}$.
62^{1}.

The above analysis of the sources can of course only be provisional until the Greek version of the original is recovered   The second source differs from the former in recognizing the judgement of the sword, 38^{5}, 48^{8-10}, and the attack of the hostile Gentiles on Jerusalem, 56, the progressive conversion of the Gentiles who had no part in oppressing Israel, 50^{2-4}, and the triumphant return of the Dispersion, 57. 55^{3}–57^{3a} looks like an independent source adapted to a new context.   There is no hint of the judgement of the sword in the first source.

These two sources had much material in common 52^{1-2} apparently belonged to both in some form.   The Elect One and the Son of Man alike judge the kings and the mighty, and the same attributes are to a great extent ascribed to each, save that of pre-existence, which, as it happens, is attributed only to the Son of Man, 48^{2} sqq

B.   Relation of 37–71 to the rest of the book. As all critics are now agreed that the Parables are distinct in origin from the rest of the book, there is no occasion for treating exhaustively the grounds for this conclusion. Accordingly, we shall give here only a few of the chief characteristics which differentiate this Section from all the other Sections of the book. (*a*) **Names of God found only in 37–71.** 'Lord of Spirits' (passim); 'Head of Days' (46^2); 'Lord of the mighty' (63^2); 'Lord of the rich' (63^2); 'Lord of wisdom' (63^2). (*b*) **Angelology.** The four chief angels in 37–71 are Michael, Raphael, Gabriel, and Phanuel. Phanuel is not mentioned elsewhere in the book, which gives Uriel instead. In 14^{11} God is surrounded by Cherubim; but in 61^{10} 71^6 by Cherubim, Seraphim, and Ophannim, angels of power, and angels of principalities. The angel of peace (40^8) is also peculiar to the Parables. (*c*) **Demonology.** In the other Sections of the book the sins of the angels consisted in their lusting after the daughters of men (6–8), but in 54^6 in their becoming subjects of Satan. In 37–71 an evil spirit-world is presupposed from the beginning, but not in the rest of the book. Satan and the Satans, 40^7 53^3 54^6, are not even mentioned in the other Sections. These have access to heaven, 40^7, whereas in the other Sections only good angels have access there. The angels of punishment also are found for the first time in 37–71. (*d*) **The Messianic doctrine** in 37–71 is unique, not only as regards the other Sections of Enoch, but also in Jewish literature as a whole. The Messiah pre-exists, 48^2 (note), from the beginning: he sits on the throne of God, 51^3, and possesses universal dominion, 62^6, all judgement is committed unto him, 69^{27}, and he slays the wicked by the word of his mouth, 62^2. Turning to the other Sections we find that there is no Messiah in 1–36 and in 91–104, while in 83–90 the Messiah is evidently human and possesses none of the great attributes belonging to the Messiah of the Parables. (*e*) **The scene of the Messianic kingdom** in 1–36 is Jerusalem and the earth purified from sin, in 83–90, a heavenly Jerusalem set up by God Himself; in 91–104, Jerusalem and the earth as they are; but in 37–70, a new heaven and a new earth, $45^{4,\,5}$ (note). Again, the duration of the Messianic kingdom in 1–36 is eternal, but the life of its members limited. The duration of the Messianic kingdom in 83–90 is eternal, and the life of its members eternal (?). The duration of the Messianic kingdom in 91–104 is limited, and the life of its members limited. (In 91–104 the real interest centres, not in the Messianic kingdom, but in the future spiritual life of the righteous.) But the duration of the Messianic kingdom in 37–71 is eternal, and the life of its members eternal.

C. Date. From a full review of the evidence, which is given and discussed in the notes on 38⁵, it appears that the kings and the mighty so often denounced in the Parables are the later Maccabean princes and their Sadducean supporters — the later Maccabean princes, on the one hand, and not the earlier, for the blood of the righteous was not shed, as the writer complains (47¹, ², ⁴), before 95 B.C : the later Maccabean princes, on the other hand, and not the Herodians; for (1) the Sadducees were not supporters of the latter, and (2) Rome was not as yet known to the writer as one of the great world-powers—a fact which necessitates an earlier date than 64 B.C., when Rome interposed authoritatively in the affairs of Judaea   Thus the date of the Parables could not have been earlier than 94 B.C. or later than 64 B C. But it is possible to define the date more precisely. As the Pharisees enjoyed un-broken power and prosperity under Alexandra 79–70 B C, the Parables must be assigned either to the years 94–79 or 70–64. Finally, if we consider that 56⁵–57³ ᵃ is an interpolation, and that this passage must have been written before 64 B C., the Parables might reasonably be referred to the years 94–79. See also Gen. Introd.

D. The Problem and its Solution. Seeing that God is a just God, how comes it that wickedness is throned in high places and that righteousness is oppressed? Is there no end to the prosperity and power of unbelieving rulers, and no recompense of reward for the suffering righteous? The author (in the genuine portions) finds the answer in a comprehensive view of the world's history only by tracing evil to its source can the present wrongness of things be understood, and only by pursuing the world's history to its final issues can its present inequalities be justified. The author has no interest save for the moral and spiritual worlds, and this is manifest even in the divine names 'Lord of Spirits', 'Head of Days', 'Most High'. Whole hierarchies of angelic beings appear in 61¹⁰⁻¹². His view is strongly apocalyptic, and follows closely in the wake of Daniel The origin of sin is traced one stage further back than in 1–36. The first authors of sin were the Satans, the adversaries of man, 40⁷ (note). The Watchers fell through becoming subject to these, and leading mankind astray, 54⁶. Punishment was at once meted out to the Watchers, and they were confined in a deep abyss, 54⁵, to await the final judgement, 54⁶ 55⁴ 64. In the meantime sin flourishes in the world : sinners deny the name of the Lord of Spirits, 38² 41². and of His Anointed, 48¹⁰; the kings and the mighty of the earth trust in their sceptre and glory, 63[7], and oppress the elect of the children of God, 62[11]. But the prayer of the righteous ascends, and their blood goes up before the Lord of Spirits crying for vengeance, 47[1]; and the angels unite in the prayer of the righteous, 47[2]. But the oppression of the kings and the mighty will not continue for ever. suddenly the Head of Days will appear and with Him the Son of Man, 46[2, 3, 4] 48[2], to execute judgement upon all alike—on the righteous and wicked, on angel and on man And to this end there will be a Resurrection of all Israel, 51[1] 61[5]; the books of the living will be opened, 47[3], all judgement will be committed unto the Son of Man, 41[9] 69[27]; the Son of Man will possess universal dominion, 62[6], and sit on the throne of his glory, 62[3, 5] 69[27, 29], which is likewise God's throne. 47[3] 51[3]. He will judge the holy angels, 61[8], and the fallen angels, 55[4], the righteous upon earth, 62[3], and the sinners, 62[2], but particularly those who oppress his saints, the kings and the mighty and those who possess the earth, 48[5, 8-9] 53[3] 62[3, 11]. All are judged according to their deeds, for their deeds are weighed in the balance, 41[1]. The fallen angels are cast into a fiery furnace, 54[6], the kings and the mighty confess their sins, and pray for forgiveness, but in vain, 63, and are given into the hands of the righteous, 38[5]; and their destruction will furnish a spectacle to the righteous as they burn and vanish for ever out of sight, 48[9, 10] 62[12] to be tortured in Gehenna by the angels of punishment, 53[3-5] 54[1, 2]. The remaining sinners and godless will be driven from off the face of the earth, 38[3] 41[2] 45[6] The Son of Man will slay them with the word of his mouth, 62[2] Sin and wrongdoing will be banished from the earth, 49[2], and heaven and earth will be transformed, 45[4, 5], and the righteous and elect will have their mansions therein, 39[5] 41[2]. And the light of the Lord of Spirits will shine upon them, 38[4] they will live in the light of eternal life, 58[3]. The Elect One will dwell amongst them, 45[4]. and they will eat and lie down and rise up with him for ever and ever, 62[14] They will be clad in garments of life, 62[15, 16], and shine as fiery lights, 39[7]. And they will seek after light and find righteousness and peace with the Lord of Spirits, 58[4]; and grow in knowledge and righteousness, 58[5].

THE PARABLES.

XXXVII. 1. The second vision which he saw, the vision of wisdom—which Enoch the son of Jared, the son of Mahalalel, the son of Cainan, the son of Enos, the son of Seth, the son of Adam, saw   2. And this is the beginning of the words of wisdom which I lifted up my voice to speak and say to those which dwell on earth : Hear, ye men of old time, and see, ye that come after, the words of the Holy One which I will speak before the Lord of Spirits.   3. It were better to declare (them only) to the men of old time, but even from those that come after we will not withhold the beginning of wisdom.   4. Till the present day such wisdom has never been given by the Lord of Spirits as I have received according to my insight, according to the good pleasure of the Lord of Spirits by whom the lot of

XXXVII. 1. The genealogy with which this Section begins agrees with many other characteristics of the Parables in marking it out as an independent work.   **The second vision.** Apparently the first vision is that referred to in 1^2 'the vision of the Holy One in the heavens'.   **2. Beginning.** The Ethiopic word here and in the next verse could be rendered 'sum'. The phrase may = ראש החכמה. But in Prov 9^{10} it is תחלת חכמה   **And say** (m, β-dy_1a). a-m, dy_1a read 'say'   **Men of old time.** These would embrace Cainan, Mahalalel, and Jared, according to the LXX chronology, which is followed in the Similitudes. See 54^7 (note) 70^4 (note).   **Words of the Holy One** (qml, fv_1b). Other MSS 'holy words'.   **Lord of Spirits.** This expression occurs in 2 Macc. 3^{24} ὁ τῶν πνευμάτων . . . δυνάστης and nowhere else in contemporary or earlier writings that I am aware of   **The way is prepared for it** in Num. 16^{22} 27^{16} 'the God of the Spirits of all flesh'. Cf. also Heb. 12^9 'the Father of Spirits'. The phrase 'Lord of Spirits' is found in 37^4 (twice) 38^2 (twice), ^{4}, ^{6} 39^2, ^{7}

(twice), ^{8}, ^{9} (twice), ^{12} 40^1, ^{2}, ^{4}, ^{5}, ^{6}, ^{7}, ^{10} 41^2 (twice), ^{5}, ^{7} 43^4 (twice) 45^1, ^{2} 46^3 (twice), ^{8}, ^{7}, ^{8} 47^1, ^{2} (twice), ^{4} 48^2, ^{3}, ^{5}, ^{7} (twice), ^{10} (twice) 49^2, ^{4} 50^2, ^{5} (twice), ^{5} 51^3 52^5, ^{9} 53^6 54^6, ^{7} 55^3, ^{4} 57^3 58^4, ^{5} (twice) 59^1, ^{2} 60^6, ^{8}, ^{24}, ^{25} (twice) 61^5, ^{6}, ^{8}, ^{9} (thrice), ^{11}, ^{13} (twice) 62^2, ^{10}, ^{12}, ^{14}, ^{16} (twice) 63^1, ^{2} (twice), ^{7}, ^{12} (twice) 65^9, ^{11} 66^2 67^8, ^{9} 68^4 (twice) 69^{24} (twice), ^{29} 70^1 71^2, ^{17}. We find it in all 104 times, and 28 of these at least in the Interpolations. In the genuine portions it stands in the closest connexion with the character of its context; cf. 39^{12} 40^{1-10} 46^{3-8}, &c ; but in the Interpolations this appropriateness is wanting; cf. 41^6, ^{7} 59^1, ^{2} where only things of the natural world are in question. This leads to the conjecture that this title was introduced into these Interpolations when they were incorporated in the Parables, with a view of adapting them to their new contexts   **3. To the men of old time.** Here for 'ἀλλά I have read la'ella. For construction cf. 95^7.   **4.** Cf. 2 Enoch 47^2 'There have been many books from the beginning of Creation . . . but none shall make things known to you like my writings'. See also our text $93^{10 \text{ sqq}}$.   **By** ^{10}, i. e. 'emqŏdma

eternal life has been given to me.   5. Now three parables
were imparted to me, and I lifted up my voice and recounted
them to those that dwell on the earth.

XXXVIII—XLIV.   The First Parable.

XXXVIII.   *The Coming Judgement of the Wicked.*

1   The first Parable.

> When the congregation of the righteous shall appear,
>
> And sinners shall be judged for their sins,
>
> And shall be driven from the face of the earth :

2.   And when the Righteous One shall appear before the eyes
> of the righteous,
>
> Whose elect works hang upon the Lord of Spirits,

מלפני =. **Eternal life** Cf. Dan 12² חיי עולם. 5. **Parables** = παραβολαί = משלים. The word has already occurred in 1². It is used pretty much in the same sense here as in Num. 32⁷, ¹³ Job 27¹, and means merely an elaborate discourse, whether in the form of a vision, prophecy, or poem. His object is generally parenetic. **Those that dwell on the earth** This phrase (except in 46⁷ and 70¹, where it is merely geographical) is used in a good ethical sense in the genuine portions of this section. Cf. 37² 40⁶, ⁷ 48⁵ So Rev. 14⁶ But in the Interpolations it calls up different associations these are bad in 54⁰ 55¹ 60⁵ 65⁶, ¹² 66¹ 67⁸ and either doubtful or merely geographical in 43⁴ 53¹ 54⁶ 55² 67⁷ 69¹ We should observe that this phrase has an evil significance in Revelation, except in 14⁶ Cf 3¹⁰ 6¹⁰ 8¹³ 11¹⁰ (twice) 13⁸, ¹⁴ 17⁸

XXXVIII. The time of requital is coming. When the kingdom of the righteous appears, and the light of the Lord of Spirits shines on the face of the righteous and elect, where will be the future habitation of the sinners and the godless ?   1 **Congregation**

of the righteous. This phrase, which is peculiar to the Parables, is explained by a comparison of 38³ 53⁶ 62³. Its equivalent occurs in Ps. 149¹ 'congregation of the saints' קהל חסידים, or rather in Ps. 1⁵ עדת צדיקים, 74² עדתך = LXX τῆς συναγωγῆς σου 111¹ Cf Pss. Sol. 17¹³ συναγωγὰς ὁσίων. **Driven from the face of the earth** This form of punishment is elsewhere mentioned in 1¹ 38³ 41² 48⁹, ¹⁰ 53². 2 **The Righteous One** (ṣâdĕq m β). a—m read sĕdĕq 'righteousness'. Though less well attested the former is preferable. Almost the same connexion of thought is found in 53⁶. The Messiah is variously named 'the Righteous and Elect One,' 53⁵, 'the Elect One of righteousness and of faith,' 39⁵, 'the Elect One,' 40⁵ 45³ 49², ⁴ 51³, ⁵ 52⁶, ⁹ 53⁶ 55⁴ 61⁵, ⁸, ¹⁰ 62¹ ; 'the Messiah,' 48¹⁰ 52⁴ For other designations see note on 48². Observe that as the members of the kingdom are 'the righteous', so the Messiah is 'the Righteous One', cf. 'The Elect', 'The Elect One' **Works** *g* reads 'hope and works'. **Hang upon the Lord of Spirits** Cf 40⁵ 46⁸. With this expression of Judith 8²⁴ ἐξ ἡμῶν κρέμαται

And light shall appear to the righteous and the elect who
dwell on the earth,

Where then will be the dwelling of the sinners,

And where the resting-place of those who have denied the
Lord of Spirits?

It had been good for them if they had not been born.

3. When the secrets of the righteous shall be revealed and the
sinners judged,

And the godless driven from the presence of the righteous
and elect,

4. From that time those that possess the earth shall no longer
be powerful and exalted:

And they shall not be able to behold the face of the holy,
For the Lord of Spirits has caused His light to appear

ἡ ψυχὴ αὐτῶν Perhaps תלא or תלה stood in the original. **Light shall appear.** Cf. Is 9² 60¹ Denied the Lord of Spirits. For 'denied' *g* reads 'outraged'. This charge is frequently brought against the sinners it is in fact 'the very head and front of their offending'. Cf. 41² 45² 46⁷ 48¹⁰ 63⁷. Cf St Jude 4. They deny likewise the heavenly world, 45¹; the Messiah, 48¹⁰, the spirit of God, 67¹⁰, the righteous judgement, 60⁶. The righteous on the other hand believe in the name of the Lord, 43¹ Observe that this phrase is taken over into the Interpolations, 67⁸, ¹⁰. **It had been good for them, &c.** A familiar Jewish expression = מוטב היה לו Wajikra R. 26 (quoted by Edersheim, *Life of Jesus the Messiah*, ii 120) Cf. 2 Bar. 10⁶ 4 Ezra 4¹² 2 Enoch 41² St. Matt 26²⁴ **3. When the secrets of the righteous shall be revealed** The blessings in store for the righteous, the heritage of faith, are still hidden, 58⁵, but they will one day be revealed. The Messiah himself is hidden with the Lord of Spirits, 62⁷. Cf. Mark 4¹¹. **And the sinners** (*g*). Other MSS om 'and'

and make this clause the apodosis 'the sinners shall be judged'. But the parallelism supports *g*, and we have seen, where the Greek is preserved, that *g* is not infrequently right when standing alone. **4. The** supremacy and oppression of the earth's rulers and great ones are speedily drawing to a close This is the constant theme of the Parables, 46⁴⁻⁸ 48⁸⁻¹⁰ 53⁵ 62¹⁻¹² 63, and has been taken over into the Interpolations, 67⁸⁻¹³, and this is one of the leading characteristics which distinguish 37–69 from 91–104. With the rulers of the earth as such the latter Section has practically no concern **From that time** The MSS. prefix 'and' which I take to be the word introducing the apodosis. **Has caused His light to appear.** I have emended tar'ěja = 'is seen' into 'ar'aja = 'has caused to appear'. This emendation is required by the fact that 'the Lord of Spirits' is in the nom. in *a, d,* and 'His light' in the acc. in *g*. *β-d* reads 'the light of the Lord of Spirits is seen'. This light is at once spiritual and physical the nearness of God's presence

On the face of the holy, righteous, and elect.

5. Then shall the kings and the mighty perish

transfigures the countenance and person of His saints. Light in all its forms is the blessing of the kingdom The righteous will have light, and joy, and peace, 5⁷, and the light of God shining upon them, 1⁸. In the Parables the heaven will be transformed into an eternal light, 45⁴; and light will appear unto the righteous, 38²; and the light of days will abide upon them, 50¹, they will abide in the light of the sun and in the light of eternal life, 58³, their faces will be illuminated with the light of the Lord of Spirits, 38⁴, and they will seek after light and find righteousness, and the light of truth will be mighty for evermore, 58³⁻⁶. This idea is still further developed in 91-108. The righteous belong to the generation of light, 108¹¹, and will be clad in light, 108¹², and will walk in eternal light, 92⁴, and will be resplendent and shine as the lights of heaven for evermore, 108¹⁸ 104². The holy, righteous, and elect. So α, *def hluyιa abcopιχ ιb* read 'the holy and righteous and elect'. The latter has the support of 48¹ where it recurs. 5 Then (q) Other MSS. 'and then'. The kings and the mighty (α t²β the mighty kings'. Cf 62¹, ³, ⁶, ⁹ 63¹, ², ¹² 67⁸, ¹² These designations are practically synonymous in the Parables. The phrase 'mighty kings' which appears often in Dillmann's text is without the support of the best MSS. except in 55⁴, and there I feel we must regard the text as corrupt, and read 'the kings and the mighty' This better text removes, as we shall find, at least one formidable difficulty in the interpretation Who then are these kings and mighty ones? The facts taken together point decidedly to unbelieving native rulers and Sadducees. They

have denied the Lord and his Anointed, 48¹⁰, and a heavenly world, 45¹, they persecute the houses of His congregations, i. e. the Theocratic community, 46⁸; and they are an offence thereto, an offence on the removal of which the Theocratic ideal will be realized, 53⁶, they do not acknowledge from whom their power is derived, 46⁵; but trust in their riches, 46⁷; and place their hope in their sceptre and glory, 63⁷, they have made the righteous their servants, 46⁷, and outraged God's children, 62¹¹, and shed their blood, 47¹, ² Accordingly they will have to stand before the Messiah whom they have denied, when He judges the angels, 61⁸ 55⁴, and the righteous, 62⁵(β)· and the sinners, 62², and they will be terrified, 62⁶; and fall down and worship the Messiah, 62⁹, and acknowledge the righteousness of their judgement, 63⁹; and pray for a respite in order to repent, 63¹, and express their thanksgiving of faith, 63⁶, but their prayer will not be heard, and the Lord of Spirits, 62¹², and the righteous, 48⁹, will execute judgement upon them, and their destruction will form a spectacle over which the righteous will rejoice, 62¹², and they will be delivered over to the angels of punishment, 62¹¹, and will descend into the tortures of hell, 63¹⁰ Only one statement seems to point to heathen rulers, i. e. 'their faith is in the gods which they have made with their hands', 46⁷ But this is only a strong expression for the heathen or Sadducean attitude of the Maccabean princes and their supporters, and with it we might aptly compare Pss Sol 1⁸ 8¹⁴ 17¹⁷, wherein the same persons are charged with surpassing the heathen in idolatries There is a like exaggeration of the

And be given into the hands of the righteous and holy.

wickedness of the Sadducees in 99⁷ 104⁹
The kings and the mighty in the text,
therefore, are native rulers and Sadducees. We thus agree with Köstlin,
Theol Jahrb 1856, 268 sqq , and Dillmann, Herzog, *R E* XII. 352, in identifying these princes with the last of the
decaying Asmonean dynasty. The
Herodian dynasty was not supported
by the Sadducees, and thus may be
left out of consideration Further,
as there are no references to Rome
in the Parables, it cannot as yet
have made its power to be felt in
Palestine , and the Parables, therefore, must have been written before
64 B C , when Rome interposed in favour
of Aristobulus II. Baldensperger, *Das
Selbstbewusstsein Jesu* (p 12), indeed,
tries to show that there are references
to the Roman power, but his main
contention, that the falling Asmoneans
could hardly be designated as ' mighty
kings ', is already answered on critical
grounds : the phrase ' mighty kings '
does not belong to the true text The
lower limit is thus 64 B C , and the
higher may be reasonably fixed at 94.
The differences between the Maccabees
and the Pharisees, which had already
grown important under John Hyrcanus
with his Sadducean policy, were further
developed under Aristobulus I, and in
the early years of Alex. Jannaeus were
intensified into an irreconcilable antagonism. This antagonism *first* issued
in bloodshed about 95 B C , when 6,000
Pharisees were put to death because
they insulted Alex. Jannaeus for failing
to comply with their views on ritual
This fact explains the writer's demand
for vengeance for the murder of the
righteous, 47¹, ², ⁴ Subsequent years
only embittered the strife between the
Pharisees and the Asmonean head of
the Sadducees, and provoked a civil
war in which 50,000 Jews fell Weary

of the struggle, Jannaeus asked the
Pharisees to name their conditions of
peace . their answer was laconic and
irreconcilable, 'Thy death', but in
the subsequent strife they were for the
time crushed into impotence. Owing to
the multitudes of Pharisees slain by
Jannaeus, he came to be called ' the
slayer of the pious '. With the accession of Alexandra 79, however, the
Pharisees became masters of the nation,
and peace prevailed till 70, when again
the nation was rent in twain and
plunged into devastating and bloody
wars, through the fraternal strife of
Hyrcanus II and Aristobulus II To
a devout Pharisee the Maccabees with
their Sadducean and Hellenic principles
might well appear as enemies of the
Theocratic community during the years
94-79 or 70-64 To one or other of
these periods, therefore, we assign the
composition of the Parables Perish
and $> q$ Be given into the
hands of the righteous. This phrase
would seem to indicate the period
of the sword, when the righteous
were themselves to slay the wicked.
But this would be unsuitable here ,
the judgement is catastrophic and
forensic The Son of Man is judge,
and his judgements are executed by the
angels of punishment, 41² 62¹¹. This
phrase recurs in 48⁹ , but there the
context requires us to understand the
casting of the kings into Gehenna In
50², where we again find this idea un-
mistakably, the difficulty is obviated
by the fact that 50 is most probably an
interpolation. Either, then, we have
here an inconsistent feature introduced
by the original writer, or else the phrase
is only to be taken in a general sense,
as expressing the triumph of the
righteous. Righteous and holy.
This designation of the members of
the kingdom is found also in 48¹, ⁴, ⁷

6. And thenceforward none shall seek for themselves mercy
from the Lord of Spirits:
For their life is at an end.

The Abode of the Righteous and of the Elect One: the Praises
of the Blessed.

XXXIX. [1. And it †shall come to pass in those days ·that
elect and holy children † will descend from the high heaven, and
their seed † will become one with the children of men.   2. And
in those days Enoch received books of zeal and wrath, and books
of disquiet and expulsion.]

And mercy shall not be accorded to them, saith the Lord of
Spirits.

3. And in those days a whirlwind carried me off from the
earth,
And set me down at the end of the heavens.

4. And there I saw another vision, the dwelling-places of the
holy,

51^2 (65^{12}).   6 Thenceforward q reads 'there'.   Seek for themselves ($a, cov_1 b$) Other MSS. 'seek'. The 'for themselves' could also be translated 'for them'; but the dative here is clearly the Hebrew *dativus ethicus*

XXXIX 1-2ª. This passage is obviously an interpolation   It has nothing to do with its present context and appears to be a fragment of the older book of Enoch, such as we find in chapters 6-36   Here manifestly 39^{2b} 'And mercy shall not be accorded to them, saith the Lord of Spirits' should follow immediately on 38^6 This interpolation refers to the descent of the Watchers to unite themselves with the daughters of men

XXXIX 1 And it shall come to pass.   Here and in the rest of this verse we should have past and not future tenses   This may be due to the interpolator who made these changes in order to adapt it to the time of the

adjoining context.   Elect and holy children . from the high heaven. For 'elect and holy' q reads 'holy and elect'.   For the idea cf. 106^{13} 'Some from the heights of heaven'.   For the epithet 'elect' cf 1 Tim. 5^{21} 'the elect angels'.   Schodde compares Tob 8^{15} **2 Enoch received books of zeal,** &c. As we shall find later, sometimes an angel dictates to Enoch, at others the angel himself writes the book and commits it to Enoch.   Zeal and wrath q trans.   3. Carried me off.   This seems to be recounted as a real translation of Enoch, as in 52^1; cf. 2 Kings 2^{11}, and not as a mere incident in a dream, as in $14^8, 9$.   **4.** Dwelling-places. This could be rendered 'dwellings' or 'abiding-places', see $39^{7,8}$ 41^2 2 Enoch 61^2 John 14^2. The vision here (39^{4-12}) set forth is prophetic, but there are many difficulties in the interpretation which we can surmount only by bearing in mind that

And the resting-places of the righteous.

5. Here mine eyes saw their dwellings with His righteous angels,
And their resting-places with the holy.

And they petitioned and interceded and prayed for the children of men,

And righteousness flowed before them as water,

And mercy like dew upon the earth :
Thus it is amongst them for ever and ever.

6 *a.* And in that place mine eyes saw the Elect One of righteousness and of faith,

7 *a.* And I saw his dwelling-place under the wings of the Lord of Spirits.

6 *b.* And righteousness shall prevail in his days,
And the righteous and elect shall be without number before Him for ever and ever

7 *b.* And all the righteous and elect before Him shall be †strong† as fiery lights,

what we have here to deal with is a *vision* of the future Messianic kingdom, and that we must not press the details; for in this, as in visions frequently, there is no exact observance of the unities of time and place. No one individual period is indicated; for the fact that the Messiah is surrounded by all His righteous and elect ones shows that the history of the world is closed, and the final judgement already passed; yet this is impossible, as the angels are still praying on behalf of men. Nor from this chapter, taken by itself, can we argue as to the locality indicated by the vision At first sight it seems to be heaven, as the Messiah and the righteous are under the wings of the Lord of Spirits, yet this is impossible, as the history of mankind is not yet consummated, and the Messiah appears only to carry out its consummation. The chief inference that we can legitimately draw is that the Messianic com-

munity will one day be composed of both angels and men, under the rule of the Messiah and the immediate protection of the Lord of Spirits.   5 His righteous angels (*a*)   *β* 'the angels'   Righteousness flowed . as water. Cf. Amos 5²⁴ See also 49¹ 97⁹.   6-7 The text is slightly confused   By placing 7ᵃ before 6ᵇ I think I have recovered the original. 6 That place (*a-m*). *m*, *t*²*β* 'those days'   The Elect One (*a-q*) *q*, *β-m* 'the place of the elect'. See note on 38². 'Elect One' = בְּחִיר. Cf Is. 41⁸, ⁹ 42¹ Luke 23³⁵.   7ᵃ His dwelling - place (*gm*) *qtuβ* 'their dwelling-place'. θᵇ In his days (*a*). *t*²*β* 'in their days'.   7ᵇ Be †strong† (jᵉthᵉjalû *a-m*) *mt*ᵃ*β-u* jetlaḥajû = 'be beautiful', not 'shine' as it has hitherto been taken. The latter is probably a correction of the former. *a-m* = יִחְקָן, which may be corrupt for יוֹהִירוּ = 'shine'. Thus 'the righteous

And their mouth shall be full of blessing,

And their lips extol the name of the Lord of Spirits,
And righteousness before Him shall never fail,
[And uprightness shall never fail before Him].

8. There I wished to dwell,
And my spirit longed for that dwelling-place:

And there heretofore hath been my portion,
For so has it been established concerning me before the Lord
of Spirits.

9. In those days I praised and extolled the name of the Lord
of Spirits with blessings and praises, because He hath destined
me for blessing and glory according to the good pleasure of the
Lord of Spirits. 10. For a long time my eyes regarded that
place, and I blessed Him and praised Him, saying 'Blessed is
He, and may He be blessed from the beginning and for evermore.
11. And before Him there is no ceasing. He knows before the
world was created what is for ever and what will be from generation unto generation. 12. Those who sleep not bless Thee ·
they stand before Thy glory and bless, praise, and extol, saying:
" Holy, holy, holy, is the Lord of Spirits: He filleth the earth
with spirits." ' 13. And here my eyes saw all those who sleep
not: they stand before Him and bless and say . ' Blessed be
Thou, and blessed be the name of the Lord for ever and

. shall shine as fiery lights ', i e the
stars; cf Dan 12⁹ This restoration
is not possible in Aramaic. And uprightness, &c Bracketed as a doublet
of the preceding line *abdwa ia*
—very second rate MSS.—omit it.
8. Enoch predestined to a place in the
kingdom. And there (*q*, *n*). Other
MSS ' there '. 9. The good
pleasure of the Lord. In 37⁴ and
here the free grace of God is brought
forward, but not exclusively, for, like
a true Pharisee, man's part in salvation
is emphasized in 37⁴ ' according to my
insight '. 11 Before Him there
is no ceasing. Past, present, and
future are before Him. 12.

Those who sleep not cf 39¹³ 40²
61¹² This designation is taken over
into the Interpolations, 71⁷. In the
note on 1⁵ I have identified them with
the ' Watchers '. Holy, holy, holy,
is the Lord of Spirits. The change
in the trisagion, ls 6³, is in keeping
with the character of the entire section.
13. All. + *q* ' the wakeful ones '.

13—XL. Enoch next sees all the
chief angels and thousands of thousands
of angels who stood before the throne
of God, and recounts this, not as a prophetic vision, but as an actual experience. 14 The change of face
here is not to be understood as a trans-
figuration, as in Ascensio Isaiae 7²⁵:

ever.'   14. And my face was changed; for I could no longer behold.

The Four Archangels.

XL. 1. And after that I saw thousands of thousands and ten thousand times ten thousand, I saw a multitude beyond number and reckoning, who stood before the Lord of Spirits.   2. And on the four sides of the Lord of Spirits I saw four presences, different from those that sleep not, and I learnt their names · for the angel who went with me made known to me their names, and showed me all the hidden things.

3. And I heard the voices of those four presences as they uttered praises before the Lord of glory.   4. The first voice blesses the Lord of Spirits for ever and ever.   5. And the

Enoch is '*blinded* by excess of light'. For (*a*). *t²β—e* 'till'

XL. 1. **Thousands of thousands and ten thousand times ten thousand** This phrase is taken over exactly into the Interpolations, 60¹ 71⁸, though the phrase was of course a current one, owing to Dan 7¹⁰ Cf Rev. 5¹¹   2 There are higher angels than those that sleep not these are the four angels of the presence—מַלְאֲכֵי הַפָּנִים—so called from Is 63⁹ Their names here are Michael, Raphael, Gabriel, and Phanuel, and the same list is carried over into the Interpolations, 71⁸ In later Judaism we find Uriel instead of Phanuel. In 9¹ the names of the four chiefs are Michael, Gabriel, Uriel, and Raphael In 20 there are seven chief angels enumerated, Uriel, Raphael, Raguel, Michael, Saraqael, Gabriel, and Remiel Thus, Michael, Raphael, and Gabriel belong in common to 20 and 40, but the functions respectively assigned them in these chapters are irreconcilable.   In 90²¹ there is a reference to seven chief angels in 81⁵ 90³¹ three angels are mentioned who were charged with the escort of Enoch in 87², ³ we find again four. It

would be a mere waste of time to attempt to reconcile the angelology of these various passages On Angelology see Schwab, *Vocabulaire de l'Angelologie*, 1897, supplement, 1899, *Jewish Encyclopaedia*, 1 583-597, Weber², *Jud Theol* 1897   **That sleep not** (*a—m*). *t²β* 'that stand' **The angel who went with me** This angel is similarly named in 43³ 46² 52⁵, ⁴ 61⁵, whereas we have the 'angel of peace' in 40⁸ 52⁵ 53⁴ 54⁴ 56², and 'the angel' in 61² 64² There is generally a certain fitness in the designation 'angel of peace' in the contexts, where it occurs in contrast to the wicked angels and the angels of punishment This designation has also been taken over into the Interpolations, 60²⁴, it is already found in the T. Dan. 6⁵ T Ash. 6⁶ T Benj. 6¹ The origin of the phrase is probably to be traced to Is 33⁷, as that verse was, according to Jerome, understood of the angels, and מַלְאֲכֵי שָׁלוֹם would in that case = 'angels of peace'. Cf Rosenmuller's *Scholia in loc*   4 The first presence, Michael, has for his task the praise of the Lord of Spirits, as his name indicates, מִיכָאֵל   In ver 9 he is 'the merciful and long-suffering'. 5 The second presence is Raphael, who

second voice I heard blessing the Elect One and the elect ones
who hang upon the Lord of Spirits.   6. And the third voice
I heard **pray and intercede** for those who dwell on the earth
and **supplicate** in the name of the Lord of Spirits.   7. And
I heard the fourth voice fending off the Satans and forbidding
them to come before the Lord of Spirits to accuse them who
dwell on the earth.   8. After that I asked the angel of peace
who went with me, who showed me everything that is hidden :
'Who are these four presences which I have seen and whose

praises the Elect and the elect ones
Conformably to his name (from רפא,
to heal) he is appointed to heal the
wounds and ills of men (ver. 9). cf
Tobit 12¹⁴ 'God sent me (Raphael) *to*
heal thee', and 3¹⁷ 'Raphael was sent
to heal them both'. In Rabbinic writings he was the power that presided
over medicine; cf. Eisenmeng *Entd.*
Jud. ii 380. See also 10⁷ 20³. **The**
Elect One. This designation of the
Messiah comes from Is. 42¹ Its later
use seems to be confined to the Parables
(see 38²) and St Luke 9³⁵ οὖτός
ἐστιν ὁ υἱός μου ὁ ἐκλελεγμένος = 'the
Elect One' (W. and H). This, the
correct text, has been preserved in the
Ethiopic N T.' St. Luke 23³⁵ 'the
Christ of God the Elect One'. **And**
the elect ones. *q* 'of the elect ones'
6 The third presence is Gabriel,
whose task is that of intercession on
behalf of the inhabiters of the earth
Of Test Lev 3⁵ 'In it are the archangels who minister and make pro-
pitiation to the Lord for all the
sins of the righteous', As the hero
or strong one of God (גבר and אל)
he is naturally set over all the powers
(ver. 9). **Pray and intercede . . .**
supplicate. These verbs are in the
plural in all MSS. but *d* **Those**
who dwell, &c.: see 37⁵.   **7.**
The fourth is Phanuel, who is set over
the repentance and hope of the inheri-

tors of eternal life (ver. 9). He pre-
vents the Satans from appearing before
the Lord of Spirits to accuse men   The
Satans appear here for the first time in
Enoch, 40⁷   They seem to belong to
a counter kingdom of evil, ruled by
a chief called Satan, 53³. They existed
as evil agencies before the fall of the
Watchers ; for the guilt of the latter
consisted in becoming subject to Satan,
54⁶   This view harmonizes exactly
with that of Gen. 3¹ combined with
6¹⁻⁴, These Satans had the right of
access into heaven, 40⁷ (cf. Job 1⁶
Zech 3)—a privilege denied to the
Watchers, 13⁵ 14⁵   Their functions
were threefold : they tempted to evil,
69⁴ ⁶, they accused the dwellers upon
earth, 40⁷, they punished the condemned.   In this last character they
are technically called 'angels of punishment', 53⁸ 56¹ 62¹¹ 63¹ ; this designation has been taken over into the
Interpolations of 66¹ (note). The Talmud (cf. Weber, *Jud. Theol* 251-254°
does not draw this clear line of demar-
cation between the Satans and the fallen
angels, but rather confuses their attributes just as in ch. 69. For the close
connexion between the Demonology of
Enoch and the N.T. see Gen. Introduction   8 Angel of peace. See
note on ver. 2 . also Test. Dan. 6⁵ note
T. Ash 6⁶ Test. Benj 6¹.   **Hidden**
+*abcdex* 'and I said unto him'.

words I have heard and written down?'   9. And he said to
me: 'This first is Michael, the merciful and long-suffering: and
the second, who is set over all the diseases and all the wounds of
the children of men, is Raphael: and the third, who is set over
all the powers, is Gabriel: and the fourth, who is set over the
repentance unto hope of those who inherit eternal life, is named
Phanuel.'   10. And these are the four angels of the Lord of
Spirits and the four voices I heard in those days.

XLI. 1. And after that I saw all the secrets of the heavens,
and how the kingdom is divided, and how the actions of men
are weighed in the balance.   2. And there I saw the mansions
of the elect and the mansions of the holy, and mine eyes saw
there all the sinners being driven from thence which deny the
name of the Lord of Spirits, and being dragged off: and they
could not abide because of the punishment which proceeds from
the Lord of Spirits.

9 Michael (a)   β 'the holy Michael'.
Gabriel (a).   β 'the holy Gabriel'.
Repentance unto hope (a–q, dghklno
vwy).   q 'repentance unto repentance',
abcex 'repentance and hope'.   Our
text = τῆς μετανοίας εἰς ἐλπίδα   Cf
Acts 11¹⁸ μετάνοιαν εἰς ζωὴν 2 Cor. 7¹⁰
μετάνοιαν εἰς σωτηρίαν   Is named
(a).   β 'is'   10. Lord of Spirits
(a)   β ' the Most High God '.

XLI 1 The kingdom is divided.
What 'the kingdom' means here is
doubtful.   Dillmann takes it to mean
the Messianic kingdom; Schodde, the
kingdom of this world. Can it refer
to the division of heaven into seven
parts?   The actions of men are
weighed: cf 61⁸   The idea is derived
from the O T, where Job (31⁶) prays
to be weighed in an even balance, and
the spirits of men are weighed by God,
Prov. 16² 21² 24¹², and the wicked are
found wanting, Ps 62⁹ Dan 5²⁷ Pss.
Sol. 5⁶.   In Enoch, as in the O T, this
idea is not incompatible with the
doctrine of divine grace; but in the

Talmud it is absolutely materialized,
and man's salvation depends on a literal
preponderance of his good deeds over
his bad ones : see Weber, *Jud Theol.*
279–284. This weighing of man's deeds
goes on daily (idem 283). But as the
results of such judgements were neces-
sarily unknown, there could not fail to
be much uneasiness, and to allay this
the doctrine of Abraham's meritorious
righteousness was in due time developed, in virtue of which all natural
descendants of Abraham through Jacob
became entitled to salvation (Weber,
292–297). This doctrine, though as
yet unknown in Enoch, was a popular
belief in N.T. times; cf. Matt. 3⁹.
2 And¹⁰ (q). > a–qβ   The sinners
being driven from thence. see 38¹.
Deny the name of the Lord of
Spirits: see 38².   3–8. These
verses are, it is obvious, alien in spirit
and position to the context; they belong in character and detail to 43¹, ²
44 59 69¹⁸⁻²⁵ : see 43. They may,
however, belong to the Parables, since

XLI. 3-9. *Astronomical Secrets.*

3. And there mine eyes saw the secrets of the lightning
and of the thunder, and the secrets of the winds, how they are
divided to blow over the earth, and the secrets of the clouds and
dew, and there I saw from whence they proceed in that place
and from whence they saturate the dusty earth.   4. And there
I saw closed chambers out of which the winds are divided, the
chamber of the hail and winds, the chamber of the mist, and of
the clouds, and the cloud thereof hovers over the earth from the
beginning of the world.   5. And I saw the chambers of the sun
and moon, whence they proceed and whither they come again, and
their glorious return, and how one is superior to the other, and
their stately orbit, and how they do not leave their orbit, and they
add nothing to their orbit and they take nothing from it, and
they keep faith with each other, in accordance with the oath

Jewish mystics were interested in these
questions   3 The lightning and
thunder are treated of repeatedly see
17³ 43¹⁻² 44 59 60¹³⁻¹⁵, cf Job 38²⁴,
²⁶, ³⁵   The secrets of the winds
On the manifold functions of the winds
in Enoch see 18¹⁻⁵ 34-36 77.   Dusty
earth (*gʲ·ᵘ*).   *mt²β* 'dust of the earth'
4 And there (*nqtβ*)   *qⁿ* 'there'.
The chamber of the winds..mist..
clouds, &c   These conceptions rest on
the poetical fancies of Job 38²²   The
writers in Enoch conceive all the
natural powers, as thunder and lightning, rain, hail, dew, sun and moon,
&c., as dwelling in their respective
chambers.   And winds (*ahovₗb*)
β-hovₗb 'and'   And of the clouds
(*qtuᵘ²β-a*) > *guᵘ²*.   The cloud thereof, *i. e* the cloud of mist.   Have we
here a reference to Gen. 1² or to 2⁶
(Beer)?   5 For the teaching of
Enoch on the sun and moon see 72⁶
Their glorious return, i. e. from west
to east on the other side of the firmament, or, according to 72⁵, round by

way of the north   The perfect regularity with which the sun and moon
traverse their orbits is here emphasized,
as in 74¹² is that of the sun and stars.
Yet in 80⁴ it is said that the moon will
become irregular.   We shall find, however, that 80 is an interpolation.   The
oath.   A certain degree of consciousness seems to be attributed to the sun,
moon, and stars. The sun and moon
are subject only to God, 41⁶; they give
thanks and praise, and rest not, for to
them thanksgiving is rest, 41⁷, cf. 69²⁴.
God calls the stars by name and they
answer, 43¹, they keep faith with each
other, 43², they are weighed, as men,
in a righteous balance, 43²; the disobedient stars are punished, 18¹³⁻¹⁶.   In
72-79 various functions regarding the
division of time are assigned to them.
In the Persian religion the stars were
regarded as embodied existences divided
into troops, each under its own leader,
*Herzog*², *R. E.* xi. 235   This theory
would suit 82⁹⁻²⁰ perfectly   It must be
confessed, however, that the conception

by which they are bound together.   6. And first the sun goes forth and traverses his path according to the commandment of the Lord of Spirits, and mighty is His name for ever and ever. 7. And after that I saw the hidden and the visible path of the moon, and she accomplishes the course of her path in that place by day and by night—the one holding a position opposite to the other before the Lord of Spirits.

And they give thanks and praise and rest not;
For unto them is their thanksgiving rest.

8. For the sun changes oft for a blessing or a curse,
And the course of the path of the moon is light to the righteous,
And darkness to the sinners in the name of the Lord,
Who made a separation between the light and the darkness,
And divided the spirits of men,
And strengthened the spirits of the righteous,
In the name of His righteousness.

9. For no angel hinders and no power is able to hinder; for He appoints a judge for them all and he judges them all before Him.

The Dwelling-places of Wisdom and of Unrighteousness.

XLII. 1. Wisdom found no place where she might dwell;

varies **By which they are bound together.** So *k* alone reading zaḥabĕrû —probably a fortunate conjecture. Very early the original reading zaḥabĕrû was corrupted into zaḥadarû (*a, ek²o ₁b*), and later into zanabarû (*abaelfkln ₁a*). Hence there is no need to assume a corrupt on in the Greek or Hebrew   **6 Traverses.** *η, ι* 'returns'.   **7. Hidden . . . path** of the moon,** ι e. when the moon is invisible : see 78-74.   **Before** + *mt¹u* 'the glory of'.   **8 The sun** (*a,py*) *m, t²β-py* read 'the shining sun'. **Divided the spirits of men.** There seems to be an actual predestination here spoken of. This division into children of light and darkness is in the past the spirits of the righteous are strengthened in the present.   **9 No angel hinders and no power** (*mη, t²uβ-y*). *gt¹, y* read 'neither angel nor power'.   **He appoints a judge for them all.** Here I follow *g* in reading 'He appoints', and ₁a in taking 'a judge' in the acc   The rest of the MSS. read 'the judge sees them all'. It would also be possible to render the latter reading 'the Judge of all sees'. The text is uncertain. If the reading adopted in the translation is right the judge appointed is the Messiah. This verse is to be read directly after 41²; cf Acts 17³¹.

XLII. As has been already recognized, this chapter is a fragment, and out

Then a dwelling-place was assigned her in the heavens.

2. Wisdom went forth to make her dwelling among the children
   of men,
   And found no dwelling-place
   Wisdom returned to her place,
   And took her seat among the angels.

3. And unrighteousness went forth from her chambers:
   Whom she sought not she found,
   And dwelt with them,
   As rain in a desert
   And dew on a thirsty land.

XLIII—XLIV. *Astronomical Secrets.*

XLIII. 1. And I saw other lightnings and the stars of heaven,
and I saw how He called them all by their names and they
hearkened unto Him.   2. And I saw how they are weighed in
a righteous balance according to their proportions of light: (I saw)
the width of their spaces and the day of their appearing, and how
their revolution produces lightning · and (I saw) their revolution

of connexion with its present context
where in the present book of Enoch it
should stand, I do not know.   1, 2
The praise of wisdom was a favourite
theme. Wisdom was regarded as having her dwelling-place in heaven, 84⁸
Job 28¹²⁻¹⁴, ²⁰⁻²⁴ Baruch 3²⁹ Sir. 24¹;
and as coming to earth and desir-
ing to make her abode with men, Prov.
1²⁰ ˢᵠᵠ· 8 9¹⁻¹⁰ Sir. 24⁷, but as men
refused to receive her, cf. 1 En. 94⁵,
she returned to heaven But in the
Messianic times she will return, and
will be poured out as water in abundance, 49¹, and the thirsty will drink
to the full of wisdom, 48¹, she will be
bestowed on the elect, 5⁸ 91¹⁰, cf. 2
Bar. 44¹⁴ 4 Ezra 8⁵², and the spirit of
Wisdom will abide in the Messiah the
Elect One, 49⁸ We are reminded in
some measure here of the Prologue of
St. John   Went forth (*a, β–
abcdrw*)   *abcr* 'came'.   3. The

different welcome which the wicked
give to unrighteousness intensifies
their guilt in respect to wisdom. They
received not wisdom when she came
unto them; but they took home unto
themselves unrighteousness though she
sought them not
  XLIII, XLIV.   These chapters
belong to the same class as 41³⁻⁸.
Though in my first edition I treated
these sections on natural phenomena as
interpolations I no longer do so Their
presence, however, frequently deranges
the context. On the other hand we
see from Job, Sirach, and Wisdom that
the wise in Israel were interested alike
in ethical and cosmic questions.
  XLIII. 1 Called them all by
their names   cf Ps. 147⁴ Is 40²⁶
Bar 3⁸⁴.   2 Weighed in a righteous balance. On the conscious
existence attributed to the stars see
41⁵.   How their revolution pro-

according to the number of the angels, and (how) they keep faith with each other.   3. And I asked the angel who went with me who showed me what was hidden: 'What are these?'   4. And he said to me: 'The Lord of Spirits hath showed thee their parabolic meaning (lit. 'their parable'): these are the names of the holy who dwell on the earth and believe in the name of the Lord of Spirits for ever and ever.'

XLIV. Also another phenomenon I saw in regard to the lightnings: how some of the stars arise and become lightnings and cannot part with their new form.

XLV—LVII. The Second Parable.

The Lot of the Apostates: the New Heaven and the New Earth.

XLV. 1. And this is the Second Parable concerning those who deny the name of the dwelling of the holy ones and the Lord of Spirits.

2. And into the heaven they shall not ascend,

And on the earth they shall not come:

Such shall be the lot of the sinners

duces lightning ($gql^1(m\kappa)$). $t^2\beta$ 'and revolution ∙ how one flash of lightning produces another'.   8. The angel who went with me who showed me what was hidden cf. 46². Taken over into the Interpolations, 60¹¹. 3, 4. There is some mysterious connexion between the stars and the holy; whereby the stars represent the holy; cf. Dan 8¹⁰. Does it mean that the holy will be as numerous as the stars' or as bright as the stars? cf. 104² Dan 12³ Matt 13⁴³. There was a close connexion between the stars and the angels in the O. T.; cf. Job 38⁷, where the morning stars are undoubtedly angels; cf. also Deut 4¹⁹.   4. Holy (a). β 'righteous'. Believe in the name: cf 39⁶ 'the Elect One . . . of faith', 58⁶ 'the inheritance of faith', 61⁴ 'the measures given to faith', 61¹¹ 'in the spirit of faith'.

Contrast the *denial* of sinners, 38²

XLIV. The reference here is to shooting stars, ἀστέρες διαθέοντες, Arist. *Meteor.* 1 4. Lightning in general is produced by the quick movement of the stars, 43²; but some of the stars at times are transformed wholly into lightning

XLV 1 It is idle to expect an accurate description of the contents of the Parable from the opening verse or superscription. We find none such in 38¹, ²; nor yet in 58¹, ². For a summary of the thought of the Parables see pp. 67-68.   Those who deny the name of the dwelling. see 38² (note).   The Lord of Spirits (a). β 'of the Lord of Spirits'.   2. And ¹⁰ (a-t). $> t$, β.   On the earth they shall not come The earth will be transformed (ver. 5) and be thenceforth the abode of the righteous only

Who have denied the name of the Lord of Spirits,
Who are thus preserved for the day of suffering and
    tribulation.

3. On that day Mine Elect One shall sit on the throne of
    glory
And shall try their works,
And their places of rest shall be innumerable.

And their souls shall grow strong within them when they
    see Mine elect ones,
And those who have called upon My glorious name:
4. Then will I cause Mine Elect One to dwell among them.

Denied the name of the Lord of Spirits see 38² (note). Day of suffering and tribulation. The final judgement is variously named—'that great day,' 54⁸, 'day of .. judgement,' 22⁴ 100⁴, 'day of ... judgement and consummation,' 10¹², 'day of the consummation,' 16¹, 'the great judgement,' 16¹ 19¹ 22⁴ 25⁴, 'day of the great judgement,' 10⁶ 19¹ 84⁴ 94⁹ 98¹⁰ 99¹⁵ 104⁵, 'great day of judgement,' 22¹¹; 'judgement which is for ever,' 104⁵; 'great judgement which is for ever,' 91¹⁵, 'judgement that is for ever and ever,' 10¹²; 'day of tribulation,' 1¹ 96², 'day of tribulation and pain,' 55³, 'day of tribulation and great shame,' 98¹⁰, 'day of suffering and tribulation,' 45² 63⁸; 'day of affliction,' 48¹⁰ 50², 'day of anguish and affliction,' 48⁸, 'day of destruction,' 98¹⁶; 'day of slaughter,' 94⁹, 'day of unceasing bloodshed,' 99⁶, 'day of darkness,' 94⁹, 'day of unrighteousness,' 97¹. As the same phrase is applied to quite different events it is necessary to observe that— (1) The Deluge or first world judgement is referred to in 10⁴, ⁵, ¹² ᵇ 54⁵, ⁷⁻¹⁰ 91⁵ 93⁴. (2) Final world judgement *at the beginning of the Messianic kingdom*, 10⁶ ¹² ᶜ 16¹ 19¹ 22⁴, ¹¹ 25⁴ 45² 54⁶ 55⁴ 90²⁰⁻²⁷ (3) Judgement of the sword *at the beginning of the Messianic*

kingdom, when the righteous slay the wicked, 50² 90¹⁹ 91¹² 95⁷ 96¹ 98¹². (4) Final world judgement *at the close of the Messianic kingdom*, 94⁹ 98¹⁰ 100⁴ 103⁸ 104⁵. In 48⁸⁻¹⁰ there seems to be a combination of (2) and (3), and in 99⁰ 99¹⁵ of (3) and (4). 3. Mine Elect One (a–m) *m*, *t²β* 'the Elect One' see 40⁵ On the throne of glory The Elect One will sit on the throne of his glory, 45³ 55⁴ 62⁵, ⁶, as Son of Man, he will sit on the throne of his glory, 69²⁷, ²⁹, being placed thereon by the Lord of Spirits, 61⁸ 62²; and his throne is likewise the throne of the Head of Days, 47³ 51³. The Elect One sits on his throne to judge, for all judgement has been committed unto him, 69²⁷. Try. Text reads jaḥari (= choose) = יבחר corrupt for יבחן If the original were Aramaic we should only have to suppose that the translator followed the wrong meaning of יבחר. Places of rest. This is not the same word as is used in 39⁴, but may be rendered similarly, as it is the Ethiopic rendering of mansio, μονή Souls (a). β 'spirits'. But as we have seen in ch 22 the Ethiopic words are often interchangeable. Elect ones (a–m, deḫinuy² ₍a₎) *m, abcfhoxy¹* 'Elect One'. Glorious (a). *t²β* 'holy and glorious'. 4. Mine Elect

And I will transform the heaven and make it an eternal
blessing and light,

5. And I will transform the earth and make it a blessing:

And I will cause Mine elect ones to dwell upon it:
But the sinners and evil-doers shall not set foot thereon.

6. For I have provided and satisfied with peace My righteous ones
And have caused them to dwell before Me.

But for the sinners there is judgement impending with Me,
So that I shall destroy them from the face of the earth.

The Head of Days and the Son of Man.

XLVI. 1. And there I saw One who had a head of days,
And His head was white like wool,
And with Him was another being whose countenance had
the appearance of a man,
And his face was full of graciousness, like one of the holy
angels.

One (*mt*, β-*en*)   *gqu*, *cy²* ' Mine elect
ones'   4, 5. After the judgement the
Messianic kingdom is established and its
scene will be a transformed heaven. 45⁴
51⁴, and earth, 41² 45⁵, its members
will be angels, 39⁴ (note), and men,
and the Elect One will abide amongst
them   This idea of the transformation
of the world was derived directly from
Is. 65¹⁷ and 66²², and probably originally from Zoroastrianism see Cheyne's
Origin of the Psalter, 404, 405 It is
found elsewhere in Enoch in 72¹ 91¹⁶
In Isaiah this idea is only adopted
eclectically, for it is incompatible with
other facts in the context, : e 65²⁰, &c ,
but in Enoch it is accepted in its entire
significance as logically involving the
immortal blessedness of man, cf. 2 Bar.
32⁶ 57² 4 Ezra 7⁷⁵   6. **Destroy
them from the face of the earth**
Cf 69²⁷.

XLVI. 1. In this and the following
chapters Daniel 7 has been laid under

contribution, and from it have been
drawn directly the expressions ' Head
of Days', and 'Son of Man' The
former means in Daniel the Everlasting, and seems to do so here likewise.
r'ésa mıwâ'él = 'the sum of days'.
Hence the first line = ' And there I
saw the Everlasting'. It is of course
awkward that the word 'head' occurs
in the next line in a literal sense. The
phrase ' Head of Days' is found in
Enoch in 46² 47³ 48², and has been
carried over into the Interpolations,
55¹ 60². The original writer uses this
expression of Daniel with much appropriateness in connexion with the supernatural Son of Man and the question
of final judgement; in fact the two expressions are correlative · observe the
question, ' Why he went with the Head
of Days ?' but this technical appropriateness is wanting in the Interpolations   Another being . . . like one
of the holy angels cf 1 Sam 29⁹

2. And I asked the **angel** who went with me and showed me all the hidden things, concerning that Son of Man, who he was,

Acts 6[15]   **2. The angel.** MSS wrongly read 'one of the angels' See note on 40[2].   **That Son of Man.** There are some difficulties connected with this expression in Enoch, as it has there three different Ethiopic renderings, = *filius hominis*, 46[2], 5, 4 48[2], *filius viri*, 62[5] 69[29] 71[14], and *filius prolis matris viventium*, 62[7], 9, 14 63[11] 69[26], 27 70[1] 71[17], and these are the greater as the Ethiopic translator can only have had one and the same phrase before him, i.e. ὁ υἱὸς τοῦ ἀνθρώπου. For the LXX invariably uses υἱὸς ἀνθρώπου as a rendering of בן־אדם and בן־אנוש, and exact Greek equivalents of the Ethiopic expressions are hardly conceivable   Are we then to suppose that these variations existed in the Hebrew, and accordingly postulate on the part of the Ethiopic translators a direct acquaintance with an Hebrew MS. (similarly, as Nöldeke, *Encyc. Brit.* xxi. 654, in the case of the Ethiopic Bible, postulates the presence of Aramaic teachers in order to explain the fact that certain religious conceptions are there expressed by Aramaic words)? These suppositions are not necessary. There is no strict uniformity of rendering in the Ethiopic Bible. υἱὸς ἀνθρώπου is rendered by 'proles matris viventium' in Num. 23[19] Ps 8[4] 144[8] 146[3] (in the last two instances, two distinct Hebrew expressions are used); but by 'filius prolis matris viventium' in Ps. 80[17]. This latter rendering is practically the authorized one in the Ethiopic as it is found throughout Ezekiel, in Dan. 7[13], and universally in the N. T. Again ·በእለ· = *vir* is frequently used where we should expect በእለ = *homo*, and vice versa. Hence *filius viri* and *filius hominis* in the Ethiopic text may be synonymous and the variation may be

due to the carelessness of the translator. Of such carelessness there are many instances in Enoch. In 89[1] we find በእለ where we should have ·በእለ· as it is correctly in vv 9 and 36. Again, in 89[45] we have twice the rendering 'sheep' where according to the context and the Greek it should be 'lamb'. Accordingly we hold that these variations were confined to the Ethiopic version, and this conclusion is confirmed by the fact that *filius viri*, 69[29], does not imply one born of man without the mediation of a mother as some have supposed, for the same phrase, as the text stands at present, is applied to Enoch in 71[14], and is therefore the equivalent of *filius hominis* in 46[2], &c. We have above remarked that the expression in the Greek version of Enoch appears to have been ὁ υἱὸς τοῦ ἀνθρώπου, and not υἱὸς ἀνθρώπου, for in Enoch it is the distinct designation of the personal Messiah   In 48[10] 52[4] he is styled the 'Messiah'   It will be observed that the demonstrative precedes the title 'Son of Man' in our text, as it does in every instance of its occurrence save in 62[7]. Wellhausen presses home the fact that the use of the demonstrative before the expression 'Son of Man' proves conclusively that 'Son of Man' cannot be a Messianic title, for that such a phrase as 'this Messiah' or 'that Messiah' is an impossibility. Since such importance is attached to the presence or absence of the demonstratives, it is well to point out that in all probability the demonstratives are here translations of the Greek article   In the earlier chapters, where the Greek version is preserved, we find that 'this' (= zě or zentû) is a rendering of the Greek article in 25[1] 27[2] 28[2] 32[5], and

and whence he was, (and) why he went with the Head of Days?
3. And he answered and said unto me:
This is the Son of Man who hath righteousness,

'that' (= w'ĕtû) in 13¹⁰ 14¹⁰. 'those' (= 'ĕlkû) in 10⁸. In 89⁴²⁻⁴⁰, where the Greek version also survives, we find that 'that' (= zekû or zektû or w'ĕtû), though occurring twelve times in these verses, is eleven times a rendering of the Greek article. Every Ethiopic scholar is aware of this fact, and attention is rightly drawn to it in Dillmann's Ethiopic Lexicon under each of the above demonstratives. Moreover we can show in the Parables in three passages undeniable instances of such renderings, i. e. in 52⁵ 62¹⁰ and 71¹³, where w'ĕtû precedes respectively the phrases 'Angel of peace', 'Lord of Spirits', and 'Head of Days'. No Jew could say 'that God'. Now turning from the above general evidence to the passages themselves we find that in two, i. e. 46⁵ and 71¹⁴, w'ĕtû serves as the copula—a frequent usage in Ethiopic, and in these passages it cannot rightly be taken otherwise. Thus there are three passages where the demonstrative is wanting, i. e. 62⁷, as we have already observed, and these two, 46⁵ 71¹⁴. These facts, combined with the usage of our translator in rendering the Greek article, as we have shown above, makes it probable in the highest degree that zekû and zentû stand for the article and nothing more in 46², ⁴ 48² 62⁹, ¹⁴ 68¹¹, and that similarly w'ĕtû in 69²⁶, ²⁹ (bis) 70¹ 71¹⁷ is a rendering of the article. For the relation between the title 'Son of Man' in Enoch and in the N. T. see Appendix on 'the Son of Man'. 3. The Son of Man. Here the w'ĕtû (= 'that') that precedes this title is a copula as in 71¹⁴. See preceding note. The Messiah is conceived in the Parables as (1) the Judge of

the world, (2) the Revealer of all things, (3) the Messianic Champion and Ruler of the righteous.   (1) As judge, he possesses (a) righteousness, (b) wisdom, and (c) power (Pss. 45⁴⁻⁵ 72 Is. 11³⁻⁵ Jer. 23⁵, ⁶).   (a) He is the Righteous One in an extraordinary sense, 38² (see note) 53⁶, he possesses righteousness, and it dwells with him, 46⁵, and on the ground of his essential righteousness, 46⁸, has he been chosen no less than according to God's good pleasure, 49⁴.   (b) Wisdom, which could find no dwelling-place on earth, 42, dwells in him and the spirit of Him who giveth knowledge, 49⁸ , and the secrets of wisdom stream forth from his mouth, 51⁸, and wisdom is poured out like water before him, 49¹.   (c) In him abides the spirit of power, 49⁸, and he possesses universal dominion, 62⁶.   (2) He is the revealer of all things. His appearance will be the signal for the revelation of good and the unmasking of evil; will bring to light everything that is hidden, alike the invisible world of righteousness and the hidden world of sin, 46⁸ 49², ⁴; and will recall to life those that have perished on land and sea, and those that are in Sheol and hell, 51¹ 61⁵. Evil when once unmasked will vanish from his presence, 49². Hence all judgement has been committed unto him, 69²⁷, and he will sit on the throne of his glory, 45³ (see note), and all men and angels will be judged before him, 51² 55⁴ 61³ 62⁴, ⁵, and no lying utterance will be possible before him, 49⁴ 62⁸, and by the mere word of his mouth will he slay the ungodly, 62². (3) He is the Messianic champion and ruler of the righteous. He is the stay of the righteous, 48⁴, and has already

With whom dwelleth righteousness,
And who revealeth all the treasures of that which is hidden,

Because the Lord of Spirits hath chosen him,
And whose lot hath the pre-eminence before the Lord of
Spirits in uprightness for ever.

4. And this Son of Man whom thou hast seen
Shall †raise up† the kings and the mighty from their seats,
[And the strong from their thrones]

And shall loosen the reins of the strong,
And break the teeth of the sinners;

5. [And he shall put down the kings from their thrones and
kingdoms]
Because they do not extol and praise Him,

been revealed to them, 62⁷, he is the avenger of their life, 48⁷, the preserver of their inheritance, 48⁷, he will vindicate the earth as their possession for ever, 51⁵, and establish the community of the righteous in unhindered prosperity, 53⁶ 62⁸, their faces will shine with joy, 51⁵, and they will be vestured with life, 62¹⁵, and be re-splendent with light, 39⁷, and he will abide in closest communion with them for ever, 62¹⁴, in the immediate presence of the Lord of Spirits, 39⁷, and his glory is for ever and ever, and his might unto all generations, 49². Who hath righteousness. On the Messiah as the possessor of righteousness cf Is 9⁶⁻⁷ 11⁹ ⁴⁹ Jer. 23⁵ Zech 9⁹ Pss Sol 17²⁵, ²⁸, ²⁹, ³¹, ⁴², ⁴⁸ 18⁸ Hath chosen him. Hence he is called 'the Elect One' see 38² (note) 40⁴ (note) Whose lot hath the pre-eminence (aefḥⁱⁱ) iⁱβ-efḥ¹ⁱ read whose lot hath surpassed everything', cf Heb 1⁴ 4 This = the Greek article See note on 46² Shall †raise up† The verb is here obviously corrupt. The clause 'shall raise up the kings .. from their thrones' and 46⁵ᵃ 'shall put down the kings from their thrones' are dittographs. One or other is corrupt

and one or other is an intrusion. The parallelism seems to be in favour of 46⁴ᵇ being retained, though the verb gives the wrong sense, whereas the right sense 'shall put down' is obviously preserved in 46⁵ᵃ. It is hard to explain with any confidence the origin of this error. Possibly ירים stood in the original, which could mean either 'shall raise up' or 'shall remove, destroy'. The present context could admit only of the latter meaning. Or we might take the former verb as = יטול—a corruption of יפיל—'shall cast down,' seeing that in 46⁵ᵃ the same verb in the Ethiopic for 'shall put down' is given. 'Shall put down the countenance' = יפיל פנים Cf 45⁸ In any case we should read 'shall put down the kings', &c It is possible that Is 14⁹ 'it hath raised up from their thrones all the kings of the nations' may have led to the above misrendering or corruption With the restored text we might compare such expressions as Sir 10¹⁴ θρόνους ἀρχόντων καθεῖλεν ὁ κύριος, Wisd. 5²³ περιτρέψει θρόνους δυναστῶν The clause in Luke 1⁵² καθεῖλε δυνάστας ἀπὸ θρόνων seems to be an echo of our text Break the teeth of the sinners, From

Nor humbly acknowledge whence the kingdom was bestowed
upon them.

6. And he shall put down the countenance of the strong,
And shall fill them with shame.

And darkness shall be their dwelling,
And worms shall be their bed,

And they shall have no hope of rising from their beds,
Because they do not extol the name of the Lord of Spirits.

7. And these are they who †judge† the stars of heaven,
[And raise their hands against the Most High],
†And tread upon the earth and dwell upon it †.

And all their deeds manifest unrighteousness,

Ps. 37 58⁶　　**5. Acknowledge
whence the kingdom**, &c　Cf. Wisd
6²⁻³ ἐνωτίσασθε οἱ κρατοῦντες πλήθους
.　ὅτι ἐδόθη παρὰ τοῦ κυρίου ἡ κράτησις
ὑμῖν, Rom 13¹　　**6 Worms shall
be their bed**　Cf Is. 14¹¹. In 2 Macc
9⁶, ⁹ it is said that Antiochus Epiphanes
died of the disease here referred to.
But the expression is best taken figuratively of the destruction awaiting the
oppressors of the righteous, cf. Is. 66²⁴
Judith 16¹⁷ Sir 7¹⁷ Mark 9⁴⁸. **Worms
. their bed . . . Because they do
not extol** Cf Acts 12²³ for a like
connexion of thought.　7 This
verse seems very corrupt　It is clearly
an echo of Dan 8¹⁰, where it is said of
Antiochus Epiphanes　'And (the little
horn) waxed great, even to the host of
heaven, and some of the host and of
the stars it cast down to the ground
and trod upon them.' Here also the
stars stand for the righteous, and the
verb 'tread' recalls 'trod' in Daniel,
and the parallel suggests that 'tread'
had the same meaning in Enoch that it
had in Daniel. In other words we
should find it stated that the oppressors
'tread down the righteous' and not
that they 'tread the earth'. Thus
46⁷ᶜ connects immediately with 46⁷ᵃ.
In other words 47⁷ᵇ is either displaced

or interpolated　That it is the latter I
conclude, since we require here, not a
tristich, but a distich like the immediate
stanzas before and after, and since
the divine designation 'Most High' does
not occur elsewhere in the Parables
I have obelized 'judge'　It = ידינו,
which may be corrupt for יורידו (or
יפילו as in Dan. 8¹⁰) = 'cast down'.
This brings our text into line with
Dan 8¹⁰ ᵇ　Finally, 'and dwell upon
the earth' may be ꞌ wrong gloss on
the preceding words, for this clause,
which has always good ethical associations in the Parables (37² note),
here a bad ethical sense.　But probably
a corruption inheres in 'and dwell
upon it'. i. e. וישבו בה corrupt for
יושביה = 'those who dwell upon it'
As for what remains, 'and they tread
upon the earth,' a glance at Dan. 8¹⁰
shows that an accusative referring to
the righteous has here been lost. 'and
tread to the earth those who dwell
upon it'　Thus this stanza should
run —

　'And these are they who cast down
　　the stars of heaven,
　And tread to the earth those who
　　dwell upon it'

Manifest, a–q, *defhklj₁*a > q₁ᵇ　t²
abcox 'and manifest'　All MSS but

And their power rests upon their riches,

And their faith is in the †gods† which they have made with
their hands,

And they deny the name of the Lord of Spirits,

8. And they persecute the houses of His congregations,

And the faithful who hang upon the name of the Lord of
Spirits.

The Prayer of the Righteous for Vengeance and their Joy at its Coming.

XLVII. 1. And in those days shall have ascended the prayer of
the righteous

And the blood of the righteous from the earth before the
Lord of Spirits.

2. In those days the holy ones who dwell above in the heavens
Shall unite with one voice

And supplicate and pray [and praise,

qu, en ₁b make a dittographic addition here · qu add 'and all their works are unrighteousness', t, abcdfhklox₁a 'their works are unrighteousness'. Their power rests upon their riches. Perhaps חֵילָם = 'their power' was a corruption of תְּהִלָּתָם = 'their glorying'. Cf 94⁸ where the rich 'trust in their riches' Their faith is in the gods, &c This is a strange expression for the idolatrous tendencies of the Sadducean court But אלילים (= 'gods') may be corrupt for מַעֲלָלִים = 'deeds'. Hence 'deeds which they have wrought', &c. For a discussion of the verse see 38⁵ note. 8 Persecute (yt) mqu, β read 'are driven forth'. The houses (gmt¹u). q, t²β read 'from the houses' Cf 53⁶.

XLVII 1 The blood of the righteous 'The righteous' is here a collective in the singular, though in the preceding phrase 'the prayer of the righteous' it is in the plural. The same juxtaposition of cases is found in 47⁴. Cf. 91¹⁰ 'the righteous one shall

arise from sleep and wisdom . . be given unto them'. Moreover, we find in the next verse 'the blood of the righteous ones'. The first of the Maccabees to shed the blood of the righteous was Alexander Jannaeus, 95 B C (see 38⁵ note). 2 On the intercession of angels see 15² note Cf Rev 6¹⁰ for a like prayer for vengeance. See 97⁵ note The text is uncertain. I have bracketed 'and praise . . . Lord of Spirits', since the context points not to thanksgiving but to prayer on behalf of the martyrs. Moreover, the words that follow 'And that the prayer of the righteous', &c depend directly on 'supplicate and pray' as their object. Furthermore, the MSS are divided on the text of 47²ᵃ. For 'unite' (gtu, β) mq read 'dwell', and for 'dwell' (a–m, β) m reads 'unite'. Finally, q, dy omit the 'and' beginning the next line. In the words 'unite' and 'dwell' there is only a difference of one letter in the Ethiopic It is just possible that they may be doublets, and that the text stood originally 'In those days the holy

And give thanks and bless the name of the Lord of Spirits]
On behalf of the blood of the righteous which has been shed,
And that the prayer of the righteous may not be in vain
 before the Lord of Spirits,
That judgement may be done unto them,
And that they may not have to suffer for ever.

3. In those days I saw the Head of Days when He seated
 himself upon the throne of His glory,
And the books of the living were opened before Him :

ones who dwell above in the heavens shall with one voice supplicate and pray'.   3. **Books of the living** The idea underlying this phrase is to be traced to the O. T.   (1) There the book of life (or its equivalents Exod. 32⁣³² ᵗ⁣ᵍ⁣. 'God's book', Ps 69²⁸ 'book of the living') was a register of the citizens of the Theocratic community. To have one's name written in the book of life implied the privilege of participating in the *temporal* blessings of the Theocracy, Is. 4³, while to be blotted out of this book, Exod. 32³² Ps. 69²⁸, meant exclusion therefrom In the O T this expression was originally confined to *temporal* blessings only, but in Dan 12¹ it is transformed through the influence of the new conception of the kingdom, and distinctly refers to an immortality of blessedness It has the same meaning in our text. A further reference to it is to be found in 104¹. The phrase again appears in the Book of Jubilees 30²⁰ ²²⁴⁻ in contrast with 'the book of those that shall be destroyed', but in the O T sense 'The holy books' in 108³ (108²⁷), cf. also 108⁷, have practically the same meaning In the N T. the phrase is of frequent occurrence, Phil. 4³ Rev. 3⁶ 13³ 17³ 20¹², ¹⁵ 21²⁷ 22¹⁹, and the idea in Luke 10²⁰ Heb 12²³ 'written in heaven' For later instances of its use see Pastor Hermae, *Vis* i 3, 2 (see Harnack *in loc*), Sim ii. 9, Mand viii. 6; 1 Clem. xlv 8.

There is no idea of absolute predestination involved in this conception. The same thought, i e. the inscription of the name in the book of life, underlies the words 'the memorial of the righteous shall be before the face of the Great One unto all the generations of the world', 103⁴.   Contrast Ps Sol. 13¹⁰ 'the memorial of the wicked shall no more be found'.   (2) Books of remembrance of good and evil deeds.   For those wherein good deeds were recorded see Ps 56⁸ Mal. 3¹⁶ Book of Jubilees 30²², wherein evil deeds were recorded, Is 65⁶ 1 En 81⁴ 89⁶¹⁻⁶⁴, ⁶⁸, ⁷⁰, ⁷¹, ⁷⁶, ⁷⁷ 90¹⁷, ²⁰ 98⁷, ⁸ 104⁷ 2 Bar 24¹, wherein good and evil deeds were recorded, Dan. 7¹⁰ Rev 20¹² Asc Is. 9²².   (3) The heavenly tablets = πλάκες τοῦ οὐρανοῦ in Test XII Patriarchs. The conception underlying this phrase is to be traced partly to Ps 139¹⁶ Exod 25⁹, ⁴⁰ 26³⁰, where we find the idea that there exist in heaven divine archetypes of certain things on earth ; partly to Dan 10²¹, where a book of God's plans is referred to, but most of all to the growing determinism of thought, for which this phrase stands as a concrete expression In Apocryphal literature historical events are not depicted according to the manifold variety of life, but are methodically arranged under artificial categories of measure, number, weight, Wisdom 11²⁰ 4 Ezra 4⁸⁶, ⁵⁷ The conception is not a hard and fixed one . in Enoch and

And all His host which is in heaven above and His counsellors
　　stood before Him,

4. And the hearts of the holy were filled with joy;

Because the number of the righteous **had been offered**,
And the prayer of the righteous had been heard,
And the blood of the righteous been required before the
　　Lord of Spirits.

Test XII Patriarchs it wavers between
an absolute determinism and prediction
pure and simple: whereas in Jubilees
in addition to these significations, it implies at times little more than a contemporary heavenly record of events. In
Enoch the idea is mainly predestinarian,
the 'heavenly tables' record all the
deeds of men to the remotest generations, 81[1, 2], and the entire history of
the earth, 93[1-3], and all the unrighteousness that will arise, 106[19] 107[1], as
well as all the blessings in store for the
righteous, 103[2, 3]. They are likewise
called the Book of the Angels, 103[2],
for they are designed also for the
perusal of the angels, 108[7], that they
may know the future recompenses of
the righteous and the wicked. In Test
XII Patriarchs I evi 5[4] Asher 7[5] (β) the
idea is predictive, in Asher 2[10] it con-
cerns a question of Levitical law. In
Jubilees the use of the phrase is very
loose, the heavenly tables are the
statute book of the Theocracy, or a
mere contemporary record, or else are
predictive or determinative. The
heavenly tables record (1) Laws Levitical and criminal, in some instances
previously observed in heaven, in
others, established for the first time on
earth. Feast of weeks, 6[17-18], Tabernacles, 16[16-29], Passover, 49, 'the
Festival of the Lord,' 18[18-19], Ceremonial cleanness, 3[8-14], Circumcision,
15[25], the Sabbath, 50[6-13], tithes, 32[2,
8, 9, 10-15], marriage of elder daughter,

28[6], destruction of him who gives his
daughter to a Gentile, 30[9], of the
murderer, 4[5], of the incestuous person,
33[10] (ordained because of Reuben);
of the seed of Lot, 16[9]; of the Philistines, 24[33]. (2) Merely a contemporary
event. the slaughter of the Shechem-
ites, 30[9 sqq.], the institution of the
'Festival of the Lord', 18[18-19], the
showing of the Seven Tables to Jacob,
32[22], Isaac's blessing of Levi and
Judah, 31[32], the naming of Abraham,
19[9], and of Levi, 30[20], as friends of
God. (3) Predictions. of the judgement of all creation, 5[13], of the Messianic kingdom, 23[30-32], of the recording of the faithful as friends of God
and the transgressors as haters, 30[21-22].
All His host. God as the Jehovah of
Hosts in His manifestations is generally
so accompanied, cf. 1[4, 9] 60[1], 4 71[9-13].
According to the Parables it is the
Messiah that judges. **4 The
number of the righteous** (m ṣādeq)
Other MSS read 'righteousness'
(ṣědēq). **Been offered** a reads
qarěba = ἤγγικε = קרב, which in
Mishnaic and late Hebrew = 'had
been offered' as well as 'had drawn
nigh'. The latter meaning is inappropriate, for the judgement is already
begun. The text means that the number of the righteous, i e the martyrs, is
complete. The martyrs were regarded
as offerings to God. Cf. Rev 6[10, 11],
and my note *in loc.* For qarěba β reads
baseha = 'has come',

The Fount of Righteousness: the Son of Man—the Stay of the Righteous: Judgement of the Kings and the Mighty.

XLVIII. 1. And in that place I saw the fountain of righteousness
Which was inexhaustible:
And around it were many fountains of wisdom;
And all the thirsty drank of them,
And were filled with wisdom,
And their dwellings were with the righteous and holy and elect.

2. And at that hour that Son of Man was named
In the presence of the Lord of Spirits,
And his name before the Head of Days.

3. Yea, before the sun and the signs were created,
Before the stars of the heaven were made,
His name was named before the Lord of Spirits.

4. He shall be a staff to the righteous whereon to stay themselves and not fall,
And he shall be the light of the Gentiles,
And the hope of those who are troubled of heart.

5. All who dwell on earth shall fall down and worship before him,

XLVIII. 1 And (*η̣t, β*). > *gπu*
Place: see 46¹ Fountains of wisdom see 42¹, ² (note) Cf Is 55¹ ꜱqq
2 At that hour, i e when Enoch was beholding these visions. **That Son of Man was named.** The preexistence of the Son of Man is plainly taught in the Parables. He (not his name) has been chosen and hidden in God's presence from before creation and unto eternity, 48⁶, ⁶, the Most High has preserved him and revealed him to the elect, 46¹⁻² 62⁷, his glory is for ever and ever, 49²; when Enoch was translated the Son of Man was already abiding with the Lord of Spirits, 70¹. This actual pre-existence of the Son of Man is in keeping with his other supernatural attributes of universal dominion,

62⁶, and unlimited judicial authority, 69²⁷ This idea of pre-existence is found also in 4 Ezra 12³² 13²⁶. Cf. Schürer, II ii. 159–162 (Eng Trans.), who agrees with the view above followed. **3. The signs.** These are the signs of the Zodiac, מזרות, Job 38³² See also 8³ 72¹³, ¹⁰ **4. Righteous** + 'and to the holy' *β*. **Whereon to stay themselves.** Cf. 61³ where the same phrase recurs **The light of the Gentiles** Is 42⁶ 49⁶ Luke 2³². **The hope of those who are troubled of heart.** Cf. Is. 61¹, ² 'The Lord hath anointed me . . . to bind up the broken-hearted' (נשברי לב). **5 All . . . shall fall down . . . before him.** Even those who denied him, 62⁶, ⁹ 63 90⁵⁷

And will praise and bless and celebrate with song the Lord
of Spirits.

6. And for this reason hath he been chosen and hidden
   before Him,
   Before the creation of the world and for evermore.

7. And the wisdom of the Lord of Spirits hath revealed him
   to the holy and righteous;
   For he hath preserved the lot of the righteous;

   Because they have hated and despised this world of un-
   righteousness,
   And have hated all its works and ways in the name of the
   Lord of Spirits:

   For in his name they are saved,
   And according to his good pleasure hath it been in regard to
   their life.

8. In these days downcast in countenance shall the kings of the
   earth have become,
   And the strong who possess the land because of the works of
   their hands;

   For on the day of their anguish and affliction they shall not
   (be able to) save themselves,

9. And I will give them over into the hands of Mine
   elect.

Phil 2¹⁰. Praise and bless (*a–q*, *cf q, β* The Lord (*a–m*) *m, β* 'the name of the Lord'. **6.** And (*q, β*) > *a–q*. For this reason, i e. that given in vv. 4, 5. Hidden Cf 4 Ezra 13⁵² Before Him. > *q* For evermore + *q, abcdl cy₁a* 'before Him'. **7.** Revealed him, i e through O. T prophecy Holy and righteous (*gmq, β–l*). *fu, l* 'righteous and holy'. Preserved the lot of the righteous. The Messiah is the stay of the righteous, and the guardian and surety of the inheritance that awaits them. Hated and despised this world cf. 108⁸, ⁹, ¹⁰ Gal 1⁴ In his name they are saved. A frequent N T expression, cf. 1 Cor 6¹¹ Acts 4¹². According to his good pleasure . . life (*g*). *mtu, β–owy₁b* 'he is the avenger of their life' *owy₁b* 'his good pleasure hath been for their life' *q* is corrupt. The difference lies between bafaqâdû (*g*) and faqâdê (*mtu*). Cf 62¹¹ on the latter reading גאל, 'avenger', is a name in later Judaism for the Messiah. See Weber, pp. 359, 362. **8.** Day of their anguish: see 45² note. **9.** Give them over into the hands, &c. Cf. 38⁵

As straw in the fire so shall they burn before the face of
   the holy;

As lead in the water shall they sink before the face of the
   righteous,

And no trace of them shall any more be found

10. And on the day of their affliction there shall be rest on the
   earth,

And before them they shall fall and not rise again

And there shall be no one to take them with his hands and
   raise them:

For they have denied the Lord of Spirits and His Anointed.

The name of the Lord of Spirits be blessed.

---

note. **As straw in the fire** Exod 15[7]
Is. 5[24] Obadiah 18 Mal. 4[1]. **Before the**
face of the holy (*gqtu*)   β 'before . .
righteous'. The reference here is to
Gehenna, cf. 27[2, 8] 90[26, 27]; but in the
Parables Gehenna undergoes transformation. In 27[2, 8] 90[26, 27] the suffer-
ings of the wicked form an ever-present
spectacle to the righteous. Cf 4 Ezra
7[36] 'Apparebit lacus tormenti, et contra
illum erit locus requietionis clibanus
gehennae ostendetur, et contra eum
iocunditatis paradisus'. But in the
Parables, where heaven and earth are
transformed on the advent of the
Messiah, this spectacle is only a temporary one, and Gehenna and its
victims vanish for ever from the
sight of the righteous, 48[9] 62[12, 13].
Cf. Rev. 20[14]   **As lead in water**
Exod. 15[10]   **Before the face of the**
righteous (α)   β 'before . . holy'.
10 **Rest** Cf 53[7]   **And** (> *q*) before them (α)   β 'and before him'.
Fall and not rise again: cf ver 4
for the opposite; cf. also Ps. 36[12].
The Lord . . . and His Anointed:
cf. Ps 2[2]   The term 'Messiah' or
'Anointed One' was applicable to any
one specially commissioned by God to

a religious or Theocratic function:
hence to David and his successors, and
even to a Gentile prince—Cyrus (Is.
45[1]); to the Jewish high-priest—'the
anointed priest', Lev 4[3, 5, 16] 6[22], to
the Servant of Jehovah, Is. 61[1]   In
the Psalms the title generally refers to
the reigning king or to the Davidic
king as such, yet its ideal aspect is
never lost sight of. When the historical kingship came to an end, the idea
still remained, and was kept prominent
through the liturgical use of the Psalms.
Its imperfect realization in the kings
of the past made Israel look forward to
the true Messianic king in whom it
should be perfectly embodied. But
the term is never used technically in
this sense in the O T. In this technical sense it is first found in the Parables,
48[10] 52[4], and a decade or so later in
Pss Sol. 17[38] 18[6, 8]   For its later
occurrences see 4 Ezra 7[29] 12[32] 2 Bar
29[3] 30[1] 39[7] 40[1] 70[9] 72[2], and N T.
passim. See Cheyne, *Origin of the*
Psalter, 338–339, Art on the Messiah,
Encyc. Bib iii. 3057 sqq. On the
question generally cf. Schürer, *Div* ii,
vol ii. 120–187.

The Power and Wisdom of the Elect One.

XLIX 1. For wisdom is poured out like water,
And glory faileth not before him for evermore.

2. For he is mighty in all the secrets of righteousness,
And unrighteousness shall disappear as a shadow,
And have no continuance;
Because the Elect One standeth before the Lord of
Spirits,
And his glory is for ever and ever,
And his might unto all generations.

3. And in him dwells the spirit of wisdom,
And the spirit which gives insight,
And the spirit of understanding and of might,
And the spirit of those who have fallen asleep in righteous-
ness.

4. And he shall judge the secret things,
And none shall be able to utter a lying word before
him;
For he is the Elect One before the Lord of Spirits according
to His good pleasure.

XLIX. That the Messiah will thus deal with the mighty ones of the earth is clear from his nature and attributes. 1 Wisdom is poured out like water cf [- 11⁹. Wisdom here = the knowledge and fear of God Cf 39⁵. Glory faileth not, &c. The Messiah is the object of endless glorification 2 Mighty in all the secrets of righteousness On the revealing and manifesting power of the Messiah see 46² (note) Disappear as a shadow, And have no continuance. The phraseology is borrowed from Job 14² The word translated 'continuance' is formed from the verb translated 'standeth': unrighteousness will have no standing ground because the Elect One standeth Glory is for ever and ever, &c cf Is 9⁶, ⁷ Mic 5⁴. 3 Further endowments of the Messiah after Is 11¹ The spirit of wisdom cf 51⁸. The spirit which gives insight (*gqtu*). *m*, *β* 'the spirit of Him who gives insight'. The spirit of those who have fallen, &c. The eschatological hopes of all the faithful in the past are realized in him 4 Judge the secret things cf. ver. 2 and 43⁵ note. A lying word Falsehood will be impossible in his presence; cf 62⁸ 67⁹ For he is the Elect One For these very purposes has he been chosen, cf 48⁵

The Glorification and Victory of the Righteous: the Repentance
of the Gentiles.

L. 1. And in those days a change shall take place for the holy
and elect,

And the light of days shall abide upon them,

And glory and honour shall turn to the holy,

2. On the day of affliction on which evil shall have been
treasured up against the sinners.

And the righteous shall be victorious in the name of the
Lord of Spirits:

And He will cause the others to witness (this)

That they may repent

L. It is very hard to decide on the character of this chapter. It seems to be an interpolation: if it is original, the writer is inconsistent with himself, and the incongruous details were due to literary reminiscence. These details belong to the same sphere of thought as 83–90 and 91–104, where the judgement of the sword forms the prelude to the Messianic kingdom, which is gradually established and attended by the conversion of the heathen $90^{30, 33}$ 91^{14}, and ultimately followed by the final judgement. And yet there is an echo of this judgement of the sword in 48^9 On the other hand 37–71 are strongly eschatological and catastrophic in character, and the kingdom is ushered in by the sudden appearing of the Son of Man, who inaugurates his reign by the two tremendous acts of the resurrection and the final judgement. This judgement is summary and forensic, 62^2 There is no place of repentance; cf 62–63 God's mercy is shown in His dealings with the righteous, 61^{13} All sinners are forthwith driven from off the earth heaven and earth are transformed and become the habitation of the righteous. Hence there is no room for the period of the

sword, or for the progressive conversion of the heathen The writer has not taken into account the destiny of the latter, save indirectly in teaching a general judgement These verses, then, may be a later addition made with the purpose of filling up a gap in the Parables. On the other hand there are greater inconsistencies in the Parables and other apocalyptic writings 1. The night of oppression will give place to the sunshine of glory and honour for the righteous with the advent of the Messianic kingdom; cf. $58^{5, 6}$. Observe that there is no mention of the Messiah in vv. 1–4, nor yet of the kings and mighty ones, both of which facts tend to confirm the conclusion we have above arrived at Holy and elect cf. 62^8 2 The period of the sword when the righteous slay the wicked is here referred to, cf $90^{19, 34}$ 91^{12} On the day (a) β 'and on the day'   Day of affliction cf. 48^{10} 45^2 (note)   On which $(gmt > qu, \beta)$ evil (q wrongly in acc) shall have been treasured up (gq; 'shall be treasured up' β–fy, 'is treasured up' ut^2)   Cause the others .. that they may repent cf $90^{30, 33, 34}$ 91^{14}.   3 The Gentiles who repent

And forgo the works of their hands.

3. They shall have no honour through the name of the Lord of
   Spirits,
   Yet through His name shall they be saved,
   And the Lord of Spirits will have compassion on them,
   For His compassion is great.

4. And He is righteous also in His judgement,
   And in the presence of His glory unrighteousness also shall
   not maintain itself
   At His judgement the unrepentant shall perish before Him.

5. And from henceforth I will have no mercy on them, saith
   the Lord of Spirits.

*The Resurrection of the Dead, and the Separation by the Judge
of the Righteous and the Wicked.*

LI. 1. And in those days shall the earth also give back that
       which has been entrusted to it,

will be saved as by fire. They will not have the abundant entering in of the Jews. Through the name of (a). *t²β* 'before'.   4, 5 When the hour of the final judgement arrives, the season of mercy for the Gentiles is past for ever. Note the affinities of thought between 50³⁻⁵ and 60⁵, ²⁵ Cf 4 Ezra 7³⁸ 2 Bar 85¹² Observe that the final judgement here is not at the beginning of the Messianic reign as in the Parables, but apparently at its close, as in 91–104 In 4 Ezra and 2 Bar, where the Messianic kingdom is of temporary duration, and brought to a close by the final judgement, a period of repentance is rightly spoken of. Cf. 2 Bar. 85¹² 4 Ezra 7³⁴.

LI. 1. The resurrection here is a resurrection of all Israel but not of the Gentiles. 51³ would indeed seem to point to the latter, and this all the more so, as 4 Ezra 7³² and 7³⁷ which are evidently based on it, and on 1 En. 60⁶, are applied to a general resurrection But the whole history of

Jewish thought points in an opposite direction. As we shall see below, no Jewish books except the T Benj 10⁶⁻⁸ and 4 Ezra teach indubitably the doctrine of a general resurrection. Individual utterances to the contrary in the Talmud will be noticed below On the question generally see Cheyne, *Origin of the Psalter*, 381–452, 'Possible Zoroastrian Influences on the Religion of Israel,' *Expository Times*, 1891, pp 224–228, 248–253, Eisenmenger, *Entdecktes Judenthum*, ii 819, 820–949; Weber, *Jud Theol* 367–371, 390–398; Schulz, *A. T. liche Theologie*, 4ᵗᵉ Aufl. 753–768, Herzog, *R E²* Art. 'Unsterblichkeit', vol xvi 189–195; Hamburger, *R. E.* ii. 98 sqq. (Art. 'Belebung der Todten'), Edersheim, *Life and Times of Jesus*, ii. 397–403, Stade, *Über d A T. lichen Vorstellungen von dem Zustande nach dem Tode*, 1877, Castelli, 'Future Life in Rabbinic Literature,' Art in *Jewish Quarterly Review*, July, 1889, pp 314–352, Montefiore, 'Doctrine of Divine

And Sheol also shall give back that which it has received,

Retribution in O T.,' Oct. 1890, 1-12; Charles, *Eschatology, Hebrew, Jewish, and Christian*, 1899 (see Index) The various forms in which the Jewish doctrine of the resurrection appeared are: (1) a resurrection of all Israelites This doctrine is first taught in Dan. 12²; but, though so powerfully attested, it did not become the prevailing belief It is the accepted faith in 1 En 1-36 (with the exception of one class of sinners in 22¹³) 37-70 83-90 Ps. 65 (title) in LXX 2 Macc. 7⁹, ¹⁴, ²³, ²⁹, ³⁰ 12⁴³, ⁴⁴ compared with 6²⁶ 2 Bar 30 50-51⁵. (2) A resurrection of the righteous Israelites. In post-Exilic Is 25² 26¹⁹ Pss. 16¹⁰, ¹¹ 17¹⁵ 49¹⁵ 73²⁴⁻²⁷ (cf Cheyne, *Origin of the Psalter*, 406-408) Job 14¹³⁻¹⁵ 19²⁵, ²⁷ 1 En 91-104 Pss Sol. 3¹⁵ 13⁹ 14⁷ 15¹⁵, Josephus, *Ant.* xviii. 1 3, *Bell. Jud.* ii. 8. 14 That the resurrection was the sole prerogative of righteous Israelites, became the accepted doctrine in Talmudic theology: Weber, *Jüd Theol* 390-391. Individual voices, however, are not wanting, who asserted the resurrection of pious Gentiles, Eisenmenger, *Entdecktes Judenthum*, 908,909 indeed, that of all the Gentiles, with some few exceptions, but only to die again, *op cit.* 908-910, Weber, 391 Even imperfect Israelites could attain to this resurrection of life after purgation in Gehenna, Weber, 391. (3) A resurrection of all mankind, 4 Ezra 7³², ³⁷ Test. XII Patriarch Benj 10⁶⁻⁸. Concurrently with the above forms of doctrine, other Jews believed only in the immortality of the soul. Wisd. 3¹ ˢᵠᵠ. 4⁷ 5¹⁶ 8²⁰ compared with 9¹⁵ 15⁸ Jub 23³⁰.   1. The earth also . . received. So *g* save that for mâhdantâ (*g,β*) = 'that which has been entrusted to it' it substitutes a gloss = 'those who are treasured up in it'. *tu* are defective . 'Sheol shall give back that which has been entrusted to it,

that which it has received ' *β* has a conflate text based partly on the original of *g* and on *tu* 'the earth shall give back that which has been entrusted to it, and Sheol shall give back that which has been entrusted to it, that which it has received.' Cf. 4 Ezra 7³² 'Et terra reddet qui in ea dormiunt, et pulvis qui in eo silentio habitant, et prumptuaria reddent quae eis commendatae sunt animae'. Our text is quoted in the Ps. Philo *Liber bibl. Antiquitatum*, an old Jewish work written originally in Hebrew soon after A D. 70 but preserved only in Latin. It was printed thrice in the sixteenth century See *Encyc. Brit*.¹¹ ii 178. The earth gives up the *body* just as Sheol and Abaddon give up the *soul* They are both reunited at the resurrection. The raising of both was subsequently justified in Sanh 91ᵃ (Lev R. iv) on the ground that the soul and body could respectively plead their innocence on the day of judgement in that neither had sinned without the other The fable of the lame man who helped the blind in robbing an orchard is here given, and as it is shown that justice can be achieved only by punishing the lame and blind together, 'so God brings the soul and puts it in the body and punishes them both together ' (מביא נשמה וזרקה בגוף ודן אותם כאחד) In 91-104 the resurrection is that of the spirit only.   Sheol and hell (haguel = ἀπώλεια = אברן) are here used in their new sense of the Intermediate State For some of the chief changes in the meaning of Sheol see 63¹⁰ note. Sheol and Abaddon are here apparently distinguished. Is Sheol the intermediate place for the righteous and Abaddon for the wicked? Or is Sheol for the righteous and the ordinary sinners, and Abaddon for only the apostates and the worst sinners? Some such idea

And hell shall give back that which it owes.

5 *a.* For in those days the Elect One shall arise,

2. And he shall choose the righteous and holy from among them :
For the day has drawn nigh that they should be saved.

3. And the Elect One shall in those days sit on My throne,
And his mouth shall **pour** forth all the secrets of wisdom
and counsel :
For the Lord of Spirits hath given (them) to him and hath
glorified him.

4. And in those days shall the mountains leap like rams,
And the hills also shall skip like lambs satisfied with milk,
And the faces of [all] the angels in heaven shall be lighted
up with joy.

seems to underlie the separate mention of the two places   They are seemingly distinguished even in Job 26[6] (28[22]) 2-5 These verses seem to be disarranged. The judge is simply mentioned as 'he' in ver. 2, and is not particularized as 'the Elect One' sitting on God's throne till ver 3   Hence it would seem at first sight that we should transpose ver. 3 before ver 2 But there appears to be a better solution of the difficulty. ver 2 has only two lines and ver 5 four This fact suggests that the missing line of ver 2 is to be found in ver 5 This idea gains confirmation when we observe that when 5[a] is restored before ver. 2, the first line of each of the first four stanzas begins with the phrase 'in those days', and the removal of 5[a] brings ver 4 and 5[bcd] into a harmony of form and subject Chapter 51, then, is found to consist of five stanzas of three lines each.   5[a]. **Shall arise**, 1 c come forward, appear   2 **The day has drawn nigh,** &c   Cf Luke 21[28] 3 The Messiah is the embodiment of wisdom, 49[3], and in this wisdom shall the members of his kingdom share, 48[1]

61[7, 11] Cf 42[2] note   **The Elect One** (*gmu, β*). *qt*[1] 'Mine Elect One'   **My throne** (*a*) *t*[2]*β* 'His throne'   **His mouth shall pour . . . counsel.** Emended.   *q, β* read 'all the secrets of wisdom shall go forth from the counsel of his mouth'. But since *a–q* put 'all the secrets' in the acc and *gu* insert 'and' after 'wisdom', I have read jâwad'ĕ (for jĕwad'ĕ) = 'shall pour forth' and omitted 'from' before 'counsel'.   4 **The mountains leap**, &c , i. e. with joy, cf Ps 114[4, 6]. **And the faces of [all] the angels .. shall be lighted up with joy.** There are two ways of taking the original text which is preserved in *yqtu,* the oldest MSS. malâ'ĕkt = 'angels' can either be taken as the subject of the verb according to *gtu* and gasômû as an accusative of limitation   '[all] the angels shall be lighted up as to their faces with joy,' or better 'angels' can be taken as a *nominativus pendens* resumed in the suffix in gasômû Hence 'the faces of [all] the angels shall ', &c The text of *m* also would admit of this rendering The text of *q* is different but gives the same sense. It reads lakuĕllû

5 *b*. And the earth shall rejoice,

   c. And the righteous shall dwell upon it,

   d. And the elect shall walk thereon.

The Seven Metal Mountains and the Elect One.

LII. 1. And after those days in that place where I had seen all the visions of that which is hidden—for I had been carried off in a whirlwind and they had borne me towards the west—

malâ'ĕkt, 'of all the angels,' and can only therefore be translated as follows · 'the faces of [all] the angels' In this verse we have the compound future jĕkawnû . jĕbarhû = 'shall be lighted up' as in 10²¹. Finally, the word 'all' is unnecessary. kuĕllû (= 'all ') I take as a corruption of 'ĕllû—a corruption that has occurred in the earlier chapters where the Greek exists, and 'ĕllû is simply a translation of the Greek article as very frequently in this book. In my former edition, with all other translators, I rendered this 'they shall all be angels in heaven their faces shall be lighted up with joy' (β) The later MSS β certainly admit of this translation, but it is wanting in sense. Who are the 'all'? Hence the idea that the righteous shall become like the angels is not found in this passage. 5 The earth rejoices, for it is transformed, 45⁵, and has at last become the inheritance of the righteous as anciently promised; cf Ps 37³, ⁹, ¹¹, ²⁹, ³⁴. Walk (η). *intu* read 'go', β 'go and walk' *g* supports β, but 5ᵇⁿ and all of 5ᵈ but the last word are written over an erasure

LII This obscure chapter seems to symbolize the various future kingdoms of the world, and to be founded on Dan 2³¹⁻⁴⁵. These kingdoms of material force, symbolized by iron and brass and silver and gold and clay, will be as the chaff of summer threshing-floors before the kingdom of the Messiah, Dan. 2³⁵; they will be broken to pieces

and consumed, Dan 2⁴⁴ So here the various world powers represented by these mountains of iron and copper and silver and gold, &c , will melt as wax before the fire in the presence of the Messiah, 52⁶, and be destroyed from off the face of the earth, 52⁹, and no earthly might will avail in that day, 52⁷, ⁸ Observe that the idea of symbolizing the world powers by mountains is drawn from the same section of Daniel In Dan 2³⁵ the Messianic kingdom is symbolized by a mountain But this chapter seems to be composed of two independent documents In 52¹⁻⁴ the mountains serve to exalt the dominion of the Messiah, whereas in 52⁶⁻⁹ they are destroyed before his presence Again, we remark that the question Enoch puts in 52³ receives two independent answers, one from the angel who went with him in 52⁴ and the other from the angel of peace in 52⁵ ˢᵠᵠ· In the Introduction to the Parables, p 64 sq , I have shown—following a suggestion of Beer—that there are two sources in the Parables, and this chapter furnishes very clear evidence in this direction. 52¹⁻² is common to both sources, 52³⁻⁴ to the Son of Man source, and 52⁶⁻⁹ to the source dealing with the Elect One Thus we have the explanation of the divergence between 52³⁻⁴ and 52⁶⁻⁹. 1. In that place, i e. in heaven where he had seen all the preceding visions. It is idle to attempt to get an exact idea of Enoch's movements In 39³ he was carried off by a whirlwind to the

2. There mine eyes saw all the secret things of heaven that shall be, a mountain of iron, and a mountain of copper, and a mountain of silver, and a mountain of gold, and a mountain of soft metal, and a mountain of lead.

3. And I asked the angel who went with me, saying, ' What things are these which I have seen in secret?' 4. And he said unto me. ' All these things which thou hast seen shall serve the dominion of His Anointed that he may be potent and mighty on the earth '

5 And that angel of peace answered, saying unto me : ' Wait a little and there shall be revealed unto thee all the secret things, which surround the Lord of Spirits.

---

ends of the heaven . here he is borne to the west. 2 There ought to be seven mountains mentioned here The six that are mentioned in this verse and in 52⁶ consist of iron, copper, silver, gold, soft metal, lead. Now if we turn to 67⁴, where these mountains are again referred to but the nature of only five of them specified, we find that these five are of gold, silver, iron, soft metal, tin. It is not improbable, therefore, that the seventh mountain, the mention of which has been lost from the text, consisted of ' tin ' This conclusion receives support from the following considerations. In 52⁷⁻⁸ there is a fresh enumeration of metals, which though not referring directly to the metal mountains yet does so indirectly. In this list the following metals are given gold, silver, iron, bronze, tin, lead Here again we find the missing metal ' tin ', though a fresh metal ' bronze' is also mentioned This ' bronze ' may be the same as the ' copper ' in the other list So much for our text Now for a myth indirectly connected with it. In Origen's *Contra Celsum,* vi 22, there is a description of a ladder with seven gates from the mysteries of Mithras The first gate consists of lead (μόλυβδος) and is assigned to Saturn, the second of tin

($κασσίτερος$), which is assigned to Venus on the ground of its splendour and softness (τὸ φαιδρόν τε καὶ μαλακὸν τοῦ κασσιτέρου), the third of copper ($χαλκός$) assigned to Jupiter, the fourth of iron ($σίδηρος$) assigned to Mercury, the fifth of a mixture of metals ($κερ.στὸν νόμισμα$) assigned to Mars, the sixth of silver ($ἄργυρον$) assigned to the Moon, and the seventh of gold ($χρυσός$) assigned to the Sun The metals in this passage and in our text are evidently the same The question now arises with which of these seven metals is the ' soft metal' in our text to be identified? If the word we have rendered ' tin ' is rightly translated, then possibly it should be identified with the $κερaστὸν νόμισμα$ On the other hand Celsus's description of ' tin as being ' soft ' might point to another conclusion. Owing to the difficulty of identifying the ancient metals we must leave this question undecided. See *K A. T* ³ 618, note 4 ' upon the earth ' ($q, t², β$). Lead 52⁶ 65⁷, ⁸ 67⁴, ⁶. 3–4. From the Son of Man source. See note at beginning of chapter 5 That angel. Here w'ětû (= that) is merely a translation of the Greek article. Wait a little + ' and thou shalt see ' β. Surround the Lord of

6. And these mountains which thine eyes have seen,
    The mountain of iron, and the mountain of copper, and the
        mountain of silver,
    And the mountain of gold, and the mountain of soft metal,
        and the mountain of lead,
    All these shall be in the presence of the Elect One,
    As wax before the fire,
    And like the water which streams down from above [upon
        those mountains],
    And they shall become powerless before his feet.

7. And it shall come to pass in those days that none shall be saved,
    Either by gold or by silver,
    And none be able to escape.

8. And there shall be no iron for war,
    Nor shall one clothe oneself with a breastplate.
    Bronze shall be of no service,
    And tin [shall be of no service and] shall not be esteemed,
    And lead shall not be desired.

9. And all these things shall be [denied and] destroyed from the
        surface of the earth,
    When the Elect One shall appear before the face of the Lord
        of Spirits.'

Spirits (*a–m*)   *m*, *t²β* ' the Lord of Spirits has established'   **6** As wax before the fire. Cf. 1⁶ Ps 97⁵ Mic 1⁴ Like the water which streams down, Mic 1⁴ MSS. add here 'upon those mountains'   The thought of this verse recurs in 53⁷   **7** From Zeph 1¹⁸ ' Neither their silver nor their gold shall be able to deliver them'. Cf. Is. 13¹⁷   **8.** Nor shall one clothe oneself with a breastplate (or 'coat of mail'). I have here read wa'lpilabēs with *q* instead of wa'llēbēs with *gt*, *cfhn₁a₁b* or wa'llebsa with *mu, aboklox* = 'nor garment for a breastplate'   I have omitted la before der'a with *u*, though the construction with la should be possible. Otherwise with *u, β* render 'garment for a coat

of mail' (or 'breastplate') In *a–u* there is a dittograph · ' nor garment ('nor shall one clothe oneself' *q*) for war nor garment for a breastplate' (or ' coat of mail '). Shall be of no service and Bracketed as a dittograph from the preceding line. *q* omits ' and shall not be esteemed'   **9** Be [denied and] destroyed. We have here two alternative renderings of יְבְחרו such as ἀπαρνηθήσονται and ἀφανισθήσονται   One was originally in the text and the other in the margin, but subsequently both were incorporated into the text. Schmidt, who advocates an Aramaic original, proposes רמא; but this verb means ' to cast down' and ' to deceive'—senses which do not explain our text

The Valley of Judgement: the Angels of Punishment. the
Communities of the Elect One.

LIII. 1. Theie mine eyes saw a deep valley with open mouths,
and all who dwell on the earth and sea and islands shall bring to
him gifts and presents and tokens of homage, but that deep
valley shall not become full.

    2. And their hands commit lawless deeds,

        And the sinners devour all whom they lawlessly **oppress**

      Yet the sinners shall be destroyed before the **face** of the
        Lord of Spirits,

      And they shall be banished from off the face of His earth,

      And they shall peiish for ever and ever.

    3. Foi I saw all the angels of punishment abiding (there) and

---

LIII. 1. The deep valley here is
that of Jehoshaphat, where, according
to Joel 3², ¹², God was to assemble and
judge the Gentiles. The valley of
Jehoshaphat (Joel 3², ¹²) is rendered in
Theodotion by the phrase τὴν χώραν τῆς
κρίσεως and by the Targ Jon. מישר
פלוג דינא (= 'the plain of the decision
of judgement'). Accoiding to the
Midrash Mishle, 68ᵈ, God will judge the
whole world in this valley (Webti,
Jud. Theol 395.) Since the fouith cent
this valley has generally been identified
with that of the Kidion. But many
scholars are of opinion that it was not
oiiginally a geographical designation.
In the Midrash Tillim, viii (Neubaner,
Geog, p 51) it is stated that no such
valley exists (אין עמק ששמו יהויעפט)
See *Encyc. Bib* ii 2353 All those
who dwell upon earth will bring gifts
and presents to the Messiah to win a
favourahle judgement, but these will
be of no avail (cf 52⁷) The idea of
the nations and the rich men of the
eaith bringing gifts to the Messiah is
a favourite one in the Talmud, Webei
(386-387). There (a-q) g, β 'and

there'. Deep valley with open
mouths (*mqlu*, β-n) g 'open and
deep-mouthed valley'. 2. Sinners
devour all whom they lawlessly
oppress So I render this line, emending jĕṣâmĕwû into jĕṣâmawû That
this is the meaning of the text appears
to follow from the last words of this
chapter, 53⁷, 'the oppression of sinners.'
The verb 'oppress', sâmawa, is formed
from the noun sâma, used in 53⁷ If
we do not emend, the sense is poor and
needs supplementing ' ' sinners lawlessly
devoui all that they (? who) produce.'
Banished from off the face of His
earth: see 38¹ (note). And they
shall perish. All MSS inseit a
negative if it is retained the text must
be rendered 'And they shall not cease '
3. Angels of punishment see 40⁷
(note). These angels apparently prepare the chains and fetters for the kings
and the mighty in the valley of Jehoshaphat where the kings are to be
judged. The chains for the fallen
angels are forged in Gehenna, 54³⁻⁵.
The kings are then taken and cast into
Gehenna, 54² Abiding (*mqt (gu*)

preparing all the instruments of Satan.   4. And I asked the angel of peace who went with me: 'For whom are they preparing these instruments?'   5. And he said unto me: 'They prepare these for the kings and the mighty of this earth, that they may thereby be destroyed.

6. And after this the Righteous and Elect One shall cause the house of his congregation to appear: henceforth they shall be no more hindered in the name of the Lord of Spirits.

7. And these mountains shall not stand as the earth before his righteousness,

But the hills shall be as a fountain of water,

And the righteous shall have rest from the oppression of sinners.'

LIV. 1. And I looked and turned to another part of the earth, and saw there a deep valley with burning fire.   2. And they brought the kings and the mighty, and began to cast them into this deep valley.   3. And there mine eyes saw how they made these their instruments, iron chains of immeasurable weight. 4. And I asked the angel of peace who went with me, saying:

---

aehk)   *bcdflnopxy₁a₁b* = 'going'.
5 **Prepare** (β) > *a*.   **These** > *qu, no*.   **This earth**   Here 'this' is probably for the Greek article.   6 **House of his congregation**   cf. 62⁸ see 38¹ (note).   The houses of his congregations are the synagogues, cf. Ps 74⁸   7 **These mountains . . the hills.**   There is a return here to the figurative language of 52   The mountains and the hills are symbols of the world powers as personated in the kings and the mighty. Before the Messiah's righteousness, the mountains (i e the kings) will not be like the earth which abideth for ever, Ps 78⁶⁹ Eccles. 1⁴, and the hills (i. e. the mighty) shall be as a fount of water, Is 64³; cf. 52⁶   The earth's great ones will become strengthless and vanish at the presence of the Messiah.   His

righteousness (*a–q*).   *q, t²β–n* 'His face'

LIV   In 53 the writer described the scene of the judgement and the fetters that were being prepared to bind the kings on their condemnation   Here he speaks of Gehenna into which the kings are cast   they are punished in the sight of the righteous, cf 62¹²   The fallen angels are cast into a furnace of fire. The idea of the fallen angels and kings being judged together is to be traced to Is 24²¹, ²²   1 **To another part of the earth.**   The writer now turns from the valley of Jehoshaphat on the north-east of Jerusalem to the valley of Hinnom lying to the south of it.   **A deep valley**   see 48⁶ (note). This valley seems to be that spoken of in 56³, ⁴   2. **This** > *q, bcdxy.*
3–5. The pre-Messianic judgement of

'For whom are these chains being prepared?' 5. And he said unto me 'These are being prepared for the hosts of Azâzêl, so that they may take them and cast them into the abyss of complete condemnation, and they shall cover their jaws with rough stones as the Lord of Spirits commanded.

6. And Michael, and Gabriel, and Raphael, and Phanuel shall take hold of them on that great day, and cast them on that day into the burning furnace, that the Lord of Spirits may take vengeance on them for their unrighteousness in becoming subject to Satan and leading astray those who dwell on the earth.'

LIV. 7—LV. 2. *Noachic Fragment on the first World Judgement.*

7. And in those days shall punishment come from the Lord of Spirits, and He will open all the chambers of waters which are

the watchers in ver 5 is that described at length in 10–16 **4 Chains** *m β-dn* read 'chains of instruments', *qt* 'chains and instruments'. I have omitted this addition with *n* **5 Abyss** Cf 10^{4}. **The abyss of complete condemnation** is not Gehenna but only the preliminary place of punishment, cf $10^{5, 12}$. We are not told by whom the chains are forged for the fallen angels, nor yet who are the agents who execute the first judgement upon them Chains are also made for the kings and the mighty, 53^{5} **And they shall cover.** *q* reads 'to cover' **6** The final judgement upon the watchers **On that great day** see 45^{2} (note). Observe that in the Parables the guilt of the watchers originated in their becoming subjects of Satan · see 40^{7} (note) · Book of Jubilees, $10^{8\ sqq}$ **And**^{50} > *q, abcde* **Cast them** (*tu, β*) > *gmq* **Furnace** (*a–q*) *q, y* 'fire', *β-y* 'furnace of fire', cf 10^{6} 18^{11} 21^{7-10} $90^{24,25}$. This is to be distinguished from Gehenna **7—LV. 2.** This digression on the first world-judgement is a Noachic fragment The Book of Noah is mentioned in the Book of Jubilees, 10^{13} 21^{10} These fragments, $39^{1, 2a}$ 54^{7}–55^{2} 60 65–69^{25}, deal mainly with the Deluge They are to be regarded as interpolations on the following grounds out of many. (1) They always disturb the context in which they occur (2) They profess to be a revelation of Noah, $60^{7-11, 24, 25}$ 65–68^{1} (3) Such a definite date as is given in 60^{1} is unknown in the Parables. (4) The demonology is different the Satans and the fallen angels which are carefully distinguished in the Parables are confused in the additions, 69 The chief, moreover, of the fallen angels in the Parables is Azazel, in the additions, Semjaza (5) The interpolator seeks to adapt his additions to their new contexts, and accordingly incorporates in them many terms and phrases from the Parables, such as 'angel of peace', 60^{24}, see 40^{2} (note), 'none shall utter an idle word,' 67^{9}, see 49^{4} (note); 'denied the Lord of Spirits,' $67^{8, 10}$, see 38^{2} (note), 'the angel who went with me and showed me what was hidden,' 60^{11}, see 43^{3} (note); *but observe that in such borrowings he misuses technical terms and phrases*, either

above the heavens, and of the fountains which are beneath the earth.   8. And all the waters shall be joined with the waters: that which is above the heavens is the masculine, and the water which is beneath the earth is the feminine.   9. And they shall destroy all who dwell on the earth and those who dwell under the ends of the heaven.   10. And when they have recognized

through ignorance or of set purpose Of 'Lord of Spirits', see 37² (note), 'Head of Days,' 55¹, see 46¹ (note); 'angels of punishment,' 40⁷ 66¹ (note), 'Son of Man,' 60¹⁰ (note); 'those who dwell on the earth,' 54⁹ 37⁵ (note). (6) The interpolator misunderstands the Parables, and combines absolutely alien elements; cf. 'the burning valley in the metal mountains in the west'— an illegitimate combination of 52¹, ² and 54¹.   (7) Finally, the Parables follow the LXX chronology, the interpolations follow the Samaritan   Thus in 61¹² Enoch speaks of the elect as being already in Paradise, and in 70⁴ on his translation he finds his forefathers already there.   This could be the case only according to the LXX reckoning, for according to the Samaritan all his forefathers survived him, and, according to the Hebrew, all except Adam   The interpolations follow the Samaritan reckoning. see 65² (note)   The object of the interpolator is clear   Although the final world judgement is treated at length, there are only the briefest references to the first   It was to supply this defect in the Parables that an existing Apocalypse of Noah was laid under contribution   7 Above the heavens All MSS but ₁b add 'and in addition to the fountains which are beneath the heavens'—an addition which originated in a dittograph of the following clause According to early Semitic views there were only waters above the heavens and below the earth.   8 We have

here a fragment of Babylonian cosmology.   According to the Babylonians water was the primeval element or elements, for there the waters were distinguished as Apsu and Tiamat—in other words as the male and female elements   From the mingling of these two arose the gods   see *KAT*³, p 492 sq, Hastings, *Encyc of Religion,* ii 814; Jastrow, *Religion of Babylonia,* 411 sqq   Traces of this myth are found in Jer Berakh ix 2 'the upper water is male and the lower water is female (המים העליונים זכרים והתחתונים נקבות)   A protest against accepting water as the primitive element is found in Chag 14ᵇ on the part of Rabbi Aqiba   This religious and philosophical idea is stated in Jer. Chag ii 1 'Originally the world consisted of water in water' (בתחלה היה העולם מים במים). 9. All who dwell on the earth see 37⁵ note   10 And¹⁰. > q When   *tu, ew* read ba'ēntaza = 'inasmuch as' = διότι, gmq, t²β-ew ba'-ēntaz = 'on this account', διὰ τοῦτο Here διότι = כי or כאשר   Thus the sentence = διότι ἔγνωσαν   καί (= the vaw of the apodosis in Hebrew) ἐν τούτοις (or τούτω) = ובאלה... כי ידעו Here the Greek translator should have rendered כי by ἐπεί and not by διότι The same confusion could arise in the case of Aramaic, for ארי = either διότι or ἐπεί   As regards the sense of the passage, we find that the kings and the mighty in 63⁴ ˢᵠᵠ· come to acknowledge their guilt before their destruction   But it is possible that the

their unrighteousness which they have wrought on the earth, then by these shall they perish.'

LV. 1. And after that the Head of Days repented and said · ' In vain have I destroyed all who dwell on the earth.' 2. And He sware by His great name : ' Henceforth I will not do so to all who dwell on the earth, and I will set a sign in the heaven and this shall be a pledge of good faith between Me and them for ever, so long as heaven is above the earth. And this is in accordance with My command.

LV. 3—LVI. 4. *Final Judgement of Azazel, the Watchers and their children.*

3. When I have desired to take hold of them by the hand of the angels on the day of tribulation and pain because of this, I will cause My chastisement and My wrath to abide upon them, saith God, the Lord of Spirits. 4. Ye †mighty kings† who dwell on the earth, ye shall have to behold Mine Elect One, how he sits on the throne of glory and judges Azâzêl, and all his associates, and all his hosts in the name of the Lord of Spirits.'

LVI. 1. And I saw there the hosts of the angels of punishment going, and they held scourges and chains of iron and bronze.

reading of *gmq*, *t²β-ew* is right and that we should render : 'And owing to this they will recognize . . and by this (i e. the deluge) shall they perish '

LV 1. **The Head of Days**. see 46¹ (note). We have here a good illustration of the method by which the interpolator seeks to assimilate his additions by incorporating technical terms from the main text. **Repented** cf Gen 8²¹. **2** So (*q*, *t²β-z*) > *qmt¹u*, *x* This is in accordance with **My command** (*gt*). *m* reads ' this is My command', *q* (ungrammatical) ' this command is according to My desire ', *u*, *t²β* 'after this according to My command' The last reading would perhaps connect best with what follows. **3** This verse connects immediately

with 54⁶. **Day of tribulation and pain** see 45² (note) **Because of this**. Text = ἔμπροσθεν τούτου, a mistranslation of מכמו זאת, **I will cause . to abide** *a-qu q*, *β-d* '(My chastisement) shall abide' **Chastisement wrath** (*a*) ᴐ *β* **4**. The kings have to witness the judgement passed on the angels · if Azazel and his hosts are judged and condemned by the Messiah, how much more likely will they ! The text should almost certainly be ' Ye kings and mighty' see 38⁵ (note), 62⁵. **Of glory** (*a-q*). *q*, *β* ' of My glory '.

LVI 1-4. These verses refer to the watchers and their children the demons The term 'beloved' is specially used of the demons in regard to their parents in 1-36 see 10¹² 14⁶ **1 They**

2. And I asked the angel of peace who went with me, saying ·
'To whom are these who hold the scourges going ? '   3. And
he said unto me : ' To their elect and beloved ones that they may
be cast into the chasm of the abyss of the valley.

>4. And then that valley shall be filled with their elect and
>beloved,
>
>>And the days of their lives shall be at an end,
>>
>>And the days of their leading astray shall not thenceforward
>>be reckoned.

LVI. 5–8. *Last struggle of heathen Powers against Israel*

>5 And in those days the angels shall return
>
>>And hurl themselves to the east upon the Parthians and Medes:

held (*gq*, β). > *mtu*.   Scourges and
(*g*). > *qt*, β   *mu* read ' and '.   2
These who (*g*, *t²*) *mqt¹u* read ' these ',
β–*n* 'who'. Scourges (*g*) > *a–g*, β
3 Chasm of > *q*.   4. And¹⁰. > *q*
Not thenceforward be reckoned,
i. e. be at an end   5—LVII 3ᵃ We
have here another section of the ' Elect
One ' source (see Introd p 65), or
rather a fresh source partially adapted
to the ' Elect One ' source. It depicts
the last struggle of the heathen powers
against the Messianic kingdom established in Jerusalem. Such a conception is quite in place in 83–90 91–104,
but is difficult to reconcile with the
ruling ideas in 37–70   A Messiah
who was only a man with his seat at
Jerusalem might well be conceived of
as assailed by the Gentile powers. But
this is impossible in the case of a superhuman Messiah, who, possessing universal dominion and attended by
legions of angels, holds universal assize,
and, supported by the actual presence
of the Almighty, destroys all his
enemies with the breath of his mouth.
Hence this section forms a harsh break
in the context   Moreover, the Parables deal only in general terms   no
names are mentioned as here, nor is

any definite information given as a
means of determining their date or the
persons against whom they are directed.
Finally, the seat of the kingdom on the
Advent of the Messiah will not be
Jerusalem merely as is here implied,
but a transformed heaven and earth.
This section may be dated with some
probability. The description is pro-
phetical, and is merely a reproduction
of the coming strife of Gog and Magog
against Israel   The latter names are
replaced by those of the Medes and
Parthians, who are the only great world
powers from whom the interpolator believes great danger may be apprehended.
Syria had ceased to be formidable from
100 B c. onward, and Rome had not
intervened in Jewish affairs practically
till 64 B c   The date therefore of this
section must be earlier than 64 B c   If
it belonged originally to the Elect One
source, then it serves to determine its
date   5   In Ezek 38¹⁴⁻¹⁷ it is said
that God will stir up the Gentiles , but
here in keeping with the views of a
later time this business is assigned to
the angels, cf Dan. 10¹³, ²⁰, ²¹ 12¹
Return (*gm¹q*). *m²tu*, β 'assemble '
The Parthians and Medes. These
are the chief nations in the league

They shall stir up the kings, so that a spirit of unrest shall
come upon them,

And they shall rouse them from their thrones,

That they may break forth as lions from their lairs,

And as hungry wolves among their flocks.

6　And they shall go up and tread under foot the land of His
elect ones,

[And the land of His elect ones shall be before them a
threshing-floor and a highway]:

7.　But the city of my righteous shall be a hindrance to their
horses.

And they shall begin to fight among themselves,

And their right hand shall be strong against themselves,

And a man shall not know his brother,

Nor a son his father or his mother,

Till there be no number of the corpses through their
slaughter,

And their punishment be not in vain.

8　In those days Sheol shall open its jaws,

And they shall be swallowed up therein,

And their destruction shall be at an end;

Sheol shall devour the sinners in the presence of the elect.'

against Israel.　　**6　And the land
. . . a highway**　Bracketed as a dittograph of the preceding line It makes
the stanza too long　Cf 58⁶ᵈ　**The
land of His elect ones**¹⁰ (*gqt*)　*mu, β-e* 'their
elect ones'.　Threshing-floor . cf. Is.
21¹⁰　**7. But** the attack on Jerusalem
will fail, Zech 12²·³, and civil strife will
break out amongst the invading nations,
Ezek. 38²¹ Zech 14¹³ Hag 2²², and they
will involve each other in common destruction, cf 100¹⁻³, to which section
these ideas rightly belong.　**But**¹⁰
(*tuβ*) > *gmq*.　**His brother** (*a*).
β 'his neighbour and his brother'.
No number . slaughter Cf. Nah. 3³.
All the MSS. read 'a number ... through

their slaughter'.　A scribe in *t* inserts a
negative before the verb—which I have
followed in my translation.　But I suggest that 'ĕmôtômû (= 'through their
slaughter') is corrupt.　It = ἐκ θανάτου
αὐτῶν = ממותם corrupt for מרבות
Hence 'the number of the corpses be
more than myriads'.　*g* omits 'ĕmôtômû.
This and the following line is read by *q* as
follows. 'For then number through their
death and chastisement shall be corpses
and it shall not be in vain'.　**8.
In those** (*a-q*).　*qβ* 'and in those'.
Sheol shall open its jaws　Cf.
Num. 16³¹⁻³³ Is 5¹⁴.　See 63¹⁰.
Shall be at an end (*g*) > *t, β*.　*q*
reads 'shall not end', *m* 'has sunk
down', *u* 'has been destroyed'.

The Return from the Dispersion.

LVII. 1. And it came to pass after this that I saw another host of wagons, and men riding thereon, and coming on the winds from the east, and from the west to the south. 2. And the noise of their wagons was heard, and when this turmoil took place the holy ones from heaven remarked it, and the pillars of the earth were moved from their place, and the sound thereof was heard from the one end of heaven to the other, in one day. 3. And they shall all fall down and worship the Lord of Spirits And this is the end of the second Parable.

LVIII—LXXI. The Third Parable

LVIII. *The Blessedness of the Saints.*

LVIII. 1. And I began to speak the third Parable concerning the righteous and elect.

2. Blessed are ye, ye righteous and elect,
   For glorious shall be your lot.

3. And the righteous shall be in the light of the sun,
   And the elect in the light of eternal life:

LVII On the destruction of the Gentile invaders, the dispersed of Israel return to Jerusalem from the East and from the West, cf Is 27^{13} 43$^{5, 6}$ 49$^{12, 22, 23}$. 1 And men (α) β 'men'. **Coming on the winds.** A figure expressing the swiftness of their return. Perhaps for 'on' we should read 'like', the mistake having arisen from a corruption of כ into כ in the Hebrew From the west *q* reads 'to the west'. 2. **The noise** was heard (*gq*, β) *mtu* 'there was the noise'. **The pillars of the earth were moved**: cf Hag. 2$^{6, 7}$ Joel 3^{16}. **One end of heaven to the other** (*a-q*). β reads 'the end of the earth to the end of the heaven'. **LVIII.** Here begins the third Parable. It is probable that a large part of it has been lost, being displaced to make room for the Noachic fragments As it stands it embraces 58 61–64 69$^{26–29}$ The introductory words, 'Concerning the righteous and the elect,' in this Parable, as in the other two, are but a very indifferent index to its contents The Parable as it has reached us, might reasonably be described as 'Concerning the final judgement held by the Son of Man over all created beings, but especially over the great ones of the earth and the final blessedness of the righteous and elect' 2. **Glorious shall be your lot** This lot is preserved for them by the Messiah, 48^7. 3 **Light of the sun** see 38^4 (note) **Eternal life**. see 37^4 (note): cf. Dan 12^3 Pss of Sol 3^{16} 4 They

The days of their life shall be unending,
And the days of the holy without number.

4. And they shall seek the light and find righteousness with
the Lord of Spirits:
There shall be peace to the righteous in the name of the
Eternal Lord.

5. And after this it shall be said to the holy in heaven
That they should seek out the secrets of righteousness, the
heritage of faith
For it has become bright as the sun upon earth,
And the darkness is past.

6. And there shall be a light that never **endeth**,
And to a limit (lit. 'number') of days they shall not come,
For the darkness shall first have been destroyed,
[And the light established before the Lord of Spirits]
And the light of uprightness established for ever before the
Lord of Spirits.

The Lights and the Thunder.

LIX. 1. In those days mine eyes saw the secrets of the
lightnings, and of the lights, and the judgements they execute
(lit. 'their judgement') and they lighten for a blessing or a

will through a natural affinity seek
after light and righteousness; cf.
38⁴ (note).   The Eternal Lord, or
'Lord of the ages'. See 81¹⁰ and note
on 1⁵. In 12³ we have 'the king of
the ages' or 'the Eternal King' Cf.
82⁷ 84².   5. They will be bidden
to seek and make their own the hidden
recompense of righteousness (cf 38⁵),
the glorious heritage which has been
ordained for them in heaven and preserved for them by the Messiah, 48⁷.
This will not be achieved once and for
all, but this will be a progress from
light to light and from righteousness to
righteousness.   Heritage of faith
cf 39⁶ 61⁴, ¹¹.   Bright as the sun,
&c. cf 1 John 1⁵.   6. That

never endeth. The MSS. read za'ï
jĕthualaquĕ (*gmqu*) or za'ï jĕthuêlaquĕ
= 'that cannot be numbered'. I have
emended this into za'ïjĕthalaq = 'that
never endeth'.   And the light
established . Spirits Bracketed
as a dittograph of the following line.
LIX. This chapter is an intrusion,
and belongs to the same class as 41³⁻⁸ 43
44   It is probably drawn from a Noah-
Apocalypse.   1. The statements
of the writer rest on Job 36³¹ 37⁵, ¹²
38²⁴⁻²⁷. He wishes to bring out the
ethical ends of the thunder and the
lightning   In those days (*a*). β
'and in those days' Of the lights
(*a, ev*) β-*ev* 'the lights'. For a
blessing or a curse . cf. Job 36³¹

curse as the Lord of Spirits willeth.   2. And there I saw the secrets of the thunder, and how when it resounds above in the heaven, the sound thereof is heard, and he caused me to see the judgements executed on the earth, whether they be for well-being and blessing, or for a curse according to the word of the Lord of Spirits.   3 And after that all the secrets of the lights and lightnings were shown to me, and they lighten for blessing and for satisfying]

Book of Noah—a Fragment.

Quaking of the Heaven : Behemoth and Leviathan : the Elements.

LX. 1. In the year five hundred, in the seventh month, on the fourteenth day of the month in the life of †Enoch†. In that Parable I saw how a mighty quaking made the heaven of heavens to quake, and the host of the Most High, and the angels, a thousand thousands and ten thousand times ten thousand, were disquieted with a great disquiet.   2. And the Head of Days sat on the throne of His glory, and the angels and the righteous stood around Him.

37^{18} 2 Cf 60^{13-15} He caused me to see (*a-u, cefhkny*) *abdovι₁a₁b* 'they caused me to see'   Judgements Text = οἰκήματα 'dwellings' corrupt for κρίματα (or οἰκητήρια corrupt for κριτήρια)   On the earth All MSS but *u* add ' and the voice of the thunder ' 'Lord of Spirits' incorporated from the adjoining context.   3. Job 38^{24-27}.

LX. This chapter is one of the Noachic fragments For the grounds on which these are regarded as interpolations see 54^7 (note) · also the following notes on $60^{1, 2, 4, 10, 11}$, &c 1. The year five hundred This date is drawn from Gen 5^{32}, and is a date in the life of Noah and not of Enoch as it stands in our text. For Enoch we should read Noah. In the seventh month, on the fourteenth day of the month This,

according to Levitical law, was the eve of the Feast of Tabernacles. In that Parable This phrase marks a clumsy attempt to connect this chapter with the main context, but betrays the hand of the interpolator A Parable in Enoch's sense is an account of a vision , but the text requires here the word ' vision '; for the writer says, ' I saw the heaven quaking ' The heaven to quake This was a token of the manifestation of divine judgement; cf. $1^{6, 7}$ Host of the Most High a thousand thousands cf. 1^9 40^1 $71^{8, 13}$ 2 Head of Days see 46^1 (note) 54^7 (note) The angels and the righteous According to this we are to regard God as accompanied by angels and *saints* The righteous here can have no other meaning. Such a conception of the

3　And a great trembling seized me,
　　'And fear took hold of me,
　　And my loins gave way,
　　And dissolved were my reins,
　　And I fell upon my face.

4. And Michael sent another angel from among the holy ones
and he raised me up, and when he had raised me up my spirit
returned; for I had not been able to endure the look of this
host, and the commotion and the quaking of the heaven.
5. And Michael said unto me: 'Why art thou disquieted with
such a vision? Until this day lasted the day of His mercy;
and He hath been merciful and long-suffering towards those
who dwell on the earth.　　6. And when the day, and the
power, and the punishment, and the judgement come, which the
Lord of Spirits hath prepared for those who worship not the
righteous law, and for those who deny the righteous judgement,

final Messianic judgement is difficult
though possible; but in the case of the
first judgement (i. e. the Flood) it is not
possible except through misconception
Here again the hand of an ignorant
interpolator is disclosed.　3 Cf
1¹⁴, ²⁴　Loins gave way. Ps 69²³
Is 45¹　Dissolved　All MSS but
u, dy add 'and'　This insertion led to
the addition of tamaswa = 'melted' in
β in order to supply a verb to 'reins'.
My reins (*mq, fnx*)　*gtu β-fnx* read
'all my being'　4 Cf Dan 8¹⁷
10⁹, ¹⁶　Michael sent another
angel. Michael is the chief archangel cf 40⁴, ⁹. The other angel is
appointed to a like duty with the angel
of peace in the Parables, and is actually
so named in 60²⁴　5 Michael (*a*)
β 'the holy Michael'　Merciful and
long-suffering of ver 25 50⁵, ⁵ 61¹³.
6 Worship not (*u*)　All other MSS
omit the negative. In my edition of
1893 I restored this negative on various
grounds when *u* was as yet unknown.
If the negative is not original, then

the corruption may have originated in
the Hebrew　The text = προσκυνοῦσι =
יִשְׁתַּחֲוּוּ, which may be corrupt for
יְשַׁחֵת = 'pervert', 'destroy'.　This
gives an excellent sense.　The righteous law　The text = 'the righteous
judgement' = מִשְׁפַּט צֶדֶק, which, as
Halévy (*Journ Asiat* 367–369, 1867)
has shown, can mean either 'the righteous law' or 'the righteous judgement'.　This phrase occurs twice in
this verse, and I have translated it
in the first instance as 'the righteous
law', and in the second as 'the righteous judgement'.　With the three
clauses in this verse we might compare
4 Ezra 7³⁷

'Videte et intellegite quem negastis,
　　Vel cui non servistis,
　　Vel cuius diligentias sprevistis'.

If the negative is not original, and
my conjecture is right, the text would
run

'Who corrupt the righteous law
And deny the righteous judgement',
　　&c.

and for those who take His name in vain—that day is prepared, for the elect a covenant, but for sinners an inquisition.

25. When the punishment of the Lord of Spirits shall rest upon them, it shall rest in order that the punishment of the Lord of Spirits may not come in vain, and it shall slay the children with their mothers and the children with their fathers. Afterwards the judgement shall take place according to His mercy and His patience.'

7. And on that day were two monsters parted, a female monster named Leviathan, to dwell in the abysses of the ocean over the fountains of the waters.   8. But the male is named Behemoth, who occupied with his breast a waste wilderness named †Dûidâin†, on the east of the garden where the elect and

---

For the elect a covenant. Cf Dan. 9⁴ 'Who keepeth covenant . with them that love Him'   25 I have restored this verse immediately after ver 6, where, if anywhere, it has some meaning   Immediately preceding it there is a dittograph   'in order that the punishment of the Lord of Spirits may not be (*lux* 'may not come' *e* . all other MSS omit negative and verb) in vain, and may slay the children with their mothers and the children with their fathers'   Again, before the final sentence beginning 'Afterwards', &c., all MSS insert the following dittograph: ' When the punishment of the Lord of Spirits shall rest upon these'   7–10 A fragment dealing with certain myths relating to the Creation but not to the Deluge.   7   This strange fancy about Behemoth and Leviathan, which are first mentioned in Job 40 41, is found by Jewish expounders also in Gen 1²¹ Ps. 50¹⁰ Is 27¹. For later allusions see 4 Ezra 6⁴⁹⁻⁵² 2 Bar 29⁴ Here they are represented as huge monsters created on the fifth day of Creation to be the food of the righteous in Messianic times (cf. B. Bathra 74ᵃ) This doctrine does not appear

in 1 Enoch   For further information see Weber, *Jud. Theol* 202, 389, 402; *Jewish Encyc* viii 38; Bousset, *Rel des Judenthums*, 271   The Talmudic view agrees with that of 4 Ezra and 2 Bar so far as to make Behemoth food for the righteous   Fountains of the waters   cf Gen 7¹¹ Job 38¹⁶ 1 En 89⁷   8   †Dûidâin† (*u*) *g* Dûnadâin, *t* Dûndâin, *in*, β–*eh* Dêndain, *h* Dêm (?)   Probably in the longer forms of the name we have a duplication of the initial letters, and Dain or Dem was the older form of the word. From the statement that the place lies to the east of Eden, it seems clear, as Kohut (*Jewish Encyc* viii. 39) has pointed out, that the word is corrupt for Naiδ or Nud , of *tu*   This is 'the land of Nod to the east of Eden' (Gen 4¹⁶). On the east of the garden, i. e the garden of Eden   The locality of Eden varies in the different sections : see notes on 18⁶ 32², ³ 70²⁻⁴ 77³   Here again the question arises have we to do here with the earthly garden of righteousness or with the heavenly ? or are they after all identical ? See note on 32¹. The garden, whichever it is, is apparently empty in

righteous dwell, where my grandfather was taken up, the seventh
from Adam, the first man whom the Lord of Spirits created.
9. And I besought the other angel that he should show me the
might of those monsters, how they were parted on one day and
cast, the one into the abysses of the sea, and the other unto
the dry land of the wilderness.   10. And he said to me.
' Thou son of man, herein thou dost seek to know what is
hidden.'

11. And the other angel who went with me and showed me
what was hidden told me, what is first and last in the heaven
in the height, and beneath the earth in the depth, and at the
ends of the heaven, and on the foundation of the heaven.
12. And the chambers of the winds, and how the winds are

Enoch's time in 32³⁻⁶, and the righteous dead are in the West, 22, it
is the abode of the righteous and
the elect in Enoch's and Noah's
times in 61¹² 60⁸, ²³, the abode of
the earliest fathers in Enoch's time,
70²⁻⁴, the abode of Enoch and Elijah
in Elijah's time, 89⁵² see 65² (note)
This passage and the LXX are the
oldest testimonies for the translation of
Enoch unto Paradise later this idea
made its way into the Latin version of
Sir 44¹⁶ and the Ethiopic version of
Gen 5²⁴. eight others shared this
honour with Enoch according to the
Talmud, Weber, 251.   Seventh from
Adam cf 93³ Jude 14 Book of
Jubilees 7³⁰   7-9, 24 4 Ezra 6⁴⁹⁻⁵²
and 2 Bar 29⁴ appear to have drawn
on our text The following citation
with references tends to prove this
4 Ezra 6⁴⁹ 'Et tunc†conservasti (= נצרת
corrupt for יצרת hence read ' creasti ')
duo animalia, nomen uni vocasti
Behemoth et nomen secundi vocasti
Leviathan' (1 Enoch 60⁷, ⁸) 6⁵⁰ ' Et
separasti ea ab alterutro (1 Enoch 60⁹),
nou enim poterat septima pars ubi erat
aqua congregata capere ea ' 6⁵¹ ' Et
dedisti Behemoth unam partem quae

siccata (1 Enoch 60⁸, ⁹) est tertio die, ut
inhabitet (60⁸) in ea ubi sunt montes
mille' 6⁵² 'Leviathan autem dedisti
septimam partem humidam (60⁸, ⁹): et
servasti ea ut fiant in devorationem
(60²⁴) quibus vis et quando vis'
2 Bar 29⁴ 'And Behemoth shall be
revealed from his place and Leviathan shall ascend from the sea, those two
great monsters (1 Enoch 60⁷, ⁸) which
I created on the fifth day of creation,
and kept until that time, and then
they shall be for food for all that are
left '.   9. The ('that ' q, β–n) other
angel . see vv. 4, 11   10. Thou
son of man This use of the phrase
is after the manner of Ezekiel, and
stands in strong contrast with the
main conception of the Son of Man
in the Parables, 46¹⁻⁹ (notes)   11.
We should expect the answer to the
question in ver 9 to follow here, but it
is not given till ver. 24, and a long
account (11-23) dealing with physical
secrets intervenes. In 60²⁴ it is the
angel of peace who gives the answer.
The other angel who went with
me and showed me, &c Borrowed
from 46², cf 43³.   12 Chambers of
the winds· cf 18¹ 41⁴. All MSS. but g

divided, and how they are weighed, and (how) the **portals** of the
winds are reckoned, each according to the power of the wind,
and the power of the lights of the moon, and according to the
power that is fitting : and the divisions of the stars according to
their names, and how all the divisions are divided.   13. And
the thunders according to the places where they fall, and all the
divisions that are made among the lightnings that it may lighten,
and their host that they may at once obey.   14. For the
thunder has †places of rest† (which) are assigned (to it) while it
is waiting for its peal, and the thunder and lightning are
inseparable, and although not one and undivided, they both go
together through the spirit and separate not.   15. For when
the lightning lightens, the thunder utters its voice, and the spirit
enforces a pause during the peal, and divides equally between
them ; for the treasury of their peals is like the sand, and each
one of them as it peals is held in with a bridle, and turned back
by the power of the spirit, and pushed forward according to the
many quarters of the earth.   16. And the spirit of the sea is
masculine and strong, and according to the might of his strength
he draws it back with a rein, and in like manner it is driven
forward and disperses amid all the mountains of the earth.

read 'in the chambers', &c   **How
they are weighed** cf. 41¹ 43² Job 28²⁵
Portals. So Flemming emends anq'eta
(a) into 'anâqda. Spirits or angels are
appointed to control the various phenomena of nature This is peculiar to these
interpolations, as in other parts of the
book the powers of nature are either
personified or are regarded as conscious
intelligences, cf 18¹⁴⁻¹⁶. The view
taken by the interpolator is followed by
the Book of Jubilees 2², where we find
' angels of the spirit of fire ', ' angels of
hail ', ' angels of hoar-frost ', ' angels of
thunder ', &c, Rev 7¹, ² 14¹⁸ (angel
of fire), 19¹⁷ (angel of the sun), Asc.
Is. iv. 18   **Lights of the moon.**
Its various phases.   13. Cf Job
37¹⁻⁵.   14 This verse is very

unintelligible Halévy's discussion of
this passage (*Journ. Asiat.* 369–372,
1867) is worth consulting. He arrives
at the following translation ' For the
thunder has fixed laws in reference to
the duration of its peal which is
assigned to it   the thunder and the
lightning are not separated in a single
instance · they both proceed with one
accord and separate not. For when
the lightning lightens, the thunder
utters its voice, and the spirit during
its peal makes its arrangements, and
divides the time equally between
them.'   16. The ebb and flow of
the sea explained. **Disperses amid
all the mountains.** With the flow of
the sea is connected its subterranean
advance into the mountains to nourish

17. And the spirit of the hoar-frost is his own angel, and the spirit of the hail is a good angel. 18. And the spirit of the snow has forsaken (his chamber) on account of his strength—there is a special spirit therein, and that which ascends from it is like smoke, and its name is frost. 19. And the spirit of the mist is not united with them in their chambers, but it has a special chamber; for its course is †glorious† both in light and in darkness, and in winter and in summer, and in its chamber is an angel. 20. And the spirit of the dew has its dwelling at the ends of the heaven, and is connected with the chambers of the rain, and its course is in winter and summer: and its clouds and the clouds of the mist are connected, and the one gives to the other. 21. And when the spirit of the rain goes forth from its chamber, the angels come and open the chamber and lead it out, and when it is diffused over the whole earth it unites with the water on the earth. And whensoever it unites with the water on the earth. . . 22. For the waters are for those who dwell on the earth; for they are nourishment for the earth from the Most High who is in heaven therefore there is a measure for the rain, and the angels take it in charge. 23. And these things I saw towards the Garden of the Righteous. 24. And the angel of peace who was with me said to me · 'These two

---

the springs So Dillmann. **17. Is his own angel**, i e. the hoar-frost has a special angel of its own **Is a good angel** Though hail is often hurtful, it is not in charge of a demon but of a good angel **19** The mist is to be distinguished from the foregoing phenomena, for it appears in all seasons and by night and day. **Is glorious** Text may = כבד If so it should have been rendered ' is oppressive'. **In its chamber is an angel** (*tu*) *gmq* 'its chamber is an angel' *β–ni* 'in its chamber is light and its angel', **20** The dew has its dwelling at the ends of the heaven: this would agree with 34¹,² 36¹ and 75⁵ **21** As the

rain is of such importance alike for the ethical and material well-being of man, Job 37¹², ¹³, its spirit is not independent but subordinated to the angels; cf Job 28²⁵ 38²⁵⁻²⁶ **And** ¹⁰. > *gq*. **And whensoever**.. on the earth (*a–q* (save that *u* omits ' with the water on the earth'), *lifhiklnx* ₁*a*) > *qacdeoy* ₁*b*. The apodosis of this sentence is lost. **22· For** ¹⁰ (*mt*, *β–doy* ₁*b*) > *u* *q*, *doy* ₁*b* read 'from the place of'· *g* a corruption of *mt* Observe that the seas and the garden adjoin in 77³⁻⁴ as here in 60²²⁻²³ **23. The Garden of the Righteous** see ver 8 (note) **24** This verse contains the answer to the question in ver 9. The appearance of the angel of peace

monsters, prepared conformably to the greatness of God, shall feed. . .

Angels go off to measure Paradise : the Judgement of the Righteous by the Elect One : the Praise of the Elect One and of God.

LXI. 1. And I saw in those days how long cords were given to those angels, and they took to themselves wings and flew, and they went towards the north.

2 And I asked the angel, saying unto him : 'Why have those (angels) taken these cords and gone off ? ' And he said unto me : 'They have gone to measure'

3. And the angel who went with me said unto me.

'These shall bring the measures of the righteous,
And the ropes of the righteous to the righteous,
That they may stay themselves on the name of the Lord of
Spirits for ever and ever.

4. The elect shall begin to dwell with the elect,

here may be due to the interpolator Elsewhere this chapter speaks of 'another angel' sent by Michael, 60⁴, ⁹, ¹¹.

LXI 1. Here the true text of the Parables is resumed, but the opening verses are very difficult.   Those angels.   *q* reads 'the two angels'.   The angels here referred to may have been definitely named in some preceding part now lost   Wings.   In the O.T. the angels are not represented as winged, unless in its latest books, cf 1 Chron. 21¹⁶.   Towards the north, i e the north-west; cf 70⁸   Paradise is the destination of the angels, cf 60⁸ (note)   2 The angel, i e the angel of peace, who is the *angelus interpres* in the sections dealing with the Elect One see Introd. p 64 sq.   Cords (α). β 'long cords'.   Have gone. > *mu, d*   To measure, ⟨q⟩luβ.   *gm* 'to begin' by *a* scribal slip   The cords which the angels take with them are

for measuring Paradise.   See the reference to this in 70³.   For this idea of angels with measuring cords see Ezek. 40³, ⁶ Zech. 2¹⁻⁸.   3–4. Here as ch 52 there are two sources   These verses belong to the 'Son of Man' source, since the *angelus interpres* is 'the angel who went with me'   See Introd p. 64 sq.   3 The measures of the righteous represent alike the blessed and their habitation.   They are an ideal representation of the community of the righteous, living and departed, and reveal especially the latter, for it matters not by what death these perished, they are alive unto the Lord of Spirits, and will return and stay themselves on the day of his Elect One   these measures are given to faith and strengthen the righteous,   To the righteous (*qqtu, n*) > *m, β-n*   Stay themselves on   Cf 48⁴ 61⁵.   4 Sinners will be driven

And those are the measures which shall be given to faith
And which shall strengthen righteousness.

5. And these measures shall reveal all the secrets of the depths
   of the earth,

   And those who have been destroyed by the desert,
   And those who have been devoured by the beasts,
   And those who have been devoured by the fish of the sea,

   That they may return and stay themselves
   On the day of the Elect One,
   For none shall be destroyed before the Lord of Spirits,
   And none can be destroyed.

6. And all who dwell above in the heaven received a command
   and power and one voice and one light like unto fire.

7. And that One (with) their first words they blessed,
   And extolled and lauded with wisdom,
   And they were wise in utterance and in the spirit of life.

8. And the Lord of Spirits placed the Elect One on the throne
   of glory.

   And he shall judge all the works of the holy above in the
   heaven,

   And in the balance shall their deeds be weighed.

from off the face of the earth, cf. 38[1] (note) **Righteousness** (a) β 'the voice of righteousness' 5 Only the resurrection of the righteous is here spoken of In 51[1,2] there is an account of the resurrection of all Israel see note After the resurrection follows the judgement **Devoured**[10]. *q* omits next nine words through hmt Hence it supports *gmtu* here **By the beasts** (*tu*). *gm* by a scribal error 'by the treasuries' Flemming, followed by Martin, abandons the text of *tu(gm)*, and gives that of β–*n*, which reads 'of the sea and by the beasts', and omits the second 'and those who have been devoured'. 6 **All who dwell above in the heaven,** i e the angels,

cf vv 10 12 47[2]. In 9[3] they are called 'the holy ones of heaven'. The angels were commanded to sing praises, and for that purpose one power and one voice are given to them. 7. **That One.** Either the Elect One or the Lord of Spirits But the translation given above is questionable For la before w'ětů read ba. Then render 'with their first words they blessed'. This seems right, though no object of the praise is definitely stated. 8. See 45[3] (note), cf Ps. 110[1] **Glory** (a). β 'His glory' **The holy above in the heaven,** i e the angels; cf. 61[6] (note). For 'the holy' *q* reads 'the righteous'. **Shall their deeds be weighed** (*mqu*, β) *g* 'they shall

9. And when he shall lift up his countenance

To judge their secret ways according to the word of the name of the Lord of Spirits,

And their, path according to the way of the righteous judgement of the Lord of Spirits,

Then shall they all with one voice speak and bless,

And glorify and extol and sanctify the name of the Lord of Spirits.

10. And He will summon all the host of the heavens, and all the holy ones above, and the host of God, the Cherubin, Seraphin, and Ophannin, and all the angels of power, and all the angels of principalities, and the Elect One, and the other powers on the earth (and) over the water   11. On that day shall raise one voice, and bless and glorify and exalt in the spirit of faith, and in the spirit of wisdom, and in the spirit of patience,

weigh their deeds', *t, abcdefhkl* ' he shall weigh their deeds' On this matter see 41¹ note   **9.** Their ... ways *t* 'their cause' According to the word of the name of the Lord of Spirits This clause is evidently parallel with the next, ' according to the way of the righteous judgement of the Lord of Spirits.' We might therefore translate nagara ' command' 'according to the command of the name of the Lord of Spirits.' Lord of Spirits ²⁰ (a)   β 'Most High God' Sanctify (a, n).   β–n 'praise' **10.** He will summon   i. e. God will summon In my text I took jesew'š as a misrendering of βοήσει. In that case we should render 'all the host of the heavens shall cry out.' Cherubin, Seraphin, and Ophannin . cf 14¹¹, ¹⁸ 20⁷ 71⁷ The Cherubim and Seraphim appear in the O T but are carefully distinguished. Schulz, *A. Tliche Theol*, p 617, says that in no instance are the Cherubim to be regarded as angels, but as symbolic figures they form God's chariot, and

are the means of revealing or concealing His presence But this does not hold of later developments. In the present passage they form an order of angels as they do in Rev 5⁸ᵟᵟ. 2 Enoch 19⁵ 20¹   The Seraphim are beings whose special duty was to serve in God's immediate presence. On the nature of these see also Delitzsch on Is 6². The Ophannim (i e. wheels) are derived from Ezek 1¹⁶. In the Talmud as here they are classed with the Cherubim and Seraphim, Weber, pp. 168, 205 On the angelology of the O. T see Schulz, *A Tliche. Theol* (606–622), *Jewish Encyc in loc* Angels of power, and all the angels of principalities These are exactly St. Paul's 'principalities and powers'; cf Rom 8³⁸ Eph. 1²¹ Col 1¹⁶. The other powers on the earth, &c., i. e the lower angel-powers over nature **11** Glorify + 'and praise', β. Exalt > g. In the spirit of faith, &c These words express the virtues which animate the angels who give praise. The virtues are seven in number; cf.

and in the spirit of mercy, and in the spirit of judgement and of peace, and in the spirit of goodness, and shall all say with one voice : " Blessed is He, and may the name of the Lord of Spirits be blessed for ever and ever."

12. All who sleep not above in heaven shall bless Him ·
All the holy ones who are in heaven shall bless him,
And all the elect who dwell in the garden of life :

And every spirit of light who is able to bless, and glorify, and extol, and hallow Thy blessed name,
And all flesh shall beyond measure glorify and bless Thy name for ever and ever.

13 For great is the mercy of the Lord of Spirits, and He is long-suffering,
And all His works and all that He has created
He has revealed to the righteous and elect
In the name of the Lord of Spirits.'

Judgement of the Kings and the Mighty. Blessedness of the Righteous.

LXII 1. And thus the Lord commanded the kings and the mighty and the exalted, and those who dwell on the earth, and

---

49³. In the spirit of patience (*il₁a*) Other MSS (perhaps rightly) 'in patience' Blessed is He, &c. cf 39¹⁰ 12 All who sleep not see 1⁵ (note). The holy ones (*a, lwxy*) β-*lwry* 'His holy ones Garden of life see 60⁸ (note) The LXX chronology is followed here as in the Parables generally ; cf 54⁷ (note) Spirit of light A phrase embracing good spirits, human and angelic. This thought (cf 108¹¹, ' generation of light') is more fully developed in the N T , 'children of light', Luke 16⁸. Blessed (*a*). β 'holy'. 13 Mercy see 60⁵ (note).

LXII Here we have a lengthened account of the judgement, particularly of the kings and of the mighty This subject has already been handled shortly, 46⁴⁻⁸ 48⁸⁻¹⁰ 53-54³ , but here the actual scene is portrayed The kings and the mighty will be filled with anguish when they behold the Messiah, and will fall down and worship, and pray for mercy at his hands But their prayers will be of no avail and they will be carried off by the angels of punishment. The blessedness of the lot of the righteous is then dwelt upon in contrast with the fate of the wicked 1. The kings and

said · ' Open your eyes and lift up your horns if ye are able to recognize the Elect One.'

2. And the Lord of Spirits seated him on the throne of His glory,
   And the spirit of righteousness was poured out upon him,
   And the word of his mouth slays all the sinners,
   And all the unrighteous are destroyed from before his face.

3. And there shall stand up in that day all the kings and the mighty,
   And the exalted and those who hold the earth,
   And they shall see and recognize
   How he sits on the throne of his glory,
   And righteousness is judged before him,
   And no lying word is spoken before him.

4. Then shall pain come upon them as on a woman in travail,
   [And she has pain in bringing forth]
   When her child enters the mouth of the womb,
   And she has pain in bringing forth.

5. And one portion of them shall look on the other,
   And they shall be terrified,
   And they shall be downcast of countenance,
   And pain shall seize them,

the mighty. see 38⁵   Lift up your horns. cf Ps 75⁴.   Recognize, i. e. recognize him to be what he is—the Messiah. The word translated 'recognize' could also be rendered 'comprehend', 'understand'   2 Seated him. MSS read nahara = 'sat' which Dillmann emended into anbarô = 'seated him'   Cf Is. 11⁴   The word of his mouth. The judgement is forensic. All the sinners, and all the unrighteous. Though the writer is chiefly concerned with the judgement of the kings, the condemnation of the sinners and godless and unrighteous

is frequently referred to; cf 38¹, ², ³ 41² 45², ⁵, ⁶ [50²] 53², ⁷ 62¹³ 69²⁷.   From before his face (α)   β 'and from before his face '.   3 The fact that even the righteous are judged opens up a terrible prospect for the kings and the mighty, cf 1 Pet. 4¹⁸.   Righteousness (α)   β–no₁b ' the righteous in righteousness ', no₁b ' the righteous '   No lying word see 49⁴ (note).   4. Cf Is 13⁸ 21³ 26¹⁷, &c   [And she has pain, &c.] Bracketed as a dittograph of the fourth line   5 One portion of them shall look on the other. With this scene cf. Wisdom

When they see that Son of Man
Sitting on the throne of his glory.

6. And the kings and the mighty and all who possess the
earth shall bless and glorify and extol him who rules over all,
who was hidden.

7. For from the beginning the Son of Man was hidden,
And the Most High preserved him in the presence of His
might,
And revealed him to the elect.

8. And the congregation of the elect and holy shall be
sown,
And all the elect shall stand before him on that day.

9. And all the kings and the mighty and the exalted and
those who rule the earth
Shall fall down before him on their faces,
And worship and set their hope upon that Son of
Man,
And petition him and supplicate for mercy at his hands.

10. Nevertheless that Lord of Spirits will so press them
That they shall hastily go forth from His presence,
And their faces shall be filled with shame,
And the darkness shall grow deeper on their faces.

5¹ˢqq. This shows that Is 13⁸ was in the mind of the writer. **Son of Man** (*a–m*) *m, β* 'Son of the woman' See 46² (note) **6.** The kings are now ready to acknowledge and worship the Son of Man, but it is too late **The kings and the mighty** (*a–u*). *u, β* 'the mighty kings'. **Rules over all.** cf Dan 7¹⁴ **Who was hidden** This could also be rendered 'that was hidden', i e the unseen universe **6, 7 Hidden** cf 48⁶. This word occasions a digression and an explanation Before he appeared to judge he was preserved by the Lord of Spirits and revealed to the elect through the spirit of pro-

phecy, 48⁷. By this means the community of the elect was founded (lit. 'sown'), but was not to behold him till the final judgement The community that is 'sown' is called the 'plant of righteousness', cf 10¹⁶ (note) **7** From the beginning (*mqt, β–₁a*). The readings of *qu₁a* are corruptions of this. **8 Congregation.** cf 38¹ (note). **Elect and holy** (*a*). *β* 'holy and elect'. **9, 10** The description of the judgement of the kings resumed they implore mercy, but in vain **10. Shame and darkness** cf 46⁶ 4 Ezra 7⁶⁵. **Darkness shall grow deeper,** &c. (*gt, β–f*). Nah. 2¹⁰ 'the

11. And He will deliver them to the angels for punishment,
    To execute vengeance on them because they have oppressed
    His children and His elect.

12. And they shall be a spectacle for the righteous and for His
    elect :
    They shall rejoice over them,
    Because the wrath of the Lord of Spirits resteth upon them,
    And His sword is drunk with their blood.

13. And the righteous and elect shall be saved on that day,
    And they shall never thenceforward see the face of the
    sinners and unrighteous.

14. And the Lord of Spirits will abide over them,
    And with that Son of Man shall they eat
    And lie down and rise up for ever and ever.

15. And the righteous and elect shall have risen from the earth,
    And ceased to be of downcast countenance.

16. And they shall have been clothed with garments of glory,
    And these shall be the garments of life from the Lord of
    Spirits :
    And your garments shall not grow old,
    Nor your glory pass away before the Lord of Spirits.

faces of all of them shall gather darkness' may be the source of our text.   11 He will deliver them to the angels, &c   I have here accepted an emendation of Flemming $m\beta$ read 'the angels of punishment shall take them in charge'   Angels for punishment   see 40[7] (note)   Cf. 53[3]-54[2].   12. Spectacle see 48[9] (note)   Sword   Used figuratively here, cf. 63[11].   Drunk . cf Is 34[6].   13 Saved   cf 48[7] 14 The kingdom is at last established and God Himself dwells amongst them, cf Is 60[19, 20] Zeph. 3[15-17] . and the Messiah will dwell with them, cf 45[4] 38[2]   The kingdom lasts for ever

Eat β-n^1 read 'abide and eat'   Eat and lie down.   From Zeph. 3[13] 15 This verse does not refer to the resurrection but signifies that all the humiliations of the righteous are at an end   16. Of glory (a, u) β-u ' of life .   Garments of life (q, β). a-q ' your garments, garments of life ' In a-q the addition seems to be drawn from the next line.   From $(a$-$t^1, t^2)$ β 'with'.   On the garments of the blessed cf 2 Cor 5[3], 4 Rev 3[4, 5, 18] 4[4] 6[11] 7[9, 13, 14] 4 Ezra 2[39, 45] Herm *Sim* 8[2] See also 1 Enoch 108[12] These garments are the spiritual bodies that await the righteous   Cf 2 Cor 5[2-5].   Shall not grow old   cf Deut 8[4] 29[5]

The unavailing Repentance of the Kings and the Mighty.

LXIII. 1. In those days shall the mighty and the kings who possess the earth implore (Him) to grant them a little respite from His angels of punishment to whom they were delivered, that they might fall down and worship before the Lord of Spirits, and confess their sins before Him.   2. And they shall bless and glorify the Lord of Spirits, and say :

' Blessed is the Lord of Spirits and the Lord of kings,
And the Lord of the mighty and the Lord of the rich,
And the Lord of glory and the Lord of wisdom,

3. And splendid in every secret thing is Thy power from generation to generation,
And Thy glory for ever and ever :

Deep are all Thy secrets and innumerable,
And Thy righteousness is beyond reckoning.

4. We have now learnt that we should glorify
And bless the Lord of kings and Him who is king over all kings.'

5. And they shall say
' Would that we had rest to glorify and give thanks
And confess our faith before His glory !

LXIII The writer again returns to the kings and the mighty in order to describe their bitter and unavailing repentance The description is not an amplification of 62⁵⁻¹², but takes up the history at a later stage after that the kings have appealed in vain to the Messiah and are already in the custody of the angels of punishment As their appeal to the Messiah has failed, they entreat the angels of punishment, to whom they are delivered, to grant them a respite to worship the Lord of Spirits and confess their sins before Him This in fact forms an indirect and last despairing appeal to the Lord of Spirits At the same time

it is a justification of God's justice. For a somewhat similar passage cf Wisdom 5³⁻⁸.   1 The **mighty and the kings** ₍a₎ *aehknvw* ' kings', *bedfilopxy*₁a₁b ' mighty kings'.   **His angels** (a–tu, β). t, q² ' the angels'. 2 Their confession acknowledges all that they formerly denied, cf 46⁵ 3 Cf 49²   **Splendid in every secret thing is Thy power** (a–mu) β ' every secret thing is lighted up and Thy power'.   5. **Would that** The Ethiopic here is a rendering of the Hebraism מִי יִתֵּן, or the Aramaism מָן יִהַב.   **Glorify and give thanks.** (a–q) q, β ' glorify Him and thank Him ' β adds ' and bless Him '

6. And now we long for a little rest but find it not :
   We follow hard upon and obtain (it) not:

   And light has vanished from before us,
   And darkness is our dwelling-place for ever and ever

7. For we have not believed before Him
   Nor glorified the name of the Lord of Spirits, [nor glorified
   our Lord]

   But our hope was in the sceptre of our kingdom,
   And in our glory.

8. And in the day of our suffering and tribulation He saves us not,
   And we find no respite for confession

   That our Lord is true in all His works, and in His judgements and His justice,
   And His judgements have no respect of persons.

9 And we pass away from before His face on account of our
   works,
   And all our sins are reckoned up in righteousness.'

10. Now they will say unto themselves . ' Our souls are full of
unrighteous gain, but it does not prevent us from descending
from the midst thereof into the †burden† of Sheol.'

---

6 And now (γβ) a–q ' now'
Follow hard upon (gt¹ ₁b = κατα-
διώκομεν) > u, ι mq, t²β–ι₁α₁b ' are
driven away' Obtain (it) not.
q omits the following ' and ' and reads
' obtain not light it has vanished,' &c
Darkness is our dwelling-place cf.
46⁶. 7 Believed, or ' confessed'
Of Spirits (gq, efv) m ' of lords',
tu, β–efv ' of kings' The following
clause is bracketed as a dittograph
Our Lord (a) β ' the Lord in all
His work' Sceptre (gm, io ₁a ₁b)
tu, fv ' throne', q, dhkln ' sceptre of
the throne' 8. There is no place
of repentance when the final judgement has come Our Lord is true,
&c. Cf. Jub 4²¹. He is ' faithful and

He is righteous beyond all and there
is no accepting of persons with Him
In His judgements (a–q) β ' in
all His judgements' 10. Riches
avail not to their salvation , cf 52⁷ 58
Ps 49⁷⁻¹² Unrighteous gain cf
Luke 16⁹· ¹¹ Sn 5⁸ From the midst
thereof (gqu). mt, β–b ' from the
flame thereof' Into the †burden†
Kěbad = βάρος, which the Ethiopic
translator may have confused with
βάριν as in Pss 47⁸· ¹² 121⁷ Lam 2⁵
If this is so, then we should render
' into the stronghold of Sheol' Though
the general sense is clear, the details
are uncertain Perhaps we should
read ' into the burden of the flame
of Sheol' Sheol. This word has

11. And after that their faces shall be filled with darkness
And shame before that Son of Man,

borne different meanings at different periods and also different meanings during the same period, owing to the coexistence of different stages in the development of thought. As these different meanings are to be found in Enoch, a short history of the conception will be the best means of explanation. (1) Sheol in the O.T. is the place appointed for all living, Job 30²³ from its grasp there is never any possibility of escape, Job 7⁶. It is situated beneath the earth, Num 16³⁰, it is the land of darkness and confusion, Job 10²¹,²², of destruction, forgetfulness, and silence, Pss 88¹¹,¹² 94¹⁷ 115¹⁷. Nevertheless the identity of the individual is in some measure preserved, Is 14¹⁰ Ezek. 32²¹ 1 Sam 28¹⁵ ˢᵠᵠ but the existence is joyless and has no point of contact with God or human interests, Pss. 6⁵ 30⁹ Is 38¹¹,¹⁸. In the conception of Sheol there is no moral or religious element involved; no moral distinctions are observed in it, good and bad fare alike. But the family, national, and social distinctions of the world above are still reproduced, and men are gathered to their fathers or people, Gen. 25⁸,⁹ 35²⁹ Ezek 32¹⁷⁻³² kings are seated on their thrones even there, Is 14⁹,¹⁰ Ezek 32²¹,²⁴. Thus the O.T Sheol does not differ essentially from the Homeric Hades, Odyss xi 488, 489. This view of Sheol was the orthodox and prevailing one till the second century B.C, cf Sir 14¹⁶ 17²²,²³ 30¹⁷ 1 Bar 3¹¹ Tob 3¹⁰ 13² 1 Enoch 102¹¹ (i.e where Sadducees are introduced as speaking). Individual voices indeed had been raised against it in favour of a religious conception of Sheol, and finally through their advocacy this higher conception gradually won its way into acceptance.

(2) This second and higher conception of Sheol was the product of the same religious thought that gave birth to the doctrine of the Resurrection—the thought that found the answer to its difficulties by carrying the idea of retribution into the life beyond the grave. The old conception thus underwent a double change. Firstly, it became essentially a place where men were treated according to their deserts, with a division for the righteous, and a division for the wicked. And, secondly, from being the unending abode of the departed, it came to be only an intermediate state ; cf En. 22 51¹ 102⁶ (?) Luke 16²² (?). (3) The conception underwent a further change, and no longer signified the intermediate state of the righteous and of the wicked, but came to be used of the abode of the wicked only, either as their preliminary abode, cf Rev 1¹⁸ 6⁸ 20¹³,¹⁴, or as their final one, En 63¹⁰ 99¹¹ 103⁷. This was probably due to the fact that the Resurrection was limited to the righteous, and thus the souls of the wicked simply remained in Sheol, which thus practically became hell or Gehenna, cf Pss Sol 14⁶ 15¹¹. In 63¹⁰ the kings are cast into Sheol, but into Gehenna in 54¹⁻². That this conception of Sheol appeared in isolated cases in the Persian period, see Cheyne, *Origin of the Psalter*, 381-412. Cf. on the question generally, Oehler, *Theol des A T* i. 253-266 ; Schulz, *A Tliche Theol.* 697-708 ; Charles, *The Doctrine of a Future Life, passim.* In the Talmud Sheol has become synonymous with Gehenna, Weber, *Jud Theol* 341-342. **11. With darkness** cf. 46⁵ 62¹⁰. **Sword.** Used figuratively here, cf. 62¹². Bousset suggests that this verse is an interpola-

And they shall be driven from his presence,
And the sword shall abide before his face in their midst.

12. Thus spake the Lord of Spirits : ' This is the ordinance and judgement with respect to the mighty and the kings and the exalted and those who possess the earth before the Lord of Spirits.'

Vision of the fallen Angels in the Place of Punishment.

LXIV. 1. And other forms I saw hidden in that place. 2. I heard the voice of the angel saying : ' These are the angels who descended to the earth, and revealed what was hidden to the children of men and seduced the children of men into committing sin.'

Enoch foretells to Noah the Deluge and his own Preservation.

LXV. 1. And in those days Noah saw the earth that it had sunk down and its destruction was nigh. 2. And he arose from thence and went to the ends of the earth, and cried aloud to his grandfather Enoch · and Noah said three times with an

---

tion. If we excise it the whole chapter refers to the judgement of the Lord of Spirits. This verse closely resembles 62¹⁰.   12 Thus (a–g)   g 'as', β ' and thus '

LXIV. A brief digression on the fallen angels whose judgement has already been described in the second Parable, 54⁹ ˢᵠᵠ 55⁸, ⁴ This chapter, if originally a part of the Parables, as it quite well can be, is in the wrong place here, for ' that place , spoken of as the place of punishment of the angels, cannot be Sheol referred to in 63¹⁰   2 I heard   m, vx ' and I heard '   Voice of the angel   m ' voice of the angels '.   Descended. + t, β ' from heaven '.

LXV—LXIX. 25. These chapters professedly and in fact belong to a Noah Apocalypse, and have no right to form a part of the text of Enoch.

The main reasons for this conclusion are to be found in the note on 54⁷. Like the other Noachic interpolations, this interpolation is of a fragmentary nature : it deals mainly with three subjects   (1) 65¹–67³, the impending Flood and the deliverance of Noah, (2) 67⁴–69¹, the punishment of the fallen angels, with a digression on the kings and the mighty, (3) 69²–²⁵, the fall of the angels and the secrets they disclosed.

LXV. 1. Observe that the vision is Noah's   The vision opens here with a subsidence of the earth, as in 60¹ with a quaking of the heavens   And (q, β). > a–q   Noah   t ' I Noah ', and in the first person throughout verses 1-2 2 The ends of the earth. The entrance to heaven is at the ends of the earth   Cf. 106⁸.   Grandfather   In reality great - grandfather , cf. 60⁸

embittered voice · 'Hear me, hear me, hear me.'   3. And I
said unto him: 'Tell me what it is that is falling out on the
earth that the earth is in such evil plight and shaken, lest per-
chance I shall perish with it.'   4. And thereupon there was
a great commotion on the earth, and a voice was heard from
heaven, and I fell on my face.   5. And Enoch my grandfather came and stood by me, and said unto me . 'Why hast
thou cried unto me with a bitter cry and weeping ?

6 And a command has gone forth from the presence of the
Lord concerning those who dwell on the earth that their ruin is
accomplished because they have learnt all the secrets of the
angels, and all the violence of the Satans, and all their powers—
the most secret ones—and all the power of those who practise
sorcery, and the power of witchcraft, and the power of those who
make molten images for the whole earth   7. And how silver
is produced from the dust of the earth, and how soft metal
originates in the earth.   8. For lead and tin are not produced
from the earth like the first   it is a fountain that produces them,
and an angel stands therein, and that angel is pre-eminent.'
9 And after that my grandfather Enoch took hold of me by my
hand and raised me up, and said unto me . 'Go, for I have asked
the Lord of Spirits as touching this commotion on the earth
10. And He said unto me . " Because of their unrighteousness

---

3. I said (*a, v*)   *t*², β–*v* ' he said '
4 A voice   This is the command in
ver 6   Fell on my face   As in
60³   6–10 ᵃ The text seems to be
in disorder   It would be clearer if
65⁹⁻¹⁰ᵃ followed immediately on 65⁵
6 Because they have learnt all
the secrets of the angels, &c   cf 7
8 6⁹.   Their powers—the most
secret ones (*gt*)   β–*an* 'their secret
powers', *m* ' the powers of their
most secret secrets ', *qu* ' their powers '
The power of witchcraft   of 7¹
The destruction of the earth is ascribed
to the corruption wrought through the
angels   8 From the earth. > *q*

An angel stands .   is pre-eminent.
I here read jĕtbadar with *t* = ' is pre-
eminent'   Other MSS. jĕbadĕr =
celer est, praecurrit (and possibly *prae-
cellit* as Dillmann assumes)   9.
My hand (*gq*)   *mtu,* β ' his hand '
10 This verse is very corrupt, but it is
possible I think to recover the original
meaning and text   The present text
runs as follows   ' Because of their unrighteousness their judgement has been
determined upon, and shall not be
reckoned before Me because of the
months which they have searched out
and learnt that (> *gtu*) the earth and
those who dwell upon it shall be

their judgement has been determined upon and shall not be withheld by Me for ever. Because of the **sorceries** which they
have searched out and learnt, the earth and those who dwell
upon it shall be destroyed."   11. And these—they have no
place of repentance for ever, because they have shown them
what was hidden, and they are the damned. but as for thee, my
son, the Lord of Spirits knows that thou art pure, and guiltless
of this reproach concerning the secrets.

12. And He has destined thy name to be among the holy,

---

destroyed.' Here first of all Halévy
has pointed out that the knowledge of
the future could hardly have been regarded by the author as criminal. He
fixes on 'months' as a corruption =
חרשים corrupt for חרשים = 'sorceries'
(Is. 3⁸). But the objection here is that
the bulk of the evidence points not to
a Hebrew but an Aramaic original
But since Aramaic speaking Jews (Jer
Taanith, iii 69) sometimes used חרשיא
instead of the regular ירחיא, it is
possible that חרשיא was here a corruption of חרשיא. But if ירחיא did
stand in the original, it may have been
a corruption of סתריא 'secrets' Next,
in my Ethiopic Text of 1906, p 118,
I pointed out that 'shall not be
reckoned' is wrong This phrase =
ולא יחשב—a corruption for ולא יחשך
'shall not be withheld'. At the same
time I pointed out in the same work,
p. xxxi, that this restoration was possible
through Aramaic Thus יתמנא =
'shall be numbered' would be a corruption of יתמנע 'shall be withheld'.
Subsequently Nathaniel Schmidt in a
reprint from *Old Testament and Semitic
Studies in Memory of W R Harper*,
pp 338-339, adopted the idea I have
above suggested but not that of Halévy
He renders. 'Because of their violence
their judgement will be carried out,
and will not be withheld by Me, on

account of the months during which
they will inquire and learn how the
earth and its inhabitants are to be
destroyed' Here 'will be reckoned'
= יתמנא corrupt for יתמנע 'will be
withheld'. So far so good, but the
rest is impossible. First 'will be carried out' and 'will inquire and learn'
should be in the past Even had these
renderings been right, the sense arrived
at is unsatisfactory The 'months' referred to are those during which Noah
preached the coming end of the world
and they remained unrepentant If
Professor Schmidt had studied my Text
he would have seen that the word
'how' is not admitted into it since
three of the best MSS gtu omit it
Bearing this fact in mind, and adopting
Halévy's emendation of 'months' and my
own of 'shall not be reckoned', we
arrive at the translation in our text
The meaning is clear and in keeping
with the teaching in the earlier chapters of the book. the world will be
destroyed because of the wickedness of
the inhabitants and the sorceries (or
secret things) they have discovered.
11 Place of repentance Text = 'return' = Aramaic תיובא, which should
here be rendered 'repentance'. The restoration is possible also in Hebrew,
since תשובה has both meanings
12. Noah is to be the founder of a

And will preserve thee amongst those who dwell on the
   earth,
And has destined thy righteous seed both for kingship and
   for great honours,
And from thy seed shall proceed a fountain of the righteous
   and holy without number for ever.'

The Angels of the Waters bidden to hold them in Check.

LXVI. 1. And after that he showed me the angels of punishment who are prepared to come and let loose all the powers of the
waters which are beneath in the earth in order to bring judgement and destruction on all who [abide and] dwell on the earth.
2. And the Lord of Spirits gave commandment to the angels
who were going forth, that they should not cause the waters to
rise but should hold them in check; for those angels were over
the powers of the waters.   3. And I went away from the
presence of Enoch

God's Promise to Noah: Places of Punishment of the Angels and
of the Kings.

LXVII. 1. And in those days the word of God came unto me,
and He said unto me: ' Noah, thy lot has come up before Me,
a lot without blame, a lot of love and uprightness.   2. And now

new and righteous generation   **Thy
righteous seed** (*gmtu(q)*) β ' thy seed
in righteousness '   Both for kingship
(*q(t)*) β ' both for kings ', *gmu* ' both
kings ' corrupt   Fountain of Deut
33²⁸ Ps 68²⁶

LXVI 1 He, i e Enoch   **Angels
of punishment.** We have here a new
use of this phrase   These angels have
to do solely with the second judgement
in the Parables, and are employed here
only through a misconception as the
agents of the Deluge or first judgement,
and as angels over the waters, cf 40⁷
(note) 54⁷   **[Abide and]** Bracketed
as a dittograph. *q* om *u, bx* omit ' and

dwell '   **2. Cause the waters to
rise.** The text here reads ' hands ' =
ידי corrupt for מים ' waters '   The
angels of the waters are here bidden to
pause in order that during the pause
the ark may be built 67²   The same
idea is found in Rev 7¹ ˢᵠᵠ, where the
four angels of the winds are bidden to
restrain the winds till the servants of
God are sealed in their foreheads
Cf 2 Bar 6⁴ ˢᵠᵠ   Angels over
the powers of the waters cf. Rev
16⁵.

LXVII. 1 The character of Noah
here is based on Gen. 6⁹   **2.** This
account differs from 89¹, where it is

the angels are making a wooden (building), and when they have
completed that task I will place My hand upon it and preserve it,
and there shall come forth from it the seed of life, and a change
shall set in so that the earth will not remain without inhabitant.   3 And I will make fast thy seed before me for ever
and ever, and I will spread abroad those who dwell with thee :
it shall not be unfruitful on the face of the earth, but it shall be
blessed and multiply on the earth in the name of the Lord.'

4. And He will imprison those angels, who have shown
unrighteousness, in that burning valley which my grandfather
Enoch had formerly shown to me in the west among the
mountains of gold and silver and iron and soft metal and tin
5. And I saw that valley in which there was a great convulsion
and a convulsion of the waters.   6. And when all this took
place, from that fiery molten metal and from the convulsion

said that Noah himself makes the ark
Have completed *t*, and *a–t* but in
a corrupt form *β* 'have gone'
3. Cf. 65¹². It shall not be unfruitful = 'ṭĕmakén, emended from
'ṭĕmakĕr (*a,β–bĕloxy₁b*). *bĕloxy₁b* omit.
Otherwise read 'ṭĕmêkĕrû 'they shall
not tempt (thy seed)' But the text
is wholly uncertain.   **4—LXIX.**
1. This section deals with the punishment of the fallen angels and its significance in regard to the kings and the
mighty It is very confused. Part of the
confusion is owing to an original confusion of thought on the part of the writer,
and much to the corruptness of the text
The latter is largely obviated by the
ascertainment of a better text   see
Crit Notes on vv 8, 11, 13   As for
the former, it has been caused by the
writer describing the first judgement in
features characteristic of the final, and
in identifying localities in the Parables
which are absolutely distinct, i e. the
burning valley of Gehenna is placed
among the metal mountains, 67⁴, though
it is definitely said to lie in another

direction, 54¹ in the Parables. It is
obvious, therefore, that no weight is
to be attached to phrases denoting
locality in this section.   4. After
treating of the judgement of mankind
through the Deluge, the writer proceeds
to describe the judgement of the angels,
who were the real cause of man's corruption   The fallen angels are cast
into a burning valley—really the
Gehenna valley of 54   There is a
twofold confusion here.   It is not said
that the angels in 54 were cast into the
valley of Gehenna, but into a 'burning
furnace', and, in the second place,
this was the final place of punishment,
not the preliminary But, again, the burning valley is here said to be amongst
the metal mountains in the west   This,
as we have shown above, is a mislead-
ing combination of utterly disparate
ideas   In the west. The mountains
mentioned are in the west according to
52¹ ˢᵠᵠ   The phrase is no real note of
locality   5, 6. These verses com
bine features of the Deluge and of
volcanic disturbances. The latter are

thereof in that place, there was produced a smell of sulphur, and it was connected with those waters, and that valley ot the angels who had led astray (mankind) burned beneath that land. 7. And through its valleys proceed streams of fire, where these angels are punished who had led astray those who dwell upon the earth.

8. But those waters shall in those days serve for the kings and the mighty and the exalted, and those who dwell on the earth, for the healing of the body, but for the punishment of the spirit, now their spirit is full of lust, that they may be punished in their body, for they have denied the Lord of Spirits and see their punishment daily, and yet believe not in His name. 9. And in proportion as the burning of their bodies becomes severe, a corresponding change shall take place in their spirit for ever and ever; for before the Lord of Spirits none shall utter an idle word   10. For the judgement shall come upon them, because they believe in the lust of their body and deny the Spirit

connected with the punishment of the angels   **Burned beneath that land.** Not merely the immediate neighbour-hood of the Gehenna valley is here designated, but, as Dillmann points out, the adjacent country down to and beyond the Dead Sea   A subterranean fire was believed to exist under the Gehenna valley, cf. 27¹ (note)   **8 Those waters shall serve . . for the healing of the body**   The hot springs resulted from the meeting of the water and fire underground by which the angels were punished   As an instance of such a hot spring Dillmann mentions Kallirhoe to the east of the Dead Sea, to which Herod the Great resorted, Jos *Ant* xvii. 6 5, *Bell Iud* 1 33 5   It has been objected that according to the latter passage these waters were sweet and not sulphurous   So far as this objection is valid, it cannot hold against the hot springs of Machaerus, *Bell Iud* vii 6 3, which were bitter, and in the neighbourhood of which

there were sulphur mines   Holtzmann (*Jahrb f. D T* xii 391) refers to the eruptions of Mount Epomeo in Ischia in 46 and 35 B C (quoted by Schodde), but, as we have seen above, there is no need to go to the west for an explanation   **In those days   Those** of the writer   **Healing of the body** (*ym, b₁*)   *gtu*, β–b₁ read 'healing of the soul and body'   **For the punishment of the spirit**, i e in the final judgement   **Punished in their body**   In Gehenna they will suffer in the body as well as in the spirit   **Denied the Lord of Spirits**   cf 3s² (note) 54⁷ (note).   **See their punishment daily.**   The hot springs are a testimony to the present punishment of the angels   a testimony likewise to the punishment that will befall the kings and the mighty.   **9** The punishment will work repentance in the kings, which will be unavailing   **An idle word**   cf 49⁴ (note)   **10. Deny the Spirit of the Lord.**

of the Lord.   11. And those same waters shall undergo a change
in those days; for when those angels are punished in these waters,
these water-springs shall change their temperature, and when the
angels ascend, this water of the springs shall change and become
cold.   12. And I heard Michael answering and saying : 'This
judgement wherewith the angels are judged is a testimony for
the kings and the mighty who possess the earth.'   13. Because
these waters of judgement minister to the healing of the body of
the kings and the lust of their body; therefore they will not see
and will not believe that those waters will change and become
a fire which burns for ever.

Michael and Raphael astonied at the Severity of the Judgement.

LXVIII. 1. And after that my grandfather Enoch gave me
the teaching of all the secrets in the book and in the Parables
which had been given to him, and he put them together for me
in the words of the book of the Parables.   2. And on that day
Michael answered Raphael and said : 'The power of the spirit
transports and makes me to tremble because of the severity of
the judgement of the secrets, the judgement of the angels · who

This expression is unique in Enoch
11. Referred to by Origen *C Celsum*
v 52 See Introd pp lxiv, lxxxv. The
removal of the angels to another place
of punishment is followed by a cooling
of the waters   In these waters (*a*)
β-*v* 'in those days'   12 Michael
(*a*)   β 'the holy Michael'   13
Kings.   Text reads 'angels' =
מלאביא corrupt for מלביא 'kings'
Lust (*m*)   *gqtu* · desire', β-*y*
'death'

LXVIII 1 According to this verse
the Parables already exist as a complete
work in the hands of the interpolator.
The verse comes from the redactor who
combined the Parables and the Noah
fragments.   The meaning of this chapter is difficult to determine   It has

probably to do with the Satans or chiefs
of the angels.   Words of the book.
g 'book of the words'.   2 The
dialogue between Michael and Raphael
is designed to set forth the severity of
the judgement over the fallen angels,
or rather the Satans.   The power of
the spirit   This is a strange expression.   I suggested in 1893 that it was
corrupt for 'the power of my spirit'
Halévy suggests that 'power' = יד
which here = 'punishment'   Makes me
to tremble   Text reads 'provokes' =
יארגיזני, which should here have been rendered 'makes me to tremble'   Because
of (*a-q*) *q*, β 'and because of'.   Judgement of the secrets.   This may mean
the judgement on account of the secrets
divulged by the angels or Satans.   Of

can endure the severe judgement which has been executed, and
before which they melt away?'　　3 And Michael answered
again, and said to Raphael · 'Who is he whose heart is not
softened concerning it, and whose reins are not troubled by this
word of judgement (that) has gone forth upon them because of
those who have thus led them out?'　　4. And it came to pass
when he stood before the Lord of Spirits, Michael said thus to
Raphael : 'I will not take their part under the eye of the Lord ;
for the Lord of Spirits has been angry with them because they
do as if they were the Lord.　　5. Therefore all that is hidden
shall come upon them for ever and ever ; for neither angel nor
man shall have his portion (in it), but alone they have received
their judgement for ever and ever.'

The Names and Functions of the (fallen Angels and) Satans : the secret Oath.

LXIX. 1. And after this judgement they shall terrify and
make them **to tremble** because they have shown this to those
who dwell on the earth.

2. And behold the names of those angels [and these are their

---

the angels (q–β) > a–q　　Executed
+ 'and abides' β.　　3 Michael
(a)　β 'the holy Michael' So also
in ver. 4.　Answered + 'me' gqu.
Is not softened (β)　a 'is not con-
victed'　The former looks like an
emendation. At the same time a does
not give a good sense　Where the Greek
exists β is hardly ever right against a,
though one or more individual MSS of
β may be　Word of judgement (that)
has gone forth (gq)　mtu, β 'word
judgement has gone forth'　Upon
them because of those who have
thus led them out　Dillmann thinks
this may mean those angels who are
conducted from the preliminary to the
final place of punishment　It might
perhaps be better to translate as I have
done above. In this case we should
have the judgement of the Satans who

are rigorously punished because they
seduced the angels into sin　The words
' They do as if they were like the Lord'
favour this interpretation ; cf. Is. 14[11–13]
5. All that is hidden (a)　β 'the
hidden judgement'.

LXIX 1 Make them to tremble
Text = 'irritate them' = יארגיזחון,
which also means 'make them to
tremble' So Schmidt has pointed out,
acting on Halévy's suggestion that text
= ירגיזם　　2 I have bracketed the
bulk of this verse and all ver 3 as an
intrusion here　These angels are the
angels who fell in the time of Jared
whereas those mentioned in 69[4 sqq] are
Satans. This list of angels is the same
as that in 6[7], but many corruptions
have taken place in the text. Ver. 4
follows naturally on the words 'Behold the names of those angels', though

names the first of them is Samjâzâ, the second Aitâqîfâ, and
the third Armên, the fourth Kôkabêl, the fifth † Tûiâêl †, the
sixth Rûmjâl, the seventh Dânjâl, the eighth † Nêqâêl †, the ninth
Barâqêl, the tenth Azâzêl, the eleventh Armârôs, the twelfth
Bataijâl, the thirteenth † Busasêjal †, the fourteenth Hanânêl,
the fifteenth † Tûiêl †, and the sixteenth Sîmâpêsîêl, the seventeenth Jetiêl, the eighteenth Tûmâêl, the nineteenth Tûrêl, the
twentieth † Rûmâêl †, the twenty-first † Azâzêl †.   3. And
these are the chiefs of their angels and their names, and their
chief ones over hundreds and over fifties and over tens.]

4. The name of the first Jeqôn · that is, the one who led
astray [all] the sons of God, and brought them down to the earth,
and led them astray through the daughters of men.   5. And
the second was named Asbeêl he imparted to the holy sons of
God evil counsel, and led them astray so that they defiled their
bodies with the daughters of men.   6. And the third was
named Gâdieêl · he it is who showed the children of men all the
blows of death, and he led astray Eve, and showed [the weapons
of death to the sons of men] the shield and the coat of mail, and
the sword for battle, and all the weapons of death to the children
of men.   7. And from his hand they have proceeded against
those who dwell on the earth from that day and for evermore.

---

probably it ran originally 'behold the
names of the Satans'   4. Jeqôn
(a–u). β reads Jeqûn   Sons of
God   Cf. Job 38[7]   The text reads
'sons of the (+ 'holy' *l*, *bedelopyx*
₁a₁b) angels', or (+ 'holy' *t*,
*bedelopy*ₗ₍a₁b) 'sons of the angels'
Schmidt thinks that this is a mistranslation of בְּנֵי אֱלֹהִיא , but, though
בֶּן אֱלֹהִים means ' angel', in the LXX
it is never so rendered. בְּנֵי אֱלֹהִים
is rendered by ἄγγελοι θεοῦ, not by
ἄγγελοι alone   Hence, I suppose a
corruption of אֱלֹהִיא into מלאביא
Led them astray, &c   In the Parables the Satans and the fallen angels
are carefully distinguished . the latter

fall in the days of Jared according to 1–36 and 91–104   In this
chapter, however, according to the
present text, the functions of these two
classes are confused   It is Azazel in
1–36 who is the cause of all the corruption upon earth, and Semjaza in 6[8] 8[3] 9[7].
Jeqûn = ' the inciter'   Asbeêl =
עֻזְבִיאל , ' the deserter from God', or
חשביאל,' the thought of God'(Schmidt)
6 Gâdieêl is evidently a Satan as he
led astray Eve   The name עדריאל
means in Aramaic ' God is my helper'
In 8[1] the making of weapons of war is
ascribed to Azazel   [The weapons
of death to the sons of men] A
dittograph from the close of the verse

8. And the fourth was named Pênêmûe : he taught the children of men the bitter and the sweet, and he taught them all the secrets of their wisdom.   9 And he instructed mankind in writing with ink and paper, and thereby many sinned from eternity to eternity and until this day.   10 For men were not created for such a purpose, to give confirmation to their good faith with pen and ink.   11. For men were created exactly like the angels, to the intent that they should continue pure and righteous, and death, which destroys everything, could not have taken hold of them, but through this their knowledge they are perishing, and through this power †it is consuming me†. 12. And the fifth was named Kâsdejâ : this is he who showed the children of men all the wicked smitings of spirits and demons, and the smitings of the embryo in the womb, that it may pass away, and [the smitings of the soul] the bites of the serpent, and the smitings which befall through the noontide heat, the son of the serpent named Tabâ'ĕt.   13. And this is the task of Kâsbeêl, the chief of the oath which he showed to the holy ones when he dwelt high above in glory, and its name

---

8 **Pênêmûe**   Perhaps, as Halévy suggests, from פנימי, 'the inside' This Satan taught the secret things of wisdom   9, 10 Though the invention of the art of writing is ascribed to an evil spirit, the writer does not seem to condemn it save in so far as it is used as a safeguard against the bad faith of men   11 **Men were created exactly like the angels**   Man was originally righteous and immortal, of Book of Wisdom, 1¹³, ¹⁴ 2²³, ²⁴   This is also the doctrine of the Talmud, Weber, *Jud Theol.* 215, 216, 222, 248 Man lost his uprightness and immortality through the envy of the devil, Wisdom 2²⁴, through the evil knowledge introduced by the Satans or angels, 1 Enoch 69¹¹, through his own evil act, 98⁴.   **Pure and righteous** (a–q).

q 'pure and holy , β 'righteous and pure'.   †It is consuming me† Perhaps we should read 'they are being consumed'   12 Cf. Rosenmuller's *Scholia* on Ps 91⁵, ⁶, which, according to ancient Jewish interpretation, treated of demonic dangers   **The serpent named Tabâ'ĕt**   I know nothing about this name   Schmidt (*op. cit* p 841) rewrites the last clause of 69¹² and the whole of 69¹³   But it is wholly hypothetical and unlikely Till the Greek version or the Aramaic original is found the passage seems beyond restoration   Schmidt finds that the name of the sixth Satan is Tabâ'ĕt and that of the seventh Hakael, fragments of the latter surviving in Biqâ and Akâe   13 Cf 41⁵   I do not pretend to interpret this and many of

is Biqâ.   14. This (angel) requested Michael to show him the
hidden name, that he might enunciate it in the oath, so that
those might quake before that name and oath who revealed all
that was in secret to the children of men.   15. And this is the
power of this oath, for it is powerful and strong, and he placed
this oath Akâe in the hand of Michael.   16. And these are the
secrets of this oath . . .

> And they are strong through his oath .
> And the heaven was suspended before the world was created,
> And for ever.

17. And through it the earth was founded upon the water,
> And from the secret recesses of the mountains come beautiful
> waters,
> From the creation of the world and unto eternity.

18. And through that oath the sea was created,
> And †as its foundation† He set for it the sand against the
> time of (its) anger,
> And it dare not pass beyond it from the creation of the
> world unto eternity.

19. And through that oath are the depths made fast,
> And abide and stir not from their place from eternity to
> eternity.

20. And through that oath the sun and moon complete their
> course,

the following verses Task The text
reads 'number' = מִנְיָן corrupt for
עִנְיָן = 'task'   14. This (a
β 'and this'   Show him (a-q)
β 'show them'   The hidden name
that + 'they might enunciate that
(+ 'evil and' m) hidden name' mu
+ 'they might see that hidden name
and' β   16 They are strong (mt,
β-d) gqu 'strengthened'   Heaven
was suspended   of Job 26⁷ for
a similar expression regarding the
earth.   17. And through it the
earth (q β)   a-q 'through it and the
earth' Earth was founded upon
the water of Pss 24² 136⁶.   From
the secret recesses of the mountains come beautiful waters   of
Ps 104¹⁰, ¹³   Beautiful waters (a-n,
aefhikp)   n, ly₁a 'waters for the
living', bcx 'beautiful waters for the
living'.   18 †As its foundation†
He set for it the sand, &c.. cf.
Jer. 5²² Job 26¹⁰ Ps 104⁹, &c Masha-
iatâ, 'its foundation,' seems corrupt for
wasinôtâ, 'to limit it.'   19 The

And deviate not from their ordinance from eternity to eternity.

21. And through that oath the stars complete their course,
And He calls them by their names,
And they answer Him from eternity to eternity.

[22 And in like manner the spirits of the water, and of the winds, and of all zephyrs, and (their) paths from all the quarters of the winds. 23. And there are preserved the voices of the thunder and the light of the lightnings : and there are preserved the chambers of the hail and the chambers of the hoar-frost, and the chambers of the mist, and the chambers of the rain and the dew. 24 And all these believe and give thanks before the Lord of Spirits, and glorify (Him) with all their power, and their food is in every act of thanksgiving they thank and glorify and extol the name of the Lord of Spirits for ever and ever.]

25. And this oath is mighty over them,
And through it [they are preserved and] their paths are preserved,
And their course is not destroyed

Close of the Third Parable.

26. And there was great joy amongst them,
And they blessed and glorified and extolled
Because the name of that Son of Man had been revealed unto them.

27 And he sat on the throne of his glory,
And the sum of judgement was given unto the Son of Man,

depths made fast of Prov 8²⁸.
20 **To eternity** ($g\beta$) $> a-q$ **21**
Calls them by their names cf 43¹
(note) **22-24** An interpolation
Ver 21 deals with the oath, and this subject is resumed in ver 25 Ver 23 seems to be an interpolation within an interpolation **22 Quarters.** So I have rendered ḥebrâta with Flemming. Otherwise 'bands' **23 Voices of the thunder** (a). β 'chambers of the voices of the thunder'. **Chambers of the hail,&c** . cf 60¹¹,¹⁹⁻²¹ **24** Cf 41⁷

for a similar thought **26-29** These verses form the conclusion of the third Parable We have again returned to the chief theme of the third Parable. It is not improbable that the interpolator omitted part of this Parable and replaced it with his own additions. **26 Because the name of that Son of Man had been revealed.** This is obscure Cf for a different use of the phrase, 48⁷ 62⁷ **27. He,** i e the Messiah **On the throne of his glory** . see 45³ (note). **The sum of**

And he caused the sinners to pass away and be destroyed
from off the face of the earth,
And those who have led the world astray.

28. With chains shall they be bound,
And in their assemblage-place of destruction shall they be
imprisoned,
And all their works vanish from the face of the earth.

29. And from henceforth there shall be nothing corruptible,

For that Son of Man has appeared,
And has seated himself on the throne of his glory,
And all evil shall pass away before his face,
And the word of that Son of Man shall go forth
And be strong before the Lord of Spirits.

This is the third Parable of Enoch.

The final Translation of Enoch

LXX. 1. And it came to pass after this that his name during
his lifetime was raised aloft to that Son of Man and to the Lord
of Spirits from amongst those who dwell on the earth.   2. And
he was raised aloft on the chariots of the spirit and his name
vanished among them.   3. And from that day I was no longer

judgement, i e all judgement, cf
St John 5²² (πᾶσαν τὴν κρίσιν). ²⁷
This meaning of רֱשׁא is found in Ps.
139¹⁷   The sinners   Though the
Parables are directed chiefly against
the kings and the mighty ones, the
author returns repeatedly to the judgement of sinners in general, cf 38¹, ², ³
41² 45², ⁵, ⁶ [50²] 53², ⁷ b2², ¹³   And
be destroyed > q   From off the
face of the earth   cf 38¹ (note)
28 Cf 53-56.   29 This verse
summarizes shortly such a chapter as 49
The word of (nagarû la t, bcehl²nᵢ)
a-t, dfil.l²opwyᵢaᵢb 'they shall say to'
    LXX There is certainly some awk-
wardness in the author making Enoch

describe his own translation , but this
in itself forms no valid reason for
obelizing the chapter, as in every other
respect it is quite in keeping with the
thought of the Parables   1 Son
of Man cf 46² (note). And to the
Lord (gqt). mu, β 'to the Lord'
Those who dwell on the earth
cf 37⁵ (note)   2 He was raised
aloft t reads 'his name was raised
aloft'   Chariots of the spirit cf
2 Kings 2¹¹ This is an account of
Enoch's translation , cf 87³, ⁸ 89⁵²
His name (mqt) gu, β 'the name'
The name here stands for the person
The actual pre-existence of the Son of
Man is here supposed, cf. 48² (note).

numbered amongst them ; and he set me between the two winds,
between the north and the west, where the angels took the
cords to measure for me the place for the elect and righteous.
4. And there I saw the first fathers and the righteous who from
the beginning dwell in that place.

Two earlier Visions of Enoch.

LXXI. 1. And it came to pass after this that my spirit was
translated

And it ascended into the heavens ·
And I saw the **holy sons of God**.

They were stepping on flames of fire :
Their garments were white [and their raiment],
And their faces shone like snow.

---

3 Numbered (*gqt, t*). *m,β-z* 'dragged'
Between the north and the west
See 18⁶ ˢᵠᵠ (note) 24¹⁻³ (note) 60⁸
(note) 67⁴　The cords. cf 61¹ ˢᵠᵠ
4. Paradise is already peopled with
his righteous forefathers　This agrees
perfectly with 61¹², which speaks of
the elect being already in Paradise

LXXI This chapter seems to belong
to the Parables, though in the first
edition I thought otherwise. A closer
study of the text as well as of Appel's
*Die Komposition des aethiopischen
Henochsbuchs*, 1906, has led me to revise
my earlier views. The chapter consists
of two visions　In the first 71¹⁻⁴
Enoch was translated in spirit into the
heavens, 71¹, where he had a vision of
God, 71², and under the guidance of
Michael was introduced into the secrets
of the spiritual, 71³, and the physical
worlds, 71⁴　The second vision consists
of 71⁵⁻¹⁷　In this vision it is said
afresh that Enoch was translated in
spirit into the heaven of heavens, 71⁵,
where he has a vision of the house
of God surrounded by angels, 71⁵⁻⁸.

Amongst these were the four archangels who came in the train of God.
Michael accordingly could not be in
attendance on Enoch as in the former
vision, 71¹⁻⁴. Moreover, the vision of
God is described afresh and in different
terms, 71¹⁰ ˢᵠᵠ·　Finally, it is to be
observed that both visions belong to
the period *before Enoch's final translation to heaven in 70*; for it could not
have been the aim of Michael to show
to Enoch, 71³, after his final translation,
what he had already seen under the
guidance of the angel of peace or the
other *angelus interpres.* That 71⁵⁻¹⁷
belongs to the same earlier period will
become clear as we advance　*First
Vision* 71¹⁻⁴　**1. Translated**　The
Ethiopic here as always renders 'hidden'　See 12¹ (note).　**Holy sons
of God**　This is practically the
same phrase as in 69⁵, cf. 69⁴ (see note)
'sons of God ', and 106⁵ 'sons of the
God of heaven '　The expression is to
be referred ultimately to בְנֵי אֱלֹהִים,
where the Elohim are interpreted as
angels　*bodσgₐb* omit 'holy '　[And

2. And I saw two streams of fire,
   And the light of that fire shone like hyacinth,
   And I fell on my face before the Lord of Spirits.

3. And the angel Michael [one of the archangels] seized me by
   my right hand,
   And lifted me up and led me forth into all the secrets,
   And he showed me all the secrets of righteousness.

4. And he showed me all the secrets of the ends of the heaven,
   And all the chambers of all the stars, and all the luminaries,
   Whence they proceed before the face of the holy ones.

5. And he translated my spirit into the heaven of heavens,
   And I saw there as it were a structure built of crystals,
   And between those crystals tongues of living fire

6. And my spirit saw the girdle which girt that house of fire,
   And on its four sides were streams full of living fire,
   And they girt that house.

7. And round about were Seraphin, Cherubin, and Ophannin ·
   And these are they who sleep not
   And guard the throne of His glory.

8 And I saw angels who could not be counted,
   A thousand thousands, and ten thousand times ten thousand,
   Encircling that house,

their raiment]. A duplicate rendering 2 Streams of fire cf 14¹⁹ Dan 7¹⁰; also ver. 6 of this chapter These streams really proceed from beneath the throne   3 And he showed me all ($>\beta$) the secrets of righteousness. All the MSS except *u* insert before this line 'And he showed me all ($>\beta$) the secrets of mercy These two lines =

καὶ ἔδειξέ μοι πάντα τὰ μυστήρια τῆς ἐλεημοσύνης

καὶ ἔδειξέ μοι πάντα τὰ μυστήρια τῆς δικαιοσύνης.

These are alternative renderings of והראני כל סודי הצדק. The context

requires a tristich.   4. This parallel treatment of ethical and natural phenomena reminds us of the appearance of such passages as 41³⁻⁸ 43 44 in the midst of contexts of a wholly ethical character   5–17 *The Second Vision.*   5 He translated my spirit (*a*). The text does not state who translated Enoch β reads 'a spirit translated him'.   There. MSS add 'in the midst of that light' as an explanatory gloss on 'there'   5, 6. Cf 14³⁻¹⁷   6 The girdle (*a*-*q*) *q*, β 'a girdle'   7. Cherubin, Seraphin, and Ophannin cf 61¹⁰, ¹² 39¹³ 40².   And³⁰ (*a*) $>\beta$ 8. A

And Michael, and Raphael, and Gabriel, and Phanuel,
And the holy angels who are above the heavens,
Go in and out of that house.

9. And they came forth from that house,
   And Michael and Gabriel, Raphael and Phanuel,
   And many holy angels without number

10. And with them the Head of Days,
    His head white and pure as wool,
    And His raiment indescribable.

11. And I fell on my face,
    And my whole body became relaxed,
    And my spirit was transfigured;

    And I cried with a loud voice,
    .   with the spirit of power,
    And blessed and glorified and extolled.

12. And these blessings which went forth out of my mouth
were well pleasing before that Head of Days.   13. And that
Head of Days came with Michael and Gabriel, Raphael and
Phanuel, thousands and ten thousands of angels without number.

[Lost passage wherein the Son of Man was described as

---

thousand thousands, &c. cf 14²²
40¹   Michael, Gabriel, &c   see
40⁴⁻⁷   Go in and out. This is not
so in 14²³   9 And²⁰ (a–t) > t β
10 The Head of Days see 46¹ (note)
Dan. 7⁹   11 And I fell . re-
laxed   Cf 60³   Spirit was transfigured   Distinguish this from 39¹⁴,
and cf Asc Is 7²⁵   Spirit of power
cf. 61¹¹   Some word or words seem to
have been lost before this phrase   13.
The following verses show, as Appel
has pointed out (p 44), that after the
Head of Days the Son of Man was
mentioned, and that Enoch asked some

question regarding him   This passage
has been lost, but the context requires
its restoration In answer to this question of Enoch an angel comes forward
and makes answer in ver 14. But
owing to the loss of this passage the
text has been changed by some scribe
in verses 14, 16 and been made to apply
to Enoch instead of to the Son of Man
The scribe, however, has fallen from
his rôle in ver. 17 and forgotten to
make the necessary changes, for that
verse as it stands refers undoubtedly
to the Son of Man and not to Enoch
'There will be length of days with

accompanying the Head of Days, and Enoch asked one of the
angels (as in 46³) concerning the Son of Man as to who
he was]

14. And he (i.e. the angel) came to me and greeted me with
His voice, and said unto me :

'This is the Son of Man who is born unto righteousness,

And righteousness abides over him,

And the righteousness of the Head of Days forsakes
him not.'

15. And he said unto me

' He proclaims unto thee peace in the name of the world to
come ,

For from hence has proceeded peace since the creation of the
world,

And so shall it be unto thee for ever and for ever and
ever.

16. And all shall walk in his ways since righteousness never
forsaketh him ·

With him will be their dwelling-places, and with him their
heritage,

And they shall not be separated from him for ever and ever
and ever.

---

that Son of Man '   14 Cf 46³.
He (*gmt*) > *u.*   *η, β* ' that angel '
This is   is. Emended as explained
in note on ver. 13   Text reads 'Thou
art .   art'   Who is born unto
righteousness   For ' unto (*gtu,*
abcfklnx) *mq, dehtouiy₁a₁b* read ' in '.
On this and the next line, wherein the ,
righteousness of the Son of Man is
dwelt on, see 46³ (note)   **Forsakes him
not.** Text ' forsakes thee not ' See note
on ver 13   15. This verse rightly
applies to Enoch   **Proclaims unto
thee peace** For the phrase cf. Mic 3⁵
1770

Zech 9¹⁰ Is 57⁷ **The world to come**
This is apparently the earliest use of
this expression = העולם הבא. See
Dalman, *Worte Jesu,* 120 sqq , Stave,
*Ueber den Einfluss des Parsismus auf
das Judentum,* 201 , Mt 12³² Mk 10³⁰
Lk, 18³⁰ 20³⁵ Eph 1²¹ Heb. 6⁵   16.
All + 'shall be and' (*β-nl₁b*) Throughout the verse I have changed the
second person into the third and so
restored the verse that it refers, as it
did originally, to the Son of Man
and not to Enoch   **With him
their dwelling-places** Cf 39⁴⁷

17. And so there shall be length of days with that Son
   of Man,
   And the righteous shall have peace and an upright way
   In the name of the Lord of Spirits for ever and ever.'

17 Length of days : ɪ ℮ an eternity.
An upright way (*m*)   *β* 'his upright
way'   *gtu* gives the reading of *m* in
a corrupt foɪm   All the MSS add
here 'to the righteous'.

   Note on 71¹⁴⁻¹⁷   From the above it
follows that I do not regard our text as
supporting the view which some modern
scholars have attached to it, ı. ℮. the
elevation of Enoch to the dignity of
the Messiah   see Bousset, *Rel des
Judenthums*, 348 , Dalman, *Woɪ te Jeɛu*,
200.   The former quotes in this con-
nexıon 2 Enoch 22⁶ 67² Targ. Jon. on
Gen. 5²⁴ , Ps Clem *Hom.* xvɪii 13 ,
Recog. ii. 47

SECTION III

(CHAPTERS LXXII—LXXXII)

THE BOOK OF THE COURSES OF THE HEAVENLY
LUMINARIES. INTRODUCTION

A. *Its Critical Structure and Object.*   B. *Its Independence of* 1-36.
C. *Its Calendar and the Knowledge therein implied.*

A. Critical Structure and Object. Chapter 72 introduces us to
a scientific treatise   In this treatise the writer attempts to bring the
many utterances in the O.T. regarding physical phenomena into one
system, and puts this forward as the genuine and biblical one as
opposed to all other systems.   The paramount and, indeed, the only
aim of this book according to 72^1, is to give the laws of the heavenly
bodies, and this object it pursues undeviatingly from its beginning
to 79^1, where it is said that the treatise is finished and all the laws
of the heavenly bodies set forth   Through all these chapters there
is not a single ethical reference. The author has no other interest
save a scientific one coloured by Jewish conceptions and beliefs.
Our author, like the author of Jubilees, upholds the accuracy of the
sun and stars as dividers of time, 74^{12}: ' The sun and stars bring
in all the years exactly, so that they do not advance or delay their
position by a single day unto eternity '. And this order is inflexible.
there will be no change in it till the new creation, 72^1. So far,
then, we have to deal with a complete and purely scientific treatise,
in which there is no breach of uniformity till the new creation
But the moment we have done with 79, we pass into a new atmo-
sphere in 80^{2-8}.   The whole interest is *ethical and nothing else*.
there is, indeed, such a thing as an order of nature, but, owing to
the sin of men, this order is more conspicuous in its breach than in
its observance, 80^{2-8}, and the moon becomes a false guide and
misleader of men, 80^4, and even the sun (80^5 see note) shines in
the furthest west at nightfall, but 80^{5a} may be interpolated.
 Chapter 80^{2-8}, therefore, is manifestly an addition, made to give
an ethical turn to a purely scientific treatise. and so furnish it with
some fitness for its present collocation.

Again, it is to be observed that this addition consists of tristichs, and is thus different in form from the rest of 72–82. It can hardly be connected with any of the other writers of our book The regularity of nature till the day of the new creation is an article of their creed. though in later apocalypses this view is partially abandoned

Nor, again, can 81 belong to this book. Before entering on this question, however, let us consider 82^{1-8}, which forms, according to most critics, the close of this treatise, vv. 9–20 being regarded as a Noachic interpolation, but wrongly see 82^9 (note) These verses, 82^{1-8}, manifestly do belong to 72–79 The same formula occurs in 82^1. 'my son Methuselah,' as in 76^{14} and in 79^1 (according to some MSS) The wisdom dealt with in 82^{1-8} is the same scientific lore as in 72–79 And the blessing of the author of 82^{1-8} is for the man who sins not in calculating the seasons, 82^4

72–79 and 82 constitute the original Book of the Heavenly Luminaries But, whereas the blessing of the author of 72–79, 82 is for the man who knows the right reckoning of the years, the blessing of 81^4 is for the man ' who dies in righteousness . concerning whom there is no book of unrighteousness written '. These two blessings, in fact, give the keynote of the respective contents of the book of the Heavenly Luminaries and 81, and disclose the motives of their respective authors This chapter did not, any more than 80, belong to this treatise originally In fact, we find on examination that it is of the nature of a mosaic, and came probably from the editor of the complete Enoch. The phrase ' those seven holy ones ', in 81^5, points to some previous statement apparently , but none such is to be found The words may be drawn from $90^{21,\ 22}$. The heavenly tablets in $81^{1,\ 2}$ may come from 93^2 103^2 The expression ' Lord of the world ', 81^{10}, may be suggested by 82^7, ' Lord of the whole creation of the world,' &c

Again, we observe that $81^{5,\ 6}$ are written with reference to $82^{1,\ 2}$ and 91^1. This latter verse introduces the Section beginning in the *present* form of Enoch with 91. We shall see later that 91 does not really form the beginning of the last book of Enoch, but that it has been dislocated from its right position by the author of 81 to serve his editorial purposes

Finally, with regard to 82, it is evident that it does not stand in its original position The Book of the Heavenly Luminaries rightly concludes with 79, which closes thus. ' Such is the picture and sketch of every luminary, which Uriel the archangel, who is their leader, showed unto me.' 82 must have preceded this chapter originally, and probably immediately. After the long disquisition on the stars in 82, the first words of 79 would come in most appropriately. 'And now, my son, I have shown thee everything, *and the law of all the stars of the heaven is completed.*' If 82 does not precede, these words have practically no justification in 72-78. The final editor of the whole book was fond of such dislocations There has been a like rearrangement of 91-93.

B. Its Independence of 1-36. (1) In 1^2 the revelation of Enoch is not for the present, but for remote generations · in 93^{10} it is to remain a secret till the seventh week of the world · in 104^{12} it is one day to be disclosed. But in 82^1 the revelations are entrusted to Methuselah to be transmitted to *the generations of the world.* (2) In 33^4 Uriel writes down everything for Enoch, but in 72^1 74^2 75^3 $79^{2, 6}$ Uriel only shows the celestial phenomena to Enoch, and Enoch himself writes them down, 82^1. (3) The description of the winds coming from different quarters in 34-36 differs from that in 76. (4) The heavenly bodies are partly conscious in 1-36; cf 18^{12-16} 21^{1-6}; but not so in 72-82 (5) The portals of the stars in 36^2 are described as *small* portals *above* the portals of the winds. As in 72-82 these portals are also those of the sun and moon, they can hardly be called 'small', being each equal to thirty degrees in width. Besides, though described at great length in 72-82, they are never said to be 'above' those of the winds. (6) The river of fire in 23, in which the luminaries set and recruit their exhausted fires, has no point of connexion with 72-82. There is undoubtedly some relationship between the later chapters of 1-36 and 72-82, but it is not that of one and undivided authorship

C. Its Calendar and the Knowledge therein implied. The chronological system of this book is most perplexing It does not in its present form present a consistent whole, and probably never did. We are not to regard it as anything more than the attempt of an individual to establish an essentially Hebrew calendar over against the heathen calendars in vogue around. In itself this calendar cannot be said to have any value. It is useful, however, as giving us some knowledge of the chronological systems more or less known to the Palestinian Jews. For (1) the writer is acquainted with the signs of the zodiac, but carefully refrains from using them, replacing them by his system of portals. (2) He is acquainted with the spring and autumn equinoxes and the summer and winter

solstices   (3) He knows apparently the length of the synodic
months (cf. 78[15, 16]), which was not published till the time of
Gamaliel II, A.D. 80–115   (4) His attempt to reconcile the lunar
year and his peculiar year of 364 days by intercalations, in the
third, fifth, and eighth years, furnishes strong presumption that he
had the Greek eight-year cycle before him, and the presumption
becomes a certainty, when we consider that, whereas every detail
in the Greek cycle is absolutely necessary to the end desired, in
the Enochian system, on the other hand, though these details are
more or less reproduced, they are absolutely idle, as Enoch's system
is really a one-year cycle, and the lunar year is reconciled to his
solar year of 364 days by the addition of ten days each year,
cf 74[13–16].   (5) He alludes to the seventy-six years' cycle of
Calippus, 79[5] (note).

The writer puts forward a year of 364 days, but this he did only
through sheer incapacity for appreciating anything better, for he
must have been acquainted with the solar year of $365\frac{1}{4}$ days.
His acquaintance with the Greek cycles shows this   Moreover,
in 2 Enoch the year of $365\frac{1}{4}$ days is distinctly taught   It is
surprising also that any writer under cloak of Enoch's name should
fix upon a year of 364 days, as Enoch was early regarded as the
teacher of the solar year of 365 days, owing to the significant
duration of his life   And our surprise is not lessened when we
consider that all the surrounding nations and peoples—the Egyptians,
Persians. Arabs, Cappadocians, Lycians, Bithynians, the inhabitants
of Gaza and Ascalon—observed a year of 365 days   But this year
was generally a movable year of 365 days exactly, and consequently
one in which New Year's day ran through all the days of the year
in the course of 1,461 such years, and the festivals continually
changed their season. Now the writer of Enoch recommends his
year of 364 days especially on the ground that the position of the
years is not prematurely advanced or delayed by a single day, 74[12].
It was, therefore, nothing but his national prejudices, and possibly
his stupidity, that prevented him, knowing as he did the Greek
systems, from seeing that only a year of $365\frac{1}{4}$ days could effect
such a result   As for Wieseler's theory that the writer held to
a year of 364 days with one intercalary day each year, and one
every fourth year, there is no evidence for it in the text. The
author's reckoning of the year at 364 days may be partly due
to his opposition to heathen systems, and partly to the fact that
364 is divisible by seven, and amounts to fifty-two weeks exactly.

The Sun.

LXXII. 1. The Book of the courses of the luminaries of the heaven, the relations of each, according to their classes, their dominion and their seasons, according to their names and places of origin, and according to their months, which Uriel, the holy angel, who was with me, who is their guide, showed me; and he showed me all their laws exactly as they are, and how it is with regard to all the years of the world and unto eternity, till the new creation is accomplished which dureth till eternity.   2. And this is the first law of the luminaries the luminary the Sun has its rising in the eastern portals of the heaven, and its setting in the western portals of the heaven.   3. And I saw six portals in which the sun rises, and six portals in which the sun sets : and the moon rises and sets in these portals, and the leaders of the stars and those whom they lead . six in the east and six in the west, and all following each other in accurately corresponding order also many windows to the right and left of these portals.

LXXII. 1 As in the Parables, the superscription of this book is far from accurately describing its contents Dominion of 75³ 82⁸⁻²⁰   **Names** · of 78¹˒²   **Places of origin.** Probably then places of rising.   **The new creation** · of 45⁴ 91¹⁵˒ ¹⁶ Is 65¹⁷ 66²² 2 Peter 3¹³ Rev 21¹ In the Yasts, xiii. 57-58 (*S B E* xxiii 194), similarly, it is stated that 'the stars, the moon, the sun and the endless lights . . . move round in their far-revolving circle for ever till they come to the time of the good restoration of the world' All the laws of the heavenly bodies given in this book are valid till the new creation.   **2** This verse introduces an account of the sun in its progress through the signs of the zodiac and the increase and decrease of the days and nights thereby occasioned. **Portals** The subject of the portals has already to some extent appeared

in 33-36 But observe that, though portals of the winds and portals of the stars are there described, there is no mention of portals of the sun and moon. According to 72-82, the sun, moon, and stars pass through the same portals can this hold true of 33-36, where the portals of the stars are said to be small and situated above the portals of the wind ? Moreover, in 72⁶ one of the sun's portals is called 'great'. **3 Portals.** These twelve portals go back ultimately to the twelve signs of the zodiac. According to the Babylonian view from which the speculations in the text are derived there were portals on both sides of the heaven in which the sun and moon rose and set   *Creation Epos,* v 9. See *K. A T.*³ 619, 630. In which (α, n). β-n 'from which'. **Leaders of the stars** see 75¹ (note). **Windows** cf ver 7, 75⁷. **Right and left,** i e.

4. And first there goes forth the great luminary, named the Sun, and his circumference is like the circumference of the heaven, and he is quite filled with illuminating and heating fire.   5. The chariot on which he ascends, the wind drives, and the sun goes down from the heaven and returns through the north in order to reach the east, and is so guided that he comes to the appropriate (lit. 'that') portal and shines in the face of the heaven.   6. In this way he rises in the first month in the great portal, which is the fourth [those six portals in the east].   7. And in that fourth portal from which the sun rises in the first month are twelve window-openings, from which proceed a flame when they are opened in their season.   8. When the sun rises in the heaven, he comes forth through that fourth portal thirty mornings

south and north, according to the familiar Hebrew use   4 Cf 41⁵⁻⁷, where the conception seems to be different   His circumference The sun is clearly circular; cf 78² 78³, also 18⁴ 78⁴   It is doubtful whether he is conceived of as a sphere or merely as a disk. I have translated on the latter supposition   5 The sun, as also the other heavenly bodies, traverses the heaven in a chariot, 78² 75³·⁸, driven by the wind, 18⁴ 78². Through the north· of 41⁵   Is guided   Possibly by an angel. In 2 Enoch several angels precede the sun on his course   In 1–36 the heavenly bodies have a semi-conscious existence; this is not so in 72–82   6. In the first month The writer begins his description of the sun's course with the first Hebrew month Abib (cf Exod 13⁴), the time of the spring equinox   This month, called generally after the Captivity Nisan (cf Neh. 2¹), was the first month of the ecclesiastical year, and corresponds to our April   The civil year began with Tishri, or October. The great portal   So called in contra-

distinction from the 'window openings' in the next verse   Yet these portals are called 'small' in 36²   7. Twelve window-openings   There are twelve such at every portal; cf 72³ 75⁷. The flame is the source of heat; cf 75⁷   8   The author's system, whereby he seeks to replace the heathen conception of the sun's revolution through the signs of the zodiac by a scheme founded as he believes on the O T., is as follows   There are six portals in the east through which the sun rises in the course of the year, and six in the west in which he sets   The first portal forms the most southern point of the sun's journey, and the sixth portal the most northern   During the first six months, from the shortest day to the longest, the sun advances from the first portal to the sixth, and conversely, from the longest day to the shortest, he returns from the sixth portal to the first.   In each portal the sun rises and sets one month in his journey northwards, and likewise rises and sets for one month in each portal on his return journey.   Thus arises the division of the year into twelve

in succession, and sets accurately in the fourth portal in the west of the heaven.   9. And during this period the day becomes daily longer and the night nightly shorter to the thirtieth morning.   10. On that day the day is longer than the night by a ninth part, and the day amounts exactly to ten parts and the night to eight parts.   11 And the sun rises from that fourth portal, and sets in the fourth and returns to the fifth portal of the east thirty mornings, and rises from it and sets in the fifth portal.   12. And then the day becomes longer by †two†

months. Moreover, during each month on his journey northwards, the day daily grows longer and the night daily shorter, and this is owing to a daily change of position on the part of the sun within each gate Of these different positions or stations of the sun there are 364 In this way the author seeks to dispense with the signs of the zodiac. The sun's northward journey from the first to the sixth portal corresponds with his course through the signs Capricornus, Aquarius, Pisces, Aries, Taurus, and Gemini, and the sun's return journey from the sixth to the first portal corresponds with his course through Cancer, Leo, Virgo, Libra, Scorpio, and Sagittarius Though perfectly acquainted with a year of 365¼ days, as we shall see later, the author reckoned it as consisting of 364 days, partly possibly on anti-heathen grounds, and partly for the attractive reason that the sum total is divisible by seven, and thus represents 52 sabbaths of days The author's solar year of 364 days is made up of eight months of 30 days each, and four months of 31 days each—these latter corresponding with the spring and autumn equinoxes and the summer and winter solstices, or, according to the system of our author, with the sun's position in the first, third, fourth, and sixth portals. These four months have each 31 days 'on account of the sign',

i e. that of the equinoxes or the sol-stices, cf 72[18], [19] The author's division of the day into eighteen parts is possibly his own device, yet it may rest on traditions derived from northern Asia of the latitude of 49°, as Krieger supposes, when the longest day is twice as long as the shortest night, as our author states it   10 On that day $(a-t)$ t, β 'and on that day' By a ninth part   The MSS read 'the day is longer by twice as much than the night', for kā'ĕbata means here 'twice as much' as in 72[14], [26]   Hence it is an interpolation This interpolation further led to the extrusion of tas ĕta 'ĕda = 'the ninth part' from the clause in mt, β But this last phrase is found in gqu, and gives the sense required by the context The ninth part = the ninth part of the whole day During six months the day grows longer and the night shorter each month by $\frac{1}{18}$th. Hence the entire difference each month amounts to $\frac{2}{18}$ths or $\frac{1}{9}$th of a day Flemming transposes the phrase before 'ĕlat, making it dependent on kā'ĕbata, and renders it 'um das Doppelte eines Neuntels', but this rendering, which Martin follows, is doubtful grammatically, and even if it were right in grammar it would be wrong in sense   **Exactly** $(a) > \beta$. 11 **In the fourth** + 'portal' $q, \beta-$ $bcd, {}_1a$ 12 **And**[o] $>bcdlopxy, {}_1a, {}_1b$ **† Two †**   We should read 'one'

parts and amounts to eleven parts, and the night becomes shorter and amounts to seven parts. 13. And it returns to the east and enters into the sixth portal, and rises and sets in the sixth portal one and thirty mornings on account of its sign. 14. On that day the day becomes longer than the night, and the day becomes double the night, and the day becomes twelve parts, and the night is shortened and becomes six parts. 15. And the sun mounts up to make the day shorter and the night longer, and the sun returns to the east and enters into the sixth portal, and rises from it and sets thirty mornings. 16. And when thirty mornings are accomplished, the day decreases by exactly one part, and becomes eleven parts, and the night seven 17. And the sun goes forth from that sixth portal in the west, and goes to the east and rises in the fifth portal for thirty mornings, and sets in the west again in the fifth western portal. 18. On that day the day decreases by †two† parts, and amounts to ten parts and the night to eight parts. 19. And the sun goes forth from that fifth portal and sets in the fifth portal of the west, and rises in the fourth portal for one and thirty mornings on account of its sign, and sets in the west. 20. On that day the day is equalised with the night, [and becomes of equal length], and the night amounts to nine parts and the day to nine parts. 21. And the sun rises from that portal and sets in the west, and returns to the east and rises thirty mornings in the third portal and sets in the west in the third portal 22. And on that day the night becomes longer than the day, and night becomes longer than night, and day shorter than day till the thirtieth morning, and the night amounts exactly to ten parts and the day to eight parts. 23. And the sun rises from that third portal and sets

13 **It returns** (a) β 'the sun returns' **Portal**[c] > a-t. On account of its sign, ι e that of the summer solstice; cf 72[19] 75[3] 78[7] 14. **On that day** (a-q) q[2]β 'and on that day' 15 **Mounts up to start on his return journey to the first portal** 18 For '†two†' read 'one' The same error occurred in ver. 12 19 **Its sign.** + 'in the fourth portal in the east', a-n. + 'in the east', a. 20 Clause bracketed as a duplicate rendering 22 **And night becomes longer than night** (a-m). β 'till the thirtieth morning' **Morning** (a-q, efln) > q. abcdhiklory

in the third portal in the west and returns to the east, and for
thirty mornings rises in the second portal in the east, and in like
manner sets in the second portal in the west of the heaven.
24. And on that day the night amounts to eleven parts and the
day to seven parts.   25. And the sun rises on that day from
that second portal and sets in the west in the second portal, and
returns to the east into the first portal for one and thirty
mornings, and sets in the first portal in the west of the heaven
26. And on that day the night becomes longer and amounts to
the double of the day: and the night amounts exactly to twelve
parts and the day to six.   27. And the sun has (therewith)
traversed the divisions of his orbit and turns again on those
divisions of his orbit, and enters that portal thirty mornings and
sets also in the west opposite to it.   28. And on that night has
the night decreased in length by a †ninth† part, and the night
has become eleven parts and the day seven parts.   29. And
the sun has returned and entered into the second portal in the
east, and returns on those his divisions of his orbit for thirty
mornings, rising and setting   30 And on that day the night
decreases in length, and the night amounts to ten parts and the
day to eight.   31. And on that day the sun rises from that
portal, and sets in the west, and returns to the east, and rises in
the third portal for one and thirty mornings, and sets in the west
of the heaven.   32. On that day the night decreases and
amounts to nine parts, and the day to nine parts, and the night
is equal to the day and the year is exactly as to its days three
hundred and sixty-four.   33. And the length of the day and
of the night, and the shortness of the day and of the night arise
—through the course of the sun these distinctions are made (lit.

₁*a*₁*b* 'day   25 In the first portal
(β-*a*)   *gq* 'in it on the first day (†)',
m 'in the sixth portal', *tu* 'on that
day'   27 That portal (*m*, β).
a–m 'all the portals'   28. On
that night (*gq,f*)   *mt*, β–*f* 'on that
day'.   A †ninth† part (*gqu*) > *m*
t, β–*a* 'one part'.   The 'ninth', if

original, must be of half the sun, for
night and day cannot decrease or
increase by more than $\frac{1}{18}$th, as in
ver. 16.   Perhaps we might emend
'ĕmnûḥâ into 'ĕm a'âlt, and translate
'has the night grown shorter than the
day by a ninth part'.   31. That
portal (*a–t*).   *t*, β 'that second portal'.

'they are separated'). 34. So it comes that its course becomes daily longer, and its course nightly shorter. 35. And this is the law and the course of the sun, and his return as often as he returns sixty times and rises, i. e the great luminary which is named the Sun, for ever and ever. 36 And that which (thus) rises is the great luminary, and is so named according to its appearance, according as the Lord commanded 37. As he rises, so he sets and decreases not, and rests not, but runs day and night, and his light is sevenfold brighter than that of the moon , but as regards size they are both equal.

The Moon and its Phases.

LXXIII. 1. And after this law I saw another law dealing with the smaller luminary, which is named the Moon. 2. And her circumference is like the circumference of the heaven, and her chariot in which she rides is driven by the wind, and light is given to her in (definite) measure. 3. And her rising and setting changes every month and her days are like the days of the sun, and when her light is uniform (i. e. full) it amounts to the seventh part of the light of the sun 4. And thus she rises. And her first phase in the east comes forth on the thirtieth

---

35. As often as he returns sixty times (a–m). m, β 'as often as he returns, he returns sixty times'. Sixty times The sun is one month in each portal on his northward journey, and one month in each portal on his southward therefore two months in each portal The author disregards for the time being the extra day in the first, third, fourth, and sixth portals The great luminary (a) β 'the great eternal luminary' 37 As he rises, so he sets (g) mqt 'so he rises and (+ 'so' qt) he sets', n 'and so he sets', β–ane 'and so he rises and sets' Day and night + 'in his chariot' t², β. Sevenfold brighter Cf 78⁴ 73² As regards size equal According to Lucretius 5⁵⁶⁴⁻⁵⁹¹ the sun, moon, and the stars are about the same

size as—possibly a little greater or less than—they appear to us This view he derived from his master Epicurus, as may be seen from comparing a letter of the latter to Pythocles in Diog Laer x 84–94. But it is not necessary to suppose any dependence on the part of our text, which gives probably the ordinary accepted view

LXXIII This and the following chapter treat of the course of the moon 2 The heaven (a–m, bedilo) m, aefhkmpu 'the sun' 3 Her rising and setting, i e the place of her rising and setting Seventh part of the light of the sun cf 72¹⁷ 78⁴. 4 Her first phase, lit. 'her beginning' The moon on the first day of her reappearance is here the new moon in the popular sense, not the morning · and on that day she becomes visible, and constitutes for you the first phase of the moon on the thirtieth day together with the sun in the portal where the sun rises   5. And the one half of her goes forth by a seventh part, and her whole circumference is empty, without light, with the exception of one-seventh part of it, (and) the fourteenth part of her light.

new moon strictly so called, which is invisible   Thirtieth morning, i e. of the solar month   Together with the sun   The sun and moon are still in the same portal on the first day after conjunction, as each portal embraces an extent of 30 degrees, and the moon advances only 13 degrees daily. 5-8 The author's account of the phases of the moon is very hard to follow. His scheme seems to be as follows. The lunar month amounts to 30 days and 29 days alternately   It is divided into two parts   during the first part the moon waxes from new moon to full moon in 14 days when the month is 29 days, and in 15 when the month is 30 days   During the second part the moon wanes from full moon till she disappears, always, it would seem, in 15 days.   Again, the author divides the moon into 14 parts, and explains the waxing of the moon by the successive lighting up of each one of the 14 parts by the sun, and the waning by the successive withdrawal of light from the 14 parts till it all disappears. But to proceed more exactly, where there are 15 days from new moon to full moon, the author supposes an additional 28th part, this part only is lighted up on the first day of such a month, whereas $\frac{1}{14}$th part is lighted up each day of the remaining 14 days, till the moon becomes full   The waning, which apparently always takes 15 days, is the reverse of this process   Again, where there are 14 days from new moon to full moon, the moon has at the end of the first day $\frac{1}{14}$th part +

$\frac{1}{28}$th part, i e $\frac{3}{28}$ths, and takes an additional 14th part of light each of the remaining 13 days   According to the text above followed, vv 5, 6 suppose the period from new to full moon to be 14 days, whereas ver 7 supposes this period to be 15 days. 5 In this verse and the next the fractions are *fractions of half the moon*. Thus, $\frac{1}{2}$th of it, i. e of the half moon = $\frac{1}{14}$th of whole moon, and $\frac{1}{14}$th of half moon = $\frac{1}{28}$th of whole moon   thus, $\frac{3}{28}$ths of whole moon are lighted on the first day of new moon, when there are but 14 days to the full moon.   Goes forth   The MSS read reḥʰq = *ἐξέχων*, which is used of the rising or appearing of the sun   *ἐξέχων* might in turn be a rendering of אצי, which is used of the rising of the sun and stars   Flemming obelizes the word and proposes rĕʼǒj = 'visible'.   One-seventh part (*gqʼu, abᵈfⁱhⁱx ₁b*)   The rest of the MSS are corrupt   (And) the fourteenth part (*gqu*)   *mt, β* 'of the fourteenth part'.   Possibly the 'em (= 'of') is a corruption of the wa (= 'and') which I have supplied.   *y* adds 'of half', but unnecessarily, since the fractions are fractions of the half of the moon.   6 Observe when the period from new moon to full moon is 14 days that it is not said that the moon receives $\frac{1}{14}$th part and $\frac{1}{28}$th, but only the former, it seems, therefore, that the moon is supposed to have this $\frac{1}{28}$th to begin with   It is different in the case of the 15-days' period   On the first day of such a period the moon receives $\frac{1}{28}$th part of light   In this

6. And when she receives one-seventh part of the half of her light, her light amounts to one-seventh part and the half thereof. 7. And she sets with the sun, and when the sun rises the moon rises with him and receives the half of one part of light, and in that night in the beginning of her morning [in the commencement of the lunar day] the moon sets with the sun, and is invisible that night with the fourteen parts and the half of one of them. 8 And she rises on that day with exactly a seventh part, and comes forth and recedes from the rising of the sun, and in her remaining days she becomes bright in the (remaining) thirteen parts

The Lunar Year.

LXXIV. 1. And I saw another course, a law for her, (and) how according to that law she performs her monthly revolution. 2. And all these Uriel, the holy angel who is the leader of them all, showed to me, and their positions, and I wrote down their positions as he showed them to me, and I wrote down their months as they were, and the appearance of their lights till fifteen days were accomplished. 3. In single seventh parts

verse there are 14 days to full moon **One seventh part** 2° (*gmqu, d*). *t, l* 'the thirteenth part', *β–dklo* 'the fourteenth part'. According to *t* and the inferior MSS the parts are fractions of the half moon in the first half of the sentence, and fractions of the whole moon in the second half. Yet Flemming and Martin follow the inferior MSS herein. 7. **Half of one part of light**, i e $\frac{1}{28}$th. See previous notes, and observe that in this verse the fractions are *fractions of the whole moon*. **Fourteen parts** (*yu, abcdefhknox₁a*). *mqt, il₁b* 'thirteen parts'. 7, 8 These verses suppose the case when there are 15 days from new to full moon On the first day the moon receives $\frac{1}{28}$th part of light, and has advanced to some slight degree out of conjunction, but still practically sets with the sun, and may be said to be invisible. On the second day she receives $\frac{1}{14}$th part of light, and becomes visible to that extent Thus the $\frac{1}{28}$th part is ignored as being practically invisible. During the remaining 13 days the moon receives daily $\frac{1}{14}$th part of light. 8. **Thirteen parts** (*a, n*) *β–n* 'fourteen parts'.

LXXIV. In this chapter the writer deals shortly with the waxing and waning of the moon, her monthly change of position with regard to the signs and the sun, and the difference between lunar and solar years. 2. **Of them all**, i e the various phases of the moon **Fifteen days**, i e from a conjunction till full moon or from full moon till a conjunction. 3.

she accomplishes all her light in the east, and in single seventh
parts accomplishes all her darkness in the west   4 And in
certain months she alters her settings, and in certain months she
pursues her own peculiar course.   5. In two months the moon sets
with the sun in those two middle portals the third and the fourth.
6. She goes forth for seven days, and turns about and returns
again through the portal where the sun rises, and accomplishes
all her light: and she recedes from the sun, and in eight days
enters the sixth portal from which the sun goes forth.   7. And
when the sun goes forth from the fourth portal she goes forth
seven days, until she goes forth from the fifth and turns back
again in seven days into the fourth portal and accomplishes all
her light: and she recedes and enters into the first portal in eight
days   8. And she returns again in seven days into the fourth
portal from which the sun goes forth.   ‘ 9. Thus I saw their
position—how the moons rose and the sun set in those days.
10. And if five years are added together the sun has an overplus
of thirty days, and all the days which accrue to it for one of
those five years, when they are full, amount to 364 days.

Cf 73 and 76. **And in single
seventh . . . darkness** > *a, an*   4
Her own peculiar course, i e a
course independent of that of the sun.
5, 6 During two months the moon
sets with the sun as new moon and as
full moon   When the sun is in Aries
and Libra, the new moon and the full
moon are in the third and fourth
portals. In verse 6 the moon goes forth
as it waxes from the third portal
through the signs to the first portal in
seven days, turns about, and returns to
the portal where the sun rises, i e the
third, in seven or eight days, and there
becomes full moon, and proceeds thence
through the fourth and fifth to the
sixth portal, where she arrives after
eight days. Thence the moon returns
to the third portal in seven days
6 And accomplishes t^y, β ‘and in
that accomplishes .   **7, 8** The

scheme with regard to the fourth portal
and the new moon   The moon proceeds
to the sixth portal and returns to the
fourth in 14 days, and thence to
the first portal and back in 15 days.
**9. How the moons rose and the
sun set** $(a-q)$ q, β ‘according to the
order of their moons the sun rising and
setting’.   **10, 11** The difference
between the lunar and the solar year
According to 78^{16}, ^{16}, in a lunar year
there are six months of 30 days, and six
months of 29 days each—in all 354 days.
In a solar year there are twelve months
of 30 days each and four intercalary
days in the equinoxes and solstices—in
all 364 days (cf. 74^{10}, ^{12} 75^2). Thus the
difference between the lunar and the
solar year amounts to 10 days   But in
ver 10^a and 11 no account is taken of
the intercalary days in the solar year,
so that the solar year is reckoned at

11. And the overplus of the sun and of the stars amounts to six days   in 5 years 6 days every year come to 30 days · and the moon falls behind the sun and stars to the number of 30 days. 12. And the sun and the stars bring in all the years exactly, so that they do not advance or delay their position by a single day unto eternity, but complete the years with perfect justice in 364 days   13. In 3 years there are 1092 days, and in 5 years 1820 days, so that in 8 years there are 2912 days   14. For the moon alone the days amount in 3 years to 1062 days, and in 5 years she falls 50 days behind : [i e. to the sum (of 1770) there is to be added (1000 and) 62 days]   15. And in 5 years there

---

360 days   Thus the difference in this case is six days.   **11. The moon** (l^2, β)   *a* has preserved the word but in the wrong context, for it has transposed it into the next sentence and made it the subject of 'bring in'   **12 And the sun**   So *gmt* save that they place 'from' before 'the sun' $> qu, \beta$ **And the stars** (*n*)   *gmt* 'and from the stars' $> t^2, \beta$ Here all MSS add 'and ($> n$) the moon'. But 'the moon' belonged to ver 11, see note   This wrong transposition was made by *a* β followed *a* herein, and at the same time preserved the word in its original setting   Our author advocates a solar and sidereal year as the author of Jubilees 6^{32-36} For 'and the sun and the stars' t^2, β read 'and the moon', thus representing the moon as the perfect time divider in glaring contradiction with verses 10–11 and Jub 6^{36} **But complete** = ἀλλὰ τελοῦσιν, which was corrupted into ἀλλὰ ἀλλάττουσιν   Whence the Ethiopic text   **13–16** We have here clearly a reference to the eight-year cycle or octaeteris   In this cycle an intercalary month of 30 days was inserted in the third, fifth, and eighth years of the cycle in order to reconcile the lunar and solar years, which were reckoned respectively at

354 and $365\frac{1}{4}$ days   As our author, however, does not reckon the solar year at $365\frac{1}{4}$ days, but at 364, he proceeds to reconcile this solar year of 364 days with the lunar year of 354. Thus (ver 13) in three such solar years there are 1092 days, in five, 1820 days, in eight, 2912 days, whereas (ver 14, 15) in three lunar years there are 1062 days, in five, 1770 days, in eight, 2832 days   Thus there is a difference of 80 days between eight solar years of 364 days and eight lunar years   As all these calculations merely amount to saying that his solar year has 10 days more than the lunar, the writer had obviously the eight-year cycle before him, for only thus can we explain the external resemblance of his system to the Greek cycle, cf. Special Introd. p 150   Unless the author had the Greek eight-year cycle before him and wished to give his own work some semblance of likeness thereto, there was no need to go through all these periods of three, five, and eight years, for they do not in fact contribute a single additional fact, but merely say over and over again that the difference between 364 and 354 days is 10 days   **14** [i e. to the sum (of 1770) there is to

are 1770 days, so that for the moon the days in 8 years amount to 2832 days. 16. [For in 8 years she falls behind to the amount of 80 days], all the days she falls behind in 8 years are 80. 17. And the year is accurately completed in conformity with their world-stations and the stations of the sun, which rise from the portals through which it (the sun) rises and sets 30 days.

LXXV. 1. And the leaders of the heads of the thousands, who are placed over the whole creation and over all the stars, have also to do with the four intercalary days, being inseparable from their office, according to the reckoning of the year, and these render service on the four days which are not reckoned in the reckoning of the year. 2. And owing to them men go wrong therein, for those luminaries truly render service on the world-stations, one in the first portal, one in the third portal of the heaven, one in the fourth portal, and one in the sixth portal, and the exactness of the year is accomplished through its separate

be added (1000 and) 62 days.] This clause is bracketed as a marginal gloss as Beer and Flemming have recognized. If it belonged to the text at all, it should be found at the close of ver 15, for it simply states that 2832 (= the days in 8 lunar years) arises from the addition of 1770 (= the days in 5 lunar years) and 1062 (= the days in 3 lunar years). The words ('1000 and') are found only in the margin of *c* 16. The bracketed clause and that which follows are duplicate renderings. 17 Their world-stations (a–m) m, β 'their stations'. Are these the *world-stations* referred to in 75² in connexion with the intercalary days, which are presided over by the four angels who are heads of thousands? In ver. 12 the stars are mentioned in connexion with the sun. In my first edition I explained it as follows 'which (i e the sun and moon) rise from the portals through which it (i. e the sun) rises and sets

thirty days' But this is very unsatisfactory

LXXV This chapter deals with the intercalary days, the stars, and the sun 1 The four intercalary days are under the charge of the highest stars, the leaders of the heads of ten thousands These are not the chiliarchs, as Dillmann supposes (p. 248), but the leaders of the chiliarchs. For further development of this subject see 82¹¹, ¹² These leaders are not angels, as might be supposed, but simply 'luminaries', cf. ver. 2   And¹⁰ (q, β) > a–q Their office (m) a–m 'its (> q) office', t², β 'their position' The reckoning¹⁰ (a). β 'all the reckoning'. Are not reckoned in the reckoning of the year. Apparently the year was popularly reckoned at 360 days, cf 82⁵. 2 Men do not know of these intercalary days, and so reckon wrongly, cf 82⁴⁻⁶. The exactness of the year (q) g 'in exactness the world', mtu, β 'the

three hundred and sixty-four stations.   3. For the signs and
the times and the years and the days the angel Uriel showed to
me, whom the Lord of glory hath set for ever over all the
luminaries of the heaven, in the heaven and in the world, that
they should rule on the face of the heaven and be seen on the
earth, and be leaders for the day and the night, i. e. the sun,
moon, and stars, and all the ministering creatures which make
their revolution in all the chariots of the heaven.   4. In like
manner twelve doors Uriel showed me, open in the circumference
of the sun's chariot in the heaven, through which the rays of the
sun break forth and from them is warmth diffused over the
earth, when they are opened at their appointed seasons.   5. [And
for the winds and the spirit of the dew† when they are opened,
standing open in the heavens at the ends.]   6. As for the
twelve portals in the heaven, at the ends of the earth, out of
which go forth the sun, moon, and stars, and all the works
of heaven in the east and in the west,   7. There are many
windows open to the left and right of them, and one window at

---

exactness of the world' In the
Ethiopic 'âm = 'year' and 'âlam
= 'world' Is accomplished (*gm, β*)
gtu 'accomplishes', i e 'the exactness', &c.   3 Yet these intercalary days are a reality, for Uriel
showed them to Enoch; cf 72¹
Signs, i e of the zodiac; cf 72¹³, ¹⁹
Lord of glory (*a–q*)   *q* 'Lord of
Spirits', *β–l* 'eternal Lord of glory'
see 84² (note)   **Chariots of the
heaven** cf 72⁵   *q* reads ' troops of
the heaven'.   4 The variation in
the amount of heat given by the sun is
explained by twelve openings in the
disk of the sun through which heat
is given forth in proportion to the number of windows opened   **Doors Uriel
showed me, open** ((*m*)*tu, ashikn*)
g 'open'   *q* 'doors and Uriel showed
me'   5 The first clause of this
verse is unintelligible, and the rest of
it looks like a dittograph of the last

clause in ver 4, and the first in ver 6
The second clause follows *a–u t²*, *β* read
' when they are opened in the seasons,
standing open', &c   The entire verse
is, with Dillmann, Beer, Martin, to be
rejected as an intrusion.   6, 7
Adjoining each one of those twelve
portals of the sun are twelve windows
open to the left and right of them; cf
72³, ⁷   These diffuse warmth over the
earth, one being open at a time, and
all differing in degree of heating
power   6 This verse begins in *a*
with a dittograph from ver 4, ' when
they are opened' Cf. ver 5   *β* has
no such dittograph, but tries to give
a meaning to the verse by inserting
' I saw', and changing the words
' twelve portals', which are a *nominativus pendens*, into the acc   But this
is manifestly wrong   These portals
have been under discussion continually
throughout the last three chapters

its (appointed) season produces warmth, corresponding (as these
do) to those doors from which the stars come forth according as
He has commanded them, and wherein they set corresponding to
their number.   8 And I saw chariots in the heaven, running
in the world, above those portals in which revolve the stars that
never set.   9. And one is larger than all the rest, and it is
that that makes its course through the entire world.

The Twelve Winds and their Portals.

LXXVI. 1. And at the ends of the earth I saw twelve portals
open to all the **quarters** (of the heaven), from which the winds
go forth and blow over the earth.   2. Three of them are open
on the face (i. e. the east) of the heavens, and three in the west,
and three on the right (i. e. the south) of the heaven, and three
on the left (i. e. the north).   3. And the three first are those of
the east, and three are of †the north, and three [after those on
the left] of the south†, and three of the west.   4. Through
four of these come winds of blessing and prosperity, and from

---

To say that Enoch saw them now
would be immeasurably inept   8
Above + 'and below' *bedflopioxy*
₁*a* ₁*b*.   9 **One** is larger. This
may be the Great Bear

   LXXVI. This chapter gives a detailed account of the twelve portals of
the winds and the nature of the winds
which issue therefrom   The short
account in 33-36 agrees with it   This
disquisition on the nature of the winds
has as much relation to reality as that
on the year of 364 days   1 The
quarters   The text has here ' wind ',
which is a rendering of רוח = ' quarter
of the heaven '   See note on 77¹
2 This method of designating the four
quarters of the earth was usual among
the Hebrews, cf. 72³   3 **And**¹⁰
> *gmt* The order of the winds in
this verse is undoubtedly wrong   First
of all the clause which I have
bracketed is nonsense in any case.

It was added after the transposition.
Martin suggests that the words translated ' north ' and ' south ', i e mas'ĕ
and 'azéb, should be rendered ' south '
and ' north ', since these words at
one period were confused together
This is quite true, but it can hardly be
the case in the Ethiopic version of
Enoch, which carefully renders βορρᾶς
by mas'ĕ in 28³ 32¹, cf. 70³, &c ,
&c , and νότος by 'azeb in 18⁶, ⁷
Hence we have simply to transpose the
text here in order to recover the
original order, i e ' And the three
first are those of the east, and three
are of the south, and three of the
north, and three of the west '   This is
the order in which the winds are dealt
with in the verses that follow   4.
Through four of these portals come
beneficial winds, i e the middle wind
of the three in each quarter   the rest
are hurtful   The winds from the four

those eight come hurtful winds · when they are sent, they bring destruction on all the earth and on the water upon it, and on all who dwell thereon, and on everything which is in the water and on the land.

5. And the first wind from those portals, called the east wind, comes forth through the first portal which is in the east, inclining towards the south : from it come forth desolation, drought, heat, and destruction.   6. And through the second portal in the middle comes what is fitting, and from it there come rain and fruitfulness and prosperity and dew ; and through the third portal which lies toward the north come cold and drought.

7. And after these come forth the south winds through three portals : through the first portal of them inclining to the east comes forth a hot wind.   8. And through the middle portal next to it there come forth fragrant smells, and dew and rain, and prosperity and health.   9 And through the third portal lying to the west come forth dew and rain, locusts and desolation.

10. And after these the north winds · from the seventh portal in the east come dew and rain, locusts and desolation.   11. And from the middle portal come in a direct direction health and rain and dew and prosperity ; and through the third portal in the west come cloud and hoar-frost, and snow and rain, and dew and locusts.

---

corners are destructive as in Rev. 7[1 sqq.] According to our author's scheme there are two destructive winds at each corner of the earth   5–6 Winds from the east, i e the ESE wind, the E and ENE winds   6 **What is fitting** or ' advantageous ' or ' right '. So I render rĕt'ĕ The same idea recurs in ver 11, where the word is rĕt'ĕt but is rendered ' in a direct direction ' Perhaps we should read iet'ĕ in the latter verse also, and render as above   7–9 Winds from the south   7 The SES wind Through the first (*gu*) *gmt.* β read

' the first through the first ' The latter form is not found in the description of any of the winds   8. The S wind.   9 The SWS wind.   10 The NEN. wind **North winds** MSS add a gloss ' which is named the sea and which came forth ' **In the east** *gtu* add ' towards the south', *m*, β–*o₁a* ' which inclines towards the south', *q* 'south'   11 The N and NWN winds. **Come in a direct direction** Perhaps we should read ' comes what is fitting ' See note on ver. 6   **Health and rain and dew** (*a*) β ' rain and dew and health '   **In the west** MSS add ' which inclines

12. And after these [four] are the west winds : through the first portal adjoining the north come forth dew and hoar-frost, and cold and snow and frost.   13. And from the middle portal come forth dew and rain, and prosperity and blessing, and through the last portal which adjoins the south come forth drought and desolation, and burning and destruction.   14. And the twelve portals of the four quarters of the heaven are therewith completed, and all their laws and all their plagues and all their benefactions have I shown to thee, my son Methuselah.

The Four Quarters of the World: the Seven Mountains, the Seven Rivers, &c.

LXXVII. 1 And the first quarter is called the east, because it is the first: and the second, the south, because the Most High will descend there, yea, there in quite a special sense will He who is blessed for ever descend.   2. And the west quarter is named the diminished, because there all the luminaries of the heaven wane and go down.   3. And the fourth quarter, named the north, is divided into three parts. the first of them is for the dwelling of men and the second contains seas of water, and the abysses and forests and rivers, and darkness and clouds, and the third part contains the garden of righteousness.

to the north'—an absurd addition
12 The WNW. wind   Dew. +
'and rain' β   13 The W. and
WSW winds.   14 Quarters.
MSS read 'portals, i e θυρῶν corrupt for μερῶν, a rendering of רוחות.
All ²⁰. > *qu*   All ³⁰ > q, β-*fhi*
My son Methuselah cf 82¹
LXXVII 1-3. These verses deal
not with the ten winds but with the
four quarters   The first quarter is the
east, i.e קֶדֶם, because it is in front or
the first, קַדְמוֹנִי. The second the south,
דָּרוֹם, 'because the Most High descends
there' from יָרַד רָם, cf. 25³. The west
is called the waning quarter, for which
probably there stood in the Hebrew
אַחֲרוֹן (not existing in Aramaic), which

the Greek translator rendered by ὑστερῶν. So Dillmann The north, צָפוֹן,
is divided into three parts one for
men, the second for waters, cf צָפָה
= 'an overflowing' for darkness and
cloud, from צָפַן, 'to render invisible'.
The third encloses Paradise, from צָפַן,
'to reserve' Paradise is the recompense *reserved* for the righteous, Ps
31¹⁹, cf Halévy, *Journal Asiat.* 1867.
1. The first quarter Here and in
verses 2, 3 the text = 'wind', which
is a rendering of רוּח, which in this
context, as in Ezek 42²⁰, should have
been rendered μέρος = 'quarter'   3
The garden of righteousness see 60⁸
(note) 70³ (note)   4 The number
seven plays a great rôle in this book,

4. I saw seven high mountains, higher than all the mountains which are on the earth and thence comes forth hoar-frost, and days, seasons, and years pass away. 5. I saw seven rivers on the earth larger than all the rivers · one of them coming from the †west† pours its waters into the Great Sea 6. And these two come from the north to the sea and pour their waters into the Erythraean Sea in the east. 7. And the remaining four come forth on the side of the north to their own sea, ⟨two of them to⟩ the Erythraean Sea, and two into the Great Sea and discharge themselves there [and some say into the desert] 8. Seven great islands I saw in the sea and in the mainland : two in the mainland and five in the Great Sea.

The Sun and Moon : the Waxing and Waning of the Moon.

LXXVIII 1. And the names of the sun are the following · the first Orjârês, and the second Tômâs 2. And the moon

and generally in Jewish writers, cf 18⁶ 24² 32¹ 61¹¹ 72⁸⁷ 91¹⁶ 93¹⁰ **Seven high mountains** These appear to have nothing to do with those of 18⁶ 24² 32¹, though originally they are derived from the same source Pass. + 'and go' *q, β*. **5 Seven** (*β*) > *a* One of them coming from the †west†. This must be the Nile, as Dillmann takes it, but the description 'from the west' cannot be right Hence I take 'ârab (= west) to be a transliteration of עֲרָבָה, which here means simply 'desert' or 'steppe', and render 'coming from the desert' Here Aramaic fails to explain the difficulty **The Great Sea,** i e the Mediterranean, cf Num 34⁶˒⁷ **6 The** Euphrates and Tigris **The Erythraean Sea** A general name for the Arabian, Persian, and Indian seas **7. The remaining four,** i e the Indus, Ganges, Oxus, and Jaxartes (Dillmann) ⟨**Two of them to** ⟩ These words must be supplied. [**And some say into the desert**] This is mani-

festly a gloss Such a second view is impossible in a vision **8 Two in the mainland and five in the Great Sea** (*bcdfrlory₁a₁b*). So also *aehkn* save that they omit 'in the mainland' after 'two' *a–m* read 'seven, and two in the Red Sea' *m* 'two in the mainland and five in the Red Sea . The text is wholly uncertain. Perhaps we might compare Jub. 8²⁰ where 'five great islands' are referred to The sevenfold division of the earth is of Babylonian origin See *K A T* ³ 618. From this source is developed the idea in 4 Ezra 6⁴² where the land is said to be ⅚ths of the earth and the sea ⅙th, the seven high mountains in our text, 77⁴, the seven streams, 77⁵, and the seven islands, 77⁸

LXXVIII, LXXIX The relations of the sun and moon are again described, as well as the waxing and the waning of the moon **LXXVIII. 1.** And¹⁰ (*a–q, ehl*) > *q, β–ehl* Halévy points out that the two names of the sun given here correspond to the two

has four names · the first name is Asônjâ, the second Eblâ, the third Benâsê, and the fourth Erâe.   3. These are the two great luminaries : their circumference is like the circumference of the heaven, and the size of the circumference of both is alike 4. In the circumference of the sun there are seven portions of light which are added to it more than to the moon, and in definite measures it is transferred till the seventh portion of the sun is exhausted.   5. And they set and enter the portals of the west, and make their revolution by the north, and come forth through the eastern portals on the face of the heaven. 6. And when the moon rises one-fourteenth part appears in the

seasons of the year in Palestine; cf. 2^5 3 4 68^{16} Orjârês from אוֹר חרס is the sun when his power is diminished in the winter season, for חרם or שרש = 'potsherd' as well as 'sun'. The second name חַמָּה in our text, altered into Tomas by change of חֹ and ‏ֿ, denotes the sun when the heat is powerful in the summer, from חמם 2 Halévy attempts to show that the four names of the moon are connected with its various phases But this seems improbable Asônjâ from אִישׁוֹן יָה where אישון is a diminutive of אישׁ and יָה merely an intensive termination This is the name of the moon in connexion with its likeness to the human face; cf ver. 17 Eblâ, corrupted from לְבָנָה = the pale star, denotes, he thinks, the moon in her waning period Ben âsê, from בַּן־כָּסָה (i e כסה, to cover), is an appropriate name of the moon in the period of conjunction when she is invisible But in Prov 7^{20} Ps 81^4 כסה means the full moon as opposed to הַחֹדֶשׁ, 'the new moon' Erâe from יָרָח (i e from ירח, 'to cast, dart,' or possibly as Martin proposes, from ארח, ' to journey,' ' go ') is suitable as a designation of the waxing or full moon.   3 Cf $72^{4, 37}$ 73^2. According to Chullin 60^b the sun and moon were originally of the same

size, but that God subsequently bade the moon to lessen her size (מַעֲטִי אֵת עַצְמֵךְ)   The size of the circumference (a) β 'the size' + ' like the circumference of the heaven' α-u— a repetition from the preceding clause. 4 From 72^{37} and 73^3 we have already learnt that the light of the sun is sevenfold that of the moon from 73^2 that light is added to the moon in due measure   Here we are further informed that $\frac{4}{7}$th of the light of the sun is gradually transferred to the moon, and that this seventh part is wholly transferred when the moon is full. Of the above Semitic words the two names for the sun חרם and חַמָּה are Hebrew and not Aramaic, while of the four names of the moon אישׁון, לְבָנָה, and בַּן־כסה are Hebrew only In Aramaic סיהרא is ' moon', and ירח ' month' or ' new moon' When our translator wishes to render 'new moon' he puts šaêq (= חדשׁ) as in 78^{12} 5. By the north cf. 72^5 6-17. These verses give a detailed description of the waxing and waning of the moon, of the length of the months, &c 6. This case where there are fourteen days from new moon to full moon has already been treated of in $73^{5, 6}$ (notes). In this verse the text follows α-u u is partly untranslatable β

heaven : [the light becomes full in her] . on the fourteenth day
she accomplishes her light.   7. And fifteen parts of light are
transferred to her till the fifteenth day (when) her light is
accomplished, according to the sign of the year, and she becomes
fifteen parts, and the moon grows by (the addition of) fourteenth
parts   8. And in her waning (the moon) decreases on the
first day to fourteen parts of her light, on the second to thirteen
parts of light, on the third to twelve, on the fourth to eleven,
on the fifth to ten, on the sixth to nine, on the seventh to eight,
on the eighth to seven, on the ninth to six, on the tenth to five,
on the eleventh to four, on the twelfth to three, on the thirteenth to two, on the fourteenth to the half of a seventh, and all
her remaining light disappears wholly on the fifteenth.   9. And
in certain months the month has twenty-nine days and once
twenty-eight.   10. And Uriel showed me another law : when
light is transferred to the moon, and on which side it is transferred to her by the sun.   11. During all the period during
which the moon is growing in her light, she is transferring it to
herself when opposite to the sun during fourteen days [her light

reads ' And when the moon rises, she
appears in the heaven, and has a fourteenth part of the light, and on the
fourteenth day she accomplishes all her
light '.   [The light becomes full in
her] (a–u)   I have bracketed this
clause as a duplicate rendering of τὸ
φῶς πληροῖ (οι τελεῖ), which the translator renders again as ' she accomplishes
her light '   7 This case, where
there are fifteen days from new moon
to full moon, has already been discussed .
see 73⁷, ⁸ (note).   8. As the moon
wanes her light decreases each day by
¹⁄₁₄th part , on the fifteenth day the
remainder, i e. ²⁄₂₈th, vanishes   Half
of a seventh (t, β)   a–t ' half and to
u seventh '   9. Twenty-nine
days   cf. 74¹⁰⁻¹⁷ 78¹⁵⁻¹⁷.   Once
twenty-eight.   As we learnt from
74¹³⁻¹⁶ that the author was acquainted
with the eight-year cycle of the Greeks,

so here, as Wieseler has already pointed
out, we find a reference to the seventy-
six year cycle of Callippus.   The cycle
of Callippus is already an emended
Metonic cycle.   According to the cycle
of Meton, to which there is no allusion
in Enoch, seven lunar months were
intercalated in nineteen lunar years,
in the third, fifth, eighth, eleventh,
thirteenth, sixteenth, nineteenth, and
thus the difference between the solar
and lunar years at the end of this cycle
was about 7½ hours   Callippus, recognizing this difference, quadrupled the
Metonic cycle and deducted one day
from the last month of this period of
seventy-six years, and thus this month
had only twenty-eight days as in our
text.   11. The moon waxes over
against the sun on the side turned to the
sun, i.e the western side   [Her light
is accomplished in the heaven]¹⁰

is accomplished in the heaven], and when she is illumined throughout, her light is accomplished in the heaven   12. And on the first day she is called the new moon, for on that day the light rises upon her   13. She becomes full moon exactly on the day when the sun sets in the west, and from the east she rises at night, and the moon shines the whole night through till the sun rises over against her and the moon is seen over against the sun.   14 On the side whence the light of the moon comes forth, there again she wanes till all the light vanishes and all the days of the month are at an end, and her circumference is empty, void of light.   15. And three months she makes of thirty days, and at her time she makes three months of twenty-nine days each, in which she accomplishes her waning in the first period of time, and in the first portal for one hundred and seventy-seven days.   16 And in the time of her going out she appears for three months (of) thirty days each, and for three months she appears (of) twenty-nine each.   17. At night she appears like a man for twenty days each time, and by day she appears like the heaven, and there is nothing else in her save her light.

Recapitulation of several of the Laws.

LXXIX. 1. And now, my son, I have shown thee everything, and the law of all the stars of the heaven is completed   2 And he showed me all the laws of these for every day, and for every season of bearing rule, and for every year, and for its going forth, and for the order prescribed to it every month and every week .   3 And the waning of the moon which takes place in the sixth portal : for in this sixth portal her light is accomplished, and after that there is the beginning of the waning : 4. ⟨And the waning⟩ which takes place in the first portal in its season, till one hundred and seventy-seven days are accomplished . reckoned according to weeks, twenty-five (weeks) and two days. 5. She falls behind the sun and the order of the stars exactly five days in the course of one period, and when this place which thou seest has been traversed.   6. Such is the picture and sketch of every luminary which Uriel the archangel, who is their leader, showed unto me.

LXXX 1. And in those days the angel Uriel answered and said to me . ‘ Behold, I have shown thee everything, Enoch, and I have revealed everything to thee that thou shouldest see this sun and this moon, and the leaders of the stars of the heaven and all those who turn them, their tasks and times and departures.

---

power ’   3, 4 Ct 78^{15}, but the verse is obscure or corrupt.   3 Of the waning (a) β ‘ of the month and of the waning ’   4 ⟨And the waning ⟩ Restored. So also Flemming and Martin   5 She falls behind (a–t) n ‘ and she falls behind ’, t, β–n ‘ and how she falls behind ’.   And the order Here I have emended wa ($>mq$) bašer'âta of a, β–bt (= ‘ and according to the order of ’) into walašer'âta For this use of la in replacing another preposition in an enumeration—in this instance ’em—see Dillmann’s *Gramm* ^{2} p 317 Our text here identifies the solar and sidereal years, as in 74^{12} Exactly five days . Cf 74$^{10-17}$ The moon falls behind five days in the half-year

LXXX. For the reasons for regarding this chapter as an interpolation see Introduction to this Book of the Heavenly Luminaries (pp. 147–8) In that Introduction we have already remarked that the moment we have done with 79 we pass into a world of new conceptions, the whole interest of which is ethical and nothing else There is absolutely no fixity in natural phenomena their laws and uniformities are always dependent on the moral action of men , cf 4 Ezra 5$^{1-13}$ This line of thought is quite alien to 72–79. See 2^1 (note).   1 The angel (gmt) $>$ qu, β I have shown (mq, β). gtu ‘ I will show ’ Leaders of the stars . cf 72^3 75$^{2, 3}$ Those who turn them These are probably the winds , cf. 72^5 73^2 And times + ‘ and they turn them ’ gmt Verses 2–5 are written as tristichs This fact helps us materially in the criticism of verses 5 and 7   2.

Perversion of Nature and the heavenly Bodies owing to the Sin of Men.

2. And in the days of the sinners the years shall be shortened,
And their seed shall be tardy on their lands and fields,
And all things on the earth shall alter,

And shall not appear in their time
And the rain shall be kept back
And the heaven shall withhold (it).

3 And in those times the fruits of the earth shall be backward,
And shall not grow in their time
And the fruits of the trees shall be withheld in their time.

4 And the moon shall alter her order,
And not appear at her time.

5. [And in those days the sun shall be seen and he shall journey
in the **evening** †on the extremity of the great chariot
in† the west]
And shall shine more brightly than accords with the order
of light.

(f Jer 3³ 5²⁶ **Shall alter** (β)
Alter' is here intransitive, but *a–u*
give the transitive tense and *t* supplies
'its ways' **Shall withhold** (*m*, β)
gqtu 'shall stand still' (by merely the
change of a vowel point) 4 Cf
for similar ideas Joel 2¹⁰ Amos 8⁹
4 Ezra 5⁴ 5 The first two lines
of this verse are very corrupt and have
been dislocated from their proper context in this chapter By their removal
verses 4–5 form a tristich relating to
the moon These corrupt clauses are
probably fragments of a tristich relating to the sun The Ethiopic reads
'And in those days the heaven (*mq*, β
gtu 'in the heaven') shall be seen,
and hunger shall come on the extremity
of the great chariot to (*a–q q*, *t²* β 'in')
the West'. Here Halévy conjectured,
and his conjecture is generally accepted, that השמים (= 'the heaven')
was corrupt for השמש (= 'the sun'),

רעב (= 'hunger') for ערב (= 'evening') But we must go further
There is no meaning in the phrase 'on
the extremity' in connexion with the
chariot of the sun This phrase =
בקץ which may be corrupt for מציק
= 'causing distress' Next there is
no point in saying 'the sun shall be
seen'. This line, moreover, is too
short, and the second too long. If we
transfer 'in the evening' to the first
line we have 'shall be seen in the
evening' The possible corruption
here is suggested by 4 Ezra 5⁴ relu-
cescet subito sol noctu' יראה ('shall
be seen') may be corrupt for יזרח =
'shall rise' Thus we arrive at the
following —

'And in those days the sun shall rise
in the evening,
'And his great chariot journey to the
west, causing distress (as it goes)'
With this we might contrast Amos 8⁹

6. And many chiefs of the stars shall transgress the order
   (prescribed).
   And these shall alter their orbits and tasks,
   And not appear at the seasons prescribed to them.

7. And the whole order of the stars shall be concealed from the
   sinners,
   And the thoughts of those on the earth shall err concerning
   them,
   [And they shall be altered from all their ways],
   Yea, they shall err and take them to be gods.

8. And evil shall be multiplied upon them,
   And punishment shall come upon them
   So as to destroy all.'

The Heavenly Tablets and the Mission of Enoch.

LXXXI. 1. And he said unto me ·
   'Observe, Enoch, these heavenly tablets,
   And read what is written thereon,
   And mark every individual fact '

2. And I observed the heavenly tablets, and read everything
which was written (thereon) and understood everything, and
read the book of all the deeds of mankind, and of all the

'I will cause the sun to go down at
noon'. The above emendations are
possible in Hebrew, but not in Aramaic.
6. Chiefs of the stars shall transgress the order (prescribed) (g^{co},
and in part by gq, o_1b) Beer conjectured this text, which differs from
that of the rest of the MSS by the
vocalization of two consonants. The
rest of the MSS = ' chiefs of the
stars of the order shall transgress '
7 Shall be concealed from the
sinners cf 75^2 82^{4-6}. Those on
the earth This phrase is used here
exactly in the sense in which it appears
in the interpolations in the Parables ;

see 37^5 (note) [And they shall be
altered ways] Bracketed as an
intrusion possibly it is a dittograph
of ver 6^b Take them to be gods ·
cf 19^1 Acts 7^{42}. 8 All (a). β
' them all '.
LXXXI For the reasons for regarding this chapter as an interpolation
see Introduction to this Book of the
Heavenly Luminaries (p 148) 1
These heavenly tablets For a complete account of this and kindred expressions see 47^3 (note) β-n reads
' the writing of the heavenly tablets '
2. The book of all the deeds (mt)
gu ' the book, all the deeds ' q, β ' the

children of flesh that shall be upon the earth to the remotest generations.   3. And forthwith I blessed the great Lord, the King of glory for ever, in that He has made all the works of the world,

> And I extolled the Lord because of His patience,
> And blessed Him because of the children of men.

4. And after that I said.

> ' Blessed is the man who dies in righteousness and goodness,
> Concerning whom there is no book of unrighteousness
>   written,
> And against whom no day of judgement shall be found.'

5. And those seven holy ones brought me and placed me on the earth before the door of my house, and said to me: ' Declare everything to thy son Methuselah, and show to all thy children that no flesh is righteous in the sight of the Lord, for He is their Creator.   6. One year we will leave thee with thy son, till thou givest thy (last) commands, that thou mayest teach thy children and record (it) for them, and testify to all thy children ; and in the second year they shall take thee from their midst.

book and all that was written therein, all the deeds'.   3 Of 22¹⁴ for a similar expression of praise. **The great Lord** (a) β ' the Lord '. **The King of glory for ever** (a). β–bc ' the eternal King of glory ' **Children of men** (a, ftloy ₁a ₁b). β–fhtlnoy ₁a ₁b ' children of the world '.   4. See Introd. (p. 148) on the contrast between this blessing and that pronounced by the writer of 72–79 **Book of unrighteousness**. see 47⁸ (note) **Day of judgement** (gmu) q, t² β ' unrighteousness ' **Shall be found** (a–m). m, t² β ' has been found '. If this clause be taken strictly, it is here taught that there is no judgement for the righteous   5 **Seven holy ones** (a). β ' three holy

ones' Cf 87² 90²¹, ²² and 20   No flesh is righteous, &c   cf Job 9² Ps 14¹.   **Creator ·** of 94¹⁰   6 **Thy son** (a) β ' thy sons ' These two verses, vv 5, 6, may be inserted to serve as an introduction to 91–104 **Till.** After ' till ' (= עד) the MSS add ' again ' = עד which is here simply a dittograph of the preceding The word ' again ' is meaningless as it stands **Givest thy (last) commands** (tĕ'ĕzĕz mt, β–cde) This is the idiomatic meaning of the Hebrew צוה. The reading of g is a corruption of mt Hence all MSS but q and three third-rate MSS support the above text q = ' comfortest him ' (tĕnâzĕzô) According to Dillmann cde read tĕ'ĕzĕz = ' growest strong ' But this gives no

7. Let thy heart be strong,
   For the good shall announce righteousness to the good ;

   The righteous with the righteous shall rejoice,
   And shall offer congratulation to one another.

8. But the sinners shall die with the sinners,
   And the apostate go down with the apostate.

9. And those who practise righteousness shall die on account of
   the deeds of men,
   And be taken away on account of the doings of the godless '
10. And in those days they ceased to speak to me, and I came
to my people, blessing the Lord of the world.

*Charge given to Enoch . the four Intercalary Days : the Stars which
lead the Seasons and the Months.*

LXXXII. 1. And now, my son Methuselah, all these things
I am recounting to thee and writing down for thee, and I have
revealed to thee everything, and given thee books concerning all
these · so preserve, my son Methuselah, the books from thy
father's hand, and (see) that thou deliver them to the generations
of the world.

suitable sense   8 The apostate
go down, i e into Gehenna   9 The
righteous die indeed, yet are they
'gathered' unto the abodes of the
blessed   The phrase is borrowed
directly from Is 57¹, where the literal
translation runs, 'the righteous is
gathered out of the way of or because of
the evil' מִפְּנֵי הָרָעָה נֶאֱסָף הַצַּדִּיק of
2 Kings 22²⁰ Book of Wisdom 4⁷⁻¹⁴.
The Hebrew verb is used of being
'gathered to one's fathers', Num 20²⁶.
In Ps 104²⁹ God is said to 'gather'
the spirit of animals when they die.
10 Lord of the world (or 'Eternal
Lord' *a–q   q, β* 'Lord of the ages'),
cf. 1³ 12³ 58⁴ 81³ 82⁷ 84²

LXXXII The conclusion of the
Book of the Heavenly Luminaries
1 In 33⁴ Uriel writes down everything
for Enoch , but in this book, cf 72¹ 74²
75³ 79²⁻⁶ 82¹, Uriel only shows the
hidden things to Enoch, and Enoch
writes them down   For thee > *gmt*
Methuselah > *gmq*   Deliver them
to the generations ('children' *g*) of
the world.   These revelations of
Enoch are for all the world from the
earliest generations: those in 1–36 are
only for the far distant generations ,
cf. 1²   See special Introd (p 149)   It
is evidently this passage that Tertullian
refers to in *De Cultu Fem* i, 3 'Cum
Enoch filio suo Matusalae nihil aliud

2. I have given wisdom to thee and to thy children,
[And thy children that shall be to thee],
That they may give it to their children for generations,
This wisdom (namely) that passeth their thought.

3 And those who understand it shall not sleep,
But shall listen with the ear that they may learn this wisdom,
And it shall please those that eat thereof better than good food.

4. Blessed are all the righteous, blessed are all those who walk in the way of righteousness and sin not as the sinners, in the reckoning of all their days in which the sun traverses the heaven, entering into and departing from the portals for thirty days with the heads of thousands of the order of the stars, together with the four which are intercalated which divide the four portions of the year, which lead them and enter with them four days. 5. Owing to them men shall be at fault and not reckon them in the **whole reckoning of the year** . yea, men shall be at fault, and not recognize them accurately.   6. For they belong to the reckoning of the year and are truly recorded (thereon) for ever, one in the first portal and one in the third, and one in the fourth and one in the sixth, and the year is completed in three hundred and sixty-four days.

mandaverit quam ut notitiam eorum posteris suis traderit'.   2 **Wisdom** The surpassing wisdom conveyed in these revelations is a frequent theme with the Enoch writers, cf 37⁴ 92¹ 93¹⁰⁻¹⁴   To thee and to thy **children** (*mqu*, β) cf Ps 78⁵⁶ *t* reads 'to thy son' · *g* corrupt As we must infer from these words that Lamech is already born, the writer has followed the Samaritan or Massoretic reckoning the former would allow of Noah being present   [And thy children . to thee.] Bracketed as an interpolation   3 **Better than good food** cf. Ps 19¹⁰   4 The four intercalary days introduced by four leaders of ver 11, 75¹,²   **Blessed are all those** (*t*, β-*y*) > *gu*, *y*   *mq* 'blessed (+ 'moreover' *q*) are all' (+ 'the righteous' *m*). **Heads of thousands,** 1 e the chiliarchs which lead these days   **Divide** (*qt*, β-*no* ₁*b*) Cf 82¹¹   *gmu*, *no* ₁*b* 'are divided'   5 Cf 75²   **Whole reckoning of the year** So with Beer I correct bahasâba kuällû 'âlam (= 'in the reckoning of the whole world') into bakuällû hasâba 'âmat.   6 On the four intercalary days, and the portals to which they belong, see 75   **The year is completed in three hundred,** &c (β)

7. And the account thereof is accurate and the recorded reckoning thereof exact; for the luminaries, and months and festivals, and years and days, has Uriel shown and revealed to me, to whom the Lord of the whole creation of the world hath subjected the host of heaven.   8. And he has power over night and day in the heaven to cause the light to give light to men—sun, moon, and stars, and all the powers of the heaven which revolve in their circular chariots   9. And these are the orders of the stars, which set in their places, and in their seasons and festivals and months.

10. And these are the names of those who lead them, who watch that they enter at their times, in their orders, in their seasons, in their months, in their periods of dominion, and in their positions.   11. Their four leaders who divide the four parts of the year enter first, and after them the twelve leaders of the orders who divide the months; and for the three hundred and sixty (days) there are heads over thousands who divide the days, and for the four inter-calary days there are the leaders which sunder the four parts of the year.   12 And these heads over thousands are inter-calated between leader and leader, each behind a station, but

---

a–gmu 'the year of three hundred and sixty-four days is completed'   7
To whom   hath subjected. The text *a–q, β* reads za'azaza (za'azazò *b efni*) lita (= 'whom He hath commanded for me') which I have emended into za'azaza lôtû = ὦ ἐπέταξε   But ἐπέταξε is corrupt for ὑπέταξε   Hence my translation   Uriel is the ruler of the starry world, 72¹   Lord of the whole creation of the world   Here only, cf 84²   9–20 Dillmann regards these verses as a later addition to the book, but without adequate reason. They are quite in harmony with all that rightly belongs to this section of the book.   Moreover, 72¹ promises an account of the stars, and 79¹ declares that the full account has now been given

This would be impossible without 82⁶⁻²⁰
10 **Who watch that they enter.** Here the Ethiopic is literally 'who watch and enter'.   But the context requires the rendering I have given   Hence it is possible that we have here the survival of the Hebrew idiom of the voluntative with waw   If so, the text would represent something like אָשֶׁר יָצְרוּ וְיָבֹאוּ.   **Times** + 'who lead them in their places' (> 'in their places' *u*) *a*
11 **For** (> *q*) **the three hundred and sixty (days) there are heads** (*gqu*) *t, β* 'for the three hundred and sixty-four (days) with the heads'   *m* supports *gqu,* but by a slip omits 'and sixty'
12 **A station.** *q, a* read 'his station'   There is no difficulty in the text of *gmqu* which we have followed here

their leaders make the division.   13. And these are the names
of the leaders who divide the four parts of the year which are
ordained : Mîlkî'êl, Hel'emmêlêk, and Mêl'êjal, and Nâiêl.
14. And the names of those who lead them · Adnâr'êl, and
Îjâsûsa'êl, and 'Êlômê'êl—these three follow the leaders of the
orders, and there is one that follows the three leaders of the
orders which follow those leaders of stations that divide the four
parts of the year

15. In the beginning of the year Melkejâl rises first and rules,
who is named †Tam'âinî, and sun† and all the days of his
dominion whilst he bears rule are ninety-one days.   16. And
these are the signs of the days which are to be seen on earth in
the days of his dominion · sweat, and heat, and calms , and all
the trees bear fruit, and leaves are produced on all the trees, and
the harvest of wheat, and the rose-flowers, and all the flowers
which come forth in the field, but the trees of the winter season
become withered.   17. And these are the names of the leaders
which are under them · Berka'êl, Zêlebs'êl, and another who is
added a head of a thousand, called Hîlûjâsĕph : and the days
of the dominion of this (leader) are at an end.

The twelve leaders of the months
divide the months; the chiliarchs
divide the 360 days, and the four
leaders which divide the year into four
parts have charge of the intercalary
days. 12 I don't understand this verse.
13 Milkiel from מלכיאל is simply an
inversion of Helemmelek from אלימלך
as Halévy has shown. Melejal =
מלאיאל (Schwab) and Narel = נראל.
These four are over the four seasons of
the year. Under each of these are
three leaders who preside over the
three months of each season   14
This verse seems unintelligible   15–
17 The period from spring to summer = 91 days under the dominion of
Meikejal.   15 Of the year (m, β)
> a–m The leader of this period is
named 'Tam'âinî' and 'sun'. As

Goldschmidt and Beer have pointed
out, these two names are one, i e.
שמש תימני = 'the southern sun' This
explanation is not possible through
Aramaic   16 Calms (zâbn ").
a–u, hazan, 'anxiety.' Rose-flowers
Not known in the O T though the
word is found in the A.V in Is 35[1]
Song of Solomon 2[1] The rose is
mentioned in Sir 24[14] 39[13] Wisdom
2[8] But in the first two passages
it is probably the oleander that is referred to. The rose in later Hebrew is
ורד and in Aramaic ורדא. Which
come forth (a–m) β 'bloom' > m
17 The leaders under them, i e.
the leaders of the three months.
Berka'el = ברכיאל Zelebs'êl = ולבשאל
= 'this is the heart of God' (Schwab).
Another who is added . . called

18. The next leader after him is Hêl'emmêlêk, whom one names the shining sun, and all the days of his light are ninety-one days.　19 And these are the signs of (his) days on the earth : glowing heat and dryness, and the trees ripen their fruits and produce all their fruits ripe and ready, and the sheep pair and become pregnant, and all the fruits of the earth are gathered in, and everything that is in the fields, and the winepress : these things take place in the days of his dominion　20. These are the names, and the orders, and the leaders of those heads of thousands · Gîdâ'ijal, Kê'êl, and Hê'êl, and the name of the head of a thousand which is added to them, Asfâ'êl and the days of his dominion are at an end.

Hilûjâsëph. There is here a play on the proper name אליוסף . . . נוסף. 18-20. The period from summer to autumn.　19 And these are the signs of (his) days (β) *gmt* 'and these are the days of his sign'. *yu* corrupt forms of *gmt*.　20 This verse is confused. The three names are those of the leaders of the three months The fourth — Asfâ'êl from יוספאל 'God adds', which is merely an inversion of Hilûjâsëph from אליוסף — is the childarch who has to do with the intercalary day under one of the four chief leaders. There is no account of the remaining six months This may have been omitted by the final redactor.

SECTION IV

(CHAPTERS LXXXIII—XC)

THE DREAM-VISIONS.   INTRODUCTION

A. *Critical Structure*.   B   *Relation of this Section to* (a) 1–36,
(b) 91–104.   C. *The Date*   D. *The Problem and its Solution*

A. Critical Structure. There is no difficulty about the critical
structure of this Section. It is the most complete and self-consistent
of all the Sections, and has suffered least from the hand of the interpolator. There seems to be only one interpolation, i. e 90^{14} b. Of
dislocations of the text there are two 89^{48} b should be read after
89^{40} see 89^{48} Crit. Note , and 90^{19} should be read before 90^{14} . see
90^{13-19} (note)   In 90 vv. 13–15 are a doublet of vv 16–18.

B. (a) **Relation of this Section to 6–36.** This question can
only be determined by giving the points of likeness as well as of
divergence. The points of likeness or identity in (1) phraseology,
and (2) in ideas, are —

(1) 'Tongue of flesh,' 84^1 14^2, 'make the earth without inhabitant,' 84^5 9^2; 'Holy and Great One,' 84^1 1^3, 'glorious land'
(i. e. Jerusalem or Palestine), 89^{40}, compared with 'blessed land ', 27^1.
The doxology in 84^2 appears to be a more rhetorical form of that
in 9^4 Finally, 88^1–89^1 presupposes 10^{1-12} See notes *in loc*

(2) There is, in the main, the same doctrine of the fallen angels .
the judgement in both is at the beginning of the Messianic kingdom ,
Gehenna is found in both, 90^{26} 27^1 the abyss of fire for the fallen
angels, 90^{24} 10^6 18^{11} 21^{7-10}, the conversion of the Gentiles, 90^{30}
10^{21}.

There is, practically, nothing that is distinctive in (2)—certainly
nothing more than would refer the two Sections to the same school
of thought   But the evidence of (1) is of a different nature, and
points, when combined with the evidence of (2), to a close connexion between the two Sections either in identity of authorship,
or in the acquaintance of one of the authors with the work of the
other. That the latter alternative is the true one, we shall find on
the following grounds —(1) In 83^{11} the sun comes forth from the

'windows of the east', a term that is never used of the sun in 1–36, nor in 72–82: see 83[11] (note). 'Windows' has a different reference altogether· see 72[3] (note) (2) In 84[4] 'the great day of judgement' = Deluge, in 1–36 and 91–104 always = final judgement. see 84[4] (note) (3) The account of the descent of the watchers in 86[1–3] differs from that in 6. (4) In 90[19] the period of the sword is an important feature, yet is not alluded to in 1–36. (5) The throne of judgement is in Palestine in 90[20–26]; whereas the throne on which God will sit when He comes to bless His people in 25[3] is the centre of the Seven Mountains see 18[8] (note). (6) Appearance of the Messiah emphasized in 90[37, 38], not alluded to in 1–36 (7) The scene of the kingdom in 83–90 is the New Jerusalem set up by God Himself, in 1–36 it is Jerusalem and the entire earth *unchanged* though purified, 10[18, 20] (8) Life of the members of the Messianic kingdom is apparently unending in 90[33–38]; but only finite in 10[17] 25[6]. Life is transfigured by the presence of the Messiah in 90[38] in the New Jerusalem. but in 25[5, 6] by the external eating of the tree of life (9) The picture on 83–90 is developed and spiritual, that in 1–36 is naive, primitive, and sensuous. (10) 83–90 are only visions assigned to Enochs earlier and unwedded life, 1–36 are accounts of actual bodily translations and are assigned to his later life If these two Sections were from the same author and that an ascetic, exactly the converse would have been the case

On these grounds, therefore, identity of authorship seems impossible, but the similarities in phraseology and idea prove that one of the authors had the work of the other before him Of the two Sections there is no room for doubt that 83–90 is the later.

(*b*) **Relation of 83–90 to 91–104.** See Special Introd. to 91–104 (pp. 220–221).

C. The Date. The fourth period began about 200 B C. (see note on 90[6–17] pp. 206 sqq) and marks the transition of supremacy over Israel from the Graeco-Egyptians to the Graeco-Syrians, as well as the rise of the Chasids. The Chasids, symbolized by the lambs that are born to the white sheep, 90[6], are already an organized party in the Maccabean revolt, 90[6–7] (note) The lambs that become horned are the Maccabean family, and the great horn is Judas Maccabeus, 90[9] (note). As this great horn is still warring at the close of the rule of the twelve shepherds, 90[10], this Section must have been written before the death of Judas, 161 B C , possibly before his purification of the temple.

As the fourth period began about 200 B. c., the author of 83–90, writing in the lifetime of Judas Maccabeus, must have expected its close between 140 and 130 B. c., for, on the analogy of the third period, each shepherd would rule between five and six years. This expectation in connexion with Judas Maccabeus was not unnatural, as his eldest brother, Simon, did not die till 135 B. c

D. The Problem and its Solution. This Section forms in short compass a philosophy of religion from the Jewish standpoint. It is divided into two visions, the former of which deals with the first world-judgement of the deluge, and the latter with the entire history of the world till the final judgement. The writer does not attempt to account for the sin that showed itself in the first generation In his view, it was not the sin of man, but the sin of the angels who fell (in the days of Jared), that corrupted the earth, 84^4 86–87, and brought upon it the first world-judgement.

In the second vision the interest centres mainly on the calamities that befall Israel from the exile onwards. Why has Israel become a byword among the nations, and the servant of one gentile power after another? Is there no recompense for the righteous nation and the righteous individual? That Israel, indeed, has sinned grievously and deserves to be punished, the author amply acknowledges, but not a punishment so immeasurably transcending its guilt But these undue severities have not come upon Israel from God's hand : they are the doing of the seventy shepherds into whose care God committed Israel, 89^{59}. These shepherds or angels have proved faithless to their trust, and treacherously destroyed those whom God willed not to destroy ; but they have not therein done so with impunity. An account has been taken of all their deeds and of all whom they have wickedly destroyed, 89^{61-64}, and for all their victims there is laid up a recompense of reward, 90^{33}. Moreover, when the outlook is darkest, and the oppression at its worst, a righteous league will be established in Israel, 90^6, and in it there will be a family from which will come forth the deliverer of Israel, i. e. Judas Maccabeus, 90^{9-16}. The Syrians and other enemies of Israel will put forth every effort to destroy him, but in vain ; for a great sword will be given to him wherewith to destroy his enemies, 90^{19}. Then all the hostile Gentiles will assemble for their final struggle against Israel, still led by Judas Maccabeus, $90^{13, 16}$; but this, their crowning act of wickedness, will also be the final act in their history and serve as the signal for their immediate judgement   God will appear in person, and the earth open its mouth and swallow them up, 90¹⁸. The wicked shepherds will then be judged and the fallen watchers, and cast into an abyss of fire, 90²⁰⁻²⁵. With the condemnation of the Apostates to Gehenna the great assize will close, 90²⁶. Then his New Jerusalem will be set up by God Himself, 90²⁸, ²⁹, and the surviving Gentiles will be converted and serve Israel, 90³⁰, and all the Jews dispersed abroad will be gathered together, and all the righteous dead will be raised to take part in the kingdom, 90³³ Then the Messiah will appear amongst them, 90³⁷; and all the righteous will be gloriously transformed after his likeness, 90³⁸, and God will rejoice over them.

87–90 were written by a Chasid in support of the Maccabean movement.

LXXXIII—LXXXIV *First Dream-Vision on the Deluge.*

LXXXIII 1. And now, my son Methuselah, I will show thee all my visions which I have seen, recounting them before thee 2 Two visions I saw before I took a wife, and the one was quite unlike the other. the first when I was learning to write. the second before I took thy mother, (when) I saw a terrible vision. And regarding them I prayed to the Lord.   3 I had laid me down in the house of my grandfather Mahalalel, (when) I saw in a vision how the heaven collapsed and was borne off and fell to the earth 4. And when it fell to the earth I saw how the earth was swallowed up in a great abyss, and mountains were suspended on mountains, and hills sank down on hills, and high trees were rent from their stems, and hurled down and sunk in the abyss. 5. And thereupon a word fell into my mouth, and I lifted up

---

LXXXIII 1 My visions (a–t) *t*, β 'visions'   **2 Before I took** a wife, i e before I was sixty-five, cf Gen 5²¹ The name of this wife was Edna, 85³, cf Book of Jubilees 4¹⁰, where these dream-visions are referred to We should observe that 83–90 are only dreams or dream-visions; whereas in the other Sections of the book Enoch has open intercourse with the angels, and is translated bodily and therein

admitted to higher privileges than in mere visions. Yet if 83–90 came from the same hand as the other Sections, the converse should have been the case on *ascetic* grounds, and Enoch should have had his bodily translations to heaven and his intercourse with the angels during his unmarried years, and his dream-visions after he had taken a wife.   **3. Mahalalel** In text it is Malâl'el   **5. Lifted up** (my

(my voice) to cry aloud, and said: 'The earth is destroyed.'
6. And my grandfather Mahalalel waked me as I lay near him,
and said unto me: 'Why dost thou cry so, my son, and why dost
thou make such lamentation?'   7. And I recounted to him
the whole vision which I had seen, and he said unto me·
'A terrible thing hast thou seen, my son, and of grave moment
is thy dream-vision as to the secrets of all the sin of the earth·
it must sink into the abyss and be destroyed with a great destruction.   8. And now, my son, arise and make petition to the
Lord of glory, since thou art a believer, that a remnant may
remain on the earth, and that He may not destroy the whole
earth.   9. My son, from heaven all this will come upon
the earth, and upon the earth there will be great destruction.'
10. After that I arose and prayed and implored and besought,
and wrote down my prayer for the generations of the world, and
I will show everything to thee, my son Methuselah.   11. And
when I had gone forth below and seen the heaven, and the sun
rising in the east, and the moon setting in the west, and a few
stars, and the whole earth, and everything as †He had known† it in
the beginning, then I blessed the Lord of judgement and extolled
Him because He had made the sun to go forth from the windows
of the east, †and he ascended and rose on the face of the heaven,
and set out and kept traversing the path shown unto him.

voice) (*mqu*, β–*n*). *g* 'arose', *t*, *n*
'began'.   **7. Secrets of all the
sin** (*tu*, β, save that *tu* ᵢb read kuéllô
for kuéllû) *gm* 'sin of all the sin', *q*
'sin of all'. Perhaps *q* is right. *gm*
could be explained as a dittograph of *q*
and *tu*, β as an emendation of *gm*.
8. Lord of glory. Cf 25³ 27³, ⁵ 36⁴
40³ 63² 75³.   **And that He may not
earth** (*t*, β) > *a–t* through bmt (?\
10 The prayer may be that given in
84²⁻⁶   **And besought** (*a–q*) > *q*, β.
My prayer (*mt*, β). *g* 'I prayed and'
> *qu*   **11. The whole earth**
(*gmq*, *cdfiloy* ᵢa ᵢb). > *t*, abehknx.
As †He had known† it. Read

'a'émaikû for 'a'emara, and translate
'as I had known it'. Otherwise it is
possible that ἐνόησεν stood before the
Ethiopic translator—a corruption of
ἐποίησεν (Flemming), or that the Greek
translator confused הבין and הכין. In
the last case render 'as He had
established'. **Lord of judgement.**
Here only. **Windows.** This term is
never used in 1–36 nor in 72–82 of the
sun Portal is the word invariably
used in connexion with the sun. For
the word 'windows' see 72³ (note).
†And he ascended This cannot be
right. What we require is 'so that
he ascended', and so all translators,

LXXXIV 1 And I lifted up my hands in righteousness and blessed the Holy and Great One, and spake with the breath of my mouth, and with the tongue of flesh, which God has made for the children of the flesh of men, that they should speak therewith, and He gave them breath and a tongue and a mouth that they should speak therewith:

2. 'Blessed be Thou, O Lord, King,
Great and mighty in Thy greatness,
Lord of the whole creation of the heaven,
King of kings and God of the whole world.

And Thy power and kingship and greatness abide for ever and ever,
And throughout all generations Thy dominion
And all the heavens are Thy throne for ever,
And the whole earth Thy footstool for ever and ever.

3. For Thou hast made and Thou rulest all things,
And nothing is too hard for Thee,
Wisdom departs not from the place of Thy throne,
Nor turns away from Thy presence.

myself included, wrongly rendered the words. Hence I assume here a wrong punctuation of the Hebrew on the part of the Greek translator Text = *καὶ ἀνέβη καὶ ἀνέτειλε* = וַיַּעַל וַיִּזְרַח, which should have been read as וַיַּעֲלֶה וַיִּזְרַח. Then we should have 'so that he ascended and rose', &c

LXXXIV. 1 *Enoch's Prayer for his Posterity* **The Holy and Great One** see 1^3 note **Tongue of flesh** see 14^2 **Children of the flesh of men** (*gmt, abcfhiknx*) *u, delopy* ${}_1a$ ${}_1b$ 'children of men'; *q* 'children of men of flesh'. **2** Cf $9^{4\ sqq.}$ **Lord of the whole creation of the heaven** Here only, cf 82^7, also 58^4 (note) **King of kings** Also in 9^4 **God of the whole world** Here only; see note on 1^3 **All the heavens are Thy throne &c** From Is 66^1 **3 Nothing is too hard for Thee** (= *ἀδυνατήσει παρὰ σοὶ οὐδέν*) This clause is drawn from Jer. $32^{17, 27}$ לֹא יִפָּלֵא מִמְּךָ כָּל דָּבָר. Here the LXX render *οὐ μὴ ἀποκρυβῇ ἀπὸ σοῦ οὐδέν*. Cf. Gen 18^{14}. After this clause the text adds a dittograph = *καὶ οὐδεμία* or earlier *καὶ οὐδέν* **Departs not** (*g*) Other MSS 'departs not from Thee'. **From the place of Thy throne, nor turns away** The text = 'nor turns away (*gqm* corrupt here) from her life (> *qu*), (+ from *mq*) Thy throne and' By the simple transposition of the verb 'nor turns away' the parallelism of the text is restored Further 'ĕmmanbartâ (= 'from her life') has been emended into 'ĕmmĕnbârâta (= 'from the place') Thus the phrase 'from the place of Thy throne' = *ἀπὸ τοῦ τόπου τοῦ θρόνου σοῦ* = מִמְּכוֹן כִּסְאֲךָ Ps 89^{15} To re-

And Thou knowest and seest and hearest everything,
And there is nothing hidden from Thee [for Thou seest
    everything]

4. And now the angels of Thy heavens are guilty of trespass,
    And upon the flesh of men abideth Thy wrath until the
    great day of judgement.

5. And now, O God and Lord and Great King,
    I implore and beseech Thee to fulfil my prayer,
    To leave me a posterity on earth.
    And not to destroy all the flesh of man,
    And make the earth without inhabitant,
    So that there should be an eternal destruction.

6. And now, my Lord, destroy from the earth the flesh which
    has aroused Thy wrath,
    But the flesh of righteousness and uprightness establish as
    a plant of the eternal seed,
    And hide not Thy face from the prayer of Thy servant,
    O Lord.'

LXXXV—XC. *The Second Dream-Vision of Enoch · the History
of the World to the Founding of the Messianic Kingdom.*

LXXXV. 1. And after this I saw another dream, and I will
show the whole dream to thee, my son.   2. And Enoch lifted

turn to the word 'ĕmmanbartâ, which
I have emended as above, we should
observe that it does not admit of any
reasonable rendering in this passage
The word means 'life', 'food', 'condition' None of these meanings suit
the passage With the above passage
we might compare Wisdom 9⁴ 'Wisdom
that sitteth by Thee on Thy throne'.
Wisdom is represented in both these
passages as the assessor or πάρεδρος of
God The idea is to be traced to Prov
8³⁰ in the LXX version ἤμην παρ'
αὐτῷ · cf. Sir 1¹ μετ' αὐτοῦ ἐστιν
εἰς τὸν αἰῶνα [For Thou seest
everything] A dittograph from the

preceding line   4. Upon the
flesh of men · cf vv. 1, 5, Job 12¹⁰
Great day of judgement Most
MSS read 'day of the great judgement' See my text, which follows in
part *q* and in part *q*, see 45² (note)
This phrase can refer here only to the
Deluge In 19¹ it refers to the final
judgement, and so always in 91–104,
cf 94⁹ 98¹⁰ 99¹⁵ 104⁵   5. Great
King Also in 91¹³   6 A plant
of the eternal seed see 10¹⁶ (note)
This idea was a very favourite one, cf.
62⁸ 93², 5, 10

LXXXV—XC The second Dream-
vision In this second vision the

up (his voice) and spake to his son Methuselah 'To thee, my
son, will I speak. hear my words—incline thine ear to the dream-
vision of thy father.   3. Before I took thy mother Edna, I saw
in a vision on my bed, and behold a bull came forth from the
earth, and that bull was white; and after it came forth a heifer,
and along with this (latter) came forth two bulls, one of them
black and the other red.   4. And that black bull gored the red
one and pursued him over the earth, and thereupon I could no
longer see that red bull.   5 But that black bull grew and
that heifer went with him, and I saw that many oxen proceeded
from him which resembled and followed him.   6. And that
cow, that first one, went from the presence of that first bull in

writer gives a complete history of the
world from Adam down to the final
judgement and the establishment of
the Messianic kingdom. After the
example of Ezekiel men are symbolized
by animals The leaders of the chosen
race are represented by domestic
animals, the patriarchs by bulls, and
the faithful of later times by sheep
(cf Ezek 34³, ⁶, ⁸ sqq.) This difference
may be intended to mark the later declension of Israel in faith and righteousness The Gentiles are symbolized by
wild beasts and birds of prey (cf Ezek
39¹⁷, where the enemies of Israel are
symbolized by the birds of the air and the
beasts of the field), the fallen watchers
by stars, unfallen angels by men At
times the author is obliged to abandon
his symbolism, and he is not always
consistent in his use of it, as the same
symbol varies in meaning Even the
divine name is adapted to the prevailing symbolism In the main the
narrative is based on the O T, but at
times mythical elements from later
Jewish exegesis are incorporated

LXXXV 2 Cf Prov 5¹   **3**
Edna cf 83²   **I saw in a vision
on my bed.** Cf Dan 4¹⁰ 'I saw
in a vision of my head upon my bed'

(also 4⁷ 7¹)   **On my bed** (*q, β*) *gmt*
'of my bed'   *u* corrupt   **Bull.**
The Ethiopic word is lâhm. This
word has various meanings in the
following chapters. In the sing it =
bull or heifer, in the plur it = bulls,
or cattle, or cows The context must
determine the sense The author uses
also the unequivocal word sôr, which
always means a bull Tâ'wâ = vitulus
or vitula in these chapters. Eve is so
designated in this verse, i e a heifer,
to denote her as a virgin In verse 6
she is called 'a cow'. **White** is the
colour that symbolizes righteousness
throughout this vision, cf 85⁸ 87², &c.
Cf Is. 1¹⁸ Ps 51⁷ Rev. 7¹⁴. **Two
bulls** (*g, n*). Other MSS 'other
young bulls'. Cain is black, as this
colour symbolizes his sin Abel is red
—the colour emblematic of his martyr-
dom   **4 Bull.** So I render tâ'wâ
when it = vitulus, as in vv 4, 5, 6
5 That heifer The same word is
used of Eve in verse 3 This heifer is
Cain's wife, and according to the Book
of Jubilees 4¹, ⁴ his sister, by name
Avan. **Oxen.** This is the rendering
of the plural of lâhm, and includes
bulls and cows   **Him**³⁰ (*q, β*). *gmt*
'them'   **6. Eve seeks Abel.**

order to seek that red one, but found him not, and lamented with
a great lamentation over him and sought him.   7 And I looked
till that first bull came to her and quieted her, and from that
time onward she cried no more.   8. And after that she bore
another white bull, and after him she bore many bulls and
black cows.

9. And I saw in my sleep that white bull likewise grow and
become a great white bull, and from him proceeded many white
bulls, and they resembled him.   10. And they began to beget
many white bulls, which resembled them, one following the other,
(even) many.

The Fall of the Angels and the Demoralization of Mankind.

LXXXVI. 1. And again I saw with mine eyes as I slept, and
I saw the heaven above, and behold a star fell from heaven,
and it arose and eat and pastured amongst those oxen.   2 And
after that I saw the large and the black oxen, and behold they all
changed their stalls and pastures and their cattle, and began to
live with each other.   3. And again I saw in the vision, and
looked towards the heaven, and behold I saw many stars descend

---

Over him (dibêhû *q*).   *g* 'with regard to him' (ḫabêhû), *mt*, *β* 'thereupon' (sôbêhâ).   According to Juh 4⁷
'Adam and Eve mourned for Abel
twenty-eight years'   In 'mourning'
there is here as in our text a play
on the word Abel, though the former
is אָבֵל and the latter הֶבֶל   8
Another white bull (*mt*, *β*)   *gqu*
'a pair of white oxen', 1 e Seth and
a sister to he his wife   On the latter
see Juh 4⁸, ¹¹   **Black cows** The
adjective 'black' belongs probably to
the 'bulls' also   9. **Bull** Rendering of *sor*, see verse 3   This bull
is Seth   The descendants of Seth are
likewise righteous like their progenitor
Many (*qmqt*). > *β*

LXXXVI 1. **A star**, 1 e Azazel
Cf 88¹ 10⁴ ˢqq   According to Jalkut

Shim. Ber. 44 (see Weber, *Jud Theol*
253) Azazel and Shemjaza descended together, but only the former was guilty
of sin with the daughters of men.
2 **And after that** (*β*).   *mq* 'and
these', *t* 'and in the midst', *u* 'and'
> *g*   To live with each other   *q*
reads jahajĕwû = 'to live one to another'; *a*-*y*, *β* ja'awajewû, 'to lament
one to ('with' *β*) another'   The
latter reading is not satisfactory   The
black bulls did not leave their pastures,
&c simply to engage in lamentation
The time for lamentation does not
arrive till verse 6   Thus ja'awajĕwû
may be an emendation of *g* jahajĕwû
But the construction that follows ' one
to another' (*a*) seems impossible.   If
we read 'to live' we must adopt the *β*
text in what follows, 1 e 'with each

and cast themselves down from heaven to that first star, and they became bulls amongst those cattle and pastured with them [amongst them]. 4. And I looked at them and saw, and behold they all let out their privy members, like horses, and began to cover the cows of the oxen, and they all became pregnant and bare elephants, camels, and asses. 5. And all the oxen feared them and were affrighted at them, and began to bite with their teeth and to devour, and to gore with their horns 6. And they began moreover to devour those oxen, and behold all the children of the earth began to tremble and quake before them and to flee from them.

The Advent of the Seven Archangels.

LXXXVII. 1. And again I saw how they began to gore each other and to devour each other, and the earth began to cry aloud 2. And I raised mine eyes again to heaven, and I saw in the vision, and behold there came forth from heaven beings who were like white men and four went forth from that place and three with them. 3. And those three that had last come forth grasped me by my hand and took me up, away from the generations of the earth, and raised me up to a lofty place, and showed me a tower raised high above the earth, and all the hills were

other' 3 Fall of the rest of the angels Became bulls amongst those cattle and pastured with them (a) β 'were amongst those cattle and bulls, pasturing with them 4 Elephants, camels, and asses Symbolizing the three kinds of giants; see 7² (note). 6 The children of the earth The writer here forgets his rôle, and uses non-symbolical language From them (gm) > other MSS.

LXXXVII 1 The conflict of the bulls and giants 2 And I saw in the vision > qu. Beings who were like white men, i e unfallen angels As men are represented by animals, the unfallen angels are naturally represented by men White· cf 85³ Four (a). β 'one'. Four . and three with them On these seven archangels see 81⁵ 90²¹,²² 20. The three are found again in 90⁵¹. With them (m) a–m, β 'with him' 3, 4. If we are to regard this high tower as Paradise, and it seems we must, as according to the universal tradition of later times Enoch was translated thither, we have in 83–90 a conception of its locality and inhabitants differing from any that has preceded, see 60⁸ (note) 3. All the hills were lower (t, β), a–t lower.   4. And one said unto me : " Remain here till thou seest everything that befalls those elephants, camels, and asses, and the stars and the oxen, and all of them."

The Punishment of the Fallen Angels by the Archangels

LXXXVIII. 1 And I saw one of those four who had come forth first, and he seized that first star which had fallen from the heaven, and bound it hand and foot and cast it into an abyss. now that abyss was narrow and deep, and horrible and dark 2. And one of them drew a sword, and gave it to those elephants and camels and asses : then they began to smite each other, and the whole earth quaked because of them.   3 And as I was beholding in the vision, lo, one of those four who had come forth stoned (them) from heaven, and gathered and took all the great stars whose privy members were like those of horses, and bound them all hand and foot, and cast them in an abyss of the earth

---

' it was built all the hills ' (sic)   4. One said (a–q, cefhih) η, β–cefhih ' they said '   Oxen and all of them (a–n) u, β 'and all the oxen.'

LXXXVIII–LXXXIX. 1 There is a very close connexion between this Section and chapter 10^{1-12} Thus 88^1, which treats of Azazel, refers to 10^{4-8}, 88^2 (of Gabriel) refers to 10^{9-10}, 88^3 (of Michael) refers to 10^{11-12}, and 89^1 (of Uriel) refers to 10^{1-8} Thus the text here clearly presupposes chapter 10, but not quite in its present form, as Lawlor, *Journal Philol*, 1897, pp 187–189 supposes For only one leader is here referred to, i e Azazel 86^1 88^1, whereas in 10^{11} a second leader is associated with Shemjaza 1. It is Raphael who here casts Azazel into the desert named Beth Chaduda See 10^{4-8} 2. Gabriel deals here with the giant offspring of the angels

and the women Cf 10^{9-10} And camels (t, β), > a–t   3 Michael deals with the fallen angels There is no mention here of any leader such as Shemjaza, whom we find specially named in 10^{11} (Cf 10^{12-13} Who had come forth stoned (them) from heaven The text seems corrupt Either emend wagara (= ' stoned ') into warada (= ' descended ') and read ' who had come forth descended from heaven ', or transpose ' from heaven ' before ' stoned ', then we have ' who had come forth from heaven (cf 87^2) stoned '. I should add here that after wagara n adds saifa = ' sword ' The phrase would then be rendered ' hurled a sword '. As regards the number of the verbs ' gathered ' and ' took ' the MSS vary β reads the singular in each case, supported in the former by tu and in the latter by mt

LXXXIX. 1–9. *The Deluge and the Deliverance of Noah.*

LXXXIX. 1. And one of those four went to that white bull and instructed him in a secret, without his being terrified: he was born a bull and became a man, and built for himself a great vessel and dwelt thereon, and three bulls dwelt with him in that vessel and they were covered in. 2. And again I raised mine eyes towards heaven and saw a lofty roof, with seven water torrents thereon, and those torrents flowed with much water into an enclosure. 3. And I saw again, and behold fountains were opened on the surface of that great enclosure, and that water began to swell and rise upon the surface, and I saw that enclosure till all its surface was covered with water. 4 And the water, the darkness, and mist increased upon it, and as I looked at the height of that water, that water had risen above the height of that enclosure, and was streaming over that enclosure, and it stood upon the earth 5. And all the cattle of that enclosure were gathered together until I saw how they sank and were swallowed up and perished in that water. 6. But that vessel floated on the water, while all the oxen and elephants and camels and asses sank to the bottom with all the animals, so that I could no longer see them, and they were not able to escape, (but) perished and sank into the depths. 7. And again I saw in the vision till those water torrents were removed from that high roof, and the chasms of the earth were levelled up and

LXXXIX 1–9. The Deluge and the Deliverance of Noah 1 Of 10¹⁻³, where Uriel visits Noah for the same end To that white bull (*m* a-*m*, β 'those white bulls' Without his being terrified (*gqu*) *mt*, β 'terrified as he was' In order to build the Ark, Noah is represented as becoming a man. **Three bulls** Noah's three sons Covered in cf Gen 7¹⁰ 1 Eu 67² 2 As men are symbolized by animals, then place of habitation is naturally called a pen, fold, or enclosure. **Seven** of 77⁴

(note) 3, 4 The Deluge 3 Saw²⁰ (= 1ᶜ'ikwo *u*). *g* 'ɑ'ᵗjo, *q* 1'ĕjŏ, *t*, β 'ijar'ajŏ = 'caused it not to be seen' 6. With all the animals, 1 e the real animals 7. The chasms of the earth, &c The writer conceived the flood as having been caused by a cleaving of the depths of the earth—cf Gen 7¹¹—and the staying of the flood as having been due to a closing or levelling up of these clefts or chasms. Cf Jub. 6²⁶ 'The mouths of the depths of the abyss . . . were closed' and Prayer of Manasses 3 ὁ κλείσας τὴν

other abysses were opened.	8. Then the water began to run down into these, till the earth became visible; but that vessel settled on the earth, and the darkness retired and light appeared. 9. But that white bull which had become a man came out of that vessel, and the three bulls with him, and one of those three was white like that bull, and one of them was red as blood, and one black — and that white bull departed from them.

LXXXIX. 10–27. *From the Death of Noah to the Exodus.*

10. And they began to bring forth beasts of the field and birds, so that there arose different genera : lions, tigers, wolves, dogs, hyenas, wild boars, foxes, squirrels, swine, falcons, vultures, kites, eagles, and ravens, and among them was born a white bull.	11. And they began to bite one another; but that white bull which was born amongst them begat a wild ass and a white bull with it, and the wild asses multiplied.	12. But that bull which was born from him begat a black wild boar and a white sheep; and the former begat many boars, but that sheep begat twelve sheep.	13. And when those twelve sheep had grown, they gave up one of them to the asses, and those asses

ἄβυσσον.	9 Noah and his three sons And one black (β) > α	That white bull departed from them, i e. Noah died	10 The necessities of his subject oblige the author to mar the naturalness of his symbolism His cattle produce all manner of four-footed beasts and birds of prey Nearly all these appear later as the enemies of Israel, cf Ezek 39¹⁷	Different genera	Here 'ahzâb means races not merely of man but of all kinds of animals. Flemming has rightly pointed out that hebr here should be written hebr, and not hebr as Dillmann takes it. 'ḗmkuĕllû ḫĕbı = διάφορα as in Deut. 22⁹	A white bull, i e Abraham 11. The wild ass is Ishmael, the progenitor of the Arabs or Midianites, who in vv 13, 16 are called the ' wild

asses', which is on the whole an apt designation, cf Gen 16¹²	The ' white bull' is Isaac	The wild asses (a, abdullnoz,a) ι efh 'the wild ass'	12 A black wild boar, i e Esau	Later Jewish hatred thus expresses itself in associating Edom with the name of the animal it detested most, cf vv 42, 43, 49, 66	In ver 72 it is used of the Samaritans	A white sheep, i e. Jacob Israel is specially in the symbolic language of the O T. the sheep of God's pasture, Pss 74¹ 79¹³ 100⁸ Jer 23¹, and hence there is a peculiar fitness in representing the individual who first bore the name as a white sheep	The idea of declension in faith (see p 186) can hardly attach to this instance of its use.	13 One of them, i e Joseph The asses, the Midianites, cf vv 11,

again gave up that sheep to the wolves, and that sheep grew up
among the wolves.   14. And the Lord brought the eleven
sheep to live with it and to pasture with it among the wolves:
and they multiplied and became many flocks of sheep.   15. And
the wolves began to fear them, and they oppressed them until
they destroyed their little ones, and they cast their young into
a river of much water: but those sheep began to cry aloud on
account of their little ones, and to complain unto their Lord.
16 And a sheep which had been saved from the wolves fled and
escaped to the wild asses; and I saw the sheep how they
lamented and cried, and besought their Lord with all their
might, till that Lord of the sheep descended at the voice of the
sheep from a lofty abode, and came to them and pastured them.
17. And He called that sheep which had escaped the wolves, and
spake with it concerning the wolves that it should admonish them
not to touch the sheep.   18 And the sheep went to the
wolves according to the word of the Lord, and another sheep
met it and went with it, and the two went and entered together
into the assembly of those wolves, and spake with them and
admonished them not to touch the sheep from henceforth.
19. And thereupon I saw the wolves, and how they oppressed
the sheep exceedingly with all their power, and the sheep cried
aloud.   20. And the Lord came to the sheep and they began
to smite those wolves and the wolves began to make lamentation, but the sheep became quiet and forthwith ceased to cry
out.   21. And I saw the sheep till they departed from
amongst the wolves; but the eyes of the wolves were blinded,
and those wolves departed in pursuit of the sheep with all their
power.   22 And the Lord of the sheep went with them, as
their leader, and all His sheep followed Him: and His face was

---

16 The wolves, i e the Egyptians—
henceforth their standing designation
in this vision   16. A sheep which
had been saved, i e Moses   Lord
of the sheep.   This title is the usual
one in this and the following chapters,
and occurs about twenty-eight times
18 Another sheep, i e Aaron   Met
it (a–t)   t, β–d 'met that sheep'.
Went and (ymy). > tu, β.   20.
The plagues of Egypt   They began
(a–m). m, β 'He began'.   21–27

dazzling and glorious and terrible to behold.   23. But the
wolves began to pursue those sheep till they reached a sea of
water.   24. And that sea was divided, and the water stood on
this side and on that before their face, and their Lord led them
and placed Himself between them and the wolves.   25. And
as those wolves did not yet see the sheep, they proceeded into
the midst of that sea, and the wolves followed the sheep, and
[those wolves] ran after them into that sea.   26. And when
they saw the Lord of the sheep, they turned to flee before His
face, but that sea gathered itself together, and became as it had
been created, and the water swelled and rose till it covered those
wolves.   27. And I saw till all the wolves who pursued those
sheep perished and were drowned.

LXXXIX. 28–40. *Israel in the Desert, the Giving of the Law,
the Entrance into Palestine.*

28. But the sheep escaped from that water and went forth into
a wilderness, where there was no water and no grass, and they
began to open their eyes and to see ; and I saw the Lord of the
sheep pasturing them and giving them water and grass, and that
sheep going and leading them.   29. And that sheep ascended
to the summit of that lofty rock, and the Lord of the sheep sent
it to them.   30. And after that I saw the Lord of the sheep
who stood before them, and His appearance was great and terrible and majestic, and all those sheep saw Him and were afraid
before His face.   31. And they all feared and trembled
because of Him, and they cried to that sheep with them [which

---

The Exodus from Egypt.   22. Glorious and terrible to behold (*gmt*). *qu*
' terrible to behold ', *β–α* ' His appearance was terrible and glorious   24
Led them (*u*).   Other MSS ' leading
them '.   In the latter MSS we must
excise the following ' and '   28
Began to open their eyes, i. e to
recover their spiritual vision and return
to God ; cf §9³², ³³, ⁴¹, ⁴⁴, ⁵⁴ 90⁶, ⁹, ¹⁰,

²⁶, ³⁵   And to see (*mtu, β*).   *gq* ' and
they saw '   29. Moses' ascent of
Sinai and return to Israel at God's
command, Exod 19.   30 Great
and (*a*) > *β–v*   31 That sheep
with them, i. e. Aaron   With
them (*gmq*)   *t, β* ' with him '
[Which was amongst them] (*gu*).
Bracketed as a dittograph.   *mqt, β* ' to
the other sheep which was among

was amongst them] " We are not able to stand before our Lord
or to behold Him." 32. And that sheep which led them again
ascended to the summit of that rock, but the sheep began to be
blinded and to wander from the way which he had showed them,
but that sheep wot not thereof. 33. And the Lord of the
sheep was wrathful exceedingly against them, and that sheep
discovered it, and went down from the summit of the rock, and
came to the sheep, and found the greatest part of them blinded
and fallen away. 34. And when they saw it they feared and
trembled at its presence, and desired to return to their folds.
35. And that sheep took other sheep with it, and came to those
sheep which had fallen away, and began to slay them, and the
sheep feared its presence, and thus that sheep brought back
those sheep that had fallen away, and they returned to their
folds. 36. And I saw in this vision till that sheep became a
man and built a house for the Lord of the sheep, and placed all
the sheep in that house. 37. And I saw till this sheep which
had met that sheep which led them fell asleep: and I saw till
all the great sheep perished and little ones arose in their place,
and they came to a pasture, and approached a stream of water.
38 Then that sheep, their leader which had become a man,
withdrew from them and fell asleep, and all the sheep sought
it and cried over it with a great crying. 39. And I saw till
they left off crying for that sheep and crossed that stream of
water, and there arose the two sheep as leaders in the place of those
which had led them and fallen asleep (lit. " had fallen asleep and

('with' *g*) them' 32 Cf Exod
24¹²⁸⁷ᵃ 32 Again ascended or 'returned and ascended' 33 Fallen
away +'from His path' β 34
It, ɪ e Moses Return to their
folds, ɪ e to abandon their errors.
35 Cf Exod 32²⁶⁻²⁹ And⁵⁶ +'after
that' *t, β* 36 In this vision
(*a–u*). β 'there a vision' That
sheep, ɪ e. Moses becomes a man to
build the tabernacle, cf. vv 1, 9.
Placed all the sheep in that house,

i e. made the tabernacle the centre of
their worship 37. Death of Aaron
and of all the generation that had
gone out of Egypt. That sheep
(*t, β*) So *g*, but corrupt *mu* defective > *q* Led them (*a*). β 'led the
sheep'. Pasture. The land to the
east of Jordan. A stream, The
Jordan 38 Death of Moses,
cf Deut, 34. 39 Two sheep as
leaders Joshua and Caleb For 'the
two' the text reads kuĕllômû (= 'all')

led them "").   40. And I saw till the sheep came to a goodly place, and a pleasant and glorious land, and I saw till those sheep were satisfied , and that house stood amongst them in the pleasant land.

LXXXIX. 41–50. *From the Time of the Judges till the Building of the Temple.*

41. And sometimes their eyes were opened, and sometimes blinded, till another sheep arose and led them and brought them all back, and their eyes were opened.

Greek fragment from Vatican MS. published by Mai, *Patrum Nova Bibliotheca*, t ii, deciphered by Gildemeister in the *ZDMG*, 1855, pp. 621, 622

42. And the dogs and the foxes and the wild boars began to devour those sheep till the Lord of the sheep raised up [another sheep] a ram from

Ἐκ τοῦ τοῦ Ἐνὼχ βιβλίου χρῆσις.

42. Καὶ οἱ κύνες ἤρξαντο κατεσθίειν τὰ πρόβατα καὶ οἱ ὕες

which I have emended into kšl'shōmū = 'the two'   **40** Palestine ; cf. 26¹ Observe that the epithet 'glorious' is used in the same connexion by Dan 11¹⁶, ⁴¹   **41–50** History of the times from the Judges to the building of the Temple Of vv 42–49 there is preserved a valuable fragment of the Greek version This was published by Mai from a Vatican MS in the *Patrum Nova Bibliotheca*, t. ii. I have given this fragment for purposes of comparison with the English version of the Ethiopic. Amongst other things the reader can observe how frequently the Greek article is translated by the Ethiopic demonstrative Furthermore, the ἑξῆς which occurs between two verses belonging immediately to each other, i e 46, 47, and the φησὶν inserted in ver 47 prove that the collector of these Greek excerpts had not the complete Enoch before him, but drew them from an author who had brought to-

gether passages from Enoch and annotated them So Gildemeister, *Zeitschrift D M. G* , 1855, pp 621 sqq. **41** Periods of religious advance and declension : work of Samuel   **42** The dogs and the foxes and the wild boars The 'dogs' are, according to vv 46, 47, the Philistines The 'foxes' are taken by Dillmann to be the Amalekites, but this interpretation will not suit ver. 55, where the foxes are still notable foes of Israel close on the time of the Exile, whereas the Amalekites practically disappear from history with the reign of David We shall most probably be right in taking the 'foxes' to mean the Ammonites. From the earliest times down to the wars of the Maccabees the Ammonites were always the unrelenting foes of Israel. This is the view also of the glosser on the Greek Fragment, vv. 42–49. The 'wild boars' are the Edomites ; cf vv. 12, 43, 49, 66   Till the

their midst, which led them. 43. And that ram began to butt on either side those dogs, foxes, and wild boars till he had destroyed them †all†. 44. And that sheep whose eyes were opened saw that ram, which was amongst the sheep, till it †forsook its gloiy† and began to butt those sheep, and trampled upon them, and behaved itself unseemly. 45. And the Lord of the sheep sent the lamb to another lamb and raised it to being a ram and leader of the sheep instead of that ram which had †for-

καὶ οἱ ἀλώπεκες κατήσθιον αὐτά, μέχρι οὗ ἤγειρεν ὁ κύριος τῶν προβάτων κριὸν ἕνα ἐκ τῶν προβάτων. 43. Καὶ ὁ κριὸς οὗτος ἤρξατο κερατίζειν καὶ ἐπιδιώκειν ἐν τοῖς κέρασιν καὶ ἐνετίνασσεν εἰς τοὺς ἀλώπεκας καὶ μετ' αὐτοὺς εἰς τοὺς ὕας καὶ ἀπώλεσεν ὕας πολλοὺς καὶ μετ' αὐτοὺς . τὸ τοὺς κύνας. 44. Καὶ τὰ πρόβατα ὧν οἱ ὀφθαλμοὶ ἠνοίγησαν ἐθεάσοντο τὸν κριὸν τὸν ἐν τοῖς προβάτοις, ἕως οὗ ἀφῆκεν τὴν ὁδὸν αὐτοῦ καὶ ἤρξατο πορεύεσθαι †ἀνοδίᾳ. 45. Καὶ ὁ κύριος τῶν προβάτων ἀπέστειλεν τὸν ἄρνα τοῦτον ἐπὶ

Lord of the sheep raised up. So *g, u* This reading is confirmed by the Greek μέχρι οὗ ἤγειρεν ὁ κύριος τῶν προβάτων κριὸν ἕνα Other MSS give 'till another sheep, the Lord of the sheep. arose' The words 'another sheep' are a gloss, and we should render 'raised up a ram from their midst'. **43. Destroyed them †all†** The Gieek text (ἀπώλεσεν πολλούς) is here decidedly better Saul by no means destroyed them all **44 That sheep whose eyes were opened** This phrase as applied to Samuel here cannot be used in the sense of spiritual awakening and return to God which it has elsewhere in this vision, cf ver 28 (note). Here it must mean the prophetic gift of insight as in 1². The Greek version certainly escapes this difficulty by applying the phrase in its usual sense to the sheep, and is probably the true text **Till** The MSS. = ὡς corrupt for ἕως.   **†For-**

sook its glory†** = ἀφῆκεν τὴν δόξαν αὐτοῦ For δόξαν the Greek rends ὁδόν If the suffix αὐτοῦ refers to the subject of the verb, 1 e Saul, then 'forsook his way' can hardly be right. Perhaps דרכו (= ὁδὸν αὐτοῦ) is corrupt for יי דרך in the earlier script, 1 e. 'the way of the Lord'. In 89⁵⁴ we have the expression 'the house of the Lord' = בית יי. Hence here and in ver 45 we should probably read 'the way of the Lord' instead of 'its glory' **45, 46.** David anointed king. Observe that in ver 45 the Gieek used ἄρνα and not πρόβατον for Samuel and for David so long as the latter is not yet king, where the Ethiopic employs the more general term 'sheep'. Observe further that Solomon previous to his coronation, ver 48ᵇ, is called 'a little sheep', 1 e a lamb. I have followed the Greek, reading 'the lamb' twice where the Ethiopic has 'the sheep'. **45. That ram.** All MSS except *d* read

saken its glory†. 46. And
it went to it and spake to it
alone, and raised it to being
a ram, and made it the prince
and leader of the sheep, but
during all these things those
dogs oppressed the sheep.
47. And the first ram pursued
that second ram, and that
second ram arose and fled
before it; and I saw till those
dogs pulled down the first ram.
48. And that second ram arose
and led the [little] sheep.
49. And those sheep grew and
multiplied; but all the dogs,
and foxes, and wild boars
feared and fled before it, and
that ram butted and killed
the wild beasts, and those

ἄρνα ἕτερον τοῦ στῆσαι αὐτὸν εἰς
κριὸν ἐν ἀρχῇ τῶν προβάτων ἀντὶ
τοῦ κριοῦ τοῦ ἀφέντος τὴν ὁδὸν
αὐτοῦ.   46. Καὶ ἐπορεύθη πρὸς
αὐτὸν καὶ ἐλάλησεν αὐτῷ σιγῇ,
κατὰ μόνας καὶ ἤγειρεν αὐτὸν εἰς
κριὸν καὶ εἰς ἄρχοντα καὶ εἰς
ἡγούμενον τῶν προβάτων καὶ οἱ
κύνες ἐπὶ πᾶσι τούτοις ἔθλιβον
τὰ πρόβατα.   47. ['Εξῆς δὲ
τούτοις γέγραπται ὅτι] ὁ κριὸς ὁ
πρῶτος τὸν κριὸν τὸν δεύτερον
ἐπεδίωκεν καὶ ἔφυγεν ἀπὸ προσώπου αὐτοῦ· εἶτ' ἐθεώρουν, [φησίν],
τὸν κριὸν τὸν πρῶτον ἕως οὗ
ἔπεσεν ἔμπροσθεν τῶν κυνῶν.
48. Καὶ ὁ κριὸς ὁ δεύτερος ἀναπη-
δήσας ἀφηγήσατο τῶν προβάτων.
49. Καὶ τὰ πρόβατα ηὐξήθησαν
καὶ ἐπληθύνθησαν· καὶ πάντες οἱ

'that sheep'. *d* 'that ram, sheep' (sic)
Greek alone right.   46. During all
these things = ἐπὶ πάντων τούτων. But
the Greek has the dative = 'in addition
to all these things'.   48. Led the
sheep. So Greek. Ethiopic MSS give
'led the little sheep' But the word
'little' should be omitted, as it is
wanting in the Greek, and the expression 'little sheep' is pointless here,
and found but once before in ver. 37.
It crept into the text from the next
line The rest of the verse, 48[b], I have
transposed after ver 49.   Ver 49
recounts the victories of David, ver. 48[b]
his death and the accession of Solomon.
This passage is wanting in the Greek,
but this is so only because the fragment ends with ver. 49, at the close of
which these words originally stood

Thus they form a natural transition
to the account of the temple. A
further and stronger reason for their
genuineness is the phrase 'a little
sheep' applied to Solomon, previous
to his becoming king This phrase has
nothing derogatory in it, but can only
be a loose rendering of ἀμνός, 'lamb,'
applied also to David previous to his
being appointed king see ver 45
Evidently the Ethiopic translator did
not feel the technical use of the word,
as he has obliterated it altogether in
ver 45 Thus, as the technical term is
not found in the Ethiopic in this con
nexion, an Ethiopic interpolator could
not have produced this manifest, though
imperfect, form of it.   48[b]. A little
sheep, i e. lamb, see vv. 45, 46 (note)
49 This is a description of the reign

wild beasts had no longer any power among the sheep and robbed them no more of aught. 48ᵇ. And that ram begat many sheep and fell asleep, and a little sheep became ram in its stead, and became prince and leader of those sheep

κύνες καὶ οἱ ἀλώπεκες ἔφυγον ἀπ' αὐτοῦ καὶ ἐφοβοῦντο αὐτόν.

50. And that house became great and broad, and it was built for those sheep ⟨and⟩ a tower lofty and great was built on the house for the Lord of the sheep, and that house was low, but the tower was elevated and lofty, and the Lord of the sheep stood on that tower and they offered a full table before Him.

LXXXIX. 51–67. *The Two Kingdoms of Israel and Judah to the Destruction of Jerusalem.*

51. And again I saw those sheep that they again erred and went many ways, and forsook that their house, and the Lord of the sheep called some from amongst the sheep and sent them to the sheep, but the sheep began to slay them. 52. And one of them was saved and was not slain, and it sped away and cried aloud over the sheep; and they sought to slay it, but the Lord of the sheep saved it from the sheep, and brought it up to me,

of David 50 That house As Dillmann shows by a comparison of vv. 56, 66 sq., 72 sq., and the passage in Test. Levi 10⁵ ὁ γὰρ οἶκος, ὃν ἂν ἐκλέξεται κύριος, Ἰερουσαλὴμ κληθήσεται, καθὼς περιέχει ἡ βίβλος Ἐνὼχ τοῦ δικαίου, this house is Jerusalem and the tower is the temple It was built for those sheep ⟨and⟩ a tower lofty and great was built on the house (*gmt, ilno* ₁a₁b, save that *mt, m* insert 'that' before 'house') β–ilno₁a₁b 'it was built for those sheep ⟨and⟩ a high tower on the house', *q* 'it was built for those sheep ⟨and⟩ a lofty tower was built'. I have added ⟨and⟩ and

yet it is after a fashion found in *m*, *ilno*₁a₁b, for after 'tower' they add 'lofty on that house *and* a tower'— a dittograph of some sort A full table, i. e offerings and sacrifices. 51–67 Gradual declension of Israel till the destruction of the Temple. 51. Forsook then house The only of the Ten Tribes That their house = τὸν οἶκον αὐτῶν. Here, as in ver 53, the Ethiopic translator renders the *mt* by a demonstrative. Called some . . . and sent them, i. e the prophets. Slay Cf 1 Kings 18⁴ 52 Escape and translation of Elijah, cf 1 Kings 19 2 Kings 2¹¹ 1 Enoch 93⁸

and caused it to dwell there.   53. And many other sheep He sent to those sheep to testify unto them and lament over them. 54. And after that I saw that when they forsook the house of the Lord and His tower they fell away entirely, and their eyes were blinded; and I saw the Lord of the sheep how He wrought much slaughter amongst them in their herds until those sheep invited that slaughter and betrayed His place.   55. And He gave them over into the hands of the lions and tigers, and wolves and hyenas, and into the hand of the foxes, and to all the wild beasts, and those wild beasts began to tear in pieces those sheep. 56. And I saw that He forsook that their house and their tower and gave them all into the hand of the lions, to tear and devour them, into the hand of all the wild beasts.   57. And I began to cry aloud with all my power, and to appeal to the Lord of the sheep, and to represent to Him in regard to the sheep that they were devoured by all the wild beasts.   58. But He remained unmoved, though He saw it, and rejoiced that they were devoured and swallowed and robbed, and left them to be devoured in the hand of all the beasts.   59. And He called seventy

From the sheep (*gm*)   Other MSS 'from the hands of the sheep'   53, 54. The fruitless activity of the prophets, and the complete apostasy of the nation owing to their abandonment of the Temple   **54 Forsook the house . . and His tower.** Judah and Benjamin did not forsake Jerusalem and the Temple, but apparently our author treats the Twelve Tribes in their solidarity.   Of the Lord + 'of the sheep' β   Invited that slaughter and betrayed His place, i. e called in heathen nations to help them and so betrayed Jerusalem.   Thus Ahaz hired Tiglath-pilezer, king of Assyria, to help him against Rezin, king of Syria, 2 Kings 16⁷ ˢᑫᑫ   55. The final fortunes of the two kingdoms and the names of their oppressors. Lions and tigers, i e. the Assyrians and Babylonians. In vv 56, 65 (?), where the lions alone are mentioned, the Babylonians are meant. The 'wolves' are the Egyptians; cf ver. 13   The 'hyenas', Martin suggests, are the Syrians, but they are symbolized by the 'ravens' in 90⁸, ⁹, ¹²   they may be the Ethiopians. 56. This verse describes how God gradually withdrew from the degraded Theocracy and gave Israel defenceless into the hands of its enemies   To . . devour   The prophets use the same figure and phraseology in regard to the destruction of Israel by the heathen; cf Jer. 12⁹ Is. 56⁹ Ezek 34⁵, ⁸   Barnabas 16⁵ refers to this verse λέγει γὰρ ἡ γραφή καὶ ἔσται ἐπ' ἐσχάτων τῶν ἡμερῶν καὶ παραδώσει κύριος τὰ πρόβατα τῆς νομῆς καὶ τὴν μάνδραν καὶ τὸν πύργον αὐτῶν εἰς καταφθοράν.   57 Lord of the sheep   *gmq* read 'Lord of the lions'.   The wild beasts. > *g*   59. Seventy (β), a 'seven'   The

shepherds, and cast those sheep to them that they might pasture them, and He spake to the shepherds and their companions: "Let each individual of you pasture the sheep henceforward, and

seventy shepherds. This is the most vexed question in Enoch. The earliest interpreters took the first thirty-seven shepherds to mean the native kings of Israel and Judah. It was Ewald's merit to point out that this was a conception impossible for a Jew, and that the seventy shepherds must represent so many heathen oppressors of Israel This interpretation has undergone many forms, but all alike have proved unsatisfactory, cf Gebhardt's 'Die 70 Hirten des Buches Henoch u. ihre Deutungen' in Merx's *Archiv f. Wissenschaftl Liforschung*, 1871, pp 163-246 To Hoffmann, *Schriftbeweis*, i. 422, is due the credit of giving the only possible and satisfactory explanation. This explanation, which has been accepted by Schurer, Drummond, Wieselei, Schodde, Thomson, and Deane, interprets the shepherds as angels and not as men, and that his interpretation is the true one there is no further room for doubt. For (1) the seventy shepherds exist *contemporaneously*, and are summoned *together* before the Lord of the sheep to receive their commission, 89⁵⁹. This could not be said of either native or Gentile rulers. (2) The shepherds are appointed to protect the sheep, 89⁷⁵, and to allow only a limited portion of them to be destroyed by the Gentiles This could not be said of heathen rulers. (3) Jews and Gentiles and their kings also are alike symbolized by animals. Hence the shepherds cannot symbolize men. If not men, they are angels. (4) In the earlier history God was the true shepherd of Israel, but on its apostasy He withdrew from it and committed its

pasturing to seventy of His angels. With the growing transcendence of God, His place was naturally taken by angels. (5) The angel who records the doings of the seventy shepherds is simply named 'another', 89⁶¹, in connexion with them, and so naturally belongs to the same category. (6) In the last judgement they are classed with the fallen angels, 90²¹⁻²⁵ (7) God speaks directly to the shepherds and not through the medium of angels as elsewhere in the book. The idea of the seventy shepherds is used by the author to explain some pressing difficulties in Israel's history. So long as God was the immediate shepherd of Israel, it was not possible for such calamities to befall it as it experienced from the Captivity onwards. Israel, therefore, during the latter period was not shepherded by God but by angels commissioned by Him. But again, though God rightly forsook Israel and committed it to the care of angels, though, further, Israel was rightly punished for its sins, yet the author and the Jews generally believed that they were punished with undue severity, indeed, twofold more grievously than they deserved (Is 40²) How was this to be accounted for? The answer was not far to seek It was owing to the faithlessness with which the angels discharged their trust. Had they only fulfilled their commission, the Gentiles could not have made havoc of Israel and apostate Jews only could have been cut off. There may be some distant connexion between the seventy angels here and the seventy guardian angels of the Gentile nations, cf Weber, 170 sq. The theory of the

everything that I shall command you that do ye   60. And
I will deliver them over unto you duly numbered, and tell you
which of them are to be destroyed—and them destroy ye." And
He gave over unto them those sheep.   61 And He called
another and spake unto him: "Observe and mark everything
that the shepherds will do to those sheep, for they will destroy
more of them than I have commanded them.   62. And every
excess and the destruction which will be wrought through the
shepherds, record (namely) how many they destroy according to my
command, and how many according to their own caprice · record
against every individual shepherd all the destruction he effects
63 And read out before me by number how many they destroy,
and how many they deliver over for destruction, that I may have
this as a testimony against them, and know every deed of the shepherds, that I may **comprehend** and see what they do, whether or

seventy shepherds is a development of
the seventy years of Jeremiah, just as
the writer of Daniel had seen in Jeremiah's seventy years seventy periods,
and the four divisions into which the
seventy shepherds fall correspond to the
four world empires in Daniel   It is
idle, however, to seek for chronological
exactness in the four periods into which
the writer of Enoch divides all history
between the fall of Jerusalem and the
Messianic kingdom   These four periods
are thus divided   12 + 23 + 23 + 12.
No system, whether of Hilgenfeld,
Volkmar, or Wieseler, which attributes
a like number of years to each shepherd, can arrive at any but a forced
explanation of these numbers   As
Schürer remarks, this division is
merely intended to denote two longer
periods coming between two shorter
The limits of these periods are on
the whole not difficult to determine.
The first period begins with the attack
of Assyria on Israel, and ends with the
return from the captivity under Cyrus,
89⁶¹⁻⁷¹. The second extends from
Cyrus to the conquests of Alexander,
332 B C, 89⁷²⁻⁷⁷   The third extends
from this date to the transference of
the supremacy over Israel from the
Graeco-Egyptian to the Graeco-Syrian
power, 90¹⁻⁵   The fourth extends
from this date, about 200 B C, to the
establishment of the Messianic kingdom, 90⁶⁻¹⁷   60 **Duly numbered**   The number in each instance
to be destroyed was a definite one.
61 **Another** According to 90¹⁴, ²²
this ' another ' is an archangel and the
guardian angel of Israel, and hence,
probably, Michael   This task of the
heavenly scribe was in the Babylonian
religion performed by Nabú, in the
Egyptian by Thot   Here it is Michael
in all probability   But in 12³ˢ⁹ 15¹ 92¹
it has devolved on Enoch, in 4 Ezra
14²²⁻²⁶ on Ezra, whereas in 2 Enoch
23¹¹ ˢᵠᵠ on Vretil (? Dabriel as in Jel-
linc's *Beth ha Midrasch*, p 180, according to Kohler)   See *K A T*³ 400 sq
63 **Destroy.** + ' of their own caprice '
bcefhnpx   **Comprehend** = 'ĕmaṭṭe-
nouû   Emended from 'ĕwaṭṭĕnouû

not they abide by my command which I have commanded them.
64. But they shall not know it, and thou shalt not declare it to
them, nor admonish them, but only record against each individual
all the destruction which the shepherds effect each in his time
and lay it all before me." 65. And I saw till those shepherds
pastured in their season, and they began to slay and to destroy
more than they were bidden, and they delivered those sheep into
the hand of the lions. 66. And the lions and tigers eat and
devoured the greater part of those sheep, and the wild boars eat
along with them; and they burnt that tower and demolished
that house 67. And I became exceedingly sorrowful over
that tower because that house of the sheep was demolished, and
afterwards I was unable to see if those sheep entered that house.

LXXXIX. 68-71. *First Period of the Angelic Rulers—from the
Destruction of Jerusalem to the Return from the Captivity.*

68. And the shepherds and their associates delivered over those
sheep to all the wild beasts, to devour them, and each one of
them received in his time a definite number: it was written by
the other in a book how many each one of them destroyed of
them. 69. And each one slew and destroyed many more than
was prescribed; and I began to weep and lament on account of
those sheep. 70 And thus in the vision I saw that one who

(gg) *int*, β read 'Cmattĕwômu (+ wa'ĕ-
manômû *m*). This emendation, suggested first in my edition of 1893, has
since been accepted by Beer, Flemming,
and Martin 64 No remonstrance
against or interference with the shepherds was to be made during their
period of dominion, but all their deeds
were to be recorded against the final
judgement. 65. Into the hand of
the lions The lions appear to be the
Assyrians and the reign of the shepherds to begin contemporaneously with
the final struggles of the northern kingdom, or possibly with a somewhat
later date, as the former may come

under the account given in vv 55,
56 66 The account in general
terms of the destruction of the
northern and southern kingdoms
by the lions and tigers, i e the
Assyrians and Babylonians. The
wild boars see ver 12 (note).
Cf Obad 10-12 Ezek 25¹² 35⁵ ˢᵃ
Is 68¹⁻⁴ Ps 137⁷. That tower
that house see ver 50 (note).
68 Was written (*u*) So already
Beer had conjectured *g* 'should
write', other MSS 'wrote'. 69
Lament +' very much' β 70
With the sealing of the book which
recorded all the doings of these shep-

wrote how he wrote down every one that was destroyed by those
shepherds, day by day, and carried up and laid down and showed
actually the whole book to the Lord of the sheep—(even) everything that they had done, and all that each one of them had
made away with, and all that they had given over to destruction.
71. And the book was read before the Lord of the sheep, and He
took the book from his hand and read it and sealed it and laid
it down.

LXXXIX. 72–77. *Second Period—from the time of Cyrus to that
of Alexander the Great.*

72. And forthwith I saw how the shepherds pastured for
twelve hours, and behold three of those sheep turned back and
came and entered and began to build up all that had fallen down
of that house, but the wild boars tried to hinder them, but they
were not able.   73. And they began again to build as before,
and they reared up that tower, and it was named the high tower,
and they began again to place a table before the tower, but all
the bread on it was polluted and not pure.   74. And as touching

herds it is implied that the first period
has come to a close   71. From
his hand (*gmt*). β 'in His hand'
72 At the close of the description of
this period the writer defines its
duration exactly as twelve hours long,
just as at the close of the third period
described in 90² ⁻⁴ he defines its duration in 90⁵ Further, we are to observe
that the term 'hour' is to be taken in
the same sense as 'time' in 90⁵, since
in the fifty-eight times there mentioned,
the twelve hours are treated exactly as
'times' In fact we may feel certain
that the variation of expression 'hour'
and 'time' originated with the Ethiopic
translator as renderings of the same
word ὥρα   Three of those sheep.
Two of these were Zerubbabel and
Joshua If the text be correct, I see
no objection to finding the third in
Ezra or Nehemiah, notwithstanding

the interval that separates these from
the former The account of the attempt of the Samaritans to prevent
the rebuilding of the temple is as true
of the latter as the former, Ezra 4–5,
Neh 4–6 In later times one of the
two was at times mentioned without
the other, Sir 49¹¹⁻¹³ 2 Macc 2¹³.
Büchler is of opinion that the three
sheep here represent not individuals but
the three tribes, Levi, Judah, and Benjamin He compares T Joseph 19⁸.
73. Named + 'as before' q   The
bread.   was polluted, i e the offerings were unclean, cf. Mal 1⁷, 'Ye
offer polluted bread upon mine altar'
These words furnish no ground for
supposing an Essene author of the
Dream-visions. they are not stronger
than Mal 1, 2, and would only express the ordinary judgement of an
old-fashioned Pharisee such as the

all this the eyes of those sheep were blinded so that they saw not, and (the eyes of) their shepherds likewise, and they delivered them in large numbers to their shepherds for destruction, and they trampled the sheep with their feet and devoured them. 75. And the Lord of the sheep remained unmoved till all the sheep were dispersed over the field and mingled with them (i e. the beasts), and they (i. e. the shepherds) did not save them out of the hand of the beasts. 76. And this one who wrote the book carried it up, and showed it and read it before the Lord of the sheep, and implored Him on their account, and besought Him on their account as he showed Him all the doings of the shepherds, and gave testimony before Him against all the shepherds 77. And he took the actual book and laid it down beside Him and departed

XC I–5. *Third Period—from Alexander the Great to the Graeco-Syrian Domination.*

XC. 1. And I saw till that in this manner thirty-five shepherds undertook the pasturing (of the sheep), and they

writer of this Section on the Persian period—a judgement certainly justified by the few details that survive of that period see Ewald's *History of Israel*, v 204–206. The author of the Assumption of Moses—a Pharisaic Quietist writing about the beginning of the Christian era—says that the two tribes grieved on their return 'because they could not offer sacrifices to the God of their fathers', 4⁸ (see my note *in loc*)— the author therein implying that the sacrifices of the second temple were no true sacrifices because the nation was under the supremacy of the heathen, and its worship was conducted by an unworthy and heathenized hierarchy. 75 Israel sinned still further in mingling

among the heathen nations This is the beginning of the 'dispersion' 76. Before the Lord (g) *mqtu* 'in the mansions of the Lord', β 'in the mansions before the Lord'. The shepherds (*gmy* t, β 'their shepherds'. Gave testimony (*mt*, β) *gy* 'it was heard' 77. Here the second period closes with the fall of the Persian power

XC 1 Thirty-five All the MSS are corrupt here *yt*, β–*ky* read 'thirty-seven' *qu* give further corruptions of 'thirty-seven' The thirty-five gives the sum of the two periods already dealt with, i.e 12 + 23, just as in 90⁵ at the close of the third period the three periods are summed together

severally completed their periods as did the first; and others
received them into their hands to pasture them for their period,
each shepherd in his own period.   2. And after that I saw in
my vision all the birds of heaven coming, the eagles, the vultures,
the kites, the ravens; but the eagles led all the birds; and they
began to devour those sheep, and to pick out their eyes and to
devour their flesh   3 And the sheep cried out because their
flesh was being devoured by the birds, and as for me I looked
and lamented in my sleep over that shepherd who pastured the
sheep.   4. And I saw until those sheep were devoured by
the dogs and eagles and kites, and they left neither flesh nor
skin nor sinew remaining on them till only their bones stood
there: and their bones too fell to the earth and the sheep became
few.   5. And I saw until that twenty-three had undertaken
the pasturing and completed in their several periods fifty-eight
times.

12 + 23 + 23 = 58   **As did the first**
As the twelve had duly completed their
times, so likewise did the rest of the
thirty-five.   **Others received them.**
These words mark the transition to the
Greek period This period extends
from the time of Alexander, 333, to
the establishment of the Messianic
kingdom. It falls into two divisions—
the first constituted by the Graeco-
Egyptian domination over Palestine,
333–200, during which twenty-three
shepherds hold sway, and the second
constituted by the Graeco-Syrian
domination over Palestine from 200
till the establishment of the Messianic
kingdom During the fourth division
twelve shepherds bear sway.   2
The new world-power—that of the
Greeks, 1 e Graeco-Egyptian and
Graeco-Syrian—is fittingly represented
by a different order of the animal
kingdom, namely, by birds of prey
The 'eagles' are the Greeks or
Macedonians The 'ravens', as we
see from vv 8, 9, 12, are the Syrians
under the Seleucidae The 'vultures'
and 'kites' must stand for the
Egyptians under the Ptolemies Verses
2-4 deal with the Graeco-Egyptian
domination. Yet the 'ravens', i e
the Syrians, are mentioned once, and
the reason is obvious, for the Syrians
frequently contested the Egyptian
supremacy over Palestine, and in all
these struggles Palestine suffered
severely. It was as Josephus says,
'like to a ship in a storm which is
tossed by the waves on both sides,'
Ant xii 3 3   **My vision** (*a–m*).
m, β 'the vision'   3 **Was being
devoured** (*a–u*) *u, β* 'was devoured'
I looked (*gqu*) *m* 'l saw', *t, β* 'I
cried out'   4. **The dogs.** According to 89[42, 46, 47], these are the
Philistines, cf Sirach 50[26] **Neither
flesh nor skin.** From Mic. 3[2, 3]
5 See ver 1 (note)   **Twenty-three**

XC. 6-12. *Fourth Period—from the Graeco-Syrian Domination to the Maccabean Revolt.*

6. But behold lambs were borne by those white sheep, and they began to open their eyes and to see, and to cry to the sheep,

+ ' shepherds ' *t, β*　　　6-17. The fourth and last period of the heathen supremacy　The beginning of this period synchronizes with the transference of the supremacy over Israel from the Graeco-Egyptian to the Graeco-Syrian power about 200 B C　Though this is not stated in so many words, it is the only legitimate interpretation For (1) the analogy of the three preceding periods points to this conclusion, as each is marked by a like transference of the supremacy over Israel from one heathen nation to another　(2) Not only does the analogy of the other periods lead to this conclusion, but also every subsequent statement in the text, and with its acceptance the traditional difficulties of interpretation vamsh　(3) This period is marked by the rise of the Chasids　As these were already an organized party (see ver 6 note) before the Maccabean rising, their first appearance must have been much earlier and possibly synchronizes with the beginning of this period.　(4) There is absolutely no ground in the text for making this period begin with the reign of Antiochus Epiphanes, as all critics have done hitherto　This misconception has naturally made a right interpretation of the subsequent details impossible, and no two critics have been able to agree on their exegesis　6 The beginning of this period is marked by the appearance of a new class or party in Israel　These were the Chasids or Asideans who existed as a party for some time before the Maccabean rising Some have identified the Chasids with

the followers of Judas Maccabeus, and have traced their origin to the efforts of that leader　But the separate mention of the Chasids as distinguished from the immediate followers of Judas, 1 Macc 8¹³, their leagued organization already existing before the Maccabean outbreak, as is clear from 1 Macc. 2⁴² 8¹³, and their action generally in support of Judas, but at times actually antagonistic to him, 1 Macc. 7¹³, make it quite manifest that this theory is without foundation　In fact, so far from its being true that Judas founded this party, the only available evidence goes to prove that he was originally merely a member of it, as we shall see presently The Chasids, while first appearing as the champions of the law against the Hellenizing Sadducees, were really the representatives of advanced forms of doctrine on the Messianic kingdom and the Resurrection　The Chasids possessed all the enthusiasm and religious faith of the nation, and though spiritual children of the Scribes, they drew within their membership the most zealous of the priestly as well as the non-priestly families　Hence our author represents (90⁹) the Maccabean family as belonging to the Chasids as well as the High-priest Onias III.　Within this party, though a diversity of eschatological views was tolerated, the most strict observance of the law was enforced, and with its requirements no political aim was allowed to interfere　On the other hand, any movement that came forward as the champion of the law naturally commanded the adhesion of the Chasids, and so they cast in their lot with the

7. Yea, they cried to them, but they did not hearken to what they said to them, but were exceedingly deaf, and their eyes were very

Maccabean party—but that only after much indecision (1 Macc 7¹³), because the Maccabean movement put them in strife with the high-priest of the time, the legitimate and religious head of the nation. By a member of this party the present Dream-visions were written This is obvious from the doctrines of the Resurrection, the final judgement, and the kingdom of the Messiah which he teaches, but especially from his severe criticism on the moral and ceremonial irregularities in the services of the second temple (89⁷³) To remedy these abuses and defeat the schemes of Antiochus the Chasids were ready to sacrifice their lives, but all their efforts were directed to one end only—the re-establishment of the Theocracy and the preparation for the Messianic kingdom To the writer of the Dream-visions all these hopes are bound up together with the success of the Maccabean leader So long then as the Maccabean family fought for these objects, so long they carried with them the support of the Chasids, but the moment they laid bands on the high-priesthood, from that moment began the alienation of the Chasids, which afterwards developed into a deadly hostility. This hostility of the Pharisees to Hyrcanus is attested by their demand that the latter should resign the high-priesthood (*Ant* xiii 10 5) and the same demand is prac-tically made in the Pss. Sol. 17. The writer who so severely criticized the temple worship under the *legitimate* line of high-priests could not regard an *illegitimate* holder of that office as the champion of the Theocracy On this ground, therefore, we hold that *chapters 83–90 must have been written before Jonathan's assumption of the high-priesthood, 153 B. C.* This in itself

makes it impossible to identify the 'great horn' with Hyrcanus—so Dill-mann, Schürer, and others, or with Alex. Jannaeus—so Hilgenfeld, and we shall find that the natural and unforced interpretation of the text will confirm the conclusion we have thus arrived at

6. Behold (*a*) β 'little   **6–7** Lambs were borne by those white sheep, &c. The 'white sheep' are the faithful adherents of the Theocracy · the 'lambs' are the Chasids, a new and distinct party amongst the Jews, as we have above seen. Schürer thinks that it is only 'stubborn prejudice which can prevent any one from seeing that by the symbolism of the lambs the Maccabees are to be understood' It seems, on the other hand to be only 'stubborn prejudice' that can hold to such a view if the text is interpreted naturally. By taking the lambs in ver 6 to symbolize the Chasids, every difficulty is removed. In vv. 6, 7 we have the unavailing appeals of the Chasids to the nation at large in ver 8 the destruction of one of them, Onias III, by the Syrians, and in ver 9 the rise of the Maccabees—the horned or powerful lambs If, with Schürer, the lambs in ver 6 are the Maccabees, what is to be made of the horned lambs in ver 9? Moreover, though the lambs or Chasids did appeal in vain to the nation, the Maccabees did not   **7.** Yea, they cried to them (*q*) That is, the lambs cried to the sheep *g* 'But they (i e the sheep) did not cry to them', *m* 'but they oppressed them', *t* 'but they did not hear them', β-*ino* 'but the sheep did not cry to them'. Only *q* has here preserved the text   Very exceed-ingly The text, which varies in the different MSS., appears to be an

exceedingly blinded.   8 And I saw in the vision how the
ravens flew upon those lambs, and took one of those lambs, and
dashed the sheep in pieces and devoured them.   9. And I saw
till horns grew upon those lambs, and the ravens cast down their
horns; and I saw till there sprouted a great horn of one of those
sheep, and their eyes were opened.   10. And it †looked at†
them [and their eyes opened], and it cried to the sheep, and the
rams saw it and all ran to it.   11. And notwithstanding all

attempt to render σφόδρα σφόδρα
but the matter is doubtful.   8
The Syrians attack Israel and put
Onias III to death, 171 B C   see
2 Macc. 4³³⁻³⁵   We are still in the
pre-Maccabean period.   We should,
perhaps, have expected Onias III to
be symbolized by a white sheep rather
than by a lamb   The writer may have
gone back for a moment to the symbolic
meaning of this term in 89⁴⁵, but it is
more likely that it is used loosely as
including Onias among the Chasids.
In any case it cannot be interpreted of
Jonathan who was chief of the nation,
and would have been symbolized by *a
horned lamb* or *a ram*, nor could it
possibly be said, as in ver 9, that the
lambs did not become horned till after
the death of Jonathan   9 Of
one *(g)*.   Other MSS. ' one '   The
horned lambs, as we have seen, must
be the Maccabees, and in the 'great
horn' it is impossible to find any
other than Judas Maccabeus.   So
Lucke, Schodde, and now Martin, but
their interpretation could not be upheld against the objection that the
period from Antiochus Epiphanes to
Judas Maccabeus is far too short
for the rule of the twelve last shepherds.   Schodde indeed tries to show
that the 'great horn' comes early in
this period, and that it is not the
'great horn' but the Messianic kingdom which forms the *terminus ad
quem*   But the text is against him

The 'great horn' is still warring in
ver 16, and the period of the twelve
shepherds' rule is closed in ver 17
But this objection does not hold against
the true conception of the period,
which dates its beginning about 200
B C.   Thus nearly forty years of this
period would have elapsed before the
writing of these chapters 83–90; for
this Section must have been written
before the death of Judas, 160 B C
The author, therefore, must have expected the Messianic kingdom to appear
within twenty years or more   This
would allow sufficient time for the rule
of the twelve shepherds, and also admit
of the 'great horn' being represented
as warring till God interposes in person
and establishes the kingdom   The
interpretation of Dillmann, Kostlin,
Schurer, and others, which takes the
' great horn ' to symbolize John Hyrcanus, does violence to the text, and
meets with the insuperable objection that thus there would not be
even the faintest reference to Judas,
the greatest of all the Maccabees.
Opened + ' and their eyes saw' *gmt*
10 And it †looked at†   For r'ĕja =
' looked at ' read i'ĕja, ' pastured with '
It cried (*m*, β–in).   α–*m* 'they cried
The eyes of the sheep are opened
through the efforts of Judas Maccabeus.   Rams   So I have rendered
dâbêlât here and in the next verse in
accordance with Dillmann's latest
views   see Lex. col 1101.   The word

this those eagles and vultures and ravens and kites still kept
tearing the sheep and swooping down upon them and devouring
them. still the sheep remained silent, but the rams lamented
and cried out. 12. And those ravens fought and battled with
it and sought to lay low its horn, but they had no power over it.

XC 13–19 *The last Assault of the Gentiles on the Jews*
(where vv. 13–15 and 16–18 are doublets).

13. And I saw till the | 16. All the eagles and vul-

rendered 'ram' in 8⁹⁴²⁻⁴⁴ is quite
a different one, and has a technical
meaning not found in this word
11, 12. **Eagles and vultures and
kites.** In the Syrian armies mer-
cenaries were enrolled from the Greek
and other nations, cf. 1 Macc 5³⁹ 6²⁹.
Syria uses every effort against Judas,
but in vain 12 With it *g, eh*
read 'with them Its horn. *q*
reads 'their horn'. 13. It would
seem that the use of some of the
symbols is not steady. The 'vultures'
and the 'kites' in ver. 2 must mean
the Graeco-Egyptians, but in this
verse and in verse 11 it is doubtful
who are to be understood by these
We have already observed that the
writer uses the same brute symbol for
different nations, i e the wild boars
represent the Edomites in 89⁶⁶, but the
Samaritans six verses later, see also
ver 16 (note) There may be a fresh
change of symbols here, and the vultures and kites may stand for Ammon
and Edom, cf 1 Macc 5 The
struggle here depicted is a life and
death one, and neither of Hyrcanus's
wars against Antiochus Sidetes and
Antiochus Cyzicenus can fairly be
described as such The latter, moreover, was conducted by Hyrcanus's
sons while Hyrcanus himself was
quietly discharging his priestly duties
in Jerusalem ; while the former occur-

ring during the first year of Hyrcanus
could not be referred to in vv. 12, 13,
as ver. 11 deals with the first attacks
of the heathen on the 'great horn
13–19. *The criticism and reconstruction of this passage.* These verses as
they stand in the text are unintelligible In my edition of 1893 I observed
in my notes that ver 19 should be read
before ver 16, since the destruction of
the Gentiles had already been accomplished in ver. 18 Next I bracketed
ver 15 as a doublet of ver 18, as both
deal with the coming of God for the
help of Israel, and only the second
coming was effectual This criticism
and reconstruction of the text are
accepted by Martin, but he suggests that
vv. 13–15 and vv. 16–18 are doublets.
This suggestion is in the right direction, but it needs to be developed It
is true that vv 13–15 correspond
respectively to vv 16–18, but it is
further true that ver 19 should be read
immediately after ver 13 (= ver 16)
In my translation I have rearranged the
text as it stood at a very early date
By this reconstruction we are enabled
to emend certain corruptions in the
text First of all in ver 13 it is quite
irregular if not impossible for 'the
shepherds' to join in the fray They
are angels. If we compare ver 16 we
see no mention of them This addition
to the text has possibly arisen through

†shepherds and† eagles and those vultures and kites came,

tures and ravens and kites were gathered together, and

---

a dittography in the Hebrew 'Shepherds' = רעים corrupt for ערבים = 'ravens', which occurs later in the text Next, it is absurd for the text to state that the eagles, vultures, and kites 'cried to the ravens' to help to break the horn of that ram, seeing that the ravens, i e. the Syrians, had begun the fighting with the sheep, and the eagles, &c , only came to assist them Now if we look at ver 16 we see that 'the ravens' are enumerated along with the eagles, vultures, and kites, and no doubt this is the right text How then are we to explain ' they cried to'? These words = ἔκραζον = יִזְעָקוּ, but the word יזעקו should have been punctuated יִזָּעֲקוּ = 'were gathered together', cf Judg 6³⁴, ³⁵ 18²² Jos 8¹⁶ 1 Sam 14²⁰, in all which passages the LXX (like the Greek translator of our text) mistranslates יִזָּעֲקוּ as if it were יִזְעָקוּ Or the confusion may have arisen similarly from a mistranslation of יִצְּעֲקוּ, which is rendered in the LXX as if it were יִצְעֲקוּ except in Judg 12¹ Hence ver 13 is to be read as follows 'And I saw till the ravens and eagles and vultures and kites were gathered together,' &c. Now if we compare ver. 16 we find that we have here recovered the original , for thus far the verses agree word for word The above facts have a further value They prove that *the doublet existed* already in Greek, and not only so but in the Hebrew. In ver. 19 there is no difficulty. The sword is given to Israel to resist the hosts of Gog and to avenge itself on its heathen oppressors. In ver. 14 the text is corrupt The original is undoubtedly preserved with more faithfulness in ver 17 Ver 17 comes at the close of the victory of

Israel over Gog and his hosts. It tells how the angel gives an account of the doings of the twelve last shepherds, just as in 89⁷⁰, ⁷⁷ he had given an account of the first two divisions of them There is no real occasion here for his intervention in behalf of Israel. Israel is already victorious in ver. 19, which precedes ver 14 Hence I bracket the words ' came and helped it and showed it everything he had come down for the help of that ram'. But these words are full of interest Before we deal further with them we must return to the first part of ver 14. It is evidently imperfect. There is no object for the verb 'carried up'. This should evidently be ' the book' mentioned in ver 17, cf 89⁷⁰, ⁷¹, ⁷⁶, ⁷⁷. Corresponding to 'carried up in ver. 14 we find 'opened' in ver. 17. It is probable that 'opened' was preceded by 'carried up' which we find in ver 14 The usage of our author seems to require the presence of this phrase ; cf 89⁷⁰ 'carried up . . and showed' and similarly in 89⁷⁶ Yet the opening of the books is not mentioned specifically till 90²⁶. This opening follows on the breaking of the seals. Hence there is just a bare possibility that ἕως τοῦ ἀνοῖξαι is corrupt for ἕως τοῦ ἀνοῖσαι (a form found in Philo i 64) Hence ver 14 so far as it survives would run 'And I saw till that man, who wrote down the names of the shepherds, carried up (the book) into the presence of the Lord of the sheep' And in ver. 17 we should read '⟨carried up⟩ and opened' or only 'carried up' for 'opened'. Now we return to the addition in ver 14 ' Came and helped it and showed it everything he had come down for the help of that ram' We have seen

and †they cried to the ravens†
that they should break the horn
of that ram, and they battled
and fought with it, and it
battled with them and cried
that its help might come.

there came with them all the
sheep of the field, yea, they
all came together, and helped
each other to break that horn
of the ram.

19. And I saw till a great sword was given to the sheep, and
the sheep proceeded against all the beasts of the field to slay
them, and all the beasts and the birds of the heaven fled before
their face.

14. And I saw till that man,
who wrote down the names of
the shepherds [and] carried up
into the presence of the Lord
of the sheep [came and helped
it and showed it everything.
he had come down for the help
of that ram]

17 And I saw that man,
who wrote the book according
to the command of the Lord,
till he opened that book concerning the destruction which
those twelve last shepherds had
wrought, and showed that they
had destroyed much more than
their predecessors, before the
Lord of the sheep.

above that the evidence points to these
doublets having already existed in the
Hebrew It is uncertain whether this
clause was added in the Hebrew or in
the Greek Its reference, however, is
clear. The words speak of the help
given by Michael to Judas Maccabaeus
According to 2 Macc 11⁶ Judas and all
the people prayed to God to send an
angel to help them, and in 11⁸ it is
recounted that 'there appeared at
their head one on horseback in white
apparel brandishing weapons of gold',
i e. Michael, the angelic patron of
Israel, who is also the heavenly scribe
in these chapters. In ver 15 the
words 'into His shadow' can hardly
be original. The corresponding phrase
in ver 18 'from among the sheep

seems | right   The former = בצלו
which may be a corruption of מוצאן
= 'from among the sheep'   In ver
18 the words 'staff' and 'smote the
earth' recall Num 20¹¹, while the
phrase 'the earth clave asunder' recalls
Num. 16³¹⁻³³.   The text = ויך הארץ
ותבקא הארץ . . . ויבלעו בארץ ותכס
עליהם.   We should observe that the
Ethiopic for 'the earth covered them',
i e kadanat dibchomu, is not Ethiopic,
but a literal reproduction of ἐκάλυψεν
ἐπ' αὐτούς, which in turn is not Greek,
but a literal reproduction of the
Hebrew ותכס עליהם (Num 16³³)
13 And eagles. g 'eagles'   14
Helped it. + 'and saved it' g.   For
the help (g). Other MSS. 'a help'

15. And I saw till the Lord of the sheep came unto them in wrath, and all who saw Him fled, and they all fell †into His shadow† from before His face

18. And 1 saw till the Lord of the sheep came unto them and took in His hand the staff of His wrath, and smote the earth, and the earth clave asunder, and all the beasts and all the birds of the heaven fell from among those sheep, and were swallowed up in the earth and it covered them.

XC. 20-27. *Judgement of the Fallen Angels, the Shepherds, and the Apostates.*

20. And I saw till a throne was erected in the pleasant land, and the Lord of the sheep sat Himself thereon, and the other took the sealed books and opened those books before the Lord of the sheep   21 And the Lord called those men the seven first

---

15. The Lord (a–y)   q, β 'that Lord'.   Into His shadow (qtu, β)   qu 'into the shadow'   16. All¹⁰   u reads 'and'.   Ravens and kites J m   Came¹⁰ (gq).   mtu β 'brought'   All the sheep (in the nom.) (g)   In the acc. nqt, β,   17 Till he opened that book concerning the destruction   u reads ' for it was opened by the command of the Lord concerning the destruction'.   Before the Lord of the sheep (mq, β)   gtu 'formerly.18ᵃ And the Lord of the sheep' 18 God Himself destroys the last enemies of Israel after the manner of Korah and his followers, Num. 16³¹ˢᵠ   This is the first act of the final judgement, but the remaining acts are of a forensic nature   And I saw till the Lord of the sheep (' of the sheep ' > m) came unto them (m, β).   > q through hmt gt and the Lord of the sheep 1 saw till He came to those sheep' (' till the Lord of the sheep came unto them ' t), u ' and

the Lord of the sheep came unto them' Covered them (mq, d) = ἐκάλυψεν ἐπ αὐτούς   t, β–d = ἐκαλύφθη ἐπ' αὐτούς y corrupt > v   20 The pleasant land. cf 89⁴⁰, i.e Palestine Cf. Dan 11¹⁰, ⁴¹, ⁴⁵ God's throne is set up in the immediate neighbourhood of Jerusalem (cf ver 29), the books are opened as in Dan 7¹⁰, see 47³ (note). The Messiah does not appear till after the judgement in 88-90   The other Here 1 read kâl'û = ' other' instead of the MSS reading kuello = 'all' ' The other ' is the angel Michael   The Lord of the sheep does not Himself read the books. Cf 89⁷⁰, ⁷¹, ⁷⁶, ⁷⁷ 90¹⁴, ¹⁷ The text reads 'and He took all the sealed books ',   21. Men (a, > β   The seven (qtu, β) > g. m 'and seven'.   Seven first white ones. This order of seven archangels is derived from the Zoroastrian Amshaspands. They are spoken of in Tobit 12¹⁵, cf Rev 1⁴ 4⁵ 8⁵, ⁶   See Cheyne,

white ones, and commanded that they should bring before Him,
beginning with the first star which led the way, all the stars
whose privy members were like those of horses, and they brought
them all before Him.   22. And He said to that man who
wrote before Him, being one of those seven white ones, and said
unto him. "Take those seventy shepherds to whom I delivered
the sheep, and who taking them on their own authority slew
more than I commanded them."   23. And behold they were
all bound, I saw, and they all stood before Him.   24. And the
judgement was held first over the stars, and they were judged
and found guilty, and went to the place of condemnation, and
they were cast into an abyss, full of fire and flaming, and full of
pillars of fire.   25. And those seventy shepherds were judged
and found guilty, and they were cast into that fiery abyss.
26. And I saw at that time how a like abyss was opened in the
midst of the earth, full of fire, and they brought those blinded
sheep, and they were all judged and found guilty and cast into
this fiery abyss, and they burned, now this abyss was to the
right of that house.   27. And I saw those sheep burning
†and their bones burning†.

Origin of the Psalter, pp. 281, 282,
323–327, 334–337 , *Jewish Encyc.* i.
590   **Bring** (*gm*, β)   *qtu* 'come'
Before Him. > *gu*, *d*.   **Star .** see
86–88   **All the stars . . . of horses**
So I render as in my edition of 1893,
emending 'ĕmna zĕkû ('ĕlkû *m*, β) into
lakuĕllû with Dillmann   Furthermore
in that edition I rejected as a dittograph the clause added after 'horses'
in the MSS , 'and the first star which
went out (*g* other MSS. 'fell') first'
Subsequent translators have accepted
both these suggestions.   22 The
seventy angels who had charge of
Israel are judged along with the fallen
watchers.   **Said** unto him (*mtu*,
β–*hox* ₁*b*).   *gq, hox* ₁*b* 'said unto them'
23. This verse reads in *g* 'and behold
they were all bound before Him '.   Cf
88⁸   **24** An abyss, full of fire

This final place of punishment is not
to be confounded with the preliminary
place of punishment in 18¹²⁻¹⁶ 19¹⁻²
21¹⁻⁶   It is that which is mentioned
in 10⁶ 18¹¹ 21⁷⁻¹⁰ 54⁶   **Flaming**, and
full of *g* reads 'flaming with'.
25. The shepherds are cast into the
same abyss ; cf. 54⁶ (note)   26
The apostates are cast into Gehenna
In the midst of the earth cf. 26¹.
To the right of that house, i. e. to
the south of Jerusalem.   27. The
apostates were punished in view of
the blessed in Jerusalem ; cf. Is. 66²⁴
1 En 48⁹ (note)   This verse seems
corrupt   It is absurd to speak of the
bones burning as distinct from the men
themselves.   Hence I suggest that we
have here a late Hebrew idiom.   The
verse would in Hebrew run וָאֵרֶא
אֶת־הַצֹּאן הָאֵת בֹּעֲרֹת וְעַצְמָה בֹּעֲרֹת

XC 28–38 *The New Jerusalem, the Conversion of the surviving Gentiles, the Resurrection of the Righteous, the Messiah.*

28. And I stood up to see till they folded up that old house; and carried off all the pillars, and all the beams and ornaments of the house were at the same time folded up with it, and they carried it off and laid it in a place in the south of the land. 29. And I saw till the Lord of the sheep brought a new house greater and loftier than that first, and set it up in the place of the first which had been folded up · all its pillars were new, and its ornaments were new and larger than those of the first, the old one which He had taken away, and all the sheep were within it

30 And I saw all the sheep which had been left, and all the beasts on the earth, and all the birds of the heaven, falling down and doing homage to those sheep and making petition to and obeying them in every thing 31 And thereafter those three who were clothed in white and had seized me by my hand [who

---

Here the second participle is probably a dittograph, and we might translate 'I saw those sheep burning, yea their very selves' Or the original may have been וארא את־הצאן עצמה בערת 'I saw the sheep themselves burning' 28, 29 The removal of the old Jerusalem and the setting up of the New Jerusalem This expectation is derived from O.T. prophecy: Ezek. 40–48 Is. 54[11, 12] 60 Hagg 2[7–9] Zech 2[8–13] The idea of a new Jerusalem coming down from heaven was a familiar one in Jewish Apocalypses, cf 4 Ezra 7[26] 13[36] Apoc Bar 32[2] Rev 21[2, 10]. 28 Folded up (ı e tawamô *np*) So practically *y. qqtu*, *β–npy* 'submerged'. Dillmann conjectured tômô = 'folded up' But the forms in *np* occur. 29 And (> *g*) all the sheep were within it (*a–m, acdiklo* ₁*ᵃˌᵇ*) *m, befknpıx* 'and (> *m*) the Lord of the sheep was within it'. The

omission of the 'and' in *qm*, which are the chief representatives of the two readings, may point to the fact of 'which He had taken away . within it' having originally constituted a single clause Simply by reading 'abâg'a instead of 'abâg'ĕ and prefixing 'ĕ to mâ'ĕkalâ we should have 'from which He had sent forth all the sheep 30 The conversion of the Gentiles— of those who took no part in the oppression of Israel, for the rest were destroyed in ver 18—and their spontaneous submission to Israel; cf Is 14[2] 66[12, 13–21], and parallel passages. Later Judaism almost universally denied even this hope to the Gentiles, cf Weber, *Jud. Theol.* 384–387, 395. **And** obeying them (*mt*, *β*) > *gqu*. In **every thing**. The Ethiopic = 'in every word' ' Word' here goes back to דבר, which here means 'matter', ' thing' **31. Those three who**

had taken me up before], and the hand of that ram also seizing
hold of me, they took me up and set me down in the midst
of those sheep †before the judgement took place†.   32. And
those sheep were all white, and their wool was abundant and
clean.   33. And all that had been destroyed and dispersed,
and all the beasts of the field, and all the birds of the heaven,
assembled in that house, and the Lord of the sheep rejoiced with
great joy because they were all good and had returned to His
house.   34 And I saw till they laid down that sword, which
had been given to the sheep, and they brought it back into the
house, and it was sealed before the presence of the Lord, and all
the sheep were invited into that house, but it held them not.
35. And the eyes of them all were opened, and they saw the
good, and there was not one among them that did not see.
36. And I saw that that house was large and broad and
very full.

37. And I saw that a white bull was born, with large horns,

were clothed in white· see 87². ³.
That ram   Same word as used in
vv. 10, 11.   This ram is the sheep
saved in 89⁵² from its enemies and
brought up to live with Enoch Paradise is only the temporary abode of
Enoch and Elijah   Before the
judgement took place.   These words
are most confusing   If they are
genuine it is hard to restore them
to their place satisfactorily.   32
The righteousness of the members of
the kingdom is expressed by the white-
ness and cleanliness of the wool of the
sheep ; and the large measure of their
righteousness by the abundance of the
wool , cf. Is 1²⁸ 4³ 60²¹   33 The
righteous dead will rise to share in
the kingdom; cf. 51² (note¹.   Likewise the dispersed of Israel will be
gathered into it , cf Mic. 4⁶, ⁷   Rejoiced : cf. Is. 62³⁻⁵ 65¹⁹   34.
The sword wherewith Israel had crushed
its enemies is sealed and preserved as a
memorial.   Into the house (g). mqt,

β 'into His house '.   Were invited
(g) Other MSS 'were enclosed'   It
held them not: cf Is 49¹⁹⁻²³ Zech
2⁴ 10¹⁰   37 A white bull, i.e
the Messiah.   We have here the Messiah coming forth from the bosom of
the community   He is a man only,
but yet a glorified man , for he is described as a white bull to mark his
superiority to the rest of the community
of the righteous who are symbolized by
sheep. So far as he is a man only, he may
be regarded as the prophetic Messiah
as opposed to the apocalyptic Messiah
of the Parables; and yet he is not really
the prophetic Messiah , for he has
absolutely no function to perform, as
he does not appear till the world's
history is finally closed.   Accordingly
his presence here must be accounted
for through literary reminiscence, and
the Messiah-hope must be regarded as
practically dead at this period.   The
nation, in fact, felt no need of such
a personality so long as they had such

and all the beasts of the field and all the birds of the air feared
him and made petition to him all the time.   38. And I saw
till all their generations were transformed, and they all became
white bulls; and the first among them became a lamb, and that
lamb became a great animal and had great black horns on

a chief as Judas. It was very different,
however, in the following century,
when the fondest enthusiast could no
longer look to the Asmoneans and the
helpless degradation of this dynasty
forced religious thinkers to give their
hopes and aspirations a different direction. Of these some returned to a
fresh study of the O T. and revived
the hopes of the Messianic Son of David
as in the Pss of Solomon (70-40 B c)·
others followed the bold and original
thinker who conceived the Messiah as
the supernatural Son of Man, who,
possessing divine attributes, should give
to every man his due and vindicate
the entire earth for the possession of the
righteous   so in the Parables (94-
70 B. c). 38. All the members
of the kingdom are transformed the
white bull (i. e. the Messiah) into a
great animal, and the sheep, beasts,
and birds into white bulls or oxen
Thus mankind is restored to the
primitive righteousness of Eden, 1 e.
Adam was symbolized by a white bull.
A lamb   The text is corrupt and
cannot be restored without the help of
Test Jos 19³⁻⁹. According to the
Ethiopic it runs 'the first became
among them (a-u, aikn: 'among
them became' bciīlox ₁a₁b) a word and
that word became a great animal'. The
term 'word' (nagar = $\dot{\rho}\hat{\eta}\mu\alpha$ not $\lambda\acute{o}\gamma os$)
here is manifestly corrupt Dillmann
suggested that nagar (= 'word') is
here a rendering of $\dot{\rho}\hat{\eta}\mu\alpha$, but that $\rho\eta\mu$
originally stood in the Greek version as
a transliteration of רֶאֵם = 'buffalo'.
1 adopted this suggestion in my first
edition, but cannot any longer accept it

The right reconstruction of the text
was made by Goldschmidt in 1892, but
I did not recognize its claims till I
had edited the Testaments XII Patriarchs. Goldschmidt (*Das Buch Henoch*,
p. 91) suggested that nagar here ulti
mately goes back to מְלֵא, which was a
corruption of טְלֵה = 'lamb'. Thus we
recover the text 'and the first became
among them a lamb, and the lamb
became a great animal and had great
black horns on its head'. This reconstruction is supported by Test Jos.
19³⁻⁹ In 19³, ⁴ the three harts (= the
three tribes of Levi, Judah, and
Benjamin) become three lambs, and
next these three with the remaining
nine harts become twelve sheep Again,
in another vision beginning with 19⁵,
the twelve tribes are symbolized by
twelve bulls, and in the third (†) tribe
(i e Levi) there arose a bull calf (probably Judas the Maccabee) who helped
the twelve bulls (19⁷). Next in the
midst of the horns of the tribe of Levi
the bull calf (probably John Hyrcanus)
became a lamb, and all the beasts and
the reptiles rushed against him and the
lamb overcame and destroyed them
(19⁸). Here we have a very close
parallel to the symbolism and trans-
formations in our text. 'The lamb'
(= $\dot{\alpha}\mu\nu\acute{o}s$) or rather the horned lamb is
clearly the head of the nation in the
Testaments, and, what is more, the
Messianic head The same idea is, I
think, clearly to be inferred from our
text, on which the Testaments in
this passage appear to be dependent
Great black horns (a) β 'great and
black horns' I cannot understand the

its head, and the Lord of the sheep rejoiced over it and over all the oxen.   39. And I slept in their midst: and I awoke and saw everything   40. This is the vision which I saw while I slept, and I awoke and blessed the Lord of righteousness and gave Him glory.   41. Then I wept with a great weeping, and my tears stayed not till I could no longer endure it: when I saw, they flowed on account of what I had seen; for everything shall come and be fulfilled, and all the deeds of men in their order were shown to me.   42. On that night I remembered the first dream, and because of it I wept and was troubled—because I had seen that vision.'

epithet 'black' here. It seems wrong. Over it All MSS read 'over them', but I have emended with Beer But possibly the following 'and' is an intrusion. In that case we should simply render 'over all the oxen'. Though nothing is said as to the duration of the life of the individual in this section, the implication is that it is eternal. If Enoch and Elijah are transferred to the Messianic kingdom from Paradise, surely it is only reasonable to conclude that the new form of existence is an eternal one, for this new form of existence is more glorious than that enjoyed by Enoch and Elijah in Paradise. In Paradise Elijah was symbolized by a *ram*, but in the Messianic kingdom by a *bull*   40 Cf. 22¹⁴   41, 42. Enoch weeps because of the woes that threaten mankind in his two visions

SECTION V

INTRODUCTION

A. *Critical Structure.* B. *Relation of* 91–104 *to* (*a*) 1–36, (*b*) 83–90. C *Authorship and Date.* D. *The Problem and its Solution.*

A. Critical Structure. This section may be regarded as complete in the main and self-consistent. It has in some degree suffered at the hands of the final editor of the book, both in the way of direct interpolation and of severe dislocations of the text. The interpolations are—91^{11} 93^{11-14} 94^{7d} 96^2. The dislocations of the text are a more important feature of the book. They are confined (with the exception of 93^{13-14}, and of 106^{17a} which should be read immediately after 106^{14}) to 91–93. All critics are agreed as to the chief of these 91^{12-17} should undoubtedly be read directly after 93. In 93 we have an account of the first seven weeks of the ten into which the world's history is divided, and in 91^{12-17} of the last three weeks. Taken together 93^{1-10} 91^{12-17} form an independent whole—the Apocalypse of Weeks—which has been incorporated in 91–104 See notes *in loc* But this is far from a full account of the matter. The remaining dislocations only need to be pointed out in order to be acknowledged. On other grounds (pp. 65 sq , 219 sqq) we find that 91–104 is a book of different authorship to the rest of the sections. Now this being so, this section obviously begins with 92—'Written by Enoch the scribe,' &c. On 92 follows $91^{1-10,}$ $^{18-19}$ as a natural sequel, where Enoch summons his children to receive his parting words. Then comes the Apocalypse of Weeks, 93^{1-10} 91^{12-17}. The original order of the text, therefore, was · 92 $91^{1-10,}$ $^{18-19}$ 93^{1-10} 91^{12-17} 94. These dislocations were the work of the editor, who put the different books of Enoch together and added 80 and 81

B. (*a*) Relation of 91–104 to 1–36. Do these sections proceed from the same author? or if not, of what nature is the manifest

relation between them ? Let us proceed to weigh the evidence on
the former question. At first sight, the evidence for unity of
authorship seems overwhelming. (1) The phrase 'ye shall have
no peace' is found in 91–104 and in 1–36, and in these sections
only—94^6 $98^{11, 16}$ 99^{13} 101^3 102^3 103^8 5^4 12^5 13^1 16^4 'Plant of
righteousness,' 93^2, $5, 10$ 10^{16}. (2) Titles of God in common. 'Holy
and Great One,' 'Holy Great One,' or 'Great Holy One,' 92^2 97^6
98^6 104^9 10^1 14^1 25^3 'The Great One,' 103^4 104^1 14^2. 'The
Great Glory,' 102^3 14^{20}. (3) References in each to the Law, 99^2 5^4;
to the eating of blood, 98^{11} 7^5; to the regularity of nature, 101^{1-7}
2^1–5^4; to the hardheartedness of men, 98^{11} 5^4. (4) No hint of
a Messiah in either. (5) The division of human history in the
Apocalypse of Weeks into ten weeks, each apparently of seven
generations, seems to agree with 10^{12}, where a period of seventy
generations is given. (6) The date of the final judgement over the
Watchers in 91^{15} at the close of the tenth week seems to agree with
the date assigned to it in 10^{12}, i. e at the end of seventy generations   (7) In both the resurrection is taught, 91^{10} 92^3 100^5 22.
(8) In both the scene of the Messianic kingdom is the earth as
it is

There are thus many points of connexion, but as we proceed
we shall see that these are mainly external   The points of divergence, on the other hand, are far more serious because internal
If we assume for the time being that the Apocalypse of Weeks,
93^{1-10} 91^{12-17}, forms a constituent part of 91–104, it follows that
(1) in the first place, the last four points of agreement mentioned
above are apparent, but not real. The seventh day of the tenth
week in 91^{15} marks *the close of the Messianic kingdom*, which began
in the eighth week. whereas the seventy generations in 10^{12} termi-
nate with the *establishment of the Messianic kingdom*. Nor do these
periods start from the same date. the Apocalypse of Weeks reckons
from the creation of Adam   the seventy generations from the
judgement of the angels. (2) The final judgement in 91^{15} is held
at the close of the Messianic kingdom, but in 10^{12} 16^1 before its
establishment. (3) Whereas the resurrection implied in 22 is only
a resuscitation to a *temporary* blessedness, 5^9 10^{17} 25^6, the resurrection in 91–104 is not to the temporary Messianic kingdom spoken
of in $91^{13, 14}$ 96^8, but to one of eternal blessedness subsequent to
the final judgement. For, from $100^{4, 5}$ we see that the righteous
do not rise till God has judged sinners and an end has been made
of all sin   Thus the resurrection of the righteous in 91–104 follows

the final judgement at the close of the temporary Messianic king-dom. Further evidence to this effect is to be found in 92³, ⁴, where the righteous are said to 'walk in eternal light'; in 104⁶, where they are to become 'companions of the hosts of heaven', in 104², where they are to 'shine as the lights', and have 'the portals of heaven open to them'. These statements could not possibly apply to the members of the temporary Messianic kingdom. (4) There is only a resurrection of the righteous in 91-104, cf. 91¹⁰ 92³ 100⁵· whereas in 22 a general resurrection with the exception of one class of sinners is taught. (5) There is no resurrection of the body in 91-104 there is a resurrection of the body in 1-36. (6) Contrast the spiritual nature of the kingdom in 91-104 with the crass materialism of 1-36, where much of the bliss consists in good eating and drinking and the begetting of large families, and life itself depends on the external eating of the tree of life. (7) Finally, contrast the answers given by 1-36 and 91-104 to the question, why do the righteous suffer?' See pp. 3 sq, 222 sq.

The lines of thought, then, being so divergent in these two sections, there is no conclusion open to us other than that they proceed from different authors; whereas the obvious points of agreement necessitate the assumption that one of the two authors had the work of the other before him, and we need feel no hesita-tion in concluding that the author of 91-104 had 1-36 or some form of this section before him—some form of this section we repeat, for it is at the best fragmentary.

B. (*b*) **Relation of 91-104 to 83-90.** There are some points of resemblance between these sections (1) Elijah's translation is referred to, 93⁸ 89⁵². God rejoices over the destruction of the wicked, 94¹⁰ 89⁵⁸. (2) Titles of God in common· 'The Great King,' 91¹³ 84⁵: 'the Holy and Great One,' 92² (note) 84¹.

But these and other superficial points of resemblance are far outweighed by the divergent lines of thought pursued in the two sections, which render the theory of one and undivided authorship impossible We should observe then, that—(1) the Messianic kingdom is finite in duration in 91-104, i.e. from the eighth to the tenth world-week inclusive: whereas in 83-90 it is eternal In 91-104 the final judgement takes place at the close of the Messianic kingdom; in 83-90 it is consummated at the beginning of the Messianic kingdom. (2) There is a resurrection of the righteous only in 91-104; but in 83-90 a resurrection of apostate Jews also (3) The period of the sword is differently dated and

conceived in the two sections   In 91–104 it is separated from the
final judgement by the whole period of the Messianic kingdom,
see 91^{12}, in 83–90 it immediately precedes the final judgement, see
90^{19}; in 91–104 it is ethical and vindictive—the destruction of
the wicked by the righteous; in 83–90 it is national and vindictive—the destruction of the hostile Gentiles by the Jews.   (4) The
building of the Temple precedes the final judgement in 91–104,
in 83–90 it is subsequent to the final judgement.   (5) The kingdom,
to which the righteous rise, in 91–104 is apparently heaven, for in
91$^{14-16}$ the former heaven and earth are destroyed and a new
heaven created, but no new earth, and in 104^2 heaven is thrown
open to the righteous.

We must therefore conclude that 91–104 and 83–90 proceed from
different authors, and this conclusion is confirmed when we observe
the forcible dislocations that 91–104 have undergone at the hands
of the final editor.   This section taken in the following order, 92
91$^{1-10,\ 18-19}$ 93$^{1-10}$ 91$^{12-17}$ 94 (see pp. 218, 224), forms a complete
book in itself, and presents a world-view peculiarly its own.   Why
then was the original order departed from, unless in order to adapt
it to a new context?   On all sides, then, the conclusion is irresistible
that 91–104 once formed an independent writing, that it was afterwards incorporated into a larger work, and underwent its present
derangements in the process of incorporation.

On the other hand, there are good grounds for regarding 93$^{1-10}$
91$^{12-17}$—the Apocalypse of Weeks, and the rest of 91–104 as proceeding from different hands though agreeing in the main in their
teaching

C. The Authorship and Date.   The author belongs to a clearly
defined party   That this party is the Pharisees is obvious, for it is
exclusive in an extreme degree, 97^4, it is an upholder of the law
against an apostate hellenizing party, 99$^{2,\ 14}$, it looks forward to
a temporal triumph over its opponents, 91^{12}, &c ; it believes in
a final judgement and resurrection of the righteou   91^{10} 92^3, and
in Sheol as the place of eternal punishment for the wicked, 99^{11}
103$^{7,\ 8}$.

The enemies of this party are rich and trust in their riches,
96^4 97$^{8-10}$ 98^2, they oppress and rob the poor of their wages, 99^{13},
they have forsaken the law. 99^2, falsified the Old Testament
writings, and led men astray through their heathen doctrines, 94^5
104^{10}, they are given up to superstition and idolatry, 99$^{7-9}$ · they
hold that God does not concern Himself with the doings of men,

98⁶, ⁷ 104⁷ As the former party are designated as the ' children of heaven ', 101¹, these are called the ' children of earth ', 100⁶ 102³.

The date of this clearly defined and developed opposition of the two parties cannot have been pre-Maccabean, nor yet earlier than the breach between John Hyrcanus and the Pharisees But a still later date must be assumed according to the literal interpretation of 103¹⁴, ¹⁵, where the rulers are said to uphold the Sadducean oppressors and to share in the murder of the righteous This charge is not justified before 95 B.C As for the later limit, the Herodian princes cannot be the rulers here mentioned, for the Sadducees were irreconcilably opposed to these, as aliens and usurpers It appears, therefore, that this section should be assigned either to the years 95–79 B.C or to 70–64 B C, during which periods the Pharisees were oppressed by both rulers and Sadducees.

If, on the other hand, we might regard the word ' murder ' as merely a strong expression for a severe persecution—and the silence elsewhere observed as to the rulers would point to this interpretation—then we should naturally refer this section to the years 107–95 B C, i e. after the breach between Hyrcanus and the Pharisees and before the savage destruction of the Pharisees by Jannaeus in 95. If the date of the book is subsequent to 95, the merely passing reference in 103¹⁵ to the cruelties of Jannaeus is hardly intelligible We should expect rather the fierce indignation against ' the kings and the mighty ', which we actually do find in 37–70, and which fittingly expresses the feelings of the Pharisees towards Jannaeus, ' the slayer of the pious.' We are inclined therefore to place 91–104 before 95 B C. and if we may regard 100² as an historical reference, these chapters are to be assigned to the years 104–95 B.C

The author is thus a Pharisee, writing between the years 104 and 95, or 95–79, or 70–64 B.C

D The Problem and its Solution The author of 1–36 solves the problem of the righteous suffering by their resuscitation to a temporary blessedness in the Messianic kingdom the wicked dead who *escaped punishment* in life, 22¹⁰, ¹¹, rise also to receive requital for their sin. What becomes of the righteous after their second death is not so much as hinted at in that section Thus in this respect the solution of the problem here presented has not advanced a single step beyond that given in Is 65 and 66

But this solution of the problem must have failed early to give satisfaction. In 91–104 we find another attempt to grapple with

this difficulty, and in this an answer immeasurably more profound
is achieved.   The wicked are seemingly sinning with impunity, yet
their evil deeds are recorded every day, 104⁷, and for these they
will suffer endless retribution in Sheol, 99¹¹; for Sheol is not a place
such as the Old Testament writers conceived, but one in which men
are requited according to their deserts, 102⁴–104⁵. From this hell
of darkness and flame their souls will never escape, 98³˒ ¹⁰. But
the time is coming when even on earth the wicked will perish and
the righteous triumph over them, on the advent of the Messianic
kingdom, at the beginning of the eighth world-week, 91¹² 95⁷ 96¹
98¹² 99⁴˒ ⁶   This kingdom will last till the close of the tenth world-
week, and during it the righteous will enjoy peace and well-being,
and see many good days on earth, 91¹³˒ ¹⁴ 96⁸   Then will ensue the
final judgement with the destruction of the former heaven and earth,
and the creation of a new heaven, 91¹⁴⁻¹⁶   And the righteous dead,
who have been specially guarded by angels all the time hitherto,
100⁵, will thereupon be raised, 91¹⁰ 92³, as spirits only, 103³˒ ⁴, and
the portals of the new heaven will be opened to them, 104², and they
shall joy as the angels, 104⁴, and become companions of the heavenly
hosts, 104⁶, and shine as the stars for ever, 104².

XCII. XCI. 1–10, 18–19 *Enoch's Book of Admonition for his Children.*

XCII. 1. The book written by Enoch—[Enoch indeed wrote this complete doctrine of wisdom, (which is) praised of all men and a judge of all the earth] for all my children who shall dwell on the earth. And for the future generations who shall observe uprightness and peace.

2. Let not your spirit be troubled on account of the times,
   For the Holy and Great One has appointed days for all
      things.

3. And the righteous one shall arise from sleep,
   [Shall arise] and walk in the paths of righteousness,
   And all his path and conversation shall be in eternal good-
      ness and grace.

XCI—XCIV. In this edition I have rearranged these chapters in what I suggested was their original order in my first edition, i e 92 91¹⁻¹⁰, ¹⁸⁻¹⁹ 93¹⁻¹⁰ 91¹²⁻¹⁷ 94, and have treated the Apocalypse of Weeks, i e. 93¹⁻¹⁰ 91¹²⁻¹⁷, as an earlier fragment incorporated by the author of 91–104 or the editor of the whole book in his work (as suggested in my first edition, p 267) Of the extent of this Apocalypse I will treat *in loc* The order of these chapters, which appears to be the original, and which is restored in this edition, is 92 (see p 218) 91¹⁻¹⁰, ¹⁸⁻¹⁹ 93¹⁻¹⁰ 91¹²⁻¹⁷ 94. Beer, on the other hand, takes 91¹⁻¹¹, ¹⁸⁻¹⁹ as forming the introduction to the Apocalypse of Weeks, and thus arranges the text 91¹⁻¹¹, ¹⁸⁻¹⁹ 93 91¹²⁻¹⁷ 92 94 Martin follows Beer in this respect, though he admits that 92 should perhaps be placed before 91¹⁻¹¹

XCII This chapter obviously forms the beginning of a new book just as 14¹ formed originally the beginning of the section 12–16, see p 27 The words 'The book written', &c evi-

dently introduce a fresh collection of visions   1 **The book   indeed wrote** (*g*) Other MSS 'written by Enoch the scribe' [**Enoch indeed all the earth**]. I have, with some hesitation, bracketed these words as an interpolation. Enoch does not attempt a complete doctrine of wisdom, and seeing that it was for the chosen race only it could hardly be said to be 'praised of all men' Wrote Cf 12³, ⁴   This **complete doctrine of wisdom, (which is) praised** (*a–t* reading *zakuello*) *t* 'of the complete doctrine', &c., *β–y* 'this complete doctrine of wisdom is praised'.   A judge, &c Wisdom is represented as the *πάρεδρος* or assessor of God in 84³ (note)   2 **The times are evil,** but these too are the ordination of God   **The Holy and Great One** (*gq, d₁a⁰ m⁰, β–el₁a* 'the Holy Great One', see 1³ (note)   3 **The righteous one** Used collectively as in 91¹⁰. Instead of 'and the righteous . from sleep, shall arise' *q* reads 'and wisdom shall arise'. **Paths** (*mwh, β* 'path . In eternal good-

4. He will be gracious to the righteous and give him eternal
   uprightness,
   And He will give him power so that he shall be (endowed)
   with goodness and righteousness,
   And he shall walk in eternal light.

5. And sin shall perish in darkness for ever,
   And shall no more be seen from that day for evermore.

XCI. 1-11, 18-19. *Enoch's Admonition to his Children.*

XCI 1. 'And now, my son Methuselah, call to me all thy
   brothers
   And gather together to me all the sons of thy mother,
   For the word calls me,
   And the spirit is poured out upon me,
   That I may show you everything
   That shall befall you for ever.'

2. And thereupon Methuselah went and summoned to him all
his brothers and assembled his relatives.   3. And he spake
unto all the children of righteousness and said

   ' Hear, ye sons of Enoch, all the words of your father,
   And hearken aright to the voice of my mouth;
   For I exhort you and say unto you, beloved

   Love uprightness and walk therein.

4. And draw not nigh to uprightness with a double heart,
   And associate not with those of a double heart,

---

ness and grace   These words are
further explained in ver 4   4
The righteous (*tu, β*)   *gq* 'righteousness'   Power   Uprightness and
power will no longer be dissevered
He shall (*mt, β*). *gqu* 'they shall'
In eternal light, see 38⁴ (note).
5 Cf 10¹⁶, ²⁰

  XCI. 1 All thy brothers . . . all
the sons of thy mother. ∞ *g*. According to 2 Enoch 1¹⁰ 57² the names of these
sons are Methuselah, Regim, Riman,

Ukhan, Khermion, Gaidal. 3 Unto all
the children of righteousness (*gq,
y₁b*). *mlu, β-ehny₁a₁b* 'to all (>*u*, + 'his
children' *t*) concerning his (> *β-ehny
₁a₁b*) righteousness'   Beloved (*a-u*)
β 'my beloved'.   Love uprightness,
&c. cf 94¹.   4 Draw not nigh to
uprightness with a double heart.
This may be derived from Sir 1²⁸
μὴ προσέλθῃς αὐτῷ (i.e. φόβῳ κυρίου)
ἐν καρδίᾳ δισσῇ. cf. Ps 12³ לֵב וָלֵב,
Jas 1⁸ δίψυχος.   Associate not, &c

But walk in righteousness, my sons.
And it shall guide you on good paths,
And righteousness shall be your companion.

5. For I know that violence must increase on the earth,
And a great chastisement be executed on the earth,
And all unrighteousness come to an end .

Yea, it shall be cut off from its roots,
And its whole structure be destroyed

6. And unrighteousness shall again be consummated on the
    earth,
And all the deeds of unrighteousness and of violence
And transgression shall prevail in a twofold degree.

7. And when sin and unrighteousness and blasphemy
And violence in all kinds of deeds increase,
And apostasy and transgression and uncleanness increase,

A great chastisement shall come from heaven upon all these,
And the holy Lord will come forth with wrath and chastise-
    ment
To execute judgement on earth.

8. In those days violence shall be cut off from its roots,
And the roots of unrighteousness together with deceit,
And they shall be destroyed from under heaven.

$>$ *gu* through hmt , cf $94^{2, 3}$ 104^6
In righteousness, my sons q ' iu uprightness and righteousness'. Good
paths There seems to be a reference
here to the Two Ways See ver 19
5 The Deluge Violence must
increase The text reads ' the state
(or ' essence') of violence shall increase'
But this is wholly unlikely. I have
therefore emended hĕlàwê (= ' state ')
into halawô, i e the substantive verb
with suffix. When we combine

halawô with jĕsan'ŭ the two =
' must increase' Cut off from its
roots cf. vv 8, 11 6 The growth
of wickedness after the Deluge 7, 8
This fresh development of wickedness
will call forth the final judgement. 7.
In all (a–q) q, β ' and all' And
transgression. $>$ *gu* From heaven
$>$ *g*. And $>$ *mjt* Lord + ' upon
earth' *g* 8 And the roots (*mtu*, β)
$>$ *gq* Roots of unrighteousness
cf. vv. 5, 11 And ($>$ *u*, *befhp*) they

9. And all the idols of the heathen shall be abandoned.
   And the temples burned with fire,
   And they shall remove them from the whole earth,

   And they (i. e. the heathen) shall be cast into the judgement
      of fire,
   And shall perish in wrath and in grievous judgement
      for ever.

10. And the righteous shall arise from their sleep,
    And wisdom shall arise and be given unto them.

[11. And after that the roots of unrighteousness shall be cut
off, and the sinners shall be destroyed by the sword . . shall be
cut off from the blasphemers in every place, and those who plan
violence and those who commit blasphemy shall perish by the
sword]

---

shall be destroyed (*mtu*, β). > *gq*
9. The absolute rejection of the heathen
seems to be taught here   This was a
prevailing though not the universal
belief of later Judaism ; see Weber,
Jud. Theol. 386 Idolatry is reprobated
in 99⁷⁻⁹, ¹⁰, as here.   And ²⁰ (*gu*, *o₁b*)
> Other MSS   They shall be cast
into the judgement of fire This repro-
bation of the heathen does not appear to
agree with the teaching of ver 14 (see
p. 233), where the conversion of the
heathen is expected   That verse, however, belongs to the Apocalypse of
Weeks which has all the appearance of
an earlier fragment incorporated in his
work by the original author of 91-104
10 The righteous The singular used
collectively as in 92⁸.   Their sleep
(*gmq*, *x*) *tu*, β-*x* 'sleep' In 91-104
only the righteous attain to the
Resurrection, see 51¹ (note) for full
discussion of the subject.   Wisdom
see 42¹, ² (note)   11 As we
have already seen (p 224), 91¹²⁻¹⁷
originally stood after 93¹⁻¹⁰. As for

this verse, we must regard it as an
interpolation added by the final editor
in order to introduce vv. 12-17 which
he had torn from their original context.
This verse is wholly out of place here.
Judgement has already been consummated, all evil works destroyed, and
all the wicked handed over to a
judgement of fire (vv. 7-9) In ver. 10
the Resurrection ensues and judgement
is now over. But in ver 11 all this is
ignored and a moral chaos is represented
as still existing—a moral chaos of
exactly the same nature as existed
before the judgement of vv. 7-9. Moreover, the period of the Sword—man's
part in the final judgement—precedes
the Resurrection, cf. 90¹⁹ 91¹² The
Resurrection follows upon the destruction of all evil and the final judgement,
100⁴, ⁵. Finally, this verse seems
modelled partly on vv 7 and 8, and
partly on ver. 12, the expressions about
blasphemers being drawn from ver. 7,
the phrase 'roots of unrighteousness
shall be cut off' from ver. 8, and the

18. And now I tell you, my sons, and show you
   The paths of righteousness and the paths of violence.
   Yea, I will show them to you again
   That ye may know what will come to pass.

19. And now, hearken unto me, my sons,
   And walk in the paths of righteousness,
   And walk not in the paths of violence;
   For all who walk in the paths of unrighteousness
       shall perish for ever'

XCIII, XCI. 12-17. *The Apocalypse of Weeks.*

XCIII. 1. And after that Enoch both †gave† and began to recount from the books. 2. And Enoch said:

reference to the Sword from ver. 12 (see p 232). **18. Will show** (*m, β*) *gqt* 'have shown'. > *u*. **19. Hearken unto me** (*qfu*). *β* 'hearken'. > *g* **And** [20] > *g* Paths of righteousness paths of violence. This theme is pressed home with great emphasis in 94[1-4] where we find the 'paths of righteousness' 94[1], 'paths of peace' 94[4], 'paths of unrighteousness' 94[1], 'paths of violence and of death' 94[2], 'paths of wickedness' and 'paths of death' 94[3]. This is one of the earliest non-canonical references to the 'Two Ways'. See T. Ash. 1[3, 5] (note in my edition) 2 Enoch 30[15] (note). Cf. Deut. 30[15, 16] Jer 21[8] Ps 1[6]

XCIII. 1-10. In these verses we have an account of the great events of the world during the first seven weeks of its history These seven belong to the past, the three last weeks described in 91[12-17] belong to the future As this Apocalypse of Weeks comes from a different author and date to the Dream-visions, 88 90 we are relieved of the task of harmonizing them, on which many critics have laboured and to no purpose. We are not to regard the

ten weeks as being definite and equal periods of 700 years each, as Wieseler, Hoffmann, and others have done; for, not to press the fact that this reckoning would place the book after Christ, the facts recorded as occurring in the individual weeks would not fall within the limits assigned them by this theory Dillmann's scheme of seventy generations of varying length, seven generations to each week, is still more unsatisfactory. In the first five weeks seven actual generations are taken for each week, but in the sixth and seventh weeks fourteen or more generations are compressed into the needful seven Rather we are to regard the ten weeks as periods of varying length, each one of which is marked, especially towards its close, by some great event—the first by the birth of Enoch; the second by the corruption of primitive man and the Flood, the third by the call of Abraham; the fourth by the revelation of the law and the occupation of Palestine; the fifth by the building of the Temple, the sixth by the apostasy of Israel and the destruction of the Temple; the seventh by the publication of Enoch's writings In the eighth

'Concerning the children of righteousness and concerning
the elect of the world,

And concerning the plant of uprightness, I will speak these
things,

Yea, I Enoch will declare (them) unto you, my sons

According to that which appeared to me in the heavenly
vision,

And which I have known through the word of the holy
angels,

And have learnt from the heavenly tablets.'

3. And Enoch began to recount from the books and said
'I was born the seventh in the first week,
While judgement and righteousness still endured.

4. And after me there shall arise in the second week great
wickedness,

the Messianic kingdom is established and lasts to the close of the tenth week. The final judgement in 91^15 is held at the close of the Messianic kingdom Cf also *Le Livre d'Henoch*, par T. G Peter, Genève, 1890.   **1.** †Gave† (a–mt) t, β 'was' I do not see how the corruption can be explained.   **And began** > a–g   **From** the books These were either written by Enoch, according to some Sections, or by the angel that accompanied him according to others, cf 33^3, 40^8 74^2 81^1,   In the next verse Enoch appeals to visions, angels, and the heavenly tablets, as the source of his revelations   **2** These disclosures are for the children of righteousness, cf 92^1.   **The elect of the world** This designation of the elect is not found elsewhere in Enoch **The plant of uprightness** see 10^16 (note) **Uprightness** (a–g) q 'righteousness', β 'righteousness and uprightness'   **Will declare** (gg, β). *intu* 'have declared'   **Heavenly tablets**

see 47^3 (note) for a complete account of this and similar expressions.   **3.** **Enoch** > mqt **Seventh in the first week.** Ewald and Dillmann find in this expression the foundation of their theory that the reckoning here is according to generations But this is to press the words too much, They mean nothing more than in Gen. 5^24, where he is the seventh of the patriarchs, or 'seventh from Adam', Jude 14. **Still endured.**   The meaning is doubtful. 'Judgement' may be taken in a favourable sense. In that case Enoch was born before the demoralization of mankind The next stanza appears to favour this view. On the other hand, the fact that the angels descended in the days of Jared, nearly sixty years before Enoch was born, Jubilees 4^15–16, is against this view, and would favour such a rendering as 'were held back' The righteous judgement of the Deluge had not yet come.   **4. Great wickedness** According to 6^9 and

And deceit shall have sprung up,
And in it there shall be the first end.

And in it a man shall be saved,
And after it is ended unrighteousness shall grow up,
And a law shall be made for the sinners

5. And after that in the third week at its close
   A man shall be elected as the plant of righteous judgement,
   And his posterity shall become the plant of righteousness
   for evermore.

6. And after that in the fourth week, at its close,
   Visions of the holy and righteous shall be seen,
   And a law for all generations and an enclosure shall be
   made for them.

7. And after that in the fifth week, at its close,
   The house of glory and dominion shall be built for ever.

106^{13} this growth of wickedness should have been assigned to Jared's days, when the fall of the angels took place This week includes the Deluge, and the Covenant made with Noah · Gen. 8^{21}–9^{17} The time order in the close of this sentence is not observed   A law shall be made (q, n Since *gmu* read 'law in the nom I take it that *jĕgabĕl* is in them corrupt for *jetgabal*—the reading of q, n   Cf ver 6 *t*,β–n read 'He will make a law' 5 Abraham and his seed chosen as the race in and through which God would reveal His righteous judgements—'the plant of righteous judgement', cf ver 2; 10^{16} (note)   His posterity. The text reads 'after him (or 'it') it shall come (or 'become', the plant of righteousness', &c But, since this is unsatisfactory however we take it, I suggest that אחריו (= 'after him' or 'it') stood before the translator but was corrupt for אחריתו = 'his posterity'   6 Visions of the holy

and righteous (*mq*, β) So u but that it omits 'and righteous'. *g* reads 'visions of the holy and righteousness', *t* 'holy and righteous visions' The divine manifestations in favour of Israel in Egypt. A law, &c The law given on Sinai This law is of eternal obligation; cf 99^2 An enclosure Dillmann thinks this refers to the Tabernacle and the hedging in of the national life by the law. It seems rather to refer to the occupation of Palestine, cf 89^2 7 The house The Temple will, according to this author, stand 'for ever', though one form of it may give place to another. If this Apocalypse of Weeks was originally an integral part of 91–104 this 'for ever' means only an indefinitely long time; for though there is an eternal law, there appears to be no Temple after the final judgement, and the risen righteous enjoy a purely spiritual existence like the angels, as in the Book of Jubilees, and possibly

8. And after that in the sixth week all who live in it shall be
blinded,

And the hearts of all of them shall godlessly forsake wisdom.

And in it a man shall ascend;

And at its close the house of dominion shall be burnt with
fire,

And the whole race of the chosen root shall be dispersed.

9. And after that in the seventh week shall an apostate
generation arise,

And many shall be its deeds,

And all its deeds shall be apostate.

10. And at its close shall be elected

The elect righteous of the eternal plant of righteousness,

To receive sevenfold instruction concerning all His creation.

[11 For who is there of all the children of men that is able
to hear the voice of the Holy One without being troubled?
And who can think His thoughts? and who is there that can
behold all the works of heaven?   12. And how should there

---

in the Pss of Solomon.   8 The
time of the divided kingdom in Israel,
of growing degeneracy and darkness.
A man, i e Elijah, cf. 89³². At
the close of this week the Temple is
destroyed and the nation carried into
captivity   **Chosen root** (*g, β*) *mql*
'root of might'.   **9.** This week
embraces the period from the Captivity
to the time of the author. It is an
apostate period.   The same judgement is passed upon it in 89⁷³⁻⁷⁵.
Apostate ¹⁰ > *gm*   **10.** The writer
here refers to his own disclosures which
will be made known at the end of the
seventh week. It might seem that it
would be impossible for any writer to
make such extravagant claims for his
productions   We find some slight approach to these in Sn. 24²⁸⁻³². **Shall
be elected** (*a, acflikn*) *bdlopuy₁a₁b*

'shall be recompensed'   **The elect
righteous** (*g, abefhikx*).   Cf. 1¹ Greek
version. *t* supports this. *g, dloy₁a₁b*
read 'the elect of righteousness', *m*
'the righteous', *u* 'the elect'. The
revelations are designed for the elect
righteous, for only these will receive
them; cf 100⁶ 104¹², ¹³   **11-14**
The verses are completely out of place
in their present context, as Laurence,
Hoffmann, and Schodde have already
remarked, and subsequently Beer and
Martin.   They would belong rather
to the Book of the Heavenly Luminaries, 72-79 82, but are foreign in
character to the whole tone of this
book, 91-104, and do not as a matter
of fact rightly describe any one of the
books of Enoch   **11. The voice
of the Holy One,** i e. the thunder;
cf. Job 37⁴, ⁵ Ps 29   **Think His**

be one who could behold the heaven, and who is there that could
understand the things of heaven and see a soul or a spirit and
could tell thereof, or ascend and see all their ends and think
them or do like them ?   13. And who is there of all men that
could know what is the breadth and the length of the earth, and
to whom has been shown the measure of all of them ?   14. Or
is there any one who could discern the length of the heaven and
how great is its height, and upon what it is founded, and how
great is the number of the stars, and where all the luminaries
rest ?]

XCI. 12–17. *The Last Three Weeks.*

12. And after that there shall be another, the eighth week, that
of righteousness,

> And a sword shall be given to it that a righteous
> judgement may be executed on the oppressors,

> And sinners shall be delivered into the hands of the
> righteous.

13. And at its close they shall acquire houses through their
righteousness,

> And a house shall be built for the Great King in glory for
> evermore,

14*d*. And all mankind shall look to the path of uprightness

thoughts . cf. Job 5^9 9^{10} 38^{33} Pss 40^5
92^5 Eccles. 11^5.   12. A soul (*ğmq*,
bזy). *t*, *β–bזy* 'His breath   A spirit
(*mtu*,*bזy*). *ğq* a corruption of text in *mtu*.
β–bזy 'His spirit'   These words would
refer to Enoch's journey through heaven
and Hades   Ascend · cf Prov. 30^4.
Their ends, i. e of the things of
heaven   But 'aknâfîhômû (= 'their
ends') may be corrupt for meknjâtîhômû
= 'their causes'   13. Cf. Job
$38^{4,6}$. Not given in Enoch.   14
The length of the heaven, &c   Jer.
31^{37} Job 11^8.   Not given in Enoch.
Founded : cf $18^{2,3}$ Number of
the stars. This is nowhere found in
Enoch.

XCI. 12-17. These verses giving
an account of the last three weeks of
the world's history are here restored to
their place after 93^{1-10} (see p. 224),
the account of the first seven weeks
12. The eighth week sees the establishment of the Messianic kingdom. It
likewise forms the first act of the final
judgement, for it is the period of the
Sword, cf 90^{19}. and the wicked are
given into the hands of the righteous
cf 95^7 96^1 98^{12} $99^{4,6}$, also 38^5.   13
On the period of strife will follow that
of rest and quiet possession of the
earth, cf. Is. $60^{21,22}$ 65^{20-23}.   A house
. . . for the Great King (*a–ğ,β*). *ğ* 'the
house of the Great King shall be built'.

14 *a*. And after that, in the ninth week, the righteous judgement shall be revealed to the whole world,

    b. And all the works of the godless shall vanish from all the earth,

    c. And the world shall be written down for destruction.

15. And after this, in the tenth week in the seventh part,
    There shall be the great eternal judgement,
    In which He will execute vengeance amongst the angels.

16. And the first heaven shall depart and pass away,
    And a new heaven shall appear,
    And all the powers of the heavens shall give sevenfold light.

17. And after that there will be many weeks without number for ever,

---

This means first of all the temple and in the next place Jerusalem.   **14.** This stanza is difficult. It is too long by one line, whereas the preceding stanza is too short   Accordingly I have transposed 14 *d* to the close of the preceding stanza   The ninth week, as Dillmann supposes, may mean the period in which true religion will spread over the earth, and the judgement described in ver 12, and executed by the righteous, will be made known to the neutral Gentile nations with a view to their conversion, cf 50²⁻⁴ 90³⁰, ³³, ³⁵. With this view the concluding words of this verse would harmonize well. Yet see ver. 15 (note)   **The works of the godless shall vanish** cf 10¹⁶, ²⁰, ²¹   **The world shall be written down for destruction** (*m, β*)   *g* 'He shall write down (i e. decree) the destruction of the world'   *t* 'He shall write down the world for destruction'   > *u*   *q* a corruption of *g* (?). The opposite phrase 'written down for life' is found in

Is. 4³ כתוב לחיים. This destination will take effect towards the close of the tenth week   **15** The tenth week ends with the final judgement on the watchers. As there is no mention of the judgement of the wicked by God in person in this verse, the preceding verse may in some measure refer to it.   **There shall be the great eternal judgement, In which . . . amongst the angels** (*a-t*). The structure of the stanza supports this text   *t, β-in* insert a gloss and read

    'There shall be the eternal judgement,
    And it shall be executed on the watchers of the eternal heaven,
    The great (judgement) in which He will execute vengeance amongst the angels.'

16 Observe that though there will be a new heaven, cf. Is 65¹⁷ 66²² Ps 102²⁶, there is no mention of a new earth, cf 104² (note). For the idea of a new creation cf. 45⁴ 72¹ (note)   **Sevenfold** cf. Is. 30²⁶ 60¹⁹, ²⁰, *mqt, β-ahk* add 'for ever'   **17.** This verse

And all shall be in goodness and righteousness,
And sin shall no more be mentioned for ever.

XCIV. 1-5. *Admonitions to the Righteous*

XCIV. 1. And now I say unto you, my sons, love righteousness
and walk therein ;
For the paths of righteousness are worthy of acceptation,
But the paths of unrighteousness shall suddenly be destroyed
and vanish.

2. And to certain men of a generation shall the paths of
violence and of death be revealed,
And they shall hold themselves afar from them,
And shall not follow them

3 And now I say unto you the righteous :
Walk not in the paths of wickedness, nor on the paths of death,
And draw not nigh to them, lest ye be destroyed

4. But seek and choose for yourselves righteousness and an
elect life,
And walk in the paths of peace,
And ye shall live and prosper

5 And hold fast my words in the thoughts of your hearts,
And suffer them not to be effaced from your hearts .

For know that sinners will tempt men to **evilly-entreat**
wisdom,

closes the Apocalypse of Weeks **And
all** (*g*). > Other MSS.

XCIV This chapter introduces the
practical part of this Section. Though
written for the righteous, it devotes as
much attention to the woes awaiting the
sinners   1 **Love righteousness,**
&c. cf 91⁵. **Worthy of acceptation** (*t*, *β*) *gmq* 'worthy and acceptable'. *u* 'worthy' Ct. 1 Tim. 1¹⁵
ἀποδοχῆς ἄξιος **Paths of unrighteousness**   **destroyed** cf P. 1⁶

On the 'two paths' see 91¹⁹ note
2 The revelations through Moses and
the Prophets **Paths of   death** cf.
Prov. 14¹² Jer 21⁸.   **3 Paths** ¹⁰
(*ymt*, *b*). *β-b* 'path' **Wickedness.** +'and of violence' *β*.   **Draw
not nigh** cf 91⁴ 104⁶.   **4. But
seek** *g* reads 'as those who seek
evil', and connects the words with
the preceding verse. **And ye shall**
(*gmq*). *t*, *β* 'that ye may'.   **5.
To evilly-entreat.** The text = 'to

So that no place may be found for her,
And no manner of temptation may minish.

XCIV 6–11. *Woes for the Sinners.*

6 Woe to those who build unrighteousness and oppression
And lay deceit as a foundation ;
For they shall be suddenly overthrown,
And they shall have no peace.

7. Woe to those who build their houses with sin ;
For from all their foundations shall they be overthrown,
And by the sword shall they fall

[And those who acquire gold and silver in judgement
suddenly shall perish.]

8 Woe to you, ye rich, for ye have trusted in your riches,
And from your riches shall ye depart,
Because ye have not remembered the Most High in the
days of your riches.

9. Ye have committed blasphemy and unrighteousness,
And have become ready for the day of slaughter,
And the day of darkness and the day of the great judgement.

10. Thus I speak and declare unto you ·
He who hath created you will overthrow you,

make . . evil', apparently a mis-rendering of κακοποιεῖν. **No place may be found for her** . cf 42¹.   **6** Some of the forms that wickedness will assume in those days   **Build** cf 91'   **Have no peace.** This recurs in 98¹¹, ¹⁶ 99¹³ 101³ 102³ 103⁸   See also 5⁴ (note)   **7 Build their houses with sin** · from Jer 22¹³ הוי בנה ביתו בלא־צדק   **They,** i. e the men who so build.   **[And those who acquire . . . perish]** I have bracketed this sentence as an interpolation. The subject of riches is not dealt with till the next woe in ver.

8   Our author does not condemn the acquisition of wealth in itself but its acquisition by wrong means   Ct. 97⁸, from which passage this interpolation may in part be drawn   The removal of this sentence sets the stanza right.   **8 Trusted in your riches.** This phrase is drawn from Prov 11²⁸ בטח בעשרו   Cf Pss 49⁶ 52⁷ In Jer. 9²³ the rich man is bidden not to glory in his riches Pss 49⁶ 52⁷ Cf also 1 En 46⁷ 63¹⁰ 96⁴ 97⁸⁻¹⁰   **9.** Through their sin and blasphemy they are now ripe for judgement. **Day of slaughter,** &c . see 45² (note)   **And the day**

And for your fall there shall be no compassion,
And your Creator will rejoice at your destruction.

11 And your righteous ones in those days shall be
A reproach to the sinners and the godless.

Enoch's Grief : fresh Woes against the Sinners.

XCV. 1. Oh that mine eyes were [a cloud of] waters
That I might weep over you,
And pour down my tears as a cloud † of † waters .
That so I might rest from my trouble of heart !

2. †Who has permitted you to practise reproaches and wickedness ?
And so judgement shall overtake you, sinners.†

3. Fear not the sinners, ye righteous ;
For again will the Lord deliver them into your hands,

---

of darkness > *g, a* 10 Your Creator will rejoice at your destruction. This sentiment has its parallels in the O T, cf Pss. 2⁵,⁴ 37¹², ¹³, and in our text 89⁶⁸ and 97² 11 Your righteous ones, i. e the righteous among his children's descendants This stanza is imperfect

XCV 1. Oh that mine eyes were [a cloud of] waters 'Cloud' here is impossible, however it may be in the next line Its genesis is, I think, clear The text = מי־יחן עיני ענן מים. Here the impossible ענן is either a dittograph of עיני , then we should have 'Oh that mine eyes were waters' or it is a corruption of עין. In that case we should have 'Oh that mine eyes were a spring of waters'. In this latter case we might compare 2 Bar 35² 'Become ye springs, O mine eyes, and ye, mine eyelids, a fount of tears' Our text, of course, is based on Jer 9¹ 'Oh that my head were waters, and mine eyes a fountain of

tears'. As a cloud of waters = כענן מים, which should probably have been translated 'as a cloud pours waters' or still better take מים as corrupt for זרם then we should have 'as a cloud (pours) rain' 2 Who has permitted (lit. 'given') you (*g,β*(=מי נתנכם)). But *a–g*(=מי יתנכם) 'Who will give you' or 'Oh that ye were' is probably right Then either omitting 'to practise' with *g*, or emending tăgabĕrû into tĕtgabarû, we should have 'Oh that ye were become a reproach and wickedness'. In that case we should in the next line adopt the subjunctive with *β* and not the indicative in *a*. The couplet would then run

'Oh that ye were become a reproach and an evil

And that so judgement might overtake you, sinners.'

3 Yet let not the righteous fear , for the period of their supremacy is at hand , cf. 91¹² Again. The writer may refer to the Maccabean victories , for

That ye may execute judgement upon them according to your desires.

4. Woe to you who fulminate anathemas which cannot be reversed ·
Healing shall therefore be far from you because of your sins.

5. Woe to you who requite your neighbour with evil ;
For ye shall be requited according to your works.

6. Woe to you, lying witnesses,
And to those who weigh out injustice,
For suddenly shall ye perish.

7. Woe to you, sinners, for ye persecute the righteous ;
For ye shall be delivered up and persecuted because of injustice,
And heavy shall its yoke be upon you.

Grounds of Hopefulness for the Righteous : Woes for the Wicked.

XCVI. 1. Be hopeful, ye righteous; for suddenly shall the sinners perish before you,
And ye shall have lordship over them according to your desires.

---

these were victories over Sadducean influences. Though the Maccabean princes are now Sadducees themselves, the period of the Sword, the time of the vengeance of the righteous, is coming. **4.** Magical practices and incantations are here referred to. **Which cannot** ('can' *gq*) be reversed (*gmq*) *t, β* 'which you cannot reverse'. Cf. 8⁸ on the reversing of incantation. **5 Requite . . with evil** For like expressions cf. Prov 17¹³ 'reward evil for good ', 20²² 'Say not, I will recompense evil' אֲשַׁלְּמָה־רָע 24²⁹ Rom.

12¹⁷ **Requited according to your works** : cf 100⁷ Judg 1⁷ **6 Weigh out injustice,** i. e. are unjust judges, but the expression is strange **7 Ye shall be delivered up** (*g*) Other MSS. 'ye shall deliver up'. **And persecuted** (*a–gt, β–a*) *gt, a* 'and ye shall persecute'. **Its yoke** (*gmq* *t, β* 'their yoke'.

XCVI. The righteous exhorted to hope in the coming Messianic kingdom, and fresh woes denounced against the sinners **1 Lordship**. cf 91¹² (note) 95³, ⁷ 98¹². **2.** This verse

[2. And in the day of the tribulation of the sinners,
   Your children shall mount and rise as eagles,
   And higher than the vultures will be your nest,

   And ye shall ascend and enter the crevices of the earth,
   And the clefts of the rock for ever as coneys before the
      unrighteous,
   And the sirens shall sigh because of you and weep.]

3. Wherefore fear not, ye that have suffered ;
   For healing shall be your portion,
   And a bright light shall enlighten you,
   And the voice of rest ye shall hear from heaven.

4. Woe unto you, ye sinners, for your riches make you appear
      like the righteous,
   But your hearts convict you of being sinners,
   And this fact shall be a testimony against you for a
      memorial of (your) evil deeds.

5. Woe to you who devour the finest of the wheat,
   And drink wine in large bowls,
   And tread under foot the lowly with your might.

must be an interpolation   it is foolish
in itself and interrupts the context   It
is the wicked who will flee to hide
themselves in secret places, 97³ 100⁴ 102¹,
and not the righteous . the latter will
not have to conceal themselves on the
day of judgement, 104². Perhaps the
first three lines may be original.   In
the day of the tribulation of the
sinners. This would naturally mean
when the sinners suffer tribulation , but
it must mean here in the day when
tribulation is caused by the sinners
Mount and rise, &c   From Is 40³¹
Higher than the vultures of Jer
49¹⁶.   Enter the crevices of the
earth, &c   These words are taken
from Is 2¹⁰, ¹⁹, ²¹, and are used there
of those who flee through fear from
the presence of the Lord. Hence they
are most inappropriate in their present

connexion.   Before the unrighteous
These words imply that the righteous
go into the clefts of the rocks to
escape the unrighteous   The sirens
Whether sirens (so the Ethiopic version
renders σειρῆνες Is 13²¹ Jer 27³⁹) or
satyrs, the meaning of the word is uncertain.   *gt*, *β* read 'as the sirens'
3 A bright light : see 38⁴ (note)   4
Your riches make you appear like
the righteous. Wealthy sinners could
appeal to their riches as a proof of their
righteousness, for according to the O T
doctrine of retribution, prosperity was
a mark of righteousness.   This fact,
i e that your riches prove you to be
righteous.   For a memorial, &c   of
ver 7   5 The finest of the
wheat Pss. 81¹⁷ (חֵלֶב חִטָּה) 147¹⁴.
†Wine in large bowls†, i e not in wine
cups Like the magnates in Samaria,

6. Woe to you who drink water from every fountain,
For suddenly shall ye be consumed and wither away,
Because ye have forsaken the fountain of life.

7. Woe to you who work unrighteousness
And deceit and blasphemy :
It shall be a memorial against you for evil

8. Woe to you, ye mighty,
Who with might oppress the righteous ,
For the day of your destruction is coming.

In those days many and good days shall come to the
righteous—in the day of your judgement.

*The Evils in Store for Sinners and the Possessors of unrighteous
Wealth*

XCVII. 1. Believe, ye righteous, that the sinners will become
a shame
And perish in the day of unrighteousness.

2. Be it known unto you (ye sinners) that the Most High is
mindful of your destruction,
And the angels of heaven rejoice over your destruction.

Amos 6⁶, these wealthy sinners drank from flagons, not from cups. The text which is here corrupt = ' the strength of the root of the fountain ' = ἰσχὺν ῥίζης πηγῆς = כֹּחַ עִיקַר עַיִן corrupt for במזרקי יין—the actual phrase used of the drinking-vessels of the luxurious nobles in Samaria   6 **Drink water from every fountain.** For 'from every fountain' the text reads literally ' at every time ' = בְּכָל־עֵת corrupt for מבְּכָל־עַיִן 'from every fountain'. The words are here used metaphorically as opposed to ' the fountain of life used at the close of the stanza. Jer 2¹³— ' they have forsaken Me the fountain of living waters ' —was in the mind of our author   Cf. Ps 36⁹   For sud-

denly shall ye be consumed (*mqt*) *g, β* 'for suddenly shall ye be requited and consumed' *u* (defective) 'suddenly'.   **Forsaken, &c.** See note on the first line of the stanza   **7** Cf 91⁸ 94⁸, ⁹.   **A memorial** Cf ver 4   **8 Many and good days** The reference here seems to be to the temporary Messianic kingdom in which the righteous who are living at the time will participate.

XCVII. This chapter mainly consists of threatenings against the wicked   **1 In the day of unrighteousness.** A peculiar expression for the day appointed for the judgement of unrighteousness see 45² (note).   **2 Angels of heaven** (*a, n*) *β–n* 'angels'   Cf.

3. What will ye do, ye sinneis,
   And whither will ye flee on that day of judgement,
   When ye heai the voice of the prayer of the righteous ?

4. Yea, ye shall fare like unto them,
   Against whom this word shall be a testimony .
   "Ye have been companions of sinners."

5. And in those days the prayer of the righteous shall reach
   unto the Lord,
   And for you the days of your judgement shall come

6 And all the words of your unrighteousness shall be read out
   before the Great Holy One,
   And your faces shall be covered with shame,
   And He will reject every work which is grounded on unrighteousness.

7. Woe to you, ye sinners, who live on the mid ocean and on
   the dry land,
   Whose remembrance is evil against you

8. Woe to you who acquire silver and gold in unrighteousness
   and say .
   "We have become rich with riches and have possessions ;
   And have acquired everything we have desired.

94¹⁰ for a similar expression of religious hate contrasted with Luke 15¹⁰   **3. Whither will ye flee** . cf 102¹. **The prayer of the righteous ·** of ver. 5. **4. Shall fare** (*gqu*). *mt, β* 'shall not fare'   **Against whom** (*g*) *t* 'for against you' *mq, β* 'ye against whom'   **This word . . . 'Ye have been companions of sinners.'** 96⁴ may be taken in this sense   The Pharisaic duty of separation from the unrighteous could not be more strongly enforced   **5 The prayer of the righteous** cf 47² 97³ 99⁸, ¹⁸ 104⁸. This cry of the righteous for vengeance on their persecutors is found in Rev 6¹⁰   **Righteous** (*a-g, β-afhikpv*). *g, afhikpv* 'holy'   **6 All the**

words of (*mqt, β-a*). *g* 'all'.   **Shall be read out,** i e. from the books of remembrance of evil deeds · see 47⁸ (note). Cf. Matt 12³⁶ πᾶν ῥῆμα ἀργόν, ὃ ἐὰν λαλήσουσιν οἱ ἄνθρωποι, ἀποδώσουσιν περὶ αὐτοῦ λόγον ἐν ἡμέρᾳ κρίσεως— which seems a reminiscence of our text   **Great Holy One** (*g₁gmq, n*) *tu, β-n₁a* 'Great and Holy One' . see 1³ (note) 92² (note)   **Covered with shame**. cf 46³ 62¹⁰ 63¹¹   **He will reject every work** (*gqt*) *mu, β* 'every work shall be rejected'   **7. On the** mid ocean and on the dry land, i e. everywhere.   **Remembrance :** of 100¹⁰, ¹¹ 104⁸   **8** Cf. 94⁷, ⁸ (note); also Sir. 11¹⁹ Luke 12¹⁹   **With riches** (*mqt, β*). >*gu*   The words of the rich,

9. And now let us do what we purposed .

For we have gathered silver,

9^d And many are the husbandmen in our houses,

9^e And our granaries are (brim)full as with water."

10. Yea and like water your lies shall flow away ,

For your riches shall not abide

But speedily ascend from you ,

For ye have acquired it all in unrighteousness,

And ye shall be given over to a great curse.

Self-indulgence of Sinners: Sin originated by Man . all Sin
recorded in Heaven · Woes for the Sinners.

XCVIII. 1. And now I swear unto you, to the wise and to the
foolish,

For ye shall have manifold experiences on the earth.

2. For ye men shall put on more adornments than a woman,

And coloured garments more than a virgin ·

In royalty and in grandeur and in power,

And in silver and in gold and in purple,

And in splendour and in food they shall be poured out as
water.

---

when retranslated into Hebrew, rhyme as they do in Lamentations 5² ˢᵍᵍ 'We have become rich with riches', &c =

וכל קנינו	עשר עשרנו
אשר אינו	ורבוש לנו
9.	ונעשה שחשבנו
	כי בסף אסף אספנו
9ᵈ.	ורבים אכרי בתינו
9ᶜ	ומלאים במים אוצרינו

9 And many (g_1g, $_1b$) ql, $\beta-_1b$ 'many'. As with water ($_1g$) Other MSS 'and as with water' 10 This verse is a rejoinder to the boasting of the sinners The writer takes up the last words and gives them a different turn Your lies . i.e. the false things in which you trust. Your riches

(u) $a-u$, β 'riches with you'. **Riches shall . . speedily ascend** cf. Prov. 23⁵. **All** (gmt, $\beta-n$) $>_1g qu$, u.

XCVIII. This chapter introduces a fresh division in 91–104 This division, 98–102³, consists mainly of a denunciation of the sinners, of their errors in life and doctrine, and announces their coming judgement **1. I swear unto you** This formula occurs here for the first time but recurs frequently, cf. vv 4, 6, 99⁶, &c. **To the wise and to the foolish.** The foolish are addressed in 98–102³, the wise in 102⁴–104. **To the foolish** (inu, β) $g_1g qt$ 'not to the foolish'. **2 Shall be poured out as water** Phrase from Ps. 22¹⁴. Their personality giving itself wholly to such external possessions will at last

3. Therefore they shall be wanting in doctrine and wisdom,
And they shall perish thereby together with their
possessions,
And with all their glory and their splendour,
And in shame and in slaughter and in great destitution,
Their spirits shall be cast into the furnace of fire.

4 I have sworn unto you, ye sinners, as a mountain has not
become a slave,
And a hill does not become the handmaid of a woman,
Even so sin has not been sent upon the earth,
But man of himself has created it,
And under a great curse shall they fall who commit it.

5. And barrenness has not been given to the woman,
But on account of the deeds of her own hands she dies
without children.

6. I have sworn unto you, ye sinners, by the Holy Great One,
That all your evil deeds are revealed in the heavens,
And that none of your deeds of oppression are covered and
hidden

7. And do not think in your spirit nor say in your heart that
ye do not know and that ye do not see that every sin is

---

lose itself in them, as water is lost in the earth. **3. In great destitution.** In contrast to their wealth in this world. Their spirits cf ver.10; 103⁸ **Into the furnace of fire** (g_1g, β). > *mqto.* Cf. Matt 13⁴², ⁵⁰. As incorporeal spirits the wicked are cast into hell. This 'furnace of fire' is the final place of punishment **4** The writer now proceeds to attack the immoral view that sin is something original and unavoidable. Sin was of man's own devising; see 69¹¹ (note) Yet the writer still ascribes the introduction of sin into the world to the fallen angels, cf. 100⁴. The contrast of mountain and slave and hill and handmaid is

suggested by the fact that הר (= 'mountain') is masculine in Hebrew and גבעה (= 'hill') is feminine. In Aramaic we have טור and רמא. **5.** And as a consequence of their sin men are punished just because sin is a voluntary thing The instance in the text is chosen as an illustration of this general law, cf. Hos 9¹⁴. Barrenness (*tu, β-n¹). g₁gmq, n¹* 'simulation', or 'excuse'. **6-8.** The writer next deals with the view that God does not concern Himself with the world or the deeds of men, cf Job 22¹³ Ps 73¹¹, and declares that the deeds of men are recorded every day in heaven. **6. Holy Great One** (*yqtu*)

every day recorded in heaven in the presence of the Most
High.   8. From henceforth ye know that all your oppression
wherewith ye oppress is written down every day till the day
of your judgement.

9. Woe to you, ye fools, for through your folly shall ye
perish : and ye transgress against the wise, and so good hap
shall not be your portion.   10 And now, know ye that
ye are prepared for the day of destruction   wherefore do not
hope to live, ye sinners, but ye shall depart and die ; for ye
know no ransom , for ye are prepared for the day of the
great judgement, for the day of tribulation and great shame
for your spirits.

11. Woe to you, ye obstinate of heart, who work wickedness
and eat blood :

Whence have ye good things to eat and to drink and to be
filled ?

From all the good things which the Lord the Most High has
placed in abundance on the earth , therefore ye shall have no
peace.   12. Woe to you who love the deeds of unrighteousness . wherefore do ye hope for good hap unto yourselves ?
know that ye shall be delivered into the hands of the righteous,
and they shall cut off your necks and slay you, and have no
mercy upon you   13. Woe to you who rejoice in the tribulation

---

ιy^m, β-n 'Holy and Great One'.
7. **Recorded .** cf. 97^6 98^8 100^{10} $104^{7, 8}$
8 From henceforth ye know, i e.
from the publication of Enoch's book
in these later times   **9** This verse
introduces a long succession of woes
directed against the sinners.   **Transgress against** $(g_1 g)$. m 'know not',
q 'tend not', t, β 'hearken not to'.
10. Prepared cf. 94^9.   **Die** This
refers not only to the loss of the life
temporal but also of the life eternal
No ransom Ps. $49^{7, 8, 9}$.   **For** $(\iota y, \beta)$.
g 'and' $> m_1 l$ **Day of the great**

judgement, &c. see 45^2 (note)   For
your spirits see ver. 3 (note).   **11**
The denunciation of individual sinners.
Obstinate of heart cf 100^8 Who
work (2nd sing t, β). In 3rd sing.
$g_1 y^m q$ The next verb 'eat' is preserved only in β in the 2nd sing   **Eat
blood** cf 7^5 Not content with enjoying the best of everything that God
gives, these sinners eat blood and break
the divine law ; cf. Book of Jubilees
7^{28-32} 21^6 Acts 15^{29}.   **The Lord** $(a$-$m)$
m, β 'our Lord'.   **Have no peace :**
see 5^4 (note).   **12 Delivered into**

of the righteous, for no grave shall be dug for you. 14. Woe to you who set at nought the words of the righteous; for ye shall have no hope of life. 15. Woe to you who write down lying and godless words; for they write down their lies that men may hear them and act godlessly towards (their) neighbour. 16. Therefore they shall have no peace but die a sudden death.

Woes pronounced on the Godless, the Lawbreakers: evil Plight of Sinners in the last Days: further Woes.

XCIX. 1. Woe to you who work godlessness,
And glory in lying, and extol them .
Ye shall perish, and no happy life shall be yours.

2. Woe to them who pervert the words of uprightness,
And transgress the eternal law,
And transform themselves into what they were not [into sinners] :
They shall be trodden under foot upon the earth.

3. In those days make ready, ye righteous, to raise your prayers
as a memorial,

the hands of the righteous see 91¹⁴ (note). **13. No grave shall be dug for you** *giy* read 'no grave of yours shall be seen' Cf. Jer 8² 22¹⁹. **14 No hope of life, &c** cf. 96¹ 98¹⁰. **15** Cf 104¹⁰. This verse attests the vigorous literary strife existing between the Sadducean or Hellenistic and the Pharisaic party. **Act godlessly** (*yqiu*, ras a = ἀσεβεῖν cf 1⁹ 5⁸ 8² &c) β inserts a negative and changes bā'ed (= 'neighbour') into 'bad = 'folly' This necessitates a change of rendering 'not forget (their) folly'. Cf ver 9. **16 Have no peace** see 5⁴ (note) **A sudden death** cf. 94¹, ⁶, ⁷ 95⁶ 96¹, ⁶.

XCIX 1 In 98¹⁵ the writers of the Hellenistic literature are denounced · here all those who sympathize with or praise them, cf 94⁵ 98¹⁵ (note) **To you** (*a–ig*) ig, β ' to them' There is a constant confusion of the second

and third persons in the MSS.—in part owing no doubt to a not infrequent change in the original from the second person to the third or vice versa I will notice only the most important **2 To them** (*gigm*) *qtu*, β 'to you' **Pervert the words of uprightness** cf 94⁵ **The eternal law**, i e the Mosaic law, 5⁴ 99¹⁴ **Transform themselves into what they were not.** This may merely mean that they adopt generally the Hellenistic customs, as I thought in my first edition; but the reference is rather the medical operation undergone by many of the young Jews of noble birth, in order that they might appear like Greeks when they undressed for the Greek games in Jerusalem Cf Ass Mos 8³, Jos *Ant* xii 5. 1 By this operation the foreskin was brought forward [**Into sinners**] Bracketed as a gloss **3. Your prayers** see 97⁵ (note)

And place them as a testimony before the angels,
That they may place the sin of the sinners for a memorial
before the Most High.

4. In those days the nations shall be stirred up,
And the families of the nations shall arise on the day of
destruction.

5. And in those days the destitute shall go forth and carry off
their children,
And they shall abandon them, so that their children shall
perish through them :
Yea, they shall abandon their children (that are still)
sucklings, and not return to them,
And shall have no pity on their beloved ones.

6. And again I swear to you, ye sinners, that sin is prepared
for a day of unceasing bloodshed.   7. And they who worship
stones, and grave images of gold and silver and wood (and stone)

Place them (α β 'ye have placed
them') . before the angels This
mediatorial function of the angels (cf.
9²⁻¹¹ note) has its root in the O T ,
cf. Job 5¹ 33²³ Zech. 1¹²; but has no
place in the N T , except in Rev. 8³, ⁴.
See my note on the mediation of angels
in T Lev 3⁵ T Dan. 6²   The Most
High   This title is found in all Sections of the book   The title ' Most
High' appears in 9³ 10¹ 46⁷ 60¹, ²² 62⁷
77¹ 94⁸ 97² 98⁷, ¹¹ 99⁸, ¹⁰ 101¹, ⁶, ⁹   4
In the last times there will be wars
and tumults among the nations of the
earth   This will be the period of the
Sword , cf. 90¹⁹ 91¹² 99⁶.   Shall be
stirred up (t, β)   a-₁gt 'are stirred
up'.   Shall arise (t, β). a-mt
' hall raise up '.   5 The terrible
results of famine are here depicted
There is no reference to miscarriages
in the verse, as has generally been supposed and so rendered   nor to rending
their children in pieces, as has been
universally supposed and translated

Abandon them (a). β ' abandon their
children'.   6—C 6 Denunciation
of the idolatry and superstition of the
wicked   In this denunciation not only
the apostates but also the actual
heathen are included.   6 Day of
unceasing bloodshed, i e. the judgement of the sword , see 91¹² (note)
45² (note)   Quoted by Tertullian, *De
Idol* iv ' Et rursus iuro vobis, peccatores, quod in diem sanguinis perditionis poenitentia parata est '.   It will
be observed here that Tertullian's 'in
diem sanguinis perditionis' = εἰς ἡμέραν αἵματος ἀπωλείας = ליום דם לאיד,
where לאיד is corrupt for לעד = ἀδιαλείπτου as in our text   Symmachus so
renders לעד in Job 16⁸ where the
Mass has לעד. Further 'poenitentia'
in Tertullian appears to be corrupt for
'impenitentia = ἀμετανοησία, of which
the word ' sin ' in our text may be a loose
rendering   7. Grave images of
gold and silver and wood (and
stone)... worship . . demons cf

and clay, and those who worship impure spirits and demons, and all kinds of idols not according to knowledge, shall get no manner of help from them.

8. And they shall become godless by reason of the folly of their hearts,
   And their eyes shall be blinded through the fear of their hearts
   And through visions in their dreams

9. Through these they shall become godless and fearful;
   For they shall have wrought all their work in a lie,
   And shall have worshipped a stone
   Therefore in an instant shall they perish.

10. But in those days blessed are all they who accept the words of wisdom, and understand them,
    And observe the paths of the Most High, and walk in the path of His righteousness,
    And become not godless with the godless;
    For they shall be saved.

11. Woe to you who spread evil to your neighbours;
    For you shall be slain in Sheol.

Rev. 9²⁰ I have added 'and stone' in accordance with Tertullian as quoted below   Impure (β, Tertullian 'infamibus') α 'evil'. Corruption is native to the Ethiopic   Demons · cf 16¹ 19¹   Not according to knowledge *gqt* (*,gu*), Tert 'non secundum scientiam'. β 'in idols' temples' The passage in Tertullian, *De Idol* iv, runs 'Qui servitis lapidibus, et qui imagines facitis aureas et argenteas et ligneas et lapideas et fictiles, et servitis phantasmatibus et daemoniis et spiritibus infamibus [MSS give *infamis*] et omnibus erroribus *non secundum scientiam*, nullum ab iis invenietis auxilium', cf Book of Jubilees 1¹¹ 11⁴   8 The victims of such superstition and idolatry will proceed from

bad to worse, cf Book of Wisdom 14¹², ²⁷ Rom 1²¹   Shall become godless cf 93⁸ 99⁹ On the relation of dreams to superstition, cf Sir. 31¹⁻⁷   9 Through these, i e dreams, Sir 40⁶   10 As sudden destruction will befall the idolaters, ver 9, so salvation will be the recompense of those who accept the true wisdom.   Of His righteousness (*a-u*) *u*, β 'of righteousness' 11 Shall be slain: cf 108⁹. This is the extreme penalty of sin a less severe punishment is eternal condemnation to Sheol, but that not attended by the 'slaying' of the soul; cf 22¹³ Sheol here means the eternal place of punishment, see 63¹⁰ (note) 103⁷ 12. Prov 11¹ Amos 8⁶ Hos 12⁷

12. Woe to you who make deceitful and false measures,
    And (to them) who cause bitterness on the earth;
    For they shall thereby be utterly consumed.

13. Woe to you who build your houses through the grievous toil
    of others,
    And all their building materials are the bricks and stones
    of sin;
    I tell you ye shall have no peace.

14. Woe to them who reject the measure and eternal heritage of
    their fathers
    And whose souls follow after idols;
    For they shall have no rest.

15. Woe to them who work unrighteousness and help oppres-
    sion,
    And slay their neighbours until the day of the great judge-
    ment.

16. For He shall cast down your glory,
    And bring affliction on your hearts,
    And shall arouse **His fierce indignation**,
    And destroy you all with the sword,
    And all the holy and righteous shall remember your
    sins.

Measures ($a-mt$, t^1). t, $\beta-i$ 'foundations'   Cause bitterness (mt, β)
gq 'know', $_1g$ 'tempt'   13 Build
. . . through the grievous toil of
others cf. Jer 22¹³, also J Enoch 94⁷
97⁸   14 The measure and eternal
heritage, i e the Mosaic law, cf
ver 2   The apostates as in that verse
are here referred to.   Whose souls
follow after ($_1gm$) $gqtu$ 'and follow
after the souls of'. β 'who cause their
souls to follow after'.   Have no
rest. see 94⁶ (note).   15. To them

($_1gu$, β) $gmqt$ ' to you .   Day of the
great judgement · see 94⁹ 98¹⁰ 45²
(note)   16. His fierce indignation
$_1g\beta$ read 'the spirit of His indignation'
= רוח אפו corrupt for חרון אפו 'His
fierce indignation' $gmqt$ read 'His
indignation and His spirit'('His spirit'
in nom in qt) + 'into your heart' $_1g$
Holy and righteous (g_1gmq) ∞
t, β Remember your sins And accordingly pray for your destruction,
see 97⁵ (note)

*The Sinners destroy each other : Judgement of the fallen Angels :
the Safety of the Righteous : further Woes for the Sinners.*

C. 1. And in those days in one place the fathers together with
their sons shall be smitten.

And brothers one with another shall fall in death

Till the streams flow with their blood.

2. For a man shall not withhold his hand from slaying his sons
and his sons' sons,

And the sinner shall not withhold his hand from his honoured
brother ·

From dawn till sunset they shall slay one another.

3. And the horse shall walk up to the breast in the blood of
sinners,

And the chariot shall be submerged to its height.

4. In those days the angels shall descend into the secret
places

And gather together into one place all those who brought
down sin,

C. 1. The thought in 99⁶ is here expanded Brothers one with another
shall fall (β). α ' brothers one with
another and shall fall '. Suggested by
Ezek 38²¹ ' Every man's sword shall be
against his brother'; Hagg 2²² Cf second line of the next stanza. Streams
flow with their blood : cf Is 34³, ⁷
Ps 58¹⁰   2 His sons' sons
(β). gmt ' his son's son ', ₁gq corrupt.
+ ' in compassion ' t, β   The sinner
(t, β) g₁gmq ' as for the sinner, he '
From his honoured brother It is very
probable that we have here a reference
to the murder of Antigonus by his
brother Aristobulus I Josephus (*Ant*
xiii 11 1, 2) tells us that Aristobulus
specially loved Antigonus, but moved
by calumnies put him to death, and
afterward died of remorse for this

deed On the internecine strife that
was to initiate the kingdom, cf 56⁷
99⁵, ⁶ Zech 14¹³ Ezek. 38²¹ Hagg. 2²²
Mic 7⁶ ' A man's enemies are the men
of his own house' In N T cf. Mt
10²¹, ³⁴, ³⁵ 24¹⁰ Mk 13¹² Luke 21¹⁶
3 Up to the breast This phraseology
reappears later in Talmudic writings ,
ct. Midrash Ech Rabb. ii ' Nor shall
they cease slaying till the horse is submerged in blood to the mouth '. Cf
Jer Taanith 69ᵃ, cf Schürer, i. 695
note , Lightfoot, *Opera*, ii 127; Rev.
14²⁰   To its height (m, β) g₁gq ' to
the day of its (>₁g) height ' (through a
dittograph), t ' for it shall be filled to
its height '.   4 The angels shall
descend   and gather. So in Matt
13³⁰, ⁴¹, ⁴⁹   Brought down sin
(a–t) t, β ' helped sin ' The reference

And the Most High will arise on that day of judgement
To execute great judgement amongst sinners.

5. And over all the righteous and holy He will appoint
   guardians from amongst the holy angels
   To guard them as the apple of an eye,
   Until He makes an end of all wickedness and all sin,
   And though the righteous sleep a long sleep, they have
   nought to fear.

6. And (then) the children of the earth shall see the wise in
   security,

in this verse can only be to the fallen angels who are here described as having 'brought down sin'. These fallen angels were temporarily buried in abysses of the earth, i.e. 'the secret places. See note on 98⁴ **Day of judgement** (a–tu) tu, β 'day **Amongst** ($_{19}gmqu$) q 'and amongst', t, β 'on all the'. **5.** This verse has always been interpreted of the righteous on earth, but wrongly The righteous here spoken of are not the living, but are righteous souls in the place of the departed. This place was afterwards called the chambers or promptuaries, as in 4 Ezra 7⁸⁵ 'videntes aliorum habitacula ab angelis conservari cum silentio magno'; and again in 7⁹⁵ the souls in their promptuaries 'requiescent cum silentio multo ab angelis conservati', cf also 4 Ezra 4³⁷ 7³² 2 Bar 30² All¹⁰ $>_1gu$ The **apple of an eye** cf Deut 32¹⁰ Ps. 17⁸ **He makes an end of all** ($q_1qmu_l²$) q^1tu, β 'all — has been made an end of'. The **righteous sleep a long sleep** The writer of 91–104 did not expect the resurrection at the beginning of the temporary Messianic kingdom The words 'sleep a long sleep' could not be said with reference to this kingdom, for the writer living at the close of the seventh

week expects its advent immediately at the beginning of the eighth week The 'long sleep' extends from his time till the close of the tenth week, when the righteous rise Again, from vv. 4, 5 we see that the righteous do not rise till God has judged sinners and an end is made of all sin Thus the resurrection of the righteous in 91–104 follows the final judgement at the close of the Messianic kingdom. **6 And (then) the children of the earth,** &c. I have here transposed the words 'the children of the earth' from the second line to the first, and with $_1qq$ taken 'the wise' in the acc, and not in the nom as in gmt, β Further. for the phrase 'in security' we find 'ěmûna (in t, β) = πιστόν οι πεποιθότα (cf Prov. 10⁹), 'emani (in g_1gm) corrupt 'ěmûna could mean also τὸ πιστόν, and accordingly all translators in the past have followed the reading of gmt, β, and taken 'the righteous' in the nom Thus they rendered —

'And the wise shall see what is to
   be believed,
   And the children of earth shall
   understand,' &c

But there is no question here as to the wise seeing *in the future* what is to be believed The judgement has

And shall understand all the words of this book,
And recognize that their riches shall not be able to save them
In the overthrow of their sins.

7. Woe to you, sinners, on the day of strong anguish,
Ye who afflict the righteous and burn them with fire:
Ye shall be requited according to your works.

8. Woe to you, ye obstinate of heart,
Who watch in order to devise wickedness:
Therefore shall fear come upon you
And there shall be none to help you.

9. Woe to you, ye sinners, on account of the words of your mouth,
And on account of the deeds of your hands which your godlessness has wrought,
In blazing flames burning worse than fire shall ye burn.

come, and whilst the righteous are secure (100⁵) nothing can save the wicked (100⁷⁻¹¹) Moreover, the lot of the wicked is aggravated by seeing the righteous in security, just as in 4 Ezra 7⁸⁵ (quoted above), while the same thought reappears in Wisdom 4¹⁷ 5¹, ²⁻⁵ Hence the stanza is to be taken as dealing with the children of the earth Next 'ĕmûna is here a rendering of πεποιθότα(s) as in Prov 10⁹, which in turn goes back to בֶּטַח (adv.) = 'in security', but used frequently = ' dwelling in security' as in Gen 34²⁵ Ezek. 30⁹. Children of the earth This title belongs to the Sadducees, sinners, apostates, paganizers, 102³, cf the Hebrew phrase עַם הָאָרֶץ the righteous are designated as the ' children of heaven', 101¹ Shall understand The sinners shall not understand till the judgement has already come upon them The same idea is in Wisdom 5³ ˢᵠᵠ Riches shall not be able to save them cf Zeph 1¹⁸ 7 The righteous underwent such per-

secution under Antiochus Epiphanes; cf 2 Macc 7, if we may trust the latter On the day of strong anguish The MSS have wrongly transposed this phrase into the next clause I have restored it as suggested in my edition of 1893 Ye who The MSS read sôba (= ' when ') corrupt for 'ĕlla (i. e. ሰበ: corrupt for አለ:) The text as it stands is very unsatisfactory ' Woe to you sinners when ye afflict on the day of strong anguish ' The woe is not felt till the judgement-day then they shall be requited according to their works, cf 45⁹ (note) Otherwise they must be taken of the time of the persecution of the righteous Requited according to your works ' cf 95⁵ 8 Obstinate of heart (a) β ' perverse of heart', cf 98¹¹ Watch cf Is 29²⁰ 9. The wicked will suffer in the flames of hell for their godless words and deeds Sinners + ' for ' ₁g, β Which your godlessness has wrought (gmu) t ' because of the work of your godless-

10. And now, know ye that from the angels He will inquire as to your deeds in heaven, from the sun and from the moon and from the stars in reference to your sins because upon the earth ye execute judgement on the righteous.   11. And He will summon to testify against you every cloud and mist and dew and rain; for they shall all be withheld because of you from descending upon you, and they shall be mindful of your sins.   12. And now give presents to the rain that it be not withheld from descending upon you, nor yet the dew, when it has received gold and silver from you that it may descend. 13. When the hoar-frost and snow with their chilliness, and all the snow-storms with all their plagues fall upon you, in those days ye shall not be able to stand before them.

Exhortation to the Fear of God : all Nature fears Him but not the Sinners

CI. 1. Observe the heaven, ye children of heaven, and every work of the Most High, and fear ye Him and work no evil in

ness ', q ' which are the work of your godlessness ', β ' which as a work ye have godlessly committed '.   In blazing flames burning worse than fire shall ye burn. Here $a-_1g$ > ' shall ye burn ', and $_1g$, β > ' burning '. The two texts appear to be complementary   10 All the heavenly powers which have witnessed the sins of the wicked will testify against them, cf. 98^{6-8}, also 97^7 104^8 In Hab 2^{11} this testimony is given by the stones and beams of the dwelling of the wicked In heaven. *g* ' from heaven '. + ' and' $a-u$ Execute judgement on = ποιεῖτε κρίσιν μετά (so *gmqt*, β)—a Hebraism   11 All the natural powers which minister to the fruitfulness of the earth will testify against sinners, as they have been withholden on account of their sins This is exactly in keeping with 80, one of the chapters interpolated in

72-82; cf. Jer 8^3 And they shall be mindful $(a-mt)$. *mt, β* ' and shall they not be mindful ' (*t, β* ' watchful ').   12. Spoken ironically.   That it may descend $(g_1gt, bilofry_1a_1b)$ *mq* ' that it should not descend '. > $u, β-bilopxy_1a_1b$ 13 Even the lesser punishments of the elements are irresistible

CI. 1. The same subject pursued, but the writer turns aside for a moment to address the righteous who are here called ' children of heaven ', as elsewhere sinners are called ' children of earth ', cf 100^6 102^3 The phrase ' children of heaven ' (cf Pirke Aboth, ni 22 בָּנִים לְמָקוֹם) is the equivalent of ' sons of God ' The designation is here limited to the righteous Israelites For the view that the individual Israelite was regarded as a son of God already in the second century B C see Test Lev. 4^2 (note) Wisd. $2^{13, 18}$.   Ye children

His presence. 2 If He closes the windows of heaven, and withholds the rain and the dew from descending on the earth on your account, what will ye do then? 3. And if He sends His anger upon you because of your deeds, ye cannot petition Him; for ye spake proud and insolent words against His righteousness: therefore ye shall have no peace. 4. And see ye not the sailors of the ships, how their ships are tossed to and fro by the waves, and are shaken by the winds, and are in sore trouble? 5. And therefore do they fear because all their goodly possessions go upon the sea with them, and they have evil forebodings of heart that the sea will swallow them and they will perish therein.

6. Are not the entire sea and all its waters, and all its movements, the work of the Most High, and has He not set limits to its doings, and confined it throughout by the sand? 7. And at His reproof it is afraid and dries up, and all its fish die and all that is in it, but ye sinners that are on the earth fear Him not 8. Has He not made the heaven and the earth, and all that is therein? Who has given understanding and wisdom to

---

(a) t^2, β 'all ye children' 2, 3. The writer resumes his address to the wicked and recurs to the subject, cf. 100[11, 12] 2 If (gt, β-enr) [1]gu, e 'for', ωq, n 'when' Windows of heaven · Gen 7[11]. 3. If (g[1]gtn, β). mq 'when' Because of (+ 'all' [1]g) your deeds ([1]gm) t, β 'and upon (+ 'all' β) your deeds' gq 'your deeds' Proud and insolent words 5[4] (note) 27[2] As instances of such insolent speech cf 98[7], 8 102[6] 4-7 They who go down to the sea in ships are filled with fear at the might of the sea how much more should not men fear God by whom the sea has been made and of whom it is sore afraid? 4. And[10] (q, β) > a-q. Sailors of the ships Text = 'kings of the ships' = מַלְכֵי הָאֳנִיּוֹת corrupt, as Halevy pointed out, for

מַלָּחֵי הָא״ = 'sailors of the ships'. For the thought of the verse cf Ps 107[23-27] 6, 7. The sea can do nothing save according to divine command 6 Has He not set limits to its doings (e, though by a slip reading 'aqama for 'aqama) The verb is rightly preserved in y though otherwise corrupt In β-y this verb is changed into hatama = 'has sealed'. gmqt 'its doings and waters', where wamâjâ (= 'its waters') may be corrupt for 'aqama With this passage cf Jer. 5[22] Job 26[10] 38[8-11] Ps. 89[9] 104[9] Prov. 8[29] 7 At His reproof it, dries up From Is 50[2] Is afraid and dries up (a-[1]g, x) β-x 'dries up and is afraid' 8 God has not only made the sea, but also heaven and earth and all that in them is He too has given instinct to animals and

every thing that moves on the earth and in the sea ?   9. Do not
the sailors of the ships fear the sea ?   Yet sinners fear not the
Most High

*Terrors of the Day of Judgement: the adverse Fortunes of the
Righteous on the Earth*

CII. 1. In those days when He hath brought a grievous fire
upon you,
Whither will ye flee, and where will ye find deliverance?
And when He launches forth His word against you,
Will you not be affrighted and fear ?

2   And all the luminaries shall be affrighted with great fear,
And all the earth shall be affrighted and tremble and be
alarmed.

3. And all the †angels shall execute their commands†
And shall seek to hide themselves from the presence of the
Great Glory,
And the children of earth shall tremble and quake ,
And ye sinners shall be accursed for ever,
And ye shall have no peace.

4   Fear ye not, ye souls of the righteous,
And be hopeful ye that have died in righteousness.

reason to man   9. The whole
argument of the chapter summed up
in a few pregnant words   Sailors of
the ships   see note on ver 4

CII. 1-3 If they now refuse to fear
God, the day will come when they will
be terrified before the awful day of the
Lord—a day so terrible that heaven
and earth will be affrighted, and even
the holy angels will seek to hide
themselves from it   What then will
become sinners ?   1 A grievous
fire, i.e. the fire of hell, cf. 99¹¹
His word, i e. word of judgement.
3. The † angels shall execute their
commands †. The text is against the
parallelism and is clearly here corrupt.

It is not good angels that will seek to
hide themselves ‘ Angels ’=מלאכים
corrupt for מלכים = ‘ kings’. We have
then a parallel here to Rev 6¹⁵ But
what is the original text behind ‘ execute their commands’ I cannot see
The Great Glory (a) β ‘ the Great in
glory ’, cf 14²⁰   Children of earth .
cf 100⁶ 101¹ (note)   Have no peace
cf 94⁶ (note)   4—CIV 9 The
discussion and condemnation of the
Sadducean views of the future life.
4, 5. The righteous are bidden to be
of good cheer though their life be such
as only sinners deserved, and their
latter end be full of grief (vv. 4, 5)
4 Ye that have died (*m, efhiklu* ₁a)

5 And grieve not if your soul into Sheol has descended in
       grief,
   And that in your life your body fared not according to
       your goodness,
   But wait for the day of the judgement of sinners
   And for the day of cursing and chastisement.

6. And yet when ye die the sinners speak over you
   " As we die, so die the righteous,
   And what benefit do they reap for their deeds ?

7. Behold, even as we, so do they die in grief and darkness,
   And what have they more than we ?
   From henceforth we are equal.

8. And what will they receive and what will they see for ever ?
   Behold, they too have died,
   And henceforth for ever shall they see no light."

9. I tell you, ye sinners, ye are content to eat and drink, and

---

gq'u ' they who have died ', *abdeox ₁b*
' the day of your death ', *g* ' the souls of
those who have died '. *q* adds ' ye who
have died in righteousness' after ' grieve
not ' in the next line.   5. The
author, given the standpoint of belief
in a blessed future for the righteous,
can readily concede that there is often
no difference in the outward lot of
the righteous and the wicked either
in life or death Such a concession
according to the O T doctrine of
retribution was impossible   If *(g ₁g)*
Other MSS ' that ' or ' because '
Soul + ' into great tribulation and
wailing and sorrow and grief ' *t ₁β*
Sheol see 63¹⁰ (note)   Wait for.
Here I emend 'enka ba (= ' moreover
on ' which is here unmean ng) into
senhû la = ' wait for ' in 108², where this
verb occurs in a like context · ' wait
for those days ', i. e the days of judgement.   Judgement of sinners
Here the text has ' ye became sinners ,

i e kônkemmû hateâna (hateân *g ₁g, u*),
which I have emended into kuenanê
hateân = ' judgement of sinners ' The
next line shows that it is the judgement
day to which this line must refer The
parallelism is thus restored.   Day of
. chastisement   From Hos 5⁹
יום תכחה.   6–8 The sinners—
the Sadducean opponents—start from
the O T. doctrine of retribution which
taught the prosperity of the righteous
in this life, and argue that as there is
no difference in the lot of the righteous
and the wicked in this life—a point
just conceded by the author in ver. 5—
so there is none in an existence beyond
this life, cf Book of Wisdom 2¹⁻⁵
3²⁻⁴ Eccles 2¹⁴⁻¹⁶ 3¹⁰⁻²¹, &c   7
In grief and darkness This refers
to the O T conception of Sheol, 63¹⁰
(note).   8 What will they receive *(mt, β)*   *q ₁gq* ' how will they
rise '.   Behold *(a–₁g)*. *₁g, β* ' for behold '   9, 10. The answer of the

10b and sin, and strip men naked, and acquire wealth and see good days   10 Have ye seen the righteous how their end falls out, that no manner of violence is found in them till their death?   11. "Nevertheless they perished and became as though they had not been, and their spirits descended into Sheol in tribulation"

Different Destinies of the Righteous and the Sinners: fresh Objections of the Sinners.

CIII. 1. Now, therefore, I swear to you, the righteous, by the glory of the Great and Honoured and Mighty One in dominion, and by His greatness I swear to you

2. I know a mystery
And have read the heavenly tablets,
And have seen the holy books,
And have found written therein and inscribed regarding them:

author. The life of the wicked is fashioned by material and temporal aims only, and so all their desires find satisfaction in this world, but the life of the righteous, as is manifest from first to last, is moulded by spiritual and eternal aims   9 See good days. So LXX of Ps 34^12, which implies a slightly different reading   10 How their end falls out (a). β 'how their end is peace'. Again, as in ver 5, the author concedes that there is no outward distinction between the righteous and the wicked in this life, but that there is a religious and ethical distinction   Death (a–19). 19, β 'day of their death'.   11 The wicked rejoin this difference in character is of no advantage—the same lot awaits good and bad alike.   Spirits (a–19). 19, β 'souls'.

CIII 1–4 The author, instead of replying directly to the wicked, turns to the righteous, and solemnly assures them that every good thing is in store for them; for so he has read in the heavenly tablets and in the holy books. Hence they were not to regard the contumely of the wicked   1 The oath is more solemn here than in 98^{1, 4, 6} 99^6 104^1   By the glory . . domin-ion (g and practically 19) niq! 'by His great glory ('by the glory of the Great One' qt) and by His honoured kingdom'. β–y 'by His great glory and honour and by His honoured kingdom'   2. The writer bases his knowledge on the heavenly tablets which he has read A mystery (a–t). t, β 'this mystery' Read the heavenly tablets (gqu) m', β 'read in the heavenly tablets'. The holy books (gq') 19m, β 'books of the holy ones', ie of the angels, cf. 108^7. See 47^3 (note) Dillmann comparing 108^3 takes the holy ones here to mean the saints or righteous.   3, 4 The blessings here depicted will be enjoyed by the righteous, both in Sheol and in the spiritual theocracy established after the final judgement The words here are vague and might apply

3. That all goodness and joy and glory are prepared for them,
And written down for the spirits of those who have died
in righteousness,

And that manifold good shall be given to you in recompense
for your labours,

And that your lot is abundantly beyond the lot of the living.

4. And the spirits of you who have died in righteousness shall
live and rejoice,

And their spirits shall not perish, nor their memorial from
before the face of the Great One

Unto all the generations of the world wherefore no longer
fear their contumely.

5. Woe to you, ye sinners, when ye have died,
If ye die in the wealth of your sins,
And those who are like you say regarding you.

"Blessed are the sinners. they have seen all their days.

6. And now they have died in prosperity and in wealth,
And have not seen tribulation or murder in their life,
And they have died in honour,
And judgement has not been executed on them during
their life."

7. Know ye, that their souls will be made to descend into Sheol
And they shall be wretched in their great tribulation.

to either There is apparently only a resurrection of the spirit. **3 For them** ($_1g$, β) $> a-_1g$ The spirits of those who (mt, β) gq 'your spirits which' **Manifold good** ($_1gmq$) gt 'things manifold and good', β 'with manifold good' **4. Spirits of you** (g_1gq, β) mt 'spirits of them' **Who have died** (2nd sing $_1g$, $t^2\beta$) $a-_1g$ 'who have died' (3rd sing) **Rejoice** + 'and be glad' (g_1g_1n, β) **And their spirits shall not perish, nor** (a) β 'their spirits and' **5-8.** A different fate awaits the wicked. These have enjoyed all the blessings which according to the O T. belonged to the righteous

Hence they vaunt themselves on their prosperity and immunity from punishment, but a sure doom awaits them in Sheol—darkness and chains and a burning flame **5. When ye have died** ($a-u$) $> \beta$. **The wealth of** ($a-q$) $> q, \beta$ The phrase 'wealth of wickedness' הון הרשע is found in the Zadokite Fragment 8^{12} **7 Sheol :** see 63^{10} (note) Sheol here is the final place of punishment. Our text here appears to be dependent on and to be a development of Jub 7^{29} :

'For unto Sheol shall they go
And into the place of condemnation
shall they descend'

8. And into darkness and chains and a burning flame where there is grievous judgement shall your spirits enter,

And the great judgement shall be for all the generations of the world.

Woe to you, for ye shall have no peace.

9 Say not in regard to the righteous and good who are in life

"In our troubled days we have toiled laboriously and experienced every trouble,

And met with much evil and been consumed,

And have become few and our spirit small.

In Jubilees Sheol is not yet associated with fire and burning, but this stage is reached in our text. It has assumed thus one of the characteristics of Gehenna, and become a place of flaming fire. See ver. 8ᵃ. Cf. the different significations it has in 102⁵, ¹¹   **8 Of the world** (a). β 'unto eternity' **Have no peace** see 5⁴ (note) 94⁶ (note). **9–15** These verses are in the mouth of the wicked an ironical description of the lot of the righteous For the time being they speak in the person of the righteous From this verse to the end of this chapter ₁g stands alone frequently, exhibiting nearly sixty variations, but these are mainly between the 1st and 3rd plurals in the verbs and the corresponding suffixes, verbal and substantival   ₁g favours throughout the 3rd pl, whereas g in the main agrees with the rest of the MSS in giving the 1st plural. The question arises on which person, the 1st or 3rd, are we to decide. The evidence of the MSS goes to prove that the *1st person was the original* For, whereas ₁g gives the 3rd person in all, except seven instances, confined to vv 14 and 15, all other MSS., with few exceptions, give the 1st person The exclusive use of the 3rd person would make the sense of the text clearer   But the evidence of the MSS is irresistible   The wicked assume the

rôle of the righteous and speak in their person   103⁹⁻¹⁵ are pronounced derisively by the sinners of the righteous For in 102⁶⁻⁸, when the sinners declare that the righteous live in trouble and darkness and have no advantage over the wicked beyond the grave, the author (102¹⁰) in reply points to the nature of their death and the purity of their life To this the sinners rejoin (102¹¹), 'despite all that they go down to Sheol in woe as we' The author now addresses himself first to the righteous (103¹⁻⁴) and then to the sinners In the case of the latter he gives their glorification of their own life (103⁵⁻⁶) and their depreciation of the life of the righteous (103⁹⁻¹⁵). In these verses the wicked describe the wretchedness and helplessness of the present life of the righteous, just as in 102⁶,⁷ they had described the wretchedness of the future of the righteous. At the close of these words the author addresses his reply (104¹⁻⁸) not directly to the sinners who have just spoken but to the righteous, just as in the opening of 103, and returns to the sinners in vv 7–9   **9. Our troubled days** (tⁿβ). *gqtˡu* 'their troubled days', ₁g 'the days of their life with their troublous toil' **We have toiled** ₁g 'they have toiled', and so on in the 3rd person except in vv 14–15   I will not record these variations so far as they

10. And we have been destroyed and have not found any to
   help us even with a word:
   We have been tortured [and destroyed], and not hoped to
   see life from day to day

11. We hoped to be the head and have become the tail:
   We have toiled laboriously and had no satisfaction in our
   toil,
   And we have become the food of the sinners and the
   unrighteous,
   And they have laid their yoke heavily upon us.

12. They have had dominion over us that hated us †and smote us;
   And to those that hated us † we have bowed our necks
   But they pitied us not

13. We desired to get away from them that we might escape
   and be at rest,
   But found no place whereunto we should flee and be safe
   from them.

14. And we complained to the rulers in our tribulation,
   And cried out against those who devoured us,
   But they did not attend to our cries
   And would not hearken to our voice.

---

consist only in a change of the person
of the verb or suffix **Been consumed**
₁g 'they have suffered from disease
Become few Cf Deut 28⁶²Ps 107³⁹
Our spirit small. Not 'humble' but
'poor spirited' (μικρόψυχος) **10**
Cf Deut 28²⁹, ⁶⁸, ⁶⁷. **We . have
not found any to help us even
with a word** (a-₁gt) So ₁g but with
a change of persons t, β there has
been none to help us in word or deed
we are powerless and have found
nothing' **11 We hoped** (a)
β 'and we hoped' **To be the
head**, &c From Deut 28¹⁸ **Laid
their yoke upon us.** From
Deut 28⁴⁸ **12 They have had**

(a–t, *deloy* ₁a₁b) t, β–*deloy* ₁a₁b 'and
they have had' **They have had
dominion** that hated us For
diction cf. Esther 9¹. **To those that
hated us** I think that this is a dittograph from the preceding line, and that
the clause which should be here has
been transposed into that line. Hence
I suggest that we should read:
  'They have had dominion over us
    that hated us,
  And to those that smote us we have
    bowed our necks,
  But they pitied us not'
13 We desired (a–₁g). ₁g,β prefix 'and'.
14. Cried out. + 'and made lamentation' g ₁g inserts this clause before

15. And they helped those who robbed us and devoured us and those who made us few; and they concealed their oppression, and they did not remove from us the yoke of those that devoured us and dispersed us and murdered us, and they concealed their murder, and remembered not that they had lifted up their hands against us."

Assurances given to the Righteous: Admonitions to Sinners and the Falsifiers of the Words of Uprightness.

CIV. 1. I swear unto you, that in heaven the angels

'in our tribulation' 14,15 These verses furnish materials towards determining the date of 91-104. In 83-90 the rulers are regarded as the divinely appointed leaders of the righteous. In this section, on the other hand, the rulers appear as the aiders and abettors of the enemies of the righteous These enemies are the Sadducees, sinners, apostates, and paganizers, while the righteous are the Pharisaic party The issues between these parties as they appear in this book could not have been so clearly defined before the Maccabean times. Nor again could this book have been written before the breach between John Hyrcanus and the Pharisees. But the date must be brought down still further, if we are to explain literally such statements as 'dispersed us and murdered us', and 'their murder', where the murder of the righteous is meant, for there was no blood spilt between the parties till the reign of Jannaeus, 94 B.C The later limit is not hard to determine The close confederacy which here prevails between the Sadducees and the rulers did not exist under the Herodian princes, but only under the later Maccabean princes Hence this section was written before 64 B C, and may be assigned either to the years 94-79 B C. or 70-64 B C, during which periods the

Pharisees were oppressed by the rulers and Sadducees. But the rest of the section is against taking the words 'murder', &c literally We should probably regard them merely as the description of a severe but not murderous persecution, see Special Introd (pp. 221, 222) 15 They helped (g, β) *gmt* 'you have helped', *q* 'thou hast helped' The yoke of those that (g_1gmt,fo_1b). *qt*, β-fo_1b 'them yoke but' Dispersed us and murdered us These words taken literally would apply well to the actual destruction and dispersion of the Pharisaic families under Jannaeus.

CIV 1-6 Instead of answering directly the wicked who have thus derisively described the lot of the righteous in this life, the author turns to the righteous and addresses them This is exactly what he did in the opening of 103 He returns to the sinners in 104⁷⁻⁹ In these verses the author practically concedes that the wicked have rightly described the lot of the righteous in this life; but he holds out a sure hope, a hope however not to be fulfilled in the transitory Messianic kingdom on earth, but to be directed to the blessed future that is awaiting them in heaven the angels are mindful of them for good even now, and in due time they will become 'companions of' the hosts of heaven'. 1. Unto you. + 'ye righteous' $t^2\beta$ The angels

remember you for good before the glory of the Great One.
and your names are written before the glory of the Great One.
2 Be hopeful, for aforetime ye were put to shame through ill
and affliction, but now ye shall shine as the lights of heaven,
ye shall shine and ye shall be seen, and the portals of heaven
shall be opened to you   3. And in your cry, cry for judgement, and it shall appear to you; for all your tribulation shall
be visited on the rulers, and on all who helped those who
plundered you   4. Be hopeful, and cast not away your
hope, for ye shall have great joy as the angels of heaven.
5. What shall ye be obliged to do ? Ye shall not have to hide
on the day of the great judgement and ye shall not be found
as sinners, and the eternal judgement shall be far from you for
all the generations of the world.   6. And now fear not, ye
righteous, when ye see the sinners growing strong and prospering in their ways be not companions with them, but keep afar

remember you Though apparently
forgotten on earth, the righteous are not
forgotten before God by the angels. On
the intercession of the angels cf. 15²
(note) 40⁵⁻⁷ 47² 89⁷⁶. And (a, z)
>β-et Names are written see 47³
(note). **The Great One** cf. 14²
103⁴   **2 Now** This word (=
עַתָּה) is used here not of the immediate
present but of the impending future
Shine as the lights: cf. Dan. 12³
4 Ezra 7⁹⁷, ¹²⁵.   Ye shall shine ²º
(a) > β **Portals of heaven shall
be opened to you,** 1 e heaven will become their dwelling-place, for they will
'shine as the lights of heaven', have
'joy as the angels', and be 'companions
of the hosts of heaven'. The author does
not hope for a new earth; cf 91¹⁰ (note)
3. Their demand for justice which they
make in vain on earth, 103¹⁴, ¹⁵ will one
day be satisfied wherefore let them
continue to make it; cf. 97³, ⁵ (note)
99⁸, ¹⁶ **The rulers** These are brought
forward very prominently here, cf
103¹⁴, ¹⁵ (note)   **4. As the angels**

of heaven of Matt 22⁸⁰ Mark 12²⁵;
also 1 En 104⁶.   **5 What shall
ye** . . **do** (a-t, e) t, β-e 'as for what ye
shall . . . do'   **Day of the great
judgement** cf 19¹ 84⁴ 94⁹ 98¹⁰ 99¹⁵.
The eternal judgement· cf 91¹⁵
'great eternal judgement' also 45²
(note) There appears to be no judgement for the righteous according to this
verse Contrast the teaching of 37–70
see 62³   **6 Prospering in their
ways** gigniqt. β 'prospering in their
lusts' Cf Jer 12¹ The Pharisaic
exclusiveness is clearly defined here,
cf 91⁸, ⁴ Observe˙ that the righteous
are not bidden to hope for blessedness
on earth through the overthrow of the
sinners No doubt the sinners will be
cut off in the period of the Sword, but
the author sets little store by the
temporary Messianic kingdom thereby
established on earth. The hopes of the
righteous can be realized in heaven alone
Be not companions, &c cf 104², ⁶.
The righteous will be companions of
the heavenly hosts, 104⁶, and rejoice as

from their violence; for ye shall become companions of the hosts of heaven.   7. And, although ye sinners say . "All our sins shall not be searched out and written down," nevertheless they shall write down all your sins every day.   8. And now I show unto you that light and darkness, day and night, see all your sins.   9 Be not godless in your hearts, and lie not and alter not the words of uprightness, nor charge with lying the words of the Holy Great One, nor take account of your idols; for all your lying and all your godlessness issue not in righteousness but in great sin.   10. And now I know this mystery, that sinners will alter and pervert the words of righteousness in many ways, and will speak wicked words, and lie, and practise great deceits, and write books concerning their words.   11 But when they write down truthfully all my

the angels in heaven, 104⁴ The idea is further developed in 2 Bar , the righteous will be transformed into the glory of the angels, 51⁹, and be made like unto them, 51¹⁰, and their surpassing splendour will exceed that of the angels, 51¹². This, too, is the teaching of the Talmud.   Be not (a) β 'and be not' Hosts So β reading harâ. Of Luke 2¹³ Rev. 19¹⁴. *ymqt* read ḫerâna = τῶν ἀγαθῶν, which Flemming takes to be a corruption of τῶν ἀγγέλων This is possible.   7–8 After showing the blessed destiny of the righteous in the future life, he turns finally to the wicked, and declares that, though they prosper and are strong, and for that reason conceive that no account is taken of their sin, nevertheless all their sins are recorded, and recorded daily 7. All our sins shall not be searched out Here I read jĕthaŝaŝ with *n* So Beer emended in 1900 without a knowledge of *n* Other MSS. read ' ye shall not search out (tĕḥĕŝĕŝû) all our sins' —which is clearly corrupt *t, β* give ' all our sins ' in the nom. *g₁gmq* in the acc. **Written down** (*t,β*) *g* 'they shall write', *mu* ' ye shall write ', *gq*

' he shall write '   8 Even the natural powers will give witness against them , cf 100¹⁰ (note)   9–13 From a reproof of the life and the attitude of the wicked towards the O T revelation, the author passes on to certain disclosures and directions regarding his own book 9. The wicked are admonished not to alter or misinterpret the O T ; cf 94⁶ 98¹⁴ 99²   **Holy Great One** see 1⁸ (note) **Take account of** (*q₁gq*) *mt, β* ' praise' **Your idols** cf 99⁷⁻⁹, ¹⁴ 10 A time will come when the words of revelation will be perverted, and books be written enforcing wicked and heathen doctrine **Sinners** **pervert** in many ways (*g₁gmt*) *q, β* ' many sinners **pervert' Books** (*t, β*) *g₁gmq* ' my books   11. But the writings of Enoch will counteract these heathen teachings, and these writings will be handed down from generation to generation and through various languages, and in the course of transmission be exposed to voluntary and involuntary perversions and changes The author speaks here from the standpoint of Enoch. **My words** (*tu, β*) *g₁gmq* ' words ' **In their** words in their languages, and do not change or minish ought from my words but write them all down truthfully—all that I first testified concerning them, 12. Then, I know another mystery, that books shall be given to the righteous and the wise to become a cause of joy and uprightness and much wisdom. 13. And to them shall the books be given, and they shall believe in them and rejoice over them, and then shall all the righteous who have learnt therefrom all the paths of uprightness be recompensed.'

God and the Messiah to dwell with Man.

CV. 1. In those days the Lord bade (them) to summon and testify to the children of earth concerning their wisdom · Show (it) unto them , for ye are their guides, and a recompense over the whole earth. 2. For I and My Son will be united with

languages. The O T. was already translated into Greek. It is probable that Aramaic and Greek are the languages here referred to 12 At last in the course of transmission these books will reach the generation for whom they were designed—a 'righteous' and 'wise' generation, and this generation will be the first to understand their worth. For this idea cf Dan. 12⁴, ⁹, ¹⁰. 13 The righteous and the wise will recognize and believe in these books , cf Dan. 12¹⁰ 'None of the wicked shall understand, but the wise shall understand' Recompensed The gift of these books with their revelations and wisdom seems to be the recompense of the righteous This is certainly the view of the writer of 105¹, cf 93¹⁰ 100⁶ 104¹², ¹³ Or is it meant that soon after their reception the Messianic kingdom will appear?

CV This chapter does not seem to belong to 91-104 For (1) the phrase 'children of earth', which in 91-104

is a synonym for the sinners or heathen, has here a good ethical signification · see 100⁶ (note) 101¹ (note). (2) The Messiah is introduced in 105², to whom there is not the faintest allusion throughout 91-104 (3) The finite duration of the lives of the saints seems to be implied in 105². This is the doctrine in 1-36, but not in 91-104 (4) The emphasis is laid in 105 on the finite life on earth : in 91-104 on the immortal life in heaven This chapter, like 56⁵-57³ ⁸, is a literary revival of O.T. thoughts and ideals 1 In those (a-m). m, β 'and in those' And testify. > m. Children of earth This phrase has a good signification here, for the books of Enoch, which only 'the righteous and the wise' will receive, are the guides of those designated 'children of earth' Contrast with this the technical meaning of this phrase in 100⁶ 102⁸. Recompense . cf. 104¹⁵. 2 I and My Son There is no difficulty about the phrase 'My Son' as applied

them for ever in the paths of uprightness in their lives;
and ye shall have peace   rejoice, ye children of uprightness.
Amen.

to the Messiah by the Jews; cf 4 Ezra
7²⁸, ²⁹ 14⁹   If the righteous are called
' God's children' in 62¹¹, the Messiah
was pre-eminently the Son of God
Moreover, the early Messianic interpretation of Ps. 2 would naturally lead
to such an expression   In 62¹⁴ above

we have practically the same thought
expressed; cf John 14²³   In their
lives   see introduction to this chapter
Ye shall have peace   This was the
special blessing of the righteous, as its
loss was the curse entailed on the
wicked, cf. 94⁶ (note).

FRAGMENT OF THE BOOK OF NOAH

LATIN FRAGMENT

CVI. 1. And after some days my son Methuselah took a wife for his son Lamech, and she became pregnant by him and bore a son.   2. And his body was white as snow and red as the blooming of a rose, and the hair of his head † and his long locks were white as wool, and his eyes beautiful |. And when he opened his eyes, he lighted up the whole house like the sun, and the whole house was very bright.   3. And thereupon he arose in the hands of the midwife, opened his mouth, and †conversed with† the Lord of

CVI 1. Factum est autem [cum esset Lamech annorum tricentorum quinquagenta] natus est ei filiu(s)

2. Cui oculi sunt sicut radii solis capilli autem eius candi-⟨di⟩ores in septies niue, corpori autem eius nemo hominum potest intueri

3. et surexit inter manus obstetricis suae et adorauit dominum uiuentem in secula [laudauit].

CVI-CVII We have here again a fragment of a Noah Apocalypse Part of this section has been preserved in a Latin version which I print side by side with the translation of the Ethiopic. 2 †And his long locks beautiful† It is rather astonishing that the new-born infant should have 'long locks'. Since there is no mention of these in the Latin, and since it is possible that děmděmâhû . šanâj 'a'ějentîhû (= 'his long locks . and (> *99*) his eyes beautiful') is corrupt for 'egarîhû ladahâj 'a'ějentîhû If this is right we should have ' was white . . and his eyes were like the rays of the

sun' This restoration is supported by the Ethiopic version in ver 5 'his eyes are as the rays of the sun' also 'septies' (ver 10) or 'in septies' (ver 2, seems corrupt for 'capitis', which depends on 'capilli'. See ver 10 (note) 3 And thereupon (.. Other MSS 'and when' Opened his mouth This phrase recurs in ver 11 The Latin is defective here †Conversed with† Here tanagara = 'conversed with' is corrupt for tagûnaja = προσεκύνησε or ἐξωμολογήσατο Hence render ' praised'. Cf 'laudavit' in the Latin But adoravit' occurs there also and=προσεκύνησε In ver 11, where the substance of ver 3

righteousness.   4. And his
father Lamech was afraid of
him and fled, and came to his
father Methuselah.   5. And
he said unto him : 'I have
begotten a strange son, diverse
from and unlike man, and
resembling the sons of the
God of heaven , and his nature
is different and he is not
like us, and his eyes are as
the rays of the sun, and his
countenance is glorious.   6.
And it seems to me that he is
not sprung from me but from
the angels, and I fear that in
his days a wonder may be
wrought on the earth.   7. And
now, my father, I am here to
petition thee and implore thee
that thou mayest go to Enoch,
our father, and learn from him
the truth, for his dwelling-
place is amongst the angels.'
8. And when Methuselah heard
the words of his son, he came
to me to the ends of the earth ;
for he had heard that I was

et timuit Lamech.   6. ne non
ex eo natus esset nisi nontius
dei.   4, 5. et uenit ad patrem
suum Mathusalem et narrauit
illi omnia.

7. dixit Mathusalem : Ego
autem non possum scire nisi
eamus ad patrem nostrum Enoc

8. quum autem uidit Enoc
filium suum Mathusalem ue-
nientem ad se [et] ait.   quid est
quod uenisti ad me nate ?

---

recurs, the Ethiopic = εὐλόγησε and the
Latin ' oravit '—evidently a corruption
for ' adoravit ' Thus the Ethiopic =
ἐξωμολογήσατο (οι προσεκύνησε) (ver. 3)
and εὐλόγησε (ver 11) and the Latin
εὐλόγησε (ver 3) and προσεκύνησε (vv.
3, 11). From this it is clear that the
Latin and the Ethiopic presuppose
different words in the Greek version

before them   Lord of Righteousness cf. 22¹⁴ 90⁴⁰   5 And²⁰ (g₁g).
> Other MSS   Sons of the God of
heaven cf. 69⁴,⁵, also 71¹ (note)   6
But from the angels The Latin gives
a somewhat different idea ' Nuntius '
=ἄγγελος.   7 Latin corrupt Observe ' eamus '   Amongst the angels,
i e. at the ends of the earth, as in 65²

there, and he cried aloud, and I heard his voice and I came to him. And I said unto him · ' Behold, here am I, my son, wherefore hast thou come to me ? ' 9. And he answered and said ' Because of a great cause of anxiety have I come to thee, and because of a disturbing vision have I approached. 10. And now, my father, hear me : unto Lamech my son there hath been born a son, the like of whom there is none, and his nature is not like man's nature, and the colour of his body is whiter than snow and redder than the bloom of a rose, and the hair of his head is whiter than white wool, and his eyes are like the rays of the sun, and he opened his eyes and thereupon lighted up the whole house. 11. And he arose in the hands of the midwife, and opened his mouth and blessed the Lord of heaven. 12. And his father Lamech became afraid

9 D₁xit

10. quod natus est filio suo [nomine] Lamech cui oculi sunt sicut radi solis capilli[s] eius candidiores septies niue, corpori autem eius nemo hominum potest intueri,

11 et surexit inter manus obstetricis suae eadem hora qua procidit de utero matris suae. orauit dominum uiuentem in secula et laudauit.

66³   8 Wherefore So Latin 'quid est quod = διὰ τί. But the Ethiopic = διότι, a corruption of the former.   9 Cause of anxiety (g₁gmt) β 'matter'.   10 And now + 'hear me ' ₁gm.   Colour of his body (₁g). Other MSS 'his colour' But the presence of 'corpori' in the Latin and of σώματα in the follow-

ing quotation appear to support ₁g The colour   rose Borrowed by Apoc. Petri τὰ μὲν γὰρ σώματα αὐτῶν ἦν λευκότερα πάσης χιόνος καὶ ἐρυθρότερα παντὸς ῥόδου Eyes   sun · cf Apoc. Petri : ἀπὸ τῆς ὄψεως αὐτῶν ἀκτὶν ὡς ἡλίου.   11. Lord of heaven Here only in Enoch. But compare the Latin ' dominum viventem in secula ,

and fled to me, and did not
believe that he was sprung
from him, but that he was in
the likeness of the angels of
heaven ; and behold I have
come to thee that thou mayest
make known to me the truth.'
13. And I, Enoch, answered
and said unto him : 'The Lord
will do a new thing on the
earth, and this I have already
seen in a vision, and make
known to thee that in the
generation of my father Jared
some of the angels of heaven
transgressed the word of the
Lord.   14. And behold they
commit sin and transgress the
law, and have united themselves with women and commit
sin with them, and have married
some of them, and have begot
children by them.   17. And
they shall produce on the earth
giants not according to the
spirit, but according to the
flesh, and there shall be a great
punishment on the earth, and
the earth shall be cleansed from
all impurity.   15. Yea, there

12. et timuit Lamech.

13. et dixit Enoc. nontia-
tum *est* mihi fili q*uia* post quin-
gentos annos

15. mitt*et* de*us* cataclismu*m*

and 5¹.   13 Do a new thing
For this phrase cf Num 16³⁰ Is 43¹⁹.
In the generation of   Jared .
cf 6⁶ Some of the angels Here
I emend 'ŏmmal'ĕlta (= 'some from
the heights') of *u*, β-*ehkn* into
emmalâ'ĕkta = 'some of the angels'

n reads 'angels'. I question whether
the rendering 'some from the heights'
is possible.   14 The law, i e the
law appointed to them as spiritual
beings, cf. 15.   17. I have restored
this verse to its original place And
(*qt*, ') > *m*, β-*w* *g*₁*g* are here defective

shall come a great destruction over the whole earth, and there shall be a deluge and a great destruction for one year 16. And this son who has been born unto you shall be left on the earth, and his three children shall be saved with him : when all mankind that are on the earth shall die [he and his sons shall be saved]. 18. And now make known to thy son Lamech that he who has been born is in truth his son, and call his name Noah, for he shall be left to you, and he and his sons shall be saved from the destruction, which shall come upon the earth on account of all the sin and all the unrighteousness, which shall be consummated on the earth in his days. 19 And after that there shall be still more unrighteousness than that which was first consummated on the earth ; for I know the mysteries of the holy ones, for He, the Lord, has showed me and informed me, and I have read (them) in the heavenly tablets

aq*uae* ut deleat omnem creatu-ra*m* [XL.] ostendit oculis n*ostr*is.

16. et erunt illi ·111· filii [et erunt nomina filioru*m* ei*us* · Sem · Cham · Iafeth]

18. et ipse uocabitu*r* Noe q*u*i i*n*te*r*pre*t*atur requies qu*i*a requiem prestabit in archam.

owing to an hint Gen 7[11] and 8[14] > Other MSS shall be saved] > *g*₁*yq* A repetition of the clause in ver 18 Unrighteousness, which shall (*mt*, β)

15 One year · of 16 And [10] (*g*₁*gq*) [He and his sons 18

*g*₁*gq* read ' unrighteousness of apostasy (which) shall '. 19. The mysteries of the holy ones Either the secrets known to the angels, or the secrets relating to the righteous in the future Heavenly tablets , see 47[3] (note).

CVII. 1. And I saw written on them that generation upon generation shall transgress, till a generation of righteousness arises, and transgression is destroyed and sin passes away from the earth, and all manner of good comes upon it.   2. And now, my son, go and make known to thy son Lamech that this son, which has been born, is in truth his son, and that (this) is no lie.'   3. And when Methuselah had heard the words of his father Enoch—for he had shown to him everything in secret—he returned and showed (them) to him and called the name of that son Noah, for he will comfort the earth after all the destruction.

CVIII. 1. Another book which Enoch wrote for his son Methuselah and for those who will come after him, and keep the law in the last days   2. Ye who have done good shall wait for those days till an end is made of those who work evil, and an end of the might of the transgressors.   3. And wait ye indeed till sin has passed away, for their names shall be blotted out of the book of life and out of the holy books,

CVII 1 The fresh growth of sin after the Deluge: its destruction and the advent of the Messianic kingdom Till (*t, β*) g_1gmq 'that'.   3 The derivation of Noah given in Gen 5²⁹ is here repeated Everything in secret (*a*). *β* 'every secret thing' Returned and showed. So *g* save that it omits two letters by hmt *t, abcdloxy₁b* 'returned after having seen'. $>_1gqu$.

CVIII This final chapter forms an independent addition Its writer was acquainted with sections 1-36 and 91-104, or at all events with parts of them. But his acquaintance with 1-36 is very inaccurate In vv 3-6 what was originally the place of punishment for the disobedient stars in chapters 18 and 21 becomes in his hands practically Gehenna. The writer is Essene in tone Observe the high honour paid to asceticism, the scorn of

gold and silver in vv 8-10, the blessed immortality of the spirit, but apparently not of the body, as well as the dualism of light and darkness so prominent in vv 11-14 108 is more nearly akin to 91-104 than any other section in the book. The object of this chapter is to encourage the righteous still to hope on despite the long delay of the advent of the kingdom 1 Keep the law, as opposed to 'fall away from the law', 99²   2 The faithful are exhorted to further patience Good (g_1g) > Other MSS Shall wait (g_1gmq) *t, β* 'and are waiting' 3 And¹⁰ (*a*) > *β* Blotted out of the book of life from Ps 69²⁸. cf 47³ (note) Out of the book of life and (g_1g) *q, r* 'out of the books of the living', *mt* 'out of the book and' Holy books ⟨*mqt, e₁b*, cf 108²) *g* 'book of the Holy One', *β-ex₁b* 'books of the holy ones'

and their seed shall be destroyed for ever, and their spirits
shall be slain, and they shall cry and make lamentation in
a place that is a chaotic wilderness, and in the fire shall they
burn . for there is no earth there   4 And I saw there something like an invisible cloud ; for by reason of its depth I could
not †look over†, and I saw a flame of fire blazing brightly, and
things like shining mountains circling and sweeping to and fro.
5. And I asked one of the holy angels who was with me and
said unto him . ' What is this shining thing ? for it is not
a heaven but only the flame of a blazing fire, and the voice of
weeping and crying and lamentation and strong pain.'   6.
And he said unto me · ' This place which thou seest—here are
cast the spirits of sinners and blasphemers, and of those who
work wickedness, and of those who pervert every thing that the
Lord hath spoken through the mouth of the prophets—(even)
the things that shall be.   7. For some of them are written
and inscribed above in the heaven, in order that the angels may

These contain the roll of the members of the kingdom , cf 103², ³
Spirits shall be slain   cf 22¹⁸ 99¹¹
(note) Though the extreme penalty
of sin, it does not imply annihilation,
for the victims of it ' cry and make
lamentation '   **In a place**, &c. This
chaotic flaming hell beyond the limits
of the earth is the place of punishment of the angels in 18¹²⁻¹⁶ 21¹⁻⁷
Chaotic Eth. = ἀόρατος, which is the
LXX rendering of תהו in Gen 1²
The rendering of בהו (Gen 1²) is found
twice in 21¹, ², i e ἀκατασκεύαστος.
In the fire shall they burn = ba'ĕsât
jĕnaddû. So I emend ba'ĕsât naddû
(g_1gmqt, β-abcx) = ' in the fire they have
burnt '   abc emend into ba'ĕsât jĕna-
dĕdû ' in fire they shall burn ' But
21⁵ ba'ĕsât . . jĕnaddû supports my
emendation.   4 This hell and its
inhabitants further described, in terms
borrowed from 18¹³ 21⁸   †**Look over**†.
We might emend lâ'ĕla (= ' over') into

lĕ'ĕlnâhû and render 'behold its height'
or emend both words into behîl ḥasĕrô
'tell its circuit' (or ' size ') But the
text is uncertain.   **Of fire** (g_1gu)
Other MSS. ' of its fire '.   **5 One
of the holy angels**, &c This phrase
is borrowed from 1-36 , cf 27². **Voice**,
&c cf 18¹³   **Weeping and crying**
(a). ∞ β.   **6** This hell which is
outside the earth is the final place of
punishment of sinners and blasphemers
and perverters of God's revelation and
action through the prophets In verses
3-6 the writer of this chapter has confounded places, i e Gehenna and the
hell of the disobedient stars, that are
most carefully distinguished in 1-36,
and yet borrowed the phraseology of
that section   **Blasphemers** . cf 91⁷.
Spoken (mtu, β). g_1yq ' done '.   **The
prophets** Here only mentioned ex-
pressly in Enoch   **7 Written
and inscribed.** This refers to the
heavenly tablet , cf. 47⁸. These records

read them and know that which shall befall the sinners, and the spirits of the humble, and of those who have afflicted their bodies, and been recompensed by God; and of those who have been put to shame by wicked men: 8. Who love God and loved neither gold nor silver nor any of the good things which are in the world, but gave over their bodies to torture. 9. Who, since they came into being, longed not after earthly food, but regarded everything as a passing breath, and lived accordingly, and the Lord tried them much, and their spirits were found pure so that they should bless His name. 10. And all the blessings destined for them I have recounted in the books. And He hath assigned them their recompense, because they have been found to be such as loved heaven more than their life in the world, and though they were trodden under foot of wicked men, and experienced abuse and reviling from them and were put to shame, yet they blessed Me. 11. And now I will summon the spirits of the good who belong to the generation of light, and

are also called the book of the holy ones, for their purpose is to acquaint the angels with the future; cf 108² See also Asc Is 7²⁷ 7-9 The humble. These are the עֲנָיִים and עֲנָוִים so often referred to in the Psalms They constitute the true Israel as opposed to the proud, the selfish, and the paganizers; see Cheyne on Ps. 9¹³ Those who have afflicted their bodies, loved neither gold nor silver, longed not after earthly food These phrases would apply well to the Essene party, cf 48⁷ 102⁵ These characteristics of the righteous have their counterpart in those of the wicked, cf. 96⁶⁻⁷ 97⁸⁻¹⁰ 98² 7 Read (*mt*, β) *giggu* 'place' 8 Loved (α, β-*cdnoyₗb*) ₁g, *cdnoyₗb* 'love' 9 Who (₁gg reading 'ĕlla') Of this g gives a corruption 'allà and *mt*¹ 'ĕllû *u* reads 'and' and β 'and who' Everything (*u*), i.e. everything in this world ₁g reads 'their bodies' But to compare their bodies to 'a passing breath' would be

rather inapt *gmqt*, β read 'themselves' But the righteous could not rightly regard themselves as a 'passing breath' Yet see James 4¹⁴ ἀτμὶς γάρ ἐστε Such language would more rightly befit the sinners, as in Wisdom 2²⁻⁴, where the sinners declare that their 'spirit shall be dispersed as thin air and their 'life shall pass away as the traces of a cloud' and 'scattered as is a mist' Similarly in Job 7⁷, ⁸ 'O remember that my life is wind . as the cloud . vanisheth away so he that goeth down to Sheol shall come up no more' How the various readings in the text arose I cannot explain The Lord tried them much, &c Cf Wisd. 3⁵ ὁ θεὸς ἐπείρασεν αὐτοὺς καὶ εὗρεν αὐτοὺς ἀξίους ἑαυτοῦ 10 Enoch speaks, and refers his hearers and readers to his books Their life in the world: cf. 48⁷ 11 Verses 11 and 12 are represented as being spoken by God Generation of light cf 61¹² (note)

I will transform those who were born in darkness, who in the flesh were not recompensed with such honour as their faithfulness deserved. 12. And I will bring forth in shining light those who have loved My holy name, and I will seat each on the throne of his honour 13. And they shall be resplendent for times without number , for righteousness is the judgement of God , for to the faithful He will give faithfulness in the habitation of upright paths 14. And they shall see those who were born in darkness led into darkness, while the righteous shall be resplendent. 15. And the sinners shall cry aloud and see them resplendent, and they indeed shall go where days and seasons are prescribed for them.'

38[4] (note) **Who were born in darkness** Of those who were born in darkness, i e in heathenism, such as were faithful and were not recompensed in the body will be transformed, but those who remain in their darkness are cast into darkness, cf. ver 14. **Were not recompensed** with (a–gu, β). g ' did not seek ' **12 In shining light**, i e clad in shining light The same idiomatic use of ba is found in Matt 7[16] The statement in the next verse ' they shall be resplendent ' calls for this translation Otherwise the text could mean ' into shining light ' Cf. 2 Enoch 22[8-10], where the garments of the blessed are said to be composed of God's glory These garments are according to our text 62[18] (see note) ' garments of life ' They are really the spiritual bodies of the blessed , cf Rev 3[4, 5, 18] 4[4] 6[11] 7[9, 13, 14] 4 Ezra 2[39, 45] Asc. Is 4[16] 7[22] 8[14, 26] **Throne of his honour** (a, u) β–n ' throne of honour, of his honour ' Cf Matt 19[28] Rev 3[21] 4[4] Asc Is 9[10, 18] **13. Resplendent, &c.** cf 39[7] 104[2] 108[14] **The habitation of upright paths** (t, β). gq ' the habitation and ($>$ q) upright paths ', m ' the habitation and uprightness ', u ' the upright paths ' **14 Led** (gmq) t, β ' cast ' 103[8] favours the former reading **15 Resplendent** (a) β ' shining ' Cf Dan 12[2, 3].

APPENDIX I

THE GIZEH GREEK FRAGMENT OF ENOCH

I. Λόγος εὐλογίας Ἐνώχ, καθὼς εὐλόγησεν ἐκλεκτοὺς δικαίους οἵτινες ἔσονται εἰς ἡμέραν ἀνάγκης ἐξᾶραι[1] πάντας τοὺς ἐχθρούς[2], ⌜καὶ σωθήσονται δίκαιοι⌝[3]

2 Καὶ ἀναλαβὼν τὴν παραβολὴν αὐτοῦ εἶπεν· Ἐνώχ, ἄνθρωπος δίκαιος, ἔστιν[4] ὅρασις[5] ἐκ θεοῦ αὐτῷ ἀνεῳγμένη, ἣν[6] † ἔχων †[7] τὴν ὅρασιν τοῦ ἁγίου *καὶ τοῦ οὐρανοῦ[8], † ἔδειξέν μοι[9] ⌜καὶ ἁγιολόγων ἁγίων ἤκουσα ἐγώ⌝, καὶ ⌜ὡς⌝ ἤκουσα παρ' αὐτῶν πάντα καὶ ἔγνων ἐγὼ θεωρῶν[10] καὶ οὐκ ἐς τὴν νῦν γενεὰν ⌜διενοούμην⌝. ἀλλὰ ἐπὶ πόρρω οὖσαν ⌜ἐγὼ λαλῶ⌝[11] 3. ⌜Καὶ⌝ περὶ τῶν ἐκλεκτῶν ⌜νῦν⌝ λέγω καὶ περὶ αὐτῶν ἀνέλαβον τὴν παραβολὴν ⌜μου⌝.

[Καὶ] ἐξελεύσεται ὁ ἅγιός † μου †[12] ὁ μέγας ἐκ τῆς κατοικήσεως αὐτοῦ,

4. καὶ ὁ θεὸς τοῦ αἰῶνος ἐπὶ γῆν[13] πατήσει ἐπὶ τὸ Σεινὰ ὄρος,
[καὶ φανήσεται *ἐκ τῆς παρενβολῆς αὐτοῦ[14]]
καὶ φανήσεται ἐν τῇ δυνάμει τῆς ἰσχύος αὐτοῦ ἀπὸ τοῦ οὐρανοῦ ⌜τῶν οὐρανῶν⌝

5 καὶ φοβηθήσονται πάντες
καὶ † πιστεύσουσιν †[15] οἱ ἐγρήγοροι

After ἐγρήγοροι the following words are interpolated. καὶ ⌜σωσιν ἀπόκρυφα ἐν πᾶσιν τοῖς ἄκροις τῆς καὶ σιοθήσονται πάντα τὰ ἄκρα τῆς γῆς[16]

[1] MS εξαρε   [2] E adds καὶ τοὺς ἀσεβεῖς.   [3] Though E omits, the clause may be genuine.   [4] To be taken with ἀνεῳγμένη or omitted   [5] E = ὀφθαλμοὶ αὐτοῦ which gives better sense, and agrees with Num 24⁴ נלוי עינים. [6] ἣν must either be written ἦν or ἦν. But the context is against the former, and ἦν is quite intelligible. It is to be taken with †ἔχων† as forming a periphrastic conjugation = 'he was †having†'   [7] = אחז, ἔχειν is found as a rendering of אחז in Job 17⁹ 18²⁰ 21⁶ 30¹⁶ Is. 12⁶, and it may be so here

It is corrupt for הזה = ὁρῶν   The passage in E = 'Ἐνώχ, ἄνθρωπος δίκαιος οὗ ἐκ Θεοῦ ὀφθαλμοὶ αὐτοῦ ἀνεῳγμένοι καὶ ἑώρα τὴν ὅρασιν τοῦ ἁγίου   [8] Corrupt (?) for κατὰ τὸν οὐρανόν as in E   [9] Text corrupt.   E = ἣν ἔδειξάν μοι οἱ ἄγγελοι   [10] MS θεορων.   [11] So Swete emends from εγω αλλω   [12] Can hardly be right   unexampled in Enoch,   E = καί.   [13] E corrupt = ἐκεῖθεν.   [14] E = σὺν or ἐν τῇ παρενβολῇ   [15] E = σαλευθήσονται Flemming suggests πτήξουσιν.   [16] This clause, which E omits, I have removed to the margin

T

καὶ λήμψεται αὐτοὺς τρόμος καὶ φόβος μέγας μέχρι τῶν περάτων τῆς γῆς

6. καὶ σεισθήσονται [καὶ πεσοῦνται καὶ διαλυθήσονται]¹ ὄρη ὑψηλά
καὶ ταπεινωθήσονται βουνοὶ ὑψηλοὶ [τοῦ διαρυῆναι ὄρη]²
καὶ τακήσονται ὡς κηρὸς ἀπὸ προσώπου πυρὸς [ἐν φλογί]³

7. καὶ διασχισθήσεται ἡ γῆ ⌐σχίσμα ⌐ῥαγάδι⌐¹⁴,
καὶ πάντα ὅσα ἐστὶν ἐπὶ τῆς γῆς ἀπολεῖται
καὶ κρίσις ἔσται κατὰ πάντων.

8. καὶ μετὰ⁵ τῶν δικαίων τὴν εἰρήνην ποιήσει,
καὶ ἐπὶ τοὺς ἐκλεκτοὺς ἔσται συντήρησις ⌐καὶ εἰρήνη⌐¹,
καὶ ἐπ᾽ αὐτοὺς γενήσεται⁶ ἔλεος.

καὶ ἔσονται πάντες τοῦ θεοῦ,
καὶ τὴν † εὐδοκίαν †⁷ δώσει αὐτοῖς,
καὶ πάντας εὐλογήσει

⌐καὶ πάντων ἀντιλήμψεται⌐¹⁸, [καὶ βοηθήσει ἡμῖν]¹
καὶ φανήσεται αὐτοῖς φῶς
[καὶ ποιήσει ἐπ᾽ αὐτοὺς εἰρήνην]⁷⁸.

9 †῞Οτι †⁹ ἔρχεται σὺν ταῖς¹⁰ μυριάσιν [αὐτοῦ καὶ τοῖς]¹¹ ἁγίοις αὐτοῦ,	JUDE 14, 15. ᾿Ιδοὺ ἦλθεν Κύριος ἐν ἁγίαις μυριάσιν αὐτοῦ
(a) ποιῆσαι κρίσιν κατὰ πάντων,	(a) ποιῆσαι κρίσιν κατὰ πάντων

as an interpolation at variance with the closing genuine words of this verse, and with all that follows on the fate of the Watchers who were imprisoned beneath the hills The scribe who added it was possibly thinking of 2 En. 18, where the singing of the Watchers is mentioned ¹ These words are omitted by E and against the parallelism. ² Bracketed because omitted by E and against sense. ³ A duplicate render-

ing ⁴ These two words look like two renderings of the same Hebrew word ⁵ MS μεγα ⁶ MS γενηται. ⁷ Corrupt for εὐοδίαν G thus = יצליהם in the active, while E gives the passive form. ⁸ This verse though omitted by E is probably genuine, being supported by the parallelism ⁹ E = καὶ ἰδού. Jude, Pseudo-Cypr and Pseudo-Vig ἰδού. ¹⁰ MS τοις. ¹¹ Interpolated against E and all other authorities Read (*b*) καὶ ἀπολέσαι[1] ⌜πάντας⌝ τοὺς ἀσεβεῖς,

(*c*) καὶ (ἐ)λέγξαι[2] πᾶσαν σάρκα

(α) περὶ πάντων ἔργων ⌜τῆς⌝ ἀσεβείας αὐτῶν⌝ ὧν ἠσέβησαν

(β) ⌜καὶ σκληρῶν ὧν ἐλάλησαν λόγων⌝[3] κατ' αὐτοῦ ἁμαρτωλοὶ ἀσεβεῖς.

(*b c*) καὶ ἐλέγξαι πάντας τοὺς ἀσεβεῖς

(α) περὶ πάντων τῶν ἔργων ἀσεβείας αὐτῶν ὧν ἠσέβησαν

(β) καὶ περὶ πάντων τῶν σκληρῶν ὧν ἐλάλησαν κατ' αὐτοῦ ἁμαρτωλοὶ ἀσεβεῖς.

PSEUDO-CYPRIAN . *Ad Novatianum*
(Hartel's Cyprian, iii. 67).

Ecce venit cum multis milibus nuntiorum suorum
(*a*) facere iudicium de omnibus
(*b*) Et perdere omnes impios
(*c*) Et arguere omnem carnem
(α) de omnibus factis impiorum quae fecerunt impie
(β) et de omnibus verbis impiis quae de | Deo | locuti sunt peccatores.

PSEUDO-VIGILIUS (Migne 62. col. 363)
Et in epistola Iudae apostoli .

Ecce veniet Dominus in millibus
(*a*) facere iudicium
(*b*) Et perdere omnes impios
(*c*) Et arguere omnem carnem
(α) de omnibus operibus impietatis eorum

II. Κατανοήσατε πάντα τὰ ἔργα ἐν τῷ οὐρανῷ, πῶς οὐκ ἠλλοίωσαν τὰς ὁδοὺς αὐτῶν, ⌜καὶ⌝ τοὺς φωστῆρας τοὺς ἐν τῷ οὐρανῷ, ὡς τὰ πάντα ἀνατέλλει καὶ δύνει, τεταγμένος ἕκαστος ἐν τῷ ⌜τεταγμένῳ⌝ καιρῷ, ⌜καὶ ταῖς ἑορταῖς αὐτῶν φαίνονται,⌝ καὶ οὐ παραβαίνουσιν τὴν ἰδίαν τάξιν. 2 ἴδετε τὴν γῆν καὶ διανοήθητε περὶ

ἁγίαις instead of ἁγίοις to agree with μυριάσιν   [1] MS ἀπολέσει, but the parallelism, Pseudo-Cypr. and Pseudo-Vig and E require ἀπολέσαι   Other edd ἀπολέσει.   [2] MS. ἐλέγξει. Parallelism and Jude, Ps-Cypi. and Ps-Vig require ἐλέγξαι   [3] Undoubtedly genuine though omitted by E. G adds

τῶν ἔργων τῶν ἐν αὐτῇ γινομένων ἀπ᾽ ἀρχῆς μέχρι τελειώσεως, ⌜ὡς¹
εἰσιν φθαρτά,⌝¹² ὡς οὐκ ἀλλοιοῦται⁸ ⌜οὐδὲν τῶν ἐπὶ γῆς, ἀλλὰ⌝ πάντα
ἔργα θεοῦ ⌜ὑμῖν⌝ φαίνεται　　3. ἴδετε τὴν θερείαν καὶ τὸν χειμῶνα
. .　III. καταμάθετε καὶ ἴδετε πάντα τὰ δένδρα⁴,

V.　　πῶς τὰ φύλλα χλωρὰ ἐν αὐτοῖς σκέπονται τὰ δένδρα⁵ καὶ
[πᾶς]* ὁ καρπὸς αὐτῶν⁶ [εἰς τιμὴν καὶ δόξαν.]　διανοήθητε ⌜καὶ
γνῶτε⌝ περὶ πάντων ⌜τῶν ἔργων⌝ αὐτοῦ, καὶ νοήσατε ὅτι [θεὸς ζῶν]
ἐποίησεν αὐτὰ οὕτως⁷, * καὶ ζῇ⁸ εἰς πάντας τοὺς αἰῶνας·　2. καὶ
τὰ ἔργα αὐτοῦ ⌜πάντα [ὅσα ἐποίησεν], εἰς τοὺς αἰῶνας⌝ ἀπὸ ἐνιαυτοῦ
εἰς ἐνιαυτὸν γινόμενα ⌜πάντα οὕτως,⌝ καὶ πάντα ὅσα ἀποτελοῦσιν
αὐτῷ τὰ ἔργα, καὶ οὐκ ἀλλοιοῦνται ⌜αὐτῶν τὰ ἔργα,⌝ ἀλλ᾽ ὡσπερεὶ
κατὰ ἐπιταγὴν⁹ τὰ πάντα γίνεται.　　3 ἴδετε πῶς ἡ θάλασσα καὶ
οἱ ποταμοὶ ὡς ὁμοίως ἀποτελοῦσιν, ⌜καὶ οὐκ ἀλλοιοῦσιν⌝ αὐτῶν τὰ
ἔργα ⌜ἀπὸ τῶν λόγων αὐτοῦ⌝.

4. Ὑμεῖς δὲ οὐκ ἐνεμείνατε οὐδὲ ἐποιήσατε κατὰ τὰς ἐντολὰς
　　αὐτοῦ¹⁰
ἀλλὰ ἀπέστητε, καὶ κατελαλήσατε μεγάλους καὶ σκληροὺς λόγους
ἐν στόματι ἀκαθαρσίας ὑμῶν κατὰ τῆς μεγαλοσύνης αὐτοῦ. [ὅτι
　　κατελαλήσατε ἐν τοῖς ψεύμασιν ὑμῶν]
σκληροκάρδιοι, οὐκ ἔστ᾽ εἰρήνη ὑμῖν.

5. τοιγὰρ τὰς ἡμέρας ὑμῶν ὑμεῖς καταράσεσθε¹¹
* καὶ τὰ ἔτη¹² τῆς ζωῆς ὑμῶν ἀπολεῖται
ϗαὶ ⌜τὰ ἔτη τῆς ἀπωλείας ὑμῶν⌝ πληθυνθήσεται ἐν κατάρᾳ
　　αἰώνων,
καὶ οὐκ ἔσται ὑμῖν ἔλεος [καὶ εἰρήνη]¹³

6 a. Τότε ἔσται¹⁴ τὰ ὀνόματα ὑμῶν εἰς κατάραν αἰώνιον πᾶσιν τοῖς
　　δικαίοις,

---

dittographic clauses καὶ περὶ πάντων ὧν
κατελάλησαν.　¹ Supplied by Swete.
² φθαρτά = נבלים corrupt foɪ נבנים
= 'steadfast'.　³ So Dillmann and
Radermacher from αλλυονται　Of
ηλλυοσαν ɪn veɪ 1 for ἠλλοίωσαν.
⁴ III. 1ᵇ—V. 1ᵃ lost thɪough hɪnt
⁵ E = τὰ δένδρα ἐν φύλλοις χλωροῖς

σκέπονται　⁶ Ŀ = καρποφοροῦσι.
⁷ = ከመዝ: of which ቅትሎሙ: may be
a corruption　⁸ E = ὁ ζῶν.　⁹ E adds
θεοῦ　¹⁰ E = τοῦ Κυρίου　¹¹ MS
κατηρασασθαι.　¹² Em. by Dillmann
and Lods fɪoɪn κατα　¹³ An interpolation, E omɪts　Εἰρήνη forɪns end of
veɪ 4.　¹⁴ E = δώσετε. ἔσται corrupt.

b. καὶ ἐν ὑμῖν καταράσονται [1] ⌜πάντες⌝ οἱ καταρώμενοι,

c. ⌜καὶ πάντες⌝ οἱ ἁμαρτωλοὶ ⌜καὶ ἀσεβεῖς⌝ ἐν ὑμῖν ὀμοῦνται,

7 *c.* ὑμῖν δὲ τοῖς ἀσεβέσιν ἔσται κατάρα.

6 *d.* ⌜καὶ πάντες οἱ † αμαρτοι [2] † χαρήσονται,

e. καὶ ἔσται [αὐτοῖς] λύσις ἁμαρτιῶν,

f. καὶ πᾶν ἔλεος καὶ εἰρήνη καὶ ἐπιείκεια,

g. ἔσται αὐτοῖς σωτηρία, φῶς ἀγαθόν.

h. [καὶ αὐτοὶ κληρονομήσουσιν τὴν γῆν] [3].

i. καὶ πᾶσιν ὑμῖν τοῖς ἁμαρτωλοῖς οὐχ ὑπάρξει σωτηρία

j. ἀλλ' ἐπὶ πάντας ὑμᾶς καταλύσει κατάρα⌝ [4]

7 *a.* καὶ τοῖς ἐκλεκτοῖς ἔσται φῶς καὶ χάρις καὶ εἰρήνη,

b. καὶ αὐτοὶ κληρονομήσουσιν τὴν γῆν.

8. τότε δοθήσεται τοῖς ἐκλεκτοῖς [5] σοφία,
   καὶ πάντες οὗτοι ζήσονται καὶ οὐ μὴ ἁμαρτήσονται ἔτι
   οὐ κατ' ἀσέβειαν [6] οὔτε ὑπερηφανίαν,
   ⌜καὶ ἔσται ἐν ἀιθρώπῳ πεφωτισμένῳ φῶς καὶ ἀνθρώπῳ ἐπι-
   στήμονι νόημα⌝ [7].

9. καὶ οὐ μὴ πλημμελήσουσιν
   οὐδὲ μὴ ἁμάρτωσιν πάσας τὰς ἡμέρας τῆς ζωῆς αὐτῶι,
   καὶ οὐ μὴ ἀποθάνωσιν ἐν ὀργῇ θυμοῦ [8],
   ἀλλὰ τὸν ἀριθμὸν αὐτῶν ζωῆς ἡμερῶν πληρώσουσιι,

   καὶ ἡ ζωὴ [9] αὐτῶν αὐξηθήσεται ἐν εἰρήνῃ,
   καὶ τὰ ἔτη τῆς χαρᾶς αὐτῶν πληθυνθήσεται
   ἐν ἀγαλλιάσει καὶ εἰρήνῃ αἰῶνος
   ἐν πάσαις ταῖς ἡμέραις τῆς ζωῆς αὐτῶι.

Gᵍ

VI. Καὶ ἐγένετο ὅταν ἐπλη-
θύνθησαν οἱ υἱοὶ τῶν ἀνθρώπων,

Gᵃ

VI. Καὶ ἐγένετο ὅτε ἐπληθύν-
θησαν οἱ υἱοὶ τῶν ὀνθρώπων,

[1] G preserves Hebrew idiom G wrongly = ὑμᾶς καταράσονται. [2] Perhaps corrupt for ἀναμάρτητοι. [3] A doublet of 7 *b*. [4] Emended by Radermacher MS reads καταλυσιν καταραν E omits 6 *d–j*. [5] Here there is a doublet of 7 *a b* and 8 *a* [φῶς καὶ χάρις, καὶ αὐτοὶ κληρονομήσουσιν τὴν γῆν, τότε δοθήσεται πᾶσιν τοῖς ἐκλεκτοῖς] [6] Emended from ἀλήθειαν with E [7] E = οἱ δὲ τὴν σοφίαν ἔχοντες πραεῖς ἔσονται [8] E = ὀργῇ καὶ θυμῷ [9] E = plural.

Gᵍ

ἐν ἐκείναις ταῖς ἡμέραις ἐγεννή-
θησαν¹ θυγατέρες ὡραῖαι ⌜καὶ
καλαί   2 καὶ ἐθεάσαντο⌝
αὐτὰς οἱ ἄγγελοι υἱοὶ οὐρανοῦ
καὶ ἐπεθύμησαν αὐτάς, καὶ εἶπαν
πρὸς ἀλλήλους Δεῦτε ἐκλεξώμεθα
ἑαυτοῖς γυναῖκας ἀπὸ τῶν ἀνθρώ-
πων², καὶ γεννήσομεν ἑαυτοῖς
τέκνα.   3 καὶ εἶπεν Σεμειαζᾶς
πρὸς αὐτούς, ὃς ἦν ἄρχων αὐτῶν,
Φοβοῦμαι μὴ οὐ θελήσετε ποιῆσαι τὸ πρᾶγμα τοῦτο, καὶ ἔσομαι
ἐγὼ μόνος ὀφειλέτης ἁμαρ-
τίας μεγάλης.   4 ἀπεκρίθησαν οὖν αὐτῷ πάντες Ὁμόσωμεν
ὅρκῳ πάντες καὶ ἀναθεματίσωμεν
πάντες ἀλλήλους μὴ ἀποστρέψαι
τὴν γνώμην ταύτην, μέχρις οὗ ἂν
[τελέσωμεν αὐτὴν καὶ]³ ποιήσω-
μεν τὸ πρᾶγμα τοῦτο.   5. τότε
ὤμοσαν πάντες ὁμοῦ καὶ ἀνεθεμάτισαν ἀλλήλους ἐν αὐτῷ .

7. Καὶ ταῦτα τὰ ὀνόματα⁵ τῶν
ἀρχόντων αὐτῶν· Σεμιαζά, οὗτος
ἦν ἄρχων αὐτῶν· Ἀραθάκ, Κιμ-
βρά, Σαμμανή, Δανειήλ, Ἀρεαρώς,
Σεμιήλ, Ἰωμειήλ, Χωχαριήλ,
Ἑζεκιήλ, Βατριήλ, Σαθιήλ, Ἀτ-
ριήλ, Ταμιήλ, Βαρακιήλ, Ἀνανθάν,

Gᴱ

ἐγεννήθησαν αὐτοῖς θυγατέρες
ὡραῖαι   2. καὶ ἐπεθύμησαν
αὐτὰς οἱ ἐγρήγοροι ⌜καὶ ἀπεπλανήθησαν ὀπίσω αὐτῶν,⌝ καὶ εἶπον
πρὸς ἀλλήλους Ἐκλεξώμεθα
ἑαυτοῖς γυναῖκας ἀπὸ τῶν θυγατέρων τῶν ἀνθρώπων τῆς γῆς.
3 καὶ εἶπε Σεμιαζᾶς ὁ ἄρχων
αὐτῶν πρὸς αὐτούς Φοβοῦμαι μὴ
οὐ θελήσητε ποιῆσαι τὸ πρᾶγμα
τοῦτο, καὶ ἔσομαι ἐγὼ μόνος
ὀφειλέτης ἁμαρτίας μεγάλης.
4 καὶ ἀπεκρίθησαν αὐτῷ πάντες
⌜καὶ εἶπον⌝ Ὁμόσωμεν ἅπαντες
ὅρκῳ καὶ ἀναθεματίσωμεν ἀλλήλους τοῦ μὴ ἀποστρέψαι τὴν
γνώμην ταύτην, μέχρις οὗ ἀποτε-
λέσωμεν αὐτήν.   5. τότε πάντες ὤμοσαν ὁμοῦ καὶ ἀνεθεμάτισαν ἀλλήλους.   6. ἦσαν δὲ
οὗτοι διακόσιοι οἱ καταβάντες ἐν
ταῖς ἡμέραις Ἰάρεδ εἰς τὴν κορυφὴν τοῦ Ἑρμονιεὶμ ὄρους, καὶ
ἐκάλεσαν τὸ ὄρος Ἑρμώμ, κα-
θότι ὤμοσαν καὶ ἀνεθεμάτισαν
ἀλλήλους ἐν αὐτῷ⁴

7. Καὶ ταῦτα τὰ ὀνόματα τῶν
ἀρχόντων αὐτῶν· αʹ Σεμιαζᾶς, ὁ
ἄρχων αὐτῶν, βʹ Ἀταρκούφ, γʹ
Ἀρακιήλ, δʹ Χωβαβιήλ, εʹ Ὁραμ-
μαμή, ϛʹ Ῥαμιήλ, ζʹ Σαμψίχ, ηʹ
Ζακιήλ, θʹ Βαλκιήλ, ιʹ Ἀζαλζήλ,
ιαʹ Φαρμαρός, ιβʹ Ἀμαριήλ ιγʹ

¹ E Gᵍ add αὐτοῖς.　　² E = υἱῶν τῶν
ἀνθρώπων.　　³ Bracketed as a doublet.　　E Gᵍ omit　　⁴ Gᵇ omits ver. 6 through
homoioteleuton　　⁵ On these names

G⁵

Θωνιήλ, ῾Ραμιήλ, ᾿Ασεάλ, ῾Ρα-
κειήλ, Τουριήλ.   8. οὗτοί εἰσιν
ἀρχαὶ αὐτῶν οἱ δέκα.[1]

VII. Καὶ[2] ἔλαβον ἑαυτοῖς
γυναῖκας· ἕκαστος αὐτῶν ἐξελέ-
ξαντο ἑαυτοῖς γυναῖκας[3], καὶ
ἤρξαντο εἰσπορεύεσθαι πρὸς
αὐτὰς καὶ μιαίνεσθαι[6] ἐν αὐταῖς·
καὶ ἐδίδαξαν αὐτὰς φαρμακείας
καὶ ἐπαοιδὰς καὶ ῥιζοτομίας, καὶ
τὰς βοτάνας ἐδήλωσαν αὐταῖς.
2. Αἱ[8] δὲ ἐν γαστρὶ λαβοῦσαι
ἐτέκοσαν γίγαντας μεγάλους ἐκ
πηχῶν τρισχιλίων, 3 οἵτινες
κατέσθοσαν τοὺς κόπους τῶν
ἀνθρώπων. ὡς δὲ[11] οὐκ ἐδυνήθησαν αὐτοῖς οἱ ἄνθρωποι ἐπιχορη-
γεῖν,   4. οἱ γίγαντες ἐτόλμησαν[12] ἐπ᾿ αὐτούς, καὶ κατεσθίοσαν
τοὺς ἀνθρώπους. 5. καὶ ἤρξαντο ἁμαρτάνειν ἐν τοῖς πετει-
νοῖς καὶ τοῖς (θ)ηρίοις καὶ ἑρπε-
τοῖς καὶ τοῖς (ἰ)χθύσιν, καὶ ἀλλή-
λων τὰς (σ)άρκας κατεσθίειν, καὶ
τὸ αἷμα (ἔ)πινον. 6. τότε ἡ γῆ
ἐνέτυχεν κατὰ τῶν ἀι ὁμων.

G⁸

᾿Αναγημάς, ιδ΄ Θαυσαήλ, ιε΄
Σαμιήλ, ις΄ Σαρινᾶς, ιζ΄ Εὐμιήλ,
ιη΄ Τυριήλ, ιθ΄ ᾿Ιουμιήλ, κ΄ Σαριήλ

VII *Οὗτοι καὶ οἱ λοιποὶ
πάντες[4] [ἐν τῷ χιλιοστῷ ἑκατο-
στῷ ἑβδομηκοστῷ ἔτει τοῦ κόσμου[5]] ἔλαβον ἑαυτοῖς γυναῖκας,
καὶ ἤρξαντο μιαίνεσθαι ἐν αὐταῖς
[ἕως τοῦ κατακλυσμοῦ].[7]   2.
καὶ ἔτεκον ⌐αὐτοῖς γένη τρία·
πρῶτον⌐[9] γίγαντας μεγάλους,
⌐οἱ δὲ Γίγαντες † ἐτέκνωσαν †[10]
Ναφηλείμ, καὶ τοῖς Ναφηλείμ
† ἐγεννήθησαν †[10] ᾿Ελιούδ. καὶ
ἦσαν αὐξανόμενοι κατὰ τὴν μεγα-
λειότητα αὐτῶν⌐[9] καὶ ἐδίδαξαν
[ἑαυτοὺς καὶ] τὰς γυναῖκας
ἑαυτῶν φαρμακείας καὶ ἐπαοιδάς.

.

VIII. ⌐Πρῶτος⌐ ᾿Αζαὴλ ⌐ὁ
δέκατος τῶν ἀρχόντων⌐ ἐδίδαξε

see pp 16, 17.   [1] The manuscript
reading seems corrupt for ἀρχαὶ αὐτῶν
τῶν δεκάδων, a literal rendering of
ראשיהן דעשריתא. We have an undoubted case of this in 19² αἱ γυναῖκες
αὐτῶν τῶν . ἀγγέλων. Radermacher
proposes ἀρχαὶ αὐτῶν οἱ (ἐπὶ) δέκα, but
this would mean ' their chiefs over ten
(angels)'   [2] See note 4   [3] E =
ἐξελέξατο ἕκαστος ἑαυτῷ μίαν.   [4] E =
καὶ οἱ λοιποὶ πάντες μετ᾿ αὐτῶν καί,
where the final καί is an intrusion
[5] Addition of Syncellus.   [6] E =
μίγνυσθαι.   [7] Addition of Syncellus
[8] MS reads ἐν.   [9] These clauses,
though omitted by E and G⁵, go back
to the original   [10] ἐτέκνωσαν and τοῖς
N″ ἐγεννήθησαν may be corrupt. We
should expect according to Jub. 7²²
ἔκτειναν and οἱ N″ ἔκτειναν.   [11] E =
ὥστε   [12] E = ἐτράπησαν, of which
ἐτόλμησαν seems a corruption.

Gᵃ

VIII. Ἐδίδαξεν τοὺς ἀνθρώπους Ἀζαὴλ μαχαίρας ποιεῖν καὶ ὅπλα καὶ ἀσπίδας καὶ θώρακας [διδάγματα ἀγγέλων], καὶ ὑπέδειξεν αὐτοῖς τὰ μέταλλα¹ καὶ τὴν ἐργασίαν αὐτῶν, καὶ ψέλια καὶ κόσμους καὶ στίβεις² καὶ τὸ καλλιβλέφαρον³ καὶ παντοίους λίθους ἐκλεκτοὺς καὶ τὰ βαφικά⁴ 2. καὶ ἐγένετο ἀσέβεια πολλή, καὶ ἐπόρνευσαν καὶ ἀπεπλανήθησαν καὶ ἠφανίσθησαν ἐν πάσαις ταῖς ὁδοῖς αὐτῶν. 3. Σεμιαζᾶς ἐδίδαξεν ἐπα(οι)δὰς καὶ ῥιζοτομίας⁵ Ἀρμαρὼς *ἐπαοιδῶν λυτήριον (Βα)ρακιὴλ⁷ ἀστρολογίας⁸ Χωχιὴλ⁷ τὰ σημειωτικά· Σαθ(ι)ὴλ⁷ ἀστεροσκοπίαν⁹ Σεριὴ(λ)⁷ σεληναγωγίας¹⁰.

Gᵃ

ποιεῖν μαχαίρας καὶ θώρακας καὶ ⌜πᾶν⌝ σκεῦος πολεμικόν, καὶ τὰ μέταλλα τῆς γῆς ⌜καὶ τὸ χρυσίον⌝ πῶς ἐργάσωνται καὶ ⌜ποιήσωσιν αὐτὰ⌝ κόσμια ⌜ταῖς γυναιξί, καὶ τὸν ἄργυρον ἔδειξε δὲ αὐτοῖς⌝ καὶ τὸ †στίλβειν†² καὶ τὸ καλλωπίζειν καὶ τοὺς ἐκλεκτοὺς λίθους καὶ τὰ βαφικά· ⌜καὶ ἐποίησαν ἑαυτοῖς οἱ υἱοὶ τῶν ἀνθρώπων καὶ ταῖς θυγατράσιν αὐτῶν, καὶ παρέβησαν καὶ ἐπλάνησαν τοὺς ἁγίους⌝. 2. καὶ ἐγένετο ἀσέβεια πολλὴ ⌜ἐπὶ τῆς γῆς,⌝ καὶ ἠφάνισαν τὰς ὁδοὺς αὐτῶν. 3. ⌜ἔτι δὲ καὶ ὁ πρώταρχος αὐτῶν⌝ Σεμιαζᾶς ἐδίδαξεν †εἶναι ὀργὰς⁶ ⌜κατὰ τοῦ νοός,⌝ καὶ ῥίζας βοτανῶν ⌜τῆς γῆς⌝. ⌜ὁ δὲ ἑνδέκατος⌝ Φαρμαρὸς ἐδίδαξε ⌜φαρμακείας, ἐπαοιδάς, σοφίας, καὶ⌝ ἐπαοιδῶν λυτήρια· ὁ ἔνατος ⌜ἐδίδαξεν⌝ ἀστροσκοπίαν· ὁ δὲ τέταρτος ⌜ἐδίδαξεν⌝ ἀστρολογίαν· ὁ δὲ ὄγδοος ἐδίδαξεν ἀεροσκοπίαν· ⌜ὁ δὲ τρίτος ἐδίδαξε τὰ σημεῖα τῆς γῆς· ὁ δὲ ἕβδομος ἐδίδαξε τὰ σημεῖα τοῦ ἡλίου⌝· ὁ δὲ εἰκοστὸς ἐδίδαξε τὰ σημεῖα τῆς σελήνης. ⌜πάντες οὗτοι ἤρξαντο ἀνακαλύπτειν τὰ μυστήρια ταῖς

---

¹ MS μεγαλα   ² Gᵃ has στίλβειν which is corrupt, Diels emends to στιβίζειν.   ³ Since Gᵃ has τὸ καλλωπίζειν the Aram may have been simply מכחל   ⁴ E adds τὰ μέταλλα τῆς γῆς—a doublet

⁶ E = ἐπαοιδοὺς καὶ ῥιζοτόμους   ⁵ Corrupt for ἐπαοιδάς (Radeim)   ⁷ See notes on pp 16, 17.   ⁸ E = ἀστρολόγους   ⁹ This word (which E translates) is corrupt for ἀεροσκοπίαν as in Gᵃ   ¹⁰ MS

Gᵍ

Gᵃ

γυναιξὶν αὐτῶν καὶ τοῖς τέκνοις
αὐτῶν. μετὰ δὲ ταῦτα⌐ [VII
4–5] ἤρξαντο οἱ γίγαντες κατεσθίειν ⌐τὰς σάρκας⌐ τῶν ἀνθρώπων ¹.

Gᵍ	Gˢ¹	Gˢ² (G Syncellus I. 42 sqq.)
4. τῶν οὖν² ἀνθρώ-πων ἀπολλυμένων ἡ βο(ὴ) εἰς οὐρανοὺς ἀνέβη.	4. καὶ ἤρξαντο οἱ ἄνθρωποι ἐλαττοῦσθαι ⌐ἐπὶ τῆς γῆς. οἱ δὲ λοιποὶ⌐ ἐβόησαν εἰς τὸν οὐρανὸν ⌐περὶ τῆς κακώσεως αὐτῶν, λέ-γοντες εἰσενεχθῆναι τὸ μνημόσυνον αὐτῶν ἐνώπιον Κυρίου⌐.	4. ⌐Τότε⌐ ἐβόησαν οἱ ἄνθρωποι εἰς τὸν οὐ-ρανὸν ⌐λέγοντες Εἰσ-αγάγετε τὴν κρίσιν ἡμῶν πρὸς τὸν ὕψι-στοι, καὶ τὴν ἀπώ-λειαν ἡμῶν ἐνώπιον τῆς δόξης τῆς μεγά-λης, ἐνώπιον τοῦ κυ-ρίου τῶν κυρίων πάν-των τῇ μεγαλωσύνῃ⌐.
IX. Τότε παρ(α)-κύψαντες Μιχαὴλ καὶ Οὐ(ρι)ὴλ καὶ Ῥαφαὴλ καὶ Γαβριή(λ), ⌐οὗτοι⌐ ἐκ τοῦ οὐρανοῦ ἐθεά-σα(ν)το αἷμα πολὺ ἐκχυννόμεν(ον) ἐπὶ τῆς γῆς³ 2. καὶ εἶπαν πρὸ(ς) ἀλλή-λους Φωνὴ βοώντω(ν) ἐπὶ τῆς γῆς· μέχρι πυλῶ(ν) τοῦ οὐρα-νοῦ⁴ 3. ἐντυγχάνου-	IX Καὶ ⌐ἀκού-σαντες οἱ τέσσαρες μεγάλοι ἀρχάγγελοι⌐, Μιχαὴλ καὶ Οὐριὴλ καὶ Ῥαφαὴλ καὶ Γα-βριὴλ παρέκυψαν⌐ἐπὶ τὴν γῆν⌐ ἐκ ⌐τῶν ἀγί-ων⌐ τοῦ οὐρανοῦ· καὶ θεασάμενοι αἷμα πολὺ ἐκκεχυμένον ἐπὶ τῆς γῆς ⌐καὶ πᾶσαν ⌐ἀσέ-βειαν καὶ⌐ ἀνομίαν ⌐γενομένην ἐπ' αὐτῆς,⌐	IX. Καὶ ⌐ἀκού-σαντες οἱ τέσσαρες μεγάλοι ἀρχάγγελοι⌐, Μιχαὴλ καὶ Οὐριὴλ καὶ Ῥαφαὴλ καὶ Γαβριὴλ παρέκυψαν ⌐ἐπὶ τὴν γῆν⌐ ἐκ ⌐τῶν ἁγίων⌐ τοῦ οὐρανοῦ· καὶ θεασάμενοι αἷμα πολὺ ἐκκεχυμένον ἐπὶ τῆς γῆς καὶ πᾶσαν ἀνομίαν καὶ ⌐ἀσέβειαν γινομένην ἐπ' αὐτῆς,⌐

σεληνοναγιας   ¹ This sentence summarizes 7⁴, ⁵ of Gᵍ   The order of nar-
ration in Gᵃ is better than in Gᵍ.
² MS. τον νουν   ³ Gᵍ omits through

hmt καὶ πᾶσαν ἀσέβειαν γινομένην ἐπ
τῆς γῆς against EGˢ¹, ²   ⁴ E adds
καὶ νῦν πρὸς ὑμᾶς τοὺς ἁγίους τοῦ
οὐρανοῦ The words μέχρι πυλῶν τ οὐρ

Gᵍ

σιν αἱ ψυχαὶ τῶν
ἀνθρώπων λεγόντων
Εἰσαγάγετε τὴν κρί-
σιν ἡμῶν πρὸς τὸν
ὕψιστ(ον). 4. Καὶ
εἶπα(ν) τῷ κυρίῳ ¹ Σὺ
εἶ κύριος τῶν κυρίων
καὶ ὁ θεὸς τῶν θεῶν
καὶ βασιλεὺς †τῶν
αἰώνων† ³ ὁ θρόνος
τῆς δόξης σου εἰς
πάσας τὰς γενεὰς τοῦ
αἰῶνος, καὶ τὸ ὄνομά
σου τὸ ἅγιον καὶ μέ-
γα⁵ καὶ εὐλογητὸν εἰς
πάντας τοὺς αἰῶνας.

Gᵃ¹

2. ⌜εἰσελθόντες⌝ εἶπον
πρὸς ἀλλήλους ⌜ὅτι
3. Τὰ πνεύματα καὶ⌝
αἱ ψυχαὶ τῶν ἀνθρώ-
πων ⌜στενάζουσιν⌝ ἐν-
τυγχάνοντα καὶ λέ-
γοντα ὅτι Εἰσαγάγετε
τὴν κρίσιν ἡμῶν πρὸς
τὸν ὕψιστον, ⌜καὶ τὴν
ἀπώλειαν ἡμῶν ἐνώ-
πιον τῆς δόξης τῆς
μεγαλωσύνης, ἐνώ-
πιον τοῦ κυρίου τῶν
κυρίων πάντων τῇ
μεγαλωσύνῃ⌝ 4. Καὶ
εἶπον τῷ κυρίῳ ⌜τῶν
αἰώνων⌝ ² Σὺ εἶ ὁ
θεὸς τῶν θεῶν καὶ
κύριος τῶν κυρίων
καὶ ὁ βασιλεὺς τῶν
βασιλευόντων ⌜καὶ
θεὸς τῶν αἰώνων⌝ ⁴,
καὶ ὁ θρόνος τῆς δόξης
σου εἰς πάσας τὰς
γενεὰς τῶν αἰώνων,
καὶ τὸ ὄνομά σου
ἅγιον ⁵ καὶ εὐλογη-
μένον εἰς πάντας τοὺς
αἰῶνας ⁶.

Gᵃ²

2. ⌜εἰσελθόντες⌝ εἶ-
πον πρὸς ἀλλήλους
⌜ὅτι 3. Τὰ πνεύματα
καὶ⌝ αἱ ψυχαὶ τῶν
ἀνθρώπων ἐντυγχά-
νουσι ⌜στενάζοντα
καὶ⌝ λέγοντα Εἰσα-
γάγετε τὴν ⌜δέησιν⌝
ἡμῶν πρὸς τὸν ὕψι-
στον. 4. Καὶ ⌜προσ-
ελθόντες οἱ τέσ-
σαρες ἀρχάγγελοι⌝
εἶπον τῷ κυρίῳ ¹ Σὺ
εἶ θεὸς τῶν θεῶν καὶ
κύριος τῶν κυρίων καὶ
βασιλεὺς τῶν βασι-
λευόντων ⌜καὶ θεὸς
τῶν ἀνθρώπων⌝, καὶ ὁ
θρόνος τῆς δόξης σου
εἰς πάσας τὰς γενεὰς
τῶν αἰώνων, καὶ τὸ
ὄνομά σου ἅγιον ⁵ καὶ
εὐλογημένον εἰς πάν-
τας τοὺς αἰῶνας

must be taken with ἐντυγχάνουσιν as
in 9¹⁰ Gᵍ   ¹ E adds τῶν βασιλέων
Gᵃ¹ has τῶν αἰώνων   ² E = τῶν
βασιλέων = מלכיא corrupt (?) for עלמיא
Hence 'Lord of the ages'   ³ Corrupt.
E Gᵃ = τῶν βασιλέων or βασιλευόντων
If this corruption is not native to Gᵍ

then we must assume a corruption in
the Aramaic, the converse of that in
note 2   ⁴ Gᵃ² has ἀνθρώπων, ι e
ανπων, corrupt for αἰώνων Converse
corruption in 11²   ⁵ E Gᵍ add καὶ μέγα
(or δεδοξασμένον).   ⁶ Here Gᵃ¹ adds
καὶ τὰ ἑξῆς. τότε ὁ ὕψιστος ἐκέλευσε

G^g

G^s (Syncellus I. 43)

5. Σὺ γὰρ ἐποίησας τὰ πάντα, καὶ πᾶσαν [1] τὴν ἐξουσίαν ἔχων, καὶ πάντα ἐνώπιόν σου φανερὰ καὶ ἀκάλυπτα, καὶ πάντα σὺ ὁρᾷς [2]

. . 6. ἃ ἐποίησεν ᾿Αζαήλ, ὃς ἐδίδαξεν πάσας τὰς ἀδικίας ἐπὶ τῆς γῆς καὶ ἐδήλωσεν τὰ μυστήρια τοῦ αἰῶνος τὰ ἐν τῷ οὐρανῷ ἃ ἐπιτηδεύουσιν †ἔγνωσαν† ἄνθρωποι [4]

7. καὶ Σεμιαζᾶς, ᾧ τὴν ἐξουσίαν ἔδωκας ἄρχειν τῶν σὺν αὐτῷ ἅμα ὄντων. 8. καὶ ἐπορεύθησαν πρὸς τὰς θυγατέρας τῶν ἀνθρώπων [7] τῆς γῆς καὶ συνεκοιμήθησαν αὐταῖς καὶ [8] . . . ἐμιάνθησαν, καὶ ἐδήλωσαν αὐταῖς πάσας τὰς ἁμαρτίας. 9. καὶ αἱ γυναῖκες ἐγέννησαν Τιτᾶνας, *ὑφ᾿ ὧν [9] ὅλη ἡ γῆ ἐπλήσθη αἵματος καὶ ἀδικίας. 10. καὶ νῦν ἰδοὺ βοῶσιν αἱ ψυχαὶ τῶν τετελευτηκότων καὶ ἐντυγχάνουσιν μέχρι τῶν πυλῶν τοῦ οὐρανοῦ, καὶ

5. Σὺ γὰρ εἶ ὁ ποιήσας τὰ πάντα καὶ πάντων [1] τὴν ἐξουσίαν ἔχων, καὶ πάντα ἐνώπιόν σου φανερὰ καὶ ἀκάλυπτα· καὶ πάντα ὁρᾷς, καὶ οὐκ ἔστιν ὃ κρυβῆναί σε δύναται. 6 ὁρᾷς ὅσα ἐποίησεν ᾿Αζαὴλ ⌜καὶ ὅσα εἰσήνεγκεν⌝, ὅσα ἐδίδαξεν, ἀδικίας ⌜καὶ ἁμαρτίας⌝ ἐπὶ τῆς γῆς καὶ ⌜πάντα δόλον ἐπὶ τῆς ξηρᾶς. ἐδίδαξε γὰρ [1] *τὰ μυστήρια καὶ ἀπεκάλυψε τῷ αἰῶνι [3] τὰ ἐν οὐρανῷ. *ἐπιτηδεύουσι δὲ ⌜τὰ ἐπιτηδεύματα αὐτοῦ,⌝ εἰδέναι ⌜τὰ μυστήρια,⌝[4] οἱ υἱοὶ τῶν ἀνθρώπων. 7. *τῷ Σεμιαζᾷ [5] τὴν ἐξουσίαν ἔδωκας †ἔχειν [6] τῶν σὺν αὐτῷ ἅμα ὄντων 8. καὶ ἐπορεύθησαν πρὸς τὰς θυγατέρας τῶν ἀνθρώπων [7] τῆς γῆς καὶ συνεκοιμήθησαν μετ᾿ αὐτῶν καὶ ἐν ταῖς θηλείαις ἐμιάνθησαν, καὶ ἐδήλωσαν αὐταῖς πάσας τὰς ἁμαρτίας, ⌜καὶ ἐδίδαξαν αὐτὰς μίσητρα ποιεῖν⌝. 9. καὶ ⌜νῦν ἰδοὺ αἱ θυγατέρες τῶν ἀνθώπων⌝ ἔτεκον ⌜ἐξ αὐτῶν υἱοὺς⌝ γίγαντας· ⌜κίβδηλα ἐπὶ τῆς γῆς τῶν ἀνθρώπων ἐκκέχυται,⌝ καὶ ὅλη ἡ γῆ ἐπλήσθη

τοῖς ἁγίοις ἀρχαγγέλοις, καὶ ἔθηκαν τοὺς ἐξάρχους αὐτῶν καὶ ἔβαλον αὐτοὺς εἰς τὴν ἄβυσσον ἕως τῆς κρίσεως, καὶ τὰ ἑξῆς Here Syncellus summarizes 10⁴, ¹² Cf end of 8³ G^s   [1] E G^g = πάντων   [4] G^g omits through hmt καὶ οὐκ ἔστιν ὁ κρυβῆναί σε δύναται ὁρᾷς against E G^s

^x E G^g = καὶ ἐδήλωσεν τὰ μυστήρια τοῦ αἰῶνος   [4] See note on p 21   [5] Corrupt E G^g = καὶ Σεμιαζᾶς   [6] Corrupt for ἄρχειν (Raderm.).   [7] E adds ἐπί   [8] Add ἐν ταῖς θηλείαις with E G^s   [9] G^s = καί

284　　　　*The Book of Enoch*

Gᵍ

ἀνέβη ὁ στεναγμὸς αὐτῶν καὶ οὐ δύναται ἐξελθεῖν ἀπὸ προσώπου τῶν ἐπὶ τῆς γῆς γινομένων ἀνομημάτων.　11. καὶ σὺ πάντα οἶδας πρὸ τοῦ αὐτὰ γενέσθαι, καὶ σὺ ὁρᾷς ταῦτα καὶ * ἐᾷς αὐτούς¹, καὶ οὐδὲ ⌜ἡμῖν⌝ λέγεις τί δεῖ ποιεῖν αὐτοὺς περὶ τούτων.

X. Τότε Ὕψιστος εἶπεν⁴ ⌜περὶ τούτων⌝, *ὁ μέγας Ἅγιος, καὶ⁵ ἐλάλησεν * καὶ εἶπεν⁶ καὶ ἔπεμψεν Ἰστραὴλ πρὸς τὸν υἱὸν Λάμεχ 2. Εἰπὸν αὐτῷ ἐπὶ τῷ ἐμῷ ὀνόματι Κρύψον σεαυτόν, καὶ δήλωσον αὐτῷ τέλος ἐπερχόμενον, ὅτι ἡ γῆ ἀπόλλυται πᾶσα, καὶ κατακλυσμὸς μέλλει γίνεσθαι πάσης τῆς γῆς καὶ ἀπολέσει πάντα ὅσα ἔστ' ἐν⁷ αὐτῇ. 3. ⌜καὶ⌝ δίδαξον αὐτὸν ὅπως ἐκφύγῃ, καὶ μενεῖ τὸ σπέρμα αὐτοῦ εἰς πάσας τὰς γενεὰς τοῦ αἰῶνος.

Gᵃ

ἀδικίας.　10. καὶ νῦν ἰδοὺ ⌜τὰ πνεύματα⌝ τῶν ψυχῶν² τῶν ἀποθανόντων ἀνθρώπων ἐντυγχάνουσι, καὶ μέχρι τῶν πυλῶν τοῦ οὐρανοῦ ἀνέβη ὁ στεναγμὸς αὐτῶν καὶ οὐ δύναται ἐξελθεῖν ἀπὸ προσώπου τῶν ἐπὶ τῆς γῆς γινομένων ἀδικημάτων.　11. καὶ σὺ αὐτὰ οἶδας πρὸ τοῦ³ αὐτὰ γενέσθαι καὶ ὁρᾷς αὐτοὺς καὶ ἐᾷς αὐτούς, καὶ οὐδὲν λέγεις, τί δεῖ ποιῆσαι αὐτοὺς περὶ τούτου.

X. Τότε ὁ Ὕψιστος εἶπε καὶ ὁ ἅγιος ὁ μέγας ἐλάλησε, καὶ ἔπεμψε τὸν Οὐριὴλ πρὸς τὸν υἱὸν Λάμεχ λέγων 2. ⌜Πορεύου πρὸς τὸν Νῶε καὶ⌝ εἰπὸν αὐτῷ τῷ ἐμῷ ὀνόματι Κρύψον σεαυτόν, καὶ δήλωσον αὐτῷ τέλος ἐπερχόμενον, ὅτι ἡ γῆ ἀπόλλυται πᾶσα· καὶ ⌜εἰπὸν αὐτῷ ὅτι⌝ κατακλυσμὸς μέλλει γίνεσθαι πάσης τῆς γῆς, ἀπολέσαι πάντα ⌜ἀπὸ προσώπου τῆς γῆς.⌝ 3. δίδαξον ⌜τὸν δίκαιον⌝⁸ τί ⌜ποιήσει, τὸν υἱὸν Λάμεχ, καὶ τὴν ψυχὴν αὐτοῦ εἰς ζωὴν συντηρήσει, καὶ⌝ ἐκφεύξεται ⌜δι' αἰῶνος⌝, καὶ ἐξ αὐτοῦ ⌜φυτευθήσεται⌝ φύτευμα ⌜καὶ⌝ σταθήσεται πάσας τὰς γενεὰς τοῦ αἰῶνος.

¹ Gᵍ E = αἱ ψυχαί.　² MS. has αιας　E = τὰ εἰς αὐτούς—a corruption　³ Emended by Raderm from τῶν　⁴ E omits wrongly　⁵ E = ὁ μέγας καὶ ὁ
ἅγιος　⁶ These words should with Gˢ E be placed after Λάμεχ　E = καὶ εἶπε πρὸς αὐτόν.　Gˢ λέγων　⁷ Emended by Raderm from εστιν　⁸ Gᵍ E = αὐ-

Gᵍ

4. Καὶ ¹ τῷ Ῥαφαὴλ εἶπεν Δῆσον
τὸν Ἀζαὴλ ποσὶν καὶ χερσίν, καὶ
βάλε αὐτὸν εἰς τὸ σκότος, καὶ
ἄνοιξον τὴν ἔρημον τὴν οὖσαν
ἐν τῷ Δαδουὴλ κἀκεῖ βάλε αὐτόν,
5. καὶ ὑπόθες² αὐτῷ λίθους τραχεῖς καὶ ὀξεῖς καὶ ἐπικάλυψον
αὐτῷ τὸ σκότος, καὶ οἰκησάτω
ἐκεῖ εἰς τοὺς αἰῶνας, καὶ τὴν
ὄψιν αὐτοῦ πώμασον καὶ φῶς
μὴ θεωρείτω· 6. καὶ ἐν τῇ
ἡμέρᾳ ⌈τῆς μεγάλης⌉ τῆς κρίσεως ἀπαχθήσεται εἰς τὸν ἐνπυρι-
σμόν. 7. καὶ ἰαθήσεται ἡ γῆ, ἣν
ἠφάνισαν οἱ ἄγγελοι, καὶ τὴν
ἴασιν τῆς γῆς⁴ δήλωσον, ἵνα
ἰάσωνται⁵ τὴν πληγήν⁶, ἵνα μὴ⁷
ἀπόλωνται πάντες οἱ υἱοὶ τῶν
ἀνθρώπων ἐν τῷ μυστηρίῳ ⌈ὅλῳ⌉
ᾧ† ἐπάταξαν †⁸ οἱ ἐγρήγοροι καὶ
ἐδί(δα)ξαν τοὺς υἱοὺς αὐτῶν,   8
καὶ ἠρημώθη πᾶσα ἡ γῆ [ἀφανι-
σθεῖσα]⁹ ἐν *τοῖς ἔργοις τῆς
διδασκαλίας¹⁰ Ἀζαήλ· καὶ ἐπ'
αὐτῷ γράψον τὰς ἁμαρτίας πάσας.
9. Καὶ τῷ Γαβριὴλ εἶπεν ὁ κύριος·
Πορεύου ἐπὶ τοὺς μαζηρέους, ἐπὶ
τοὺς κιβδήλους¹² καὶ τοὺς υἱοὺς
τῆς πορνείας¹³, καὶ ἀπόλεσον¹⁴

Gᵃ

4. Καὶ τῷ Ῥαφαὴλ εἶπε ⌈Πο-
ρεύου, Ῥαφαήλ, καὶ⌉ δῆσον τὸν
Ἀζαὴλ χερσὶ καὶ ποσὶ [συμπό-
δισον αὐτόν], καὶ ἔμβαλε αὐτὸν
εἰς τὸ σκότος καὶ ἄνοιξον τὴν
ἔρημον τὴν οὖσαν ἐν τῇ [ἐρήμῳ]
Δουδαήλ, καὶ ἐκεῖ ⌈πορευθεὶς⌉
βάλε αὐτόν· 5 καὶ ὑπόθες αὐτῷ
λίθους ὀξεῖς καὶ ⌈λίθους⌉ τραχεῖς
καὶ ἐπικάλυψον αὐτῷ σκότος, καὶ
οἰκησάτω ἐκεῖ εἰς τὸν αἰῶνα· καὶ
τὴν ὄψιν αὐτοῦ πώμασον καὶ φῶς
μὴ θεωρείτω· 6. καὶ ἐν τῇ ἡμέρᾳ
τῆς κρίσεως ἀπαχθήσεται εἰς τὸν
ἐμπυρισμὸν ⌈τοῦ πυρός⌉. 7. καὶ
ἴασαι τὴν γῆν ἣν ἠφάνισαν οἱ
ἐγρήγοροι⁹, καὶ τὴν ἴασιν τῆς
πληγῆς⁴ δήλωσον, ἵνα * ἰάσωνται
τὴν πληγὴν⁶ καὶ μὴ ἀπόλωνται
πάντες οἱ υἱοὶ τῶν ἀνθρώπων ἐν
τῷ μυστηρίῳ ὃ εἶπον οἱ ἐγρήγοροι
καὶ ἐδίδαξαν τοὺς υἱοὺς αὐτῶν,
8 καὶ ἠρημώθη πᾶσα ἡ γῆ ἐν τοῖς
ἔργοις τῆς διδασκαλίας Ἀζαήλ·
καὶ ἐπ' αὐτῇ¹¹ γράψον πάσας τὰς
ἁμαρτίας. 9. Καὶ τῷ Γαβριὴλ
εἶπε· Πορεύου, ⌈Γαβριήλ⌉, ἐπὶ
τοὺς γίγαντας. ἐπὶ τοὺς κιβδήλους,
ἐπὶ τοὺς υἱοὺς τῆς πορνείας, καὶ

τόν   ¹ E adds πάλιν ὁ κύριος   ² E
= ἐπίθες.   ³ Gᵍ E = ἄγγελοι.   ⁴ = E
Gᵃ πληγῆς   ⁵ MS ιασονται   ⁸ E =
τὴν γῆν   ⁷ MS μην   ⁸ Here
ἐπάταξαν = אברד corrupt for אמרו =
εἶπον as we have in Gᵃ.   ⁹ Gᵍ E omit
¹⁰ E = τῇ διδασκαλίᾳ τῶν ἔργων   ¹¹ Gᵍ

αὐτῷ   ¹² κίβδηλος here seems to
represent שעטני (cf Lev 19¹⁹ Deut
22¹¹) or some derivative of it as representing beings who are derived from
two distinct classes of creatures E
took it as = ἀδόκιμος   ¹³ E = πόρνης,
corrupt for πορνείας   ¹⁴ E adds τοὺς

G^g

τοὺς υἱοὺς τῶν ἐγρηγόρων ἀπὸ τῶν ἀνθρώπων·[1] πέμψον αὐτοὺς[2] ἐν πολέμῳ ἀπωλείας. μακρότης γὰρ ἡμερῶν οὐκ ἔστιν αὐτῶν, 10. καὶ πᾶσα ἐρώτησις[4] (οὐκ) ἔσται τοῖς πατράσιν αὐτῶν [καὶ] ⌜περὶ αὐτῶν⌝, ὅτι ἐλπίζουσιν ζῆσαι ζωὴν αἰώνιον, καὶ ὅτι ζήσεται ἕκαστος αὐτῶν ἔτη πεντακόσια 11. Καὶ εἶπεν (τῷ) Μιχαὴλ Πορεύου καὶ †δήλωσον†[5] Σεμιαζᾷ καὶ τοῖς λοιποῖς τοῖς σὺν αὐτῷ ταῖς γυναιξὶν μιγέντας, μιανθῆναι ἐν αὐταῖς ἐν[6] τῇ ἀκαθαρσίᾳ αὐτῶν· 12. καὶ ὅταν κατασφαγῶσιν οἱ υἱοὶ αὐτῶν καὶ ἴδωσιν τὴν ἀπώλειαν τῶν ἀγαπητῶν, [καὶ] δῆσον αὐτοὺς ἑβδομήκοντα γενεὰς εἰς τὰς νάπας τῆς γῆς μέχρι ἡμέρας κρίσεως αὐτῶν καὶ συντελεσμοῦ, ἕως τελεσθῇ τὸ κρίμα τοῦ αἰῶνος τῶν αἰώνων. 13. τότε ἀπαχθήσονται εἰς τὸ χάος τοῦ πυρὸς καὶ[7] εἰς τὴν βάσανον καὶ εἰς τὸ δεσμωτήριον * συνκλείσεως αἰῶνος[8]. 14 καὶ * ὃς ἂν[9] †κατακαυσθῇ†[10] καὶ ἀφανισθῇ, ἀπὸ τοῦ νῦν μετ' αὐτῶν ὁμοῦ δεθήσονται μέχρι τελειώσεως γενεᾶς.[11]

G^s

ἀπόλεσον τοὺς υἱοὺς τῶν ἐγρηγόρων ἀπὸ τῶν υἱῶν τῶν ἀνθρώπων· πέμψον αὐτοὺς * εἰς ἀλλήλους, ἐξ αὐτῶν εἰς αὐτούς[3], ἐν πολέμῳ καὶ ἐν ἀπωλείᾳ. καὶ μακρότης ἡμερῶν οὐκ ἔσται αὐτοῖς, 10. καὶ πᾶσα ἐρώτησις οὐκ ἔστι τοῖς πατράσιν αὐτῶν, ὅτι ἐλπίζουσι ζῆσαι ζωὴν αἰώνιον, καὶ ὅτι ζήσεται ἕκαστος αὐτῶν ἔτη πεντακόσια. 11. Καὶ τῷ Μιχαὴλ εἶπε· Πορεύου, ⌜Μιχαήλ⌝, δῆσον[5] Σεμιαζᾶν καὶ τοὺς ἄλλους σὺν αὐτῷ τοὺς συμμιγέντας ταῖς θυγατράσι τῶν ἀνθρώπων τοῦ μιανθῆναι ἐν αὐταῖς ἐν[6] τῇ ἀκαθαρσίᾳ αὐτῶν 12. καὶ ὅταν κατασφαγῶσιν οἱ υἱοὶ αὐτῶν καὶ ἴδωσι τὴν ἀπώλειαν τῶν ἀγαπητῶν αὐτῶν, δῆσον αὐτοὺς ἐπὶ ἑβδομήκοντα γενεὰς εἰς τὰς νάπας τῆς γῆς μέχρι ἡμέρας κρίσεως αὐτῶν, μέχρι ἡμέρας τελειώσεως [τελεσμοῦ], ἕως συντελεσθῇ κρίμα τοῦ αἰῶνος τῶν αἰώνων. 13. τότε ἀπενεχθήσονται εἰς τὸ χάος τοῦ πυρὸς καὶ[7] εἰς τὴν βάσανον καὶ εἰς τὸ δεσμωτήριον τῆς συγκλείσεως τοῦ αἰῶνος[8]. 14. καὶ ὃς ἂν κατακριθῇ καὶ ἀφανισθῇ,

υἱοὺς τῆς πόρνης καί [1] E adds ἐξαπόστειλον αὐτοὺς καί—a dittographic rendering [2] Add εἰς ἀλλήλους with G^s E [3] So also E G^g omits [4] MS ἐργεσις Em by Lods [5] G^g = E. G^s is right [6] E adds πάσῃ [7] E omits [8] E = καὶ συγκλειθήσονται εἰς τοὺς αἰῶνας—a free rendering of the text [9] Em with G^s from οταν. E = ὅταν. [10] = E. Corrupt for

G⁸   Gᵇ

ἀπὸ τοῦ νῦν μετ᾽ αὐτῶν δεθήσεται

μέχρι τελειώσεως γενεᾶς αὐτῶν[11].

15. Ἀπόλεσον πάντα τὰ πνεύματα τῶν κιβδήλων καὶ τοὺς υἱοὺς τῶν ἐγρηγόρων διὰ τὸ ἀδικῆσαι τοὺς ἀνθρώπους. 16. καὶ ἀπόλεσον τὴν ἀδικίαν πᾶσαν ἀπὸ τῆς γῆς, καὶ πᾶν ἔργον πονηρίας ἐκλειπέτω, καὶ ἀναφανήτω τὸ φυτὸν τῆς δικαιοσύνης καὶ τῆς ἀληθείας[1] εἰς τοὺς αἰῶνας . . . μετὰ χαρᾶς φυτευ(θή)σεται.

17 Καὶ νῦν πάντες οἱ δίκαιοι ἐκφεύξονται,

καὶ ἔσονται ζῶντες ἕως γεννήσωσιν χιλιάδας,

καὶ πᾶσαι αἱ ἡμέραι νεότητος αὐτῶν, καὶ † τὰ σάββατα αὐτῶν[2]

μετὰ εἰρήνης πληρώσουσιν[3]

18 τότε ἐργασθήσεται πᾶσα ἡ γῆ ἐν δικαιοσύνῃ καὶ καταφυτευθήσεται * δένδρον ἐν αὐτῇ[4], καὶ πλησθήσεται εὐλογίας 19 καὶ πάντα τὰ δένδρα τῆς †γῆς ἀγαλλιάσονται †[5] φυτευθήσεται, καὶ ἔσονται φυτεύοντες ἀμπέλους, (κ)αὶ ἡ ἄμπελος ἣν ἂν φυτεύσωσιν, ποιήσουσιν προχοὺς οἴνου· *χιλιάδας καὶ σπόρου ποιήσει καθ᾽ ἕκαστον μέτρον[6], ἐλαίας ποιήσει ἀνὰ βάτους δέκα. 20. καὶ σὺ καθάρισον τὴν γῆν ἀπὸ πάσης ἀκαθαρσίας[7] καὶ ἀπὸ πάσης ἀδικίας καὶ ἀπὸ (πά)σης ἁμαρτίας καὶ[8] ἀσεβείας, καὶ πάσας τὰς ἀκαθαρσίας τὰς γινομένας ἐπὶ τῆς γῆς ἐξάλειψον[9] 21. καὶ ἔσονται πάντες λατρεύοντες οἱ λαοὶ καὶ εὐλογοῦντες πάντες ἐμοὶ καὶ προσκυνοῦντες 22. καὶ καθαρισθήσεται ⌜πᾶσα⌝ ἡ γῆ ἀπὸ παντὸς μιάσματος καὶ ἀπὸ πάσης ἀκαθαρσίας καὶ ὀργῆς καὶ μάστιγος, καὶ οὐκέτι πέμψω ἐπ᾽ αὐτοὺς εἰς πάσας τὰς γενεὰς τοῦ αἰῶνος XI καὶ τότε ἀνοίξω τὰ ταμεῖα τῆς εὐλογίας τὰ ὄντα ἐν τῷ οὐρανῷ, καὶ κατενεγκεῖν αὐτὰ[10] ἐπὶ

κατακριθῇ as in Gᵃ   [11] E = πασῶν γενεῶν.   [1] Add with E καὶ ἔσται εὐλογία τὰ ἔργα τῆς δικαιοσύνης καὶ τῆς ἀληθείας lost through hmt.   [2] = שַׁבְּתְהוֹן in which the word is wrongly vocalized for שִׁבְתְהוֹן = 'their old age.' The error is explicable in Heb also ı e שְׁבָתָם instead of שִׂבָתָם. Hence read τὸ γῆρας αὐτῶν.   [3] Appears to be intransitive heıe E renders ıt transı tively and puts the preceding nomi-

natives ın the accusatıve   [4] E = πᾶσα δένδροıς   [5] Coıı upt. E = 'and all desırable trees.'   [6] Text ıs translate-able but seems curruµt E = καὶ πᾶς ὁ σπόρος ὁ σπαρεὶς ἐν αὐτῇ ἕκαστον μέτρον ποιήσει χιλιάδας καὶ ἕκαστον μέτρον Here πᾶς αὐτῇ ıs a nominatıvus pendens.   [7] E = 'oppressıon'   [8] E adds πάσης   [9] E adds ἀπὸ τῆς γῆς.   21 καὶ ἔσονται πάντες οἱ υἱοὶ τῶν ἀνθρώπων δίκαιοı   [10] E adds ἐπὶ τὴν γῆν.

τὰ ἔργα, ἐπὶ τὸν κόπον τῶν υἱῶν τῶν ἀνθρώπων.　2. καὶ ⌈τότε⌉
* ἀλήθεια καὶ εἰρήνη [1] κοινωνήσουσιν ὁμοῦ εἰς πάσας τὰς ἡμέρας τοῦ
αἰῶνος καὶ εἰς πάσας τὰς γενεὰς τῶν ἀνθρώπων [2]

XII. Πρὸ τούτων τῶν λόγων ἐλήμφθη Ἐνώχ, καὶ οὐδεὶς [3] τῶν
ἀνθρώπων ἔγνω ποῦ ἐλήμφθη καὶ ποῦ ἐστιν καὶ τί ἐγένετο αὐτῷ.
2. καὶ τὰ ἔργα αὐτοῦ [4] μετὰ τῶν ἐγρηγόρων, καὶ μετὰ τῶν ἁγίων * αἱ
ἡμέραι [5] αὐτοῦ.　3. Καὶ ⌈ἑστὼς⌉ ἤμην Ἐνὼχ εὐλογῶν τῷ κυρίῳ [6] τῆς
μεγαλοσύνης, τῷ βασιλεῖ τῶν αἰώνων　καὶ ἰδοὺ οἱ ἐγρήγοροι ⌈τοῦ
ἁγίου τοῦ μεγάλου⌉ ἐκάλουν με Ἐνώχ [7], ...　4. ὁ γραμματεὺς τῆς
δικαιοσύνης Πορεύου καὶ εἰπὲ τοῖς ἐγρηγόροις τοῦ οὐρανοῦ οἵτινες
ἀπολιπόντες τὸν οὐρανὸν τὸν ὑψηλόν, τὸ ἁγίασμα τῆς στάσεως τοῦ
αἰῶνος, μετὰ τῶν γυναικῶν ἐμιάνθησαν, καὶ ὥσπερ οἱ υἱοὶ τῆς γῆς
ποιοῦσιν, οὕτως καὶ αὐτοὶ ποιοῦσιν [8], καὶ ἔλαβον ἑαυτοῖς γυναῖκας·
ἀφανισμὸν μέγαν †κατῃφανίσατε [9] τὴν γῆν,　5. καὶ οὐκ ἔσται ὑμῖν [10]
εἰρήνη οὔτε ἄφεσις. καὶ περὶ ὧν χαίρουσιν τῶν υἱῶν αὐτῶν [11],　6. τὸν
φόνον τῶν ἀγαπητῶν αὐτῶν ὄψονται, καὶ ἐπὶ τῇ ἀπωλείᾳ τῶν υἱῶν
αὐτῶν στενάξουσιν καὶ δεηθήσονται εἰς τὸν αἰῶνα. καὶ οὐκ ἔσται
αὐτοῖς εἰς ἔλεον καὶ εἰρήνην [12]

XIII Ὁ δὲ Ἐνὼχ †τῷ Ἀζαὴλ εἶπεν Πορεύου † [13] οὐκ ἔσται σοι
εἰρήνη κρίμα μέγα ἐξῆλθεν κατὰ σοῦ δῆσαί σε,　2. καὶ ἀνοχὴ καὶ
ἐρώτησίς σοι οὐκ ἔσται περὶ ὧν ἔδειξας ἀδικημάτων καὶ περὶ πάντων
τῶν ἔργων τῶν ἀσεβειῶν καὶ τῆς ἀδικίας καὶ τῆς ἁμαρτίας, ὅσα
ὑπέδειξας τοῖς ἀνθρώποις.

3. Τότε πορευθεὶς εἴρηκα πᾶσιν αὐτοῖς, καὶ αὐτοὶ πάντες ἐφοβή-
θησαν, καὶ ἔλαβεν αὐτοὺς τρόμος καὶ φόβος.　4. καὶ ἠρώτησαν [14]

---

[1] E trans　[2] E = αιωνων a wrong expansion of α̅π̅ω̅ν̅ which appears in G　[3] E
adds τῶν υἱῶν.　[4] MS αὐτῶν.　[5] E
corrupt = ἐν ταῖς ἡμέραις. [6] Εὐλογεῖν
used with dat in Sn 50²², 51¹² &c.
[7] Add with E τὸν γραμματέα καὶ εἶπον
ἐμοί Ἐνώχ lost through hmt　[8] E =
ἐποίησαν οι πεποιήκεσαν.　[9] MS. και-
ηφανισατε　E = καὶ ἀφ. μέγ ἠφανίσθησαν　[10] E = αὐτοῖς which appears
wrong　[11] Read ὑμῶν and ὑμῖν fοι
αὐτῶν and αὐτοῖς here and in the next

verse.　[12] A strange construction.
[13] Corrupt for πορευθεὶς εἶπεν Ἀζαὴλ as
is shown by E, and G 13². The corruption in G may have originated in
the Aram.　G = אֵלִיל corrupt for
אוֹל וָאמֵר　Here we may conclude
either to a happy emendation of the
Ethiopic translator of G or of the scribe
of the Greek MS. used by E or to the
existence in the Aramaic of both forms,
the corrupt in the text and the true
reading in the margin.　[14] E adds

ὅπως γράψω αὐτοῖς ὑπομνήματα ἐρωτήσεως, ἵνα γένηται¹ αὐτοῖς ἄφεσις, καὶ ἵνα ἐγὼ ἀναγνῶ² αὐτοῖς τὸ ὑπόμνημα τῆς ἐρωτήσεως ἐνώπιον Κυρίου τοῦ οὐρανοῦ,   5. ὅτι αὐτοὶ οὐκέτι δύνανται λαλῆσαι, οὐδὲ ἐπᾶραι αὐτῶν τοὺς ὀφθαλμοὺς εἰς τὸν οὐρανὸν ἀπὸ αἰσχύνης *περὶ ὧν ἡμαρτήκεισαν καὶ κατεκρίθησαν³.   6. Τότε ἔγραψα τὸ ὑπόμνημα τῆς ἐρωτήσεως αὐτῶν καὶ τὰς δεήσεις περὶ τῶν πνευμάτων αὐτῶν⁴ καὶ περὶ ὧν δέονται, ὅπως αὐτῶν γένωνται ἄφεσις καὶ μακρότης.   7. καὶ πορευθεὶς ἐκάθισα ἐπὶ τῶν ὑδάτων Δὰν ἐν γῇ⁵ Δάν, ἥτις ἐστὶν ἐκ *δεξιῶν Ἑρμωνειεὶμ δύσεως⁶· ἀνεγίνωσκον τὸ ὑπόμνημα τῶν δεήσεων αὐτῶν ἕως⁷ ἐκοιμήθην.   8 καὶ ἰδοὺ ὄνειροι ἐπ' ἐμὲ ἦλθον καὶ ὁράσεις ἐπ' ἐμὲ ἐπέπιπτον, καὶ ἴδον ὁράσεις ὀργῆς, ⌜καὶ ἦλθεν φωνὴ λέγουσα⌝ Εἰπὸν⁸ τοῖς υἱοῖς τοῦ οὐρανοῦ *τοῦ ἐλέγξαι⁹ αὐτούς.   9 καὶ ἔξυπνος γενόμενος ἦλθον πρὸς αὐτούς, καὶ πάντες συνηγμένοι ἐκάθηντο πενθοῦντες [σ]ἐν Ἐβελσατά¹⁰, ἥτις ἐστὶν ἀνὰ μέσον τοῦ Λιβάνου καὶ Σενισήλ¹¹, περικεκαλυμμένοι τὴν ὄψιν.   10 ἐνώπιον αὐτῶν καὶ¹² ἀνήγγειλα αὐτοῖς πάσας τὰς ὁράσεις ἃς εἶδον κατὰ τοὺς ὕπνους, καὶ ἠρξάμην λαλεῖν τοὺς λόγους τῆς δικαιοσύνης, ἐλέγχων¹³ τοὺς ἐγρηγόρους τοῦ οὐρανοῦ.

XIV. Βίβλος λόγων δικαιοσύνης καὶ ἐλέγξεως ἐγρηγόρων τῶν ἀπὸ τοῦ αἰῶνος, κατὰ τὴν ἐντολὴν τοῦ ἁγίου¹⁴ τοῦ μεγάλου ἐν ταύτῃ τῇ ὁράσει.   2. Ἐγὼ εἶδον κατὰ τοὺς ὕπνους μου ὃ¹⁵ νῦν λέγω ἐν γλώσσῃ σαρκίνῃ *ἐν τῷ πνεύματι τοῦ στόματός μου, ὃ ἔδωκεν ὁ μέγας¹⁶ τοῖς ἀνθρώποις λαλεῖν ἐν αὐτοῖς καὶ *νοήσει καρδίας¹⁷·   3. ὃς¹⁸ ἔκτισεν καὶ ἔδωκεν¹⁹ ἐλέγξασθαι²⁰ ἐγρηγόρους τοὺς υἱοὺς τοῦ οὐρανοῦ.   4 Ἐγὼ τὴν ἐρώτησιν ὑμῶν [τῶν ἀγγέλων]²¹ ἔγραψα, καὶ

ἐμέ.   ¹ MS. γένονται.   ² MS. αναγνοι. E = ἀνάγω corrupt for ἀναγνῶ   ³ E = περὶ τῶν ἁμαρτιῶν αὐτῶν περὶ ὧν κατεκρίθησαν   ⁴ E adds 'and their deeds individually'   ⁵ E wrongly omits.   ⁶ E gives the right order = δεξιῶν δύσεως Ἑρ   ⁷ Em with E from ως.   ⁸ E = ἵνα εἴπω.   ⁹ E = καὶ ἐλέγξω.   ¹⁰ E = Ἀβελσιαήλ.   ¹¹ E = Sénêsêr = the O.T. Senir, a name of Hermon (Deut 3³) or of a part of it (Cant 4⁸)   ¹² Trans before ἐνώπιον with E   ¹³ E = καὶ ἐλέγχειν   ¹⁴ E adds καί   ¹⁵ MS ων   ¹⁶ E = καὶ ἐν τῷ πνεύματί μου ὃ ἔδωκεν ὁ μέγας εἰς τὸ στόμα, but is easily emended   ¹⁷ If the text were right νοήσει should be taken as under the same government as γλώσσῃ E = νοῆσαι καρδίᾳ.   ¹⁸ Read ὡς with E.   ¹⁹ Add with E the following words which have been lost through hmt. νοεῖν τοὺς λόγους τῆς γνώσεως, καὶ ἐμὲ ἔκτισεν καὶ ἔδωκεν   ²⁰ MS. ἐκλεξασθαι   ²¹ A gloss   E omits.

ἐν τῇ ὁράσει μου τοῦτο¹ ἐδείχθη   * καὶ οὔτε² ἡ ἐρώτησις ὑμῶν παρεδέχθη³,   5. *ἴνα μηκέτι⁴ εἰς τὸν οὐρανὸν ἀναβῆτε ἐπὶ πάντας τοὺς αἰῶνας, καὶ * ἐν τοῖς † δεσμοῖς † τῆς γῆς⁵ ἐρρέθη δῆσαι ὑμᾶς εἰς πάσας τὰς γενεὰς⁶ τοῦ αἰῶνος,   6. καὶ ⌜ἴνα⌝ πρὸ⁷ τούτων ἴδητε τὴν ἀπώλειαν τῶν υἱῶν ὑμῶν τῶν ἀγαπητῶν, καὶ ὅτι οὐκ ἔσται ὑμῖν ὄνησις αὐτῶν, ἀλλὰ πεσοῦνται ἐνώπιον ὑμῶν ἐν μαχαίρᾳ.   7. καὶ ἡ ἐρώτησις ὑμῶν περὶ αὐτῶν οὐκ ἔσται οὐδὲ περὶ ὑμῶν· * καὶ ὑμεῖς κλαίοντες⁸ καὶ δεόμενοι καὶ μὴν⁹ λαλοῦντες πᾶν ῥῆμα ἀπὸ τῆς γραφῆς ἧς ἔγραψα.   8. Καὶ ἐμοὶ * ἐφ᾽ ὁράσει¹⁰ οὕτως ἐδείχθη· ἰδοὺ νεφέλαι ἐν τῇ ὁράσει ἐκάλουν καὶ ὁμίχλαι με ἐφώνουν, καὶ διαδρομαὶ τῶν ἀστέρων καὶ διαστραπαί με κατεσπούδαζον καὶ †ἐθορύβαζόν†¹¹ με, καὶ ἄνεμοι ἐν τῇ ὁράσει μου †ἐξεπέτασάν†¹² με καὶ ἐπῆράν¹³ με ἄνω¹⁴ καὶ εἰσήνεγκάν με εἰς τὸν οὐρανόν.   9. καὶ εἰσῆλθον μέχρις ἤγγισα τείχους οἰκοδομῆς¹⁵ ἐν λίθοις χαλάζης καὶ γλώσσαις¹⁶ πυρὸς κύκλῳ αὐτῶν καὶ ἤρξαντο ἐκφοβεῖν με.   10 Καὶ εἰσῆλθον εἰς τὰς γλώσσας τοῦ πυρός, καὶ ἤγγισα εἰς οἶκον μέγαν οἰκοδομημένον ἐν λίθοις χαλάζης, καὶ οἱ τοῖχοι τοῦ οἴκου ὡς λιθόπλακες, καὶ πᾶσαι ἦσαν ἐκ χιόνος¹⁷, καὶ ἐδάφη χιονικά,   11. καὶ αἱ στέγαι ὡς διαδρομαὶ ἀστέρων καὶ ἀστραπαί, καὶ μεταξὺ αὐτῶν χερουβὶν πύρινα, καὶ οὐρανὸς αὐτῶν ὕδωρ,   12. καὶ πῦρ φλεγόμενον κύκλῳ τῶν τοίχων, καὶ θύραι πυρὶ καιόμεναι.   13. εἰσῆλθον¹⁸ εἰς τὸν οἶκον ἐκεῖνον, θερμὸν¹⁸ ὡς πῦρ καὶ ψυχρὸν ὡς χιών¹⁹, καὶ πᾶσα τροφὴ²⁰ ζωῆς οὐκ ἦν ἐν αὐτῷ· φόβος με ἐκάλυψεν καὶ τρόμος με ἔλαβεν.   14. καὶ ἤμην σειόμενος καὶ τρέμων, καὶ ἔπεσον * ἐπὶ πρόσωπόν μου καὶ²¹ ἐθεώρουν * ἐν τῇ ὁράσει ⌜μου⌝²²,   15. καὶ ἰδοὺ * ἄλλην θύραν ἀνεῳγμένην κατέναντί μου,

---

¹ E = κατὰ τοῦτο, ² E = ὅτι. ³ E = οὐκ ἔσται ὑμῖν, and adds εἰς πάσας τὰς ἡμέρας τοῦ αἰῶνος καὶ ἡ κρίσις ἐτελειώθη ἐφ᾽ ὑμᾶς καὶ οὐκ ἔσται ὑμῖν ⁴ E = καὶ ἀπὸ τοῦ νῦν ⁵ For δεσμοῖς τῆς γῆς we should probably read δεσμοῖς ἐν τῇ γῇ E has ἐν τῇ γῇ only ⁶ E = ἡμέρας. ⁷ MS περί ⁸ We should expect καὶ κλαιόντων ⁹ Em from MS μη, which E follows. ¹⁰ E = ὅρασις ¹¹ This word (= perturbabant, and so E) cannot be right We require a synonym of κατεσπούδαζον ¹² This may be an attempt to render אֶפְרַח = 'caused to fly' E = ἀνεπτέρωσαν. Or rather it may be corrupt for ἐξεπέρασαν (Lods) ¹³ E = κατεσπούδαζον, or possibly ἔπαιρον ¹⁴ E wrongly trans into next clause ¹⁵ E = οἰκοδομημένου ¹⁶ MS γλωσσης. ¹⁷ E = ἐν λίθοις τοῖς ἐκ χιόνος. ¹⁸ E prefixes καί. ¹⁹ E = κρύσταλλος ²⁰ E = τρυφή These words are frequently confused ²¹ Added from E ²² E = ὅρασιν

καὶ ὁ οἶκος μείζων τούτου, καὶ ὅλος¹ οἰκοδομημένος ἐν γλώσσαις πυρός,
16. καὶ ὅλος διαφέρων ἐν δόξῃ καὶ ἐν τιμῇ καὶ ἐν μεγαλοσύνῃ, ὥστε μὴ
δύνασθαί με ἐξειπεῖν ὑμῖν περὶ τῆς δόξης καὶ περὶ τῆς μεγαλοσύνης
αὐτοῦ.   17. τὸ² ἔδαφος αὐτοῦ ἦν πυρός, τὸ δὲ ἀνώτερον αὐτοῦ
ἦσαν ἀστραπαὶ καὶ διαδρομαὶ ἀστέρων, καὶ ἡ στέγη αὐτοῦ ἦν πῦρ
φλέγον.   18. Ἐθεώρουν δὲ καὶ εἶδον³ θρόνον ὑψηλόν⁴, καὶ τὸ
εἶδος αὐτοῦ ὡσεὶ κρυστάλλινον, καὶ *τροχὸς ὡς ἡλίου λάμποντος⁵ καὶ
† ὄρος †⁶ χερουβίν.   19. καὶ ὑποκάτω τοῦ θρόνου ἐξεπορεύοντο
ποταμοὶ πυρὸς φλεγόμενοι⁷, καὶ οὐκ ἐδυνάσθην ἰδεῖν.   20. καὶ ἡ
δόξα ἡ μεγάλη ἐκάθητο ἐπ' αὐτῷ· τὸ περιβόλαιον αὐτοῦ [ὡς εἶδος]⁸
ἡλίου λαμπρότερον καὶ λευκότερον πάσης χιόνος.   21. καὶ οὐκ
ἐδύνατο πᾶς ἄγγελος παρελθεῖν ⌈εἰς τὸν οἶκον τοῦτον⌉ καὶ ἰδεῖν τὸ
πρόσωπον αὐτοῦ * διὰ τὸ ἔντιμον καὶ ἔνδοξον⁹, καὶ οὐκ ἐδύνατο
πᾶσα σὰρξ ἰδεῖν αὐτόν.   22. τὸ πῦρ φλεγόμενον κύκλῳ· καὶ πῦρ
μέγα παρειστήκει αὐτῷ, καὶ οὐδεὶς ἐγγίζει αὐτῷ (τῶν)¹⁰ κύκλῳ, μυρίαι
μυριάδες ἑστήκασιν ἐνώπιον αὐτοῦ, * καὶ πᾶς λόγος αὐτοῦ ἔργον¹¹.
23. καὶ οἱ ἅγιοι τῶν ἀγγέλων¹² οἱ ἐγγίζοντες αὐτῷ οὐκ ἀποχωροῦσιν
νυκτὸς οὔτε ἀφίστανται αὐτοῦ.   24. Κἀγὼ ἤμην ἕως τούτου ἐπὶ
πρόσωπόν μου βεβλημένος¹³ καὶ τρέμων, καὶ ὁ κύριος τῷ στόματι
αὐτοῦ ἐκάλεσέν με καὶ εἶπέν μοι Πρόσελθε ὧδε, Ἐνώχ, καὶ τὸν
λόγον μου ἄκουσον¹⁴.   25. ⌈καὶ προσελθών μοι εἷς τῶν ἁγίων
ἤγειρέν με⌉ καὶ ἔστησέν με, καὶ προσήγαγέν με μέχρι τῆς θύρας·
ἐγὼ δὲ τὸ πρόσωπόν μου κάτω ἔκυφον.

XV. Καὶ ἀποκριθεὶς εἶπέν μοι [Ὁ ἄνθρωπος ὁ ἀληθινός, ἄνθρωπος
τῆς ἀληθείας ὁ γραμματεύς]¹⁵ καὶ τῆς φωνῆς αὐτοῦ ἤκουσα· μὴ

---

¹ Seems corrupt. E which gives good
sense = ἄλλος οἶκος μείζων τούτου καὶ
ὅλη ἡ θύρα αὐτοῦ ἀνεῳγμένη κατέναντί
μου καί   Gᵍ appears to be a dislocated
form of E   ² E = καὶ τό.   ³ E
adds ἐν αὐτῷ   ⁴ g m q of E = ὑψηλοῦ
⁵ E = τροχὸς αὐτοῦ ὡς ἥλιος λάμπων
⁹ Corrupt for ὅρασις E seems to have
had οροσ before it and emended it into
ὀπός (from ὄψ) ' the voice '.   ⁷ Better
read φλεγομένου with E : cf Dan. 7¹⁰.
⁸ Bracketed as an interpolation.   ⁹ E
= τοῦ ἐντίμου, καὶ ἐνδόξου.   ¹⁰ τῶν

supplied from E. So Diels and Flemming. κύκλῳ cannot be connected
with the next clause owing to the
words ἐνώπιον αὐτοῦ   ¹¹ E = οὐδὲ
προσδεῖται οὐδεμᾶς συμβυνλῆς. It is
probable that this clause, or some
equivalent, is lost in G   ¹² E = ἁγίων
¹³ E = περίβλημα which is corrupt.
¹⁴ E = ἅγιον corrupt.   ¹⁵ Bracketed
as an interpolation. They occur in
their correct form and place two lines
later. If they are in any sense au-
thentic the second ἄνθρωπος must be

φοβηθῆς, Ἐνώχ, ἄνθρωπος ἀληθινὸς καὶ γραμματεὺς τῆς ἀληθείας·
πρόσελθε ὧδε, καὶ τῆς φωνῆς μου ἄκουσον   2. πορεύθητι¹ καὶ¹
εἰπὲ² τοῖς πέμψασίν σε³ .... Ἐρωτῆσαι ὑμᾶς ἔδει περὶ τῶν
ἀνθρώπων, καὶ μὴ τοὺς ἀνθρώπους περὶ ὑμῶν.   3. διὰ τί ἀπελίπετε
τὸν οὐρανὸν τὸν ὑψηλὸν τὸν ἅγιον τοῦ αἰῶνος, καὶ μετὰ τῶν γυναικῶν
ἐκοιμήθητε καὶ μετὰ τῶν θυγατέρων τῶν ἀνθρώπων ἐμιάνθητε καὶ
ἐλάβετε ἑαυτοῖς γυναῖκας ;⁴ ὥσπερ υἱοὶ τῆς γῆς ἐποιήσατε καὶ ἐγεννήσατε ἑαυτοῖς [τέκνα]⁵ υἱοὺς γίγαντας.   4 καὶ ὑμεῖς ἦτε ἅγιοι
*καὶ πνεύμα(τα)⁶ ζῶντα αἰώνια· ἐν τῷ αἵματι τῶν γυναικῶν ἐμιάνθητε,
καὶ ἐν αἵματι σαρκὸς ἐγεννήσατε καὶ † ἐν αἵματι ἀνθρώπων ἐπεθυμή-
σατε⁷, καθὼς καὶ αὐτοὶ ποιοῦσιν, σάρκα καὶ αἷμα, οἵτινες ἀποθνή-
σκουσιν καὶ ἀπόλλυνται.   5. διὰ τοῦτο ἔδωκα αὐτοῖς θηλείας, ἵνα
σπερματίσουσιν⁸ εἰς αὐτὰς καὶ τεκνώσουσιν ἐν αὐταῖς⁹ τέκνα οὕτως,
ἵνα μὴ ἐκλείπῃ¹⁰ αὐτοῖς¹¹ πᾶν ἔργον ἐπὶ τῆς γῆς.   6. ὑμεῖς δὲ
ὑπήρχετε πνεύμα(τα)¹² ζῶντα αἰώνια καὶ¹³ οὐκ ἀποθνήσκοντα εἰς
πάσας τὰς γενεὰς τοῦ αἰῶνος.   7 καὶ διὰ τοῦτο οὐκ ἐποίησα ἐν
ὑμῖν θηλείας τὰ¹⁴ πνεύμα(τα)¹² τοῦ οὐρανοῦ, ἐν τῷ οὐρανῷ ἡ κατοίκησις αὐτῶν.

G^g	**G⁸**

Gᵍ

8 καὶ νῦν οἱ γίγαντες οἱ γεν-
νηθέντες ἀπὸ τῶν πνευμάτων καὶ
σαρκὸς πνεύμα(τα) † ἰσχυρὰ †¹⁵
⟨κληθήσονται⟩¹⁶ ἐπὶ τῆς γῆς καὶ ἐν
τῇ γῇ ἡ κατοίκησις αὐτῶν ἔσται.
9. πνεύμα(τα) πονηρὰ ἐξῆλθον
ἀπὸ τοῦ σώματος αὐτῶν, διότι
ἀπὸ τῶν † ἀνωτέρων †¹⁷ ἐγένοντο,

G⁸

8. Καὶ νῦν οἱ γίγαντες οἱ γεν-
νηθέντες ἀπὸ πνευμάτων καὶ
σαρκὸς πνεύματα πονηρὰ ἐπὶ τῆς
γῆς καλέσουσιν αὐτούς¹⁶, ὅτι ἡ
κατοίκησις αὐτῶν ἔσται ἐπὶ τῆς
γῆς.   9. πνεύματα πονηρὰ
⌜ἔσονται, τὰ πνεύματα⌝ ἐξεληλυ-
θότα ἀπὸ τοῦ σώματος ⌜τῆς σαρ-

regarded as an intrusion   ¹ E trans
² E adds τοῖς ἐγρηγόροις τοῦ οὐρανοῦ.
³ Add with E the following words
lost through hmt. . ἐρωτῆσαι περὶ αὐτῶν
⁴ E adds καί.   ⁵ Bracketed as a
dittographic rendering   ⁶ E = πνευ-
ματικοί.   ⁷ The error appears to lie
in ἐν αἵματι ἀνθρώπων. This = ברם
אֲנָשֵׁי which may be corrupt (?) for
כבני אֲנָשֵׁי = ὥσπερ υἱοὶ τῶν ἀνθρώπων.

In that case the object of ἐπεθυμήσατε
is σαρκα καὶ αἷμα.   ⁸ MS. σπερματί-
ζουσιν   ⁹ MS. αυτοις   ¹⁰ MS.
εκλειπει   ¹¹ E = ἐν αὐταῖς   ¹² E =
πνευματικά   ¹³ E = τά   ¹⁴ E prefixes διότι.   ¹⁵ May be corrupt for
σκληρά see ver 11   E Gˢ = πονηρά.
¹⁶ Added with E   Gˢ has καλέσουσιν
αὐτούς   ¹⁷ So also E   Corrupt for
ἀνθρώπων as in Gˢ

G⁸

καὶ ἐκ τῶν ἁγίων ἐγρηγόρων ἡ
ἀρχὴ *τῆς κτίσεως ¹ αὐτῶν *καὶ
ἀρχὴ θεμελίου ². *πνεύματα
πονηρὰ κληθήσεται ³. [10.
πνεύμα(τα) οὐρανοῦ, ἐν τῷ οὐρανῷ
ἡ κατοίκησις αὐτῶν ἔσται· καὶ τὰ
πνεύματα ἐπὶ τῆς γῆς τὰ γεννη-
θέντα, ἐπὶ τῆς γῆς ἡ κατοίκησις
αὐτῶν ἔσται.⁴] 11. καὶ τὰ
πνεύματα τῶν γιγάντων † νεφέλας † ⁵ ἀδικοῦντα, ἀφανίζοντα
καὶ ἐνπίπτοντα καὶ συνπαλαίοντα
καὶ συνρίπτοντα ἐπὶ τῆς γῆς
[πνεύματα σκληρὰ γιγάντων] ⁶
καὶ δρόμους ⁷ ποιοῦντα καὶ μηδὲν
ἐσθίοντα, ⌐ἀλλ' ἀσιτοῦντα⌐ ⁸ καὶ
διψῶντα καὶ προσκόπτοντα ⁹.
12. καὶ ἐξαναστήσει ταῦτα (τὰ)
πνεύμα(τα) ¹⁰ εἰς τοὺς υἱοὺς τῶν
ἀνθρώπων καὶ *τῶν γυναικῶν ¹¹,
ὅτι ἐξεληλύθασιν ⌐ἀπ' αὐτῶν⌐,
XVI. ἀπὸ ἡμέρας σφαγῆς καὶ
ἀπωλείας καὶ θανάτου ¹², ἀφ'
ὧν ¹³ τὰ πνεύματα ἐκπορευόμενα
ἐκ τῆς ψυχῆς τῆς σαρκὸς αὐτῶν

G⁸

κὸς⌐ αὐτῶν, διότι ἀπὸ τῶν ἀνθρώπων ἐγένοντο, καὶ ἐκ τῶν ἁγίων
τῶν ἐγρηγόρων ἡ ἀρχὴ *τῆς κτίσεως ¹ αὐτῶν καὶ ἀρχὴ θεμελίου ²· πνεύματα πονηρὰ ἐπὶ τῆς
γῆς ἔσονται ³ 11. τὰ πνεύματα
τῶν γιγάντων νεμόμενα, ἀδικοῦντα, ἀφανίζοντα, ἐμπίπτοντα
καὶ συμπαλαίοντα καὶ ῥιπτοῦντα
ἐπὶ τῆς γῆς καὶ δρόμους ποιοῦντα,
καὶ μηδὲν ἐσθίοντα, ⌐ἀλλ' ἀσιτοῦντα ⁸ *καὶ φάσματα ποιοῦντα⌐
καὶ διψῶντα καὶ προσκόπτοντα ⁹.
12. καὶ ἐξαναστήσονται τὰ πνεύματα ἐπὶ τοὺς υἱοὺς τῶν ἀνθρώπων καὶ *τῶν γυναικῶν ¹¹, ὅτι ἐξ
αὐτῶν ἐξεληλύθασι, XVI. καὶ
ἀπὸ ἡμέρας ⌐καιροῦ⌐ σφαγῆς καὶ
ἀπωλείας καὶ θανάτου τῶν γιγάντων [Ναφηλείμ, οἱ ἰσχυροὶ τῆς
γῆς, οἱ μεγάλοι ὀνομαστοί,] τὰ
πνεύματα τὰ ἐκπορευόμενα ἀπὸ
τῆς ψυχῆς αὐτῶν, ⌐ὡς ἐκ⌐ τῆς
σαρκὸς ἔσονται ἀφανίζοντα χωρὶς
κρίσεως· οὕτως ἀφανίσουσι μέ-

---

¹ E omits ² The phrase is possibly a dittography. ἀρχὴ τῆς κτίσεως = ראש מולדת
which could easily be corrupted into
ר״ = מוסדה = ἀρχὴ θεμελίου. In Aram
we may suppose ראש ילדותא corrupted
into ר״ יסודא. ³ E = πνεύματα πονηρὰ
ἔσονται ἐπὶ τῆς γῆς καὶ πνεύματα πονηρὰ
κληθήσεται Add with G⁵ E καὶ πνεύματα πονηρὰ κληθήσεται. ⁴ This verse
is merely a repetition of phrases in
verses 7, 8 G⁸ rightly omits. ⁵ So
also E = עניין. G⁸ has νεμόμενα, which

in the sense of 'laying waste' may =
רעעין which was corrupted into עניין
⁶ A gloss. G³ E omit. ⁷ E = τρόμους ⁸ So also G⁵. E omits. It
may be a doublet of μηδὲν ἐσθίοντα
⁹ E corrupt = ἀόρατα ¹⁰ MS. wrongly
trans before καὶ ἐξαναστήσει ¹¹ E =
εἰς τὰς γυναῖκας ¹² Add τῶν γιγάντων
with G⁸ E. It is required by ἀφ' ὧν.
¹³ ἀφ' ὧν must be taken with ἐκ τῆς
ψυχῆς τῆς σαρκὸς αὐτῶν It is the
Semitic idiom די מנפש בבשרהן = 'from

G^g

ἔσται ἀφανίζοντα χωρὶς κρίσεως·
οὕτως ἀφανίσουσιν μέχρις ἡμέρας
τελειώσεως, *τῆς κρίσεως ¹ τῆς
μεγάλης, ἐν ᾗ ὁ αἰὼν *ὁ μέγας ¹
τελεσθήσεται ².

G^s

χρις ἡμέρας τῆς τελειώσεως, ἕως
τῆς κρίσεως τῆς μεγάλης, ἐν ᾗ ὁ
αἰὼν *ὁ μέγας ¹ τελεσθήσεται
ἐφάπαξ ὁμοῦ τελεσθήσεται.

2. Καὶ νῦν ἐγρηγόροις τοῖς πέμψασίν σε ἐρωτῆσαι περὶ αὐτῶν,
οἵτινες ³ ἐν οὐρανῷ ἦσαν   3. Ὑμεῖς ἐν τῷ οὐρανῷ ἦτε, καὶ πᾶν
μυστήριον [ὁ] ⁴ οὐκ ἀνεκαλύφθη ὑμῖν καὶ μυστήριον* τὸ ἐκ τοῦ θεοῦ
γεγενημένον ⁵ ἔγνωτε, καὶ τοῦτο ἐμηνύσατε ταῖς γυναιξὶν ἐν ταῖς
σκληροκαρδίαις ὑμῶν, καὶ ἐν τῷ μυστηρίῳ τούτῳ πληθύνουσιν αἱ
θήλειαι καὶ οἱ ἄνθρωποι τὰ κακὰ ἐπὶ τῆς γῆς.   4 εἶπον οὖν αὐτοῖς ⁶
Οὐκ ἔστιν εἰρήνη.

XVII.   Καὶ παραλαβόντες με εἴς τινα τόπον ⌈ἀπήγαγον⌉, ἐν ᾧ οἱ
ὄντες ἐκεῖ γίνονται ὡς πῦρ φλέγον καί, ὅταν θέλωσιν, φαίνονται
ὡσεὶ ἄνθρωποι.   2. Καὶ ἀπήγαγόν με εἰς ζοφώδη ⁷ τόπον καὶ εἰς
ὄρος οὗ *ἡ κεφαλὴ ⁸ ἀφικνεῖτο εἰς τὸν οὐρανόν.   3. καὶ ἴδον
τόπον τῶν φωστήρων ⌈καὶ τοὺς θησαυροὺς τῶν ἀστέρων⌉ καὶ τῶν
βροντῶν, ⌈καὶ⌉ εἰς τὰ ἀεροβαθῆ ⁹, ὅπου τόξον πυρὸς καὶ τὰ βέλη καὶ
αἱ θῆκαι αὐτῶν ¹⁰ καὶ αἱ ἀστρωπαὶ πᾶσαι.   4. Καὶ ἀπήγαγόν με
μέχρι ὑδάτων ζώντων καὶ μέχρι πυρὸς δύσεως, ὅ ἐστιν καὶ παρέχον ¹¹
πάσας τὰς δύσεις τοῦ ἡλίου.   5. καὶ ἦλθο[με]ν μέχρι ποταμοῦ
πυρός, ἐν ᾧ κατατρέχει τὸ πῦρ ὡς ὕδωρ καὶ ῥέει εἰς θάλασσαν μεγάλην
δύσεως.   6. ἴδον ¹² τοὺς μεγάλους ποταμού(ς), καὶ μέχρι τοῦ
μεγάλου ⌈ποταμοῦ καὶ μέχρι τοῦ μεγάλου⌉ ¹³ σκότους κατήντησα, καὶ
ἀπῆλθον ὅπου πᾶσα σὰρξ ⌈οὐ⌉ περιπατεῖ.   7. ἴδον τοὺς ἀνέμους τῶν
γνόφων † ¹⁴ τοὺς χειμερινοὺς καὶ τὴν ἔκχυσιν* τῆς ἀβύσσου πάντων
ὑδάτων ¹⁵.   8. ἴδον ¹² τὸ στόμα τῆς γῆς πάντων τῶν ποταμῶν καὶ τὸ

---

the souls of whose flesh'   ¹ E wrongly
omits.   ² Add with E ἐπὶ τοῖς ἐγρηγόροις καὶ τοῖς ἀσεβέσιν ὅλως τελεσθήσεται   ³ E adds πρότερον   ⁴ Interpolated (?)   E omits   ⁵ E = ἐξου-
θενημένα.   ⁶ E adds Ὑμῖν.   ⁷ E =
γνοφώδη taking γνόφος in the sense of
'whirlwind' or 'tempest', as in Job

27²⁰ (LXX).   ⁸ E = ἡ κορυφὴ τῆς
κεφαλῆς   ⁹ E seems corrupt, but
may point back to ἄκρα βάθη.   ¹⁰ E
adds καὶ μάχαιραν πυρός   ¹¹ E = παρα-
δεχόμενον I don't understand παρέχον
in this clause   ¹² E = καὶ ἴδον.
¹³ E omits through hmt   ¹⁴ E = τὰ
ὄρη τῶν γνόφων.   ¹⁵ E = ὑδάτων τῆς

στόμα τῆς ἀβύσσου. XVIII. ἴδον[1] τοὺς θησαυροὺς τῶν ἀνέμων πάντων, ἴδον[1] ὅτι ἐν αὐτοῖς ἐκόσμησεν πάσας τὰς κτίσεις καὶ τὸν θεμέλιον τῆς γῆς, 2. καὶ τὸν λίθον ἴδον τῆς γωνίας τῆς γῆς. ἴδον τοὺς τέσσαρας ἀνέμους [τὴν γῆν][2] βαστάζοντας, καὶ τὸ στερέωμα τοῦ οὐρανοῦ, 3. καὶ[3] αὐτοὶ ἱστᾶσιν μεταξὺ γῆς καὶ οὐρανοῦ[4]. 4. ἴδον[1] ἀνέμους *τῶν οὐραι ῶν[5] στρέφοντας καὶ †διανεύοντας†[6] τὸν τροχὸν τοῦ ἡλίου, καὶ πάντας τοὺς ἀστέρας 5. ἴδον τοὺς ἐπὶ τῆς γῆς ἀνέμους βαστάζοντας †ἐν νεφέλῃ†[7]. ἴδον[8] ⟨παρὰ⟩[9] πέρατα τῆς γῆς, τὸ στήριγμα τοῦ οὐρανοῦ ἐπάνω 6. Παρῆλθον[10] ⌜καὶ ἴδον τόπον⌝ καιόμενον νυκτὸς καὶ ἡμέρας, ὅπου τὰ ἑπτὰ ὄρη ἀπὸ λίθων πολυτελῶν, ⟨τρία⟩[11] εἰς ἀνατολὰς καὶ τρία[11] εἰς νότον ⌜βάλλοντα.⌝[12] 7. καὶ τὰ μὲν πρὸς ἀνατολὰς[13] ἀπὸ λίθου χρώματος, τὸ δὲ ἦν ἀπὸ λίθου μαργαρίτου, καὶ τὸ ἀπὸ λίθου †ταθέν†[14], τὰ[15] δὲ κατὰ νότον ἀπὸ λίθου πυρροῦ· 8 τὸ δὲ μέσον αὐτῶν ἦν εἰς οὐρανόν, ὥσπερ θρόνος θεοῦ ἀπὸ λίθου φουκά[16], καὶ ἡ κορυφὴ τοῦ θρόνου ἀπὸ λίθου σαπφείρου 9. καὶ πῦρ καιόμενον ἴδον. κὰ(πέ)κεινα τῶν ὀρέων τούτων 10. τόπος ἐστὶν πέρας[17] τῆς μεγάλης γῆς ἐκεῖ συντελεσθήσονται[18] οἱ οὐρανοί. 11. καὶ ἴδον χάσμα μέγα ἐν τοῖς στύλοις[19] τοῦ πυρὸς καταβαίνοντας καὶ οὐκ ἦν μέτρον οὔτε εἰς βάθος οὔτε εἰς ὕψος. 12. καὶ ἐπέκεινα τοῦ χάσματος τούτου[20] ἴδον τόπον ὅπου οὐδὲ στερέωμα οὐρανοῦ ἐπάνω, οὔτε γῆ[21] ἡ[21] τεθεμελιωμένη[21] ὑποκάτω αὐτοῦ οὔτε ὕδωρ ἦν ὑπ᾽ αὐτῷ[22] οὔτε πετεινόν, ἀλλὰ τόπος ἦν ἔρημος καὶ φοβερός. 13. ἐκεῖ ἴδον ἑπτὰ ἀστέρας ὡς ὄρη μεγάλα καιόμενα, *περὶ ὧν πυνθανομένῳ μοι[23] 14. εἶπεν ὁ ἄγγελος Οὗτός ἐστιν ὁ τόπος τὸ τέλος τοῦ οὐρανοῦ καὶ γῆς· δεσμω-

---

ἀβύσσου πάσης. [1] E = καὶ ἴδον
[2] So also E, corruptly. [3] Before
καὶ E adds καὶ ἴδον ὡς οἱ ἄνεμοι ἐξέτεινον
τὸ ὕψος τοῦ οὐρανοῦ—lost through hmt.
[4] Add with E καὶ οὗτοί εἰσιν οἱ στύλοι
τοῦ οὐρανοῦ—lost through hmt. [5] We
should probably emend into τὸν οὐρανόν
with E. [6] E = δύνοντας in an active
sense, and this is probably the right
reading here. [7] So also *gmqu* of E
t, β = τὰς νεφέλας [8] Add with E
τὰς ὁδοὺς τῶν ἀγγέλων ἴδον—lost through
hmt [9] Added with E. Lost before

πέρατα. Radermacher and Diels add
περὶ τά. [10] E adds πρὸς νότον.
[11] MS τρις [12] MS. βαλλοντας
[13] Add τὸ μέν (Radermacher) [14] E
= ιασιω: corrupt for ιασπιδος. [15] MS.
το [16] An Aramaic form of פוך.
[17] E = πέραν. [18] E = συνετελέσθησαν.
[19] MS εις τους στυλους Add with E
τοῦ πυρὸς τοῦ οὐρανοῦ καὶ ἴδον ἐν αὐτοῖς
στύλους—lost through hmt. [20] E =
ἐκείνου. [21] MS puts in acc [22] MS.
αυτο. [23] MS. πυθανομαιον μοι. E
corrupt = καὶ ὡς πνεύματα πυνθανόμενα

τήριον τοῦτο ἐγένετο τοῖς ἄστροις καὶ *ταῖς δυνάμεσιν τοῦ οὐρανοῦ[1]. 15. καὶ οἱ ἀστέρες οἱ κυλιόμενοι *ἐν τῷ πυρί[2], οὗτοί εἰσιν οἱ παραβάντες πρόσταγμα Κυρίου[3] ἐν ἀρχῇ τῆς ἀνατολῆς αὐτῶν [ὅτι τόπος ἔξω τοῦ οὐρανοῦ κενός ἐστιν][4], ὅτι οὐκ ἐξῆλθαν ἐν τοῖς καιροῖς αὐτῶν· 16. καὶ ὀργίσθη αὐτοῖς καὶ ἔδησεν αὐτοὺς μέχρι καιροῦ τελειώσεως [αὐτῶν] ἁμαρτίας αὐτῶν, *ἐνιαυτῶν μυρίων[5].

XIX   καὶ εἰπέν μοι Οὐριήλ Ἐνθάδε οἱ μιγέντες ἄγγελοι ταῖς γυναιξὶν στήσονται, καὶ τὰ πνεύματα αὐτῶν πολύμορφα γενόμενα λυμαίνεται τοὺς ἀνθρώπους καὶ πλανήσει αὐτοὺς ἐπιθύειν τοῖς δαιμονίοις[6] μέχρι[7] τῆς μεγάλης κρίσεως, ἐν ᾗ κριθήσονται εἰς ἀποτελείωσιν   2. *καὶ αἱ γυναῖκες αὐτῶν τῶν παραβάντων ἀγγέλων[8] εἰς σειρῆνας γενήσονται

Ge1	Ga2
3. κἀγὼ Ἐνὼχ ἴδον τὰ θεωρήματα μόνος, τὰ πέρατα πάντων, καὶ οὐ μὴ ἴδῃ οὐδὲ εἷς ἀνθρώπων ὡς ἐγὼ ἴδον	3. . . . . ἀνθρώπων ὡς ἐγὼ εἶδον.
XX. Ἄγγελοι τῶν δυνάμεων[9] 2. Οὐριήλ, ὁ εἷς τῶν ἁγίων ἀγγέλων ὁ ἐπὶ τοῦ κόσμου[10] καὶ τοῦ ταρτάρου[11]. 3. Ῥαφαήλ, ὁ εἷς τῶν ἁγίων ἀγγέλων ὁ ἐπὶ τῶν πνευμάτων τῶν ἀνθρώπων. 4 Ῥαγουήλ, ὁ εἷς τῶν ἁγίων ἀγγέλων ὁ ἐκδικῶν[13] τὸν κόσμον *τῶν φωστήρων[15]. 5. Μιχαήλ,	XX. . . . . . 2. ὁ εἷς τῶν ἁγίων ἀγγέλων ὁ ἐπὶ τοῦ κόσμου καὶ τοῦ ταρτάρου 3. Ῥαφαήλ ὁ εἷς τῶν ἁγίων ἀγγέλων ὁ ἐπὶ τῶν πνευμάτων τῶν ἀνθρώπων. 4. Ῥαγουήλ ὁ εἷς τῶν[12] ἁγίων ἀγγέλων ὁ ἐκδικῶν[14] τὸν κόσμον τῶν φωστήρων 5 Μιχαήλ, *ὁ εἷς τῶν[16] ἁγίων ἀγγέλων ὃς ἐπὶ

μου   [1] = צְבָא הַשָּׁמַיִם.   [2] E = ὑπὲρ τοῦ πυρός.   [3] E = θεοῦ   [4] A gloss in Gᵍ.   [5] E corrupt = ἐνιαυτῷ μυστηρίου Cf 21⁶   [6] E adds ὡς θεοῖς   [7] E adds τῆς ἡμέρας.   [8] This phrase reproduces literally an Aramaic idiom.   [9] This verse is defective Its complement is found at the close of the chapter Gᵏ¹ ἀρχαγγέλων ὀνόματα ἑπτά which should, however, be read as in Gᵍ² ὀνόματα ζ' ἀρχαγγέλων Taken together these point to ὀνόματα τῶν

ἑπτὰ ἀρχαγγέλων τῶν δυνάμεων   E = καὶ ταῦτά ἐστιν ὀνόματα τῶν ἐγρηγόρων τῶν ἁγίων ἀγγέλων.   [10] If the original were Hebrew we might with Lods take κόσμος here to be a rendering of צְבָא as in LXX, (Gen 2¹ Deut. 4¹⁹ 17⁵ Isa. 24²¹.   [11] E corrupt = τρόμου   [12] MS τον   [13] MS. εκδικων I have emended in accordance with E.   [14] MS. εκεκων.   [15] E = καὶ τοὺς φωστῆρας, but G is right.   [16] MS. ο εις τον

G^{g1}

ὁ εἷς τῶν ἁγίων ἀγγέλων ὁ ἐπὶ
τῶν τοῦ λαοῦ ἀγαθῶν τεταγμένος
καὶ[1] ἐπὶ τῷ χάῳ[2]. 6. Σαριήλ,
ὁ εἷς τῶν ἁγίων ἀγγέλων ὁ ἐπὶ
τῶν πνευμάτων οἵτινες *ἐπὶ τῷ
πνεύματι[3] ἁμαρτάνουσιν. 7. Γα-
βριήλ, ὁ εἷς τῶν ἁγίων ἀγγέλων
ὃς ἐπὶ τοῦ παραδείσου καὶ τῶν
δρακόντων καὶ χερουβείν[4].
*ἀρχαγγέλων ὀνόματα ἑπτά[5].

XXI. Καὶ ἐφώδευσα ἕως τῆς
ἀκατασκευάστου. 2. κἀκεῖ ἐθεασάμην ἔργον φοβερόν· ἑώρακα
οὔτε οὐρανὸν ἐπάνω, οὔτε γῆν
τεθέαμαι τεθεμελιωμένην, ἀλλὰ
τόπον ἀκατασκεύαστον καὶ φοβερόν. 3. καὶ ἐκεῖ τεθέαμαι ἑπτὰ
τῶν ἀστέρων τοῦ οὐρανοῦ δεδεμένους καὶ ἐρριμμένους[6] ἐν αὐτῷ[7],
ὁμοίους ὄρεσιν μεγάλοις καὶ ἐν
πυρὶ καιομένους. 4. τότε εἶπον
Διὰ ποίαν αἰτίαν ἐπεδέθησαν, καὶ
διὰ τί ὧδε ἐρίφησαν ; 5. τότε
εἶπέν μοι Οὐριήλ, ὁ εἷς τῶν ἁγίων
ἀγγέλων ὃς μετ' ἐμοῦ ἦν καὶ αὐτὸς
ἡγεῖτο αὐτῶν, καὶ εἶπέν ⌜μοι⌝
Ἑνώχ, περὶ τίνος ἐρωτᾷς, ἢ περὶ

G^{g2}

τῶν τοῦ λαοῦ ἀγαθῶν τέτακται
καὶ ἐπὶ τῷ χάῳ[1]. 6. Σαριήλ,
ὁ εἷς τῶν ἁγίων ἀγγέλων ὁ ἐπὶ
τῶν πνευμάτων οἵτινες ἐπὶ τῷ
πνεύματι ἁμαρτάνουσιν. 7. Γα-
βριήλ, ὁ εἷς τῶν ἁγίων ἀγγέλων
ὁ ἐπὶ τοῦ παραδείσου καὶ τῶν
δρακόντων καὶ χερουβίν. 8. ⌜Ῥε-
μειήλ, ὁ εἷς τῶν ἁγίων ἀγγέλων
ὃν ἔταξεν ὁ θεὸς ἐπὶ τῶν ἀνιστα-
μένων.⌝ *ὀνόματα ζ΄ ἀρχαγγέλων.

XXI. Καὶ ἐφώδευσα μέχρι
τῆς ἀκατασκευάστου. 2. καὶ ἐκεῖ
ἐθεασάμην ἔργον φοβερόν· ἑώρακα οὔτε οὐρανὸν ἐπάνω οὔτε
γῆν τεθεμελιωμένην, ἀλλὰ τόπον
ἀκατασκεύαστον καὶ φοβερόν. 3.
καὶ ἐκεῖ τεθέαμαι ζ΄ ἀστέρας τοῦ
οὐρανοῦ δεδεμένους καὶ ἐρριμμένους ἐν αὐτῷ[7], ὁμοίους †ὁράσει
μεγάλη[8] καὶ ἐν πυρὶ καιομένους.
4. τότε εἶπον Διὰ ποίαν αἰτίαν
ἐπεδέθησαν, καὶ *διὰ ποίαν
αἰτίαν[9] ἐρίφησαν ὧδε ; 5. καὶ[10]
εἶπέν μοι Οὐριήλ, ὁ εἷς τῶν ἁγίων
ἀγγέλων ὁ μετ' ἐμοῦ ὢν καὶ αὐτὸς
αὐτῶν ἡγεῖτο, καὶ εἶπέν ⌜μοι⌝
Ἑνώχ, περὶ τίνος ἐρωτᾷς, ἢ περὶ

---

[1] E wrongly omits. [2] Though E =
λαῷ, the above is right. Uriel presides
over Chaos . see 21[3], [2] (18[12]). The καί
which G^g preserves before ἐπὶ τῷ λαῷ
supports this view. [3] E gives acc
of limitation [4] See G^{b2} for ver. 8
omitted here and in E. [5] On these

words see note on verse 1 above. [6] This
phrase goes badly with τεθέαμαι E
omits it. Is it a gloss due to ver 4 ?
[7] E adds ὁμοῦ, which goes well with
δεδεμένους, and could easily fall out
before ὁμοίους. [8] Corrupt [9] G^{g1}
E = διὰ τί [10] G^{g1} E = τότε

G^{g1}

τίνος *τὴν ἀλήθειαν φιλοσπου-
δεῖς¹ ; 6. οὗτοί εἰσιν τῶν ἀστέρων ⌜τοῦ οὐρανοῦ⌝ οἱ παραβάντες
τὴν ἐπιταγὴν τοῦ κυρίου², καὶ
ἐδέθησαν ὧδε μέχρι τοῦ πληρῶ-
σαι³ μύρια ἔτη, τὸν χρόνον⁴ τῶν
ἀμαρτημάτων αὐτῶν.

7. Κἀκεῖθεν ἐφώδευσα εἰς
ἄλλον τόπον τούτου φοβερώτερον,
καὶ τεθέαμαι ἔργα φοβερώτερα⁵,
πῦρ μέγα ἐκεῖ καιόμενον καὶ
φλεγόμενον, καὶ διακοπὴν εἶχεν
ὁ τόπος ἕως τῆς ἀβύσσου, πλήρης
στύλων πυρὸς μεγάλου⁶ κατα-
φερομένων· οὔτε μέτρον οὔτε
πλάτος⁷ ἠδυνήθην ἰδεῖν οὐδὲ
εἰκάσαι 8. τότε εἶπον Ὡς φοβερὸς ὁ⁸ τόπος⁹ καὶ ὡς δεινὸς¹⁰
τῇ ὁράσει. 9. τότε ἀπεκρίθη
μοι¹¹ ὁ εἷς τῶν ἁγίων ἀγγέλων
ὃς μετ' ἐμοῦ ἦν, καὶ εἶπέν μοι
⌜Ἐνώχ⌝, διὰ τί ἐφοβήθης οὕτως

G^{g2}

τίνος τὴν ἀλήθειαν φιλοσπου-
δεῖς¹ ; 6. οὗτοί εἰσιν τῶν ἀστέρων
⌜τοῦ οὐρανοῦ⌝ οἱ παραβάντες τὴν
ἐπιταγὴν τοῦ κυρίου², καὶ ἐδέθησαν ὧδε μέχρι πληρωθῆναι
μύρια ἔτη, τὸν χρόνον τῶν ἀμαρτημάτων αὐτῶν.

7. Κἀκεῖθεν ἐφώδευσα εἰς ἄλλον τόπον τούτου φοβερώτερον,
καὶ τεθέαμαι ἔργα φοβερά· πῦρ
μέγα ἐκεῖ καιόμενον καὶ φλεγόμενον, καὶ διακοπὴν εἶχεν ὁ
τόπος ἕως τῆς ἀβύσσου, πλήρης
στύλων πυρὸς μεγάλου⁶ κατα-
φερομένων· οὔτε μέτρον οὔτε
μέγεθος ἠδυνήθην ἰδεῖν οὔτε εἰκάσαι. 8. τότε εἶπον Ὡς φοβερὸς
ὁ τόπος οὗτος καὶ ὡς δεινὸς τῇ
ὁράσει 9. τότε ἀπεκρίθη μοι
καὶ εἶπεν . .

καὶ ἐπτοήθης , * καὶ ἀπεκρίθη(ν)¹² Περὶ τούτου τοῦ φοβεροῦ (τόπου)
καὶ περὶ τῆς προσόψεως *τῆς δεινῆς¹³. 10 καὶ εἶπεν Οὗτος ὁ τόπος
δεσμωτήριον ἀγγέλων· ὧδε¹⁴ συνσχεθήσονται [μέχρι ἑνὸς]¹⁵ εἰς τὸν
αἰῶνα

XXII. Κἀκεῖθεν ἐφώδευσα εἰς ἄλλον τόπον, καὶ ἔδειξέν μοι πρὸς
δυσμὰς ⌜ἄλλο⌝ ὄρος μέγα καὶ ὑψηλὸν¹⁶ πέτρας στερεᾶς¹⁷. 2 καὶ

---

¹ = חצבא יציבא Cf. Dan 7¹⁰, ¹⁹　² E
= θεοῦ.　⁰ G^{g2} E = πληρωθῆναι
⁴ E = τὸν ἀριθμὸν τῶν ἡμερῶν.　⁵ G^{g2} E
= φοβερά.　⁶ Read μεγάλων with E.
⁷ G^{g2} E = μέγεθος which is better than
πλάτος as is clear from μέτρον which
precedes.　⁸ E gives חז̈ז̈: and thus
agrees with G^{g2}　⁹ E G^{g2} add οὗτος

¹⁰ E = ὀδυνηρός　¹¹ E adds Οὐριήλ.
¹² E wrongly trans. before καὶ εἶπέν
μοι and changes into 3rd sing.　¹³ E
= τῆς ὀδύνης　¹⁴ E = καὶ ὧδε　¹⁵ This
phrase forms a doublet with εἰς τὸν
αἰῶνα. Here ενος is a corruption of
αἰῶνος　¹⁶ E adds καί　¹⁷ Here in
genitive. But if we follow E we must

†τέσσαρες† [1] τόποι ἐν αὐτῷ κοῖλοι, βάθος [2] ἔχοντες καὶ λίαν λεῖοι, ⌐τρεῖς αὐτῶν σκοτεινοὶ καὶ εἷς φωτεινός, καὶ πηγὴ ὕδατος ἀνὰ μέσον αὐτοῦ. καὶ εἶπον⌐ [3] †Πῶς† [1] λεῖα τὰ κοιλώματα [1] ταῦτα καὶ ὁλοβαθῆ καὶ σκοτεινὰ τῇ ὁράσει. 3. τότε ἀπεκρίθη Ῥαφαήλ, ὁ εἷς τῶν ἁγίων ἀγγέλων ὃς μετ᾽ ἐμοῦ ἦν, καὶ εἶπέν μοι Οὗτοι οἱ τόποι οἱ κοῖλοι, ἵνα ἐπισυνάγωνται εἰς αὐτοὺς τὰ πνεύματα τῶν ψυχῶν τῶν νεκρῶν, εἰς αὐτὸ τοῦτο ἐκρίθησαν, ὧδε ἐπισυνάγεσθαι πάσας τὰς ψυχὰς [4] τῶν ἀνθρώπων. 4. καὶ οὗτοι οἱ τόποι εἰς ἐπισύνσχεσι(ν) αὐτῶν ἐποι(ήθ)ησαν [5] μέχρι τῆς ἡμέρας τῆς κρίσεως αὐτῶν καὶ μέχρι τοῦ διορισμοῦ [6] [καὶ διωρισμένου χρόνου,] ἐν ᾧ ἡ κρίσις ἡ μεγάλη ἔσται ἐν αὐτοῖς. 5. Τεθέαμαι †ἀνθρώπους νεκροὺς ⌐ἐντυγχάνοντος⌐, καὶ ἡ φωνὴ αὐτοῦ† [7] μέχρι τοῦ οὐρανοῦ προέβαινεν καὶ ἐνετύγχανεν. 6. καὶ [8] ἠρώτησα [9] Ῥαφαὴλ τὸν ἄγγελον ὃς μετ᾽ ἐμοῦ ἦν, καὶ εἶπα αὐτῷ Τοῦτο τὸ πνεῦμα ⌐τὸ ἐντυγχάνον⌐ τίνος ἐστίν, οὗ [10] οὕτως [11] ἡ φωνὴ αὐτοῦ προβαίνει καὶ ἐντυγχάνει ⌐ἕως τοῦ οὐρανοῦ⌐ ; 7 καὶ ἀπεκρίθη μοι λέγων Τοῦτο τὸ πνεῦμά ἐστιν τὸ ἐξελθὸν ἀπὸ Ἄβελ ὃν ἐφόνευσεν Κάειν ὁ ἀδελφός, καὶ ⌐Ἄβελ⌐ ἐντυγχάνει περὶ αὐτοῦ μέχρι τοῦ ἀπολέσαι τὸ σπέρμα αὐτοῦ ἀπὸ προσώπου τῆς γῆς, καὶ ἀπὸ τοῦ σπέρματος τῶν ἀνθρώπων ἀφανισθῇ τὸ σπέρμα αὐτοῦ. 8. Τότε ἠρώτησα [12] περὶ τῶν κοιλωμάτων [13] πάντων, διὰ τί ἐχωρίσθησαν *ἐν ἀπὸ τοῦ ἑνός [14]. 9. καὶ ἀπεκρίθη μοι λέγων Οὗτοι οἱ τρὶς ἐποιήθησαν χωρίζεσθαι τὰ πνεύματα τῶν νεκρῶν· καὶ οὕτως [15] (ἐ)χωρίσθη εἰς τὰ πνεύματα τῶν δικαίων, οὗ [16] ἡ πηγὴ τοῦ ὕδατος ἐν αὐτῷ [16]

---

read στερεάς ιn acc MS. εἰστερεας. [1] See notes ιn text [2] E adds καὶ πλάτος. [3] E omits. For σκοτεινοί MS gives εισκοτινοι [4] E adds τῶν υἱῶν. [5] The impossible ἐποιησαν ιs accurately reproduced by E. The οὖτοι οἱ τύποι (also ιn nominative ιn E) may be of course be a nominativus pendens. [6] E adds αὐτῶν [7] Text corrupt. also that of E which = τὰ πνεύματα ἀνθρώπων νεκρῶν καὶ ἡ φωνὴ αὐτῶν As Lods has pointed out, vers 5 b and 6 of G show that only a single spirit is referred to. Moreover G has lost πνεῦμα which is preserved by E. Hence read

πνεῦμα ἀνθρώπου νεκροῦ ἐντυγχάνοντος καὶ ἡ φωνὴ αὐτοῦ [8] E = τότε [9] MS ηρωτησεν [10] Em. with E from διο Thus ιn οὗ .. ἡ φωνὴ αὐτοῦ we have the Semitic idiom קלה . . . . ד. [11] E omits [12] E adds περὶ αὐτοῦ καὶ but wrongly, apparently. [13] Em. from κυκλωματων. The translator of E found κυκλώματα ιn ver. 2 for a corruption of κοιλώματα preserved ιn G, and here κριμάτων another corruption of κοιλωμάτων. [14] Em. by Dillmann and Lods from ην απο του αιωνος. [15] Corrupt for οὗτος. See note ιn text. [16] Semitic idiom = בו . . . אשר or די . . . בה.

φωτινή[1]　　　10. καὶ οὕτως ἐκτίσθη *τοῖς ἁμαρτωλοῖς[2], ὅταν ἀποθάνωσιν καὶ ταφῶσιν εἰς τὴν γῆν, καὶ κρίσις οὐκ ἐγενήθη ἐπ' αὐτῶν ἐν
τῇ ζωῇ αὐτῶν.　　11. ὧδε χωρίζεται τὰ πνεύματα αὐτῶν εἰς τὴν μεγάλην
βάσανον ταύτην, μέχρι τῆς μεγάλης ἡμέρας τῆς κρίσεως, τῶν μαστίγων
καὶ τῶν βασάνων τῶν κατηραμένων[3] *μέχρι αἰῶνος[4] *ἵν' ἀνταπό-
δοσις[5] τῶν πνευμάτων· ἐκεῖ δήσει αὐτοὺς μέχρις αἰῶνος.　　12. καὶ
οὕτως ἐχωρίσθη τοῖς πνεύμασιν τῶν ἐντυγχανόντων, οἵτινες ἐνφανί-
ζουσιν περὶ τῆς ἀπωλείας, ὅταν φονευθῶσιν ἐν ταῖς ἡμέραις τῶν
ἁμαρτωλῶν.　　13 καὶ οὕτως ἐκτίσθη τοῖς πνεύμασιν τῶν ἀνθρώπων,
ὅσοι οὐκ ἔσονται[6] ὅσιοι ἀλλὰ ἁμαρτωλοί, ὅσοι[7] ἀσεβεῖς, καὶ μετὰ
τῶν ἀνόμων ἔσονται μέτοχοι. τὰ δὲ πνεύματα [ὅτι οἱ ἐνθάδε θλιβέντες
ἔλαττον κολάζονται][8] αὐτῶν, οὐ τιμωρηθήσονται[9] ἐν ἡμέρᾳ τῆς κρίσεως,
οὐδὲ μὴ μετεγερθῶσιν ἐντεῦθεν.　14. Τότε ηὐλόγησα τὸν κύριον τῆς
δόξης, καὶ εἶπα Εὐλογητὸς *εἶ, Κύριε ὁ τῆς δικαιοσύνης[10], κυριεύων
*τοῦ αἰῶνος[11].

XXIII. Κἀκεῖθεν ἐφώδευσα εἰς ἄλλον τόπον πρὸς δυσμὰς[12] τῶν
περάτων τῆς γῆς.　　2. καὶ ἐθεασάμην πῦρ[13] διατρέχον καὶ οὐκ
ἀναπαυόμενον οὐδὲ ἐνλεῖπον τοῦ δρόμου, ἡμέρας καὶ νυκτὸς †ἅμα†[14]
διαμένον.　　3. καὶ ἠρώτησα λέγων Τί ἐστὶν τὸ μὴ ἔχον ἀνάπαυσιν,
4. τότε ἀπεκρίθη μοι Ῥαγουήλ, ὁ εἷς τῶν ἁγίων ἀγγέλων ὃς μετ' ἐμοῦ
ἦν[15] Οὗτος ὁ δρόμος τοῦ πυρὸς[16] τὸ πρὸς δυσμὰς πῦρ τὸ ἐκδιῶκόν ἐστιν
πάντας τοὺς φωστῆρας τοῦ οὐρανοῦ.　　XXIV. Καὶ[17] ἔδειξέν μοι
ὄρη πυρὸς καιόμενα[18]　.　.　νυκτός.　　2. καὶ ἐπέκεινα αὐτῶν
ἐπορεύθην καὶ ἐθεασάμην ἑπτὰ ὄρη ἔνδοξα, πάντα ἑκάτερα τοῦ
ἑκατέρου διαλλάσσοντα, *ὧν οἱ λίθοι ἔντιμοι τῇ καλλονῇ[19], καὶ
πάντα ἔντιμα καὶ ἔνδοξα καὶ εὐειδῆ, ⟨τρία ἐπ'⟩ ἀνατολὰς ἐστηριγμένα
⟨ἐν⟩ ἐν τῷ ἑνί, καὶ τρία ἐπὶ νότον ⟨ἐν⟩ ἐν τῷ ἑνί. καὶ φάραγγες βαθεῖαι
καὶ τραχεῖαι[20], μία τῇ μιᾷ οὐκ ἐγγίζουσαι,　　3. καὶ [τῷ ὄρει][21]

---

[1] E = 'brightness'　　[2] Em with E
from των αμαρτωλώ.　　[3] E takes this
transitively: but it is to be taken
passively　　[4] E = μέχρι αἰῶνος καί
[5] So Radermacher emends from ην
ανταποδοσεις　E = καὶ τῆς ἀνταποδόσεως
[6] E = ἦσαν　　[7] Add ὅλοι with E.
[8] An explanatory gloss.　　[9] E = ἀναιρεθήσονται or ἀποθανοῦνται　　[10] E
= κύριός μου, ὁ κύριος τῆς δικαιοσύνης

[11] = 'the world'　E = μέχρι τοῦ αἰῶνος.
[12] E adds μέχρι　　[13] E adds φλεγόμενον.　[14] Read ἀλλά with E.　　[15] E
adds καὶ εἶπέν μοι.　　[16] E adds ὃν εἶδες.
[17] Before καί insert with E κἀκεῖθεν
ἐφώδευσα εἰς ἄλλον τόπον τῆς γῆς.　[18] E
adds ἡμέρας καί.　　[19] E = καὶ τοὺς λίθους
ἐντίμους καὶ καλούς or by a slight change
the nom. can be read.　　[20] E = σκολιαί
[21] An intrusion

ἔβδομον ὄρος ἀνὰ μέσον τούτων, καὶ *ὑπερεῖχεν τῷ ὕψει, ὅμοιον [1] καθέδρᾳ θρόνου, καὶ περιεκύκλου δένδρα αὐτὸ [2] εὐειδῆ [3]. 4. καὶ ἦν ἐν αὐτοῖς δένδρον ὃ οὐδέποτε ὤσφρανμαι καὶ οὐδεὶς ἕτερος αὐτῶν ⌜εὐφράνθη⌝, καὶ οἶδὲν ἕτερον ὅμοιον αὐτῷ [4]· ὀσμὴν εἶχεν εὐωδεστέραν πάντων ἀρωμάτων, καὶ τὰ φύλλα αὐτοῦ καὶ τὸ ἄνθος καὶ τὸ δένδρον οὐ φθίνει [5] εἰς τὸν αἰῶνα· *οἱ δὲ περὶ τὸν καρπὸν [6] ὡσεὶ βότρυες φοινίκων. 5. τότε εἶπον ⌜Ὠς⌝ καλὸν τὸ δένδρον τοῦτό ἐστιν καὶ εὐῶδες [7], καὶ ὡραῖα τὰ φύλλα, καὶ τὰ ἄνθη αὐτοῦ ὡραῖα [8] τῇ ὁράσει. 6. τότε ἀπεκρίθη μοι Μιχαήλ, εἷς τῶν ἁγίων [9] ἀγγέλων ὃς μετ᾽ ἐμοῦ ἦν καὶ αὐτὸς αὐτῶν ἡγεῖτο, XXV. καὶ εἶπέν μοι Ἑνώχ, τί ἐρωτᾷς [10] ⌜καὶ τί ἐθαύμασας⌝ ἐν τῇ ὀσμῇ τοῦ δένδρου, καὶ ⌜διὰ τί⌝ *θέλεις τὴν ἀλήθειαν μαθεῖν; 2. τότε ἀπεκρίθην [11] αὐτῷ [12] Περὶ πάντων εἰδέναι θέλω, μάλιστα δὲ περὶ τοῦ δένδρου τούτου σφόδρα. 3. καὶ ἀπεκρίθη λέγων Τοῦτο τὸ ὄρος τὸ ὑψηλόν [13], οὗ ἡ κορυφὴ ὁμοία θρόνου θεοῦ, καθέδρα [14] ἐστὶν οὗ καθίζει [15] *ὁ μέγας κύριος, ὁ ἅγιος τῆς δόξης [16], ὁ βασιλεὺς *τοῦ αἰῶνος [17], ὅταν καταβῇ ἐπισκέψασθαι τὴν γῆν ἐπ᾽ ἀγαθῷ. 4. καὶ τοῦτο τὸ δένδρον εὐωδίας, καὶ οὐδεμία σὰρξ ἐξουσίαν ἔχει ἅψασθαι αὐτοῦ μέχρι τῆς μεγάλης κρίσεως, ἐν [18] ᾗ ἐκδίκησις πάντων καὶ τελείωσις μέχρις αἰῶνος· τότε [19] δικαίοις καὶ ὁσίοις δοθήσεται. 5. *ὁ καρπὸς αὐτοῦ τοῖς ἐκλεκτοῖς †εἰς ζωὴν† εἰς βοράν, καὶ [20] μεταφυτευθήσεται ἐν τόπῳ ἁγίῳ παρὰ τὸν οἶκον τοῦ θεοῦ [21] βασιλέως [22] * τοῦ αἰῶνος [23].

6 τότε εὐφρανθήσονται εὐφραινόμενοι καὶ χαρήσονται
καὶ [24] * εἰς τὸ ἅγιον εἰσελεύσονται·
αἱ ὀσμαὶ αὐτοῦ [25] ἐν τοῖς ὀστέοις αὐτῶν,
καὶ ζωὴν πλείονα [26] ζήσονται ἐπὶ γῆς

---

[1] E (i.e. h o, b) = ὑπερεῖχεν (a, β-h o, b = καὶ τὸ ὕψος) αὐτῶν ἦσαν ὅμοια πάντα, but πάντα is an intrusion [2] MS. αυτω [3] E = εὐώδη which is right Cf vers. 4, 5, 25⁴. [4] For οὐδεὶς .. αὐτῷ E gives οὐδὲν (or οὐδεὶς) αὐτῶν καὶ οὐδὲν ἕτερον ὅμοιον αὐτῷ ἦν. [5] MS φθεινι ᵏ E = ὁ δὲ καρπὸς καλὸς καὶ ὁ καρπός. [7] E = εὐειδές but text is better. [8] E adds σφόδρα. [9] E adds καὶ ἐντίμων. [10] E adds με. [11] MS απεκρειθη [12] E adds λέγων [13] E

[14] E adds αὐτοῦ. [15] E = καθίσει. [16] Text confused. E = ὁ ἅγιος καὶ ὁ μέγας ὁ κύριος τῆς δόξης. ὁ κύριος τῆς δόξης is supported by 27⁵. [17] E = αἰώνιος. [18] MS. ει. [19] E = τόδε [20] This text seems right save the phrase εἰς ζωήν = לחיי or possibly לאלהים corrupt for לאלה ἔσται [21] E = κυρίου. [22] MS βασιλεὺς. [23] E = αἰωνίου. [24] E trans. after ἅγιον, and perhaps rightly. [25] See notes on text, pp. 53, 54. [26] This seems to

ἣν ἔζησαν οἱ πατέρες σου,
καὶ ἐν ταῖς ἡμέραις αὐτῶν¹ καὶ βάσανοι
καὶ πληγαὶ καὶ μάστιγες οὐχ ἅψονται αὐτῶν.

7. Τότε ηὐλόγησα² τὸν θεὸν τῆς δόξης, τὸν βασιλέα *τοῦ αἰῶνος³, ὃς
ἡτοίμασεν *ἀνθρώποις τὰ τοιαῦτα δικαίοις⁴, καὶ αὐτὰ ἔκτισεν καὶ
εἶπεν δοῦναι αὐτοῖς.

XXVI. Καὶ ἐκεῖθεν ἐφώδευσα εἰς τὸ μέσον τῆς γῆς, καὶ ἴδου
τόπον ηὐλογημένον, ἐν ᾧ ⌜δένδρα ἔχοντα⌝ παραφυάδας μενούσας καὶ
βλαστούσας [τοῦ δένδρου ἐκκοπέντος]. 2. κἀκεῖ τεθέαμαι ὄρος
ἅγιον⁵. ὑποκάτω τοῦ ὄρους ὕδωρ ἐξ ἀνατολῶν, καὶ τὴν † δύσιν †⁶
εἶχεν πρὸς νότον. 3. καὶ ἴδου πρὸς ἀνατολὰς ἄλλο ὄρος ὑψηλό-
τερον τούτου, καὶ ἀνὰ μέσον αὐτοῦ⁷ φάραγγα βαθεῖαν, οὐκ ἔχουσαν
πλάτος, καὶ δι᾽ αὐτῆς ὕδωρ πορεύεται ⌜ὑποκάτω⌝ ὑπὸ τὸ ὄρος. 4
καὶ πρὸς δυσμὰς τούτου ἄλλο ὄρος ταπεινότερον αὐτοῦ καὶ οὐκ ἔχον
ὕψος, καὶ φάραγγα ⌜βαθεῖαν καὶ ξηρὰν⌝⁸ ἀνὰ μέσον αὐτῶν, καὶ
ἄλλην φάραγγα βαθεῖαν καὶ ξηρὰν ἐπ᾽ ἄκρων τῶν τριῶν ⌜ὀρέων.⌝ 5.
καὶ *πᾶσαι φάραγγές⁹ εἰσιν βαθεῖαι¹⁰ ἐκ πέτρας στερεᾶς, καὶ δένδρον
οὐκ ἐφυτεύετο ἐπ᾽ αὐτάς. 6. καὶ ἐθαύμασα¹¹ περὶ τῆς φάραγγος,
καὶ λίαν ἐθαύμασα. XXVII. καὶ¹² εἶπον Διὰ τί ἡ γῆ αὕτη ἡ
εὐλογημένη καὶ πᾶσα πλήρης δένδρων, αὕτη δὲ ἡ φάραγξ κεκατηραμένη ἐστίν¹³ ; . . . 2. γῆ¹⁴ κατάρατος τοῖς κεκαταραμένοις
ἐστὶν μέχρι αἰῶνος. ὧδε ἐπισυναχθήσονται πάντες ⌜οἱ κεκατηρα-
μένοι⌝ οἵτινες¹⁵ ἐροῦσιν τῷ στόματι αὐτῶν κατὰ Κυρίου φωνὴν
ἀπρεπῆ, καὶ περὶ τῆς δόξης αὐτοῦ σκληρὰ λαλήσουσιν ὧδε ἐπισυναχθήσονται, καὶ ὧδε ἔσται τὸ οἰκητήριον¹⁶, 3 ἐπ᾽ ἐσχάτοις
αἰῶσιν, *ἐν ταῖς ἡμέραις¹⁷ τῆς κρίσεως τῆς ἀληθινῆς ἐναντίον τῶν

---

require us to read ἤ before ἤν. ¹ E
adds καὶ λύπη. ² MS ηυλογησαν.
³ E = αἰώνιον. ⁴ This order is
preserved in E. ⁵ E adds καί.
⁶ Corrupt E = ῥύσιν which is right.
⁷ Better αὐτῶν with E. ⁸ Instead
of this phrase E reads ὑποκάτω ⁹ MS.
ποσε φαραγγες ¹⁰ E adds καὶ ουκ
ἔχουσαι πλάτος ¹¹ Add with E περὶ
τῶν πετρῶν καὶ ἐθαύμασα—lost through
hmt. ¹² E = τότε. ¹³ Add with E

ἐν μέσω; τότε ἀπεκρίθη Οὐριήλ, ὁ εἷς
τῶν ἁγίων ἀγγέλων ὃς μετ᾽ ἐμοῦ ἦν, καὶ
εἶπεν. ¹⁴ A transliteration of גיא. The
translator of E understood it rightly as
= φάραγξ. Before γῆ add with E αὕτη
ἡ. ¹⁵ E τινες ¹⁶ E = κριτήριον
αὐτῶν E is corrupt. ¹⁷ E = ἔσται
ἡ ὅρασις. Thus E makes the sentence
begin with this verse, whereas G makes
the first half of this verse part of the
sentence which immediately precedes.

δικαίων εἰς τὸν ἅπαντα χρόνον. ὧδε εὐλογήσουσιν οἱ εὐσεβεῖς[1] τὸν κύριον τῆς δόξης, τὸν βασιλέα *τοῦ αἰῶνος[2], 4. ἐν ταῖς ἡμέραις τῆς κρίσεως αὐτῶν εὐλογήσουσιν ἐν ἐλέει[3], ὡς ἐμέρισεν αὐτοῖς. 5. Τότε ηὐλόγησα τὸν κύριον τῆς δόξης, καὶ ⌈τὴν δόξαν⌉ αὐτοῦ ἐδήλωσα καὶ ὕμνησα μεγαλοπρεπῶς.

XXVIII. Καὶ ἐκεῖθεν ἐπορεύθην[4] εἰς τὸ μέσον[5], Μανδοβαρά[6], καὶ ἴδον αὐτὸ[7] ἔρημον καὶ αὐτὸ μόνον, πλήρης δένδρων † καὶ ἀπὸ τῶν σπερμάτων †[8] 2. ὕδωρ[9] ἀνομβροῦν[10], ἄνωθεν 3. φερόμενον[11] ὡς ὑδραγωγὸς δαψιλὴς[12] ὡς[13] *πρὸς βορρᾶν ἐπὶ δυσμῶν[14] πάντοθεν *ἀνάγει †ὕδωρ† καὶ δρόσον[15]. XXIX. *῎Ετι ἐκεῖθεν[16] ἐπορεύθην εἰς ἄλλον τόπον *ἐν τῷ[17] Βαβδηρά[18], καὶ[19] πρὸς ἀνατολὰς τοῦ ὄρους τούτου ᾠχόμην, 2. καὶ[20] ἴδον κρίσεως[21] δένδρα πνέοντα[22] ἀρωμάτων λιβάνων καὶ ζμύρνης[23], καὶ τὰ δένδρα αὐτῶν ὅμοια καρύαις[24] XXX. Καὶ *ἐπέκεινα[25] τούτων ᾠχόμην[26] πρὸς ἀνατολὰς[27] μακράν, καὶ ἴδον τόπον ἄλλον ⌈μέγαν⌉, φάραγγα ὕδατος[28], 2. *ἐν ᾧ καὶ δένδρον[29] χρόα[30] ἀρωμάτων ὁμοίων σχίνῳ, 3. καὶ τὰ παρὰ τὰ χείλη τῶν φαράγγων τούτων ἴδον *κιννάμωμον ἀρωμάτων·[31] καὶ *ἐπέκεινα[25] τούτων ᾠχόμην πρὸς ἀνατολάς. XXXI. καὶ ἴδον ἄλλα ὄρη καὶ ἐν αὐτοῖς ⌈ἄλση⌉ δένδρων, καὶ ἐκ-

---

[1] MS ασεβεις [2] E = αἰώνιον [3] E = ὑπὲρ ἐλέους [4] E adds πρὸς ἀνατολάς. [5] E adds τοῦ ὄρους, which G wrongly omits [6] A faulty transliteration of מַדְבְּרָא, more faulty as Βαβδηρά in 29[1]. Though מדברא is Aramaic it does not prove that the original was Aramaic, for ᴍᴀᴅᴡᴀᴇᴡ: (= madbarâ), which is an Ethiopic transliteration of the same Hebrew word מִדְבָּר in Jos. 5[6], implies an Aramaic form For other forms see Jos. 5[6] 18[12] μαδβαρῖτις or μαβδαρῖτις. The Greek translators were often Aramaic-speaking Jews, and introduced Aramaisms probably unconsciously. [7] E omits αὐτό rightly. [8] E = ἀπὸ τῶν σπερμάτων καί [9] E adds ἐν αὐτῷ. [10] Em. with E from ανομβρον which gives no good sense. [11] E = φαινόμενον, but G is right. MS. φαιρομενον. [12] E adds ὡς ὑδραγωγεῖ [13] ὡς is redundant [14] North-West A Semitic idiom. Cf Hebrew צְפוֹנָה מַעֲרָבָה or צְפֹנִית מַעֲרָבִית in this sense [15] E = ἀνάγεται ὕδωρ καὶ δρόσος, but by a slight change in vocalization becomes = G. [16] E = καὶ ἐκεῖθεν which it has transposes into previous verse [17] E =᾿ ἀπὸ τοῦ. [18] See note on 28[1]. [19] E corrupt. [20] E adds ἐκεῖ [21] Here we should have εὐώδη instead of κρίσεως. [22] E corrupt [23] = מר. MS Ζμυρνα. [24] E omits, but see note on p. 58. [25] MS. Καρσηης. [26] E misrenders by ἐπὶ ἐκείνων, cf. 18[9]. [26] E = ὄρη. [27] E adds οὔ. [26] E adds ἀενάου, a gloss. [29] E = καὶ ἴδον δένδρον καλόν. [30] E = ὅμοιον. χρόα may be corrupt for χλόα (Radermacher). [31] See

πορευόμενον ἐξ αὐτῶν¹ νέκταρ τὸ καλούμενον σαρρὰν² καὶ χαλ-
βάνη³.　　2. καὶ ἐπέκεινα⁴ τῶν ὀρέων τούτων⁵ ἴδον ἄλλο ὄρος
⌜πρὸς ἀνατολὰς τῶν περάτων τῆς γῆς⌝⁶, καὶ πάντα τὰ δένδρα
πλήρης⁷ στακτῆς⁸ ἐν ὁμοιώματι ἀμυγδάλων.　　3. ὅταν τρίβωσιν⁹,
διὸ¹⁰ εὐωδέστερον ὑπὲρ πᾶν ἀρωμά[των]. . . . . . XXXII.
*εἰς βορρᾶν¹¹ ⌜πρὸς ἀνατολὰς⌝ τεθέαμαι ἑπτὰ ὄρη πλήρη νάρδου
χρηστοῦ καὶ * σχίνου¹² καὶ κινναμώμου καὶ πιπέρεως.

2. Καὶ ἐκεῖθεν ἐφόδευσα ἐπὶ¹³ τὰς ἀρχὰς ⌜πάντων⌝ τῶν ὀρέων
τούτων, μακρὰν ἀπέχων πρὸς ἀνατολὰς ⌜της γῆς⌝, καὶ διέβην ἐπάνω
τῆς ἐρυθρᾶς θαλάσσης, καὶ ᾠχόμην *ἐπ' Ἄκρων, καὶ ἀπὸ τούτου¹⁴
διέβην ἐπάνω¹⁵ τοῦ Ζωτιήλ.　　3. καὶ ἦλθον¹⁶ πρὸς τὸν παράδεισον
τῆς δικαιοσύνης, καὶ ἴδον *μακρόθεν τῶν δένδρων τούτων¹⁷ δένδρα
πλείονα¹⁸ καὶ μεγάλα * δύο μὲν¹⁹ ἐκεῖ²⁰, μεγάλα σφόδρα καλὰ καὶ
ἔνδοξα ⌜καὶ μεγαλοπρεπῆ²¹, καὶ τὸ δένδρον τῆς φρονήσεως, οὗ²²
ἐσθίουσιν ⌜ἁγίου τοῦ καρποῦ αὐτοῦ⌝²² καὶ ἐπίστανται φρόνησιν
μεγάλην.　　4. ὅμοιον ⌜τὸ δένδρον ἐκεῖνο στροβιλέᾳ τὸ ὕψος, τὰ
δὲ φύλλα αὐτοῦ⌝²³ κερατίᾳ²⁴ ὅμοια, ὁ δὲ καρπὸς αὐτοῦ ὡσεὶ βότρυες
ἀμπέλου ἱλαροὶ λίαν, ἡ δὲ ὀσμὴ αὐτοῦ διέτρεχεν πόρρω ἀπὸ τοῦ
δένδρου.　　5. τότε²⁵ εἶπον ⌜Ὡς⌝ καλὸν τὸ δένδρον, καὶ ὡς ἐπίχαρι²⁶
τῇ ὁράσει.　　6. τότε ἀπεκρίθη Ῥαφαήλ, ὁ ἅγιος ἄγγελος ὁ μετ'
ἐμοῦ ὤν, Τοῦτο τὸ δένδρον φρονήσεως, ἐξ οὗ ἔφαγεν ὁ πατήρ σου.

---

note on p 58.　¹ E adds ὡς　² = צְרִי.
³ = חֶלְבְּנָה.　⁴ E misrenders by ἐπὶ ἐκείνων, cf. 18⁹　⁵ E = ἐκείνων.　⁶ This
clause defines the habitat of the tree.
E omits this, but gives the name καὶ ἐν
αὐτῷ δένδρα ἀλόης.　⁷ Indeclinable
as in 28¹.　⁸ Em from ἐξαυτης E
corrupt = στερεός. στακτή = לֹט Gen.
37²⁵ 43¹¹. It also translates אֲהָלוֹת,
נטף, מֹר in the LXX　⁹ E =
λάβωσιν, and adds ἐκεῖνον τὸν καρπόν,
and connects this clause with what
follows.　For τρίβωσιν we should read
καύσωσιν.　¹⁰ E omits.　¹¹ E = καὶ
μετὰ ταῦτα τὰ ἀρώματα εἰς βορρᾶν ὁρῶν
ὑπὲρ τὰ ὄρη the first five words of which
were lost through hmt.　¹² E = δένδρων

εὐωδῶν a free rendering　¹³ E = ὑπέρ
¹⁴ E = μακρὰν ἀπὸ τούτου καί　¹⁵ E adds
τοῦ ἀγγέλου.　¹⁶ MS ελθων　¹⁷ E
takes μακρόθεν as = μακρὰν governing
the following words in the genitive
¹⁸ E = πολλά　¹⁹ E = φυόμενα　²⁰ E
adds εὐώδη.　²¹ Can the Greek before
the translator of E have been εὐειδή ?
If so, it is a corruption of the εὐώδη
found in E after ἐκεῖ　²² = the
Aramaic idiom פירה . . . . רי. See also
16¹ 22⁶, ⁹　²³ This clause is lost in
E through hmt., though the order such
a loss presumes must have been different
such as : ὅμοιον ⌜τὸ δένδρον ἐκεῖνο .
ὅμαια⌝ κερατίᾳ　²⁴ MS κερατι　²⁵ E =
καί. ²⁶ E adds καλὸν καί before this word.

ADDITIONAL FRAGMENT PRESERVED IN
SYNCELLUS' CHRONOGRAPHIA

(ed. Dindorf, 1829, vol. ι. p. 47.)

Καὶ αὖθις· παρὰ δὲ τοῦ ὄρους ἐν ᾧ ὤμοσαν καὶ ὀνεθεμάτισαν πρὸς
τὸν πλησίον αὐτῶν, ὅτι εἰς τὸν αἰῶνα οὐ μὴ ἀποστῇ ἀπ' αὐτοῦ ψῦχος
καὶ χιὼν καὶ πάχνη καὶ δρόσος οὐ μὴ καταβῇ εἰς οὐτό, εἰ μὴ εἰς
κατάραν καταβήσεται ἐπ' αὐτό, μέχρις ἡμέρας κρίσεως τῆς μεγάλης
ἐν τῷ κπιρῷ ἐκείνῳ κατακανθήσεται καὶ ταπεινωθήσεται καὶ ἔσται
κατακαιόμενον καὶ τηκόμενον ὡς κηρὸς ἀπὸ πυρός, οὕτως κατακαήσεται
περὶ πάντων τῶν ἔργων αὐτοῦ. καὶ νῦν ἐγὼ λέγω ὑμῖν υἱοῖς ἀνθρώπων, ὀργὴ μεγάλη καθ' ὑμῶν, κατὰ τῶν υἱῶν ὑμῶν, καὶ οὐ παύσεται
ἡ ὀργὴ αὕτη ἀφ' ὑμῶν, μέχρι καιροῦ σφαγῆς τῶν υἱῶν ὑμῶν. καὶ
ἀπολοῦνται οἱ ἀγαπητοὶ ὑμῶν καὶ ἀποθανοῦνται οἱ ἔντιμοι ὑμῶν ἀπὸ
πάσης τῆς γῆς, ὅτι πᾶσαι αἱ ἡμέραι τῆς ζωῆς αὐτῶν ἀπὸ τοῦ νῦν οὐ
μὴ ἔσονται πλείω τῶν ἑκατὸν εἴκοσιν ἐτῶν. καὶ μὴ δόξητε ἔτι ζῆσαι
ἐπὶ πλείονα ἔτη· οὐ γὰρ ἐστὶν ἐπ' αὐτοῖς πᾶσα ὁδὸς ἐκφεύξεως ἀπὸ
τοῦ νῦν διὰ τὴν ὀργὴν ἣν ὠργίσθη ὑμῖν ὁ βασιλεὺς πάντων τῶν
αἰώνων· μὴ νομίσητε ὅτι ἐκφεύξεσθε ταῦτα.

Καὶ ταῦτα μὲν ἐκ τοῦ πρώτου βιβλίου Ἐνὼχ περὶ τῶν ἐγρηγόρων·

APPENDIX II

THE SON OF MAN. ITS MEANING IN JEWISH APOCALYPTIC AND THE NEW TESTAMENT

WITHIN the last eighteen years a vast literature [1] has been written on the above Messianic title, which started with the publication of the first edition of the present work. I have followed with much interest the various attempts to explain the origin and meaning of this title or else to prove that it had no part originally in 1 Enoch or in the N.T. Into a discussion of these hypotheses I cannot enter here, and will only state my present position on the question, and this position is the same as regards the meaning of the title in 1 Enoch and the N.T. as in 1893 However scholars may differ as to the origin of the title, its meaning in the N T. is to my mind free from such ambiguities. If the title has a long history behind it, it does not in the least follow that what was its meaning in O T. times persisted in later Judaism or Christianity. In fact every analogy teaches us to expect an entire transformation. I will here republish with a few verbal corrections what I wrote in 1892.

The true interpretation of the N.T. title 'Son of Man' will, we believe, be found *if we start with the conception as found in 1 Enoch and trace its enlargement and essential transformation in the usage of our Lord. In this transformation it is reconciled to and takes over into itself its apparent antithesis, the conception of the Servant of Jehovah, while it betrays occasional reminiscences of Dan. 7, the ultimate source of this designation.*

First, shortly, as to the facts of the problem. The expression is found in St. Matthew thirty times, in St. Mark fourteen, in

---

[1] See the Articles in the Encyc Bib and Hastings, *B D.* for the fairly exhaustive bibliography on this question

St. Luke twenty-five, in St. John twelve. Outside the Gospels, in Acts 7^{56} Rev. 1^{13} 14^{14}. In all these cases we find ὁ υἱὸς τοῦ ἀνθρώπου, except in St. John 5^{27} and Rev 1^{13} 14^{14} The two passages in Rev. may be disregarded, since the phiase is different, i. e. ὅμοιον υἱὸν ἀνθρώπου Even there they are real designations of the Messiah. As for St John 5^{27} I can find no satisfactory explanation of the absence of the article.

Our interpretation of this title is as follows · (1) *Its source in Daniel and its differentiation therefrom.* The title 'Son of Man' in Enoch was undoubtedly derived from Dan. 7, but a whole world of thought lies between the suggestive words in Daniel and the definite rounded conception as it appears in Enoch In Daniel the phrase seems merely symbolical of Israel, but in Enoch it denotes a supernatural person. In the formei, moreover, the title is indefinite, 'like a son of man,' but in Enoch it is perfectly definite and distinctive, 'the Son of Man.'

(2) *The first occasion of its use.* As the Parables are pre-Christian, they furnish the first instance in which the definite personal title appears in literature.

(3) *Its supernatural import in Enoch.* The Son of Man as portrayed in the Parables is a supernatural being and not a mere man. He is not even conceived as being of human descent, as the Messiah in 1 En. 90^{37}. He sits on God's throne, 51^{3}, which is likewise His own throne, 62$^{3,\ 5}$ 69$^{27,\ 29}$, possesses universal dominion, 62^{6}, and all judgement is committed unto Him, 41^{9} 69^{27}.

(4) *Its import in the New Testament.* This title, with its supernatural attributes of superhuman glory, of universal dominion and supreme judicial powers, was adopted by our Lord. The Son of Man has come down from heaven, St. John 3^{13} (cf 1 En. 48^{2} note); He is Lord of the Sabbath, St. Matt 12^{8},[1] can forgive sins, St. Matt. 9^{6}, and all judgement is committed unto Him, St. John 5$^{22,\ 27}$ (cf. 1 En. 69^{27}). But while retaining its supernatural associations, this title underwent transformation

---

[1] The text in St Matt. here is doubtful Originally it may only have meant that ' man was Lord of the Sabbath '

in our Lord's use of it, a transformation that all Pharisaic ideas, so far as He adopted them, likewise underwent. And just as His kingdom in general formed a standing protest against the prevailing Messianic ideas of temporal glory and dominion, so the title 'the Son of Man' assumed a deeper spiritual significance, and this change we shall best apprehend if we introduce into the Enoch conception of the Son of Man the Isaiah conception of the Servant of Jehovah *These two conceptions, though outwardly antithetic, are through the transformation of the former reconciled and fulfilled in a deeper unity—in the New Testament Son of Man.* This transformation flowed naturally from the object of Jesus' coming, the revelation of the Father The Father could be revealed not through the self-assertion of the Son, not through His grasping at self-display in the exhibition of superhuman majesty and power, but through His self-emptying, self-renunciation and service (Phil 2⁶). Whilst, therefore, in adopting the title 'the Son of Man' from Enoch, Jesus made from the outset supernatural claims, yet these supernatural claims were to be vindicated not after the external Judaistic conceptions of the Book of Enoch, but in a revelation of the Father in a sinless and redemptive life, death, and resurrection. Thus in the life of the actual Son of Man the Father was revealed in the Son, and supernatural greatness in universal service.   He that was greatest was likewise Servant of all.   This transformed conception of the Son of Man is thus permeated throughout by the Isaiah conception of the Servant of Jehovah ; but though the Enochic conception is fundamentally transformed, the transcendant claims underlying it are not for a moment foregone. *If then we bear in mind the inward synthesis of these two ideas of the past in an ideal, nay in a Personality transcending them both, we shall find little difficulty in understanding the startling contrasts that present themselves in the New Testament in connexion with this designation.* We can understand how on the one hand the Son of Man hath not where to lay His head (St. Matt. 8²⁰) and yet release men from their sins (St. Matt. 9⁶), how He is to be despised and rejected of the elders and chief priests and scribes and be put to death (St. Luke 9²²), and yet be the Judge of all mankind (St. John 5²⁷).

It has been objected that St. Matt. 16¹³ St. John 12³⁴ prove that the Son of Man was not a current designation of the Messiah in the time of Christ, but no such conclusion can be drawn from these passages; for in the older form of the question given in St. Matt. 16¹³ the words 'the Son of Man' are not found: see St. Mark 8²⁷ St. Luke 9¹⁸. In St. John 12³⁴ it is just the strangeness of this *new* conception of this current phrase of a Messiah who was to suffer death, that makes the people ask 'Who is this Son of Man? we have heard of the law that the Christ abideth for ever'.

On the other hand, though the phrase was to some extent a current one,[1] our Lord's use of it must have been an enigma, not only to the people generally, but also to His immediate disciples, so much so that they shrank from using it; for, as we know, it is used in the Gospels only by our Lord in speaking of Himself.

---

[1] On the survival of its use as a Messianic designation see Jer. Taanith ii. 1 · 'R. Abbahu said, If a man says to thee—I am God, he lies; I am the Son of Man, he will at last repent it · I ascend to heaven, if he said it he will not prove it'

INDEX I

PASSAGES FROM THE SCRIPTURES AND OTHER ANCIENT BOOKS DIRECTLY CONNECTED OR CLOSELY PARALLEL WITH THE TEXT

(a) THE OLD TESTAMENT

Phil.	4^3	1 En. 47^3	Jude 14, 15	1 En. $1^9\ 5^4$
Col	1^{16}	61^{10}	Rev. 3^4 &c.	62^{16}
1 Tim	1^{15}	94^{1b}	3^5	47^3
	6^{16}	14^{21}	9^{20}	99^7
Jas.	1^8	91^4	13^5	5^4
2 Pet	3^{13}	$45^4\ 91^{18}$	14^6	37^5
Jude	4	38^2	14^{20}	100^9
	6	10^{12}	20^{12}	47^3
	14	60^8	21^1	$45^4\ 91^{16}$

INDEX II

NAMES AND SUBJECTS

Angels
spiritual ones of the heaven, 15[7]
spirits of the heaven, 15[10]
who fell, 6[1-6] (*n.*) 15[8] 69[4, 6] 86[1, 8]
106[18]
punishment of, 10[4-16] 12[4-6] 14[4-6] 19[1]
21[7-10] 55[4] 67[4, 6, 7, 11, 12] 90[21-24] 91[15].
See also 'Gabriel', 'Michael', 'Phan-
nel', 'Raguel', 'Raphael', 'Rem-
iel', 'Saraqael', 'Uriel'; 'Spirits'
Anger. See 'Wrath'.
Anguish See 'Day'
Antigonus, 100[2] (*n*)
Antiochus Cyzicenus, 90[18] (*n.*).
Antiochus Epiphanes, 46[6] (*n*) 90[8] (*n*)
100[7] (*n*).
Antiochus Sidetes, 90[18] (*n*)
Apostasy, 91[7] See 'Sin'
Apostate deeds, 93[8]
generation, 93[9]
Apostolic Constitutions, xcii.
Arakiba, 6[7].
Aramaic original of 1 Enoch, lvii-lxx
Araqiel, 8[8]
Archelaus, Disputation of, with Manes,
xciii.
Aristobulus I, 38[5] (*n.*) 100[2] (*n*)
Aristobulus II, 38[5] (*n*).
Armaros, 6[7] 8[3] 64[2]
Armen, 69[2]
Artaqifa, 69[2]
Asael, 6[7]
Asbeel, 69[6]
Asfa'el, 82[20]
Asonja 78[2]
Ass, wild = Ishmael, 89[11].
Asses = a species of giants, 86[4].
wild = Midianites, 89[11, 13, 16].
Assyrians = tigers in 89[55, 66].
Athenagoras, lxxxii-lxxxiii, 13[5] (*n*)
Augustine, xcii, 6[2] (*n*).
Azazel, 6[0] (*n.*) 8[1, 2] 8[8] (G[s]) 9[6] 10[4, 8] 13[1]
54[5] 55[4] 69[2] 86[1] (*n*) 88[1] (*n*); all sin
ascribed to, 10[8], bound in desert of
Dudael, 10[4], hosts of, judged, 54[5]
55[4]
†Azazel†, 69[2] 6[7] (*n.*).

Babylonians = lions in 89[56, 66, 65, 60].
Baraqel, 69[2]
Baraqijal, 6[7] 8[5].

Bardesanes (?), lxxxv
Barnabas, Epistle of, lxxxi, 89[56] (*n*)
Baruch, Apocalypse of, influence of
1 Enoch on, lxxvii-lxxviii.
Batarel, 6[7]
Batarjal, 69[2].
Beasts, wild = Gentiles, 85-90 (*n.*)
Behemoth and Leviathan, 60[7, 8, 24]
Benase, 78[2]
Berka'el, 82[17]
Biqa, 69[18]
Blasphemy, 91[7, 11] 94[9] 96[7]. See 'Sin'
Blessing, 10[16, 18] 41[8] 45[4, 5] 59[1, 2, 8] 76[4, 18]
Blood, 9[1, 9] 15[4] 100[1]
of flesh, 15[4]
righteous, 47[2, 4]
sinners, 100[8]
women, 15[4]
drink, 7[5].
eat, 9b[11]
shed, 9[1] 99[6].
Boar, black wild = Esau, 89[12]
Boars, wild = Edomites, 89[12] (*n*) [42, 43,]
[49, 66], = Samaritans, 89[72] 90[19] (*n*).
Book, the (of the Seventy Shepherds),
89[68, 70, 71, 76, 77] 90[17, 20].
Book, sealed, 89[70, 71]
Book of life, 108[3]
of the words of righteousness, 14[1]
of unrighteousness, 81[4] Cf 9b[7, 8]
104[7].
of zeal and wrath, disquiet and
expulsion, 39[1].
Books, of heathen writers, 104[10], the
holy, 103[2] 108[3] See also 'heavenly
tablets', and cf 108[7].
Books of the living, 47[3] Cf 104[1]
Books, opened, 90[20]
Bull, symbolically used, 85[8-9] 86[8] 89[1,]
[9-12]
white = Messiah, 90[87]
†Busasejal†, 69[2].

Cain, 22[7] 85[8-5].
Cainan, 37[1]
Camels = a class of giants, 86[4]
Carob tree, 32[4]
Cassianus, xci
Chambers, 41[4, 5] 60[12, 18].
Chaos, 18[12] 20[8] 21[1, 2] 108[8]
Chasids, existed as a party before the

OXFORD: HORACE HART, M A.
PRINTER TO THE UNIVERSITY

Printed in the USA
CPSIA information can be obtained
at www.ICGtesting.com
LVHW021928240124
769841LV00003B/38